LANDMARKS OF IRISH DRAMA

BERNARD SHAW: JOHN BULL'S OTHER ISLAND

J. M. SYNGE: THE PLAYBOY OF THE WESTERN WORLD

W. B. YEATS: ON BAILE'S STRAND

SEAN O'CASEY: THE SILVER TASSIE

DENIS JOHNSTON: THE OLD LADY SAYS 'NO'!

SAMUEL BECKETT: ALL THAT FALL

BRENDAN BEHAN: THE QUARE FELLOW

in the same series

Landmarks of Modern British Drama:
The Plays of the Sixties

Landmarks of Modern British Drama:
The Plays of the Seventies

Landmarks of French Classical Drama

LANDMARKS OF IRISH DRAMA

Bernard Shaw: John Bull's Other Island
J. M. Synge: The Playboy of the Western World
W. B. Yeats: On Baile's Strand
Sean O'Casey: The Silver Tassie
Denis Johnston: The Old Lady Says 'No'!
Samuel Beckett: All That Fall
Brendan Behan: The Quare Fellow

with an introduction by
Brendan Kennelly

METHUEN DRAMA

This collection first published in 1988
as a Methuen Paperback
in Great Britain by Methuen London Ltd
Reprinted in 1991 by Methuen Drama,
Michelin House, 81 Fulham Road, London SW3 6RB

On Baile's Strand first published by Macmillan London Ltd in 1964
John Bull's Other Island first published 1907
Copyright © 1957, The Public Trustee as Executor of
the Estate of George Bernard Shaw
The Playboy of the Western World first published
in this edition by Methuen & Co., 1961
The Silver Tassie first published by The Macmillan Press Ltd, in 1928
Copyright © Eileen O'Casey
The Quare Fellow first published by Methuen & Co. Ltd., in 1956
Copyright © 1956 by Brendan Behan and Theatre Workshop
All That Fall first published by Faber & Faber Ltd., in 1957
Copyright © 1957 Samuel Beckett
The Old Lady Says 'No'! first published by Colin Smythe Ltd in 1977
Copyright © 1983 Denis Johnston
In all cases the text used here was that currently in print in 1987.
Introduction copyright © Brendan Kennelly 1988
This collection copyright © Methuen London Ltd 1988

Acknowledgements

I wish to thank my colleagues,
Professor Nicholas Grene and
Professor Terence Brown for their help.
– Brendan Kennelly

Printed in Great Britain
by Cox & Wyman Ltd, Reading

British Library and Library of Congress Cataloging-in-Publication Data
Landmarks of Irish Drama. – (Landmarks).
1. English Drama – Irish authors
I. Series
822'.8'08094515   PR8865
ISBN 0-413-40290-8

CAUTION

Contents

Introduction

There are many reasons for the distinctive character of Irish drama. The first is obvious: Ireland is a small, poorish island in the Atlantic, close to Britain, with which country it has had a long and troubled relationship (is that the proper word?) for almost a thousand years. One would hardly think that a rather impoverished insularity would help to breed a world-renowned drama, but it has, because drama thrives on that trouble and conflict which are as much a tragic part of Irish life today as they have ever been. During the past fifteen years, several fine plays have been written about the 'Northern troubles'. Irish drama presents an ongoing re-creation of Irish history.

This insularity breeds a particular kind of intensity in talk, humour and human relationships. It nourishes gossip rather than thought, encourages anecdotes rather than philosophy. It creates an atmosphere of congestion that is frequently bitter and, more often than not, bitterly articulate. It helps to spawn what is known in Ireland as 'begrudgery', that is the state of envying other people whatever progress they may make in their lives, particularly in Ireland. One may be forgiven for improving one's lot abroad, but not at home. An oppressed people for centuries, we Irish frequently give evidence of that vicious slave-mentality noted, in different but definite ways, by all the dramatists in this anthology. Much of this begrudgery is accompanied by humour that is often savage and derisive or even downright destructive. Anything for a laugh, as the man said. This is also noted by our seven dramatists. The quality and consequences of the laughter in most Irish plays should be closely looked at.

It may be an aspect of this insularity that there is a sense in which these plays seem at times to be the work of inevitable outsiders. Reality is often viewed and explored from an odd perspective, an arrestingly different angle. Not being of the 'chief' or 'pure' tradition in English drama, these plays will strike readers for the freshness of their perspectives, the athletic freedom of their language, the articulate oddness of many of the human relationships they depict.

There is a considerable amount of drama in Irish life itself. The impulse to dramatise experience is especially noticeable in the *talk* of people on our damp island. Whoever said that Ireland is an open-air debating society wasn't far off the mark. This sense of a furiously talkative people is especially strong in the plays of Shaw, Synge, O'Casey, Johnston and Behan. Much of the talk is concerned with complaint, scandal, abuse, judgements of spontaneous and varying severity. Much of it is remarkable for its spirit of banter, for its word-play, for its light, rippling mockery. Some of it is a striking mixture of cleverness and bitterness, as if one's waking hours were at best an opportunity to hone one's satirical intelligence. And much of it is incisively, memorably funny, packed with merry poisons and smiling jibes.

These talkative people are too busy talking, it seems, to prevent the pollution of their landscape just now. It is one of the most beautiful, landscapes in the world and its presence is real and pervasive in most of the following plays. In Synge's drama, for example, the landscape seems as much a character as any of the people on stage. Language and landscape reflect each other.

Ireland's economic poverty has had, and continues to have, a deep influence on its dramatists. Writers like Congreve, Wilde, Shaw, O'Casey and Beckett left Ireland for several reasons; and it's a safe bet that the casual, insidious degradations of poverty were one strong reason for their deliberate exile. Poverty too plays an important part in nearly all plays in this volume.

But the most important influence on Irish drama is the way the Irish people live their lives, or are seen to live their lives, by individual playwrights. When Synge said that art is a collaboration I believe he meant, among other things, that the writer is the people's truest voice, and probably never more so than when his art offends his people. All the writers in this anthology draw inspiration from the lives of the people among whom they themselves lived and grew and changed. 'A people alone', Yeats said, 'are a great river'. There is a deep sense in which Irish life, or more particularly Irish lives, flow through these plays.

The pressures of history and mythology are further factors to be taken into account when one is trying to describe or define the special character of these works. Political and religious realities are present everywhere and at nearly all times. The 'relationship' with Britain, or more particularly with England, is vital and is perhaps most obvious in the work of Shaw, Synge, O'Casey and Behan.

Even these few reasons will help us to appreciate both the background and the content of our seven plays. If, taken together, they suggest a collectively distinctive character, it is hardly surprising to find that each writer included here has his own individual voice and vision, ensuring that each play is a compelling imaginative creation.

John Bull's Other Island

John Bull's Other Island is about Ireland or, more precisely, about Irelands – the different Irelands in the minds of the various characters. For Broadbent, the Englishman whose 'first duty is his duty to Ireland', that country is the stage on which he can witness charm and wit, comedy and fecklessness, humour, captivating feminine innocence and lyrical natural beauty in an unpolluted landscape. It is also the place where he can grab a seat in Parliament and plan to turn that same lyrical landscape into a lively tourist area in which even the most interesting and complex figure in the play, Peter Keegan, will become a tourist attraction. For Broadbent, Ireland is a stage. His English naïveté, his 'eupeptic jollity', breezily automatic sense of superiority and invincible sentimentality, are equalled only by his shrewd business instinct for turning not merely wild beauty into exploitable territory but for presenting a visionary human being as a colourful local eccentric. The entrepreneur in Broadbent is powered by the sentimentalist. Most forms of sentimentality are repugnant because the sentimentalist is not only committed to the cheapest form of self-deception (it literally costs him nothing) but also because sentimentality is usually a mask for cruelty, callousness and instinctive exploitation. Broadbent proposing to Nora Riley is a slobbering lump of sentimentality; Broadbent using Nora's attractiveness as a way of getting votes is a cold-blooded politician who is, one feels certain, on the threshold of developing a passion for kissing babies in public. Broadbent is aptly named by Shaw; he is certainly broad in the scope of his ambition, and undeniably if acceptably bent in his manner of achieving it. 'What I really dread,' he says, 'is misunderstanding.' His capacity for sentimental misunderstanding is, however, the real source of his strength because it prepares the way for his ruthless vision of power in the magnificent final scene with Larry Doyle and Peter Keegan.

For Larry Doyle, Ireland is a more complex matter. Broadbent's power derives from his ignorance of Ireland; Doyle's strength comes from his knowledge of it. He has genuine insight into certain crippling aspects of Irish life. Such insight must result from self-knowledge; hence the savage, self-loathing violence of Doyle's expression when he lashes out to Broadbent about Irish dreaming. This is the dreaming that Doyle escaped from as a youngster; yet there is an element of fascination running through his fierce denunciation.

Oh, the dreaming! the dreaming! the torturing, heart-scalding, never satisfying dreaming, dreaming, dreaming, dreaming! No debauchery that ever coarsened and brutalized an Englishman can take the worth and usefulness out of him like that dreaming. An Irishman's imagination never lets him alone, never convinces him, never satisfies him; but it makes him that he can't face reality nor deal with it nor handle it nor conquer it: he can only sneer at them that do, and be 'agreeable to strangers', like a good-for-nothing woman on the streets. It's all dreaming, all imagination. He can't be religious. The inspired Churchman that teaches him the sanctity of life and the importance of conduct is sent away empty; while the poor village priest that gives him a miracle or a sentimental story of a saint, has cathedrals built for him out of the pennies of the poor. He can't be intelligently political: he dreams of what the Shan Van Vocht said in ninety-eight. If you want to interest him in Ireland you've got to call the unfortunate island Kathleen ni Hoolihan and pretend she's a little old woman. It saves thinking. It saves working. It saves everything except imagination, imagination, imagination; and imagination's such a torture that you can't bear it without whisky.

Even more perceptive on Doyle's part is his statement about the nature of some Irish laughter. This same mocking, derisive laughter was noted by Joyce in *Dubliners* and *Ulysses*, by Yeats in poetry ('Come let us mock at the good'), by O'Casey in his plays and autobiography, as well as by Flann O'Brien, Patrick Kavanagh and others including Synge, Denis Johnston and Brendan Behan. Shaw must have had some bitter personal experience of this laughing derision when he lived in Ireland because Doyle's words are haunted, authentic and unmistakably personal.

And all the while there goes on a horrible, senseless, mischievous laughter. When you're young, you exchange drinks with other young men; and you exchange vile stories with them; and as you're too futile to be able to help or cheer them, you chaff and sneer and taunt them for not doing the things you daren't do yourself. And all the time you laugh! laugh! laugh! eternal derision, eternal envy, eternal folly, eternal fouling and staining and degrading, until, when you come at last to a country where men take a question seriously and give a serious answer to it, you deride them for having no sense of humor, and plume yourself on your own worthlessness as if it made you better than them.

Though Doyle has left Ireland, Ireland has not left Doyle; and when he returns with Broadbent to effect a commercial conquest as well as to see Nora Riley, his relationship with country and woman defines him as an intelligent, eloquent, perceptive man who can best cope with Ireland by rather crudely cutting Nora out of his life and by endorsing and sharing Broadbent's vision of a tourist emerald isle. Shaw never quite presents Doyle as being scared of sexual contact; and yet it is impossible not to see in Doyle the kind of Irish flight from sexuality that actually gives a certain acid to his eloquence, a bitchy venom to his invective.

Both Broadbent and Doyle are, in their different ways, essentially cold fish impassioned by ambition. Peter Keegan is a passionate man made thoughtfully detached by his experience. Keegan is a visionary, perhaps a saintly one; he is tolerant, loving, critical, jocular in his special way: 'My way of joking is to tell the truth. It's the funniest joke in the world'. Keegan is, above all, sane in that his insistence on detecting and practising what seem to him to be the most worthwhile human values leads to his being an outsider, a defrocked priest in a society that pays lip-service to these values but often treats them with that derisive laughter so well described by Larry Doyle. In such a society, Keegan's sanity is what makes him a 'madman'; and his final confrontation with Doyle and Broadbent, in which he expresses his vision of heaven, a vision connected with his conviction that 'this world is hell', is in his own words 'the dream of a madman'. On the contrary, it is the dream of a deeply humane person with a vision of unity necessarily 'mad' to those whose lives are deliberately and savagely fragmented in the pursuit of self-interest. And yet, Keegan's dream *is* impossible; but is Shaw not implying that a passionate dream sharpens the sense of reality, broadens and invigorates the mind's horizons, and vitalises rather than deadens the potential of the individual? The dream, in this sense, pushes a person's capacity for self-knowledge towards its limits. Keegan's Ireland may well be hell, but it is also the raw material of his dream of heaven. As well as that, his final words reveal the dramatic power of Shaw's innate capacity for paradox. The Irish 'hell of littleness and monotony' begets the heaven-dream of magnanimity and justice. Heaven and hell, and the Ireland that symbolises both, dwell in Peter Keegan's heart and mind.

In my dreams it is a country where the State is the Church and the Church the people: three in one and one in three. It is a commonwealth in which work is play and play is life: three in one and one in three. It is a temple in which the priest is the worshipper and the worshipper the worshipped: three in one and one in three. It is a godhead in which all life is human and all humanity divine: three in one and one in three. It is, in short, the dream of a madman.

As the curtain falls on Broadbent's 'I feel sincerely obliged to Keegan: he has made me feel a better man: distinctly better. I feel now as I never did before that I am right in devoting my life to the cause of Ireland', we feel that Keegan's dream must yield before the combined energies of Broadbent and Doyle; and yet it lingers vividly in the memory.

The other characters, too, are pre-occupied in their varying minor yet important ways with Ireland. For some, Ireland echoes with the wrongs and sufferings of history, the evils of absentee landlordism. For others, it is a small stage where life is a struggle and the struggle gives value to life. For others, Ireland is land, land to be fought for, to be owned and worked; and as the land is worked, it clarifies the workers' capacity for industry and greed, for enlightened co-operation and rapacious individualism. For all, Ireland is an image that absorbs their days, moulds their dreams and defines their notions of, and capacity for, success and failure. Silent Ireland defines its speaking people. Like Godot in Beckett's play, like the wild duck in Ibsen's, and like the quare fellow himself of Behan, Ireland never speaks in *John Bull's Other Island*; and yet its silence measures and judges the value and consequence of the words of all those whose lives are entangled with the rich, mysterious life of that 'other island' which fascinated Shaw throughout his entire life. Written out of the deepest recesses of his nature, this is one of Shaw's finest plays. It is beautifully structured, the large cast of characters is effectively orchestrated, the Irish-English problem of the tragedies and comedies of mutual misunderstanding is deftly and penetratingly handled, political issues are seen as part of the characters' everyday lives not as remote parliamentary abstractions, and the language, always lucid and pertinent, does justice to Shaw's complex relationship with the land of his birth and, to a lesser extent, with the land that enabled him to explore and develop his cheeky, compassionate genius. An essential element of that genius is Shaw's need to explain himself, his world, himself in relation to his world, his ideas, beliefs, disbeliefs, attitudes, opinions, prejudices, judgements and hopes. Hence his prefaces, that vast bulk of explanatory literature which is an eloquent indication of Shaw's terror of being misunderstood, and also, perhaps, of misunderstanding himself, his work and the meaning of his work for other people. He wrote four prefaces to *John Bull's Other Island*. Readers of these and other prefaces can hardly be blamed for thinking that in Shaw the passion to explain might well have stifled the impulse to dramatise. It has not. Shaw's energy of mind, body and imagination is such that one can only marvel at the fact that far from stifling his dramatic impulse, his tireless preface-writing deepened and enriched it. *John*

Bull's Other Island is a fully realised dramatic achievement; and the preface to it is a model of lucid, urgent prose.

The Playboy of the Western World

J. M. Synge is one of the most poetic dramatists of this century; he creates complex imaginative worlds which are genuinely rich and strange. The word 'rich' is, in fact, one of Synge's favourite words whenever he seeks to describe his view of drama (the italics are mine):

> . . . there is little doubt that in the happy ages of literature, striking and beautiful phrases were as ready to the story-teller's or the playwright's hand, as the *rich* cloaks and dresses of his time.

or again:

> . . . where the imagination of the people, and the language they use, is *rich* and living, it is possible for a writer to be *rich* and copious in his words, and at the same time to give the reality, which is the root of all poetry, in a comprehensive and natural form.

Synge's determination to embody reality in a richly copious language led to his desire to create plays marked by the kind of '*rich* joy' which is found 'only in what is superb and wild in reality'.

This 'richness' has several fascinating ingredients. Two of its most essential elements are its musicality and its health. The musicality of Synge's language is inseparable from his view of art as 'collaboration'; he literally draws his inspiration from the people he meets and observes. Synge, like Pinter, has a tape-recorder in his brain; and he is quick to acknowledge the help which he, as a patient, vigilant, listening outsider, gets from the community in which he moves. He constantly acknowledges this in his prose works, *The Aran Islands* and *In Wicklow, West Kerry and Connemara*. And he states it bluntly in the opening sentence of the preface to *The Playboy of the Western World*:

> In writing *The Playboy of the Western World*, as in my other plays, I have used one or two words only that I have not heard among the

country people of Ireland, or spoken in my own nursery before I could read the newspapers.

It is not sufficient, at the same time, to present Synge's drama merely as a kind of distilled collaborative music. This musicality has deeper sources in Synge; it is profoundly personal; it is inseparable from his view of life itself. His brief *Autobiography* begins:

Every life is a symphony, and the translation of this life into music, and from music back to literature or sculpture or painting is the real effort of the artist. The emotions which pass through us have neither end nor beginning – are a part of the sequence of existence – and as the laws of the world are in harmony it is this almost cosmic element in the person which gives great art, as that of Michelangelo or Beethoven, the dignity of nature.

This is very different from Pater's neat dictum that 'All art aspires to the condition of music'. Synge's conviction is that each human life *is* music. The dramatist who would present that human life must, therefore, discover and perfect an appropriate music. An examination of the various drafts of Synge's plays reveals precisely this: the scrupulous struggle of a writer to discover and reveal the minutely appropriately heart-music, mind-music and soul-music of *each* of his characters. In this struggle, Synge is nearly always successful; his output of plays is small but his work is as close to perfection as that of the greatest modern dramatists.

The second element of Synge's 'richness' is his sense of the drama as being a source of imaginative and spiritual health, of giving us a certain 'nourishment' which, he says, is 'not very easy to define'; but it is precisely this 'nourishment' that helps our imaginations to 'live'. It is significant that Synge himself was in poor health for many years; and there is what amounts to an obsession with sickness and death in his plays. But there is also a passionate concern with the opposite; with robust health, vigorous well-being, and a kind of emotional exuberance which, when expressed in Synge's soaring but always appropriate language, is nothing short of electrifying.

'We should not' writes Synge in his preface to *The Tinker's Wedding*, 'go to the theatre as we go to a chemist's or a dram-shop, but as we go to a dinner where the food we need is taken with pleasure and excitement'.

It is hardly surprising that in these uniquely musical plays of which *The Playboy* is the most consistently sublime, Synge sees humour as a necessary ingredient in that 'nourishment' which he considered vital for the healthy life of the imagination. Synge's belief in the power of humour is more relevant in our polluted, nuclear-bomb-threatened world than it has ever been. Across the years, his words ring with sanity and a kind of singing common sense.

> Of the things which nourish the imagination humour is one of the most needful, and it is dangerous to limit or destroy it. Baudelaire calls laughter the greatest sign of the Satanic element in man; and where a country loses its humour, as some towns in Ireland are doing, there will be morbidity of mind, as Baudelaire's mind was morbid.

Morbid images abound in *The Playboy of the Western World*, yet the overall effect is of a marvellously comic play. Jimmy Farrell may talk of 'the skulls they have in the city of Dublin, ranged out like blue jugs in a cabin of Connaught', and Philly O'Cullen may speak of the 'remnants of a man' whose 'shiny bones' he puts together for fun on 'many a fine Sunday', but the imagery of skulls and bones is more a vivid part of the story being told than it is evidence of a morbid preoccupation with death and its work.

One feels, on reflection, that *The Playboy* should, in fact, be morbid. It is set in a poor, remote, severed if self-contained community; and it concerns the fate of a tired, frightened, dirty little man who tells how he killed his father with the blow of a loy. Far from being morbid, however, this is an exhilarating play, a genuinely complex comedy. When it was first produced it led to riots in the Abbey Theatre, proof that it cut to the bone with Irish audiences. After the riots an interview appeared in which Synge was represented as saying that the play was merely an 'extravaganza' and that he 'did not care a rap' for the public's reaction. In a letter to *The Irish Times* in January 1907, Synge said of that interview:

... The interview took place in conditions that made it nearly impossible for me – in spite of the patience and courtesy of the interviewer – to give a clear account of my views about the play, and the lines I followed in writing it. *The Playboy of the Western World* is not a play with 'a purpose' in the modern sense of the word, but although parts of it are, or are meant to be, extravagant comedy, still a great deal more that is behind it is perfectly serious when looked at in a certain light. That is often the case, I think, with comedy, and no one is quite sure today whether 'Shylock' and 'Alceste' should be played seriously or not. There are, it may be hinted, several sides to 'The Playboy'.

The more one reads and sees this play, the more one realises the truth of Synge's statement that 'there are several sides to "The Playboy"'. It can be seen in different ways. One may say, for example, that it is a play about an outsider (a recurring figure in Synge's plays) whose presence in a small, tightly-knit society has, because of the story he tells and the way he tells it, profound and far-reaching consequences. To this extent, it is a play about the transfiguring power of the imagination itself, the ways in which the story creates the man with a power as wonderful and effective as that of the man creating the story; the fact that the story is one of patricide merely adds to our sense of Synge's ability to involve his audience in the fabulous skill and wonder of the story itself; morality is burned up in Christy's fiery poetry; the audience, as well as the other characters in the play, are lifted beyond the accepted fact of murder into the marvel of a tale captivatingly told by Christy Mahon who changes from being a dirty, frightened weakling into a towering champion capable of shaping his own destiny. We are witnessing the growth of a poet's imagination; and we delight in that rare, inspiring spectacle.

We may also say that the play is a lyrical and moving love-story with a sad, almost tragic ending, certainly an ending marked by a deeply cutting and consciously felt sense of loss. Or it may be asserted that *The Playboy* vividly demonstrates that the world evoked by the poetic imagination is both fabulous and fragile; fabulous, because it has an enchanting, liberating effect on all who permit it to touch their hearts; fragile, because the magical world evoked by the story is diminished, even destroyed by an action which fulfils in dreary fact what had been mesmerically narrated in fiction. When Christy finally kills his father (only he doesn't), he turns to Pegeen, his love and his inspiration, and he asks:

> And what is it you'll say to me, and I after doing it this time in the face of all?

Pegeen's reply is not only a dismissal of a man capable of murderous action, 'a dirty deed'; it is also a defence of the poetry which had won her heart.

> I'll say, a strange man is a marvel, with his mighty talk;
> but what's a squabble in your back yard, and the blow of a loy, have taught me that there's a great gap between a gallous story and a dirty deed.

There is a genuine feeling of let-down, of sadness, disappointment and loss, at the end of *The Playboy*. In his preface to the play, Synge wrote: 'On the stage, one must have reality and one must have joy.' Much of *The Playboy* is deeply thrilling because of the joyful reality of its poetry and the exuberant reality of its comedy; but the reality of its final lines from Pegeen is stinging and sad; and that final sadness, pithy and undeniable, seems, as we contemplate this play of 'many sides', to enrich and deepen its many moments of comic vigour and lyrical beauty.

> PEGEEN: Oh, my grief, I've lost him surely. I've lost the only Playboy of the Western World.

That word 'only' may be the key to the nature and extent of Pegeen's loss. She has indeed lost somebody unique, somebody she will never replace. Her consciousness of the loss of a unique human being, her 'only playboy', adds to the 'richness' of Synge's comedy, throwing back on the preceding action a dark shadow that stresses the wild laughter, the abandoned but accurate language of so many memorable scenes. Ultimately, *The Playboy of the Western World* defies strict categorisation; but its swirling energies of imagination and language make it an increasingly fascinating play. Like a great poem, it turns the reader's sense of familiarity into a deepening sense of freshness and wonder.

On Baile's Strand

When in January, 1907, rioting crowds disrupted the first production of Synge's play at the Abbey Theatre, W. B. Yeats came quickly to the dramatist's defence. Yeats, a passionate lover of freedom and a ruthless champion of what he believed to be artistic excellence, showed heroic grit in defending Synge's work against some of the most repressive forces in Irish society. That word 'heroic' can never be far from the lips of any critic trying to assess Yeats's achievement in poetry and drama. In fact, right from the start of his career, Yeats was concerned, even obsessed, with the idea and image of the hero, the man who leads a brief, passionate, egotistical, free, adventurous life, scorning a long lifetime of secure mediocrity and pensionable caution. In art, Synge was one of Yeats's heroes, living and writing with the fiery simplicity and integrity that Yeats admired.

In his quest for the heroic, a quest that implied a scorn for realistic art, Yeats turned to Irish mythology where, thanks to the translations by scholars such as Standish O'Grady and by other writers like Lady Gregory, he discovered the heroic figure of Cuchulain, the Achilles of Ireland, the focal character of the old Irish epic, Táin Bó Cuailgne. Yeats determined to create a number of plays based on incidents in Cuchulain's life. Writing about his play *On Baile's Strand*, he says in his preface to *Plays in Prose and Verse*: 'It makes one of a series of plays upon events in the life of Cuchulain, and if placed in the order of these events the plays would run: 1. 'The Hawk's Well' (*Four Plays for Dancers*); 2. 'The Green Helmet'; 3. 'On Baile's Strand'; 4. 'The Only Jealousy of Emer' (*Four Plays for Dancers*): but they were so little planned for performance upon one evening that they should be at their best on three different kinds of stage.' There is a fifth play, *The Death of Cuchulain*, which Yeats finished near the end of his life.

These Cuchulain plays may, as Yeats says, be performed separately, but they are also an intriguing dramatic unity which Yeats may not have consciously intended. In the late fifties, I saw a production of the five plays in the course of a delightfully lengthy evening in the Players' Theatre, Trinity College, Dublin. It was an unforgettable theatrical experience. The five plays fused into a single, multi-faceted, heroic-dramatic image. At the centre of that image stood the proud, passionate and ultimately tragic figure of Cuchulain.

Our concern here is with *On Baile's Strand* in which the High King Conchubar, desiring to harness Cuchulain's individual bravery and strength in the interest of firm government, persuades Cuchulain to swear an oath of obedience to him as a result of which the hero is forced to fight and kill his own son although, at the moment of combat, Cuchulain does not know his son's identity. This son is the child of Aoife, a warrior-woman of Scotland, whom Cuchulain had overcome in battle and then loved. When he *does* discover his son's identity, Cuchulain goes mad and fights the waves of the sea, believing in his madness that the foamy crown of every wave is the crown on King Conchubar's crafty head.

On Baile's Strand is a tragic drama. Yeats saw tragedy as 'a moment of intense life'; he held that passion and not thought makes tragedy, and that tragedy, in fact, 'is passion alone'. Indeed, for Yeats, 'the subject of all art is passion, and a passion can only be contemplated when separated by itself, purified of all but itself, and aroused into a perfect intensity by opposition with some other passion.' In *On Baile's Strand*, Cuchulain's passion for self-assertion is brought into conflict with Conchubar's passion for strong government, for the need to establish and maintain a reliable defence of his country, and above all, perhaps, for the desire, at once civilised and primitive, to pass on to his children a stable and well-ordered society. Yeats saw this kind of passionate conflict as being essential to tragedy which 'must always be a drowning and breaking of the dykes that separate man from man'. The tragic experience carries one 'beyond time and persons to where passion, living through its thousand purgatorial years, as in the wink of an eye becomes wisdom; as though we too have touched and felt and seen a disembodied thing.'

On Baile's Strand is indeed a play of extraordinary passion. This passionate effect is achieved through a deliberate, coherent structure. Although the play is a continuous rhythmical entity, undivided into scenes, I suggest that a helpful way to see how Yeats achieves his passionate effect is to strip the play into the different sections or scenes that constitute its peculiar rhythm.

1. A Fool and a Blind Man open the play. (They will end it also.) From the beginning, we realise that the Blind Man, clever and resourceful, harnesses and directs the Fool's energy so that he, the Blind Man, will not be short of food. The Fool's energy is necessary for the Blind Man's survival just as Cuchulain's heroic drive is essential to Conchubar's vision of strong government. Not a word is wasted in this play: each word works for the next, each scene echoes and deepens preceding and following scenes.

In this opening section we learn that the Blind Man knows the identity of the Young Man who is challenging Conchubar's warriors. Indeed, the Blind Man knows who the Young Man's father is.

BLIND MAN: Listen. I know who the young man's father is, but I won't say. I would be afraid to say. Ah, Fool, you would forget everything if you could know who the young man's father is.

Much of the impact of this opening section is due to the Fool's soaring fantasies. Yeats, indeed, dedicated the play to the actor William Fay 'because of the beautiful fantasy of his playing in the character of the Fool'.

2. This second section, tense with the sense of the High King's determination to make the hero swear an oath of obedience to him, is a kind of passionate debate between Conchubar and Cuchulain. As the debate proceeds we become aware of the conflict between the man who believes in government, succession and heredity and the man who lives gloriously and unapologetically for himself, out of a real passion for the thrills of open, adventurous living. The High King's aim is clear:

CONCHUBAR: I would leave
A strong and settled country to my children.

Cuchulain refuses to be bound. He'll dance or hunt, or quarrel or make love, wherever and whenever he has a mind to. He says he has no need of children; he is even glad he has none.

CUCHULAIN:
> I think myself most lucky that I leave
> No pallid ghost or mockery of a man
> To drift and mutter in the corridors
> Where I have laughed and sung.

This is the proud boast of Cuchulain the son-killer. When his son does turn up, Cuchulain is immediately attracted to him. But that is not yet.

3. All the Kings gather to try to persuade Cuchulain to take the oath of obedience to Conchubar. Three women attend who will sing their strange prayer-song when the hero finally agrees to take the oath.

4. Cuchulain has scarcely taken the oath when the Young Man turns up and challenges the hero. Cuchulain immediately feels affection for the Young Man and plans to make him his friend. Conchubar will not permit this friendship; Cuchulain, angry, lays hands on the High King. The other Kings say this violence done to the High King's person is a result of witchcraft. Cuchulain accepts this and, throwing aside his instant, instinctive affection for the Young Man, insists on fighting him. He kills him.

5. The women predict Cuchulain's death. This brief scene sends the most gripping reverberations backwards and forwards through the play. When, for example, the First Woman says:

> Life drifts between a fool and a blind man
> To the end, and nobody can know his end.

We realise the same could be said of the play itself.

6. Cuchulain learns from the Fool's prattle that he has killed his own son. He goes mad with grief for his deed and with rage against the High King, and he goes to fight the sea. The Fool describes to

the Blind Man how the hero cuts the head off each wave. The use of repetition in this final scene is hypnotically effective, clarifying the ironic fact that the hero's death prepares the way for thieving opportunism.

> FOOL: There, he is down! He is up again. He is going out in the deep water. There is a big wave. It has gone over him. I cannot see him now. He has killed kings and giants, but the waves have mastered him!
>
> BLIND MAN: Come here, Fool!
>
> FOOL: The waves have mastered him.
>
> BLIND MAN: Come here.
>
> FOOL: The waves have mastered him.
>
> BLIND MAN: Come here, I say.
>
> FOOL: (*coming towards him, but looking backwards towards the door*). What is it?
>
> BLIND MAN: There will be nobody in the houses. Come this way; come quickly! The ovens will be full. We will put our hands into the ovens. (*They go out.*)

Each of these six scenes or sections plays its part in creating that passionate rhythm, initiated and completed by the hunger and rapacity of the Fool and the Blind Man, which makes *On Baile's Strand* such a compelling play. Yeats's preoccupation with re-writing his poems and plays is almost legendary among scholars and critics; but the real point of all his re-writing is to establish an inner resonance in his work which adds greatly to its appeal. This becomes clearer each time one reads or sees *On Baile's Strand*. Also, far from being an obscure writer, Yeats is forever struggling to make difficult yet lucid connections between different parts of his poems and plays. If, for example, we read *On Baile's Strand* and then read his poem *The Circus Animals' Desertion*, we can think about not only the deep themes of this play itself, or its relationship with certain other of Yeats's plays, but also its place in Yeats's entire work. So we can appreciate both its special significance for Yeats and its status as a poetic play about heroism in an age when poetry is at a low ebb in the theatre.

And when the Fool and Blind Man stole the bread
Cuchulain fought the ungovernable sea;
Heart-mysteries there, and yet when all is said
It was the dream itself enchanted me . . .

Well, 'when all is said', what matters most about *On Baile's Strand*
is that it is a many-layered, well-structured play by a great dramatic
poet. For its language alone, *On Baile's Strand* is worth reading and
re-reading. Here, for example, is Cuchulain's description of Aoife,
mother of the son he kills. Aoife is both the source of his love and of
his madness.

CUCHULAIN: Ah! Conchubar, had you seen her
With that high, laughing, turbulent head of hers
Thrown backward, and the bowstring at her ear,
Or sitting at the fire with those grave eyes
Full of good counsel as it were with wine,
Or when love ran through all the lineaments
Of her wild body – although she had no child,
None other had all beauty, queen or lover,
Or was so fitted to give birth to kings.

Yeats is not just a distinguished poet who wrote plays with the
intention of adding dramatic fire and fibre to his lyric verse. He is an
important dramatist who spent much of his life trying to bring poetry
back into the theatre. I believe that Yeats's plays, with their profound
insights, tight structures and distinctive language will become more
and more significant with time.

The Silver Tassie

Fighting and war play an important part in Yeats's plays about
Cuchulain. Sean O'Casey's drama *The Silver Tassie* is also about war.
Yeats's rejection of that play for the Abbey Theatre is now part of
theatrical history. O'Casey had given three excellent, popular plays to
the Abbey – *The Shadow of a Gunman*, *Juno and the Paycock* and *The
Plough and the Stars*. These plays had dealt with war, drunkenness,

ignorance and poverty in the Dublin slums. They were boisterous, tender, comic, tragic and extremely powerful. The Dublin crowds rioted against *The Plough and the Stars* as they had against *The Playboy of the Western World*. And, just as he had defended Synge, Yeats now defended O'Casey. When, however, O'Casey submitted his anti-war play, *The Silver Tassie*, to the Abbey, Yeats rejected it. O'Casey, living in England at this stage, did not write for the Abbey again, although he produced many more plays.

What sort of dramatist is this Sean O'Casey, child of the Dublin slums, self-educated socialist, actor, docker, stone-breaker, builders' labourer, opinionated hater of injustice and cant? I would say that first and foremost he is a writer who believes in the dignity and courage of ordinary men and women even as he witnesses apparently endless human suffering and pain. In an essay called 'Immanuel', O'Casey writes:

Man's real fight has always been against sorrow of every kind, a fight to banish it out of sight, out of feeling, out of the earth altogether: to abolish the weariness of hard work, the sorrows of insufficient food, the misery of cold clothing, of misery-making homes, of the pains of illnesses, and, when possible, the unhappiness of death to life before life is ripe enough to discard the care of going.

We are immediately into what is central to O'Casey's dramatic vision: a spirit of fighting gaiety, a profound awareness of human misery and sorrow equalled only by a fierce determination to make laughter triumph over trouble and despair. It is difficult to avoid calling O'Casey an emotional idealist; that in fact is what he is. This man who had seen human misery somewhere near its worst in the slums of Dublin had an unshakeable faith in the power of gaiety and laughter to help people survive all kinds of misfortune. O'Casey's genius lies in his ability to make his audience accept and admire those powerful surges of feeling that show people waging an incessant war 'against sorrow of every kind'. O'Casey consciously and aggressively gives us a passionate, personal Theatre of Feeling. He responds

strongly to what he considers over-intellectualised writing and eloquently re-states his view of the primacy of feeling in life.

Feeling, rather than thought or detachment, seems to dominate the
world of life. It was not thought but feeling that led the way to
human development, for the meaning of the word is based on the
word 'to grope', and life, in its first stage of withdrawal from the
world's waters, must have felt, groped its way in to the land. When
hands grew handier, we groped our way forward more accurately,
and, even today, with all our knowledge and our dependence on
mind, the fingers retain an amazingly delicate sense of touch. We
usually trust our feelings. How does one feel towards this or that?
How often the question is asked! 'I felt sympathy towards him or
her: I felt obliged to do that or this; I felt it was time to go; I feel
something is bound to happen': the examples of the use of feeling
are a multitude, and there is no escape from them, even in a snarl
of a poem or snarl of a play, for cynicism itself is prompted by the
feeling that there is little or no hope in humanity.

Any poem or play that ignores or lessens the importance of feeling
is to O'Casey an act of artistic perversion, a heartless attempt to turn
the theatre into a morgue.

Feeling is a faculty common to all living things ... So since we
can't take this feeling away, this emotion that is common to all
things – even to those who taboo them – to banish it from poem or
play is to banish it, not from life, but to banish life from the poem
and the play.

It follows from this that O'Casey will try to create a drama in which
there is as much 'life' and 'feeling' as possible. It follows too that he
must be fascinated by whatever force or forces cripple or kill this
feeling and life. War is such a force, 'the one great calamity,' according
to O'Casey, 'fashioned by the stupid mind and fumbling hand of
Man.' O'Casey rails against war:

Life becomes a tale of an idiot when nation is set against nation, and war flames in our face to a clamor of sound and fury, signifying nothing; and life becomes an idiot's babble when we watch the few having so much, while many have so little.

In his three early Abbey Theatre plays, O'Casey had demonstrated the tragic futility and waste of war as he had witnessed it in Ireland during the 1916 Uprising, the War of Independence and the Civil War. But now, O'Casey wanted to show the horror, carnage and consequences of the First World War. In his *Autobiographies*, he tells how he first heard the song, 'The Silver Tassie', and how that song became the title of his new anti-war play.

> The Silver Tassie
> Gae fetch to me a pint o' wine,
> An' full it in a sulver tossie;
> That I may drink before I gae
> A service tae my bonnie lossie . . .
>
> But it's no' the roar of sea or shore
> Wad mak' me langer wish tae tarry;
> Nor shout o' war that's heard afar –
> It's leavin' thee, my bonnie lossie.

Sean was startled. Aaron's rod had budded. A riotous and romantic song had drifted up . . . He hummed it in his tiny flat in South Kensington; he hummed it in the dead of night, strolling down the Cromwell Road. He would give the title of the song to his next play. He would set down without malice or portly platitude the shattered enterprise of life to be endured by many of those who, not understanding the bloodied melody of war, went forth to fight, to die, or to return again with tarnished bodies and complaining minds. He would show a wide expanse of war in the midst of timorous hope and overweening fear; amidst a galaxy of guns; silently show the garlanded horror of war. However bright and haughty be the burning of a town; however majestic be the snapping thunder of the cannon-fire, the consummation is the ruin of an ordered, sheltering city, with the odious figure of war astride the tumbled buildings, sniffing up the evil smell of the burning ashes. The ruin, the squeal of the mangled, the softening moan of the badly rended are horrible, be the battle just or unjust; be the fighters striving for the good or manifesting faith in evil.

And he would do it in a new way.

Doing it 'in a new way' meant that O'Casey no longer gave audiences the kind of play that had packed the Abbey Theatre when *The Shadow of a Gunman*, *Juno and the Paycock* and *The Plough and the Stars* had appeared there. This departure from his early style was a conscious decision on O'Casey's part.

There was no importance in trying to do the same thing again, letting the second play imitate the first, and the third the second. He wanted a change from what the Irish critics had called burlesque, photographic realism, or slices of life, though the manner and method of two of the plays were as realistic as the scents stealing from a gaudy bunch of blossoms.

The conscious throwing-aside of 'photographic realism' allows O'Casey a whole range of exciting new possibilities in *The Silver Tassie*. Most significant of the new developments is the use of a dramatic chant in the play, especially in the powerful second Act, set in the war zone, in the 'jagged and lacerated ruin of what was once a monastery'. This is where we hear 'the bloodied melody of war' and witness 'the garlanded horror of war'.

What an apt phrase is 'the bloodied melody of war' to describe, for example, the strong misery-chant of the wounded soldiers in Act Two. This full, musical expression of misery would be unthinkable in a realistic play. O'Casey's 'bloodied melody' is a sensuous, disciplined chant that reveals horror in a ritualised word-music. The chant gives an ironic religious dimension to the horror, as if the soldiers were maimed but articulate celebrants at some High Mass of destruction and death in this old ruined monastery, this broken relic of Christianity.

The Wounded on the Stretchers chanting:

> Carry on, carry on to the place of pain,
> Where the surgeon spreads his aid, aid, aid.
> And we show man's wonderful work, well done,
> To the image God hath made, made, made,
> And we show man's wonderful work well done
> To the image God hath made!
>
> When the future hours have all been spent,
> And the hand of death is near, near, near,
> Then a few, few moments and we shall find
> There'll be nothing left to fear, fear, fear,
> Then a few, few moments and we shall find
> There'll be nothing left to fear.
>
> The power, the joy, the pull of life,
> The laugh, the blow, and the dear kiss,
> The pride and hope, the gain and loss,
> Have been tempered down to this, this, this.
> The pride and hope, the gain and loss,
> Have been tempered down to this.

The Silver Tassie, in four Acts, has an effective structural rhythm. Act One is vibrant with the boisterous enjoyment of a victorious football team of which the hero is Harry Heegan. Here is what O'Casey calls 'the sweet and innocent insanity of a fine achievement'; but all this celebration, this drinking from the Silver Tassie, takes place on the threshold of hell, the edge of war. Act Two plunges us into that hell; we go swiftly from the spectacle of joyous victory to a weirdly effective music of war's obscenity and abomination. If there is music in hell, this is it.

In Act Three, set in hospital, we meet some of the men who have returned from war 'with tarnished bodies and complaining minds'. The football-hero, Harry Heegan, is a bitter cripple in a wheelchair, sexually frustrated, jealous and hopeless. His friend Teddy Foran, the frightening bully of Act One, is a blind shadow of himself. Sylvester Heegan and Simon Norton who have *not* been to war provide the kind of mild comedy that underlines the bitterness of the war-victims. Harry's bitterness has a black, lyrical intensity.

> HARRY (*with intense bitterness*). I'll say to the pine, 'Give me the grace and beauty of the beech'; I'll say to the beech, 'Give me the strength and stature of the pine.' In a net I'll catch butterflies in bunches; twist and mangle them between my fingers and fix them wriggling on to mercy's banner. I'll make my chair a Juggernaut, and wheel it over the neck and spine of every daffodil that looks at me, and strew them dead to manifest the mercy of God and the justice of man!

In the final Act, set in a room of the dance hall of the Avondale Football Club, that crippled bitterness is contrasted mercilessly with the health and gaiety of the dancers. Although at the end both Harry Heegan and Teddy Foran resolve to 'face like men' whatever lies before them, it is Susie who, changing throughout the play from self-righteous hot-gospeller to self-consciously sensuous beauty, is given the hard, necessary words of truth by O'Casey. The bloodied melody of war must always be replaced by the sweet music of continuing life.

> SUSIE (*to Jessie*). . . . Teddy Foran and Harry Heegan have gone to live their own way in another world. Neither I nor you can lift them out of it. No longer can they do the things we do. We can't give sight to the blind or make the lame walk. We would if we could. It is the misfortune of war. As long as wars are waged, we shall be vexed by woe; strong legs shall be made useless and bright eyes made dark. But we, who have come through the fire unharmed, must go on living.

Most important of all, however, is the fierce, surging, musical power with which O'Casey's hatred of war and his love of humanity come through. The deepest war in this play is between the forces of destruction and the forces of creativity. O'Casey presents both, but there is no doubt as to which side he is on. The mature dramatist who had as a boy witnessed in the Dublin slums various kinds of human misery extracted from that youthful hardship an unshakeable appreciation of human grit and gaiety, and a kind of fierce goodwill towards all creative power.

O'Casey is not a subtle thinker; his use of language often proves this; he cannot handle an argument like Shaw or achieve the pure lyricism of Synge; but he has the whole-hearted faith and the warm affections of an instinctive celebrant of life's irrepressible beauty and strength. He is a flawed, lovable writer whose heartening wish for humanity's welfare and happiness is more needed and pertinent today than it has ever been.

The Old Lady Says 'No!'

When Denis Johnston submitted his play, *Shadowdance*, to the Abbey Theatre, it was returned to the playwright with the words 'The Old Lady Says No' scribbled across the manuscript's front page. The 'old lady' in question was Lady Gregory; and her rejection provided Johnston with a new, and more striking, title for his play.

Johnston's readiness to change the scrawled rejection into the play's title gives us a good idea as to the actual nature of the play itself. One thing that the four plays we have already looked at have in common is that they each have a plot, a definite narrative line which leads with firm dramatic logic to a conclusion. In his delightful play, Denis Johnston seems more to anticipate Samuel Beckett than to echo Shaw, Synge, Yeats and O'Casey, although in fact *The Old Lady Says 'No!'* owes a lot to these writers in the sense that their achievements, readily acknowledged and applauded by Johnston, are also the objects of his considerable genius for parody and satire. A tradition begins to be mature when its masterpieces are mocked with sharp perception and critical affection; and while *The Old Lady Says 'No!'* is a distinguished addition to the Irish dramatic tradition it is also a tribute to the achievements of most of the writers it satirises. This play is written out of that restless and fertile frame of mind which rebels against what it most admires. It *is* a rebel's play — vivacious, experimental, satirical, mocking, consciously having a go at the sacred cows and the enthroned gods not only of the theatre but also of society and its institutions. It is one of those rare plays in which the spirit of fun and mischief is quite inseparable from the more serious satirical purposes and meth-

ods of the drama. *The Old Lady Says 'No!'* is quite zany at times, full
of moments of inspired nonsense and uproarious confusion; anything
can happen and there are moments when anything *does*; but all this is
not to obscure or deny the deep-lying seriousness of the play. I say
this despite Johnston's stated reservations concerning plays which are
'About' something:

> In English-speaking countries . . . the tradition of Pinero, Barker
> and Shaw, culminating in the 'Problem Play', is still well entrenched
> in the path of any further development of the theatre. We have the
> Play that leaves you with a Thought. What would I do if I met an
> Escaped Convict? How would I like it if Father married a Prostitute?
> Is War Right? I need hardly say that as a natural consequence
> nobody can go to an ostensibly serious play without feeling that he
> must concentrate upon what it is all About.
>
> But surely this is all wrong, just as it would be in the case of
> music! All that is needed to enjoy and appreciate a work, such as
> e.e. cummings' *Him*, is a simple faith, a little human experience,
> and a receptive state of mind attained by a process the reverse of
> concentration. This being the normal condition of my own mind I
> need hardly say that I find little difficulty in preferring Strindberg's
> *Dream Play*, to *Emperor and Galilean*.

For Johnston, it is only a short step from this to say that 'the real
play must be regarded as what goes on in the mind of the audience.
What, therefore, a play is about depends entirely on who is listening
to it.'

The audience is a vital aspect of the play itself, playing its part in
that atmosphere of animated experiment, ultimately controlled, which
enables weird and wonderful things, as well as cynical and sinister
things, to happen. Johnston has always stressed the importance of the
role played by the director in the play's success.

> It is, of course, a director's play written very much in the spirit of
> 'Let's see what would happen' if we did this or that. We were tired
> of the conventional three-act shape, of conversational dialogue, and
> of listening to the tendentious social sentiments of the stage of the

twenties, and we wanted to know whether the emotional appeal of music could be made use of in terms of theatrical prose, and an opera constructed that did not have to be sung. Could dialogue be used in lieu of some for the scenery, or as a shorthand form of character-delineation? Could the associations and thought-patterns already connected with the songs and slogans of our city be used deliberately to evoke a planned reaction from a known audience?

The 'city' referred to is, of course, Dublin. Johnston says 'This play, if plays must be about something, is about what Dublin has made a good many of us feel.'

In *The Old Lady Says 'No!'* the actor playing the part of Robert Emmet, a famous, romantic young patriot executed for his part in the rebellion in 1803, gets a blow on the head which leaves him concussed. This concussed actor/patriot, known as the Speaker, slipping from one identity to another with stunned and stunning unpredictability, fumbles and orates his way through the play, finding himself in all sorts of situations, quoting from poems and speeches. The Speaker is at once dazed and articulate, but always a determined, somewhat ludicrous Romantic seeking the love of his heart, one Sarah Curran of The Priory, Rathfarnham, a village outside Dublin.

Both Irish life and literature are myth-haunted. Shaw, Synge, Yeats and O'Casey acknowledge this fact, in different ways, in their plays. None of these writers, however, has the mischievous attitude to myth that Denis Johnston has. Johnston has a deeply ironic intelligence; and he is profoundly aware of the Irish tendency to mythologise the past, to glamourise its famous figures, to put patriots on pedestals. This is, of course, a human tendency and is not confined to Ireland. But Johnston believes that this tendency has a special power and prominence in Ireland; and he questions the effects and consequences of that tendency. His comments on one of Ireland's most Romantic patriots are ironic and, one feels, true:

So we all love Robert Emmet. Yeats and De Valera loved him, each in his own fashion. I do too; and so did Sarah Curran . . . We all agree that it was a pity that some of his supporters had to murder one of the most liberal judges on the bench, Lord Kilwarden, and that the only practical outcome of his affray was to confirm the Union with England for about a hundred and twenty years. Our affection is not affected by these details.

Johnston writes of his myth-riddled, myth-haunted city of Dublin with an irony at once blistering and affectionate. In doing so, he shows a deep, intimate knowledge of Ireland's literature, and he makes effective dramatic use of that knowledge. He writes:

The play with which the first part opens, and which crops up again at intervals, is almost entirely composed of well-known lines from Mangan, Moore, Callanan, Blacker, Griffin, Ferguson, Kickham, Todhunter and a dozen more. The voices of the Shadows are the easily recognisable words of some of Dublin's greatest contributors to the World's knowledge of itself. The long speech with which the play concludes contains suggestions from Emmet's speech from the dock, the resurrection thesis of the Litany, and the magnificent though sadly neglected Commination Service of the Anglican Church.

By what is literally a stroke of genius, Johnston treats his contributing audience to a most revealing view of Irish life, history and mythology as experienced and expressed by a concussed actor. So the play is not only a hilarious send-up of everything and everybody it encounters, it is also a satirical swipe at the theatre itself, at the very notion of theatrical illusion, the willing suspension of disbelief for which we pay our hard-earned cash to look at people pretending to be other people while we pretend to believe the entire illusory exercise. By setting aside 'the long predominance of narrative drama', by allowing the receptive audience to be active participants, by simultaneously undercutting and extending the peculiar nature of the theatrical illusion, Johnston enjoys all the advantages of an irreverent approach to drama. Does he also, one wonders, suffer from its disadvantages?

Is *The Old Lady Says 'No!'* an inbred play, demanding a prior knowledge of Irish life, literature, mythology and history? Is it provincial in its assumptions? Is it too 'literary'? Is it indulgently pedantic?

I cannot pretend to answer for others but while I would say that the knowledge mentioned above would be an asset to anybody viewing the play for the first time, I would add that the deeper life of the play lies in the marvellously daft ways in which the concussed speaker, dazed and drunk as history itself is when you try to grasp it in its bewildering complexity, meets and tries to cope with people and situations. This is the only comedy I know where the 'hero' is both semi-stunned and expressive. Whether he is talking with the Statue of Grattan or the old Flower Woman or conversing with Joe whom he has shot or making a singular mess of an encounter with two girls or simply trying to catch the bus to Rathfarnham, we find ourselves delighted by this dazed, glamorous, romantic figure. Concussed patriots are excellent company.

Satirical though much of the play is, it has a very touching, lyrical ending, a love-poem to the city of Dublin, city of Joyce, Shaw, Synge, Yeats, O'Casey and Behan. And, of course, of the bold Robert Emmet, the dazed darling of Erin!

SPEAKER:
>Strumpet city in the sunset
>Suckling the bastard brats of Scots,
>>of Englishry, of Hugenot.
>Brave sons breaking from the womb, wild
>>sons fleeing from their Mother.
>Wilful city of savage dreamers,
>So old, so sick with memories!
>Old Mother
>Some they say are damned,
>But you, I know, will walk the streets of Paradise
>Head high, and unashamed.

The Old Lady Says 'No!' is a proud, ironic, loving hymn to a city and its people; a rebellious, irreverent appraisal of the culture of that city and that people; a satirical stab at 'narrative' drama. But, it is also, in its own right, a most enjoyable, youthful play, packed with critical laughter and thoughtful comedy.

All That Fall

Among the reasons why Samuel Beckett is widely considered one of the most important writers of the twentieth century is the fact that his works give evidence of unusual courage and unusual comedy. Harold Pinter has noted Beckett's courage:

> The further he goes the more good it does me. I don't want philosophies, tracts, dogmas, creeds, way outs, truths, answers, *nothing from the bargain basement.* He is the most courageous, remorseless writer going and the more he grinds my nose in the shit the more I am grateful to him.

Beckett is sometimes referred to as a gloomy, even a despairing writer. He is not. He writes of gloom and despair but not in a despairing, gloomy way. He writes of pain, distress, suffering, hardship, various forms of affliction; and yet a sensitive person will come away with a profound sense of the value of human grit and endurance. Beckett was once asked by an American critic, Tom Driver, if his plays were concerned with those aspects of human experience with which religion is also involved. Beckett's reply was:

> Yes, for they deal with distress. Some people object to this in my writing. At a party an English intellectual – so-called – asked me why I write always about distress. As if it were perverse to do so! He wanted to know if my father had beaten me or my mother had run away from home to give me an unhappy childhood. I told him no, that I had had a very happy childhood. Then he thought me more perverse than ever. I left the party as soon as possible and got into a taxi. On the glass partition between me and the driver were three signs: one asked for help for the blind, another help for orphans, and the third for relief for the war refugees. One does not have to look for distress. It is screaming at you even in the taxis of London.

This is one of the most important things to grasp about Beckett. His entire being is saturated in a consciousness of human distress.

Waiting For Godot is the creation of a writer whose awareness of that distress in so many painful and bewildering ways is close to being Christ-like. A friend of mine who recently spent some time with Beckett said to me, 'The man is a saint'. I have never met Beckett but I know from his writing that he, of all the modern writers I know, has allowed into his being a truly shattering awareness of the agonies, disasters, tragedies and humiliations of the twentieth century. I would say to anybody approaching Beckett that he or she should sit in a darkened room, alone, for a considerable while and think about the many appalling horrors of our 'civilisation'. Then that person should ask himself or herself, 'which writer most truthfully reflects the reality of the world we and our ancestors have created?' Many people would, I believe, come up with the name of Samuel Beckett.

But it is never enough for a writer simply to be aware of horror and distress; he must create and communicate his vision of it. And he must do that in the way most appropriate to his genius. Beckett's way is comedy – but a very special kind of comedy, and *All That Fall* is a good example of Beckett's comedy of distress.

All That Fall was first written for radio, commissioned by the BBC and first broadcast in the Third Programme on 13 January 1957. The play is made of sounds, silences, words, pauses. Beckett is as much a poet of silence as he is of sound. Very few dramatists equal him in his cunning and effective uses of silence. Such uses of silence give an added intensity to the sounds of *All That Fall*. Primary among these sounds is that of shuffling human feet, shuffling onward, ever onward through wind and rain and all weathers. It is the sound of human pain and human endurance. But there are many other sounds; the sound of sheep, bird, cock, cow, music, cartwheels, trains, a man welting a horse, bicycle-bell, squeal of brakes, thunderous rattles of a motor-van, cooing of ringdoves, woman sobbing, bumping bicycle, wild laughter, panting, violent slapping, hard breathing, slamming doors, violent unintelligible muttering, motor starter, roaring engine, grinding gears, feet quickening receding ceasing, handkerchief loudly applied, hymn-humming, nose-blowing, guffaws stifled and unleashed, bells, whistles, hissing of steam and clashing of couplings, blind man's stick thumping ground, ejaculations, curses, braying of donkey, children's cries, and always the dragging steps of the blind couple, Mr and Mrs

Rooney trudging home from the station where Mrs Rooney has gone to meet her husband off the train.

The other major sound in this play is the sound of words, the sound of language. Mrs Rooney is dissatisfied with her language. She says to Christy the dung-carter:

> Do you find anything . . . bizarre about my way of speaking? (*Pause.*) I do not mean the voice. (*Pause.*) No, I mean the words. (*Pause. More to herself:*) I use none but the simplest words, I hope, and yet I sometimes find my way of speaking very . . . bizarre.

Shortly afterwards, Mrs Rooney says 'I am not half alive nor anything approaching it.'

Mrs Rooney's consciousness of her half-livingness extends to her uses of language. As so often in Beckett, *All That Fall* is riddled with the sense of deadness of language in people's mouths. It's as if Beckett were saying that a person *is* language; therefore, if a person suffers pain and depression, his language must suffer depression and pain also. This sense of language being afflicted, even crippled at times, is one of Beckett's chief obsessions.

The vitality of Beckett's language springs from his awareness of the ways in which language is brutalised, fatigued, corrupted and endlessly abused by most of us today. It's as though he were so aware of the appallingly normal *deadness* of language in our society that his imagination, in recording and exploring that deadness, discovered a paradoxical freshness, even beauty, in the battered carcase of language. Lilies sprout from the guts of corpses.

Sounds of affliction fill *All That Fall*; yet it is essentially a comic play. If people and language are afflicted or crippled, language and people are made to speak of that fact in a specially eloquent way. It is a stilted, arch eloquence, even ludicrously pedantic at times, rooted in desperation, unleashing a deep sense of frustration with a dogged, ironic fluency, refusing to give in to the sense of being battered, refusing to shrivel up and expire in the face of incessant insult and injury, refusing to die, refusing to live, just going on and on with an obstinacy laced with despair, with a persistence mingled with futility.

MRS ROONEY: I feel very cold and faint. The wind – (*whistling wind*) – is whistling through my summer frock as if I had nothing on over my bloomers. I have had no solid food since my elevenses.

MR ROONEY: You have ceased to care. I speak – and you listen to the wind.

MRS ROONEY: No no, I am agog, tell me all, then we shall press on and never pause, never pause, till we come home to haven.

Pause.

MR ROONEY: Never pause ... safe to haven ... Do you, know, Maddy, sometimes one would think you were struggling with a dead language.

MRS ROONEY: Yes indeed, Dan, I know full well what you mean, I often have that feeling, it is unspeakably excruciating.

MR ROONEY: I confess I have it sometimes myself, when I happen to overhear what I am saying.

MRS ROONEY: Well, you know, it will be dead in time, just like our own poor dear Gaelic, there is that to be said. (*Urgent baa.*)

MR ROONEY (*startled*): Good God!

MRS ROONEY: Oh the pretty little woolly lamb, crying to suck its mother! Theirs has not changed, since Arcady.

That is not, given Mr and Mrs Rooney's situation, realistic language; nor was it meant to be. Beckett's comedy far outstrips the aggressive grime and abundant blood of realism, and yet he makes hilarious and effective use of slapstick and music-hall antics. The feat of getting Mrs Rooney into the car, and then getting her out again, is a nice example of Beckett's love of rumpus.

The dark comic intricacies of *All That Fall* form the core of the drama. There is something sinister in it all, expecially towards the end. Mrs Rooney speaks of attending a lecture 'by one of these new mind doctors', hoping 'he might shed a little light on my lifelong preoccupation with horses' buttocks.' She speaks of 'the troubled mind' and 'mental distress'. The tone is bitingly light. Mr Rooney, a little earlier, had asked her:

Did you ever wish to kill a child?
(*Pause.*) Nip some young doom in the bud.

At the end of the play we learn that Mr Rooney's train was late because, as young Jerry tells Mrs Rooney, 'It was a little child fell out of the carriage, Ma'am. (*Pause.*) On to the line, Ma'am. (*Pause.*) Under the wheels, Ma'am.'

And that is it. No more words. No more explanation. Nothing but the *sound* of dragging steps as Mr and Mrs Rooney trudge homewards through a 'tempest of wind and rain'. Horrors of all kinds come and go but the old blind couple must try to drag on home together. We get a tempestuous elemental conclusion to a drama so deeply human it brings home to all of us a painful sense of the reality of our situations. *All That Fall* is a blistering revelation of human inadequacy in many forms; it also contains some dark suggestions about the nature of evil; but it is above all a comic hymn to human endurance in a savage, crass, battering world.

The Quare Fellow

It would be hard to imagine a more striking contrast than that between the austere, remote Samuel Beckett and the boisterous figure of Brendan Behan, poet, drinker, talker, hell-raiser and gifted if ultimately undisciplined playwright. Much of Behan's early life was spent in English and Irish jails. An active member of the IRA at one stage of his brief and turbulent life, he frequently fell foul of the law and because of his outrageous behaviour and quick wit appeared regularly in newspapers and on television. Born in 1923, he died forty-one years later in Dublin, a broken man, a total legend, a writer whose work is marked by honesty, humour, intelligence and compassion. *The Quare Fellow* is his best play.

When it was first produced in London in 1956 Kenneth Tynan wrote in the *Observer*:

The English hoard words like misers, the Irish spend them like sailors and in Brendan Behan's tremendous new play language is out on a spree, ribald, dauntless and spoiling for a fight. In a sense of course this is scarcely amazing. It is Ireland's sacred duty to send over every few years a playwright who will save the English theatre from inarticulate dumbness. And Irish dialogue almost invariably sparkles.

Tynan puts his finger on one of the most vital aspects of Behan's genius – his ability to write sparkling dialogue. And this sparkle is deeply comic, for the most part. As in Beckett, it is the nature of the comedy which, on reflection, strikes us as being appallingly, heart-breakingly funny.

A man is about to be hanged in a Dublin prison. Some other prisoners and a number of warders talk about that fact, among various other matters. There are tensions among both the prisoners and the warders. There is a visit from an official of the Department of Justice, named Holy Healey. The Chief Warder and Governor of the prison appear and contribute to the atmosphere. So do the hangman, slightly drunk, and his assistant, remarkably sober. The quare fellow is hanged amid a ferocious, howling hullaballoo.

The theme is grim. The treatment of the theme is, for the most part, humorous and humane. When Kenneth Tynan wrote that Behan could 'move wild laughter in the throat of death' he was pinpointing Behan's ability to extract the most energetic comedy from characters literally on the edge of the grave. During the entire second Act, prisoners hop in and out of the grave being dug for the quare fellow. The situation is bizarre; but the secret of Behan's comic genius is that all his characters behave with complete 'normality', doing on the edge of the grave, or even *in* it, what they would do in a pub if they were free in the city. They bet, boast, taunt, banter, smoke, are kind, cruel, lying, truthful. It is this air of unquestioned normality in a bizarre situation that seduces the audience to laugh at what, in their own concept of 'normal' circumstances, would horrify them. An important part of Behan's genius is his ability to turn the appalling into the hilarious without letting his audience forget how appalling the situation really is. However, with Behan, the more horrifying the situation the more comic the language. Far from creating confusion, this unlikely mixture drives home to the audience the horrors of hanging; and yet there's not a moment of obvious or aggressive propaganda in the play. Behan works through implication, suggestion, conversation and laugh-ter. But there is no doubting the humanity of his message. Hanging the quare fellow is merely murdering the murderer. And we, laughing our heads off, are all involved. Our sense of responsibility sharpens as our laughter deepens.

This play has a deep and abiding effect on readers and audiences. The dialogue and peculiar comic tone of the work are two important reasons. So is the characterisation. Each of the prisoners, though simply named A, B, C etc., comes vividly alive, particularly the pair known as Neighbour and Dunlavin. So do the warders, especially Regan who performs his duties scrupulously but whose mind and heart are steeped in that understanding and compassion which form one of the most attractive aspects of Behan's writing. Warder Regan has seen many hangings. He will be present too, along with a new young warder, Crimmin, at the hanging of the quare fellow. Many people, from the Chief to the most seasoned old prisoners, have a strange reliance on Warder Regan.

CHIEF: I don't know what we'd do without you, Regan, on these jobs. Is there anything the Governor or I could do to make things easier?

WARDER REGAN: You could say a decade of the rosary.

CHIEF: I could hardly ask the Governor to do that.

WARDER REGAN: His prayers would be as good as anyone else's.

CHIEF: Is there anything on the practical side we could send down?

WARDER REGAN: A bottle of malt.

CHIEF: Do you think he'd drink it?

WARDER REGAN: No, but I would.

CHIEF: Regan, I'm surprised at you.

WARDER REGAN: I was reared among people that drank at a death or prayed. Some did both. You think the law makes this man's death someway different, not like anyone else's. Your own, for instance.

CHIEF: I wasn't found guilty of murder.

WARDER REGAN: No, nor no one is going to jump on you in the morning and throttle the life out of you, but it's not him I'm thinking of. It's myself. And you're not going to give me that stuff about just shoving over the lever and bob's your uncle. You forget the times the fellow gets caught and has to be kicked off the edge of the trap hole. You never heard of the warders below swinging on his legs the better to break his neck, or jumping on his back when the drop was too short.

CHIEF: Mr Regan, I'm surprised at you.

WARDER REGAN: That's the second time to-night.

Tapping. Enter Crimmin.

CRIMMIN: All correct, sir.

CHIEF: Regan, I hope you'll forget these things you mentioned just now. If talk the like of that got outside the prison . . .

WARDER REGAN: (*almost shouts*): I think the whole show should be put on in Croke Park; after all, it's at the public expense and they let it go on. They should have something more for their money than a bit of paper stuck up on the gate.

CHIEF: Good night, Regan. If I didn't know you, I'd report what you said to the Governor.

WARDER REGAN: You will anyway.

CHIEF: Good night, Regan.

As well as the dialogue, comic tone and characterisation, there is another factor which plays an important part in creating the astonishing effect of this play. The character at the centre of all the talk and all the action, the quare fellow himself, never actually appears on stage. And yet his presence dominates this play just as comprehensively as Godot, who never makes an appearance in Beckett's drama, dominates the atmosphere of *Waiting for Godot*. Both these characters figure in the titles of these two plays; and though they are physically absent throughout, they are the most crucial figures in both works. Their very invisibility is the deepest source of their fascination for audiences. The quare fellow has committed a terrible crime; and the law is about to kill him in the name of the people. But he is nowhere to be seen, his voice cannot be heard. Who will speak for the quare fellow? Will anyone plead for the helpless, condemned man? Such are the thoughts born in the minds of the audience as they realise they will not see the man about to be hanged; they will only hear the other characters, unforgettably visible and audible, speak of the invisible victim.

This invisibility gives almost unbearable dramatic tension to the play. Details sustain this tension – details like the digging of the grave, the hangman's calculations about the height of the drop, the likely strength and thickness of the quare fellow's neck, his weight, 'twelve stone, fine pair of shoulders on him', the stratagems necessary to avoid telling him the time, the slitting of the hood, the holy oils used for anointing a Catholic, the procession to the place of execution, the Gaelic song the quare fellow asked for. All these details associated with the hanging of the invisible man are searingly present and memorable. They haunt the audience with a peculiar intensity, as does the entire play itself, as boisterous as it is compassionate.

This anthology begins and ends with plays by two remarkable humanists – Shaw and Behan. Ireland was and is a poorish country in economic terms, but it has produced writers who have made rich contributions to literature in the English language. Brendan Behan, like Sean O'Casey, knew all about poverty. Lacking O'Casey's discipline and self-restraint, Behan embraced life with ultimately self-destructive passion and gusto. Imprisoned for many years, he knew and cherished the value of every living moment. That sense of value throbs through every word of *The Quare Fellow*, one of the most moving of all Irish plays and a searching contribution to world drama.

                                                     Brendan Kennelly.

Selected Bibliography

BACKGROUND READING

Lady Augusta Gregory, *Our Irish Theatre*, Gerrards Cross, Colin Smythe, (1973)

Sean O'Casey, *Autobiographies*, London, Macmillan, (1963) – see particularly *Inishfallen Fare Thee Well*, London, Macmillan, (1949)

J. M. Synge *Collected Works*, II, *Prose*, London, Oxford University Press, (1966) – see especially *The Aran Islands* and *In Wicklow, West Kerry and Connemara*

W. B. Yeats, *Essays and Introductions*, London, Macmillan, (1961)

CRITICAL READING

Nicholas Grene, *Bernard Shaw: a Critical View*, London, Macmillan, (1984)

A. N. Jeffares and A. S. Knowland, *A Commentary on the Collected Plays of W. B. Yeats*, London, (1975)

Peter Ure, *Yeats the Playwright*, London, Routledge, (1963)

Daniel Corkery, *Synge and Anglo-Irish Literature*, London, (1931)

Nicholas Grene, *Synge: A Critical Study of the Plays*, London, (1975)

Declan Kiberd, *Synge and The Irish Language*, London, Macmillan, (1979)

James Simmons, *Sean O'Casey*, London, (1983)

David Krause, *Sean O'Casey: the Man and His Work*, London, McGibbon & Kee, (1960)

Joseph Ronsley (ed.), *Denis Johnston: a Retrospective*, Gerrards Cross, Colin Smythe, (1981)

Colbert Kearney, *The Writings of Brendan Behan*, Dublin, Gill & Macmillan, (1977)

Ulick O'Connor, *Brendan Behan*, London, Hamish Hamilton, (1970)

Hugh Kenner, *A Reader's Guide to Samuel Beckett*, London, Thames & Hudson, (1973)

Vivian Mercier, *Beckett - Beckett: the Truth of Contradictions*, New York, Oxford, University Press, (1977)

Philip Edwards, *Threshold of a Nation*, Cambridge, Cambridge University Press, (1983)

James Flannery, *W. B. Yeats and the Idea of a Theatre*, Toronto, Macmillan of Canada, (1976)

G. J. Watson, *Irish Identity and the Literary Revival*, London, (1979)

Katharine Worth, *The Irish Drama of Europe from Yeats to Beckett*, Atlantic Highlands, Humanities Press, (1978)

D. E. S. Maxwell, *A Critical History of Modern Irish Drama 1891–1980*, Cambridge, Cambridge University Press, (1984)

BERNARD SHAW

John Bull's Other Island

Bernard Shaw (1856–1950)

Bernard Shaw was born in Dublin in 1856. Essentially shy, he yet created the persona of G.B.S., the showman, satirist, controversialist, critic, pundit, wit, intellectual buffoon and dramatist. Commentators brought a new adjective into English: Shavian, a term used to embody all his brilliant qualities.

After his arrival in London in 1876 he became an active socialist and a brilliant platform speaker. He wrote on many social aspects of the day; on *Common Sense about the War* (1914), *How to Settle the Irish Question* (1917) and *The Intelligent Woman's Guide to Socialism and Capitalism* (1928). He undertook his own education at the British Museum and consequently became keenly interested in cultural subjects. His prolific output included music, art and theatre reviews, which were collected into several volumes, published as *Music in London 1890–1894* (3 vols., 1931); *Pen Portraits and Reviews* (1931); and *Our Theatres in the Nineties* (3 vols., 1931). Among his five novels, *Cashel Byron's Profession* and some shorter fiction including *The Black Girl in Search of God and Some Lesser Tales* are published by Penguin.

He conducted a strong attack on the London theatre and was closely associated with the intellectual revival of British theatre. His many plays fall into several categories: his 'Plays Unpleasant', 'Plays Pleasant', comedies, chronicle-plays, 'metabiological Pentateuch' (*Back to Methuselah*, a series of plays) and 'political extravagazas'. G.B.S. died in 1950.

John Bull's Other Island

On 12 March 1900, W. B. Yeats wrote to Lady Gregory: 'I saw Shaw to-day. He talks of a play on the contrast between Irish and English character which sounds amusing.' Yeats was keen to have a Shaw play put on at the Abbey Theatre, but *John Bull's Other Island* was first produced at the Royal Court Theatre, London, on 1 November 1904, with the following cast:

BROADBENT	Louis Calvert
LARRY DOYLE	F. L. Shine
TIM HAFFIGAN	Percival Stevens
HODSON	Nigel Playfair
PETER KEEGAN	Granville Barker
PATSY FARRELL	Graham Browne
FATHER DEMPSEY	Charles Daly
CORNEY DOYLE	F. Cremlin
BARNEY DORAN	Wilfred Shine
MATTHEW HAFFIGAN	A. E. George
AUNT JUDY	Agnes Thomas
NORA	Ellen O'Malley

John Bull's Other Island was produced at the Abbey theatre in 1916 and was an instant success with Dublin critics and audiences. Between 1917 and 1931 it was put on at the Abbey every year for at least a week at a time – a total of 135 performances. In 1969, Micheál MacLiammóir and Hilton Edwards produced it at the Gate Theatre, Dublin. The most recent performance in Dublin was during the Theatre Festival of 1987, at the Gaiety Theatre.

A Select Bibliography

Where no publisher is named, in the following list, the work was issued by Constable, Shaw's usual publisher during his lifetime. Place of publication is mentioned only when it was not London.

Before 1930, Shaw's plays appeared serially in small collections, or singly, in order of composition. These texts were reprinted, commonly in revised form, and others were added, in the main subsequent collections. Short titles, used for reference in other sections, are given first.

Principal Collected Editions (all vols. with authorial Prefaces): Limited edition, *Collected Works*, 30 vols. (1930–32) + 3 more (1934, 1938, 1938). Standard edition, *Collected Works*, 37 vols. (1931–50). Authorised edition, *Collected Plays and Their Prefaces*, 7 vols, The Bodley Head Shaw, Max Reinhardt, 1970–74. Editorial supervision by Dan H. Laurence. Previously unpublished texts in vol. 7. Ephemeral writings by Shaw, relating to specific plays, one included in all vols.

Paperback editions: All the plays have now been published in Penguin Books, Harmondsworth, 1946–1985, and are in print. A substantial number of the plays, including educational texts, has been published by Longman in paperback.

One-volume collection of plays (without Prefaces): *Complete Plays*, 1931. New Edition published by Hamlyn, 1960, repr. 1965. Enlarged in successive reprints up to 1950. Also issued by Odhams Press for readers of *The Daily Herald*, 1934. *Companion volume Prefaces*, 1934; enlarged, Odhams Press, 1938; *The Collected Screenplays*, ed. Bernard F. Dukore. George Prior, 1980.

Facsimile edition for scholars: Shaw: *Early Texts*, *Play Manuscripts in Facsimile*. New York: Garland Publishing, 1981. 12 vols., with individual editions under General Editorship of Dan H. Laurence.

John Bull's Other Island

Preface for Politicians

(written in 1906)

John Bull's Other Island was written in 1904 at the request of Mr William Butler Yeats, as a patriotic contribution to the repertory of the Irish Literary Theatre. Like most people who have asked me to write plays, Mr Yeats got rather more than he bargained for. The play was at that time beyond the resources of the new Abbey Theatre, which the Irish enterprise owed to the public spirit of Miss A. E. F. Horniman (an Englishwoman, of course), who, twelve years ago, played an important part in the history of the modern English stage as well as in my own personal destiny by providing the necessary capital for that memorable season at the Avenue Theatre which forced my Arms and The Man and Mr Yeats's Land of Heart's Desire on the recalcitrant London playgoer, and gave a third Irish playwright, Dr John Todhunter, an opportunity which the commercial theatres could not have afforded him.

There was another reason for changing the destination of John Bull's Other Island. It was uncongenial to the whole spirit of the neo-Gaelic movement, which is bent on creating a new Ireland after its own ideal, whereas my play is a very uncompromising presentment of the real old Ireland. The next thing that happened was the production of the play in London at the Court Theatre by Messrs Vedrenne and Barker, and its immediate and enormous popularity with delighted and flattered English audiences. This constituted it a successful commercial play, and made it unnecessary to resort to the special machinery or tax the special resources of the Irish Literary Theatre for its production.

HOW TOM BROADBENT TOOK IT

Now I have a good deal more to say about the relations between the Irish and the English than will be found in my play. Writing the play for an Irish audience, I thought it would be good for them to be shewn very clearly that the loudest laugh they could raise at the expense of the absurdest Englishman was not really a laugh on their side; that he would succeed where they would fail; that he could inspire strong affection and loyalty in an Irishman who knew the world and was moved only to dislike, mistrust, impatience and even exasperation by his own countrymen; that his power of taking himself seriously, and his insensibility to anything funny in danger and destruction, was the first condition of economy and concentration of force, sustained purpose, and rational conduct. But the need for this lesson in Ireland is the measure of its demoralizing superfluousness in England. English audiences very naturally swallowed it eagerly and smacked their lips over it, laughing all the more heartily because they felt that they were taking a caricature of themselves with the most tolerant and large-minded goodhumor. They were perfectly willing to allow me to represent Tom Broadbent as infatuated in politics, hypnotized by his newspaper leader-writers and parliamentary orators into an utter paralysis of his common sense, without moral delicacy or social tact, provided I made him cheerful, robust, goodnatured, free from envy, and above all, a successful muddler-through in business and love. Not only did no English critic allow that the success in business of Messrs English Broadbent and Irish Doyle might possibly have been due to some extent to Doyle, but one writer actually dwelt with much feeling on the pathos of Doyle's failure as an engineer (a circumstance not mentioned nor suggested in my play) in contrast with Broadbent's solid success. No doubt, when the play is performed in Ireland, the Dublin critics will regard it as self-evident that without Doyle Broadbent would have become bankrupt in six months. I should say, myself, that the combination was probably much more effective than either of the partners would have been alone. I am persuaded further – without pretending to know more about it than anyone else – that Broadbent's special contribution was simply the strength, self-satisfaction, social confidence and cheerful bumptiousness that money, comfort, and good feeding bring to all healthy people; and that Doyle's special contribution was the freedom from illusion, the power of facing facts, the nervous industry, the sharpened wits, the sensitive pride of the imaginative man who has fought his way up through social persecution and poverty. I do not say that the confidence of the Englishman in Broadbent is not for the moment justified. The virtues of the English soil are not less real because they consist of coal and iron, not of metaphysical sources of character. The virtues of Broadbent are not less real because they are the virtues of the money that coal and iron have produced. But as the mineral virtues are being discovered and developed in other soils, their derivative virtues are appearing so rapidly in other nations that Broadbent's relative advantage is vanishing. In truth I am afraid (the misgiving is natural to a by-this-time slightly elderly playwright) that Broadbent is out of date. The successful Englishman of today, when he is not a transplanted Scotchman or Irishman, often turns out on investigation to be, if not an American, an Italian, or a Jew, at least to be depending on the brains, the nervous energy, and the freedom from romantic illusions (often called cynicism) of such foreigners for the management of his sources of income. At all events I am persuaded that a modern nation that is satisfied with Broadbent is in a dream. Much as I like him, I object to be governed by him, or entangled in his political destiny. I therefore propose to give him a piece of my mind here, as an Irishman, full of an instinctive pity for those of my fellow-creatures who are only English.

WHAT IS AN IRISHMAN?

When I say that I am an Irishman I mean that I was born in Ireland, and that my native language is the English of Swift and not the unspeakable jargon of the mid-XIX century London newspapers. My extraction is the extraction of most Englishmen: that is, I have no trace in me of the commercially imported North Spanish strain which passes for aboriginal Irish: I am a genuine typical Irishman of the Danish, Norman, Cromwellian, and (of course) Scotch invasions. I am violently and arrogantly Protestant by family tradition; but let no English Government therefore count on my allegiance: I am English enough to be an inveterate Republican and Home Ruler. It is true that one of my grandfathers was an Orangeman; but then his sister was an abbess; and his uncle, I am proud to say, was hanged as a rebel. When I look round me on the hybrid cosmopolitans, slum poisoned or square pampered, who call themselves Englishmen today, and see them bullied by the Irish Protestant garrison as no Bengalee now lets himself be bullied by an Englishman; when I see the Irishman everywhere standing clearheaded, sane, hardily callous to the boyish sentimentalities, susceptibilities, and credulities that make the Englishman the dupe of every charlatan and the idolater of every numskull, I perceive that Ireland is the only spot on earth which still produces the ideal Englishman of history. Blackguard, bully, drunkard, liar, foulmouth, flatterer, beggar, backbiter, venal functionary, corrupt judge, envious friend, vindictive opponent, unparalleled political traitor: all these your Irishman may easily be, just as he may be a gentleman (a species extinct in England, and nobody a penny the worse); but he is never quite the hysterical, nonsense-crammed, fact-proof, truth-terrified, un-ballasted sport of all the bogey panics and all the silly enthusiasms that now calls itself 'God's Englishman'. England cannot do without its Irish and its Scots today, because it cannot do without at least a little sanity.

THE PROTESTANT GARRISON

The more Protestant an Irishman is – the more English he is, if it flatters you to have it put that way, the more intolerable he finds it to be ruled by English instead of Irish folly. A 'loyal' Irishman is an abhorrent phenomenon, because it is an unnatural one. No doubt English rule is vigorously exploited in the interests of the property, power, and promo-tion of the Irish classes as against the Irish masses. Our delicacy is part of a keen sense of reality which makes us a very practical, and even, on occasion, a very coarse people. The Irish soldier takes the King's shilling and drinks the King's health; and the Irish squire takes the title deeds of the English settlement and rises uncovered to the strains of the English national anthem. But do not mistake this cupboard loyalty for anything deeper. It gains a broad base from the normal attachment of every reasonable man to the established government as long as it is bearable; for we all, after a certain age, prefer peace to revolution and order to chaos, other things being equal. Such considerations produce loyal Irishmen as they produce loyal Poles and Fins, loyal Hindoos, loyal Filipinos, and faithful slaves. But there is nothing more in it than that. If there is an entire lack of gall in the feeling of the Irish gentry towards the English, it is because the Englishman is always gaping admiringly at the Irishman as at some clever child prodigy. He overrates him with a generosity born of a traditional conviction of his own superiority in the deeper aspects of human character. As the Irish gentleman, tracing his pedigree to the conquest or one of the invasions, is equally convinced that if this superiority really exists, he is the genuine true blue heir to it, and as he is easily able to hold his own in all the superficial social accomplishments, he finds English society agreeable, and English houses very comfortable, Irish establishments being generally straitened by an attempt to keep a park and a stable on an income which would not justify an Englishman in venturing upon a wholly detached villa.

OUR TEMPERAMENTS CONTRASTED

But however pleasant the relations between the Protestant garrison and the English gentry may be, they are always essentially of the nature of an *entente cordiale* between foreigners. Personally I like Englishmen much better than Irishmen (no doubt because they make more of me) just as many Englishmen like Frenchmen better than Englishmen, and never go on board a Peninsular and Oriental steamer when one of the ships of the Messageries Maritimes is available. But I never think of an Englishman as my countryman. I should as soon think of applying that term to a German. And the Englishman has the same feeling. When a Frenchman fails to make the distinction, we both feel a certain disparagement involved in the misapprehension. Macaulay, seeing that the Irish had in Swift an author worth stealing, tried to annex him by contending that he must be classed as an Englishman because he was not an aboriginal Celt. He might as well have refused the name of Briton to Addison because he did not stain himself blue and attach scythes to the poles of his sedan chair. In spite of all such trifling with facts, the actual distinction between the idolatrous Englishman and the fact-facing Irishman, of the same extraction though they be, remains to explode those two hollowest of fictions, the Irish and English 'races'. There is no Irish race any more than there is an English race or a Yankee race. There *is* an Irish climate, which will stamp an immigrant more deeply and durably in two years, apparently, than the English climate will in two hundred. It is reinforced by an artificial economic climate which does some of the work attributed to the natural geographic one; but the geographic climate is eternal and irresistible, making a mankind and a womankind that Kent, Middlesex, and East Anglia cannot produce and do not want to imitate.

How can I sketch the broad lines of the contrast as they strike me? Roughly I should say that the Englishman is wholly at the mercy of his imagination, having no sense of reality to check it. The Irishman, with a ´r subtler and more fastidious imagination, has one eye always on things as they are. If you compare Moore's visionary Minstrel Boy with Mr Rudyard Kipling's quasi-realistic Soldiers Three, you may yawn over Moore or gush over him, but you will not suspect him of having had any illusions about the contemporary British private; whilst as to Mr Kipling, you will see that he has not, and unless he settles in Ireland for a few years will always remain constitutionally and congenitally incapable of having, the faintest inkling of the reality which he idolizes as Tommy Atkins. Perhaps you have never thought of illustrating the contrast between English and Irish by Moore and Mr Kipling, or even by Parnell and Gladstone. Sir Boyle Roche and Shakespear may seem more to your point. Let me find you a more dramatic instance. Think of the famous meeting between the Duke of Wellington, that intensely Irish Irishman, and Nelson, that intensely English Englishman. Wellington's contemptuous disgust at Nelson's theatricality as a professed hero, patriot, and rhapsode, a theatricality which in an Irishman would have been an insufferably vulgar affectation, was quite natural and inevitable. Wellington's formula for that kind of thing was a well-known Irish one: 'Sir: dont be a damned fool.' It is the formula of all Irishmen for all Englishmen to this day. It is the formula of Larry Doyle for Tom Broadbent in my play, in spite of Doyle's affection for Tom. Nelson's genius, instead of producing intellectual keenness and scrupulousness, produced mere delirium. He was drunk with glory, exalted by his fervent faith in the sound British patriotism of the Almighty, nerved by the vulgarest anti-foreign prejudice, and apparently unchastened by any reflections on the fact that he had never had to fight a technically capable and properly equipped enemy except on land, where he had never been successful. Compare Wellington, who had to fight Napoleon's armies, Napoleon's marshals, and finally Napoleon himself, without one moment of illusion as to the human material he had to command, without one gush of the 'Kiss me, Hardy' emotion which enabled Nelson to idolize his crews and his staff, without forgetting even in his dreams that the normal British officer of that time was an incapable amateur (as he still is) and the normal British soldier a never-do-well (he is now a depressed and respectable young man). No wonder Wellington became an accomplished comedian in the art of anticlimax, scandalizing the unfortunate Croker, responding to the demand for glorious sentiments by the most disenchanting touches of realism, and, generally, pricking the English windbag at its most explosive crises of distention. Nelson, intensely nervous and theatrical, made an enormous fuss about victories so cheap that he would have deserved shooting if he had lost them, and, not content with lavishing splendid fighting on helpless adversaries like the heroic De Brueys or Villeneuve (who had not even the illusion of heroism when he went like a lamb to the slaughter), got himself killed by his passion for exposing himself to death in that sublime defiance of it which was perhaps the supreme tribute of the exquisite coward to the King of Terrors (for, believe me, you cannot be a hero without being a coward: supersense cuts both ways), the result being a tremendous effect on the gallery. Wellington, most capable of captains, was neither a hero nor a patriot: perhaps not even a coward; and had it not been for the Nelsonic anecdotes invented for him – 'Up guards, and at em' and so forth – and the fact that the antagonist with whom he finally closed was such a master of theatrical effect that Wellington could not fight him without getting into his limelight, nor overthrow him (most unfortunately for us all) without drawing the eyes of the whole world to the catastrophe, the Iron Duke would have been almost forgotten by this time. Now that contrast is English against Irish all over, and is the more delicious because the real Irishman in it is the Englishman of tradition, whilst the real Englishman is the traditional theatrical foreigner.

The value of the illustration lies in the fact that Nelson and Wellington were both in the highest degree efficient, and both in the highest degree incompatible with one another on any other footing than one of independence. The government of Nelson by Wellington or of Wellington by Nelson is felt at once to be a dishonorable outrage to the governed and a finally impossible task for the governor.

I daresay some Englishman will now try to steal Wellington as Macaulay tried to steal Swift. And he may plead with some truth that though it seems impossible that any other country than England could produce a hero so utterly devoid of common sense, intellectual delicacy, and international chivalry as Nelson, it may be contended that Wellington was rather an eighteenth century aristocratic type, than a specifically Irish type. George IV and Byron, contrasted with Gladstone, seem Irish in respect of a certain humorous blackguardism, and a power of appreciating art and sentiment without being duped by them into mistaking romantic figments for realities. But faithlessness and the need for carrying off the worthlessness and impotence that accompany it, produce in all nations a gay, sceptical, amusing, blaspheming, witty fashion which suits the flexibility of the Irish mind very well; and the contrast between this fashion and the energetic infatuations that have enabled intellectually ridiculous men, without wit or humor, to go on crusades and make successful revolutions, must not be confused with the contrast between the English and Irish idiosyncrasies. The Irishman makes a distinction which the Englishman is too lazy intellectually (the intellectual laziness and slovenliness of the English is almost beyond belief) to make. The Englishman, impressed with the dissoluteness of the faithless wits of the Restoration and the Regency, and with the victories of the wilful zealots of the patriotic, religious, and revolutionary wars, jumps to the conclusion that wilfulness is the main thing. In this he is right. But he overdoes his jump so far as to conclude also that stupidity and wrong-headedness are better guarantees of efficiency and trustworthiness than intellectual vivacity, which he mistrusts as a common symptom of worthlessness, vice, and instability. Now in this he is most dangerously wrong. Whether the Irishman grasps the truth as firmly as the Englishman may be open to question; but he is certainly comparatively free from the error. That affectionate and admiring love of sentimental stupidity for its own sake, both in men and women, which shines so steadily through the novels of Thackeray would hardly be possible in the works of an Irish novelist. Even Dickens, though too vital a genius and too severely educated in the school of shabby-genteel poverty to have any doubt of the national danger of fatheadedness in high places, evidently assumes rather too hastily the superiority of Mr Meagles to Sir John Chester and Harold Skimpole. On the other hand, it takes an Irishman years of residence in England to learn to respect and like a blockhead. An Englishman will not respect nor like anyone else. Every English statesman has to maintain his popularity by pretending to be ruder, more ignorant, more sentimental, more super-stitious, more stupid than any man who has lived behind the scenes of public life for ten minutes can possibly be. Nobody dares to publish really intimate memoirs of him or really private letters of his until his whole generation has passed away, and his party can no longer be compromised by the discovery that the platitudinizing twaddler and hypocritical opportunist was really a man of some perception as well as of strong constitution, pegaway industry, personal ambition, and party keenness.

ENGLISH STUPIDITY EXCUSED

I do not claim it as a natural superiority in the Irish nation that it dislikes and mistrusts fools, and expects its political leaders to be clever and humbug-proof. It may be that if our resources included the armed force and virtually unlimited money which push the political and military figureheads of England through bungled enterprises to a muddled success, and create an illusion of some miraculous and divine innate English quality that enables a general to become a conqueror with abilities that would not suffice to save a cabman from having his license marked, and a member of parliament to become Prime Minister with the outlook on life of a sporting country solicitor educated by a private governess, we should lapse into gross intellectual sottishness, and prefer leaders who encouraged our vulgarities by sharing them, and flattered us by associating them with purchased successes, to our betters. But as it is, we cannot afford that sort of encouragement and flattery in Ireland. The odds against which our leaders have to fight would be too heavy for the fourth-rate Englishmen whose leadership consists for the most part in marking time ostentatiously until they are violently shoved, and then stumbling blindly forward (or backward) wherever the shove sends them. We cannot crush England as a Pickford's van might crush a perambulator. We are the perambulator and England the Pickford. We must study her and our real weaknesses and real strength; we must practise upon her slow conscience and her quick terrors; we must deal in ideas and political principles since we cannot deal in bayonets; we must outwit, outwork, outstay her; we must embarrass, bully, even conspire and assassinate when nothing else will move her, if we are not all to be driven deeper and deeper into the shame and misery of our servitude. Our leaders must be not only determined enough, but clever enough to do this. We have no illusions as to the existence of any mysterious Irish pluck, Irish honesty, Irish bias on the part of Providence, or sterling Irish solidity of character, that will enable an Irish blockhead to hold his own against England. Blockheads are of no use to us: we were compelled to follow a supercilious, unpopular, tongue-tied, aristocratic Protestant Parnell, although there was no lack among us of fluent imbeciles, with majestic presences and oceans of dignity and sentiment, to promote into his place could they have done his work for us. It is obviously convenient that Mr Redmond should be a better speaker and rhetorician than Parnell; but if he began to use his powers to make himself agreeable instead of making himself reckoned with by the enemy; if he set to work to manufacture and support English shams and hypocrisies instead of exposing and denouncing them; if he constituted himself the permanent apologist of doing nothing, and, when the people insisted on his doing something, only roused himself to discover how to pretend to do it without really changing anything, he would lose his leadership as certainly as an English politician would, by the same course, attain a permanent place on the front bench. In short, our circumstances place a premium on political ability whilst the circumstances of England discount it; and the quality of the supply naturally follows the demand. If you miss in my writings that hero-worship of dotards and duffers which is planting England with statues of disastrous statesmen and absurd generals, the explanation is simply that I am an Irishman and you an Englishman.

IRISH PROTESTANTISM REALLY PROTESTANT

When I repeat that I am an Irish Protestant, I come to a part of the relation between England and Ireland that you will never understand unless I insist on explaining it to you with that Irish insistence on intellectual clarity to which my English critics are so intensely recalcitrant.

First, let me tell you that in Ireland Protestantism is really Protestant. It is true that there is an Irish Protestant Church (disestablished some 35 years ago) in spite of the fact that a Protestant Church is, fundamentally, a contradiction in terms. But this means only that the Protestants use the word Church to denote their secular organization, without troubling themselves about the metaphysical sense of Christ's famous pun, 'Upon this rock I will build my church.' The Church of England, which is a reformed Anglican Catholic Anti-Protestant Church, is quite another affair. An Anglican is acutely conscious that he is not a Wesleyan; and many Anglican clergymen do not hesitate to teach that all Methodists incur damnation. In Ireland all that the member of the Irish Protestant Church knows is that he is not a Roman Catholic. The decorations of even the 'lowest' English Church seem to him to be extravagantly Ritualistic and Popish. I myself entered the Irish Church by baptism, a ceremony performed by my uncle in 'his own church'. But I was sent, with many boys of my own denomination, to a Wesleyan school where the Wesleyan catechism was taught without the least protest on the part of the parents, although there was so little presumption in favor of any boy there being a Wesleyan that if all the Church boys had been withdrawn at any moment, the school would have become bankrupt. And this was by no means analogous to the case of those working class members of the Church of England in London, who send their daughters to Roman Catholic schools rather than to the public elementary schools. They do so for the definite reason that the nuns teach girls good manners and sweetness of speech, which have no place in the County Council curriculum. But in Ireland the Church parent sends his son to a Wesleyan school (if it is convenient and socially eligible) because he is indifferent to the form of Protestantism provided it is Protestantism. There is also in Ireland a characteristically Protestant refusal to take ceremonies and even sacraments very seriously except by way of strenuous objection to them when they are conducted with candles or incense. For example, I was never confirmed, although the ceremony was specially needed in my case as the failure of my appointed godfather to appear at my baptism had led to his responsibilities being assumed on the spot, at my uncle's order, by the sexton. And my case was a very common one, even among people quite untouched by modern scepticisms. Apart from the weekly churchgoing, which holds its own as a respectable habit, the initiations are perfunctory, the omissions regarded as negligible. The distinction between churchman and dissenter, which in England is a class distinction, a political distinction, and even occasionally a religious distinction, does not exist. Nobody is surprised in Ireland to find that the squire who is the local pillar of the formerly established Church is also a Plymouth Brother, and, except on certain special or fashionable occasions, attends the Methodist meeting-house. The parson has no priestly character and no priestly influence: the High Church curate of course exists and has his vogue among religious epicures of the other sex; but the general attitude of his congregation towards him is that of Dr Clifford. The clause in the Apostles' creed professing belief in a Catholic Church is a standing puzzle to Protestant children; and when they grow up they dismiss it from their minds more often than they solve it, because they really are not Catholics but Protestants to the extremest practicable degree of individualism. It is true that they talk of church and chapel with all the Anglican contempt for chapel; but in Ireland the chapel means the Roman Catholic church, for which the Irish Protestant reserves all the class rancor, the political hostility, the religious bigotry, and the bad blood generally that in England separates the Establishment from the non-conforming Protestant organizations. When a vulgar Irish Protestant speaks of a 'Papist' he feels exactly as a vulgar Anglican vicar does when he speaks of a Dissenter. And when the vicar is Anglican enough to call himself a Catholic priest, wear a cassock, and bless his flock with two fingers, he becomes horrifically incomprehensible to the Irish Protestant Churchman, who, on his part, puzzles the Anglican by regarding a Methodist as tolerantly as an Irishman who likes grog regards an Irishman who prefers punch.

A FUNDAMENTAL ANOMALY

Now nothing can be more anomalous, and at bottom impossible, than a Conservative Protestant party standing for the established order against a revolutionary Catholic party. The Protestant is theoretically an anarchist as far as anarchism is practicable in human society: that is, he is an individualist, a freethinker, a self-helper, a Whig, a Liberal, a mistruster and vilifier of the State, a rebel. The Catholic is theoretically a Collectivist, a self-abnegator, a Tory, a Conservative, a supporter of Church and State one and undivisible, an obeyer. This would be a statement of fact as well as of theory if men were Protestants and Catholics by temperament and adult choice instead of by family tradition. The peasant who supposed that Wordsworth's son would carry on the business now the old gentleman was gone was not a whit more foolish than we who laugh at his ignorance of the nature of poetry whilst we take it as a matter of course that a son should 'carry on' his father's religion. Hence, owing to our family system, the Catholic Churches are recruited daily at the font by temperamental Protestants, and the Protestant organizations by temperamental Catholics, with consequences most disconcerting to those who expect history to be deducible from the religious professions of the men who make it.

Still, though the Roman Catholic Church may occasionally catch such Tartars as Luther and Voltaire, or the Protestant organizations as Newman and Manning, the general run of mankind takes its impress from the atmosphere in which it is brought up. In Ireland the Roman Catholic peasant cannot escape the religious atmosphere of his Church. Except when he breaks out like a naughty child he is docile; he is reverent; he is content to regard knowledge as something not his business; he is a child before his Church, and accepts it as the highest authority in science and philosophy. He speaks of himself as a son of the Church, calling his priest father instead of brother or Mister. To rebel politically, he must break away from tutelage and follow a Protestant leader on national questions. His Church naturally fosters his submissiveness. The British Government and the Vatican may differ very vehemently as to whose subject the Irishman is to be; but they are quite agreed as to the propriety of his being a subject. Of the two, the British Government allows him more liberty, giving him as complete a democratic control of local government as his means will enable him to use, and a voice in the election of a formidable minority in the House of Commons, besides allowing him to read and learn what he likes – except when it makes a tufthunting onslaught on a seditious newspaper. But if he dared to claim a voice in the selection of his parish priest, or a representative at the Vatican, he would be denounced from the altar as an almost inconceivable blasphemer; and his educational opportunities are so restricted by his Church that he is heavily handicapped in every walk of life that requires any literacy. It is the aim of his priest to make him and keep him a submissive Conservative; and nothing but gross economic oppression and religious persecution could have produced the strange phenomenon of a revolutionary movement not only tolerated by the Clericals, but, up to a certain point, even encouraged by them. If there is such a thing as political science, with natural laws like any other science, it is certain that only the most violent external force could effect and maintain this unnatural combination of political revolution with Papal reaction, and of hardy individualism and independence with despotism and subjugation.

That violent external force is the clumsy thumb of English rule. If you would be good enough, ladies and gentlemen of England, to take your thumb away and leave us free to do something else than bite it, the unnaturally combined elements in Irish politics would fly asunder and recombine according to their proper nature with results entirely satisfactory to real Protestantism.

THE NATURE OF POLITICAL HATRED

Just reconsider the Home Rule question in the light of that very English characteristic of the Irish people, their political hatred of priests. Do not be distracted by the shriek of indignant denial from the Catholic papers and from those who have witnessed the charming relations between the Irish peasantry and their spiritual fathers. I am perfectly aware that the Irish love their priests as devotedly as the French loved them before the Revolution or as the Italians loved them before they imprisoned the Pope in the Vatican. They love their landlords too: many an Irish gentleman has found in his nurse a foster-mother more interested in him than his actual mother. They love the English, as every Englishman who travels in Ireland can testify. Please do not suppose that I speak satirically: the world is full of authentic examples of the concurrence of human kindliness with political rancor. Slaves and schoolboys often love their masters; Napoleon and his soldiers made desperate efforts to save from drowning the Russian soldiers under whom they had broken the ice with their cannon; even the relations between nonconformist peasants and country parsons in England are not invariably unkindly; in the southern States of America planters are often traditionally fond of negroes and kind to them, with substantial returns in humble affection; soldiers and sailors often admire and cheer their officers sincerely and heartily; nowhere is actual personal intercourse found compatible for long with the intolerable friction of hatred and malice. But people who persist in pleading these amiabilities as political factors must be summarily bundled out of the room when questions of State are to be discussed. Just as an Irishman may have English friends whom he may prefer to any Irishman of his acquaintance, and be kind, hospitable, and serviceable in his intercourse with Englishmen, whilst being perfectly prepared to make the Shannon run red with English blood if Irish freedom could be obtained at that price; so an Irish Catholic may like his priest as a man and revere him as a confessor and spiritual pastor whilst being implacably determined to seize the first opportunity of throwing off his yoke. This is political hatred: the only hatred that civilization allows to be mortal hatred.

THE REVOLT AGAINST THE PRIEST

Realize, then, that the popular party in Ireland is seething with rebellion against the tyranny of the Church. Imagine the feelings of an English farmer if the parson refused to marry him for less than £20, and if he had virtually no other way of getting married! Imagine the Church Rates revived in the form of an unofficial Income Tax scientifically adjusted to your taxable capacity by an intimate knowledge of your affairs verified in the confessional! Imagine being one of a peasantry reputed the poorest in the world, under the thumb of a priesthood reputed the richest in the world! Imagine a Catholic middle class continually defeated in the struggle of professional, official, and fashionable life by the superior education of its Protestant competitors, and yet forbidden by its priests to resort to the only efficient universities in the country! Imagine trying to get a modern education in a seminary of priests, where every modern book worth reading is on the index, and the earth is still regarded, not perhaps as absolutely flat, yet as being far from so spherical as Protestants allege! Imagine being forbidden to read this preface because it proclaims your own grievance! And imagine being bound to submit to all this because the popular side must hold together at all costs in the face of the Protestant enemy! That is, roughly, the predicament of Roman Catholic Ireland.

PROTESTANT LOYALTY: A FORECAST

Now let us have a look at Protestant Ireland. I have already said that a 'loyal' Irishman is an abhorrent phenomenon, because he is an unnatural one. In Ireland it is not 'loyalty' to drink the English king's health and stand uncovered to the English national anthem: it is simply exploitation of English rule in the interests of the property, power, and promotion of the Irish classes as against the Irish masses. From any other point of view it is cowardice and dishonor. I have known a Protestant go to Dublin Castle to be sworn in as a special constable, quite resolved to take the baton and break the heads of a patriotic faction just then upsetting the peace of the town, yet back out at the last moment because he could not bring himself to swallow the oath of allegiance tendered with the baton. There is no such thing as genuine loyalty in Ireland. There is a separation of the Irish people into two hostile camps: one Protestant, gentlemanly, and oligarchical: the other Roman Catholic, popular, and democratic. The oligarchy governs Ireland as a bureaucracy deriving authority from the king of England. It cannot cast him off without casting off its own ascendancy. Therefore it naturally exploits him sedulously, drinking his health, waving his flag, playing his anthem, and using the foolish word 'traitor' freely in its cups. But let the English Government make a step towards the democratic party, and the Protestant garrison revolts at once, not with tears and prayers and anguish of soul and years of trembling reluctance, as the parliamentarians of the XVII century revolted against Charles I, but with acrid promptitude and strident threatenings. When England finally abandons the garrison by yielding to the demand for Home Rule, the Protestants will not go under, nor will they waste much time in sulking over their betrayal, and comparing their fate with that of Gordon left by Gladstone to perish on the spears of heathen fanatics. They cannot afford to retire into an Irish Faubourg St Germain. They will take an energetic part in the national government, which will be sorely in need of parliamentary and official forces independent of Rome. They will get not only the Protestant votes, but the votes of Catholics in that spirit of toleration which is everywhere extended to heresies that happen to be politically serviceable to the orthodox. They will not relax their determination to hold every inch of the government of Ireland that they can grasp; but as that government will then be a national Irish government instead of as now an English government, their determination will make them the vanguard of Irish Nationalism and Democracy as against Romanism and Sacerdotalism, leaving English Unionists grieved and shocked at their discovery of the true value of an Irish Protestant's loyalty.

But there will be no open break in the tradition of the party. The Protestants will still be the party of Union, which will then mean, not the repeal of Home Rule, but the maintenance of the Federal Union of English-speaking commonwealths, now theatrically called the Empire. They will pull down the Union Jack without the smallest scruple; but they know the value of the Channel Fleet, and will cling closer than brothers to that and any other Imperial asset that can be exploited for the protection of Ireland against foreign aggression or the sharing of expenses with the British taxpayer. They know that the Irish coast is for the English invasion-scaremonger the heel of Achilles, and that they can use this to make him pay for the boot.

PROTESTANT PUGNACITY

If any Englishman feels incredulous as to this view of Protestantism as an essentially Nationalist force in Ireland, let him ask himself which leader he, if he were an Irishman, would rather have back from the grave to fight England: the Catholic Daniel O'Connell or the Protestant Parnell. O'Connell organized the Nationalist movement only to draw its teeth, to break its determination, and to declare that Repeal of the Union was not worth the shedding of a drop of blood. He died in the bosom of his Church, not in the bosom of his country. The Protestant leaders, from Lord Edward Fitzgerald to Parnell, have never divided their devotion. If any Englishman thinks that they would have been more sparing of blood than the English themselves are, if only so cheap a fluid could have purchased the honor of Ireland, he greatly mistakes the Irish Protestant temper. The notion that Ireland is the only country in the world not worth shedding a drop of blood for is not a Protestant one, and certainly not countenanced by English practice. It was hardly reasonable to ask Parnell to shed blood *quant. suff.* in Egypt to put an end to the misgovernment of the Khedive and replace him by Lord Cromer for the sake of the English bondholders, and then to expect him to become a Tolstoyan or an O'Connellite in regard to his own country. With a wholly Protestant Ireland at his back he might have bullied England into conceding Home Rule; for the insensibility of the English governing classes to philosophical, moral, social considerations – in short, to any considerations which require a little intellectual exertion and sympathetic alertness – is tempered, as we Irish well know, by an absurd susceptibility to intimidation.

For let me halt a moment here to impress on you, O English reader, that no fact has been more deeply stamped into us than that we can do nothing with an English Government unless we frighten it, any more than you can yourself. When power and riches are thrown haphazard into children's cradles as they are in England, you get a governing class without industry, character, courage, or real experience; and under such circumstances reforms are produced only by catastrophes followed by panics in which 'something must be done'. Thus it costs a cholera epidemic to achieve a Public Health Act, a Crimean War to reform the Civil Service, and a gunpowder plot to disestablish the Irish Church. It was by the light, not of reason, but of the moon, that the need for paying serious attention to the Irish land question was seen in England. It cost the American War of Independence and the Irish Volunteer movement to obtain the Irish parliament of 1782, the constitution of which far overshot the nationalist mark of today in the matter of independence.

It is vain to plead that this is human nature and not class weakness. The Japanese have proved that it is possible to conduct social and political changes intelligently and providentially instead of drifting along helplessly until public disasters compel a terrified and inconsiderate rearrangement. Innumerable experiments in local government have shewn that when men are neither too poor to be honest nor too rich to understand and share the needs of the people – as in New Zealand, for example – they can govern much more providently than our little circle of aristocrats and plutocrats.

THE JUST ENGLISHMAN

English Unionists, when asked what they have to say in defence of their rule of subject peoples, often reply that the Englishman is just, leaving us divided between our derision of so monstrously inhuman a pretension, and our impatience with so gross a confusion of the mutually exclusive functions of judge and legislator. For there is only one condition on which a man can do justice between two litigants, and that is that he shall have no interest in common with either of them, whereas it is only by having every interest in common with both of them that he can govern them tolerably. The indispensable preliminary to Democracy is the representation of every interest: the indispensable preliminary to justice is the elimination of every interest. When we want an arbitrator or an umpire, we turn to a stranger: when we want a government, a stranger is the one person we will not endure. The Englishman in India, for example, stands, a very statue of justice, between two natives. He says, in effect, 'I am impartial in your religious disputes because I believe in neither of your religions. I am impartial in your conflicts of custom and sentiment because your customs and sentiments are different from, and abysmally inferior to, my own. Finally, I am impartial as to your interests because they are both equally opposed to mine, which is to keep you both equally powerless against me in order that I may extract money from you to pay salaries and pensions to my self and my fellow Englishmen as judges and rulers over you. In return for which you get the inestimable benefit of a government that does absolute justice as between Indian and Indian, being wholly preoccupied with the maintenance of absolute injustice as between India and England.'

It will be observed that no Englishman, without making himself ridiculous, could pretend to be perfectly just or disinterested in English affairs, or would tolerate a proposal to establish the Indian or Irish system in Great Britain. Yet if the justice of the Englishman is sufficient to ensure the welfare of India or Ireland, it ought to suffice equally for England. But the English are wise enough to refuse to trust to English justice themselves, preferring democracy. They can hardly blame the Irish for taking the same view.

In short, dear English reader, the Irish Protestant stands outside that English Mutual Admiration Society which you call the Union or the Empire. You may buy a common and not ineffective variety of Irish Protestant by delegating your powers to him, and in effect making him the oppressor and you his sorely bullied and bothered catspaw and military maintainer; but if you offer him nothing for his loyalty except the natural superiority of the English character, you will – well, try the experiment, and see what will happen! You would have a ten-times better chance with the Roman Catholic; for he has been saturated from his youth up with the Imperial idea of foreign rule by a spiritually superior international power, and is trained to submission and abnegation of his private judgment. A Roman Catholic garrison would take its orders from England and let her rule Ireland if England were Roman Catholic. The Protestant garrison simply seizes on the English power; uses it for its own purposes; and occasionally orders the English Government to remove an Irish secretary who has dared to apply English ideas to the affairs of the garrison. Whereupon the English Government abjectly removes him, and implores him, as a gentleman and a loyal Englishman, not to reproach it in the face of the Nationalist enemy.

Such incidents naturally do not shake the sturdy conviction of the Irish Protestant that he is more than a match for any English Government in determination and intelligence. Here, no doubt, he flatters himself; for his advantage is not really an advantage of character, but of comparative directness of interest, concentration of force on one narrow issue, simplicity of aim, with freedom from the scruples and responsibilities of world-politics. The business is Irish business, not English; and he is Irish. And his object, which is simply to secure the dominance of his own caste and creed behind the power of England, is simpler and clearer than the confused aims of English Cabinets struggling ineptly with the burdens of empire, and biassed by the pressure of capital anywhere rather than in Ireland. He has no responsibility, no interest, no status outside his own country and his own movement, which means that he has no conscience in dealing with England; whereas England, having a very uneasy conscience, and many hindering and hampering responsibilities and interests in dealing with him, gets bullied and driven by him, and finally learns sympathy with Nationalist aims by her experience of the tyranny of the Orange party.

IRISH CATHOLICISM FORECAST

Let us suppose that the establishment of a national government were to annihilate the oligarchic party by absorbing the Protestant garrison and making it a Protestant National Guard. The Roman Catholic laity, now a cipher, would organize itself; and a revolt against Rome and against the priesthood would ensue. The Roman Catholic Church would become the official Irish Church. The Irish parliament would insist on a voice in the promotion of churchmen; fees and contributions would be regulated; blackmail would be resisted; sweating in conventual factories and workshops would be stopped; and the ban would be taken off the universities. In a word, the Roman Catholic Church, against which Dublin Castle is powerless, would meet the one force on earth that can cope with it victoriously. That force is Democracy, a thing far more Catholic than itself. Until that force is let loose against it, the Protestant garrison can do nothing to the priesthood except consolidate it and drive the people to rally round it in defence of their altars against the foreigner and the heretic. When it *is* let loose, the Catholic laity will make as short work of sacerdotal tyranny in Ireland as it has done in France and Italy. And in doing so it will be forced to face the old problem of the relations of Church and State. A Roman Catholic party must submit to Rome: an anti-clerical Catholic party must of necessity become an Irish Catholic party. The Holy Roman Empire, like the other Empires, has no future except as a Federation of national Catholic Churches; for Christianity can no more escape Democracy than Democracy can escape Socialism. It is noteworthy in this connection that the Anglican Catholics have played and are playing a notable part in the Socialist movement in England in opposition to the individualist Secularists of the urban proletariat; but they are quit of the preliminary dead lift that awaits the Irish Catholic. Their Church has thrown off the yoke of Rome, and is safely and permanently Anglicized. But the Catholic Church in Ireland is still Roman. Home Rule will herald the day when the Vatican will go the way of Dublin Castle, and the island of the saints assume the headship of her own Church. It may seem incredible that long after the last Orangeman shall lay down his chalk for ever, the familiar scrawl on every blank wall in the north of Ireland 'To hell with the Pope!' may reappear in the south, traced by the hands of Catholics who shall have forgotten the traditional counter legend, 'To hell with King William!' (of glorious, pious, and immortal memory); but it may happen so. 'The island of the saints' is no idle phrase. Religious genius is one of our national products; and Ireland is no bad rock to build a Church on. Holy and beautiful is the soul of Catholic Ireland: her prayers are lovelier than the teeth and claws of Protestantism, but not so effective in dealing with the English.

ENGLISH VOLTAIREANISM

Let me familiarize the situation by shewing how closely it reproduces the English situation in its essentials. In England, as in France, the struggle between the priesthood and the laity has produced a vast body of Voltaireans. But the essential identity of the French and English movements has been obscured by the ignorance of the ordinary Englishman, who, instead of knowing the distinctive tenets of his church or sect, vaguely believes them to be the eternal truth as opposed to the damnable error of all the other denominations. He thinks of Voltaire as a French 'infidel', instead of as the champion of the laity against the official theocracy of the State Church. The Nonconformist leaders of our Free Churches are all Voltaireans. The warcry of the Passive Resisters is Voltaire's warcry, 'Écrasez l'infâme.' No account need be taken of the technical difference between Voltaire's 'infâme' and Dr Clifford's. One

was the unreformed Roman Church of France; the other is the reformed
Anglican Church; but in both cases the attack has been on a priestly
tyranny and a professional monopoly. Voltaire convinced the Genevan
ministers that he was the philosophic champion of their Protestant,
Individualistic, Democratic Deism against the State Church of Roman
Catholic France; and his heroic energy and beneficence as a philan-
thropist, which now only makes the list of achievements on his monument
at Ferney the most impressive epitaph in Europe, then made the most
earnest of the Lutheran ministers glad to claim a common inspiration
with him. Unfortunately Voltaire had an irrepressible sense of humor.
He joked about Habakkuk; and jokes about Habakkuk smelt too strongly
of brimstone to be tolerated by Protestants to whom the Bible was not
a literature but a fetish and a talisman. And so Voltaire, in spite of the
church he 'erected to God', became in England the bogey-atheist of
three generations of English ignoramuses, instead of the legitimate
successor of Martin Luther and John Knox.

Nowadays, however, Voltaire's jokes are either forgotten or else fall
flat on a world which no longer venerates Habakkuk; and his true position
is becoming apparent. The fact that Voltaire was a Roman Catholic
layman, educated at a Jesuit college, is the conclusive reply to the shallow
people who imagine that Ireland delivered up to the Irish democracy –
that is, to the Catholic laity – would be delivered up to the tyranny of
the priesthood.

SUPPOSE!

Suppose, now, that the conquest of France by Henry V of England had
endured, and that France in the XVIII century had been governed by
an English viceroy through a Huguenot bureaucracy and a judicial bench
appointed on the understanding that loyalty for them meant loyalty to
England, and patriotism a willingness to die in defence of the English
conquest and of the English Church, would not Voltaire in that case
have been the meanest of traitors and self-seekers if he had played the
game of England by joining in its campaign against his own and his
country's Church? The energy he threw into the defence of Calas and
Sirven would have been thrown into the defence of the Frenchmen
whom the English would have called 'rebels'; and he would have been

forced to identify the cause of freedom and democracy with the cause of 'l'infâme'. The French revolution would have been a revolution against England and English rule instead of against aristocracy and ecclesiasticism; and all the intellectual and spiritual forces in France, from Turgot to De Tocqueville, would have been burnt up in mere anti-Anglicism and nationalist dithyrambs instead of contributing to political science and broadening the thought of the world.

What would have happened in France is what has happened in Ireland; and that is why it is only the small-minded Irish, incapable of conceiving what religious freedom means to a country, who do not loathe English rule. For in Ireland England is nothing but the Pope's policeman. She imagines she is holding the Vatican cardinals at bay when she is really strangling the Voltaires, the Foxes and Penns, the Cliffords, Hortons, Campbells, Walters, and Silvester Hornes, who are to be found among the Roman Catholic laity as plentifully as among the Anglican Catholic laity in England. She gets nothing out of Ireland but infinite trouble, infinite confusion and hindrance in her own legislation, a hatred that circulates through the whole world and poisons it against her, a reproach that makes her professions of sympathy with Finland and Macedonia ridiculous and hypocritical, whilst the priest takes all the spoils, in money, in power, in pride, and in popularity.

IRELAND'S REAL GRIEVANCE

But it is not the spoils that matter. It is the waste, the sterilization, the perversion of fruitful brain power into flatulent protest against unnecessary evil, the use of our very entrails to tie our own hands and seal our own lips in the name of our honor and patriotism. As far as money or comfort is concerned, the average Irishman has a more tolerable life – especially now that the population is so scanty – than the average Englishman. It is true that in Ireland the poor man is robbed and starved and oppressed under judicial forms which confer the imposing title of justice on a crude system of bludgeoning and perjury. But so is the Englishman. The Englishman, more docile, less dangerous, too lazy intellectually to use such political and legal power as lies within his reach, suffers more and makes less fuss about it than the Irishman. But at least he has nobody to blame but himself and his fellow countrymen. He does not doubt that if an effective majority of the English people made up their minds to alter the Constitution, as the majority of the Irish people have made up their minds to obtain Home Rule, they could alter it without having to fight an overwhelmingly powerful and rich neighboring nation, and fight, too, with ropes round their necks. He can attack any institution in his country without betraying it to foreign vengeance and foreign oppression. True, his landlord may turn him out of his cottage if he goes to a Methodist chapel instead of to the parish church. His customers may stop their orders if he votes Liberal instead of Conservative. English ladies and gentlemen who would perish sooner than shoot a fox do these things without the smallest sense of indecency and dishonor. But they cannot muzzle his intellectual leaders. The English philosopher, the English author, the English orator can attack every abuse and expose every supersitition without strengthening the hands of any common enemy. In Ireland every such attack, every such exposure, is a service to England and a stab to Ireland. If you expose the tyranny and rapacity of the Church, it is an argument in favor of Protestant ascendency. If you denounce the nepotism and jobbery of the new local authorities, you are demonstrating the unfitness of the Irish to govern themselves, and the superiority of the old oligarchical grand juries.

And there is the same pressure on the other side. The Protestant must stand by the garrison at all costs: the Unionist must wink at every bureaucratic abuse, connive at every tyranny, magnify every official blockhead, because their exposure would be a victory for the Nationalist enemy. Every Irishman is in Lancelot's position: his honor rooted in dishonor stands; and faith unfaithful keeps him falsely true.

THE CURSE OF NATIONALISM

It is hardly possible for an Englishman to understand all that this implies. A conquered nation is like a man with cancer: he can think of nothing else, and is forced to place himself, to the exclusion of all better company, in the hands of quacks who profess to treat or cure cancer. The windbags of the two rival platforms are the most insufferable of all windbags. It requires neither knowledge, character, conscience, diligence in public affairs, nor any virtue, private or communal, to thump the Nationalist or Orange tub: nay, it puts a premium on the rancor or callousness that has given rise to the proverb that if you put an Irishman on a spit you can always get another Irishman to baste him. Jingo oratory in England is sickening enough to serious people: indeed one evening's mafficking in London produced a determined call for the police. Well, in Ireland all political oratory is Jingo oratory; and all political demonstrations are maffickings. English rule is such an intolerable abomination that no other subject can reach the people. Nationalism stands between Ireland and the light of the world. Nobody in Ireland of any intelligence likes Nationalism any more than a man with a broken arm likes having it set. A healthy nation is as unconscious of its nationality as a healthy man of his bones. But if you break a nation's nationality it will think of nothing else but getting it set again. It will listen to no reformer, to no philosopher, to no preacher, until the demand of the Nationalist is granted. It will attend to no business, however vital, except the business of unification and liberation.

That is why everything is in abeyance in Ireland pending the achievement of Home Rule. The great movements of the human spirit which sweep in waves over Europe are stopped on the Irish coast by the English guns of the Pigeon House Fort. Only a quaint little offshoot of English pre-Raphaelitism called the Gaelic movement has got a footing by using Nationalism as a stalking horse, and popularizing itself as an attack on the native language of the Irish people, which is most fortunately also the native language of half the world, including England. Every election is fought on nationalist grounds; every appointment is made on nationalist grounds; every judge is a partisan in the nationalist conflict; every speech is a dreary recapitulation of nationalist twaddle; every lecture is a corruption of history to flatter nationalism or defame it; every school is a recruiting station; every church is a barrack; and every Irishman is unspeakably tired of the whole miserable business, which nevertheless is and perforce must remain his first business until Home Rule makes an end of it, and sweeps the nationalist and the garrison hack together into the dustbin.

There is indeed no greater curse to a nation than a nationalist movement, which is only the agonizing symptom of a suppressed natural function. Conquered nations lose their place in the world's march because they can do nothing but strive to get rid of their nationalist movements by recovering their national liberty. All demonstrations of the virtues of a foreign government, though often conclusive, are as useless as demonstrations of the superiority of artificial teeth, glass eyes, silver windpipes, and patent wooden legs to the natural products. Like Democracy, national self-government is not for the good of the people: it is for the satisfaction of the people. One Antonine emperor, one St Louis, one Richelieu, may be worth ten democracies in point of what is called good government; but there is no satisfaction for the people in them. To deprive a dyspeptic of his dinner and hand it over to a man who can digest it better is a highly logical proceeding; but it is not a sensible one. To take the government of Ireland away from the Irish and hand it over to the English on the ground that they can govern better would be a precisely parallel case if the English had managed their own affairs so well as to place their superior faculty for governing beyond question. But as the English are avowed muddlers – rather proud of it, in fact – even the logic of that case against Home Rule is not complete. Read Mr Charles Booth's account of London, Mr Rowntree's account of York, and the latest official report on Dundee; and then pretend, if you can, that Englishmen and Scotchmen have not more cause to hand over their affairs to an Irish parliament than to clamor for another nation's cities to devastate and another people's business to mismanage.

A NATURAL RIGHT

The question is not one of logic at all, but of natural right. English universities have for some time past encouraged an extremely foolish academic exercise which consists in disproving the existence of natural rights on the ground that they cannot be deduced from the principles of any known political system. If they could, they would not be natural rights but acquired ones. Acquired rights are deduced from political constitutions; but political constitutions are deduced from natural rights. When a man insists on certain liberties without the slightest regard to demonstrations that they are not for his own good, nor for the public good, nor moral, nor reasonable, nor decent, nor compatible with the existing constitution of society, then he is said to claim a natural right to that liberty. When, for instance, he insists on living, in spite of the irrefutable demonstrations of many able pessimists, from the author of the book of Ecclesiastes to Schopenhauer, that life is an evil, he is asserting a natural right to live. When he insists on a vote in order that his country may be governed according to his ignorance instead of the wisdom of the Privy Council, he is asserting a natural right to self-government. When he insists on guiding himself at 21 by his own inexperience and folly and immaturity instead of by the experience and sagacity of his father, or the well-stored mind of his grandmother, he is asserting a natural right to independence. Even if Home Rule was as unhealthy as an Englishman's eating, as intemperate as his drinking, as filthy as his smoking, as licentious as his domesticity, as corrupt as his elections, as murderously greedy as his commerce, as cruel as his prisons, and as merciless as his streets, Ireland's claim to self-government would still be as good as England's. King James the First proved so cleverly and conclusively that the satisfaction of natural rights was incompatible with good government that his courtiers called him Solomon. We, more enlightened, call him Fool, solely because we have learnt that nations insist on being governed by their own consent – or, as they put it, by themselves and for themselves – and that they will finally upset a good government which denies them this even if the alternative be a bad government which at least creates and maintains an illusion of democracy. America, as far as one can ascertain, is much worse governed, and has a much more disgraceful political history than England under Charles I; but the American Republic is the stabler government because it starts from a formal concession of natural rights, and keeps up an illusion of safeguarding them by an elaborate machinery of democratic election. And the final reason why Ireland must have Home Rule is that she has a natural right to it.

A WARNING

Finally, some words of warning to both nations. Ireland has been deliberately ruined again and again by England. Unable to compete with us industrially, she has destroyed our industries by the brute force of prohibitive taxation. She was perfectly right. That brute force was a more honorable weapon than the poverty which we used to undersell her. We lived with and as our pigs, and let loose our wares in the Englishman's market at prices which he could compete with only by living like a pig himself. Having the alternative of stopping our industry altogether, he very naturally and properly availed himself of it. We should have done the same in his place. To bear malice against him on that score is to poison our blood and weaken our constitutions with unintelligent rancor. In wrecking all the industries that were based on the poverty of our people England did us an enormous service. In omitting to do the same on her own soil, she did herself a wrong that has rotted her almost to the marrow. I hope that when Home Rule is at last achieved, one of our first legislative acts will be to fortify the subsistence of our people behind the bulwark of a standard wage, and to impose crushing import duties on every English trade that flourishes in the slum and fattens on the starvation of our unfortunate English neighbors.

DOWN WITH THE SOLDIER!

Now for England's share of warning. Let her look to her Empire; for unless she makes it such a Federation for civil strength and defence that all free peoples will cling to it voluntarily, it will inevitably become a military tyranny to prevent them from abandoning it; and such a tyranny will drain the English taxpayer of his money more effectually than its worst cruelties can ever drain its victims of their liberty. A political scheme that cannot be carried out except by soldiers will not be a permanent one. The soldier is an an anachronism of which we must get rid. Among people who are proof against the suggestions of romantic fiction there can no longer be any question of the fact that military service produces moral imbecility, ferocity, and cowardice, and that the defence of nations must be undertaken by the civil enterprise of men enjoying all the rights and liberties of citizenship, and trained by the exacting discipline of democratic freedom and responsibility. For permanent work the soldier is worse than useless: such efficiency as he has is the result of dehumanization and disablement. His whole training tends to make him a weakling. He has the easiest of lives: he has no freedom and no responsibility. He is politically and socially a child, with rations instead of rights, treated like a child, punished like a child, dressed prettily and washed and combed like a child, excused for outbreaks of naughtiness like a child, forbidden to marry like a child, and called Tommy like a child. He has no real work to keep him from going mad except housemaid's work: all the rest is forced exercise, in the form of endless rehearsals for a destructive and terrifying performance which may never come off, and which, when it does come off, is not like the rehearsals. His officer has not even housekeeper's work to keep him sane. The work of organizing and commanding bodies of men, which builds up the character and resource of the large class of civilians who live by it, only demoralizes the military officer, because his orders, however disastrous or offensive, must be obeyed without regard to consequences: for instance, if he calls his men dogs, and perverts a musketry drill order to make them kneel to him as an act of personal humiliation, and thereby provokes a mutiny among men not yet thoroughly broken in to the abjectness of the military condition, he is not, as might be expected, shot, but, at worst, reprimanded, whilst the leader of the mutiny, instead of getting the Victoria Cross and a public testimonial, is condemned to five years' penal servitude by Lynch Law (technically called martial law) administered by a trade union of officers. Compare with this the position of, for instance, our railway managers or our heads of explosive factories. They have to handle large bodies of men whose carelessness or insubordination may cause wholesale destruction of life and property; yet any of these men may insult them, defy them, or assault them without special penalties of any sort. The military commander dares not face these conditions: he lives in perpetual terror of his men, and will undertake their command only when they are stripped of all their civil rights, gagged, and bound hand and foot by a barbarous slave code. Thus the officer learns to punish, but never to rule; and when an emergency like the Indian Mutiny comes, he breaks down; and the situation has to be saved by a few untypical officers with character enough to have retained their civilian qualities in spite of the messroom. This, unfortunately, is learnt by the public, not on the spot, but from Lord Roberts fifty years later.

Besides the Mutiny we have had the Crimean and South African wars, the Dreyfus affair in France, the incidents of the anti-militarist campaign by the Social-Democrats in Germany, and now the Denshawai affair in the Nile delta, all heaping on us sensational demonstrations of the fact that soldiers pay the penalty of their slavery and outlawry by becoming, relatively to free civilians, destructive, cruel, dishonest, tyrannical, hysterical, mendacious, alarmists at home and terrorists abroad, politically reactionary, and professionally incapable. If it were humanly possible to militarize all the humanity out of a man, there would be absolutely no defence to this indictment. But the military system is so idiotically academic and impossible, and renders its victims so incapable of carrying it out with any thoroughness except when, in an occasional hysterical outburst of terror and violence, that hackneyed comedy of civil life, the weak man putting his foot down, becomes the military tragedy of the armed man burning, flogging, and murdering in a panic, that a body of soldiers and officers is in the main, and under normal circumstances, much like any other body of laborers and gentlemen. Many of us count among our personal friends and relatives officers whose amiable and honorable character seems to contradict everything I have just said about the military character. You have only to describe Lynch courts and acts of terrorism to them as the work of Ribbonmen, Dacoits, Moonlighters, Boxers, or – to use the general term most familiar to them – 'natives', and their honest and generous indignation knows no bounds: they feel about them like men, not like soldiers. But the moment you bring the professional side of them uppermost by describing precisely the same proceedings to them as the work of regular armies, they defend them, applaud them, and are ready to take part in them as if their humanity had been blown out like a candle. You find that there is a blind spot on their moral retina, and that this blind spot is the military spot.

The excuse, when any excuse is made, is that discipline is supremely important in war. Now most soldiers have no experience of war; and to assume that those who have are therefore qualified to legislate for it, is as absurd as to assume that a man who has been run over by an omnibus is thereby qualified to draw up wise regulations for the traffic of London. Neither our military novices nor our veterans are clever enough to see that in the field, discipline either keeps itself or goes to pieces; for humanity under fire is a quite different thing from humanity in barracks: when there is danger the difficulty is never to find men who will obey, but men who can command. It is in time of peace, when an army is either a police force (in which case its work can be better done by a civilian constabulary) or an absurdity, that discipline is difficult, because the wasted life of the soldier is unnatural, except to a lazy man, and his servitude galling and senseless, except to a docile one. Still, the soldier is a man, and the officer sometimes a gentleman in the literal sense of the word; and so, what with humanity, laziness, and docility combined, they manage to rub along with only occasional outbursts of mutiny on the one side and class rancor and class cowardice on the other.

They are not even discontented; for the military and naval codes simplify life for them just as it is simplified for children. No soldier is asked to think for himself, to judge for himself, to consult his own honor and manhood, to dread any consequence except the consequence of punishment to his own person. The rules are plain and simple; the ceremonies of respect and submission are as easy and mechanical as a prayer wheel; the orders are always to be obeyed thoughtlessly, however inept or dishonorable they may be. As the late Laureate said in the two stinging lines in which he branded the British soldier with the dishonor of Esau, 'theirs not to reason why, theirs but to do and die.' To the moral imbecile and political sluggard these conditions are as congenial and attractive as they are abhorrent and intolerable to the William Tell temperament. Just as the most incorrigible criminal is always, we are told, the best behaved convict, so the man with least conscience and initiative makes the best behaved soldier, and that not wholly through mere fear of punishment, but through a genuine fitness for and consequent happiness in the child-like military life. Such men dread freedom and responsibility as a weak man dreads a risk or a heavy burden; and the objection to the military system is that it tends to produce such men by a weakening disuse of the moral muscles. No doubt this weakness is just what the military system aims at, its ideal soldier being, not a complete man, but a docile unit of cannon-fodder which can be trusted to respond promptly and certainly to the external stimulus of a shouted order, and is intimidated to the pitch of being afraid to run away from a battle. It may be doubted whether even in the Prussian heyday of the system, when floggings of hundreds and even thousands of lashes were matters of ordinary routine, this detestable ideal was ever realized; but your courts-martial are not practical enough to take that into account: it is characteristic of the military mind continually to ignore human nature and cry for the moon instead of facing modern social facts and accepting modern democratic conditions. And when I say the military mind, I repeat that I am not forgetting the patent fact that the military mind and the humane mind can exist in the same person; so that an officer who will take all the civilian risks, from city traffic to foxhunting, without uneasiness, and who will manage all the civil employees on his estate and in his house and stables without the aid of a Mutiny Act, will also, in his military capacity, frantically declare that he dare not walk about in a foreign country unless every crime of violence against an Englishman in uniform is punished by the bombardment and destruction of a whole

village, or the wholesale flogging and execution of every native in the
neighborhood, and also that unless he and his fellow-officers have power,
without the intervention of a jury, to punish the slightest self-assertion or
hesitation to obey orders, however grossly insulting or disastrous those
orders may be, with sentences which are reserved in civil life for the worst
crimes, he cannot secure the obedience and respect of his men, and the
country will accordingly lose all its colonies and dependencies, and be
helplessly conquered in the German invasion which he confidently
expects to occur in the course of a fortnight or so. That is to say, in so far
as he is an ordinary gentleman he behaves sensibly and courageously; and
in so far as he is a military man he gives way without shame to the grossest
folly, cruelty and poltroonery. If any other profession in the world had
been stained by these vices, and by false witness, forgery, swindling,
torture, compulsion of men's families to attend their executions, digging
up and mutilation of dead enemies, all wantonly added to the devastation
proper to its own business, as the military profession has been within
recent memory in England, France, and the United States of America (to
mention no other countries), it would be very difficult to induce men of
capacity and character to enter it. And in England it is, in fact, largely
dependent for its recruits on the refuse of industrial life, and for its officers
on the aristocratic and plutocratic refuse of political and diplomatic life,
who join the army and pay for their positions in the more or less
fashionable clubs which the regimental messes provide them with – clubs
which, by the way, occasionally figure in ragging scandals as circles of
extremely coarse moral character.

Now in countries which are denied Home Rule: that is, in which the
government does not rest on the consent of the people, it must rest on
military coercion; and the bureaucracy, however civil and legal it may be
in form and even in the character of its best officials, must connive at all
the atrocities of military rule, and become infected in the end with the
chronic panic characteristic of militarism. In recent witness whereof, let
me shift the scene from Ireland to Egypt, and tell the story of the
Denshawai affair of June 1906 by way of object-lesson.

THE DENSHAWAI HORROR

Denshawai is a little Egyptian village in the Nile delta. Besides the dilapidated huts among the reeds by the roadside, and the palm trees, there are towers of unbaked brick, as unaccountable to an English villager as a Kentish oast-house to an Egyptian. These towers are pigeon-houses; for the villagers keep pigeons just as an English farmer keeps poultry.

Try to imagine the feelings of an English village if a party of Chinese officers suddenly appeared and began shooting the ducks, the geese, the hens, and the turkeys, and carried them off, asserting that they were wild birds, as everybody in China knew, and that the pretended indignation of the farmers was a cloak for hatred of the Chinese, and perhaps for a plot to overthrow the religion of Confucius and establish the Church of England in its place! Well, that is the British equivalent of what happened at Denshawai when a party of English officers went pigeon-shooting there the year before last. The inhabitants complained and memorialized; but they obtained no redress: the law failed them in their hour of need. So one leading family of pigeon farmers, Mahfouz by name, despaired of the law; and its head, Hassan Mahfouz, aged 60, made up his mind not to submit tamely to a repetition of the outrage. Also, British officers were ordered not to shoot pigeons in the villages without the consent of the Omdeh, or headman, though nothing was settled as to what might happen to the Omdeh if he ventured to refuse.

Fancy the feelings of Denshawai when on the 13th of June last there drove to the village four khaki-clad British officers with guns, one of them being a shooter of the year before, accompanied by one other officer on horseback, and also by a dragoman and an Ombashi, or police official! The oriental blood of Hassan Mahfouz boiled; and he warned them that they would not be allowed to shoot pigeons; but as they did not understand his language, the warning had no effect. They sent their dragoman to ask the Omdeh's permission to shoot; but the Omdeh was away; and all the interpreter could get from the Omdeh's deputy, who knew better than to dare an absolute refusal, was the pretty obvious reply that they might shoot if they went far enough away from the village. On the strength of this welcome, they went from 100 to 300 yards away from the houses (these distances were afterwards officially averaged at 500 yards), and began shooting the villagers' pigeons. The villagers remonstrated and finally seized the gun of the youngest officer. It went off in the struggle, and wounded three men and the wife of one Abd-el-Nebi, a young man of 25. Now the lady, though, as it turned out, only temporarily disabled by a charge of pigeon shot in the softest part of her person, gave herself up for dead; and the feeling in the village was much as if our imaginary Chinese officers, on being interfered with in their slaughter of turkeys, had killed an English farmer's wife. Abd-el-Nebi, her husband, took the matter to heart, not altogether without reason, we may admit. His threshing-floor also caught fire somehow (the official English theory is that he set it on fire as a signal for revolt to the entire Moslem world); and all the lads and loafers in the place were presently on the spot. The other officers, seeing their friend in trouble, joined him. Abd-el-Nebi hit the supposed murderer of his wife with a stick; Hassan Mahfouz used a stick also; and the lads and loafers began to throw stones and bricks. Five London policemen would have seen that there was nothing to be done but fight their way out, as there is no use arguing with an irritated mob, especially if you do not know its language. Had the shooting party been in the charge of a capable non-commissioned officer, he would perhaps have got it safely off. As it was, the officers tried propitiation, making their overtures in pantomime. They gave up their guns; they offered watches and money to the crowd, crying Baksheesh; and the senior officer actually collared the junior and pretended to arrest him for the murder of the woman. Naturally they were mobbed worse than before; and what they did not give to the crowd was taken from them, whether as payment for the pigeons, blood money, or simple plunder was not gone into. The officers, two Irishmen and three Englishmen, having made a hopeless mess of it, and being now in serious danger, made for their carriages, but were dragged out of them again, one of the coachmen being knocked senseless. They then 'agreed to run', the arrangement being that the Englishmen, being the juniors, should run away to camp and bring help to the Irishmen. They bolted accordingly; but the third, the youngest, seeing the two Irishmen hard put to it, went back and stood by them. Of the two fugitives, one, after a long race in the Egyptian afternoon sun, got to the next village and there dropped, smitten by sunstroke, of which he died. The other ran on and met a patrol, which started to the rescue.

Meanwhile, the other three officers had been taken out of the hands of the lads and the loafers, of Abd-el-Nebi and Hassan Mahfouz, by the elders and watchmen, and saved from further injury, but not before they had been severely knocked about, one of them having one of the bones of his left arm broken near the wrist – simple fracture of the thin end of the ulna. They were also brought to the threshing-floor; shewn the wounded woman; informed by gestures that they deserved to have their throats cut for murdering her; and kicked (with naked feet, fortunately); but at this point the elders and constables stopped the mobbing. Finally the three were sent off to camp in their carriages; and the incident ended for that day.

No English mob, under similar provocation, would have behaved any better; and few would have done as little mischief. It is not many months since an old man – not a foreigner and not an unbeliever – was kicked to death in the streets of London because the action of a park constable in turning him out of a public park exposed him to suspicion of misconduct. At Denshawai, the officers were not on duty. In their private capacity as sportsmen, they committed a serious depredation on a very poor village by slaughtering its stock. In an English village they would have been tolerated because the farmers would have expected compensation for damage, and the villagers coals and blankets and employment in country house, garden and stable, or as beaters, huntsmen and the like, from them. But Denshawai had no such inducements to submit to their thoughtless and selfish aggression. One of them had apparently killed a woman and wounded three men with his gun: in fact his own comrade virtually convicted him of it before the crowd by collaring him as a prisoner. In short, the officers had given outrageous provocation; and they had shewn an amiable but disastrous want of determination and judgment in dealing with the riot they provoked. They should have been severely reprimanded and informed that they had themselves to thank for what happened to them; and the villagers who assaulted them should have been treated with leniency, and assured that pigeon-shooting would not be allowed in future.

That is what should have ensued. Now for what actually did ensue.

Abd-el-Nebi, in consideration of the injury to his wife, was only sentenced to penal servitude for life. And our clemency did not stop there. His wife was not punished at all – not even charged with stealing the shot which was found in her person. And lest Abd-el-Nebi should feel lonely at 25 in beginning penal servitude for the rest of his days, another young man, of 20, was sent to penal servitude for life with him.

No such sentimentality was shewn to Hassan Mahfouz. An Egyptian pigeon farmer who objects to Brtish sport; threatens British officers and gentlemen when they shoot his pigeons; and actually hits those officers with a substantial stick, is clearly a ruffian to be made an example of. Penal servitude was not enough for a man of 60 who looked 70, and might not have lived to suffer five years of it. So Hassan was hanged; but as a special mark of consideration for his family, he was hanged in full view of his own house, with his wives and children and grandchildren enjoying the spectacle from the roof. And lest this privilege should excite jealousy in other households, three other Denshavians were hanged with him. They went through the ceremony with dignity, professing their faith ('Mahometan, I regret to say,' Mr Pecksniff would have said). Hassan, however, 'in a loud voice invoked ruin upon the houses of those who had given evidence against him'; and Darweesh was impatient and presumed to tell the hangman to be quick. But then Darweesh was a bit of a brigand: he had been imprisoned for bearing false witness; and his resistance to the British invasion is the only officially recorded incident of his life which is entirely to his credit. He and Abd–el–Nebi (who had been imprisoned for theft) were the only disreputable characters among the punished. Ages of the four hanged men respectively, 60, 50, 22 and 20.

Hanging, however, is the least sensational form of public execution: it lacks those elements of blood and torture for which the military and bureaucratic imagination lusts. So, as they had room for only one man on the gallows, and had to leave him hanging half an hour to make sure work and give his family plenty of time to watch him swinging ('slowly turning round and round on himself', as the local papers described it), thus having two hours to kill as well as four men, they kept the entertainment going by flogging eight men with fifty lashes each: eleven more than the utmost permitted by the law of Moses in times which our Army of Occupation no doubt considers barbarous. But then Moses conceived his law as being what he called the law of God, and not simply an instrument for the gratification of his own cruelty and terror. It is unspeakably reassuring to learn from the British official reports laid before parliament that 'due dignity was observed in carrying out the executions', and 'all possible humanity was shewn in carrying them out', and that 'the arrangements were admirable, and reflect great credit on all concerned'. As this last testimonial apparently does not refer to the victims, they are evidently officially considered not to have been concerned in the proceedings at all. Finally, Lord Cromer certifies that the Englishman in charge of the proceedings is 'a singularly humane man, and is very popular amongst the natives of Egypt by reason of the great sympathy he has always shewn for them'. It will be seen that Pariamentary Papers, Nos. 3 and 4, Egypt, 1906, are not lacking in unconscious humor. The official walrus pledges himself in every case for the kindliness of the official carpenter.

One man was actually let off, to the great danger of the British Empire perhaps. Still, as he was an epileptic, and had already had several fits in the court of Judge Lynch, the doctor said Better not; and he escaped. This was very inconvenient; for the number of floggees had been made up solely to fill the time occupied by the hangings at the rate of two floggings per hanging; and the breakdown of the arrangement through Said Suleiman Kheirallah's inconsiderate indisposition made the execution of Darweesh tedious, as he was hanging for fully quarter of an hour without any flogging to amuse his fellow villagers and the officers and men of the Inniskilling Dragoons, the military mounted police, and the mounted infantry. A few spare sentences of flogging should have been kept in hand to provide against accidents.

In any case there was not time to flog everybody, not to flog three of the floggees enough; so these three had a year's hard labor apiece in addition to their floggings. Six others were not flogged at all, but were sent to penal servitude for seven years each. One man got fifteen years. Total for the morning's work: four hanged, two to penal servitude for life, one to fifteen years penal servitude, six to seven years penal servitude, three to imprisonment for a year with hard labor and fifty lashes, and five to fifty lashes.

Lord Cromer certifies that these proceedings were 'just and necessary'. He also gives his reasons. It appears that the boasted justice introduced into Egypt by the English in 1882 was imaginary, and that the real work of coping with Egyptian disorder was done by Brigandage Commissions, composed of Egyptians. These Commissions, when an offence was reported, descended on the inculpated village; seized everybody concerned; and plied them with tortures, mentionable and unmentionable, until they accused everybody they were expected to accuse. The accused were in turn tortured until they confessed anything and everything they were accused of. They were then killed, flogged, or sent to penal servitude.

This was the reality behind the illusion that soothed us after bombarding Alexandria. The bloodless, white-gloved native courts set up to flatter our sense of imperial justice had, apparently, about as much to do with the actual government of the fellaheen as the annual court which awards the Dunmow flitch of bacon has to do with our divorce court. Eventually a Belgian judge, who was appointed Procureur-Général, exposed the true state of affairs.

Then the situation had to be faced. Order had to be maintained somehow; but the regular native courts which saved the face of the British Occupation were useless for the purpose; and the Brigandage Commissions were so abominable and demoralizing that they made more mischief than they prevented. Besides, there was Mr Wilfrid Scawen Blunt on the warpath against tyranny and torture, threatening to get questions asked in parliament. A new sort of tribunal in the nature of a court-martial had therefore to be invented to replace the Brigandage Commissions; but simple British military courts-martial, though probably the best available form of official Lynch Law, were made impossible by the jealousy of the 'loyal' (to England) Egyptians, who, it seems, rule the Occupation and bully England exactly as the 'loyal' Irish rule the Garrison and bully the Unionists nearer home. That kind of loyalty, not being a natural product, has to be purchased; and the price is an official job of some sort with a position and a salary attached. Hence we got, in 1895, a tribunal constituted in which three English officials sat with two Egyptian officials, exercising practically unlimited powers of punishment without a jury and without appeal. They represent the best of our judicial and military officialism. And what that best is may be judged by the sentences on the Denshawai villagers.

Lord Cromer's justification of the tribunal is practically that, bad as it is, the Brigandage Commissions were worse. Also (lest we should propose to carry our moral superiority any further) that the Egyptians are so accustomed to associate law and order with floggings, executions, torture and Lynch Law, that they will not respect any tribunal which does not continue these practices. This is a far-reaching argument: for instance, it suggests that Church of England missionaries might do well to adopt the rite of human sacrifice when evangelizing tribes in whose imagination that practice is inseparably bound up with religion. It suggests that the sole reason why the Denshawai tribunal did not resort to torture for the purpose of extorting confessions and evidence was that parliament might not stand it – though really a parliament which stood the executions would, one would think, stand anything. The tribunal had certainly no intention of allowing witnesses to testify against British officers; for, as it happened, the Ombashi who accompanied them on the two shooting expeditions, one Ahmed Hassan Zakzouk, aged 26, was rash enough to insist that after the shot that struck the woman, the officers fired on the mob twice. This appears in the parliamentary paper; but the French newspaper *L'Égypte* is quoted by Mr Wilfrid Scawen Blunt as reporting that Zakzouk, on being asked by one of the English judges whether he was not afraid to say such a thing, replied 'Nobody in the world is able to frighten me: the truth is the truth,' and was promptly told to stand down. Mr Blunt adds that Zakzouk was then tried for his conduct in connection with the affair before a Court of Discipline, which awarded him two years imprisonment and fifty lashes. Without rudely calling this a use of torture to intimidate anti-British witnesses, I may count on the assent of most reasonable people when I say that Zakzouk probably regards himself as having received a rather strong hint to make his evidence agreeable to the Occupation in future.

Not only was there of course no jury at the trial, but considerably less than no defence. Barristers of sufficient standing to make it very undesirable for them to offend the Occupation were instructed to 'defend' the prisoners. Far from defending them, they paid high compliments to the Occupation as one of the choicest benefits rained by Heaven on their country, and appealed for mercy for their miserable clients, whose conduct had 'caused the unanimous indignation of all Egyptians'. 'Clemency,' they said, 'was above equity.' The Tribunal in delivering judgment remarked that 'the counsel for the defence had a full hearing: nevertheless the defence broke down completely, and all that their counsel could say on behalf of the prisoners practically amounted to an appeal to the mercy of the Court'.

Now the proper defence, if put forward, would probably have convinced Lord Cromer that nothing but the burning of the village and the crucifixion of all its inhabitants could preserve the British Empire. That defence was obvious enough: the village was invaded by five armed foreigners who attempted for the second time to slaughter the villagers' farming stock and carry it off; in resisting an attempt to disarm them four villagers had been wounded; the villagers had lost their tempers and knocked the invaders about; and the older men and watchmen had finally rescued the aggressors and sent them back with no worse handling than they would have got anywhere for the like misconduct.

One can imagine what would have happened to the man, prisoner or advocate, who should have dared to tell the truth in this fashion. The prisoners knew better than to attempt it. On the scaffold, Darweesh turned to his house as he stood on the trap, and exclaimed 'May God compensate us well for this world of meanness, for this world of injustice, for this world of cruelty.' If he had dared in court thus to compare God with the tribunal to the disadvantage of the latter, he would no doubt have had fifty lashes before his hanging, to teach him the greatness of the Empire. As it was, he kept his views to himself until it was too late to do anything worse to him than hang him. In court, he did as all the rest did. They lied; they denied; they set up desperate alibis; they protested they had been in the next village, or tending cattle a mile off, or threshing, or what not. One of them, when identified, said 'All men are alike.' He had only one eye. Darweesh, who had secured one of the officers' guns, declared that his enemies had come in the night and buried it in his house, where his mother sat on it, like Rachel on Laban's stolen teraphim, until she was dragged off. A pitiable business, yet not so pitiable as the virtuous indignation with which Judge Lynch, himself provable by his own judgment to be a prevaricator, hypocrite, tyrant, and coward of the first water, preened himself at its expense. When Lord Cromer, in his official apology for Judge Lynch, says that 'the prisoners had a perfectly fair trial' – not, observe, a trial as little unfair as human frailty could make it, which is the most that can be said for any trial on earth, but 'a *perfectly* fair trial' – he no doubt believes what he says; but his opinion is interesting mainly as an example of the state of his mind, and of the extent to which, after thirty years of official life in Egypt, one loses the plain sense of English words.

Lord Cromer recalls how, in the eighties, a man threatened with the courbash by a Moudir in the presence of Sir Claude MacDonald, said 'You dare not flog me now that the British are here.' 'So bold an answer,' says Lord Cromer, 'was probably due to the presence of a British officer.' What would that man say now? What does Lord Cromer say now? He deprecates 'premature endeavors to thrust Western ideas on an Eastern people', by which he means that when you are in Egypt you must do as the Egyptians do: terrorize by the lash and the scaffold. Thus does the East conquer its conquerors. In 1883 Lord Dufferin was abolishing the bastinado as 'a horrible and infamous punishment'. In 1906 Lord Cromer guarantees ferocious sentences of flogging as 'just and necessary', and can see 'nothing reprehensible in the manner in which they were carried out'. 'I have,' he adds, 'passed nearly thirty years of my life in an earnest endeavor to raise the moral and material condition of the people of Egypt. I have been assisted by a number of very capable officials, all of whom, I may say, have been animated by the same spirit as myself.' Egypt may well shudder as she reads those words. If the first thirty years have been crowned by the Denshawai incident, what will Egypt be like at the end of another thirty years of moral elevation 'animated by the same spirit'?

It is pleasanter to return to Lord Cromer's first letter on Denshawai, written to Sir Edward Grey the day after the shooting party. It says that 'orders will shortly be issued by the General prohibiting officers in the army from shooting pigeons in the future under any circumstances whatever'. But pray why this prohibition, if, as the tribunal declared, the officers were 'guests [actually *guests!*] who had done nothing to deserve blame'?

Mr Findlay is another interesting official correspondent of Sir Edward. Even after the trial, at which it had been impossible to push the medical evidence further than to say that the officer who died of sunstroke had been predisposed to it by the knocking about he had suffered and by his flight under the Egyptian sun, whilst the officers who had remained defenceless in the hands of the villagers were in court, alive and well, Mr Findlay writes that the four hanged men were 'convicted of a brutal and premeditated murder', and complains that 'the native press disregards the fact' and 'is being conducted with such an absolute disregard for the truth as to make it evident that large sums of money have been expended'. Mr Findlay is also a bit of a philosopher. 'The Egyptian, being a fatalist,' he says, 'does not greatly fear death, and there is therefore much to be said for flogging as a judicial punishment in Egypt.' Logically, then, the four hanged men ought to have been flogged instead. But Mr Findlay does not draw that conclusion. Logic is not his strong point: he is a man of feeling, and a very nervous one at that. 'I do not believe that this brutal attack on British officers had anything directly to do with political animosity. It

is, however, due to the insubordinate spirit which has been sedulously
fostered during the last year by unscrupulous and interested agitators.'
Again, 'it is my duty to warn you of the deplorable effect which is being
produced in Egypt by the fact that Members of Parliament have seriously
called in question the unanimous sentence passed by a legally constituted
Court, of which the best English and the best native Judge were members.
This fact will, moreover, supply the lever which has, up to the present,
been lacking to the venal agitators who are at the head of the so-called
patriotic party.' I find Mr Findlay irresistible, so exquisitely does he give
us the measure and flavor of officialism. 'A few days after the Denshawai
affray some native stoned and severely injured an irrigation inspector.
Two days ago three natives knocked a soldier off his donkey and kicked
him in the stomach: his injuries are serious. In the latter case theft appears
to have been the motive. My object in mentioning these instances is to
shew the results to be expected if once respect for the law is shaken. Should
the present state of things continue, and, still more, should the agitation
in this country find support at home, the date is not far distant when the
necessity will arise for bringing in a press law and for considerably
increasing the army of occupation.' Just think of it! In a population of
nearly ten million, one irrigation inspector is stoned. The Denshawai
executions are then carried out to make the law respected. The result is
that three natives knock a soldier off his donkey and rob him. Thereupon
Mr Findlay, appalled at the bankruptcy of civilization, sees nothing for it
now but suppression of the native newspapers and a considerable increase
in the army of occupation! And Lord Cromer writes 'All I need say is that
I concur generally in Mr Findlay's remarks, and that, had I remained in
Egypt, I should in every respect have adopted the same course as that
which he pursued.'

But I must resolutely shut this rich parliamentary paper. I have
extracted enough to paint the picture, and enforce my warning to England
that if her Empire means ruling the world as Denshawai has been ruled
in 1906 – and that, I am afraid, is what the Empire does mean to the main
body of our aristocratic-military caste and to our Jingo plutocrats – then
there can be no more sacred and urgent political duty on earth than the
disruption, defeat, and suppression of the Empire, and, incidentally, the
humanization of its supporters by the sternest lessons of that adversity
which comes finally to institutions which make themselves abhorred by

the aspiring will of humanity towards divinity. As for the Egyptians, any man cradled by the Nile who, after the Denshawai incident, will ever voluntarily submit to British rule, or accept any bond with us except the bond of a Federation of free and equal states, will deserve the worst that Lord Cromer can consider 'just and necessary' for him. That is what you get by attempting to prove your supremacy by the excesses of frightened soldiers and denaturalized officials instead of by courageous helpfulness and moral superiority.

In any case let no Englishman who is content to leave Abd-el-Nebi and his twenty-year-old neighbor in penal servitude for life, and to plume himself on the power to do it, pretend to be fit to govern either my country or his own. The responsibility cannot be confined to the tribunal and to the demoralized officials of the Occupation. The House of Commons had twentyfour hours clear notice, with the telegraph under the hand of Sir Edward Grey, to enable it to declare that England was a civilized Power and would not stand these barbarous lashings and vindictive hangings. Yet Mr Dillon, representing the Irish party, which well knows what British Occupation and Findlay 'loyalism' mean, protested in vain. Sir Edward, on behalf of the new Liberal Government (still simmering with virtuous indignation at the flogging of Chinamen and the military executions in South Africa in the forced presence of the victims' families under the late Imperialist Government), not only permitted and defended the Denshawai executions, but appealed to the House almost passionately not to criticize or repudiate them, on the ground – how incredible it now appears! – that Abd-el-Nebi and Hassan Mahfouz and Darweesh and the rest were the fuglemen of a gigantic Moslem plot to rise against Christendom in the name of the Prophet and sweep Christendom out of Africa and Asia by a colossal second edition of the Indian Mutiny. That this idiotic romance, gross and ridiculous as the lies of Falstaff, should have imposed on any intelligent and politically experienced human being, is strange enough – though the secret shame of revolted humanity will make cabinet ministers snatch at fantastic excuses – but what humanity will not forgive our foreign secretary for is his failure to see that even if such a conspiracy really existed, England should have faced it and fought it bravely by honorable means, instead of wildly lashing and strangling a handful of poor peasants to scare Islam into terrified submission. Were I abject enough to grant to Sir Edward Grey as valid that main asset of 'thinking Imperially', the conviction that we are all going to be murdered, I should still suggest to him that we can at least die like gentlemen? Might I even be so personal as to say that the reason for giving him a social position and political opportunities that are denied to his tradesmen is that he is supposed to understand better than they that honor is worth its danger and its cost, and that life is worthless without honor? It is true that Sir John Falstaff did not think so; but Sir John is hardly a model for Sir Edward. Yet even Sir John would have had enough gumption to see that the Denshawai panic was more dangerous to the Empire than the loss of ten pitched battles.

As cowardice is highly infectious, would it not be desirable to supersede officials who, after years of oriental service, have lost the familiar art of concealing their terrors? I am myself a sedentary literary civilian, constitutionally timid; but I find it possible to keep up appearances, and can even face the risk of being run over, or garotted, or burnt out in London without shrieking for martial law, suppression of the newspapers, exemplary flogging and hanging of motor-bus drivers, and compulsory police service. Why are soldiers and officials on foreign service so much more cowardly than citizens? Is it not clearly because the whole Imperial military system of coercion and terrorism is unnatural, and that the truth formulated by William Morris that 'no man is good enough to be another man's master' is true also of nations, and very specially true of those plutocrat-ridden Powers which have of late stumbled into an enormous increase of material wealth without having made any intelligent provision for its proper distribution and administration?

However, the economic reform of the Empire is a long business, whereas the release of Abd-el-Nebi and his neighbors is a matter of the stroke of a pen, once public opinion is shamed into activity. I fear I have stated their case very unfairly and inadequately, because I am hampered, as an Irishman, by my implacable hostility to English domination. Mistrusting my own prejudices, I have taken the story from the two parliamentary papers in which our officials have done their utmost to whitewash the tribunals and the pigeon-shooting party, and to blackwash the villagers. Those who wish to have it told to them by an Englishman of unquestionable personal and social credentials, and an intimate knowledge of Egypt and the Egyptians, can find it in Mr Wilfrid Scawen Blunt's pamphlet entitled 'Atrocities of British Rule in Egypt'. When they have read it they will appreciate my forbearance; and when I add that English rule in Ireland has been 'animated by the same spirit' (I thank Lord Cromer for the phrase) as English rule in Egypt, and that this is the inevitable spirit of all coercive military rule, they will perhaps begin to understand why Home Rule is a necessity not only for Ireland, but for all constituents of those Federations of Commonwealths which are now the only permanently practicable form of Empire.

POSTSCRIPT. These sheets had passed through the press when the news came of Lord Cromer's resignation. As he accuses himself of failing health, he will perhaps forgive me for accusing him of failing judgment, and for suggesting that his retirement from office might well be celebrated in Egypt by the retirement, at his intercession, of Abd-el-Nabi and the rest from penal servitude.

A YEAR LATER

It may be a relief to some of my readers to learn that very shortly after the publication of the above account of the Denshawai atrocity, I received a private assurance that Abd-el-Nebi and his fellow-prisoners would be released on the following New Year's Day, which is the customary occasion in Egypt for such acts of grace and clemency as the Occupation may allow the Khedive to perform, and that in the meantime their detention would not be rigorous. As the hanged men could not be un-hanged nor the flogged men unflogged, this was all that could be done. I am bound to add, in justice to the Government, that this was, as far as I could ascertain, an act of pure conscience on the part of the Cabinet; for there was no sign of any serious pressure of public opinion. One or two newspapers seemed to be amused at my calling the Denshawai villagers Denshavians; but they shewed no other interest in the matter: another illustration of how hopeless it is to induce one modern nation, pre-occupied as it necessarily is with its own affairs, to take any real interest in the welfare of another, even when it professes to govern that other in a superior manner for its good. Sir Edward Grey's reputation as a great Minister for Foreign Affairs was not shaken in the least: the eulogies which were heaped on him by both parties increased in volume; and an attempt which I made to call attention to the real character of the Anglo-Russian agreement as to Persia, which was held up as a masterpiece of his diplomacy (I was apparently the only person who had taken the trouble to read it) had no effect. Not until Sir Edward ventured to threaten a really formidable European Power in 1911, and threatened it successfully from his point of view, did a sudden and violent agitation against him spring up. Until then, men of both parties idolized him without knowing why, just as they had formerly idolized Lord Cromer and Lord Milner without knowing why. They will now very possibly turn on him and rend him, also without knowing why. The one thing they will not do is to blame themselves, which is the only blaming that can be of any profit to them.

Preface to the
Home Rule Edition of
1912

[When Shaw reprinted this Preface in the Collected Edition of his works in 1930, he placed it before the original Preface and added an explanatory note. The text has now been placed in its proper chronological order. The prefatory note has been retained without editorial revision.]

(I reprint this interim preface after much hesitation. It is based on two confident political assumptions that have since been not merely disproved but catastrophically shattered.

The first was that Parliament in 1912 was still what it had been in the heyday of Gladstonian Liberalism, when it was utterly inconceivable that an Act of constitutional reform which had been duly passed and assented-to by the Crown could be dropped into the waste paper basket because a handful of ladies and gentlemen objected to it, and the army officers' messes blustered mutinously against it.

The second assumption was that Ireland was politically one and indivisible, and, consequently, that when Home Rule came, as it was evident it must come, the Protestants of Ireland must stand together and make the best of it. The possibility of a Partition by which Belfast Protestantism should accept Home Rule for itself in a concentration camp and thus abandon its co-religionists outside the camp to what must then inevitably become a Roman Catholic Home Rule Government of the rest of Ireland, was undreamt of.

How both these things nevertheless happened I have described in a postscript to the original preface which will be found on a later page. Readers who skip to that preface will lose nothing by missing this one except a possibly instructive example of how our eternal march into the future must always be a blindfold march. I guessed ahead, and guessed wrongly, whilst stupider and more ignorant fellow-pilgrims guessed rightly.)

John Bull's Other Island was written when a Unionist Government was in power, and had been in power with one brief interval for twenty years. The reason for this apparent eclipse of Home Rule was that the Liberal Party had during that period persisted in assuring the English people anxiously that it had no intention of doing anything for England (its object being to shew its abhorrence of Socialism) and that it cared for nothing but Home Rule in Ireland. Now as the English electors, being mostly worse off than the Irish, were anxious to have something done to alleviate their own wretched condition, they steadily voted for the Unionist Party (not because it was Unionist, but because it cared more for England than for Ireland), except on one occasion in 1893, when the Liberals put all their Home Rule tracts in the fire, and fought on a program of English Social Reform, known as the Newcastle Program, drawn up by my friend and Fabian colleague, Mr Sidney Webb, and ingeniously foisted on the Liberals by myself and other Fabians disguised as artless Gladstonian members of certain little local caucuses which called themselves Liberal and Radical Associations, and were open to any passer-by who might astonish them by seeming to take an interest in their routine of bleeding candidates for registration expenses and local subscriptions. The program won the election for the Home Rulers. It was a close thing; but it won it. The Liberals then dropped it; and Lord Rosebery made his famous discovery that programs are a mistake, a view which, though supported with deep conviction by his Party, which still had no desire to do or mean or understand anything that could conceivably benefit anyone in England, had the immediate effect of extinguishing its noble author politically, and sending his party back into opposition for another ten years, at the end of which the Unionists, quite as ignorant of what the people of England were thinking about as Lord Rosebery, entered upon an impassioned defence of the employment of Chinese labor in South Africa without considering the fact that every one of their arguments was equally valid for the introduction of Chinese labor into Lancashire. And as the people of Lancashire were concerned about Lancashire and not at all about South Africa, the Unionist Party followed Lord Rosebery into the shades.

One consequence of this political swing of the pendulum was that John Bull's Other Island, which had up to that moment been a topical play, immediately became a historical one. Broadbent is no longer up-to-date. His *bête noir*, Mr Joseph Chamberlain, has retired from public life. The controversies about Tariff Reform, the Education and Licensing Bills, and the South African war, have given way to the far more vital questions raised by Mr Lloyd George's first unskilful essays in Collectivism, and to the agitation for Votes for Women. Broadbent is still strong on the question of Persia: stronger than he was on that of Armenia (probably because Persia is further off); but there is little left of the subjects that excited him in 1904 except Home Rule. And Home Rule is to be disposed of this year.

The Government will no doubt be glad to get rid of it. The English people, with prices up and wages down, care less, if possible, than they ever did about it. Even the governing classes are feeling the pressure of the Home Rule agitations in Egypt and India more than in Ireland; for the Irish, now confident that their battle is won, are keeping comparatively quiet, whilst in the East the question is in the acute stage in which the Government has to explain that really very few people have had confessions extorted by torture in the police stations, and that if the natives would only be reasonable and recognize the advantages of British rule, and their own utter unfitness for self-government, there would be no need to imprison nationalists either in India or Egypt; so that, in effect, the natives have themselves to thank for whatever unpleasantness may happen to them.

The only considerable body of Englishmen really concerned about Home Rule except as a Party question, are those members of the Free Churches, vulgarly called Dissenters or Nonconformists, who believe that the effect of Home Rule would be to deliver Ireland into the hands of the Roman Catholic Church, which they regard as The Scarlet Woman. It is clearly not a very deeply considered apprehension, because there is not a country in the world, not even Spain, where the people are so completely in the hands of the Roman Catholic Church as they are in Ireland under English rule and because of English rule. In the non-Protestant Christian countries which are politically independent, the clericals are struggling, not to regain their lost supremacy (that survives only in Ireland), but for their houses, their property, their right to live in the country they were born in, and to have the political weight due to their merits; for they have merits: the priest is not so black as he is painted in all free countries nowadays. But our Free Churchmen are too much afraid of the Pope, and of the confessional, and of the priest in the house, to see how weak these forces are in the face of democracy. Also, they are not all well off enough to buy plays in six-shilling, or even in eighteenpenny volumes. Therefore, I think it opportune to issue this cheap edition of John Bull's Other Island this Home Rule Year, because its preface was written by an Irishman of Protestant family and Protestant prejudices, and shews that the one way in which the power of the priest can be kept within its proper limits in Ireland is by setting the Irish people free to take it in hand themselves without seeming to be treacherously taking the side of England against their own country.

Still more needed is this cheap edition in Ireland, where nobody can well afford to pay more than sixpence for anything, since, if I may put it elliptically, the only people in Ireland who can afford more than sixpence are those who live in England. I should like to call the attention of my nervous fellow Protestants in Ireland to the fact that in Italy, the centre of Roman Catholicism, the Pope is in a position closely resembling what that of Louis XVI would have been during the first years of the French Revolution if he, like the Pope, had had no wife to bring him to the scaffold by tempting him to betray his country to a foreign foe. Also that in France, in spite of the revocation of the Edict of Nantes by the Roman Catholic Church at the height of its power, the Huguenots have always wielded, and still wield today, a power that is out of all proportion to their comparative numbers, and even, I am afraid I must add, to their merits. The Huguenot of Ulster is a coward only when he breaks his own backbone by taking the part of a foreign country against his own. Shut him up in Derry with an English King besieging him, and he does not shriek for the Germans to come and help him as if the thumbscrews of the Spanish Armada were already on his hands; he chalks up No Surrender merrily, and puts up one of the famous fights of history. After all, what is the use of protesting that you will not be governed from Rome if the alternative is to be governed from London? The great Protestant Irishmen have been all the more powerful because they loved Ireland better, not only than Rome, but than England. Why was it that the priests had no power to impose a Roman Catholic Leader on the Home Rule movement instead of Parnell? Simply because Parnell was so proud of his Irish birthright that he would rather have been one of even a persecuted minority in an Irish parliament than the Premier of an English Cabinet. He was not afraid of his countrymen: he knew that Protestantism could hold its own only too well in a free Ireland; and even if he had not known it he would have taken his chance rather than sell his birthright and his country. It is the essential dishonor of acting as a foreign garrison in a land where they are not foreigners that makes the position of the Orangemen so impossible, and breaks in them the spirit that animates every man in Europe who is fighting for a minority; and what man of any dignity today is not one of a minority that cries in the wilderness against one or other of the manifold iniquities and falsehoods of our civilization? I think if I as a Home Ruler (and many other less orthodox things) can live in England and hold my own in a minority which on some very sensitive points reaches the odds of about 1 to 48,000,000, an Ulster Orangeman should be able to face Home Rule without his knees knocking shamefully in the face of a contemptuous England which despises him none the less because his cowardice seems to serve her own turn.

There are, I know, men and women who are political perverts by nature. The supreme misfortune of being born with one's natural instincts turned against nature by a freak of nature is a phenomenon that occurs politically as well as physiologically. There are Poles who are devoted with all their soul to Russia and the maintenance of Russian rule in Poland, Persians who are risking their lives to introduce it in Persia, Indians and Egyptians who are ready to sacrifice all they possess for England and English rule. And it is not to be denied that among these are persons of high character and remarkable ability, comparing very favorably with the dregs of the nationalist movements, which, just because they are national and normal, are made up of all sorts, and consequently have dregs: pretty nasty ones too. For that matter, if ever a Book of Spies be written, it will include examples of courage, conviction, perseverance, and ability, that will almost persuade shallow people that spies are the real heroes of military history. Even in more personal relations, natural passion cannot pretend to inspire more intense devotion than perverted passion. But when all is said, the pervert, however magnificently he may conduct his campaign against nature, remains abhorrent. When Napoleon, though he boasted of having made peers and marshals of peasants and ostlers, drew the line at promoting a spy, he followed a universal instinct and a sound one. When the Irish Catholic who, feeling bitterly that the domination of the priest is making his own lot hopeless, nevertheless stands shoulder to shoulder with the priest for Home Rule against Dublin Castle, he is behaving naturally and rightly. When the Orangeman sacrifices his nationality to his hatred of the priest, and fights against his own country for its conqueror, he is doing something for which, no matter how bravely he fights, history and humanity will never forgive him: English history and humanity, to their credit be it said, least of all.

Please do not suppose for a moment that I propose that the Irish Protestant should submit to the Irish Roman Catholic. I reproach the Irish Roman Catholic for his submission to Rome exactly as I reproach the Orangeman for his submission to England. If Catholicism is to be limited in Ireland by any geographical expression (in which case it ceases to be Catholic) let it be Irish Catholicism, not Italian Catholicism. Let us maintain our partnership with Rome as carefully as our partnership with England; but let it be, in the one case as in the other, a free partnership. But the Irish Catholics are not Italian in their politics. They do not oppose Home Rule; and that gives them the right to the support of every Irish Protestant until Home Rule is achieved. After that, let us by all means begin a civil war next day if we are fools enough. A war for an idea may be a folly; but it is not a dishonor. Both parties would be fighting for Ireland; and though the slaying of an Irishman by an Irishman for Ireland may be a tragedy — may be even a crime to those who think that all war is crime — at least it is not unnatural crime, like the slaying of an Irishman by an Irishman for England's sake. There will, of course, be no war of religion: I have shewn in this book that the Protestant under Home Rule will be far safer and stronger than he is today; but even if there were, that is the way to look at it.

The question is still more important for England than for Ireland, in spite of England's indifference to it. In Ireland we are still sane: we do not sneer at our country as 'Little Ireland', and cheer for a doubtful commercial speculation called The Empire which we could not point out accurately on the map, and which is populated by such an overwhelming majority of what an Irish peasant would call 'black heathens', that they force us to punish our own missionaries for asking them to buy and read The Bible, and compel the Protestant Passive Resisters, who will be sold up rather than pay a rate to maintain a Church school, to pay without a murmur for the establishment of the Roman Catholic Church in Malta. Formerly 'Little England', the 'right little, tight little Island', despised Spain for her imperial policy, and saw her lose her place, not only among the empires, but even among the nations, with self-satisfied superiority. Today England is letting herself be dragged into the path of Spain. She dreams of nothing but the old beginning: an Invincible Armada. Spain reckoned without the Lord of Hosts, who scattered that Invincible Armada for Little England. The modern Imperialist does not believe in the Lord of Hosts; but the Armada was defeated for all that, though England's fleet was far more inferior to it than the German fleet will ever again be to the English fleet. The Lord of Hosts may not be quite the sort of power that Philip of Spain conceived it to be: many of us are dropping the personal pronoun, as I have just dropped it lest I should be prosecuted for superstition by the Society for the Encouragement of Cruelty to Animals; but it can still send bigger fleets to the bottom than England can build, and exalt smaller nations than England ever was above drifting congeries of derelict regions held desperately together by terrified soldiers trying to wave half a dozen flags all at once in the name of Empire: a name that every man who has ever felt the sacredness of his own native soil to him, and thus learnt to regard that feeling in other men as something holy and inviolable, spits out of his mouth with enormous contempt.

Not that I have any delusions about Drake and his Elizabethan comrades: they were pirates and slave-traders, not a whit better than the Algerine corsair who shared with them what modern idiots call 'the command of the sea' (much the sea cares about their command!); but it is better to be a pirate trading in slaves out of sheer natural wickedness than a bankrupt in a cocked hat, doing the same things, and worse, against your own conscience, because you are paid for it and are afraid to do anything else. Drake thought nothing of burning a Spanish city; but he was not such a fool as to suppose that if he told off some of his crew to stay and govern that Spanish city by force when it was rebuilt, all the reasonable inhabitants of that town would recognize the arrangement as an enormous improvement, and be very much obliged to him, which is the modern Imperial idea. To singe the King of Spain's beard; pick his pocket; and run away, was, in the absence of any international police, a profitable bit of sport, if a rascally one; but if Drake had put a chain round the King's neck and led him round a prisoner for the rest of his life, he would have suffered as much by such a folly as the King, and probably died sooner of worry, anxiety, expense, and loss through the neglect of his own proper affairs, than the King would have died of captivity. Bermondsey goes to the dogs whilst those whose business it is to govern it are sitting on Bengal;

and the more Bengal kicks, the more Bermondsey is neglected, except by the tax collector. The notion that the way to prosper is to insist on managing everybody else's affairs is, on the face of it, a fool's notion. It is at bottom the folly of the ignorant simpletons who long to be kings and chiefs because they imagine that a king or chief is an idle voluptuary with lots of money, leisure, and power over others, to use irresponsibly for his own amusement.

In short, then, the future is not to the empires, but to federations of self-governing nations, exactly as, within these nations, the future is not to Capitalist Oligarchies, but to Collectivist organizations of free and equal citizens. In short, to Commonwealths.

In expressing this irresistible sentiment of nationality with all the rhetoric to which it lends itself, I am not forgetting that there are international rights as well as national ones. We are not only natives within our own frontiers but inheritors of the earth. England has rights in Ireland as Ireland has rights in England. I demand of every nation right of ingress and egress, roads, police, an efficient post office, and, in reason, freedom of conscience. I am prepared to steam-roller Tibet if Tibet persist in refusing me my international rights. If the Moors and Arabs cannot or will not secure these common human conditions for me in North Africa, I am quite prepared to co-operate with the French, the Italians, and the Spaniards in Morocco, Algeria, Tunisia, and Tripoli, with the Russians in Siberia, with all three and the English and Germans as well in Africa, or with the Americans in the hunting grounds of the red man, to civilize these places; though I know as well as anyone that there are many detestable features in our civilization, many virtues in village and tribal communities, and a very large alloy indeed of brigandage in our explorations and colonizations.

I know also that what compels us to push our frontiers farther and farther into regions we call barbarous is the necessity of policing, not the barbarians, but the European dregs and riffraff who set up little hells of anarchy and infamy just beyond the border, and thus compel us to advance and rope them in, step by step, no matter how much we are adding to that 'white man's burden', which is none the less a real thing because it is not specially a white man's burden any more than it is specially an Englishman's burden, as most of Mr Kipling's readers seem to interpret it. Tribes must make themselves into nations before they can claim the rights of nations; and this they can do only by civilization.

Also I cannot deny that the exclusion of the Chinese from America and Australia is a violation of international right which the Chinese will be perfectly justified in resisting by arms as soon as they feel strong enough. If nations are to limit immigration, inter-marriage with foreigners, and even international trade by tariffs, it had better be done by international law than by arbitrary national force as at present. It will be seen that I am under no delusion as to the freedom of Nationalism from abuse. I know that there are abuses in England which would not exist if she were governed by Germany, and that there will no doubt be abuses in Ireland under Home Rule which do not exist under English rule, just as things have been done under the Irish Local Government Act that the old oligarchical grand juries would not have tolerated. There are, indeed, a hundred horses on which I could ride off if I wished to shirk the main issue. But when all is said, it is so certain that in the long run all civilized nations must at the same time become more dependent one on another and do their own governing work themselves, that if Ireland refused Home Rule now, it would sooner or later be forced on her by England because England will need all her time and political energy for her own affairs when once she realizes that the day for letting them slide and muddling through is past.

LONDON
19th January 1912

TWENTYFOUR YEARS LATER

The sequel to these events confirmed my unheeded warning with a sanguinary completeness of which I had no prevision. At Easter 1916 a handful of Irishmen seized the Dublin Post Office and proclaimed an Irish Republic, with one of their number, a schoolmaster named Pearse, as President. If all Ireland had risen at this gesture it would have been a serious matter for England, then up to her neck in the war against the Central Empires. But there was no response: the gesture was a complete failure. All that was necessary was to blockade the Post Office until its microscopic republic was starved out and made ridiculous. What actually happened would be incredible if there were not so many living witnesses of it. From a battery planted at Trinity College (the Irish equivalent of Oxford University), and from a warship in the river Liffey, a bombardment was poured on the centre of the city which reduced more than a square mile of it to such a condition that when, in the following year, I was taken through Arras and Ypres to shew me what the German artillery had done to these cities in two and a half years, I laughed and said, 'You should see what the British artillery did to my native city in a week.' It would not be true to say that not one stone was left upon another; for the marksmanship was so bad that the Post Office itself was left standing amid a waste of rubbish heaps; and enough scraps of wall were left for the British Army, which needed recruits, to cover with appeals to the Irish to remember Belgium lest the fate of Louvain should befall their own hearths and homes.

Having thus worked up a harebrained romantic adventure into a heroic episode in the struggle for Irish freedom, the victorious artillerists proceeded to kill their prisoners of war in a drawn-out string of executions. Those who were executed accordingly became not only national heroes, but the martyrs whose blood was the seed of the present Irish Free State. Among those who escaped was its first President. Nothing more blindly savage, stupid, and terror-mad could have been devised by England's worst enemies. It was a very characteristic example of the mentality produced by the conventional gentleman-militarist education at Marlborough and Sandhurst and the conventional gentleman-diplomatist education at Eton and Oxford, Harrow and Cambridge. Is it surprising that the Russian Soviet Government, though fanatically credulous as to the need for popular education, absolutely refused to employ as teachers anyone who had been touched by the equivalent public school and university routine in Russia, and stuck to its resolution even at the cost of carrying on for some years with teachers who were hardly a day ahead of their pupils?

But the Post Office episode was eclipsed by an event which was much more than an episode, as it shattered the whole case for parliamentary government throughout the world. The Irish Nationalists, after thirty years of constitutional procedure in the British Parliament, had carried an Act to establish Irish Home Rule, as it was then called, which duly received the royal assent and became a statute of the realm. Immediately the British officers on service in Ireland mutinied, refusing to enforce the

Act or operate against the northern Orangemen who were openly arming themselves to resist it. They were assured of support by their fellow-officers at home. The Act was suspended after prominent English statesmen had taken part in the military manoeuvres of the Orangemen. The Prime Minister publicly pledged himself that Belfast, the Orange capital, would not in any case be coerced. In short, the Act was shelved under a threat of civil war; and the Clan na Gael, which in America had steadfastly maintained that the constitutional movement was useless, as England would in the last resort repudiate the constitution and hold Ireland against the Irish by physical force, and had been rebuked, lectured, and repudiated by the parliamentary Home Rulers for a whole generation for saying so, was justified. The Catholic Irish accordingly armed themselves and drilled as Volunteers in spite of the hostility of the Government, which meanwhile gave every possible assistance to the parallel preparations of the Orangemen. An Irish parliament (or Dail) sat in Dublin and claimed to be the national government. Irish courts were set up for the administration of Irish justice; Irish order was kept by Irish police; Irish taxes were collected by Irish officials; and British courts were boycotted. Upon this interesting but hopeless attempt to ignore British rule the Government let loose a specially recruited force (known to history as the Black and Tans) with *carte blanche* to kill, burn, and destroy, save only that they must stop short of rapine. They wrecked the Irish courts and produced a state of anarchy. They struck at the Irish through the popular co-operative stores and creameries, which they burnt. The people found a civil leader in Arthur Griffiths and a military one in Michael Collins. The Black and Tans had the British Government at their back: Collins had the people at his back. He threatened that for every creamery or co-operative store or cabin or cottage burnt by the Black and Tans he would burn two country houses of the Protestant gentry. The country houses that were not burnt were raided at night and laid under contribution for needed supplies. If the occupants reported the raid, the house was burnt. The Black and Tans and the ordinary constabulary were treated as enemies in uniform: that is, they were shot at sight and their stations burnt; or they were ambushed and killed in petty battles. Those who gave warnings or information of any helpful kind to them were mercilessly executed without privilege of sex or benefit of clergy. Collins, with allies in every street and hamlet, proved able to carry out his threat.

He won the crown of the Reign of Terror; and the position of the Protestant gentry became unbearable.

Thus by fire and bullet, murder and torture and devastation, a situation was produced in which the British Government had either to capitulate at the cost of a far more complete concession of self-government to Ireland than that decreed by the repudiated Home Rule Act, or to let loose the military strength of England in a Cromwellian reconquest, massacre, and replantation which it knew that public opinion in England and America would not tolerate; for some of the most conspicuous English champions of Ulster warned the Government that they could stand no more of the Black and Tan terrorism. And so we settled the Irish Question, not as civilized and reasonable men should have settled it, but as dogs settle a dispute over a bone.

Future historians will probably see in these catastrophes a ritual of human sacrifice without which the savages of the twentieth century could not effect any redistribution of political power or wealth. Nothing was learnt from Denshawai or the Black and Tan terror. In India, which is still struggling for self-government, and obviously must finally have it, a military panic led to the cannonading of a forbidden public meeting at Amritsar, the crowd being dealt with precisely as if it were a body of German shocktroops rushing the British trenches in Flanders. In London the police would have broken a score or two of heads and dragged a handful of ringleaders to the police courts. And there was the usual combination of mean spite with hyperbolical violence. Indians were forced to crawl past official buildings on their hands and knees. The effect was to make British imperial rule ridiculous in Europe, and implacably resented in India.

In Egypt the British domination died of Denshawai; but at its deathbed the British Sirdar was assassinated, whereupon the British Government, just then rather drunk after a sweeping election victory secured by an anti-Russian scare, announced to an amazed world that it was going to cut off the Nile at its source and destroy Egypt by stopping its water supply. Of course nothing happened but an ignominious climb down; but the incident illustrates my contention that our authority, when it is too far flung (as our patriotic rhapsodists put it), goes stark mad at the periphery if a pin drops. As to what further panics and atrocities will ensue before India is left to govern itself as much as Ireland and Egypt now are I am in the dark until the event enlightens me. But on the folly of allowing military counsels to prevail in political settlements I may point to the frontiers established by the victors after the war of 1914–18. Almost every one of these frontiers has a new war implicit in it, because the soldier recognizes no ethnographical, linguistic, or moral boundaries: he demands a line that he can defend, or rather that Napoleon or Wellington could have defended; for he has not yet learnt to think of offence and defence in terms of airplanes which ignore his Waterloo ridges. And the inevitable nationalist rebellions against these military frontiers, and the atrocities by which they are countered, are in full swing as I write.

Meanwhile, John Bull's Other Island, though its freedom has destroyed all the romantic interest that used to attach to it, has become at last highly interesting to the student of political science as an experiment in political structure. Protestant Ulster, which armed against the rest of Ireland and defied the British Parliament to the cry of 'We wont have it,' meaning that they would die in the last ditch singing 'O God, our help in ages past' rather than suffer or tolerate Home Rule, is now suffering and indeed hugging Home Rule on a much more homely scale than the Home Rulers ever demanded or dreamt of; for it has a Belfast Home Rule Parliament instead of an Irish one. And it has allowed Catholic Ireland to secure the Irish parliament. Thus, of the two regional parliaments which have been established on a sectarian basis, Protestant Ulster has been left with the smaller. Now it happens that Protestant Ulster is industrial Ireland and Catholic Ireland agricultural Ireland. And throughout the world for a century past the farmer, the peasant, and the Catholic have been the bulwark of the industrial capitalists against the growing political power of the industrial proletariat organized in trade unions, Labor parties, and the ubiquitous sodalities of that new ultra-Catholic Church called Socialism.

From this defensive alliance the Ulster employers, blinded by an obsolete bigotry and snobbery, have deliberately cut themselves off. In my preface of 1906, and again in my 1912 preface to a sixpenny edition of this play called the Home Rule edition, I exhorted the Protestants to take their chance, trust their grit, and play their part in a single parliament ruling an undivided Ireland. They did not take my advice. Probably they did not even read it; being too deeply absorbed in the History of Maria Monk, or the latest demonstration that all the evil in the world is the work of an underground conspiracy entitled by them 'the Jesuits'. It is a pity they did not begin their political education, as I began mine, by reading Karl Marx. It is true that I had occasion to point out that Marx was not infallible; but he left me with a very strong disposition to back the economic situation to control all the other situations, religious, nationalist, or romantic, in the long run. And so I do not despair of seeing Protestant Ulster seeking the alliance it repudiated. The Northern Parliament will not merge into the Oireachtas; for until both of them are superseded by a completely modernized central government, made for action and not for obstruction, they will remain more effective as regional parliaments than they would be as national ones; but they will soon have to take counsel together through conferences which will recur until they become a permanent institution and finally develop into what the Americans call Congress, or Federal Government of the whole island. No doubt this will be received in Belfast (if noticed at all) with shouts of 'We wont have it.' But I have heard that cry before, and regard it as a very hopeful sign that they will have it gladly enough when they have the luck to get it.

AYOT ST LAWRENCE,
November 1929

Persons in the Play

BROADBENT
LARRY DOYLE
TIM HAFFIGAN
HODSON
PETER KEEGAN
PATSY FARRELL
FATHER DEMPSEY
CORNEY DOYLE
BARNEY DORAN
MATTHEW HAFFIGAN
AUNT JUDY
NORA

Period – The Present. London and Ireland

ACT I *Office of Broadbent and Doyle, Civil Engineers, Great George Street, Westminster*

ACT II Scene 1: *Roscullen Hill*
Scene 2: *The Round Tower*

ACT III *The Grass Plot before Corney Doyle's House*

ACT IV Scene 1: *The Parlor at Corney Doyle's*
Scene 2: *Roscullen Hill*

Composition begun 17 June 1904; completed 23 August 1904. Published in *John Bull's Other Island, How He Lied to Her Husband, Major Barbara*, 1907. Revised text in Collected Edition, 1930. First presented at the Royal Court Theatre, London, on 1 November 1904, for six matinées.

ACT I

Great George Street, Westminster, is the address of Doyle and Broadbent, civil engineers. On the threshold one reads that the firm consists of Mr Laurence Doyle and Mr Thomas Broadbent, and that their rooms are on the first floor. Most of these rooms are private; for the partners, being bachelors and bosom friends, live there; and the door marked Private, next the clerks' office, is their domestic sitting room as well as their reception room for clients. Let me describe it briefly from the point of view of a sparrow on the window sill. The outer door is in the opposite wall, close to the right hand corner. Between this door and the left hand corner is a hatstand and a table consisting of large drawing boards on trestles, with plans, rolls of tracing paper, mathematical instruments, and other draughtsman's accessories on it. In the left hand wall is the fireplace, and the door of an inner room between the fireplace and our observant sparrow. Against the right hand wall is a filing cabinet, with a cupboard on it, and, nearer, a tall office desk and stool for one person. In the middle of the room a large double writing table is set across, with a chair at each end for the two partners. It is a room which no woman would tolerate, smelling of tobacco, and much in need of repapering, repainting, and recarpeting; but this is the effect of bachelor untidiness and indifference, not want of means; for nothing that Doyle and Broadbent themselves have purchased is cheap; nor is anything they want lacking. On the walls hang a large map of South America, a pictorial advertisement of a steamship company, an impressive portrait of Gladstone, and several caricatures of Mr Balfour as a rabbit and Mr Chamberlain as a fox by Francis Carruthers Gould.

At twenty minutes to five o'clock on a summer afternoon in 1904, the room is empty. Presently the outer door is opened, and a valet comes in laden with a large Gladstone bag and a strap of rugs. He carries them into the inner room. He is a respectable valet, old enough to have lost all alacrity and acquired an air of putting up patiently with a great deal of trouble and indifferent health. The luggage belongs to Broadbent, who enters after the valet. He pulls off his overcoat and hangs it with his hat on the stand. Then he comes to the writing table and looks through the letters waiting there for him. He is a robust, full-blooded, energetic man in the prime of life, sometimes eager and credulous, sometimes shrewd and roguish, sometimes portentously solemn, sometimes jolly

*and impetuous, always buoyant and irresistible, mostly likeable, and
enormously absurd in his most earnest moments. He bursts open his letters with
his thumb, and glances through them, flinging the envelopes about the floor
with reckless untidiness whilst he talks to the valet.*

BROADBENT [*calling*] Hodson.

HODSON [*in the bedroom*] Yes sir.

BROADBENT. Dont unpack. Just take out the things Ive worn; and put in
clean things.

HODSON [*appearing at the bedroom door*] Yes sir. [*He turns to go back into the
bedroom*].

BROADBENT. And look here! [*Hodson turns again*]. Do you remember
where I put my revolver?

HODSON. Revolver, sir! Yes sir. Mr Doyle uses it as a paperweight, sir,
when he's drawing.

BROADBENT. Well, I want it packed. Theres a packet of cartridges
somewhere, I think. Find it and pack it as well.

HODSON. Yes sir.

BROADBENT. By the way, pack your own traps too. I shall take you with
me this time.

HODSON [*hesitant*] Is it a dangerous part youre going to, sir? Should I be
expected to carry a revolver, sir?

BROADBENT. Perhaps it might be as well. I'm going to Ireland.

HODSON [*reassured*] Yes sir.

BROADBENT. You dont feel nervous about it, I suppose?

HODSON. Not at all, sir. I'll risk it, sir.

BROADBENT. Ever been in Ireland?

HODSON. No sir. I understand it's a very wet climate, sir. I'd better pack
your india-rubber overalls.

BROADBENT. Do. Wheres Mr Doyle?

HODSON. I'm expecting him at five, sir. He went out after lunch.

BROADBENT. Anybody been looking for me?

HODSON. A person giving the name of Haffigan has called twice today, sir.

BROADBENT. Oh, I'm sorry. Why didnt he wait? I told him to wait if I
wasnt in.

HODSON. Well sir, I didnt know you expected him; so I thought it best to —
to — not to encourage him, sir.

BROADBENT. Oh, he's all right. He's an Irishman, and not very particular about his appearance.

HODSON. Yes sir: I noticed that he was rather Irish.

BROADBENT. If he calls again let him come up.

HODSON. I think I saw him waiting about, sir, when you drove up. Shall I fetch him, sir?

BROADBENT. Do, Hodson.

HODSON. Yes sir [*He makes for the outer door*].

BROADBENT. He'll want tea. Let us have some.

HODSON [*stopping*] I shouldnt think he drank tea, sir.

BROADBENT. Well, bring whatever you think he'd like.

HODSON. Yes sir [*An electric bell rings*]. Here he is, sir. Saw you arrive, sir.

BROADBENT. Right. Shew him in. [*Hodson goes out. Broadbent gets through the rest of his letters before Hodson returns with the visitor*].

HODSON. Mr Affigan.

Haffigan is a stunted, shortnecked, smallheaded man of about 30, with a small bullet head, a red nose, and furtive eyes. He is dressed in seedy black, almost clerically, and might be a tenth-rate schoolmaster ruined by drink. He hastens to shake Broadbent's hand with a show of reckless geniality and high spirits, helped out by a rollicking stage brogue. This is perhaps a comfort to himself, as he is secretly pursued by the horrors of incipient delirium tremens.

HAFFIGAN. Tim Haffigan, sir, at your service. The top o the mornin to you, Misther Broadbent.

BROADBENT [*delighted with his Irish visitor*] Good afternoon, Mr Haffigan.

TIM. An is it the afthernoon it is already? Begorra, what I call the mornin is all the time a man fasts afther breakfast.

BROADBENT. Havnt you lunched?

TIM. Divil a lunch!

BROADBENT. I'm sorry I couldnt get back from Brighton in time to offer you some; but –

TIM. Not a word, sir, not a word. Sure itll do tomorrow. Besides, I'm Irish, sir: a poor aither, but a powerful dhrinker.

BROADBENT. I was just about to ring for tea when you came. Sit down, Mr Haffigan.

TIM. Tay is a good dhrink if your nerves can stand it. Mine cant.

Haffigan sits down at the writing table, with his back to the filing cabinet. Broadbent sits opposite him. Hodson enters empty-handed; takes two glasses, a siphon, and a tantalus from the cupboard: places them before Broadbent on the writing table; looks ruthlessly at Haffigan, who cannot meet his eye; and retires.

BROADBENT. Try a whisky and soda.

TIM [*sobered*] There you touch the national wakeness, sir. [*Piously*] Not that I share it meself. Ive seen too much of the mischief of it.

BROADBENT [*pouring the whisky*] Say when.

TIM. Not too sthrong. [*Broadbent stops and looks inquiringly at him*]. Say half-an-half. [*Broadbent, somewhat startled by this demand, pours a little more, and again stops and looks*]. Just a dhrain more: the lower half o the tumber doesnt hold a fair half. Thankya.

BROADBENT [*laughing*] You Irishmen certainly know how to drink. [*Pouring some whisky for himself*] Now thats my poor English idea of a whisky and soda.

TIM. An a very good idea it is too. Dhrink is the curse o me unhappy counthry. I take it meself because Ive a wake heart and a poor digestion; but in principle I'm a teetoatler.

BROADBENT [*suddenly solemn and strenuous*] So am I, of course. I'm a Local Optionist to the backbone. You have no idea, Mr Haffigan, of the ruin that is wrought in this country by the unholy alliance of the publicans, the bishops, the Tories, and The Times. We must close the public-houses at all costs [*he drinks*].

TIM. Sure I know. It's awful [*he drinks*]. I see youre a good Liberal like meself, sir.

BROADBENT. I am a lover of liberty, like every true Englishman, Mr Haffigan. My name is Broadbent. If my name were Breitstein, and I had a hooked nose and a house in Park Lane, I should carry a Union Jack handkerchief and a penny trumpet, and tax the food of the people to support the Navy League, and clamor for the destruction of the last remnants of national liberty —

TIM. Not another word. Shake hands.

BROADBENT. But I should like to explain —

TIM. Sure I know every word youre goin to say before yev said it. *I* know the sort o man yar. An so youre thinkin o comin to Ireland for a bit?

BROADBENT. Where else can I go? I am an Englishman and a Liberal; and now that South Africa has been enslaved and destroyed, there is no country left to me to take an interest in but Ireland. Mind: I dont say that an Englishman has not other duties. He has a duty to Finland and a duty to Macedonia. But what sane man can deny that an Englishman's first duty is his duty to Ireland? Unfortunately, we have politicians here more unscrupulous than Bobrikoff, more bloodthirsty than Abdui the Damned; and it is under their heel that Ireland is now writhing.

TIM. Faith, theyve reckoned up with poor oul Bobrikoff anyhow.

BROADBENT. Not that I defend assassination: God forbid! However strongly we may feel that the unfortunate and patriotic young man who avenged the wrongs of Finland on the Russian tyrant was perfectly right from his own point of view, yet every civilized man must regard murder with abhorrence. Not even in defence of Free Trade would I lift my hand against a political opponent, however richly he might deserve it.

TIM. I'm sure you wouldnt; and I honor you for it. Youre goin to Ireland, then, out o sympithy: is it?

BROADBENT. I'm going to develop an estate there for the Land Development Syndicate, in which I am interested. I am convinced that all it needs to make it pay is to handle it properly, as estates are handled in England. You know the English plan, Mr Haffigan, dont you?

TIM. Bedad I do, sir. Take all you can out of Ireland and spend it in England: thats it.

BROADBENT [not quite liking this] My plan, sir, will be to take a little money out of England and spend it in Ireland.

TIM. More power to your elbow! an may your shadda never be less! for youre the broth of a boy entirely. An how can I help you? Command me to the last dhrop o me blood.

BROADBENT. Have you ever heard of Garden City?

TIM [doubtfully] D'ye mane heavn?

BROADBENT. Heaven! No: it's near Hitchin. If you can spare half an hour I'll go into it with you.

TIM. I tell you hwat. Gimme a prospectus. Lemmy take it home and reflect on it.

BROADBENT. Youre quite right: I will [He gives him a copy of Ebenezer Howard's book, and several pamphlets]. You understand that the map of the city – the circular construction – is only a suggestion.

TIM. I'll make a careful note o that [looking dazedly at the map].

BROADBENT. What I say is, why not start a Garden City in Ireland?

TIM [*with enthusiasm*] Thats just what was on the tip o me tongue to ask you. Why not? [*Defiantly*] Tell me why not.

BROADBENT. There are difficulties. I shall overcome them; but there are difficulties. When I first arrive in Ireland I shall be hated as an Englishman. As a Protestant, I shall be denounced from every altar. My life may be in danger. Well, I am prepared to face that.

TIM. Never fear, sir. We know how to respict a brave innimy.

BROADBENT. What I really dread is misunderstanding. I think you could help me to avoid that. When I heard you speak the other evening in Bermondsey at the meeting of the National League, I saw at once that you were – You wont mind my speaking frankly?

TIM. Tell me all me faults as man to man. I can stand anything but flatthery.

BROADBENT. May I put it in this way? that I saw at once that you are a thorough Irishman, with all the faults and all the qualities of your race: rash and improvident but brave and goodnatured; not likely to succeed in business on your own account perhaps, but eloquent, humorous, a lover of freedom, and a true follower of that great Englishman Gladstone.

TIM. Spare me blushes. I mustnt sit here to be praised to me face. But I confess to the goodnature: it's an Irish wakeness. I'd share me last shillin with a friend.

BROADBENT. I feel sure you would, Mr Haffigan.

TIM [*impulsively*] Damn it! call me Tim. A man that talks about Ireland as you do may call me anything. Gimmy a howlt o that whisky bottle [*he replenishes*].

BROADBENT [*smiling indulgently*] Well, Tim, will you come with me and help to break the ice between me and your warmhearted, impulsive countrymen?

TIM. Will I come to Madagascar or Cochin China wid you? Bedad I'll come to the North Pole wid you if yll pay me fare; for the divil a shillin I have to buy a third class ticket.

BROADBENT. Ive not forgotten that, Tim. We must put that little matter on a solid English footing, though the rest can be as Irish as you please. You must come as my – my – well, I hardly know what to call it. If we call you my agent, theyll shoot you. If we call you a bailiff, theyll duck you in the horsepond. I have a secretary already; and –

TIM. Then we'll call him the Home Secretary and me the Irish Secretary. Eh?

BROADBENT [*laughing industriously*] Capital. Your Irish wit has settled the first difficulty. Now about your salary —

TIM. A salary, is it? Sure I'd do it for nothin, only me cloes ud disgrace you; and I'd be dhriven to borra money from your friends: a thing thats agin me nacher. But I wont take a penny more than a hundherd a year. [*He looks with restless cunning at Broadbent, trying to guess how far he may go*].

BROADBENT. If that will satisfy you —

TIM [*more than reassured*] Why shouldnt it satisfy me? A hundherd a year is twelve pound a month, isnt it?

BROADBENT. No. Eight pound six and eightpence.

TIM. Oh murdher! An I'll have to sind five timmy poor oul mother in Ireland. But no matther: I said a hundherd; and what I said I'll stick to, if I have to starve for it.

BROADBENT [*with business caution*] Well, let us say twelve pounds for the first month. Afterwards, we shall see how we get on.

TIM. Youre a gentleman, sir. Whin me mother turns up her toes, you shall take the five pounds off; for your expinses must be kep down wid a sthrong hand; an — [*He is interrupted by the arrival of Broadbent's partner*].

Mr Laurence Doyle is a man of 36, with cold grey eyes, strained nose, fine fastidious lips, critical brows, clever head, rather refined and goodlooking on the whole, but with a suggestion of thinskinnedness and dissatisfaction that contrasts strongly with Broadbent's eupeptic jollity.

He comes in as a man at home there, but on seeing the stranger shrinks at once, and is about to withdraw when Broadbent reassures him. He then comes forward to the table, between the two others.

DOYLE [*retreating*] Youre engaged.

BROADBENT. Not at all, not at all. Come in. [*to Tim*] This gentleman is a friend who lives with me here: my partner, Mr Doyle. [*To Doyle*] This is a new Irish friend of mine, Mr Tim Haffigan.

TIM [*rising with effusion*] Sure it's meself thats proud to meet any friend o Misther Broadbent's. The top o the mornin to you, sir! Me heart goes out teeye both. It's not often I meet two such splendid speciments iv the Anglo-Saxon race.

BROADBENT [*chuckling*] Wrong for once, Tim. My friend Mr Doyle is a countryman of yours.

Tim is noticeably dashed by this announcement. He draws in his horns at once, and scowls suspiciously at Doyle under a vanishing mask of goodfellowship: cringing a little, too, in mere nerveless fear of him.

DOYLE [*with cool disgust*] Good evening. [*He retires to the fireplace, and says to Broadbent in a tone which conveys the strongest possible hint to Haffigan that he is unwelcome*] Will you soon be disengaged?

TIM [*his brogue decaying into a common would-be genteel accent with an unexpected strain of Glasgow in it*] I must be going. Avnmpoartnt engeegement in the west end.

BROADBENT [*rising*] It's settled, then, that you come with me.

TIM. Ashll be verra pleased to accompany ye, sir.

BROADBENT. But how soon? Can you start tonight? from Paddington? We go by Milford Haven.

TIM [*hesitating*] Well – A'm afraid – A [*Doyle goes abruptly into the bedroom, slamming the door and shattering the last remnant of Tim's nerve. The poor wretch saves himself from bursting into tears by plunging again into his role of daredevil Irishman. He rushes to Broadbent; plucks at his sleeve with trembling fingers; and pours forth his entreaty with all the brogue he can muster, subduing his voice lest Doyle should hear and return*]. Misther Broadbent: dont humiliate me before a fella counthryman. Look here: me cloes is up the spout. Gimmy a fypounnote – I'll pay ya nex Choosda whin me ship comes home – or you can stop it out o me month's sallery. I'll be on the platform at Paddnton punctial an ready. Gimmy it quick, before he comes back. You wont mind me axin, will ye?

BROADBENT. Not at all. I was about to offer you an advance for travelling expenses. [*He gives him a bank note*].

TIM [*pocketing it*] Thank you. I'll be there half an hour before the thrain starts. [*Larry is heard at the bedroom door, returning*]. Whisht: he's comin back. Goodbye and God bless ye. [*He hurries out almost crying, the £5 note and all the drink it means to him being too much for his empty stomach and overstrained nerves*].

DOYLE [*returning*] Where the devil did you pick up that seedy swindler? What was he doing here? [*He goes up to the table where the plans are, and makes a note on one of them, referring to his pocket book as he does so*].

BROADBENT. There you go! Why are you so down on every Irishman you meet, especially if he's a bit shabby? poor devil! Surely a fellow-countryman may pass you the top of the morning without offence, even if his coat is a bit shiny at the seams.

DOYLE [*contemptuously*] The top of the morning! Did he call you the broth of a boy? [*He comes to the writing table*].

BROADBENT [*triumphantly*] Yes.

DOYLE. And wished you more power to your elbow?

BROADBENT. He did.

DOYLE. And that your shadow might never be less?

BROADBENT. Certainly.

DOYLE [*taking up the depleted whisky bottle and shaking his head at it*] And he got about half a pint of whisky out of you.

BROADBENT. It did him no harm. He never turned a hair.

DOYLE. How much money did he borrow?

BROADBENT. It was not borrowing exactly. He shewed a very honorable spirit about money. I believe he would share his last shilling with a friend.

DOYLE. No doubt he would share his friend's last shilling if his friend was fool enough to let him. How much did he touch you for?

BROADBENT. Oh, nothing. An advance on his salary – for travelling expenses.

DOYLE. Salary! In Heaven's name, what for?

BROADBENT. For being my Home Secretary, as he very wittily called it.

DOYLE. I dont see the joke.

BROADBENT. You can spoil any joke by being cold blooded about it. I saw it all right when he said it. It was something – something really very amusing – about the Home Secretary and the Irish Secretary. At all events, he's evidently the very man to take with me to Ireland to break the ice for me. He can gain the confidence of the people there, and make them friendly to me. Eh? [*He seats himself on the office stool, and tilts it back so that the edge of the standing desk supports his back and prevents his toppling over*].

DOYLE. A nice introduction, by George! Do you suppose the whole population of Ireland consists of drunken begging letter writers, or that even if it did, they would accept one another as references?

BROADBENT. Pooh! nonsense! he's only an Irishman. Besides, you dont seriously suppose that Haffigan can humbug me, do you?

DOYLE. No: he's too lazy to take the trouble. All he has to do is to sit there and drink your whisky while you humbug yourself. However, we neednt argue about Haffigan, for two reasons. First, with your money in his pocket he will never reach Paddington: there are too many public houses on the way. Second, he's not an Irishman at all.

BROADBENT. Not an Irishman! [*He is so amazed by the statement that he straightens himself and brings the stool bolt upright*].

DOYLE. Born in Glasgow. Never was in Ireland in his life. I know all about him.

BROADBENT. But he spoke — he behaved just like an Irishman.

DOYLE. Like an Irishman!! Man alive, dont you know that all this top-o-the-morning and broth-of-a-boy and more-power-to-your-elbow business is got up in England to fool you, like the Albert Hall concerts of Irish music? No Irishman ever talks like that in Ireland, or ever did, or ever will. But when a thoroughly worthless Irishman comes to England, and finds the whole place full of romantic duffers like you, who will let him loaf and drink and sponge and brag as long as he flatters your sense of moral superiority by playing the fool and degrading himself and his country, he soon learns the antics that take you in. He picks them up at the theatre or the music hall. Haffigan learnt the rudiments from his father, who came from my part of Ireland. I knew his uncles, Matt and Andy Haffigan of Rosscullen.

BROADBENT [*still incredulous*] But his brogue?

DOYLE. His brogue! A fat lot you know about brogues! Ive heard you call a Dublin accent that you could hang your hat on, a brogue. Heaven help you! you dont know the difference between Connemara and Rathmines. [*With violent irritation*] Oh, damn Tim Haffigan! lets drop the subject: he's not worth wrangling about.

BROADBENT. Whats wrong with you today, Larry? Why are you so bitter? *Doyle looks at him perplexedly; comes slowly to the writing table; and sits down at the end next the fireplace before replying.*

DOYLE. Well: your letter completely upset me, for one thing.

BROADBENT. Why?

DOYLE. Your foreclosing this Rosscullen mortgage and turning poor Nick

Lestrange out of house and home has rather taken me aback; for I liked the old rascal when I was a boy and had the run of his park to play in. I was brought up on the property.

BROADBENT. But he wouldnt pay the interest. I had to foreclose on behalf of the Syndicate. So now I'm off to Rosscullen to look after the property myself. [*He sits down at the writing table opposite Larry, and adds, casually, but with an anxious glance at his partner*] Youre coming with me, of course?

DOYLE [*rising nervously and recommencing his restless movements*] Thats it. Thats what I dread. Thats what has upset me.

BROADBENT. But dont you want to see your country again after 18 years absence? to see your people? to be in the old home again? to –

DOYLE [*interrupting him very impatiently*] Yes, yes: I know all that as well as you do.

BROADBENT. Oh well, of course [*with a shrug*] if you take it in that way, I'm sorry.

DOYLE. Never you mind my temper: it's not meant for you, as you ought to know by this time. [*He sits down again, a little ashamed of his petulance; reflects a moment bitterly; then bursts out*] I have an instinct against going back to Ireland· an instinct so strong that I'd rather go with you to the South Pole than to Rosscullen.

BROADBENT. What! Here you are, belonging to a nation with the strongest patriotism! the most inveterate homing instinct in the world! and you pretend youd rather go anywhere than back to Ireland. You dont suppose I believe you, do you? In your heart –

DOYLE. Never mind my heart: an Irishman's heart is nothing but his imagination. How many of all those millions that have left Ireland have ever come back or wanted to come back? But whats the use of talking to you? Three verses of twaddle about the Irish emigrant 'sitting on the stile, Mary', or three hours of Irish patriotism in Bermondsey or the Scotland Division of Liverpool, go further with you than all the facts that stare you in the face. Why, man alive, look at me! You know the way I nag, and worry, and carp, and cavil, and disparage, and am never satisfied and never quiet, and try the patience of my best friends.

BROADBENT. Oh, come, Larry! do yourself justice. Youre very amusing and agreeable to strangers.

DOYLE. Yes, to strangers. Perhaps if I was a bit stiffer to strangers, and a bit easier at home, like an Englishman, I'd be better company for you.

BROADBENT. We get on well enough. Of course you have the melancholy of the Keltic race —

DOYLE [bounding out of his chair] Good God!!!

BROADBENT [slyly] — and also its habit of using strong language when theres nothing the matter.

DOYLE. Nothing the matter! When people talk about the Celtic race, I feel as if I could burn down London. That sort of rot does more harm than ten Coercion Acts. Do you suppose a man need be a Celt to feel melancholy in Rosscullen? Why, man, Ireland was peopled just as England was; and its breed was crossed by just the same invaders.

BROADBENT. True. All the capable people in Ireland are of English extraction. It has often struck me as a most remarkable circumstance that the only party in parliament which shews the genuine old English character and spirit is the Irish party. Look at its independence, its determination, its defiance of bad Governments, its sympathy with oppressed nationalities all the world over! How English!

DOYLE. Not to mention the solemnity with which it talks old fashioned nonsense which it knows perfectly well to be a century behind the times. Thats English, if you like.

BROADBENT. No, Larry, no. You are thinking of the modern hybrids that now monopolize England. Hypocrites, humbugs, Germans, Jews, Yankees, foreigners, Park Laners, cosmopolitan riffraff. Dont call them English. They dont belong to the dear old island, but to their confounded new empire; and by George! theyre worthy of it; and I wish them joy of it.

DOYLE [unmoved by this outburst] There! You feel better now, dont you?

BROADBENT [defiantly] I do. Much better.

DOYLE. My dear Tom, you only need a touch of the Irish climate to be as big a fool as I am myself. If all my Irish blood were poured into your veins, you wouldnt turn a hair of your constitution and character. Go and marry the most English Englishwoman you can find, and then bring up your son in Rosscullen; and that son's character will be so like mine and so unlike yours that everybody will accuse me of being the father. [With sudden anguish] Rosscullen! oh, good Lord, Rosscullen! The dullness! The hopelessness! the ignorance! the bigotry!

BROADBENT [*matter-of-factly*] The usual thing in the country, Larry. Just the same here.

DOYLE [*hastily*] No, no: the climate is different. Here, if the life is dull, you can be dull too, and no great harm done. [*Going off into a passionate dream*] But your wits cant thicken in that soft moist air, on those white springy roads, in those misty rushes and brown bogs, on those hillsides of granite rocks and magenta heather. Youve no such colors in the sky, no such lure in the distances, no such sadness in the evenings. Oh, the dreaming! the dreaming! the torturing, heart-scalding, never satisfying dreaming, dreaming, dreaming, dreaming! [*Savagely*] No debauchery that ever coarsened and brutalized an Englishman can take the worth and usefulness out of him like that dreaming. An Irishman's imagination never lets him alone, never convinces him, never satisfies him; but it makes him that he cant face reality nor deal with it nor handle it nor conquer it: he can only sneer at them that do, and [*bitterly, at Broadbent*] be 'agreeable to strangers', like a good-for-nothing woman on the streets. [*Gabbling at Broadbent across the table*] It's all dreaming, all imagination. He cant be religious. The inspired Churchman that teaches him the sanctity of life and the importance of conduct is sent away empty; while the poor village priest that gives him a miracle or a sentimental story of a saint, has cathedrals built for him out of the pennies of the poor. He cant be intelligently political: he dreams of what the Shan Van Vocht said in ninetyeight. If you want to interest him in Ireland youve got to call the unfortunate island Kathleen ni Hoolihan and pretend she's a little old woman. It saves thinking. It saves working. It saves everything except imagination, imagination, imagination; and imagination's such a torture that you cant bear it without whisky. [*With fierce shivering self-contempt*] At last you get that you can bear nothing real at all: youd rather starve than cook a meal; youd rather go shabby and dirty than set your mind to take care of your clothes and wash yourself; you nag and squabble at home because your wife isnt an angel, and she despises you because youre not a hero; and you hate the whole lot round you because theyre only poor slovenly useless devils like yourself. [*Dropping his voice like a man making some shameful confidence*] And all the while there goes on a horrible, senseless, mischievous laughter. When youre young, you exchange vile stories with them; and as youre too futile to be able to help or cheer them, you chaff and sneer and taunt them for not doing the things you darent do yourself. And all the time you laugh! laugh! laugh! eternal derision, eternal envy, eternal folly, eternal fouling and staining and degrading, until, when you come at last to a country where men take a question seriously and give a serious answer to it, you deride them for having no sense of humor, and plume yourself on your own worthlessness as if it made you better than them.

BROADBENT [*roused to intense earnestness by Doyle's eloquence*] Never despair, Larry. There are great possibilities for Ireland. Home Rule will work wonders under English guidance.

DOYLE [*pulled up short, his face twitching with a reluctant smile*] Tom: why do you select my most tragic moments for your most irresistible strokes of humor?

BROADBENT. Humor! I was perfectly serious. What do you mean? Do you doubt my seriousness about Home Rule?

DOYLE. I am sure you are serious, Tom, about the English guidance.

BROADBENT [*quite reassured*] Of course I am. Our guidance is the important thing. We English must place our capacity for government without stint at the service of nations who are less fortunately endowed in that respect; so as to allow them to develop in perfect freedom to the English level of self-government, you know. You understand me?

DOYLE. Perfectly. And Rosscullen will understand you too.

BROADBENT [*cheerfully*] Of course it will. So thats all right. [*He pulls up his chair and settles himself comfortably to lecture Doyle*]. Now Larry, Ive listened carefully to all youve said about Ireland; and I can see nothing whatever to prevent your coming with me. What does it all come to? Simply that you were only a young fellow when you were in Ireland. Youll find all that chaffing and drinking and not knowing what to be at in Peckham just the same as in Donnybrook. You looked at Ireland with a boy's eyes and saw only boyish things. Come back with me and look at it with a man's; and get a better opinion of your country.

DOYLE. I daresay youre partly right in that: at all events I know very well that if I had been the son of a laborer instead of the son of a country landagent, I should have struck more grit than I did. Unfortunately I'm not going back to visit the Irish nation, but to visit my father and Aunt Judy and Nora Reilly and Father Dempsey and the rest of them.

BROADBENT. Well, why not? Theyll be delighted to see you, now that England has made a man of you.

DOYLE [*struck by this*] Ah! you hit the mark there, Tom, with true British inspiration.

BROADBENT. Common sense, you mean.

DOYLE [*quickly*] No I dont: youve no more common sense than a gander. No Englishman has any common sense, or ever had, or ever will have. Youre going on a sentimental expedition for perfectly ridiculous reasons with your head full of political nonsense that would not take in any ordinarily intelligent donkey; but you can hit me in the eye with the simple truth about myself and my father.

BROADBENT [*amazed*] I never mentioned your father.

DOYLE [*not heeding the interruption*] There he is in Rosscullen, a landagent who's always been in a small way because he's a Catholic, and the landlords are mostly Protestants. What with land courts reducing rents and Land Purchase Acts turning big estates into little holdings, he'd be a beggar if he hadnt taken to collecting the new purchase instalments instead of the old rents. I doubt if he's been further from home than Athenmullet for twenty years. And here am I, made a man of, as you say, by England.

BROADBENT [*apologetically*] I assure you I never meant –

DOYLE. Oh, dont apologize: it's quite true. I daresay Ive learnt something in America and a few other remote and inferior spots; but in the main it is by living with you and working in double harness with you that I have learnt to live in a real world and not in an imaginary one. I owe more to you than to any Irishman.

BROADBENT [*shaking his head with a twinkle in his eye*] Very friendly of you, Larry, old man, but all blarney. I like blarney; but it's rot, all the same.

DOYLE. No it's not. I should never have done anything without you; though I never stop wondering at that blessed old head of yours with all its ideas in watertight compartments, and all the compartments warranted impervious to anything it doesnt suit you to understand.

BROADBENT [*invincible*] Unmitigated rot, Larry, I assure you.

DOYLE. Well, at any rate you will admit that all my friends are either Englishmen or men of the big world that belongs to the big Powers. All the serious part of my life has been lived in that atmosphere: all the serious part of my work has been done with men of that sort. Just think of me as I am now going back to Rosscullen! to that hell of littleness and monotony! How am I to get on with a little country landagent that ekes out his 5 per cent with a little farming and a scrap of house property in the nearest country town? What am I to say to him? What is he to say to me?

BROADBENT [*scandalized*] But youre father and son, man!

DOYLE. What difference does that make? What would you say if I proposed a visit to your father?

BROADBENT [*with filial rectitude*] I always made a point of going to see my father regularly until his mind gave way.

DOYLE [*concerned*] Has he gone mad? You never told me.

BROADBENT. He has joined the Tariff Reform League. He would never have done that if his mind had not been weakened. [*Beginning to declaim*] He has fallen a victim to the arts of a political charlatan who –

DOYLE [*interrupting him*] You mean that you keep clear of your father because he differs from you about Free Trade, and you dont want to quarrel with him. Well, think of me and my father! He's a Nationalist and a Separatist. I'm a metallurgical chemist turned civil engineer. Now whatever else metallurgical chemistry may be, it's not national. It's international. And my business and yours as civil engineers is to join countries, not to separate them. The one real political conviction that our business has rubbed into us is that frontiers are hindrances and flags confounded nuisances.

BROADBENT [*still smarting under Mr Chamberlain's economic heresy*] Only when there is a protective tariff –

DOYLE [*firmly*] Now look here, Tom: you want to get in a speech on Free Trade; and youre not going to do it: I wont stand it. My father wants to make St George's Channel a frontier and hoist a green flag on College Green; and I want to bring Galway within 3 hours of Colchester and 24 of New York. I want Ireland to be the brains and imagination of a big Commonwealth, not a Robinson Crusoe island. Then theres the religious difficulty. My Catholicism is the Catholicism of Charlemagne or Dante, qualified by a great deal of modern science and folklore which Father Dempsey would call the ravings of an Atheist. Well, my father's Catholicism is the Catholicism of Father Dempsey.

BROADBENT [*shrewdly*] I dont want to interrupt you, Larry; but you know this is all gammon. These differences exist in all families; but the members rub on together all right. [*Suddenly relapsing into portentousness*] Of course there are some questions which touch the very foundations of morals; and on these I grant you even the closest relationships cannot excuse any compromise or laxity. For instance –

DOYLE [*impatiently springing up and walking about*] For instance, Home Rule, South Africa, Free Trade, and putting the Church schools on the Education Rate. Well, I should differ from my father on every one of them, probably, just as I differ from you about them.

BROADBENT. Yes; but you are an Irishman; and these things are not serious to you as they are to an Englishman.

DOYLE. What! not even Home Rule!

BROADBENT [*steadfastly*] Not even Home Rule. We owe Home Rule not to the Irish, but to our English Gladstone. No, Larry: I cant help thinking that theres something behind all this.

DOYLE [*hotly*] What is there behind it? Do you think I'm humbugging you?

BROADBENT. Dont fly out, old chap. I only thought –

DOYLE. What did you think?

BROADBENT. Well, a moment ago I caught a name which is new to me: a Miss Nora Reilly, I think. [*Doyle stops dead and stares at him with something like awe*]. I dont wish to be impertinent, as you know, Larry; but are you sure she has nothing to do with your reluctance to come to Ireland with me?

DOYLE [*sitting down again, vanquished*] Thomas Broadbent: I surrender. The poor silly-clever Irishman takes off his hat to God's Englishman. The man who could in all seriousness make that recent remark of yours about Home Rule and Gladstone must be simply the champion idiot of all the world. Yet the man who could in the very next sentence sweep away all my special pleading and go straight to the heart of my motives must be a man of genius. But that the idiot and the genius should be the same man! how is that possible? [*Springing to his feet*] By Jove, I see it all now. I'll write an article about it, and send it to Nature.

BROADBENT [*staring at him*] What on earth –

DOYLE. It's quite simple. You know that a caterpillar –

BROADBENT. A caterpillar!!!

DOYLE. Yes, a caterpillar. Now give your mind to what I am going to say; for it's a new and important scientific theory of the English national character. A caterpillar —

BROADBENT. Look here, Larry: dont be an ass.

DOYLE [*insisting*] I say a caterpillar and I mean a caterpillar. Youll understand presently. A caterpillar [*Broadbent mutters a slight protest, but does not press it*] when it gets into a tree, instinctively makes itself look exactly like a leaf; so that both its enemies and its prey may mistake it for one and think it not worth bothering about.

BROADBENT. Whats that got to do with our English national character?

DOYLE. I'll tell you. The world is as full of fools as a tree is full of leaves. Well, the Englishman does what the caterpillar does. He instinctively makes himself look like a fool, and eats up all the real fools at his ease while his enemies let him alone and laugh at him for being a fool like the rest. Oh, nature is cunning! cunning! [*He sits down, lost in contemplation of his word-picture*].

BROADBENT [*with hearty admiration*] Now you know, Larry, that would never have occurred to me. You Irish people are amazingly clever. Of course it's all tommy rot; but it's so brilliant, you know! How the dickens do you think of such things! You really must write an article about it: they'll pay you something for it. If Nature wont have it, I can get it into Engineering for you: I know the editor.

DOYLE. Lets get back to business. I'd better tell you about Nora Reilly.

BROADBENT. No: never mind. I shouldnt have alluded to her.

DOYLE. I'd rather. Nora has a fortune.

BROADBENT [*keenly interested*] Eh? How much?

DOYLE. Forty per annum.

BROADBENT. Forty thousand?

DOYLE. No forty. Forty pounds.

BROADBENT [*much dashed*] Thats what you call a fortune in Rosscullen, is it?

DOYLE. A girl with a dowry of five pounds calls it a fortune in Rosscullen. Whats more, £40 a year is a fortune there; and Nora Reilly enjoys a good deal of social consideration as an heiress on the strength of it. It has helped my father's household through many a tight place. My father was her father's agent. She came on a visit to us when he died, and has lived with us ever since.

BROADBENT [*attentively, beginning to suspect Larry of misconduct with Nora, and resolving to get to the bottom of it*] Since when? I mean how old were you when she came?

DOYLE. I was seventeen. So was she: if she'd been older she'd have had more sense than to stay with us. We were together for 18 months before I went up to Dublin to study. When I went home for Christmas and Easter, she was there. I suppose it used to be something of an event for her; though of course I never thought of that then.

BROADBENT. Were you at all hard hit?

DOYLE. Not really. I had only two ideas at that time: first, to learn to do something; and then to get out of Ireland and have a chance of doing it. She didnt count. I was romantic about her, just as I was romantic about Byron's heroines or the old Round Tower of Rosscullen; but she didnt count any more than they did. Ive never crossed St George's Channel since for her sake – never even landed at Queenstown and come back to London through Ireland.

BROADBENT. But did you ever say anything that would justify her in waiting for you?

DOYLE. No, never. But she is waiting for me.

BROADBENT. How do you know?

DOYLE. She writes to me – on her birthday. She used to write on mine, and send me little things as presents; but I stopped that by pretending that it was no use when I was travelling, as they got lost in the foreign post-offices. [*He pronounces post-offices with the stress on offices, instead of on post*].

BROADBENT. You answer the letters?

DOYLE. Not very punctually. But they get acknowledged at one time or another.

BROADBENT. How do you feel when you see her handwriting?

DOYLE. Uneasy. I'd give £50 to escape a letter.

BROADBENT [*looking grave, and throwing himself back in his chair to intimate that the cross-examination is over, and the result very damaging to the witness*] Hm!

DOYLE. What d'ye mean by Hm!

BROADBENT. Of course I know that the moral code is different in Ireland. But in England it's not considered fair to trifle with a woman's affections.

DOYLE. You mean that an Englishman would get engaged to another woman and return Nora her letters and presents with a letter to say he was unworthy of her and wished her every happiness?

BROADBENT. Well, even that would set the poor girl's mind at rest.

DOYLE. Would it? I wonder! One thing I can tell you; and that is that Nora would wait until she died of old age sooner than ask my intentions or condescend to hint at the possibility of my having any. You dont know what Irish pride is. England may have knocked a good deal of it out of me; but she's never been in England; and if I had to choose between wounding that delicacy in her and hitting her in the face, I'd hit her in the face without a moment's hesitation.

BROADBENT [*who has been nursing his knee and reflecting, apparently rather agreeably*] You know, all this sounds rather interesting. Theres the Irish charm about it. Thats the worst of you: the Irish charm doesnt exist for you.

DOYLE. Oh yes it does. But it's the charm of a dream. Live in contact with dreams and you will get something of their charm: live in contact with facts and you will get something of their brutality. I wish I could find a country to live in where the facts were not brutal and the dreams not unreal.

BROADBENT [*changing his attitude and responding to Doyle's earnestness with deep conviction: his elbows on the table and his hands clenched*] Dont despair, Larry, old boy: things may look black; but there will be a great change after the next election.

DOYLE [*jumping up*] Oh, get out, you idiot!

BROADBENT [*rising also, not a bit snubbed*] Ha! Ha! you may laugh; but we shall see. However, dont let us argue about that. Come now! you ask my advice about Miss Reilly?

DOYLE [*reddening*] No I dont. Damn your advice! [*Softening*] Lets have it, all the same.

BROADBENT. Well, everything you tell me about her impresses me favorably. She seems to have the feelings of a lady; and though we must face the fact that in England her income would hardly maintain her in the lower middle class –

DOYLE [*interrupting*] Now look here, Tom. That reminds me. When you go to Ireland, just drop talking about the middle class and bragging of belonging to it. In Ireland youre either a gentleman or youre not. If you want to be particularly offensive to Nora, you can call her a Papist; but if you call her a middle-class woman, Heaven help you!

BROADBENT [*irrepressible*] Never fear. Youre all descended from the ancient kings: I know that. [*Complacently*] I'm not so tactless as you think, my boy. [*Earnest again*] I expect to find Miss Reilly a perfect lady; and I strongly advise you to come and have another look at her before you make up your mind about her. By the way, have you a photograph of her?

DOYLE. Her photographs stopped at twenty-five.

BROADBENT [*saddened*] Ah yes, I suppose so. [*With feeling, severely*] Larry: youve treated that poor girl disgracefully.

DOYLE. By George, if she only knew that two men were talking about her like this –!

BROADBENT. She wouldnt like it, would she? Of course not. We ought to be ashamed of ourselves, Larry. [*More and more carried away by his new fancy*]. You know, I have a sort of presentiment that Miss Reilly is a very superior woman.

DOYLE [*staring hard at him*] Oh! you have, have you?

BROADBENT. Yes I have. There is something very touching about the history of this beautiful girl.

DOYLE. Beau –! Oho! Heres a chance for Nora! and for me! [*Calling*] Hodson.

HODSON [*appearing at the bedroom door*] Did you call, sir?

DOYLE. Pack for me too. I'm going to Ireland with Mr Broadbent.

HODSON. Right sir. [*He retires into the bedroom*].

BROADBENT [*clapping Doyle on the shoulder*] Thank you, old chap. Thank you.

ACT II

Rosscullen. Westward a hillside of granite rock and heather slopes upward across the prospect from south to north. A huge stone stands on it in a naturally impossible place, as if it had been tossed up there by a giant. Over the brow, in the desolate valley beyond, is a round tower. A lonely white high road trending away westward past the tower loses itself at the foot of the far mountains. It is evening; and there are great breadths of silken green in the Irish sky. The sun is setting.

A man with the face of a young saint, yet with white hair and perhaps 50 years on his back, is standing near the stone in a trance of intense melancholy, looking over the hills as if by mere intensity of gaze he could pierce the glories of the sunset and see into the streets of heaven. He is dressed in black, and is rather more clerical in appearance than most English curates are nowadays; but he does not wear the collar and waistcoat of a parish priest. He is roused from his trance by the chirp of an insect from a tuft of grass in a crevice of the stone. His face relaxes; he turns quietly, and gravely takes off his hat to the tuft, addressing the insect in a brogue which is the jocular assumption of a gentleman and not the natural speech of a peasant.

THE MAN. An is that yourself, Misther Grasshopper? I hope I see you well this fine evenin.

THE GRASSHOPPER [*prompt and shrill in answer*] X.X.

THE MAN [*encouragingly*] Thats right. I suppose now youve come out to make yourself miserable be admyerin the sunset?

THE GRASSHOPPER [*sadly*] X.X.

THE MAN. Aye, youre a thrue Irish grasshopper.

THE GRASSHOPPER [*loudly*] X.X.X.

THE MAN. Three cheers for ould Ireland, is it? That helps you to face out the misery and the poverty and the torment, doesnt it?

THE GRASSHOPPER [*plaintively*] X.X.

THE MAN. Ah, it's no use, me poor little friend. If you could jump as far as a kangaroo you couldnt jump away from your own heart an its punishment. You can only look at Heaven from here: you cant reach it. There! [*pointing with his stick to the sunset*] thats the gate o' glory, isnt it?

THE GRASSHOPPER [*assenting*] X.X.

THE MAN. Sure it's the wise grasshopper yar to know that. But tell me this, Misther Unworldly Wiseman: why does the sight of Heaven wring your heart an mine as the sight of holy wather wrings the heart o the divil? What wickedness have you done to bring that curse on you? Here! where are you jumpin to? Wheres your manners to go skyrocketing like that out o the box in the middle o your confession [*he threatens it with his stick*]?

THE GRASSHOPPER [*penitently*] X.

THE MAN. [*lowering the stick*] I accept your apology; but dont do it again. And now tell me one thing before I let you go home to bed. Which would you say this country was: hell or purgatory?

THE GRASSHOPPER. X.

THE MAN. Hell! Faith I'm afraid youre right. I wondher what you and me did when we were alive to get sent here.

THE GRASSHOPPER [*shrilly*] X.X.

THE MAN [*nodding*] Well, as you say, it's a delicate subject; and I wont press it on you. Now off widja.

THE GRASSHOPPER. X.X. [*It springs away*].

THE MAN [*waving his stick*] God speed you! [*He walks away past the stone towards the brow of the hill. Immediately a young laborer, his face distorted with terror, slips round from behind the stone*].

THE LABORER [*crossing himself repeatedly*] Oh glory be to God! glory be to God! Oh Holy Mother an all the saints! Oh murdher! murdher! [*Beside himself, calling*] Fadher Keegan! Fadher Keegan!

THE MAN [*turning*] Who's there? What's that? [*He comes back and finds the laborer, who clasps his knees*] Patsy Farrell! What are you doing here?

PATSY. Oh for the love o God dont lave me here wi dhe grasshopper. I hard it spakin to you. Dont let it do me any harm, Father darlint.

KEEGAN. Get up, you foolish man, get up. Are you afraid of a poor insect because I pretended it was talking to me?

PATSY. Oh, it was no pretendin, Fadher dear. Didnt it give three cheers n say it was a divil out o hell? Oh say youll see me safe home, Fadher; n put a blessin on me or somethin [*he moans with terror*].

KEEGAN. What were you doin there, Patsy, listnin? Were you spyin on me?

PATSY. No, Fadher: on me oath an soul I wasnt: I was waitn to meet

Masther Larry n carry his luggage from the car; n I fell asleep on the grass; n you woke me talking to the grasshopper; n I hard its wicked little voice. Oh, d'ye think I'll die before year's out, Fadher?

KEEGAN. For shame, Patsy! Is that your religion, to be afraid of a little deeshy grasshopper? Suppose it was a divil, what call have you to fear it? If I could ketch it, I'd make you take it home widja in your hat for a penance.

PATSY. Sure, if you wont let it harm me, I'm not afraid, your riverence. [*He gets up, a little reassured. He is a callow, flaxen polled, smoothfaced, downy chinned lad, fully grown but not yet fully filled out, with blue eyes and an instinctively acquired air of helplessness and silliness, indicating, not his real character, but a cunning developed by his constant dread of a hostile dominance, which he habitually tries to disarm and tempt into unmasking by pretending to be a much greater fool than he really is. Englishmen think him half-witted, which is exactly what he intends them to think. He is clad in corduroy trousers, unbuttoned waistcoat, and coarse blue striped shirt*].

KEEGAN [*admonitorily*] Patsy: what did I tell you about callin me Father Keegan an your reverence? What did Father Dempsey tell you about it?

PATSY. Yis, Fadher.

KEEGAN. Father!

PATSY [*desperately*] Arra, hwat am I to call you? Fadher Dempsey sez youre not a priest; n we all know youre not a man: n how do we know what ud happen to us if we shewed any disrespect to you? N sure they say wanse a priest always a priest.

KEEGAN [*sternly*] It's not for the like of you, Patsy, to go behind the instruction of your parish priest and set yourself up to judge whether your Church is right or wrong.

PATSY. Sure I know that, sir.

KEEGAN. The Church let me be its priest as long as it thought me fit for its work. When it took away my papers it meant you to know that I was only a poor madman, unfit and unworthy to take charge of the souls of the people.

PATSY. But wasnt it only because you knew more Latn than Father Dempsey that he was jealous of you?

KEEGAN [*scolding him to keep himself from smiling*] How dar you, Patsy

Farrell, put your own wicked little spites and foolishnesses into the heart of your priest? For two pins I'd tell him what you just said.

PATSY [*coaxing*] Sure you wouldnt —

KEEGAN. Wouldnt I? God forgive you! youre little better than a heathen.

PATSY. Deedn I am, Fadher: it's me bruddher the tinsmith in Dublin youre thinkin of. Sure he had to be a free-thinker when he larnt a thrade and went to live in the town.

KEEGAN. Well, he'll get to Heaven before you if youre not careful, Patsy. And now you listen to me, once and for all. Youll talk to me and pray for me by the name of Pether Keegan, so you will. And when youre angry and tempted to lift your hand agen the donkey or stamp your foot on the little grasshopper, remember that the donkey's Pether Keegan's brother, and the grasshopper Pether Keegan's friend. And when youre tempted to throw a stone at a sinner or a curse at a beggar, remember that Pether Keegan is a worse sinner and a worse beggar, and keep the stone and the curse for him the next time you meet him. Now say God bless you, Pether, to me before I go, just to practise you a bit.

PATSY. Sure it wouldnt be right, Fadher, I cant —

KEEGAN. Yes you can. Now out with it; or I'll put this stick into your hand an make you hit me with it.

PATSY [*throwing himself on his knees in an ecstasy of adoration*] Sure it's your blessin I want, Fadher Keegan. I'll have no luck widhout it.

KEEGAN [*shocked*] Get up out o that, man. Dont kneel to me: I'm not a saint.

PATSY [*with intense conviction*] Oh in throth yar, sir. [*The grasshopper chirps. Patsy, terrified, clutches at Keegan's hands*] Dont set it on me, Fadher: I'll do anythin you bid me.

KEEGAN [*pulling him up*] You bosthoon, you! Dont you see that it only whistled to tell me Miss Reilly's comin? There! Look at her and pull yourself together for shame. Off widja to the road: youll be late for the car if you dont make haste [*bustling him down the hill*]. I can see the dust of it in the gap already.

PATSY. The Lord save us! [*He goes down the hill towards the road like a haunted man*].

Nora Reilly comes down the hill. A slight weak woman in a pretty muslin print gown (her best), she is a figure commonplace enough to Irish eyes; but on the inhabitants of fatter-fed, (crowded, hustling and bustling modern

*countries she makes a very different impression. The absence of any symptoms
of coarseness or hardness or appetite in her, her comparative delicacy of
manner and sensibility of apprehension, her fine hands and frail figure, her
novel accent, with the caressing plaintive Irish melody of her speech, give her
a charm which is all the more effective because, being untravelled, she is
unconscious of it, and never dreams of deliberately dramatizing and exploiting
it, as the Irishwomen in England do. For Tom Broadbent therefore, an
attractive woman, whom he would even call ethereal. To Larry Doyle, an
everyday woman fit only for the eighteenth century, helpless, useless, almost
sexless, an invalid without the excuse of disease, an incarnation of everything
in Ireland that drove him out of it. These judgments have little value and
no finality; but they are the judgments on which her fate hangs just at present.
Keegan touches his hat to her: he does not take it off.*

NORA. Mr Keegan: I want to speak to you a minute if you dont mind.

KEEGAN [*dropping the broad Irish vernacular of his speech to Patsy*] An hour
if you like, Miss Reilly: youre always welcome. Shall we sit down?

NORA. Thank you. [*They sit on the heather. She is shy and anxious; but she
comes to the point promptly because she can think of nothing else*]. They
say you did a gradle o travelling at one time.

KEEGAN. Well, you see I'm not a Mnooth man [*he means that he was not a
student at Maynooth College*]. When I was young I admired the older
generation of priests that had been educated in Salamanca. So when I
felt sure of my vocation I went to Salamanca. Then I walked from
Salamanca to Rome, an sted in a monastery there for a year. My
pilgrimage to Rome taught me that walking is a better way of travelling
than the train; so I walked from Rome to the Sorbonne in Paris; and
I wish I could have walked from Paris to Oxford; for I was very sick
on the sea. After a year of Oxford I had to walk to Jerusalem to walk
the Oxford feeling off me. From Jerusalem I came back to Patmos, and
spent six months at the monastery of Mount Athos. From that I came
to Ireland and settled down as a parish priest until I went mad.

NORA [*startled*] Oh dont say that.

KEEGAN. Why not? Dont you know the story? how I confessed a black man
and gave him absolution? and how he put a spell on me and drove me
mad?

NORA. How can you talk such nonsense about yourself? For shame!

KEEGAN. It's not nonsense at all: it's true – in a way. But never mind the

black man. Now that you know what a travelled man I am, what can
I do for you? [*She hesitates and plucks nervously at the heather. He stays
her hand gently*]. Dear Miss Nora: dont pluck the little flower. If it was
a pretty baby you wouldnt want to pull its head off and stick it in a vawse
o water to look at. [*The grasshopper chirps: Keegan turns his head and
addresses it in the vernacular*]. Be aisy, me son: she wont spoil the swing-
swong in your little three. [*To Nora, resuming his urbane style*] You see
I'm quite cracked; but never mind: I'm harmless. Now what is it?

NORA [*embarrassed*] Oh, only idle curiosity. I wanted to know whether you
found Ireland – I mean the country part of Ireland, of course – very
small and backwardlike when you came back to it from Rome and
Oxford and all the great cities.

KEEGAN. When I went to those great cities I saw wonders I had never seen
in Ireland. But when I came back to Ireland I found all the wonders
there waiting for me. You see they had been there all the time; but my
eyes had never been opened to them. I did not know what my own house
was like, because I had never been outside it.

NORA. D'ye think thats the same with everybody?

KEEGAN. With everybody who has eyes in his soul as well as in his head.

NORA. But really and truly now, werent the people rather disappointing? I
should think the girls must have seemed rather coarse and dowdy after
the foreign princesses and people? But I suppose a priest wouldnt notice
that.

KEEGAN. It's a priest's business to notice everything. I wont tell you all I
noticed about women; but I'll tell you this. The more a man knows,
and the farther he travels, the more likely he is to marry a country girl
afterwards.

NORA [*blushing with delight*] Youre joking, Mr Keegan: I'm sure yar.

KEEGAN. My way of joking is to tell the truth. It's the funniest joke in
the world.

NORA [*incredulous*] Galong with you!

KEEGAN [*springing up actively*] Shall we go down to the road and meet the
car? [*She gives him her hand and he helps her up*]. Patsy Farrell told me
you were expecting young Doyle.

NORA [*tossing her chin up at once*] Oh, I'm not expecting him particularly.
It's a wonder he's come back at all. After staying away eighteen years
he can harly expect us to be very anxious to see him: can he now?

KEEGAN. Well, not anxious perhaps; but you will be curious to see how much he's changed in all these years.

NORA [*with a sudden bitter flush*] I suppose thats all that brings him back to look at us just to see how much we've changed. Well, he can wait and· see me by candlelight: I didnt come out to meet him: I'm going to walk to the Round Tower [*going west across the hill*].

KEEGAN. You couldnt do better this fine evening. [*Gravely*] I'll tell him where youve gone. [*She turns as if to forbid him; but the deep understanding in his eyes makes that impossible; and she only looks at him earnestly and goes. He watches her disappear on the other side of the hill; then says*] Aye, he's come to torment you; and youre driven already to torment him. [*He shakes his head, and goes slowly away across the hill in the opposite direction, lost in thought*].

By this time the car has arrived, and dropped three of its passengers on the high road at the foot of the hill. It is a monster jaunting car, black and dilapidated, one of the last survivors of the public vehicles known to earlier generations as Beeyankiny cars, the Irish having laid violent tongues on the name of their projector, one Bianconi, an enterprising Italian. The three passengers are the parish priest, Father Dempsey; Cornelius Doyle, Larry's father; and Broadbent, all in overcoats and as stiff as only an Irish car could make them.

The priest, stout and fatherly, falls far short of that finest type of countryside pastor which represents the genius of priesthood; but he is equally far above the base type in which a strongminded unscrupulous peasant uses the Church to extort money, power, and privilege. He is a priest neither by vocation nor ambition, but because the life suits him. He has boundless authority over his flock, and taxes them stiffly enough to be a rich man. The old Protestant ascendency is now too broken to gall him. On the whole, an easygoing, amiable, even modest man as long as his dues are paid and his authority and dignity fully admitted.

Cornelius Doyle is an elder of the small wiry type, with a hardskinned, rather worried face, clean shaven except for sandy whiskers blanching into a lustreless pale yellow and quite white at the roots. His dress is that of a country-town man of business: that is, an oldish shooting suit, with elastic sided boots quite unconnected with shooting. Feeling shy with Broadbent, he is hasty, which is his way of trying to appear genial.

Broadbent, for reasons which will appear later, has no luggage except a field glass and a guide book. The other two have left theirs to the unfortunate Patsy Farrell, who struggles up the hill after them, loaded with a sack of potatoes, a hamper, a fat goose, a colossal salmon, and several paper parcels.

Cornelius leads the way up the hill, with Broadbent at his heels. The priest follows. Patsy lags laboriously behind.

CORNELIUS. This is a bit of a climb, Mr Broadbent; but it's shorter than goin round be the road.

BROADBENT [*stopping to examine the great stone*] Just a moment, Mr Doyle: I want to look at this stone. It must be Finian's die-cast.

CORNELIUS [*in blank bewilderment*] Hwat?

BROADBENT. Murray describes it. One of your great national heroes — I cant pronounce the name — Finian Somebody, I think.

FATHER DEMPSEY [*also perplexed, and rather scandalized*] Is it Fin McCool you mean?

BROADBENT. I daresay it is. [*Referring to the guide book*] Murray says that a huge stone, probably of Druidic origin, is still pointed out as the die cast by Fin in his celebrated match with the devil.

CORNELIUS [*dubiously*] Jeuce a word I ever heard of it!

FATHER DEMPSEY [*very seriously indeed, and even a little severely*] Dont believe any such nonsense, sir. There never was any such thing. When people talk to you about Fin McCool and the like, take no notice of them. It's all idle stories and superstition.

BROADBENT [*somewhat indignantly; for to be rebuked by an Irish priest for superstition is more than he can stand*] You dont suppose I believe it, do you?

FATHER DEMPSEY. Oh, I thought you did. D'ye see the top of the Roun Tower there? thats an antiquity worth lookin at.

BROADBENT [*deeply interested*] Have you any theory as to what the Round Towers were for?

FATHER DEMPSEY [*a little offended*] A theory? Me! [*Theories are connected in his mind with the late Professor Tyndall, and with scientific scepticism generally: also perhaps with the view that the Round Towers are phallic symbols*].

CORNELIUS [*remonstrating*] Father Dempsey is the priest of the parish, Mr Broadbent. What would he be doing with a theory?

FATHER DEMPSEY [*with gentle emphasis*] I have a k n o w l e d g e of what

the Round Towers were, if thats what you mean. They are the fore-
fingers of the early Church, pointing us all to God.

*Patsy, intolerably overburdened, loses his balance, and sits down involun-
tarily. His burdens are scattered over the hillside. Cornelius and Father
Dempsey turn furiously on him, leaving Broadbent beaming at the stone and
the tower with fatuous interest.*

CORNELIUS. Oh, be the hokey, the sammin's broke in two! You schoopid
ass, what d'ye mean?

FATHER DEMPSEY. Are you drunk, Patsy Farrell? Did I tell you to carry
that hamper carefully or did I not?

PATSY [*rubbing the back of his head, which has almost dinted a slab of granite*]
Sure me fut slipt. Howkn I carry three men's luggage at wanst?

FATHER DEMPSEY. You were told to leave behind what you couldnt
carry, an go back for it.

PATSY. An whose things was I to lave behind? Hwat would your reverence
think if I left your hamper behind in the wet grass; n hwat would the
masther say if I left the sammin and the goose be the side o the road
for annywan to pick up?

CORNELIUS. Oh, youve a dale to say for yourself, you butther-
fingered omadhaun. Waitll Ant Judy sees the state o that sammin:
she'll talk to you. Here! gimmy that birdn that fish there; an take
Father Dempsey's hamper to his house for him; n then come back for the
rest.

FATHER DEMPSEY. Do, Patsy. And mind you dont fall down again.

PATSY. Sure I –

CORNELIUS [*bustling him up the hill*] Whisht! heres Ant Judy. [*Patsy goes
grumbling in disgrace, with Father Dempsey's hamper*].

*Aunt Judy comes down the hill, a woman of 50, in no way remarkable, lively
and busy without energy or grip, placid without tranquillity, kindly without
concern for others: indeed without much concern for herself: a contented
product of a narrow, strainless life. She wears her hair parted in the middle
and quite smooth, with a flattened bun at the back. Her dress is a plain brown
frock, with a woollen pelerine of black and aniline mauve over her shoulders,
all very trim in honor of the occasion. She looks round for Larry; is puzzled;
then stares incredulously at Broadbent.*

AUNT JUDY. Surely to goodness thats not you, Larry!

CORNELIUS. Arra how could he be Larry, woman alive? Larry's in no hurry home, it seems. I havnt set eyes on him. This is his friend, Mr Broadbent. Mr Broadbent: me sister Judy.

AUNT JUDY [*hospitably: going to Broadbent and shaking hands heartily*] Mr Broadbent! Fancy me takin you for Larry! Sure we havn't seen a sight of him for eighteen years, n he ony a lad when he left us.

BROADBENT. It's not Larry's fault: he was to have been here before me. He started in our motor an hour before Mr Doyle arrived, to meet us at Athenmullet, intending to get here long before me.

AUNT JUDY. Lord save us! do you think he's had n axidnt?

BROADBENT. No: he's wired to say he's had a breakdown and will come on as soon as he can. He expects to be here at about ten.

AUNT JUDY. There now! Fancy him trustn himself in a motor and we all expectn him! Just like him! he'd never do anything like anybody else. Well, what cant be cured must be injoored. Come on in, all of you. You must be dyin for your tea, Mr Broadbent.

BROADBENT [*with a slight start*] Oh, I'm afraid it's too late for tea [*he looks at his watch*].

AUNT JUDY. Not a bit: we never have it airlier than this. I hope they gave you a good dinner at Athenmullet.

BROADBENT [*trying to conceal his consternation as he realizes that he is not going to get any dinner after his drive*] Oh – ei – excellent, excellent. By the way, hadnt I better see about a room at the hotel? [*They stare at him*].

CORNELIUS. The hotel!

FATHER DEMPSEY. Hwat hotel?

AUNT JUDY. Indeedn youre not going to a hotel. Youll stay with us. I'd have put you into Larry's room, ony the boy's pallyass is too short for you; but we'll make a comfortable bed for you on the sofa in the parlor.

BROADBENT. Youre very kind, Miss Doyle; but really I'm ashamed to give you so much trouble unnecessarily. I shant mind the hotel in the least.

FATHER DEMPSEY. Man alive! theres no hotel in Rosscullen.

BROADBENT. No hotel! Why, the driver told me there was the finest hotel in Ireland here. [*They regard him joylessly*].

AUNT JUDY. Arra would you mind what the like of him would tell you? Sure he'd say hwatever was the least trouble to himself and the pleasantest to you, thinkin you might give him a thruppeny bit for himself or the like.

BROADBENT. Perhaps theres a public house.

FATHER DEMPSEY [*grimly*] Theres seventeen.

AUNT JUDY. Ah then, how could you stay at a public house? theyd have no place to put you even if it was a right place for you to go. Come! is it the sofa youre afraid of? If it is, you can have me own bed. I can sleep with Nora.

BROADBENT. Not at all: I should be only too delighted. But to upset your arrangements in this way —

CORNELIUS [*anxious to cut short the discussion, which makes him ashamed of his house; for he guesses Broadbent's standard of comfort a little more accurately than his sister does*] Thats all right; itll be no trouble at all. Hweres Nora?

AUNT JUDY. Oh, how do I know? She slipped out a little while ago: I thought she was going to meet the car.

CORNELIUS [*dissatisfied*] It's a queer thing of her to run out o the way at such a time.

AUNT JUDY. Sure she's a queer girl altogether. Come. Come in: come in.

FATHER DEMPSEY. I'll say good night, Mr Broadbent. If theres anything I can do for you in this parish, let me know. [*He shakes hands with Broadbent*].

BROADBENT [*effusively cordial*] Thank you, Father Dempsey. Delighted to have met you, sir.

FATHER DEMPSEY [*passing on to Aunt Judy*] Good night, Miss Doyle.

AUNT JUDY. Wont you stay to tea?

FATHER DEMPSEY. Not tonight, thank you kindly: I have business to do at home. [*He turns to go, and meets Patsy Farrell returning unloaded*]. Have you left that hamper for me?

PATSY. Yis, your reverence.

FATHER DEMPSEY. Thats a good lad [*going*].

PATSY [*to Aunt Judy*] Fadher Keegan sez —

FATHER DEMPSEY [*turning sharply on him*] Whats that you say?

PATSY [*frightened*] Fadher Keegan —

FATHER DEMPSEY. How often have you heard me bid you call Mister Keegan in his proper name, the same as I do? Father Keegan indeed! Cant you tell the difference between your priest and any ole madman in a black coat?

PATSY. Sure I'm afraid he might put a spell on me.

FATHER DEMPSEY [*wrathfully*] You mind what I tell you or I'll put a spell on you thatll make you lep. D'ye mind that now? [*He goes home*].
Patsy goes down the hill to retrieve the fish, the bird, and the sack.

AUNT JUDY. Ah, hwy cant you hold your tongue, Patsy, before Father Dempsey?

PATSY. Well, hwat was I to do? Father Keegan bid me tell you Miss Nora was gone to the Roun Tower.

AUNT JUDY. An hwy couldnt you wait to tell us until Father Dempsey was gone?

PATSY. I was afeerd o forgetn it; and then may be he'd a sent the grasshopper or the little dark looker into me at night to remind me of it. [*The dark looker is the common grey lizard, which is supposed to walk down the throats of incautious sleepers and cause them to perish in a slow decline*].

CORNELIUS. Yah, you great gaum, you! Widjer grasshoppers and dark lookers! Here: take up them things and let me hear no more o your foolish lip. [*Patsy obeys*]. You can take the sammin under your oxther. [*He wedges the salmon into Patsy's axilla*].

PATSY. I can take the goose too, sir. Put it on me back n gimmy the neck of it in me mouth. [*Cornelius is about to comply thoughtlessly*].

AUNT JUDY [*feeling that Broadbent's presence demands special punctiliousness*] For shame, Patsy! to offer to take the goose in your mouth that we have to eat after you! The masterll bring it in for you.

PATSY. Arra what would a dead goose care for me mouth? [*He takes his load up the hill*].

CORNELIUS. Hwats Nora doin at the Roun Tower?

AUNT JUDY. Oh, the Lord knows! Romancin, I suppose. Praps she thinks Larry would go there to look for her and see her safe home.

BROADBENT. Miss Reilly must not be left to wait and walk home alone at night. Shall I go for her?

AUNT JUDY [*contemptuously*] Arra hwat ud happen to her? Hurry in now, Corny. Come, Mr Broadbent: I left the tea on the hob to draw; and itll be black if we dont go in and drink it.
They go up the hill. It is dusk by this time.

Broadbent does not fare so badly after all at Aunt Judy's board. He gets not only tea and bread-and-butter, but more mutton chops than he has ever conceived it possible to eat at one sitting. There is also a most filling substance called potato cake. Hardly have his fears of being starved been replaced by his first misgiving that he is eating too much and will be sorry for it tomorrow, when his appetite is revived by the production of a bottle of illicitly distilled whisky, called potcheen, which he has read and dreamed of (he calls it pottine) and is now at last to taste. His goodhumor rises almost to excitement before Cornelius shows signs of sleepiness. The contrast between Aunt Judy's table service and that of the south and east coast hotels at which he spends his Fridays-to-Tuesdays when he is in London, seems to him delightfully Irish. The almost total atrophy of any sense of enjoyment in Cornelius, or even any desire for it or toleration of the possibility of life being something better than a round of sordid worries, relieved by tobacco, punch, fine mornings, and petty successes in buying and selling, passes with his guest as the whimsical affectation of a shrewd Irish humorist and incorrigible spendthrift. Aunt Judy seems to him an incarnate joke. The likelihood that the joke will pall after a month or so, and is probably not apparent at any time to born Rossculleners, or that he himself unconsciously entertains Aunt Judy by his fantastic English person-ality and English mispronunciations, does not occur to him for a moment. In the end he is so charmed, and so loth to go to bed and perhaps dream of prosaic England, that he insists on going out to smoke a cigar and look for Nora Reilly at the Round Tower. Not that any special insistence is needed; for the English inhibitive instinct does not seem to exist in Rosscullen. Just as Nora's liking to miss a meal and stay out at the Round Tower is accepted as a sufficient reason for her doing it, and for the family going to bed and leaving the door open for her, so Broadbent's whim to go out for a late stroll provokes neither hospitable remonstrance nor surprise. Indeed Aunt Judy wants to get rid of him whilst she makes a bed for him on the sofa. So off he goes, full fed, happy and enthusiastic, to explore the valley by moonlight.

The Round Tower stands about half an Irish mile from Rosscullen, some fifty yards south of the road on a knoll with a circle of wild greensward on it. The road once ran over this knoll; but modern engineering has tempered the level to the Beeyankiny car by carrying the road partly round the knoll and partly through a cutting; so that the way from the road to the tower is a footpath up the embankment through furze and brambles.

On the edge of this slope, at the top of the path, Nora is straining her eyes in the moonlight, watching for Larry. At last she gives it up with a sob of impatience, and retreats to the hoary foot of the tower, where she sits down discouraged and cries a little. Then she settles herself resignedly to wait, and hums a song — not an Irish melody, but a hackneyed English drawing room ballad of the season before last — until some slight noise suggests a footstep, when she springs up eagerly and runs to the edge of the slope again. Some moments of silence and suspense follow, broken by unmistakable footsteps. She gives a little gasp as she sees a man approaching.

NORA. Is that you, Larry? [*Frightened a little*] Who's that?

BROADBENT'S *voice from below her on the path.* Dont be alarmed.

NORA. Oh, what an English accent youve got!

BROADBENT [*rising into view*] I must introduce myself —

NORA [*violently startled, retreating*] It's not you! Who are you? What do you want?

BROADBENT [*Advancing*] I'm really so sorry to have alarmed you, Miss Reilly. My name is Broadbent. Larry's friend, you know.

NORA [*chilled*] And has Mr Doyle not come with you?

BROADBENT. No. Ive come instead. I hope I am not unwelcome.

NORA [*deeply mortified*] I'm sorry Mr Doyle should have given you the trouble, I'm sure.

BROADBENT. You see, as a stranger and an Englishman, I thought it would be interesting to see the Round Tower by moonlight.

NORA. Oh, you came to see the tower. I thought — [*confused, trying to recover her manners*] Oh, of course. I was so startled. It's a beautiful night, isnt it?

BROADBENT. Lovely. I must explain why Larry has not come himself.

NORA. Why should he come? He's seen the tower often enough: it's no attraction to him [*Genteelly*] An what do you think of Ireland, Mr Broadbent? Have you ever been here before?

BROADBENT. Never.

NORA. An how do you like it?

BROADBENT [*suddenly betraying a condition of extreme sentimentality*] I can hardly trust myself to say how much I like it. The magic of this Irish scene, and — I really dont want to be personal, Miss Reilly; but the charm of your Irish voice —

NORA [*quite accustomed to gallantry, and attaching no seriousness whatever to it*] Oh, get along with you, Mr Broadbent! Youre breaking your heart about me already, I daresay, after seeing me for two minutes in the dark.

BROADBENT. The voice is just as beautiful in the dark you know. Besides, Ive heard a great deal about you from Larry.

NORA [*with bitter indifference*] Have you now? Well, thats a great honor, I'm sure.

BROADBENT. I have looked forward to meeting you more than to anything else in Ireland.

NORA [*ironically*] Dear me! did you now?

BROADBENT. I did really. I wish you had taken half as much interest in me.

NORA. Oh, I was dying to see you, of course. I daresay you can imagine the sensation an Englishman like you would make among us poor Irish people.

BROADBENT. Ah, now youre chaffing me, Miss Reilly: you know you are. You mustnt chaff me. I'm very much in earnest about Ireland and everything Irish. I'm very much in earnest about you and about Larry.

NORA. Larry has nothing to do with me, Mr Broadbent.

BROADBENT. If I really thought that, Miss Reilly, I should – well, I should let myself feel that charm of which I spoke just now more deeply than I – than I –

NORA. Is it making love to me you are?

BROADBENT [*scared and much upset*] On my word I believe I am, Miss Reilly. If you say that to me again I shant answer for myself: all the harps of Ireland are in your voice. [*She laughs at him. He suddenly loses his head and seizes her arms, to her great indignation*]. Stop laughing: do you hear? I am in earnest: in English earnest. When I say a thing like that to a woman, I mean it. [*Releasing her and trying to recover his ordinary manner in spite of his bewildering emotion*] I beg your pardon.

NORA. How dare you touch me?

BROADBENT. There are not many things I would not dare for you. That does not sound right perhaps; but I really – [*he stops and passes his hand over his forehead, rather lost*].

NORA. I think you ought to be ashamed. I think if you were a gentleman, and me alone with you in this place at night, you would die rather than do such a thing.

BROADBENT. You mean that it's an act of treachery to Larry?

NORA. Deed I dont. What has Larry to do with it? It's an act of disrespect and rudeness to me: it shews what you take me for. You can go your way now; and I'll go mine. Good night, Mr Broadbent.

BROADBENT. No, please, Miss Reilly. One moment. Listen to me. I'm serious: I'm desperately serious. Tell me that I'm interfering with

Larry; and I'll go straight from this spot back to London and never see you again. Thats on my honor: I will. Am I interfering with him?

NORA [answering in spite of herself in a sudden spring of bitterness] I should think you ought to know better than me whether youre interfering with him. Youve seen him oftener than I have. You know him better than I do, by this time. Youve come to me quicker than he has, havnt you?

BROADBENT. I'm bound to tell you, Miss Reilly, that Larry has not arrived in Rosscullen yet. He meant to get here before me; but his car broke down; and he may not arrive until tomorrow.

NORA [her face lighting up] Is that the truth?

BROADBENT. Yes: thats the truth. [She gives a sigh of relief]. Youre glad of that?

NORA [up in arms at once] Glad indeed! Why should I be glad? As weve waited eighteen years for him we can afford to wait a day longer, I should think.

BROADBENT. If you really feel like that about him, there may be a chance for another man yet. Eh?

NORA [deeply offended] I suppose people are different in England, Mr Broadbent; so perhaps you dont mean any harm. In Ireland nobody'd mind what a man'd say in fun, nor take advantage of what a woman might say in answer to it. If a woman couldnt talk to a man for two minutes at their first meeting without being treated the way youre treating me, no decent woman would ever talk to a man at all.

BROADBENT. I dont understand that. I dont admit that. I am sincere; and my intentions are perfectly honorable. I think you will accept the fact that I'm an Englishman as a guarantee that I am not a man to act hastily or romantically; though I confess that your voice had such an extraordinary effect on me just now when you asked me so quaintly whether I was making love to you –

NORA [flushing] I never thought –

BROADBENT [quickly] Of course you didnt: I'm not so stupid as that. But I couldnt bear your laughing at the feeling it gave me. You – [again struggling with a surge of emotion] you dont know what I – [he chokes for a moment and then blurts out with unnatural steadiness] Will you be my wife?

NORA [promptly] Deed I wont. The idea! [Looking at him more carefully] Arra, come home, Mr Broadbent; and get your senses back again. I think youre not accustomed to potcheen punch in the evening after your tea.

BROADBENT [*horrified*] Do you mean to say that I – I – I – my God! that I appear **drunk** to you, Miss Reilly?

NORA [*compassionately*] How many tumblers had you?

BROADBENT [*helplessly*] Two.

NORA. The flavor of the turf prevented you noticing the strength of it. Youd better come home to bed.

BROADBENT [*fearfully agitated*] But this is such a horrible doubt to put into my mind – to – to – For Heaven's sake, Miss Reilly, am I really drunk?

NORA [*soothingly*] Youll be able to judge better in the morning. Come on now back with me, an think no more about it. [*She takes his arm with motherly solicitude and urges him gently towards the path*].

BROADBENT [*yielding in despair*] I must be drunk: frightfully drunk; for your voice drove me out of my senses – [*he stumbles over a stone*]. No: on my word, on my most sacred word of honor, Miss Reilly, I tripped over that stone. It was an accident: it was indeed.

NORA. Yes, of course it was. Just take my arm, Mr Broadbent, while we're going down the path to the road. Youll be all right then.

BROADBENT [*submissively taking it*] I cant sufficiently apologize, Miss Reilly, or express my sense of your kindness when I am in such a disgusting state. How could I be such a bea – [*he trips again*] damn the heather! my foot caught in it.

NORA. Steady now, steady. Come along: come. [*He is led down to the road in the character of a convicted drunkard. To him there is something divine in the sympathetic indulgence she substitutes for the angry disgust with which one of his own countrywomen would resent his supposed condition. And he has no suspicion of the fact, or of her ignorance of it, that when an Englishman is sentimental he behaves very much as an Irishman does when he is drunk*].

ACT III

*Next morning Broadbent and Larry are sitting at the ends of a breakfast
table in the middle of a small grass plot before Cornelius Doyle's house. They
have finished their meal, and are buried in newspapers. Most of the crockery
is crowded upon a large square black tray of japanned metal. The teapot
is of brown delft ware. There is no silver; and the butter, on a dinner plate,
is en bloc. The background to this breakfast is the house, a small white slated
building, accessible by a half-glazed door. A person coming out into the garden
by this door would find the table straight in front of him, and a gate leading
to the road half-way down the garden on his right; or, if he turned sharp
to his left, he could pass round the end of the house through an unkempt
shrubbery. The mutilated remnant of a huge plaster statue, nearly dissolved
by the rains of a century, and vaguely resembling a majestic female in Roman
draperies, with a wreath in her hand, stands neglected amid the laurels. Such
statues, though apparently works of art, grow naturally in Irish gardens.
Their germination is a mystery to the oldest inhabitants, to whose means
and tastes they are totally foreign.*

*There is a rustic bench, much soiled by the birds, and decorticated and
split by the weather, near the little gate. At the opposite side, a basket lies
unmolested because it might as well be there as anywhere else. An empty
chair at the table was lately occupied by Cornelius, who has finished his
breakfast and gone into the room in which he receives rents and keeps his
books and cash, known in the household as 'the office'. This chair, like the
two occupied by Larry and Broadbent, has a mahogany frame and is up-
holstered in black horsehair.*

*Larry rises and goes off through the shrubbery with his newspaper. Hodson
comes in through the garden gate, disconsolate. Broadbent, who sits facing
the gate, augurs the worst from his expression.*

BROADBENT. Have you been to the village?

HODSON. No use, sir. We'll have to get everything from London by
parcel post.

BROADBENT. I hope they made you comfortable last night.

HODSON. I was no worse than you were on that sofa, sir. One expects to rough it here, sir.

BROADBENT. We shall have to look out for some other arrangement. [*Cheering up irrepressibly*] Still, it's no end of a joke. How do you like the Irish, Hodson?

HODSON. Well, sir, theyre all right anywhere but in their own country. Ive known lots of em in England, and generally liked em. But here, sir, I seem simply to hate em. The feeling come over me the moment we landed at Cork, sir. It's no use my pretendin, sir: I cant bear em. My mind rises up agin their ways, somehow: they rub me the wrong way all over.

BROADBENT. Oh, their faults are on the surface: at heart they are one of the finest races on earth. [*Hodson turns away, without affecting to respond to his enthusiasm*]. By the way, Hodson —

HODSON [*turning*] Yes, sir.

BROADBENT. Did you notice anything about me last night when I came in with that lady?

HODSON [*surprised*] No, sir.

BROADBENT. Not any — er —? You may speak frankly.

HODSON. I didnt notice nothing, sir. What sort of thing did you mean, sir?

BROADBENT. Well — er — er — well, to put it plainly, was I drunk?

HODSON [*amazed*] No, sir.

BROADBENT. Quite sure?

HODSON. Well, I should a said rather the opposite, sir. Usually when youve been enjoying yourself, youre a bit hearty like. Last night you seemed rather low, if anything.

BROADBENT. I certainly have no headache. Did you try the pottine, Hodson?

HODSON. I just took a mouthful, sir. It tasted of peat: oh! something horrid, sir. The people here call peat turf. Potcheen and strong porter is what they like, sir. I'm sure I dont know how they can stand it. Give me beer, I say.

BROADBENT. By the way, you told me I couldnt have porridge for breakfast; but Mr Doyle had some.

HODSON. Yes, sir. Very sorry, sir. They call it stirabout, sir: thats how it was. They know no better, sir.

BROADBENT. All right: I'll have some tomorrow.

Hodson goes to the house. When he opens the door he finds Nora and Aunt Judy on the threshold. He stands aside to let them pass, with the air of a well trained servant oppressed by heavy trials. Then he goes in. Broadbent rises. Aunt Judy goes to the table and collects the plates and cups on the tray. Nora goes to the back of the rustic seat and looks out at the gate with the air of a woman accustomed to have nothing to do. Larry returns from the shrubbery.

BROADBENT. Good morning, Miss Doyle.

AUNT JUDY [*thinking it absurdly late in the day for such a salutation*] Oh, good morning. [*Before moving his plate*] Have you done?

BROADBENT. Quite, thank you. You must excuse us for not waiting for you. The country air tempted us to get up early.

AUNT JUDY. N d'ye call this airly, God help you?

LARRY. Aunt Judy probably breakfasted about half past six.

AUNT JUDY. Whisht, you! draggin the parlor chairs out into the gardn n giving Mr Broadbent his death over his meals out here in the cold air. [*To Broadbent*] Why d'ye put up with his foolishness, Mr Broadbent?

BROADBENT. I assure you I like the open air.

AUNT JUDY. Ah galong! How can you like whats not natural? I hope you slept well.

NORA. Did anything wake yup with a thump at three o'clock? I thought the house was falling. But then I'm a very light sleeper.

LARRY. I seem to recollect that one of the legs of the sofa in the parlor had a way of coming out unexpectedly eighteen years ago. Was that it, Tom?

BROADBENT [*hastily*] Oh, it doesnt matter: I was not hurt — at least — er —

AUNT JUDY. Oh now what a shame! An I told Patsy Farrll to put a nail in it.

BROADBENT. He did, Miss Doyle. There was a nail, certainly.

AUNT JUDY. Dear oh dear!

An oldish peasant farmer, small, leathery, peat-faced, with a deep voice and a surliness that is meant to be aggressive, and is in effect pathetic — the voice of a man of hard life and many sorrows — comes in at the gate. He is old enough to have perhaps worn a long tailed frieze coat and knee breeches in his time; but now he is dressed respectably in a black frock coat, tall hat, and pollard colored trousers; and his face is as clean as washing can make it, though that is not saying much, as the habit is recently acquired and not yet congenial.

THE NEW-COMER [*at the gate*] God save all here! [*He comes a little way into the garden*].

LARRY [*patronizingly, speaking across the garden to him*] Is that yourself, Matt Haffigan? Do you remember me?

MATTHEW [*intentionally rude and blunt*] No. Who are you?

NORA. Oh, I'm sure you remember him, Mr Haffigan.

MATTHEW [*grudgingly admitting it*] I suppose he'll be young Larry Doyle that was.

LARRY. Yes

MATTHEW [*to Larry*] I hear you done well in America.

LARRY. Fairly well.

MATTHEW. I suppose you saw me brother Andy out dhere.

LARRY. No. It's such a big place that looking for a man there is like looking for a needle in a bundle of hay. They tell me he's a great man out there.

MATTHEW. So he is, God be praised. Wheres your father?

AUNT JUDY. He's inside, in the office, Mr Haffigan, with Barney Doarn n Father Dempsey.

Matthew, without wasting further words on the company, goes curtly into the house.

LARRY [*staring after him*] Is anything wrong with old Matt?

NORA. No. He's the same as ever. Why?

LARRY. He's not the same to me. He used to be very civil to Masther Larry: a deal too civil, I used to think. Now he's as surly and stand-off as a bear.

AUNT JUDY. Oh sure he's bought his farm in the Land Purchase. He's independent now.

NORA. It's made a great change, Larry. Youd harly know the old tenants now. Youd think it was a liberty to speak t'dhem — some o dhem. [*She goes to the table, and helps to take off the cloth, which she and Aunt Judy fold up between them*].

AUNT JUDY. I wonder what he wants to see Corny for. He hasnt been here since he paid the last of his old rent; and then he as good as threw it in Corny's face, I thought.

LARRY. No wonder! Of course they all hated us like the devil. Ugh!
[*Moodily*] Ive seen them in that office, telling my father what a fine
boy I was, and plastering him with compliments, with your honor
here and your honor there, when all the time their fingers were itching
to be at his throat.

AUNT JUDY. Deedn why should they want to hurt poor Corny? It was
he that got Matt the lease of his farm, and stood up for him as an
industrious decent man.

BROADBENT. Was he industrious? Thats remarkable, you know, in an
Irishman.

LARRY. Industrious! That man's industry used to make me sick, even
as a boy. I tell you, an Irish peasant's industry is not human: it's
worse than the industry of a coral insect. An Englishman has some
sense about working: he never does more than he can help – and hard
enough to get him to do that without scamping it; but an Irishman
will work as if he'd die the moment he stopped. That man Matthew
Haffigan and his brother Andy made a farm out of a patch of stones
on the hillside: cleared it and dug it with their own naked hands and
bought their first spade out of their first crop of potatoes. Talk of
making two blades of wheat grow where one grew before! those two
men made a whole field of wheat grow where not even a furze bush
had ever got its head up between the stones.

BROADBENT. That was magnificent, you know. Only a great race is
capable of producing such men.

LARRY. Such fools, you mean! What good was it to them? The moment
theyd done it, the landlord put a rent of £5 a year on them, and turned
them out because they couldnt pay it.

AUNT JUDY. Why couldnt they pay as well as Billy Byrne that took it
after them?

LARRY [*angrily*] You know very well that Billy Byrne never paid it. He
only offered it to get possession. He never paid it.

AUNT JUDY. That was because Andy Haffigan hurt him with a brick
so that he was never the same again. Andy had to run away to America
for it.

BROADBENT [*glowing with indignation*] Who can blame him, Miss Doyle?
Who can blame him?

LARRY [*impatiently*] Oh, rubbish! whats the good of the man thats starved out of a farm murdering the man thats starved into it? Would you have done such a thing?

BROADBENT. Yes. I – I – I – I – [*stammering with fury*] I should have shot the confounded landlord, and wrung the neck of the damned agent, and blown the farm up with dynamite, and Dublin Castle along with it.

LARRY. Oh yes: youd have done great things; and a fat lot of good youd have got out of it, too! Thats an Englishman all over! make bad laws and give away all the land, and then, when your economic incompetence produces its natural and inevitable results, get virtuously indignant and kill the people that carry out your laws.

AUNT JUDY. Sure never mind him, Mr Broadbent. It doesnt matter, anyhow, because theres harly any landlords left; and therll soon be none at all.

LARRY. On the contrary, therll soon be nothing else; and the Lord help Ireland then!

AUNT JUDY. Ah, youre never satisfied, Larry. [*To Nora*] Come on, alanna, an make the paste for the pie. We can leave them to their talk. They dont want us [*she takes up the tray and goes into the house*].

BROADBENT [*rising and gallantly protesting*] Oh, Miss Doyle! Really, really –

Nora, following Aunt Judy with the rolled-up cloth in her hands, looks at him and strikes him dumb. He watches her until she disappears; then comes to Larry and addresses him with sudden intensity.

BROADBENT. Larry.

LARRY. What is it?

BROADBENT. I got drunk last night, and proposed to Miss Reilly.

LARRY. You hwat??? [*He screams with laughter in the falsetto Irish register unused for that purpose in England*].

BROADBENT. What are you laughing at?

LARRY [*stopping dead*] I dont know. Thats the sort of thing an Irishman laughs at. Has she accepted you?

BROADBENT. I shall never forget that with the chivalry of her nation, though I was utterly at her mercy, she refused me.

LARRY. That was extremely improvident of her. [*Beginning to reflect*] But look here: when were you drunk? You were sober enough when you came back from the Round Tower with her.

BROADBENT. No, Larry, I was drunk, I am sorry to say. I had two tumblers of punch. She had to lead me home. You must have noticed it.

LARRY. I did not.

BROADBENT. She did.

LARRY. May I ask how long it took you to come to business? You can hardly have known her for more than a couple of hours.

BROADBENT. I am afraid it was hardly a couple of minutes. She was not here when I arrived; and I saw her for the first time at the tower.

LARRY. Well, you are a nice infant to be let loose in this country! Fancy the potcheen going to your head like that!

BROADBENT. Not to my head, I think. I have no headache; and I could speak distinctly. No: potcheen goes to the heart, not to the head. What ought I to do?

LARRY. Nothing. What need you do?

BROADBENT. There is rather a delicate moral question involved. The point is, was I drunk enough not to be morally responsible for my proposal? Or was I sober enough to be bound to repeat it now that I am undoubtedly sober?

LARRY. I should see a little more of her before deciding.

BROADBENT. No, no. That would not be right. That would not be fair. I am either under a moral obligation or I am not. I wish I knew how drunk I was.

LARRY. Well, you were evidently in a state of blithering sentimentality, anyhow.

BROADBENT. That is true, Larry: I admit it. Her voice has a most extraordinary effect on me. That Irish voice!

LARRY [*sympathetically*] Yes, I know. When I first went to London I very nearly proposed to walk out with a waitress in an Aerated Bread shop because her Whitechapel accent was so distinguished, so quaintly touching, so pretty –

BROADBENT [*angrily*] Miss Reilly is not a waitress, is she?

LARRY. Oh, come! The waitress was a very nice girl.

BROADBENT. You think every Englishwoman an angel. You really have coarse tastes in that way, Larry. Miss Reilly is one of the finer types: a type rare in England, except perhaps in the best of the aristocracy.

LARRY. Aristocracy be blowed! Do you know what Nora eats?

BROADBENT. Eats! what do you mean?

LARRY. Breakfast: tea and bread-and-butter, with an occasional rasher, and an egg on special occasions: say on her birthday. Dinner in the middle of the day, one course and nothing else. In the evening, tea and bread-and-butter again. You compare her with your English-women who wolf down from three to five meat meals a day; and naturally you find her a sylph. The difference is not a difference of type: it's the difference between the woman who eats not wisely but too well, and the woman who eats not wisely but too little.

BROADBENT [*furious*] Larry: you – you – you disgust me. You are a damned fool. [*He sits down angrily on the rustic seat, which sustains the shock with difficulty*].

LARRY. Steady! stead-eee! [*He laughs and seats himself on the table*].

Cornelius Doyle, Father Dempsey, Barney Doran, and Matthew Haffigan come from the house. Doran is a stout bodied, short armed, roundheaded, red haired man on the verge of middle age, of sanguine temperament, with an enormous capacity for derisive, obscene, blasphemous, or merely cruel and senseless fun, and a violent and impetuous intolerance of other temperaments and other opinions, all this representing energy and capacity wasted and demoralized by want of sufficient training and social pressure to force it into beneficent activity and build a character with it; for Barney is by no means either stupid or weak. He is recklessly untidy as to his person; but the worst effects of his neglect are mitigated by a powdering of flour and mill dust; and his unbrushed clothes, made of a fashionable tailor's sack-cloth, were evidently chosen regardless of expense for the sake of their appearance.

Matthew Haffigan, ill at ease, coasts the garden shyly on the shrubbery side until he anchors near the basket, where he feels least in the way. The priest comes to the table and slaps Larry on the shoulder. Larry, turning quickly, and recognizing Father Dempsey, alights from the table and shakes the priest's hand warmly. Doran comes down the garden between Father Dempsey and Matt; and Cornelius, on the other side of the table, turns to Broadbent, who rises genially.

CORNELIUS. I think we all met last night.

DORAN. I hadnt that pleasure.

CORNELIUS. To be sure, Barney: I forgot. [*To Broadbent, introducing Barney*] Mr Doran. He owns that fine mill you noticed from the car.

BROADBENT [*delighted with them all*] Most happy, Mr Doran. Very pleased indeed.

Doran, not quite sure whether he is being courted or patronized, nods independently.

DORAN. Hows yourself, Larry?

LARRY. Finely, thank you. No need to ask you [*Doran grins; and they shake hands*].

CORNELIUS. Give Father Dempsey a chair, Larry.

Matthew Haffigan runs to the nearest end of the table and takes the chair from it, placing it near the basket; but Larry has already taken the chair from the other end and placed it in front of the table. Father Dempsey accepts that more central position.

CORNELIUS. Sit down, Barney, will you; and you, Matt.

Doran takes the chair Matt is still offering to the priest; and poor Matthew, outfaced by the miller, humbly turns the basket upside down and sits on it. Cornelius brings his own breakfast chair from the table and sits down on Father Dempsey's right. Broadbent resumes his seat on the rustic bench. Larry crosses to the bench and is about to sit down beside him when Broadbent holds him off nervously.

BROADBENT. Do you think it will bear two, Larry?

LARRY. Perhaps not. Dont move. I'll stand. [*He posts himself behind the bench*].

They are all now seated, except Larry; and the session assumes a portentous air, as if something important were coming.

CORNELIUS. Praps youll explain, Father Dempsey.

FATHER DEMPSEY. No, no: go on, you: the Church has no politics.

CORNELIUS. Were yever thinkin o goin into parliament at all, Larry?

LARRY. Me!

FATHER DEMPSEY [*encouragingly*] Yes, you. Hwy not?

LARRY. I'm afraid my ideas would not be popular enough.

CORNELIUS. I dont know that. Do you, Barney?

DORAN. Theres too much blatherumskite in Irish politics: a dale too much.

LARRY. But what about your present member? Is he going to retire?

CORNELIUS. No: I dont know that he is.

LARRY [*interrogatively*] Well? then?

MATTHEW [*breaking out with surly bitterness*] Weve had enough of his foolish talk agen landlords. Hwat call has he to talk about the lan, that never was outside of a city office in his life?

CORNELIUS. We're tired of him. He doesnt know hwere to stop. Every man cant own land; and some men must own it to employ them. It was all very well when solid men like Doran an Matt were kep from ownin land. But hwat man in his senses ever wanted to give land to Patsy Farrll an dhe like o him?

BROADBENT. But surely Irish landlordism was accountable for what Mr Haffigan suffered.

MATTHEW. Never mind hwat I suffered. I know what I suffered adhout you tellin me. But did I ever ask for more dhan the farm I made wid me own hans? tell me that, Corny Doyle, and you that knows. Was I fit for the responsibility or was I not? [*Snarling angrily at Cornelius*] Am I to be compared to Patsy Farrll, that doesnt harly know his right hand from his left? What did he ever suffer, I'd like to know?

CORNELIUS. Thats just what I say. I wasnt comparin you to your disadvantage.

MATTHEW [*implacable*] Then hwat did you mane be talking about giving him lan?

DORAN. Aisy, Matt, aisy. Youre like a bear with a sore back.

MATTHEW [*trembling with rage*] An who are you, to offer to taitch me manners?

FATHER DEMPSEY [*admonitorily*] Now, now, now, Matt! none o dhat. How often have I told you youre too ready to take offence where none is meant? You dont understand: Corny Doyle is saying just what you want to have said. [*To Cornelius*] Go on, Mr Doyle; and never mind him.

MATTHEW [*rising*] Well, if me lan is to be given to Patsy and his like, I'm goin oura dhis. I —

DORAN [*with violent impatience*] Arra who's going to give your lan to Patsy, yowl fool ye?

FATHER DEMPSEY. Aisy, Barney, aisy. [*Sternly, to Matt*] I told you, Matthew Haffigan, that Corny Doyle was sayin nothin against you. I'm sorry your priest's word is not good enough for you. I'll go, sooner than stay to make you commit a sin against the Church. Good morning, gentlemen. [*He rises. They all rise, except Broadbent*].

DORAN [*to Matt*] There! Sarve you dam well right, you cantankerous oul noodle.

MATTHEW [*appalled*] Dont say dhat, Fadher Dempsey. I never had a thought agen you or the Holy Church. I know I'm a bit hasty when I think about the lan. I axe your pardon for it.

FATHER DEMPSEY [*resuming his seat with dignified reserve*] Very well: I'll overlook it this time. [*He sits down. The others sit down, except Matthew. Father Dempsey, about to ask Corny to proceed, remembers Matthew and turns to him, giving him just a crumb of graciousness*]. Sit down, Matt [*Matthew, crushed, sits down in disgrace, and is silent, his eyes shifting piteously from one speaker to another in an intensely mistrustful effort to understand them*]. Go on, Mr Doyle. We can make allowances. Go on.

CORNELIUS. Well, you see how it is, Larry. Round about here, weve got the land at last; and we want no more Government meddlin. We want a new class o man in parliament: one dhat knows dhat the farmer's the real backbone o the country, n doesnt care a snap of his fingers for the shoutn o the riff-raff in the towns, or for the foolishness of the laborers.

DORAN. Aye; and dhat can afford to live in London and pay his own way until Home Rule comes, instead of wantin subscriptions and the like.

FATHER DEMPSEY. Yes: thats a good point, Barney. When too much money goes to politics, it's the Church that has to starve for it. A member of parliament ought to be a help to the Church instead of a burden on it.

LARRY. Heres a chance for you, Tom. What do you say?

BROADBENT [*deprecatory, but important and smiling*] Oh, I have no claim whatever to the seat. Besides, I'm a Saxon.

DORAN. A hwat?

BROADBENT. A Saxon. An Englishman.

DORAN. An Englishman. Bedad I never heard it called that before.

MATTHEW [*cunningly*] If I might make so bould, Fadher, I wuldnt say but an English Prodestn mightnt have a more indepindent mind about the lan, an be less afeerd to spake out about it dhan an Irish Catholic.

CORNELIUS. But sure Larry's as good as English: arnt you, Larry?

LARRY. You may put me out of your head, father, once for all.

CORNELIUS. Arra why?

LARRY. I have strong opinions which wouldnt suit you.

DORAN [*rallying him blatantly*] Is it still Larry the bould Fenian?

LARRY. No: the bold Fenian is now an older and possibly foolisher man.

CORNELIUS. Hwat does it matter to us hwat your opinions are? You know that your father's bought his place here, just the same as Matt's farm n Barney's mill. All we ask now is to be let alone. Youve nothin against that, have you?

LARRY. Certainly I have. I dont believe in letting anybody or anything alone.

CORNELIUS [*losing his temper*] Arra what d'ye mean, you young fool? Here Ive got you the offer of a good seat in parliament; n you think yourself mighty smart to stand there and talk foolishness to me. Will you take it or leave it?

LARRY. Very well: I'll take it with pleasure if youll give it to me.

CORNELIUS [*subsiding sulkily*] Well, why couldnt you say so at once? It's a good job youve made up your mind at last.

DORAN [*suspiciously*] Stop a bit: stop a bit.

MATTHEW [*writhing between his dissatisfaction and his fear of the priest*] It's not because he's your son that he's to get the sate. Fadher Dempsey: wouldnt you think well to ask him what he manes about the lan?

LARRY [*coming down on Matt promptly*] I'll tell you, Matt. I always thought it was a stupid, lazy, good-for-nothing sort of thing to leave the land in the hands of the old landlords without calling them to a strict account for the use they made of it, and the condition of the people on it. I could see for myself that they thought of nothing but what they could get out of it to spend in England; and that they mortgaged and mortgaged until hardly one of them owned his own property or could have afforded to keep it up decently if he'd wanted to. But I tell you plump and plain, Matt, that if anybody thinks things will be any better now that the land is handed over to a lot of little men like you, without calling you to account either, theyre mistaken.

MATTHEW [*sullenly*] What call have you to look down on me? I suppose you think youre everybody because your father was a landagent.

LARRY. What call have you to look down on Patsy Farrell? I suppose you think youre everybody because you own a few fields.

MATTHEW. Was Patsy Farrll ever ill used as I was ill used? tell me dhat.

LARRY. He will be, if ever he gets into your power as you were in the power of your old landlord. Do you think, because youre poor and ignorant and half-crazy with toiling and moiling morning noon and night, that youll be any less greedy and oppressive to them that have no land at all than old Nick Lestrange, who was an educated travelled gentleman that would not have been tempted as hard by a hundred pounds as youd be by five shillings? Nick was too high above Patsy Farrell to be jealous of him; but you, that are only one little step above him, would die sooner than let him come up that step; and well you know it.

MATTHEW [black with rage, in a low growl] Lemmy oura dhis. [He tries to rise; but Doran catches his coat and drags him down again] I'm goin, I say. [Raising his voice] Leggo me coat, Barney Doran.

DORAN. Sit down, yowl omadhaun, you. [Whispering] Dont you want to stay an vote agen him?

FATHER DEMPSEY [holding up his finger] Matt! [Matt subsides]. Now, now, now! come, come! Hwats all dhis about Patsy Farrll? Hwy need you fall out about him?

LARRY. Because it was by using Patsy's poverty to undersell England in the markets of the world that we drove England to ruin Ireland. And she'll ruin us again the moment we lift our heads from the dust if we trade in cheap labor; and serve us right too! If I get into parliament, I'll try to get an Act to prevent any of you from giving Patsy less than a pound a week [they all start, hardly able to believe their ears] or working him harder than youd work a horse that cost you fifty guineas.

DORAN. Hwat!!!

CORNELIUS [aghast] A pound a – God save us! the boy's mad.

Matthew, feeling that here is something quite beyond his powers, turns openmouthed to the priest, as if looking for nothing less than the summary excommunication of Larry.

LARRY. How is the man to marry and live a decent life on less?

FATHER DEMPSEY. Man alive, hwere have you been living all these years? and hwat have you been dreaming of? Why, some o dhese honest men here cant make that much out o the land for dhemselves, much less give it to a laborer.

LARRY [now thoroughly roused] Then let them make room for those who can. Is Ireland never to have a chance? First she was given to the rich; and now that they have gorged on her flesh, her bones are to be flung to the poor, that can do nothing but suck the marrow out of her. If we cant have men of honor own the land, lets have men of ability. If we cant have men with ability, let us at least have men with capital. Anybody's better than Matt, who has neither honor, nor ability, nor capital, nor anything but mere brute labor and greed in him, Heaven help him!

DORAN. Well, we're not all foostherin oul doddherers like Matt. [*Pleasantly, to the subject of his description*] Are we, Matt?

LARRY. For modern industrial purposes you might just as well be, Barney. Youre all children: the big world that I belong to has gone past you and left you. Anyhow, we Irishmen were never made to be farmers; and we'll never do any good at it. We're like the Jews: the Almighty gave us brains, and bid us farm them and leave the clay and the worms alone.

FATHER DEMPSEY [*with gentle irony*] Oh! is it Jews you want to make of us? I must catechize you a bit meself, I think. The next thing youll be proposing is to repeal the disestablishment of the so-called Irish Church.

LARRY. Yes: why not? [*Sensation*].

MATTHEW [*rancorously*] He's a turncoat.

LARRY. St Peter, the rock on which our Church was built, was crucified head downwards for being a turncoat.

FATHER DEMPSEY [*with a quiet authoritative dignity which checks Doran, who is on the point of breaking out*] Thats true. You hold your tongue as befits your ignorance, Matthew Haffigan; and trust your priest to deal with this young man. Now, Larry Doyle, whatever the blessed St Peter was crucified for, it was not for being a Prodestan. Are you one?

LARRY. No. I am a Catholic intelligent enough to see that the Protestants are never more dangerous to us than when they are free from all alliances with the State. The so-called Irish Church is stronger today than ever it was.

MATTHEW. Fadher Dempsey: will you tell him dhat me mother's ant was shot and kilt dead in the sthreet o Rosscullen be a soljer in the tithe war? [*Frantically*] He wants to put the tithes on us again. He —

LARRY [*interrupting him with overbearing contempt*] Put the tithes on you again! Did the tithes ever come off you? Was your land any dearer when you paid the tithe to the parson than it was when you paid the same money to Nick Lestrange as rent, and he handed it over to the Church Sustentation Fund? Will you always be duped by Acts of Parliament that change nothing but the necktie of the man that picks your pocket? I'll tell you what I'd do with you, Matt Haffigan; I'd make you pay tithes to your own Church. I want the Catholic Church established in Ireland: thats what I want. Do you think that I, brought up to regard myself as the son of a great and holy Church, can bear to see her begging her bread from the ignorance and superstition of men like you? I would have her as high above worldly want as I would have her above worldly pride or ambition. Aye; and I woul·¹ have Ireland compete with Rome itself for the chair of St Peter and the citadel of the Church; for Rome, in spite of all the blood of the martyrs, is pagan at heart to this day, while in Ireland the people is the Church and the Church the people.

FATHER DEMPSEY [*startled but not at all displeased*] Whisht, man! youre worse than mad Pether Keegan himself.

BROADBENT [*who has listened in the greatest astonishment*] You amaze me, Larry. Who would have thought of your coming out like this! [*Solemnly*] But much as I appreciate your really brilliant eloquence, I implore you not to desert the great Liberal principle of Disestablishment.

LARRY. I am not a Liberal: Heaven forbid! A disestablished Church is the worst tyranny a nation can groan under.

BROADBENT [*making a wry face*] Dont be paradoxical, Larry. It really gives me a pain in my stomach.

LARRY. Youll soon find out the truth of it here. Look at Father Dempsey! he is disestablished: he has nothing to hope or fear from the State; and the result is that he's the most powerful man in Rosscullen. The member for Rosscullen would shake in his shoes if Father Dempsey looked crooked at him. [*Father Dempsey smiles, by no means averse to this acknowledgment of his authority*]. Look at yourself! you would defy the established Archbishop of Canterbury ten times a day; but catch you daring to say a word that would shock a Nonconformist! not you. The Conservative party today is the only one thats not priest-ridden – excuse the expression, Father [*Father Dempsey nods tolerantly*]

– because it's the only one that has established its Church and can prevent a clergyman becoming a bishop if he's not a Statesman as well as a Churchman.

He stops. They stare at him dumbfounded, and leave it to the priest to answer him.

FATHER DEMPSEY [*judicially*] Young man: youll not be the member for Rosscullen; but dheres more in your head than the comb will take out.

LARRY. I'm sorry to disappoint you, Father; but I told you it would be no use. And now I think the candidate had better retire and leave you to discuss his successor. [*He takes a newspaper from the table and goes away through the shrubbery amid dead silence, all turning to watch him until he passes out of sight round the corner of the house*].

DORAN [*dazed*] Hwat sort of a fella is he at all at all?

FATHER DEMPSEY. He's a clever lad: dheres the making of a man in him yet.

MATTHEW [*in consternation*] D'ye mane to say dhat yll put him into parliament to bring back Nick Lesthrange on me, and to put tithes on me, and to rob me for the like o Patsy Farrll, because he's Corny Doyle's son?

DORAN [*brutally*] Arra hould your whisht: who's going to send him into parliament? Maybe youd like us to send you dhere to thrate dhem to a little o your anxiety about dhat dirty little podato patch o yours.

MATTHEW [*plaintively*] Am I to be towld dhis afther all me sufferins?

DORAN. Och, I'm tired o your sufferins. Weve been hearin nothin else ever since we was childher but sufferins. Hwen it wasnt yours it was somebody else's; and hwen it was nobody else's it was ould Irelan's. How the divil are we to live on wan anodher's sufferins?

FATHER DEMPSEY. Thats a thrue word, Barney Doran; only your tongue's a little too familiar wi dhe divil. [*To Matt*] If youd think a little more o the sufferins of the blessed saints, Matt, an a little less o your own, youd find the way shorter from your farm to heaven [*Matt is about to reply*] Dhere now! dhats enough! we know you mean well; an I'm not angry with you.

BROADBENT. Surely, Mr Haffigan, you can see the simple explanation of all this. My friend Larry Doyle is a most brilliant speaker; but he's a Tory: an ingrained old-fashioned Tory.

CORNELIUS. N how d'ye make dhat out, if I might ask you, Mr Broadbent?

BROADBENT [*collecting himself for a political deliverance*] Well, you know, Mr Doyle, theres a strong dash of Toryism in the Irish character. Larry himself says that the great Duke of Wellington was the most typical Irishman that ever lived. Of course thats an absurd paradox; but still theres a great deal of truth in it. Now I am a Liberal. You know the great principles of the Liberal Party. Peace –

FATHER DEMPSEY [*piously*] Hear! hear!

BROADBENT [*encouraged*] Thank you. Retrenchment – [*he waits for further applause*].

MATTHEW [*timidly*] What might rethrenchment mane now?

BROADBENT. It means an immense reduction in the burden of the rates and taxes.

MATTHEW [*respectfully approving*] Dhats right. Dhats right, sir.

BROADBENT [*perfunctorily*] And, of course, Reform.

CORNELIUS
FATHER DEMPSEY } [*conventionally*] Of course.
DORAN

MATTHEW [*still suspicious*] Hwat docs Reform mane, sir? Does it mane altherin annythin dhats as it is now?

BROADBENT [*impressively*] It means, Mr Haffigan, maintaining those reforms which have already been conferred on humanity by the Liberal Party, and trusting for future developments to the free activity of a free people on the basis of those reforms.

DORAN. Dhats right. No more meddlin. We're all right now: all we want is to be let alone.

CORNELIUS. Hwat about Home Rule?

BROADBENT [*rising so as to address them more imposingly*] I really cannot tell you what I feel about Home Rule without using the language of hyperbole.

DORAN. Savin Fadher Dempsey's presence, eh?

BROADBENT [*not understanding him*] Quite so – er – oh yes. All I can say is that as an Englishman I blush for the Union. It is the blackest stain on our national history. I look forward to the time – and it cannot be far distant, gentlemen, because Humanity is looking forward to it too, and insisting on it with no uncertain voice – I look forward to the time when an Irish legislature shall arise once more on the emerald pasture of College Green, and the Union Jack – that detestable symbol of a decadent Imperialism – be replaced by a flag as green as the island over which it waves: a flag on which we shall ask for England only a modest quartering in memory of our great party and of the immortal name of our grand old leader.

DORAN [*enthusiastically*] Dhats the style, begob! [*He smites his knee, and winks at Matt*].

MATTHEW. More power to you, sir!

BROADBENT. I shall leave you now, gentlemen, to your deliberations. I should like to have enlarged on the services rendered by the Liberal Party to the religious faith of the great majority of the people of Ireland; but I shall content myself with saying that in my opinion you should choose no representative who – no matter what his personal creed may be – is not an ardent supporter of freedom of conscience, and is not prepared to prove it by contributions, as lavish as his means will allow, to the great and beneficent work which you, Father Dempsey [*Father Dempsey bows*], are doing for the people of Rosscullen. Nor should the lighter, but still most important question of the sports of the people be forgotten. The local cricket club –

CORNELIUS. The hwat!

DORAN. Nobody plays bat n ball here, if dhats what you mane.

BROADBENT. Well, let us say quoits. I saw two men, I think, last night – but after all, these are questions of detail. The main thing is that your candidate, whoever he may be, shall be a man of some means, able to help the locality instead of burdening it. And if he were a countryman of my own, the moral effect on the House of Commons would be immense! tremendous! Pardon my saying these few words: nobody feels their impertinence more than I do. Good morning, gentlemen.

He turns impressively to the gate, and trots away, congratulating himself, with a little twist of his head and cock of his eye, on having done a good stroke of political business.

MATTHEW [*awestruck*] Good morning, sir.

THE REST. Good morning. [*They watch him vacantly until he is out of earshot*].

CORNELIUS. Hwat d'ye think, Father Dempsey?

FATHER DEMPSEY [*indulgently*] Well, he hasnt much sense, God help him; but for the matter o that, neether has our present member.

DORAN. Arra musha he's good enough for parliament: what is there to do there but gas a bit, an chivy the Government, an vote wi dh Irish party?

CORNELIUS [*ruminatively*] He's the queerest Englishman *I* ever met. When he opened the paper dhis mornin the first thing he saw was that an English expedition had been bet in a battle in Inja somewhere; an he was as pleased as Punch! Larry told him that if he'd been alive when the news o Waterloo came, he'd a died o grief over it. Bedad I dont think he's quite right in his head.

DORAN. Divil a matther if he has plenty o money. He'll do for us right enough.

MATTHEW [*deeply impressed by Broadbent, and unable to understand their levity concerning him*] Did you mind what he said about rethrenchment? That was very good, I thought.

FATHER DEMPSEY. You might find out from Larry, Corny, what his means are. God forgive us all! it's poor work spoiling the Egyptians, though we have good warrant for it; so I'd like to know how much spoil there is before I commit meself. [*He rises. They all rise respectfully*].

CORNELIUS [*ruefully*] I'd set me mind on Larry himself for the scat; but I suppose it cant be helped.

FATHER DEMPSEY [*consoling him*] Well, the boy's young yet; an he has a head on him. Goodbye, all. [*He goes out through the gate*].

DORAN. I must be goin, too. [*He directs Cornelius's attention to what is passing in the road*]. Look at me bould Englishman shakin hans wid Fadher Dempsey for all the world like a candidate on election day. And look at Fadher Dempsey givin him a squeeze an a wink as much as to say It's all right, me boy. You watch him shakin hans with me too: he's waitn for me. I'll tell him he's as good as elected. [*He goes, chuckling mischievously*].

CORNELIUS. Come in with me, Matt. I think I'll sell you the pig after all. Come in an wet the bargain.

MATTHEW [*instantly dropping into the old whine of the tenant*] I'm afeerd I cant afford the price, sir. [*He follows Cornelius into the house*].

Larry, newspaper still in hand, comes back through the shrubbery. Broadbent returns through the gate.

LARRY. Well? What has happened?

BROADBENT [*hugely self-satisfied*] I think Ive done the trick this time. I just gave them a bit of straight talk; and it went home. They were greatly impressed: everyone of those men believes in me and will vote for me when the question of selecting a candidate comes up. After all, whatever you say, Larry, they like an Englishman. They feel they can trust him, I suppose.

LARRY. Oh! theyve transferred the honor to you, have they?

BROADBENT [*complacently*] Well, it was a pretty obvious move, I should think. You know, these fellows have plenty of shrewdness in spite of their Irish oddity. [*Hodson comes from the house. Larry sits in Doran's chair and reads*]. Oh, by the way, Hodson —

HODSON [*coming between Broadbent and Larry*] Yes, sir?

BROADBENT. I want you to be rather particular as to how you treat the people here.

HODSON. I havnt treated any of em yet, sir. If I was to accept all the treats they offer me I shouldnt be able to stand at this present moment, sir.

BROADBENT. Oh well, dont be too stand-offish, you know, Hodson. I should like you to be popular. If it costs anything I'll make it up to you. It doesnt matter if you get a bit upset at first: theyll like you all the better for it.

HODSON. I'm sure youre very kind, sir; but it dont seem to matter to me whether they like me or not. I'm not going to stand for parliament here, sir.

BROADBENT. Well, I am. Now do you understand?

HODSON [*waking up at once*] Oh, I beg your pardon, sir, I'm sure. I understand, sir.

CORNELIUS [*appearing at the house door with Matt*] Patsy'll drive the pig over this evenin, Matt. Goodbye. [*He goes back into the house. Matt makes for the gate. Broadbent stops him. Hodson, pained by the derelict basket, picks it up and carries it away behind the house*].

BROADBENT [*beaming candidatorially*] I must thank you very particularly, Mr Haffigan, for your support this morning. I value it because I know that the real heart of a nation is the class you represent, the yeomanry.

MATTHEW [*aghast*] The yeomanry!!!

LARRY [*looking up from his paper*] Take care, Tom! In Rosscullen a yeoman means a sort of Orange Bashi-Bazouk. In England, Matt, they call a freehold farmer a yeoman.

MATTHEW [*huffily*] I dont need to be insthructed be you, Larry Doyle. Some people think no one knows anythin but dhemselves. [*To Broadbent, deferentially*] Of course I know a gentleman like you would not compare me to the yeomanry. Me own granfather was flogged in the sthreets of Athenmullet be them when they put a gun in the thatch of his house and then went and found it there, bad cess to them!

BROADBENT [*with sympathetic interest*] Then you are not the first martyr of your family, Mr Haffigan?

MATTHEW. They turned me out o the farm I made out of the stones o Little Rosscullen hill wid me own hans.

BROADBENT. I have heard about it; and my blood still boils at the thought. [*Calling*] Hodson –

HODSON [*behind the corner of the house*] Yes, sir. [*He hurries forward*].

BROADBENT. Hodson: this gentleman's sufferings should make every Englishman think. It is want of thought rather than want of heart that allows such iniquities to disgrace society.

HODSON [*prosaically*] Yes, sir.

MATTHEW Well, I'll be goin. Good mornin to you kindly, sir.

BROADBENT. You have some distance to go, Mr Haffigan: will you allow me to drive you home?

MATTHEW. Oh sure it'd be throublin your honor.

BROADBENT. I insist: it will give me the greatest pleasure, I assure you. My car is in the stable: I can get it round in five minutes.

MATTHEW. Well, sir, if you wouldnt mind, we could bring the pig Ive just bought from Corny –

BROADBENT [*with enthusiasm*] Certainly, Mr Haffigan: it will be quite delightful to drive with a pig in the car: I shall feel quite like an Irishman. Hodson: stay with Mr Haffigan; and give him a hand with the pig if necessary. Come, Larry; and help me. [*He rushes away through the shrubbery*].

LARRY [*throwing the paper ill-humoredly on the chair*] Look here, Tom! here, I say! confound it! – [*he runs after him*].

MATTHEW [*glowering disdainfully at Hodson, and sitting down on Cornelius's chair as an act of social self-assertion*] N are you the valley?

HODSON. The valley? Oh, I follow you: yes: I'm Mr Broadbent's valet.

MATTHEW. Ye have an aisy time of it: you look purty sleek. [*With suppressed ferocity*] Look at me! Do *I* look sleek?

HODSON [*sadly*] I wish I ad your ealth: you look as ard as nails. I suffer from an excess of uric acid.

MATTHEW. Musha what sort o disease is zhourag-assid? Didjever suffer from injustice and starvation? Dhats the Irish disease. It's aisy for you to talk o sufferin, and you livin on the fat o the land wid money wrung from us.

HODSON [*suddenly dropping the well-spoken valet, and breaking out in his native cockney*] Wots wrong with you, aold chep? Ez ennybody been doin ennythink to you?

MATTHEW. Anythin timmy! Didnt your English masther say that the blood biled in him to hear the way they put a rint on me for the farm I made wid me own hans, an turned me out of it to give it to Billy Byrne?

HODSON. Ow, Tom Broadbent's blad boils pretty easy over ennything that eppens aht of his aown cantry. Downt you be tiken in by my aowl men, Peddy.

MATTHEW [*indignantly*] Paddy yourself! How dar you call me Paddy?

HODSON [*unmoved*] You jast keep your air on and listen to me. You Awrish people are too well off: thets wots the metter with you. [*With sudden passion*] You talk of your rotten little fawm cause you mide it by chackin a few stowns dahn a ill! Well, wot prawce maw grenfawther, Oi should lawk to knaow, that fitted ap a fust clawss shop and built ap a fust clawss dripery business in Landon by sixty years work, and then was chacked aht of it on is ed at the end of is lease withaht a penny for his goodwill. You talk of evictions! you that cawnt be moved until youve ran ap ighteen months rent. Oi once ran ap four weeks in Lembeth wen Oi was aht of a job in winter. They took the door off its inges and the winder aht of its seshes on me, and gev maw wawf pnoomownia. Oi'm a widower nah. [*Between his teeth*] Gawd! when Oi think of the things we Englishmen as to pat ap with, and eah you Awrish ahlin abaht your silly little grievances, and see the wy you mike it worse for haz by the rotten wiges youll cam over and tike and the rotten plices youll sleep in, I jast feel that I could tike the aowl bloomin British awland and mike you a present of it, jast to let you fawnd aht wot reel awdship's lawk.

MATTHEW [*starting up, more in scandalized incredulity than in anger*] D'ye have the face to set up England agen Ireland for injustices an wrongs an disthress an sufferin?

HODSON [*with intense disgust and contempt*] Ow, chack it, Paddy. Cheese it. You danno wot awdship is owver eah: all you knaow is ah to ahl abaht it. You tike the biscuit at thet, you do. Oi'm a Owm Ruler, Oi em. Do you knaow woy?

MATTHEW [*equally contemptuous*] D'ye know, yourself?

HODSON. Yus Oi do. It's because Oi want a little attention pide to my aown cantry; and thetll never be as long as your cheps are ollerin at Westminster as if nowbody mettered but your own bloomin selves. Send em back to ell or C'naught, as good aowld English Cramwell said. I'm jast sick of Awrland. Let it gow. Cat the caible. Mike it a present to Germany to keep the aowl Kyzer busy for a wawl; and give poor aowld England a chawnce: thets wot Oi sy.

MATTHEW [*full of scorn for a man so ignorant as to be unable to pronounce the word Connaught, which practically rhymes with bonnet in Ireland, though in Hodson's dialect it rhymes with untaught*] Take care we dont cut the cable ourselves some day, bad scran to you! An tell me dhis: have yanny Coercion Acs in England? Have yanny Removable magisthruts? Have you Dublin Castle to suppress every newspaper dhat takes the part o your own counthry?

HODSON. We can beyive ahrselves withaht sich things.

MATTHEW. Bedad youre right. It'd ony be waste o time to muzzle a sheep. Here! wheres me pig? God forgimmy for talkin to a poor ignorant craycher like you!

HODSON [*grinning with good-humored malice, too convinced of his own superiority to feel his withers wrung*] Your pig'll ev a rare doin in that car, Peddy. Forty mawl an ahr dahn that rocky line will strawk it pretty pink, you bet.

MATTHEW [*scornfully*] Hwy cant you tell a raisonable lie whcn youre about it? What horse can go forty mile an hour?

HODSON. Orse! Wy, you silly aowl rotter, it's not a orse: it's a mowtor. Do you spowse Tom Broadbent ud gow himself to fetch a orse?

MATTHEW [*in consternation*] Holy Moses! dont tell me it's the ingine he wants to take me on.

HODSON. Wot else?

MATTHEW. Your sowl to Morris Kelly! why didnt you tell me that before? The divil an ingine he'll get me on this day. [*His ear catches an approaching teuf-teuf*]. Oh murdher! it's comin afther me: I hear the puff-puff of it. [*He runs away through the gate, much to Hodson's amusement. The noise of the motor ceases; and Hodson, anticipating Broadbent's return, throws off the cockney and recomposes himself as a valet. Broadbent and Larry come through the shrubbery. Hodson moves aside to the gate*].

BROADBENT. Where is Mr Haffigan? Has he gone for the pig?

HODSON. Bolted, sir. Afraid of the motor, sir.

BROADBENT [*much disappointed*] Oh, thats very tiresome. Did he leave any message?

HODSON. He was in too great a hurry, sir. Started to run home, sir, and left his pig behind him.

BROADBENT [*eagerly*] Left the pig! Then it's all right. The pig's the thing: the pig will win over every Irish heart to me. We'll take the pig home to Haffigan's farm in the motor: it will have a tremendous effect. Hodson!

HODSON. Yes, sir?

BROADBENT. Do you think you could collect a crowd to see the motor?

HODSON. Well, I'll try, sir.

BROADBENT. Thank you, Hodson: do.

Hodson goes out through the gate.

LARRY [*desperately*] Once more, Tom, will you listen to me?

BROADBENT. Rubbish! I tell you it will be all right.

LARRY. Only this morning you confessed how surprised you were to find that the people here shewed no sense of humor.

BROADBENT [*suddenly very solemn*] Yes: their sense of humor is in abeyance: I noticed it the moment we landed. Think of that in a country where every man is a born humorist! Think of what it means! [*Impressively*] Larry: we are in the presence of a great national grief.

LARRY. Whats to grieve them?

BROADBENT. I divined it, Larry: I saw it in their faces. Ireland has never smiled since her hopes were buried in the grave of Gladstone.

LARRY. Oh, whats the use of talking to such a man? Now look here, Tom. Be serious for a moment if you can.

BROADBENT [*stupent*] Serious! I!!!!

LARRY. Yes, you. You say the Irish sense of humor is in abeyance. Well, if you drive through Rosscullen in a motor car with Haffigan's pig, it wont stay in abeyance. Now I warn you.

BROADBENT [*breezily*] Why, so much the better! I shall enjoy the joke myself more than any of them. [*Shouting*] Hallo, Patsy Farrell, where are you?

PATSY [*appearing in the shrubbery*] Here I am, your honor.

BROADBENT. Go and catch the pig and put it into the car: we're going to take it to Mr Haffigan's. [*He gives Larry a slap on the shoulders that sends him staggering off through the gate, and follows him buoyantly, exclaiming*] Come on, you old croaker! I'll shew you how to win an Irish seat.

PATSY [*meditatively*] Bedad, if dhat pig gets a howlt o the handle o the machine – [*He shakes his head ominously and drifts away to the pigsty*].

ACT IV

The parlor in Cornelius Doyle's house. It communicates with the garden by a half glazed door. The fireplace is at the other side of the room, opposite the door and windows, the architect not having been sensitive to draughts. The table, rescued from the garden, is in the middle; and at it sits Keegan, the central figure in a rather crowded apartment. Nora, sitting with her back to the fire at the end of the table, is playing backgammon across its corner with him, on his left hand. Aunt Judy, a little further back, sits facing the fire knitting, with her feet on the fender. A little to Keegan's right, in front of the table, and almost sitting on it, is Barney Doran. Half a dozen friends of his, all men, are between him and the open door, supported by others outside. In the corner behind them is the sofa, of mahogany and horsehair, made up as a bed for Broadbent. Against the wall behind Keegan stands a mahogany sideboard. A door leading to the interior of the house is near the fireplace, behind Aunt Judy. There are chairs against the wall, one at each end of the sideboard. Keegan's hat is on the one nearest the inner door; and his stick is leaning against it. A third chair, also against the wall, is near the garden door.

There is a strong contrast of emotional atmosphere between the two sides of the room. Keegan is extraordinarily stern: no game of backgammon could possibly make a man's face so grim. Aunt Judy is quietly busy. Nora is trying to ignore Doran and attend to her game.

On the other hand Doran is reeling in an ecstasy of mischievous mirth which has infected all his friends. They are screaming with laughter, doubled up, leaning on the furniture and against the walls, shouting, screeching, crying.

AUNT JUDY [*as the noise lulls for a moment*] Arra hold your noise, Barney. What is there to laugh at?

DORAN. It got its fut into the little hweel – [*he is overcome afresh: and the rest collapse again*].

AUNT JUDY. Ah, have some sense: youre like a parcel o childher. Nora: hit him a thump on the back: he'll have a fit.

DORAN [*with squeezed eyes, exsufflicate with cachinnation*] Frens, he sez to dhem outside Doolan's: I'm takin the gintleman that pays the rint for a dhrive.

AUNT JUDY. Who did he mean be that?

DORAN. They call a pig that in England. Thats their notion of a joke.

AUNT JUDY. Musha God help them if they can joke no better than that!

DORAN [*with renewed symptoms*] Thin –

AUNT JUDY. Ah now dont be tellin it all over and settin yourself off again, Barney.

NORA. Youve told us three times, Mr Doran.

DORAN. Well but whin I think of it –!

AUNT JUDY. Then dont think of it, alanna.

DORAN. Dhere was Patsy Farrll in the back sate wi dhe pig between his knees, n me bould English boyoh in front at the machinery, n Larry Doyle in the road startin the injine wid a bed winch. At the first puff of it the pig lep out of its skin and bled Patsy's nose wi dhe ring in its snout. [*Roars of laughter: Keegan glares at them*]. Before Broadbint knew hwere he was, the pig was up his back and over into his lap; and bedad the poor baste did credit to Corny's thrainin of it; for it put in the fourth speed wid its right crubeen as if it was enthered for the Gordn Bennett.

NORA [*reproachfully*] And Larry in front of it and all! It's nothin to laugh at, Mr Doran.

DORAN. Bedad, Miss Reilly, Larry cleared six yards sideways at wan jump if he cleared an inch; and he'd a cleared seven if Doolan's granmother hadnt cotch him in her apern widhout intindin to. [*Immense merriment*].

AUNT JUDY. Ah, for shame, Barney! the poor old woman! An she was hurt before, too, when she slipped on the stairs.

DORAN. Bedad, maam, she's hurt behind now; for Larry bouled her over like a skittle. [*General delight at this typical stroke of Irish Rabelaisianism*].

NORA. It's well Mr Doyle wasnt killed.

DORAN. Faith it wasnt o Larry we were thinkin jus dhen, wi dhe pig takin the main sthreet o Rosscullen on market day at a mile a minnit. Dh ony thing Broadbint could get at wi dhe pig in front of him was a fut brake; n the pig's tail was undher dhat; so that whin he thought he was putn non the brake he was ony squeezin the life out o the pig's tail. The more he put the brake on the more the pig squealed n the fasther he dhruv.

AUNT JUDY. Why couldnt he throw the pig out into the road?

DORAN. Sure he couldnt stand up to it, because he was spanchelled-like between his seat and dhat thing like a wheel on top of a stick between his knees.

AUNT JUDY. Lord have mercy on us!

NORA. I dont know how you can laugh. Do you, Mr Keegan?

KEEGAN [grimly] Why not? There is danger, destruction, torment! What more do we need to make us merry? Go on, Barney: the last drops of joy are not squeezed from the story yet. Tell us again how our brother was torn asunder.

DORAN [puzzled] Whose bruddher?

KEEGAN. Mine.

NORA. He means the pig, Mr Doran. You know his way.

DORAN [rising gallantly to the occasion] Bedad I'm sorry for your poor bruddher, Misther Keegan; but I recommend you to thry him wid a couple o fried eggs for your breakfast tomorrow. It was a case of Excelsior wi dhat ambitious baste; for not content wid jumpin from the back seat into the front wan, he jumped from the front wan into the road in front of the car. And —

KEEGAN. And everybody laughed!

NORA. Dont go over that again, please, Mr Doran.

DORAN. Faith be the time the car went over the poor pig dhere was little left for me or anywan else to go over except wid a knife an fork.

AUNT JUDY. Why didnt Mr Broadbent stop the car when the pig was gone?

DORAN. Stop the car! He might as well ha tried to stop a mad bull. First it went wan way an made fireworks o Molly Ryan's crockery stall; an dhen it slewed round an ripped ten fut o wall out o the corner o the pound. [With enormous enjoyment] Begob, it just tore the town in two and sent the whole dam market to blazes. [Nora offended, rises].

KEEGAN [indignantly] Sir!

DORAN [quickly] Savin your presence, Miss Reilly, and Misther Keegan's. Dhere! I wont say anuddher word.

NORA. I'm surprised at you, Mr Doran. [She sits down again].

DORAN [reflectively] He has the divil's own luck, that Englishman, anny-

way; for hwen they picked him up he hadnt a scratch on him, barrn
hwat the pig did to his cloes. Patsy had two fingers out o jynt; but
the smith pulled them sthraight for him. Oh, you never heard such
a hullaballoo as there was. There was Molly cryin Me chaney, me
beautyful chaney! n oul Matt shoutin Me pig, me pig! n the polus
takin the number o the car, n not a man in the town able to speak for
laughin —

KEEGAN [*with intense emphasis*] It is hell: it is hell. Nowhere else could
such a scene be a burst of happiness for the people.

*Cornelius comes in hastily from the garden, pushing his way through the
little crowd.*

CORNELIUS. Whisht your laughin, boys! Here he is. [*He puts his hat
on the sideboard, and goes to the fireplace, where he posts himself with
his back to the chimneypiece*].

AUNT JUDY. Remember your behavior now.

*Everybody becomes silent, solemn, concerned, sympathetic. Broadbent
enters, soiled and disordered as to his motoring coat: immensely important
and serious as to himself. He makes his way to the end of the table nearest
the garden door, whilst Larry, who accompanies him, throws his motoring
coat on the sofa bed, and sits down, watching the proceedings.*

BROADBENT [*taking off his leather cap with dignity and placing it on the
table*] I hope you have not been anxious about me.

AUNT JUDY. Deedn we have, Mr Broadbent. It's a mercy you werent
killed.

DORAN. Kilt! It's a mercy dheres two bones of you left houldin together.
How dijjescape at all at all? Well, I never thought I'd be so glad to
see you safe and sound again. Not a man in the town would say less
[*murmurs of kindly assent*]. Wont you come down to Doolan's and have
a dhrop o brandy to take the shock off?

BROADBENT. Youre all really too kind; but the shock has quite passed
off.

DORAN [*jovially*] Never mind. Come along all the same and tell us about
it over a frenly glass.

BROADBENT. May I say how deeply I feel the kindness with which I
have been overwhelmed since my accident? I can truthfully declare that
I am glad it happened, because it has brought out the kindness and
sympathy of the Irish character to an extent I had no conception of.

SEVERAL
PRESENT
{
Oh, sure youre welcome!
Sure it's only natural.
Sure you might have been kilt.
}

A young man, feeling that he must laugh or burst, hurries out. Barney puts an iron constraint on his features.

BROADBENT. All I can say is that I wish I could drink the health of everyone of you.

DORAN. Dhen come an do it.

BROADBENT [*very solemnly*] No: I am a teetotaller.

AUNT JUDY [*incredulously*] Arra since when?

BROADBENT. Since this morning, Miss Doyle. I have had a lesson [*he looks at Nora significantly*] that I shall not forget. It may be that total abstinence has already saved my life; for I was astonished at the steadiness of my nerves when death stared me in the face today. So I will ask you to excuse me. [*He collects himself for a speech*]. Gentlemen: I hope the gravity of the peril through which we have all passed – for I know that the danger to the bystanders was as great as to the occupants of the car – will prove an earnest of closer and more serious relations between us in the future. We have had a somewhat agitating day: a valuable and innocent animal has lost its life: a public building has been wrecked: an aged and infirm lady has suffered an impact for which I feel personally responsible, though my old friend Mr Laurence Doyle unfortunately incurred the first effects of her very natural resentment. I greatly regret the damage to Mr Patrick Farrell's fingers; and I have of course taken care that he shall not suffer pecuniarily by his mishap. [*Murmurs of admiration at his magnanimity, and A Voice* 'Youre a gentleman, sir']. I am glad to say that Patsy took it like an Irishman, and, far from expressing any vindictive feeling, declared his willingness to break all his fingers and toes for me on the same terms [*subdued applause, and* 'More power to Patsy!']. Gentlemen: I felt at home in Ireland from the first [*rising excitement among his hearers*]. In every Irish breast I have found that spirit of liberty [*A cheery voice* 'Hear hear'], that instinctive mistrust of the Government [*A small pious voice, with intense expression*, 'God bless you, sir!'], that love of independence [*A defiant voice*, 'Thats it! Independence!'], that indignant sympathy with the cause of oppressed nationalities abroad [*A threatening growl from all: the ground-swell of patriotic passion*] and with the resolute assertion of personal rights at home, which is all but extinct in my own country. If it were legally possible I should become a naturalized Irishman; and if ever it be my good fortune to represent an Irish constituency in parliament, it shall be my first care to introduce a Bill legalizing such an operation. I believe a large section of the Liberal party would avail themselves of it. [*Momentary scepticism*] I do. [*Convulsive cheering*]. Gentlemen: I have said enough. [*Cries of* 'Go on']. No: I have as yet no right to address you at all on political subjects; and we must not abuse the warm-hearted Irish hospitality of Miss Doyle by turning her sitting room into a public meeting.

DORAN [*energetically*] Three cheers for Tom Broadbent, the future member for Rosscullen!

AUNT JUDY [*waving a half knitted sock*] Hip hip hurray!

The cheers are given with great heartiness, as it is by this time, for the more humorous spirits present, a question of vociferation or internal rupture.

BROADBENT. Thank you from the bottom of my heart, friends.

NORA [*whispering to Doran*] Take them away, Mr Doran [*Doran nods*].

DORAN. Well, good evenin, Mr Broadbent; an may you never regret the day you wint dhrivin wid Haffigan's pig! [*They shake hands*]. Good evenin, Miss Doyle.

General handshaking, Broadbent shaking hands with everybody effusively. He accompanies them to the garden and can be heard outside saying Good night in every inflexion known to parliamentary candidates. Nora, Aunt Judy, Keegan, Larry, and Cornelius are left in the parlor. Larry goes to the threshold and watches the scene in the garden.

NORA. It's a shame to make game of him like that. He's a gradle more good in him than Barney Doran.

CORNELIUS. It's all up with his candidature. He'll be laughed out o the town.

LARRY [*turning quickly from the doorway*] Oh no he wont: he's not an Irishman. He'll never know theyre laughing at him; and while theyre laughing he'll win the seat.

CORNELIUS. But he cant prevent the story getting about.

LARRY. He wont want to. He'll tell it himself as one of the most providential episodes in the history of England and Ireland.

AUNT JUDY. Sure he wouldnt make a fool of himself like that.

LARRY. Are you sure he's such a fool after all, Aunt Judy? Suppose you had a vote! which would you rather give it to? the man that told the story of Haffigan's pig Barney Doran's way or Broadbent's way?

AUNT JUDY. Faith I wouldnt give it to a man at all. It's a few women they want in parliament to stop their foolish blather.

BROADBENT [*bustling into the room, and taking off his damaged motoring overcoat, which he puts down on the sofa*] Well thats over. I must apologize for making a speech, Miss Doyle; but they like it, you know. Everything helps in electioneering.

Larry takes the chair near the door; draws it near the table; and sits astride it, with his elbows folded on the back.

AUNT JUDY. I'd no notion you were such an orator, Mr Broadbent.

BROADBENT. Oh, it's only a knack. One picks it up on the platform. It stokes up their enthusiasm.

AUNT JUDY. Oh, I forgot. Youve not met Mr Keegan. Let me introjoosha.

BROADBENT [*shaking hands effusively*] Most happy to meet you, Mr Keegan. I have heard of you, though I have not had the pleasure of shaking your hand before. And now may I ask you – for I value no man's opinion more – what you think of my chances here.

KEEGAN [*coldly*] Your chances, sir, are excellent. You will get into parliament.

BROADBENT [*delighted*] I hope so. I think so. [*Fluctuating*] You really think so? You are sure you are not allowing your enthusiasm for our principles to get the better of your judgment?

KEEGAN. I have no enthusiasm for your principles, sir. You will get into parliament because you want to get into it enough to be prepared to take the necessary steps to induce the people to vote for you. That is how people usually get into that fantastic assembly.

BROADBENT [*puzzled*] Of course. [*Pause*]. Quite so. [*Pause*]. Er – yes. [*Buoyant again*] I think they will vote for me. Eh? Yes?

AUNT JUDY. Arra why shouldnt they? Look at the people they do vote for!

BROADBENT [*encouraged*] Thats true: thats very true. When I see the windbags, the carpet-baggers, the charlatans, the – the – the fools and ignoramuses who corrupt the multitude by their wealth, or seduce them by spouting balderdash to them, I cannot help thinking that an Englishman with no humbug about him, who will talk straight common sense and take his stand on the solid ground of principle and public duty, must win his way with men of all classes.

KEEGAN [*quietly*] Sir: there was a time, in my ignorant youth, when I should have called you a hypocrite.

BROADBENT [*reddening*] A hypocrite!

NORA [*hastily*] Oh I'm sure you dont think anything of the sort, Mr Keegan.

BROADBENT [*emphatically*] Thank you, Miss Reilly: thank you.

CORNELIUS [*gloomily*] We all have to stretch it a bit in politics: hwats the use o pretendin we dont?

BROADBENT [*stiffly*] I hope I have said or done nothing that calls for any such observation, Mr Doyle. If there is a vice I detest – or against which my whole public life has been a protest – it is the vice of hypocrisy. I would almost rather be inconsistent than insincere.

KEEGAN. Do not be offended, sir: I know that you are quite sincere. There is a saying in the Scripture which runs – so far as the memory of an oldish man can carry the words – Let not the right side of your brain know what the left side doeth. I learnt at Oxford that this is the secret of the Englishman's strange power of making the best of both worlds.

BROADBENT. Surely the text refers to our right and left hands. I am somewhat surprised to hear a member of your Church quote so essentially Protestant a document as the Bible; but at least you might quote it accurately.

LARRY. Tom: with the best intentions youre making an ass of yourself. You dont understand Mr Keegan's peculiar vein of humor.

BROADBENT [*instantly recovering his confidence*] Ah! it was only your delightful Irish humor, Mr Keegan. Of course, of course. How stupid of me! I'm so sorry. [*He pats Keegan consolingly on the back*]. John Bull's wits are still slow, you see. Besides, calling me a hypocrite was too big a joke to swallow all at once, you know.

KEEGAN. You must also allow for the fact that I am mad.

NORA. Ah, dont talk like that, Mr Keegan.

BROADBENT [*encouragingly*] Not at all, not at all. Only a whimsical Irishman, eh?

LARRY. Are you really mad, Mr Keegan?

AUNT JUDY [*shocked*] Oh, Larry, how could you ask him such a thing?

LARRY. I dont think Mr Keegan minds. [*To Keegan*] Whats the true version of the story of that black man you confessed on his deathbed?

KEEGAN. What story have you heard about that?

LARRY. I am informed that when the devil came for the black heathen, he took off your head and turned it three times round before putting it on again; and that your head's been turned ever since.

NORA [*reproachfully*] Larry!

KEEGAN [*blandly*] That is not quite what occurred. [*He collects himself for a serious utterance: they attend involuntarily*]. I heard that a black man was dying, and that the people were afraid to go near him. When I went to the place I found an elderly Hindoo, who told me one of those tales of unmerited misfortune, of cruel ill luck, of relentless persecution by destiny, which sometimes wither the commonplaces of consolation on the lips of a priest. But this man did not complain of his misfortunes. They were brought upon him, he said, by sins committed in a former existence. Then without a word of comfort from me, he died with a clear-eyed resignation that my most earnest exhortations have rarely produced in a Christian, and left me sitting there by his bedside with the mystery of this world suddenly revealed to me.

BROADBENT. That is a remarkable tribute to the liberty of conscience enjoyed by the subjects of our Indian Empire.

LARRY. No doubt; but may we venture to ask what is the mystery of this world?

KEEGAN. This world, sir, is very clearly a place of torment and penance, a place where the fool flourishes and the good and wise are hated and persecuted, a place where men and women torture one another in the name of love; where children are scourged and enslaved in the name of parental duty and education; where the weak in body are poisoned and mutilated in the name of healing, and the weak in character are put to the horrible torture of imprisonment, not for hours but for years, in the name of justice. It is a place where the hardest toil is a welcome refuge from the horror and tedium of pleasure, and where charity and good works are done only for hire to ransom the souls of the spoiler and the sybarite. Now, sir, there is only one place of horror and torment known to my religion; and that place is hell. Therefore it is plain to me that this earth of ours must be hell, and that we are all here, as the Indian revealed to me – perhaps he was sent to reveal it to me – to expiate crimes committed by us in a former existence.

AUNT JUDY [*awestruck*] Heaven save us, what a thing to say!

CORNELIUS [*sighing*] It's a queer world: thats certain.

BROADBENT. Your idea is a very clever one, Mr Keegan: really most brilliant: *I* should never have thought of it. But it seems to me – if I may say so – that you are overlooking the fact that, of the evils you describe, some are absolutely necessary for the preservation of society, and others are encouraged only when the Tories are in office.

LARRY. I expect you were a Tory in a former existence; and that is why you are here.

BROADBENT [*with conviction*] Never, Larry, never. But leaving politics out of the question, I find the world quite good enough for me: rather a jolly place, in fact.

KEEGAN [*looking at him with quiet wonder*] You are satisfied?

BROADBENT. As a reasonable man, yes. I see no evils in the world – except, of course, natural evils – that cannot be remedied by freedom, self-government, and English institutions. I think so, not because I am an Englishman, but as a matter of common sense.

KEEGAN. You feel at home in the world, then?

BROADBENT. Of course. Dont you?

KEEGAN [*from the very depths of his nature*] No.

BROADBENT [*breezily*] Try phosphorus pills. I always take them when my brain is overworked. I'll give you the address in Oxford Street.

KEEGAN [*enigmatically: rising*] Miss Doyle: my wandering fit has come on me: will you excuse me?

AUNT JUDY. To be sure: you know you can come in n nout as you like.

KEEGAN. We can finish the game some other time, Miss Reilly. [*He goes for his hat and stick*].

NORA. No: I'm out with you [*she disarranges the pieces and rises*]. I was too wicked in a former existence to play backgammon with a good man like you.

AUNT JUDY [*whispering to her*] Whisht, whisht, child! Dont set him back on that again.

KEEGAN [*to Nora*] When I look at you, I think that perhaps Ireland is only purgatory, after all. [*He passes on to the garden door*].

NORA. Galong with you!

BROADBENT [*whispering to Cornelius*] Has he a vote?

CORNELIUS [*nodding*] Yes. An theres lotsle vote the way he tells them.

KEEGAN [*at the garden door, with gentle gravity*] Good evening, Mr Broadbent. You hae set me thinking. Thank you.

BROADBENT [*delighted, hurrying across to him to shake hands*] No, really? You find that contact with English ideas is stimulating, eh?

KEEGAN. I am never tired of hearing you talk, Mr Broadbent.

BROADBENT [*modestly remonstrating*] Oh come! come!

KEEGAN. Yes, I assure you. You are an extremely interesting man. [*He goes out*].

BROADBENT [*enthusiastically*] What a nice chap! What an intelligent, broadminded character, considering his cloth! By the way, I'd better have a wash [*He takes up his coat and cap, and leaves the room through the inner door*].

Nora returns to her chair and shuts up the backgammon board.

AUNT JUDY. Keegan's very queer today. He has his mad fit on him.

CORNELIUS [*worried and bitter*] I wouldnt say but he's right after all. It's a contrairy world. [*To Larry*] Why would you be such a fool as to let Broadbent take the seat in parliament from you?

LARRY [*glancing at Nora*] He will take more than that from me before he's done here.

CORNELIUS. I wish he'd never set foot in my house, bad luck to his fat face! D'ye think he'd lend me £300 on the farm, Larry? When I'm so hard up, it seems a waste o money not to mortgage it now it's me own.

LARRY. *I* can lend you £300 on it.

CORNELIUS. No, no; I wasnt putn in for that. When I die and leave you the farm I should like to be able to feel that it was all me own, and not half yours to start with. Now I'll take me oath Barney Doarn's going to ask Broadbent to lend him £500 on the mill to put in a new hweel; for the old one'll harly hol together. An Haffigan cant sleep with covetn that corner o land at the foot of his medda that belongs to Doolan. He'll have to mortgage to buy it. I may as well be first as last. D'ye think Broadbent'd len me a little?

LARRY. I'm quite sure he will.

CORNELIUS. Is he as ready as that? Would he len me five hunderd, d'ye think?

LARRY. He'll lend you more than the landll ever be worth to you; so for Heaven's sake be prudent.

CORNELIUS [*judicially*] All right, all right, me son: I'll be careful. I'm goin into the office for a bit. [*He withdraws through the inner door, obviously to prepare his application to Broadbent*].

AUNT JUDY [*indignantly*] As if he hadnt seen enough o borryin when he was an agent without beginning borryin himself! [*She rises*]. I'll borry him, so I will. [*She puts her knitting on the table and follows him out, with a resolute air that bodes trouble for Cornelius*].

Larry and Nora are left together for the first time since his arrival. She looks at him with a smile that perishes as she sees him aimlessly rocking his chair, and reflecting, evidently not about her, with his lips pursed as if he were whistling. With a catch in her throat she takes up Aunt Judy's knitting, and makes a pretence of going on with it.

NORA. I suppose it didnt seem very long to you.

LARRY [*starting*] Eh? What didnt?

NORA. The eighteen years youve been away.

LARRY. Oh, that! No: it seems hardly more than a week. I've been so busy – had so little time to think.

NORA. Ive had nothing else to do but think.

LARRY. That was very bad for you. Why didnt you give it up? Why did you stay here?

NORA. Because nobody sent for me to go anywhere else, I suppose. Thats why.

LARRY. Yes: one does stick frightfully in the same place, unless some external force comes and routs one out. [*He yawns slightly; but as she looks up quickly at him, he pulls himself together and rises with an air of waking up and setting to work cheerfully to make himself agreeable*]. And how have you been all this time?

NORA. Quite well, thank you.

LARRY. Thats right. [*Suddenly finding that he has nothing else to say, and being ill at ease in consequence, he strolls about the room humming distractedly*].

NORA [*struggling with her tears*] Is that all you have to say to me, Larry?

LARRY. Well, what is there to say? You see, we know each other so well.

NORA [*a little consoled*] Yes: of course we do. [*He does not reply*]. I wonder you came back at all.

LARRY. I couldnt help it. [*She looks up affectionately*]. Tom made me. [*She looks down again quickly to conceal the effect of this blow. He whistles another stave; then resumes*] I had a sort of dread of returning to Ireland. I felt somehow that my luck would turn if I came back. And now here I am, none the worse.

NORA. Praps it's a little dull for you.

LARRY. No: I havnt exhausted the interest of strolling about the old places and remembering and romancing about them.

NORA [*hopefully*] Oh! You do remember the places, then?

LARRY. Of course. They have associations.

NORA [*not doubting that the associations are with her*] I suppose so.

LARRY. M'yes. I can remember particular spots where I had long fits of thinking about the countries I meant to get to when I escaped from Ireland. America and London, and sometimes Rome and the east.

NORA [*deeply mortified*] Was that all you used to be thinking about?

LARRY. Well, there was precious little else to think about here, my dear Nora, except sometimes at sunset, when one got maudlin and called Ireland Erin, and imagined one was remembering the days of old, and so forth. [*He whistles Let Erin Remember*].

NORA. Did jever get a letter I wrote you last February?

LARRY. Oh yes; and I really intended to answer it. But I havnt had a moment; and I knew you wouldnt mind. You see, I am so afraid of boring you by writing about affairs you dont understand and people you dont know! And yet what else have I to write about? I begin a letter; and then I tear it up again. The fact is, fond as we are of one another, Nora, we have so little in common – I mean of course the things one can put in a letter – that correspondence is apt to become the hardest of hard work.

NORA. Yes: it's hard for me to know anything about you if you never tell me anything.

LARRY [*pettishly*] Nora: a man cant sit down and write his life day by day when he's tired enough with having lived it.

NORA. I'm not blaming you.

LARRY [*looking at her with some concern*] You seem rather out of spirits. [*Going closer to her, anxiously and tenderly*] You havnt got neuralgia, have you?

NORA. No.

LARRY [*reassured*] I get a touch of it sometimes when I am below par.

[Absently, again strolling about] Yes, yes. *[He gazes through the doorway at the Irish landscape, and sings, almost unconsciously, but very expressively, an air from Offenbach's Whittington]*.

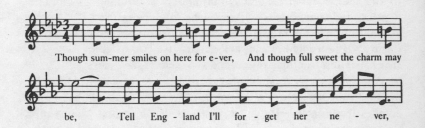

Though sum-mer smiles on here for e-ver, And though full sweet the charm may be, Tell Eng-land I'll for-get her ne - ver,

[Nora, who has been at first touched by the tenderness of his singing, puts down her knitting at this very unexpected sentiment, and stares at him. He continues until the melody soars out of his range, when he trails off into whistling Let Erin Remember].

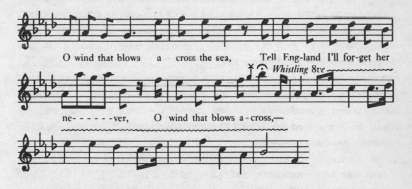

O wind that blows a cross the sea, Tell Eng-land I'll for-get her
Whistling 8ve
ne - - - - - -ver, O wind that blows a-cross,—

I'm afraid I'm boring you, Nora, though youre too kind to say so.

NORA. Are you wanting to get back to England already?

LARRY. Not at all. Not at all.

NORA. Thats a queer song to sing to me if youre not.

LARRY. The song! Oh, it doesnt mean anything: it's by a German Jew, like most English patriotic sentiment. Never mind me, my dear: go on with your work; and dont let me bore you.

NORA [*bitterly*] Rosscullen isnt such a lively place that I am likely to be bored by you at our first talk together after eighteen years, though you dont seem to have much to say to me after all.

LARRY. Eighteen years is a devilish long time, Nora. Now if it had been eighteen minutes, or even eighteen months, we should be able to pick up the interrupted thread, and chatter like two magpies. But as it is, I have simply nothing to say; and you seem to have less.

NORA. I – [*her tears choke her; but she keeps up appearances desperately*].

LARRY [*quite unconscious of his cruelty*] In a week or so we shall be quite old friends again. Meanwhile, as I feel that I am not making myself particularly entertaining, I'll take myself off. Tell Tom Ive gone for a stroll over the hill.

NORA. You seem very fond of Tom, as you call him.

LARRY [*the triviality going suddenly out of his voice*] Yes: I'm fond of Tom.

NORA. Oh, well, dont let me keep you from him.

LARRY. I know quite well that my departure will be a relief. Rather a failure, this first meeting after eighteen years, eh? Well, never mind: these great sentimental events always are failures; and now the worst of it's over anyhow. [*He goes out through the garden door*].

Nora, left alone, struggles wildly to save herself from breaking down, and then drops her face on the table and gives way to a convulsion of crying. Her sobs shake her so that she can hear nothing; and she has no suspicion that she is no longer alone until her head and breast are raised by Broadbent who, returning newly washed and combed through the inner door, has seen her condition, first with surprise and concern, and then with an emotional disturbance that quite upsets him.

BROADBENT. Miss Reilly. Miss Reilly. Whats the matter? Dont cry: I cant stand it: you mustnt cry. [*She makes a choked effort to speak, so painful that he continues with impulsive sympathy*] No: dont try to speak: it's all right now. Have your cry out: never mind me: trust me. [*Gathering her to him, and babbling consolatorily*] Cry on my chest: the only really comfortable place for a woman to cry is a man's chest: a real man, a real friend. A good broad chest, eh? not less than forty-two inches – no: dont fuss: never mind the conventions: we're two

friends, arnt we? Come now, come, come! It's all right and comfortable
and happy now, isnt it?

NORA [*through her tears*] Let me go. I want me hankerchief.

BROADBENT [*holding her with one arm and producing a large silk handkerchief from his breast pocket*] Heres a handkerchief. Let me [*he dabs
her tears dry with it*]. Never mind your own: it's too small: it's one
of those wretched little cambric handkerchiefs –

NORA [*sobbing*] Indeed it's a common cotton one.

BROADBENT. Of course it's a common cotton one – silly little cotton
one – not good enough for the dear eyes of Nora Cryna –

NORA [*spluttering into a hysterical laugh and clutching him convulsively
with her fingers while she tries to stifle her laughter against his collar
bone*] Oh dont make me laugh: please dont make me laugh.

BROADBENT [*terrified*] I didnt mean to, on my soul. What is it? What
is it?

NORA. Nora Creena, Nora Creena.

BROADBENT [*patting her*] Yes, yes, of course, Nora Creena, Nora acushla
[*he makes cush rhyme to plush*] –

NORA. Acushla [*she makes cush rhyme to bush*].

BROADBENT. Oh, confound the language! Nora darling – my Nora –
the Nora I love –

NORA [*shocked into propriety*] You mustnt talk like that to me.

BROADBENT [*suddenly becoming prodigiously solemn and letting her go*]
No, of course not. I dont mean it. At least I do mean it, but I know
it's premature. I had no right to take advantage of your being a little
upset; but I lost my self-control for a moment.

NORA [*wondering at him*] I think youre a very kind-hearted man, Mr
Broadbent; but you seem to me to have no self-control at all [*she turns
her face away with a keen pang of shame and adds*] no more than myself.

BROADBENT [*resolutely*] Oh yes, I have: you should see me when I am
really roused: then I have TREMENDOUS self-control. Remember: we
have been alone together only once before; and then, I regret to say,
I was in a disgusting state.

NORA. Ah no, Mr Broadbent: you wernt disgusting.

BROADBENT [*mercilessly*] Yes I was: nothing can excuse it: perfectly
beastly. It must have made a most unfavorable impression on you.

NORA. Oh, sure it's all right. Say no more about that.

BROADBENT. I must, Miss Reilly: it is my duty. I shall not detain you long. May I ask you to sit down. [*He indicates her chair with oppressive solemnity. She sits down wondering. He then, with the same portentous gravity, places a chair for himself near her; sits down; and proceeds to explain*]. First, Miss Reilly, may I say that I have tasted nothing of an alcoholic nature today.

NORA. It doesnt seem to make as much difference in you as it would in an Irishman, somehow.

BROADBENT. Perhaps not. Perhaps not. I never quite lose myself.

NORA [*consolingly*] Well, anyhow, youre all right now.

BROADBENT [*fervently*] Thank you, Miss Reilly: I am. Now we shall get along. [*Tenderly, lowering his voice*] Nora: I was in earnest last night. [*Nora moves as if to rise*]. No: one moment. You must not think I am going to press you for an answer before you have known me for 24 hours. I am a reasonable man, I hope; and I am prepared to wait as long as you like, provided you will give me some small assurance that the answer will not be unfavorable.

NORA. How could I go back from it if I did? I sometimes think youre not quite right in your head, Mr Broadbent, you say such funny things.

BROADBENT. Yes: I know I have a strong sense of humor which sometimes makes people doubt whether I am quite serious. That is why I have always thought I should like to marry an Irishwoman. She would always understand my jokes. For instance, you would understand them, eh?

NORA [*uneasily*] Mr Broadbent: I couldnt.

BROADBENT [*soothingly*] Wait: let me break this to you gently, Miss Reilly: hear me out. I daresay you have noticed that in speaking to you I have been putting a very strong constraint on myself, so as to avoid wounding your delicacy by too abrupt an avowal of my feelings. Well, I feel now that the time has come to be open, to be frank, to be explicit. Miss Reilly: you have inspired in me a very strong attachment. Perhaps, with a woman's intuition, you have already guessed that.

NORA [*rising distractedly*] Why do you talk to me in that unfeeling nonsensical way?

BROADBENT [*rising also, much astonished*] Unfeeling! Nonsensical!

NORA. Dont you know that you have said things to me that no man ought to say unless – unless – [*she suddenly breaks down again and hides her face on the table as before*] Oh, go away from me: I wont get married at all: what is it but heartbreak and disappointment?

BROADBENT [*developing the most formidable symptoms of rage and grief*] Do you mean to say that you are going to refuse me? that you dont care for me?

NORA [*looking at him in consternation*] Oh, dont take it to heart, Mr Br—

BROADBENT [*flushed and almost choking*] I dont want to be petted and blarneyed. [*With childish rage*] I love you. I want you for my wife. [*In despair*] I cant help your refusing. I'm helpless: I can do nothing. You have no right to ruin my whole life. You – [*a hysterical convulsion stops him*].

NORA [*almost awestruck*] Youre not going to cry, are you? I never thought a man could cry. Dont.

BROADBENT. I'm not crying. I – I – I leave that sort of thing to your damned sentimental Irishmen. You think I have no feeling because I am a plain unemotional Englishman, with no powers of expression.

NORA. I dont think you know the sort of man you are at all. Whatever may be the matter with you, it's not want of feeling.

BROADBENT [*hurt and petulant*] It's you who have no feeling. Youre as heartless as Larry.

NORA. What do you expect me to do? Is it to throw meself at your head the minute the word is out o your mouth?

BROADBENT [*striking his silly head with his fists*] Oh, what a fool! what a brute I am! It's only your Irish delicacy: of course, of course. You mean Yes. Eh? What? Yes? yes? yes?

NORA. I think you might understand that though I might choose to be an old maid, I could never marry anybody but you now.

BROADBENT [*clasping her violently to his breast, with a crow of immense relief and triumph*] Ah, thats right, thats right: thats magnificent. I knew you would see what a first-rate thing this will be for both of us.

NORA [*incommoded and not at all enraptured by his ardor*] Youre dreadfully strong, an a gradle too free with your strength. An I never thought o whether it'd be a good thing for us or not. But when you found me here that time, I let you be kind to me, and cried in your arms, because I was too wretched to think of anything but the comfort of it. And how could I let any other man touch me after that?

BROADBENT [*moved*] Now thats very nice of you, Nora: thats really most delicately womanly [*he kisses her hand chivalrously*].

NORA [*looking earnestly and a little doubtfully at him*] Surely if you let one woman cry on you like that youd never let another touch you.

BROADBENT [*conscientiously*] One should not. One ought not, my dear girl. But the honest truth is, if a chap is at all a pleasant sort of chap, his chest becomes a fortification that has to stand many assaults: at least it is so in England.

NORA [*curtly, much disgusted*] Then youd better marry an Englishwoman.

BROADBENT [*making a wry face*] No, no: the Englishwoman is too prosaic for my taste, too material, too much of the animated beefsteak about her. The ideal is what I like. Now Larry's taste is just the opposite: he likes em solid and bouncing and rather keen about him. It's a very convenient difference; for weve never been in love with the same woman.

NORA. An d'ye mean to tell me to me face that youve ever been in love before?

BROADBENT. Lord! yes.

NORA. I'm not your first love!

BROADBENT. First love is only a little foolishness and a lot of curiosity: no really self-respecting woman would take advantage of it. No, my dear Nora: Ive done with all that long ago. Love affairs always end in rows. We're not going to have any rows: we're going to have a solid four-square home: man and wife: comfort and common sense. And plenty of affection, eh [*he puts his arm round her with confident proprietorship*]?

NORA [*coldly, trying to get away*] I dont want any other woman's leavings.

BROADBENT [*holding her*] Nobody asked you to, maam. I never asked any woman to marry me before.

NORA [*severely*] Then why didnt you if youre an honorable man?

BROADBENT. Well, to tell you the truth, they were mostly married already. But never mind! there was nothing wrong. Come! dont take a mean advantage of me. After all, you must have had a fancy or two yourself, eh?

NORA [*conscience-stricken*] Yes. I suppose Ive no right to be particular.

BROADBENT [*humbly*] I know I'm not good enough for you, Nora. But no man is, you know, when the woman is a really nice woman.

NORA. Oh, I'm no better than yourself. I may as well tell you about it.

BROADBENT. No, no: lets have no telling: much better not. *I* shant tell you anything: dont you tell me anything. Perfect confidence in one another and no tellings: thats the way to avoid rows.

NORA. Dont think it was anything I need be ashamed of.

BROADBENT. I dont.

NORA. It was only that I'd never known anybody else that I could care for; and I was foolish enough once to think that Larry –

BROADBENT [*dispcsing of the idea at once*] Larry! Oh, that wouldnt have done at all, not at all. You dont know Larry as I do, my dear. He has absolutely no capacity for enjoyment: he couldnt make any woman happy. He's as clever as be-blowed; but life's too earthly for him: he doesnt really care for anything or anybody.

NORA. I've found that out.

BROADBENT. Of course you have. No, my dear: take my word for it, youre jolly well out of that. There! [*swinging her round against his breast*] thats much more comfortable for you.

NORA [*with Irish peevishness*] Ah, you mustnt go on like that. I dont like it.

BROADBENT [*unabashed*] Youll acquire the taste by degrees. You mustnt mind me: it's an absolute necessity of my nature that I should have somebody to hug occasionally. Besides, it's good for you: itll plump out your muscles and make em elastic and set up your figure.

NORA. Well, I'm sure! if this is English manners! Arnt you ashamed to talk about such things?

BROADBENT [*in the highest feather*] Not a bit. By George, Nora, it's a tremendous thing to be able to enjoy oneself. Lets go off for a walk out of this stuffy little room. I want the open air to expand in. Come along. Co-o-ome along. [*He puts her arm into his and sweeps her out into the garden as an equinoctial gale might sweep a dry leaf*].

Later in the evening, the grasshopper is again enjoying the sunset by the great stone on the hill; but this time he enjoys neither the stimulus of Keegan's conversation nor the pleasure of terrifying Patsy Farrell. He is alone until Nora and Broadbent come up the hill arm in arm. Broadbent is still breezy and confident; but she has her head averted from him and is almost in tears.

BROADBENT [*stopping to snuff up the hillside air*] Ah! I like this spot.

I like this view. This would be a jolly good place for a hotel and a golf links. Friday to Tuesday, railway ticket and hotel all inclusive. I tell you, Nora, I'm going to develop this place. [*Looking at her*] Hallo! Whats the matter? Tired?

NORA [*unable to restrain her tears*] I'm ashamed out o me life.

BROADBENT [*astonished*] Ashamed! What of?

NORA. Oh, how could you drag me all round the place like that, telling everybody that we're going to be married, and introjoocing me to the lowest of the low, and letting them shake hans with me, and encouraging them to make free with us? I little thought I should live to be shaken hans with be Doolan in broad daylight in the public street of Rosscullen.

BROADBENT. But, my dear, Doolan's a publican: a most influential man. By the way, I asked him if his wife would be at home tomorrow. He said she would; so you must take the motor car round and call on her.

NORA [*aghast*] Is it me call on Doolan's wife!

BROADBENT. Yes, of course: call on all their wives. We must get a copy of the register and a supply of canvassing cards. No use calling on people who havnt votes. Youll be a great success as a canvasser, Nora: they call you the heiress; and theyll be flattered no end by your calling, especially as youve never cheapened yourself by speaking to them before — have you?

NORA [*indignantly*] Not likely, indeed.

BROADBENT. Well, we mustnt be stiff and stand-off, you know. We must be thoroughly democratic, and patronize everybody without distinction of class. I tell you I'm a jolly lucky man, Nora Cryna. I get engaged to the most delightful woman in Ireland; and it turns out that I couldnt have done a smarter stroke of electioneering.

NORA. An would you let me demean meself like that, just to get yourself into parliament?

BROADBENT [*buoyantly*] Aha! Wait till you find out what an exciting game electioneering is: youll be mad to get me in. Besides, youd like people to say that Tom Broadbent's wife had been the making of him? that she got him into parliament? into the Cabinet, perhaps, eh?

NORA. God knows I dont grudge you me money! But to lower meself to the level of common people —

BROADBENT. To a member's wife, Nora, nobody is common provided he's on the register. Come, my dear! it's all right: do you think I'd let you do it if it wasnt? The best people do it. Everybody does it.

NORA [*who has been biting her lip and looking over the hill, disconsolate and unconvinced*] Well, praps you know best what they do in England. They must have very little respect for themselves. I think I'll go in now. I see Larry and Mr Keegan coming up the hill; and I'm not fit to talk to them.

BROADBENT. Just wait and say something nice to Keegan. They tell me he controls nearly as many votes as Father Dempsey himself.

NORA. You little know Peter Keegan. He'd see through me as if I was a pane o glass.

BROADBENT. Oh, he wont like it any the less for that. What really flatters a man is that you think him worth flattering. Not that I would flatter any man: dont think that. I'll just go and meet him. [*He goes down the hill with the eager forward look of a man about to greet a valued acquaintance. Nora dries her eyes, and turns to go as Larry strolls up the hill to her*].

LARRY. Nora. [*She turns and looks at him hardly, without a word. He continues anxiously, in his most conciliatory tone*]. When I left you that time, I was just as wretched as you. I didnt rightly know what I wanted to say; and my tongue kept clacking to cover the loss I was at. Well, Ive been thinking ever since; and now I know what I ought to have said. Ive come back to say it.

NORA. Youve come too late, then. You thought eighteen years was not long enough, and that you might keep me waiting a day longer. Well, you were mistaken. I'm engaged to your friend Mr Broadbent; and I'm done with you.

LARRY [*naïvely*] But that was the very thing I was going to advise you to do.

NORA [*involuntarily*] Oh you brute! to tell me that to me face!

LARRY [*nervously relapsing into his most Irish manner*] Nora, dear, dont you understand that I'm an Irishman, and he's an Englishman. He wants you; and he grabs you. *I* want you; and I quarrel with you and have to go on wanting you.

NORA. So you may. Youd better go back to England to the animated beefsteaks youre so fond of.

LARRY [*amazed*] Nora! [*Guessing where she got the metaphor*] He's been talking of me, I see. Well, never mind: we must be friends, you and I. I dont want his marriage to you to be his divorce from me.

NORA. You care more for him than you ever did for me.

LARRY [*with curt sincerity*] Yes of course I do: why should I tell you lies about it? Nora Reilly was a person of very little consequence to me or anyone else outside this miserable little hole. But Mrs Tom Broadbent will be a person of very considerable consequence indeed. Play your new part well, and there will be no more neglect, no more loneliness, no more idle regrettings and vain-hopings in the evenings by the Round Tower, but real life and real work and real cares and real joys among real people: solid English life in London, the very centre of the world. You will find your work cut out for you keeping Tom's house and entertaining Tom's friends and getting Tom into parliament; but it will be worth the effort.

NORA. You talk as if I was under obligation to him for marrying me.

LARRY. I talk as I think. Youve made a very good match, let me tell you.

NORA. Indeed! Well, some people might say he's not done so badly himself.

LARRY. If you mean that you will be a treasure to him, he thinks so now; and you can keep him thinking so if you like.

NORA. I wasnt thinking o meself at all.

LARRY. Were you thinking of your money, Nora?

NORA. I didnt say so.

LARRY. Your money will not pay your cook's wages in London.

NORA [*flaming up*] If thats true – and the more shame for you to throw it in me face if it is true – at all events itll make us independent; for if the worst comes to the worst, we can always come back here and live on it. An if I have to keep his house for him, at all events I can keep you out of it; for Ive done with you; and I wish I'd never seen you. So goodbye to you, Mister Larry Doyle. [*She turns her back on him and goes home*].

LARRY [*watching her as she goes*] Goodbye. Goodbye. Oh, thats so Irish! Irish both of us to the backbone: Irish! Irish! Iri—

Broadbent arrives, conversing energetically with Keegan.

BROADBENT. Nothing pays like a golfing hotel, if you hold the land instead of the shares, and if the furniture people stand in with you, and if you are a good man of business.

LARRY. Nora's gone home.

BROADBENT [*with conviction*] You were right this morning, Larry. I must feed up Nora. She's weak; and it makes her fanciful. Oh, by the way, did I tell you that we're engaged?

LARRY. She told me herself.

BROADBENT [*complacently*] She's rather full of it, as you may imagine. Poor Nora! Well, Mr Keegan, as I said, I begin to see my way here. I begin to see my way.

KEEGAN [*with a courteous inclination*] The conquering Englishman, sir. Within 24 hours of your arrival you have carried off our only heiress, and practically secured the parliamentary seat. And you have promised me that when I come here in the evenings to meditate on my madness; to watch the shadow of the Round Tower lengthening in the sunset; to break my heart uselessly in the curtained gloaming over the dead heart and blinded soul of the island of the saints, you will comfort me with the bustle of a great hotel, and the sight of the little children carrying the golf clubs of your tourists as a preparation for the life to come.

BROADBENT [*quite touched, mutely offering him a cigar to console him, at which he smiles and shakes his head*] Yes, Mr Keegan: youre quite right. Theres poetry in everything, even [*looking absently into the cigar case*] in the most modern prosaic things, if you know how to extract it [*he extracts a cigar for himself and offers one to Larry, who takes it*]. If I was to be shot for it I couldnt extract it myself; but thats where you come in, you see. [*Roguishly, waking up from his reverie and bustling Keegan goodhumoredly*] And then *I* shall wake you up a bit. Thats where *I* come in: eh? d'ye see? Eh? eh? [*He pats him very pleasantly on the shoulder, half admiringly, half pityingly*]. Just so, just so. [*Coming back to business*] By the way, I believe I can do better than a light railway here. There seems to be no question now that the motor boat has come to stay. Well, look at your magnificent river there, going to waste.

KEEGAN [*closing his eyes*]

'Silent, O Moyle, be the roar of thy waters.'

BROADBENT. You know, the roar of a motor boat is quite pretty.

KEEGAN. Provided it does not drown the Angelus.

BROADBENT [*reassuringly*] Oh no: it wont do that: not the least danger. You know, a church bell can make a devil of a noise when it likes.

KEEGAN. You have an answer for everything, sir. But your plans leave one question still unanswered: how to get butter out of a dog's throat.

BROADBENT. Eh?

KEEGAN. You cannot build your golf links and hotels in the air. For that you must own our land. And how will you drag our acres from the ferret's grip of Matthew Haffigan? How will you persuade Cornelius Doyle to forgo the pride of being a small landowner? How will Barney Doran's millrace agree with your motor boats? Will Doolan help you to get a licence for your hotel?

BROADBENT. My dear sir: to all intents and purposes the syndicate I represent already owns half Rosscullen. Doolan's is a tied house; and the brewers are in the syndicate. As to Haffigan's farm and Doran's mill and Mr Doyle's place and half a dozen others, they will be mortgaged to me before a month is out.

KEEGAN. But pardon me, you will not lend them more on their land than the land is worth; so they will be able to pay you the interest.

BROADBENT. Ah, you are a poet, Mr Keegan, not a man of business.

LARRY. We will lend every one of these men half as much again on their land as it is worth, or ever can be worth, to them.

BROADBENT. You forget, sir, that we, with our capital, our knowledge, our organization, and may I say our English business habits, can make or lose ten pounds out of land that Haffigan, with all his industry, could not make or lose ten shillings out of. Doran's mill is a superannuated folly: I shall want it for electric lighting.

LARRY. What is the use of giving land to such men? they are too small, too poor, too ignorant, too simpleminded to hold it against us: you might as well give a dukedom to a crossing sweeper.

BROADBENT. Yes, Mr Keegan: this place may have an industrial future, or it may have a residential future: I cant tell yet; but it's not going to be a future in the hands of your Dorans and Haffigans, poor devils!

KEEGAN. It may have no future at all. Have you thought of that?

BROADBENT. Oh, I'm not afraid of that. I have faith in Ireland. Great faith, Mr Keegan.

KEEGAN. And we have none: only empty enthusiasms and patriotisms, and emptier memories and regrets. Ah yes: you have some excuse for believing that if there be any future, it will be yours; for our faith seems dead, and our hearts cold and cowed. An island of dreamers who wake up in your jails, of critics and cowards whom you buy and tame for your own service, of bold rogues who help you to plunder us that they may plunder you afterwards.

BROADBENT [*a little impatient of this unbusinesslike view*] Yes, yes; but you know you might say that of any country. The fact is, there are only two qualities in the world: efficiency and inefficiency, and only two sorts of people: the efficient and the inefficient. It dont matter whether theyre English or Irish. I shall collar this place, not because I'm an Englishman and Haffigan and Co are Irishmen, but because theyre duffers, and I know my way about.

KEEGAN. Have you considered what is to become of Haffigan?

LARRY. Oh, we'll employ him in some capacity or other, and probably pay him more than he makes for himself now.

BROADBENT [*dubiously*] Do you think so? No no: Haffigan's too old. It really doesnt pay now to take on men over forty even for unskilled labor, which I suppose is all Haffigan would be good for. No: Haffigan had better go to America, or into the Union, poor old chap! He's worked out, you know: you can see it.

KEEGAN. Poor lost soul, so cunningly fenced in with invisible bars!

LARRY. Haffigan doesnt matter much. He'll die presently.

BROADBENT [*shocked*] Oh come, Larry! Dont be unfeeling. It's hard on Haffigan. It's always hard on the inefficient.

LARRY. Pah! what does it matter where an old and broken man spends his last days, or whether he has a million at the bank or only the work-house dole? It's the young men, the able men, that matter. The real tragedy of Haffigan is the tragedy of his wasted youth, his stunted mind, his drudging over his clods and pigs until he has become a clod and a pig himself – until the soul within him has smouldered into nothing but a dull temper that hurts himself and all around him. I say let him die, and let us have no more of his like. And let young Ireland take care that it doesnt share his fate, instead of making another empty grievance of it. Let your syndicate come –

BROADBENT. Your syndicate too, old chap. You have your bit of the stock.

LARRY. Yes: mine if you like. Well, our syndicate has no conscience:

it has no more regard for your Haffigans and Doolans and Dorans than it has for a gang of Chinese coolies. It will use your patriotic blatherskite and balderdash to get parliamentary powers over you as cynically as it would bait a mousetrap with toasted cheese. It will plan, and organize, and find capital while you slave like bees for it and revenge yourselves by paying politicians and penny newspapers out of your small wages to write articles and report speeches against its wickedness and tyranny, and to crack up your own Irish heroism, just as Haffigan once paid a witch a penny to put a spell on Billy Byrne's cow. In the end it will grind the nonsense out of you, and grind strength and sense into you.

BROADBENT [out of patience] Why cant you say a simple thing simply, Larry, without all that Irish exaggeration and talky-talky? The syndicate is a perfectly respectable body of responsible men of good position. We'll take Ireland in hand, and by straightforward business habits teach it efficiency and self-help on sound Liberal principles. You agree with me, Mr Keegan, dont you?

KEEGAN. Sir: I may even vote for you.

BROADBENT [sincerely moved, shaking his hand warmly] You shall never regret it, Mr Keegan: I give you my word for that. I shall bring money here: I shall raise wages: I shall found public institutions: a library, a Polytechnic (undenominational, of course), a gymnasium, a cricket club, perhaps an art school. I shall make a Garden City of Rosscullen: the Round Tower shall be thoroughly repaired and restored.

KEEGAN. And our place of torment shall be as clean and orderly as the cleanest and most orderly place I know in Ireland, which is our poetically named Mountjoy prison. Well, perhaps I had better vote for an efficient devil that knows his own mind and his own business than for a foolish patriot who has no mind and no business.

BROADBENT [stiffly] Devil is rather a strong expression in that connection, Mr Keegan.

KEEGAN. Not from a man who knows that this world is hell. But since the word offends you, let me soften it, and compare you simply to an ass. [Larry whitens with anger].

BROADBENT [reddening] An ass!

KEEGAN [gently] You may take it without offence from a madman who calls the ass his brother — and a very honest, useful and faithful brother, too. The ass, sir, is the most efficient of beasts, matter-of-fact, hardy, friendly when you treat him as a fellow-creature, stubborn when you abuse him, ridiculous only in love, which sets him braying, and in politics, which move him to roll about in the public road and raise a dust about nothing. Can you deny these qualities and habits in yourself, sir?

BROADBENT [*goodhumoredly*] Well, yes, I'm afraid I do, you know.

KEEGAN. Then perhaps you will confess to the ass's one fault.

BROADBENT. Perhaps so: what is it?

KEEGAN. That he wastes all his virtues – his efficiency, as you call it – in doing the will of his greedy masters instead of doing the will of Heaven that is in himself. He is efficient in the service of Mammon, mighty in mischief, skilful in ruin, heroic in destruction. But he comes to browse here without knowing that the soil his hoof touches is holy ground. Ireland, sir, for good or evil, is like no other place under heaven; and no man can touch its sod or breathe its air without becoming better or worse. It produces two kinds of men in strange perfection: saints and traitors. It is called the island of the saints; but indeed in these later years it might be more fitly called the island of the traitors; for our harvest of these is the fine flower of the world's crop of infamy. But the day may come when these islands shall live by the quality of their men rather than by the abundance of their minerals; and then we shall see.

LARRY. Mr Keegan: if you are going to be sentimental about Ireland, I shall bid you good evening. We have had enough of that, and more than enough of cleverly proving that everybody who is not an Irishman is an ass. It is neither good sense nor good manners. It will not stop the syndicate; and it will not interest young Ireland so much as my friend's gospel of efficiency.

BROADBENT. Ah, yes, yes: efficiency is the thing. I dont in the least mind your chaff, Mr Keegan; but Larry's right on the main point. The world belongs to the efficient.

KEEGAN [*with polished irony*] I stand rebuked, gentlemen. But believe me, I do every justice to the efficiency of you and your syndicate. You are both, I am told, thoroughly efficient civil engineers; and I have no doubt the golf links will be a triumph of your art. Mr Broadbent will get into parliament most efficiently, which is more than St Patrick could do if he were alive now. You may even build the hotel efficiently if you can find enough efficient masons, carpenters, and plumbers, which I rather doubt. [*Dropping his irony, and beginning to fall into the attitude of the priest rebuking sin*] When the hotel becomes insolvent [*Broadbent takes his cigar out of his mouth, a little taken aback*] your English business habits will secure the thorough efficiency of the liquidation. You will reorganize the scheme efficiently; you will liquidate its second bankruptcy efficiently [*Broadbent and Larry look quickly at one another; for this, unless the priest is an old financial hand, must be inspiration*]; you will get rid of its original shareholders efficiently after efficiently ruining them; and you will finally profit very efficiently by getting that hotel for a few shillings in the pound. [*More and more sternly*] Besides these efficient operations, you will foreclose your mortgages most efficiently [*his rebuking forefinger goes up in spite of himself*]; you will drive Haffigan to America very efficiently; you will find a use for Barney Doran's foul mouth and bullying temper by employing him to slave-drive your laborers very efficiently; and [*low and bitter*] when at last this poor desolate country-side becomes a busy mint in which we shall all slave to make money for you, with our Polytechnic to teach us how to do it efficiently, and our library to fuddle the few imaginations your distilleries will spare, and our repaired Round Tower with admission sixpence, and refreshments and penny-in-the-slot mutoscopes to make it interesting, then no doubt your English and American shareholders will spend all the money we make for them very efficiently in shooting and hunting, in operations for cancer and appendicitis, in gluttony and gambling; and you will devote what they save to fresh land development schemes. For four wicked centuries the world has dreamed this foolish dream of efficiency; and the end is not yet. But the end will come.

BROADBENT [*seriously*] Too true, Mr Keegan, only too true. And most eloquently put. It reminds me of poor Ruskin: a great man, you know. I sympathize. Believe me, I'm on your side. Dont sneer, Larry: I used to read a lot of Shelley years ago. Let us be faithful to the dreams of our youth [*he wafts a wreath of cigar smoke at large across the hill*].

KEEGAN. Come, Mr Doyle! is this English sentiment so much more efficient than our Irish sentiment, after all? Mr Broadbent spends his life inefficiently admiring the thoughts of great men, and efficiently serving the cupidity of base money hunters. We spend our lives efficiently sneering at him and doing nothing. Which of us has any right to reproach the other?

BROADBENT [*coming down the hill again to Keegan's right hand*] But you know, something must be done.

KEEGAN. Yes: when we cease to do, we cease to live. Well, what shall we do?

BROADBENT. Why, what lies to our hand.

KEEGAN. Which is the making of golf links and hotels to bring idlers to a country which workers have left in millions because it is a hungry land, a naked land, an ignorant and oppressed land.

BROADBENT. But, hang it all, the idlers will bring money from England to Ireland!

KEEGAN. Just as our idlers have for so many generations taken money from Ireland to England. Has that saved England from poverty and degradation more horrible than we have ever dreamed of? When I went to England, sir, I hated England. Now I pity it. [*Broadbent can hardly conceive an Irishman pitying England; but as Larry intervenes angrily, he gives it up and takes to the hill and his cigar again*].

LARRY. Much good your pity will do it!

KEEGAN. In the accounts kept in heaven, Mr Doyle, a heart purified of hatred may be worth more than even a Land Development Syndicate of Anglicized Irishmen and Gladstonized Englishmen.

LARRY. Oh, in heaven, no doubt. I have never been there. Can you tell me where it is?

KEEGAN. Could you have told me this morning where hell is? Yet you know now that it is here. Do not despair of finding heaven: it may be no farther off.

LARRY [*ironically*] On this holy ground, as you call it, eh?

KEEGAN [*with fierce intensity*] Yes, perhaps, even on this holy ground which such Irishmen as you have turned into a Land of Derision.

BROADBENT [*coming between them*] Take care! you will be quarrelling presently. Oh, you Irishmen, you Irishmen! Toujours Ballyhooly, eh? [*Larry, with a shrug, half comic, half impatient, turns away up the hill, but presently strolls back on Keegan's right. Broadbent adds, confidentially to Keegan*] Stick to the Englishman, Mr Keegan: he has a bad name here; but at least he can forgive you for being an Irishman.

KEEGAN. Sir: when you speak to me of English and Irish you forget that I am a Catholic. My country is not Ireland nor England, but the whole mighty realm of my Church. For me there are but two countries: heaven and hell; but two conditions of men: salvation and damnation. Standing here between you the Englishman, so clever in your foolishness, and this Irishman, so foolish in his cleverness, I cannot in my ignorance be sure which of you is the more deeply damned; but I should be unfaithful to my calling if I opened the gates of my heart less widely to one than to the other.

LARRY. In either case it would be an impertinence, Mr Keegan, as your approval is not of the slightest consequence to us. What use do you suppose all this drivel is to men with serious practical business in hand?

BROADBENT. I dont agree with that, Larry. I think these things cannot be said too often: they keep up the moral tone of the community. As you know, I claim the right to think for myself in religious matters: in fact, I am ready to avow myself a bit of a – of a – well, I dont care who knows it – a bit of a Unitarian; but if the Church of England contained a few men like Mr Keegan, I should certainly join it.

KEEGAN. You do me too much honor, sir. [*With priestly humility to Larry*] Mr Doyle: I am to blame for having unintentionally set your mind somewhat on edge against me. I beg your pardon.

LARRY [*unimpressed and hostile*] I didnt stand on ceremony with you; you neednt stand on it with me. Fine manners and fine words are cheap in Ireland: you can keep both for my friend here, who is still imposed on by them. *I* know their value.

KEEGAN. You mean you dont know their value.

LARRY [*angrily*] I mean what I say.

KEEGAN [*turning quietly to the Englishman*] You see, Mr Broadbent, I only make the hearts of my countrymen harder when I preach to them: the gates of hell still prevail against me. I shall wish you good evening. I am better alone, at the Round Tower, dreaming of heaven. [*He goes up the hill*].

LARRY. Aye, thats it! there you are! dreaming! dreaming! dreaming! dreaming!

KEEGAN [*halting and turning to them for the last time*] Every dream is a prophecy: every jest is an earnest in the womb of Time.

BROADBENT [*reflectively*] Once, when I was a small kid, I dreamt I was in heaven. [*They both stare at him*]. It was a sort of pale blue satin place, with all the pious old ladies in our congregation sitting as if they were at a service; and there was some awful person in the study at the other side of the hall. I didnt enjoy it, you know. What is it like in your dreams?

KEEGAN. In my dreams it is a country where the State is the Church and the Church the people: three in one and one in three. It is a commonwealth in which work is play and play is life: three in one and one in three. It is a temple in which the priest is the worshipper and the worshipper the worshipped: three in one and one in three. It is a godhead in which all life is human and all humanity divine: three in one and one in three. It is, in short, the dream of a madman. [*He goes away across the hill*].

BROADBENT [*looking after him affectionately*] What a regular old Church and State Tory he is! He's a character: he'll be an attraction here. Really almost equal to Ruskin and Carlyle.

LARRY. Yes; and much good they did with all their talk!

BROADBENT. Oh tut, tut, Larry! They improved my mind: they raised my tone enormously. I feel sincerely obliged to Keegan: he has made me feel a better man: distinctly better. [*With sincere elevation*] I feel now as I never did before that I am right in devoting my life to the cause of Ireland. Come along and help me to choose the site for the hotel.

To the Audience
at the Kingsway Theatre

A Personal Appeal from the Author of
John Bull's Other Island

Dear Sir or Madam,

It is your custom to receive my plays with the most generous and unrestrained applause. You sometimes compel the performers to pause at the end of every line until your laughter has quieted down. I am not ungrateful; but may I ask you a few questions?

Are you aware that you would get out of the Theatre half an hour earlier if you listened to the play in silence and did not applaud until the fall of the curtain?

Do you really consider that a performance is improved by continual interruptions, however complimentary they may be to the actors and the author?

Do you not think that the naturalness of the pre-presentation must be destroyed, and therefore your own pleasure greatly diminished, when the audience insists on taking part in it by shouts of applause and laughter, and the actors have repeatedly to stop acting until the noise is over?

Have you considered that in all good plays tears and laughter lie very close together, and that it must be very distressing to an actress who is trying to keep her imagination fixed on pathetic emotions to hear bursts of laughter breaking out at something she is supposed to be unconscious of?

Do you know that even when there is no such conflict of comic and tragic on the stage, the strain of performing is greatly increased if the performers have to attend to the audience as well as to their parts at the same time?

Can you not imagine how a play which has been rehearsed to perfection in dead silence without an audience must be upset, disjointed, and spun out to a wearisome length by an audience which refuses to enjoy it silently?

Have you noticed that if you laugh loudly and repeatedly for two hours, you get tired and cross, and are sorry next morning that you did not stay at home?

Will you think me very ungrateful and unkind if I tell you that though you cannot possibly applaud my plays too much at each fall of the curtain to please me, yet the more applause there is during the performance the angrier I feel with you for spoiling your enjoyment and my own?

Would you dream of stopping the performance of a piece of music to applaud every bar that happened to please you? and do you not know that an act of a play is intended, just like a piece of music, to be heard without interruption from beginning to end?

Have you ever told your sons and daughters that little children should be seen and not heard? And have you ever thought how nice theatrical performances would be, and how much sooner you would get away to supper, if parents in the theatre would follow the precepts they give to their children at home?

Have you noticed that people look very nice when they smile or look pleased, but look shockingly ugly when they roar with laughter or shout excitedly or sob loudly? Smiles make no noise.

Do you know that what pleases actors and authors most is not your applauding them but your coming to see the play again and again, and that if you tire yourselves out and spoil the play with interruptions you are very unlikely to come again?

Do you know that my plays, as rehearsed, are just the right length: that is, quite as long as you can bear; and that if you delay the performances by loud laughter you will make them half an hour too long?

Can I persuade you to let the performance proceed in perfect silence just this once to see how you like it. The intervals will give you no less than five opportunities of expressing your approval or disapproval, as the case may be.

And finally, will you believe me to be acting sincerely in your own interests in this matter as

your faithful servant,

THE AUTHOR.

New Year, 1913

Author's Note

(From the programme of the production at the
Regent Theatre, London, 15 February 1926)

John Bull's Other Island was written in 1904, when the Irish Free State
was unborn and undreamt of, and when Liberals like Mr Thomas Broadbent, still smarting from their recent unpopularity as pro-Boers, were
ardent advocates of Home Rule for Ireland, the emancipation of
Macedonia from the Turkish yoke, and, generally, an implacable resistance to oppression everywhere except at home. They believed that freedom would come to Ireland from the Gladstonian tradition; and if an
enchanter had shown them in a magic mirror the Easter rebellion, the
ruins of bombarded Dublin, the sanguinary campaign in which the Black-
and-Tans and Sinn Fein tried which could burn most houses until
Michael Collins won, and the armistice which established the Irish Free
State only to inaugurate a purely Irish civil war in which every bridge
in Ireland was broken, they would have regarded that enchanter as the
most ridiculous romancer that ever showed the grossest ignorance of the
modern, sensible, matter-of-fact, parliamentary world he was living in.
As to these events passing almost unnoticed in England because England
was fighting hard for her own life, and Broadbent's and several other
London houses had been blown to bits by the bombs of a foreign enemy,
that would have seemed too silly to be even funny.

The play you are about to see takes you back to that state of innocence
and false security. As no attempt has been made to bring it up to date,
the younger members of the audience must listen as patiently as they
can to Mr Broadbent delivering a few speeches which will make them
wonder what on earth he is talking about. But, in the main, human nature,
though it has changed its catchwords a little, is very much what it was
then. There are still Rosscullens in Ireland and still Broadbents in
England. I do not believe there is a single character in the play that you
may not find today not perceptibly different from what he or she was
then. The Macdona Players therefore present the play just as it was,
feeling confident that its few discrepancies with the world just as it is

will not prevent you from enjoying it, and may even add to your amusement.

G. B. S.

J. M. SYNGE

The Playboy of the
Western World

J. M. Synge (1871–1909)

John Millington Synge was born in 1871, of Anglo-Irish Protestant landowning stock. He graduated at Trinity College, Dublin, and then spent a few years wandering on the continent. Synge went to the Aran Islands in 1898, and subsequently revisited them several times. *In the Shadow of the Glen* and *Riders to the Sea* were both completed in the summer of 1902, and both were taken from material he had collected on the islands. *The Playboy of the Western World*, published in 1907, aroused a prolonged and bitter controversy, which lasted until his death in 1909. His other works include poems and two books of travels, *The Aran Islands* and *In Wicklow, West Kerry and Connemara*. *Deirdre of the Sorrows* was published posthumously.

The Playboy of the Western World

The first production of *The Playboy of the Western World* was given in Dublin by the National Theatre Society Ltd., at the Abbey Theatre on Saturday, 26 January 1907. It was directed by W. G. Fay, with the following cast:

CHRISTOPHER MAHON	W. G. Fay
OLD MAHON, *his father, a squatter*	A. Power
MICHAEL JAMES FLAHERTY	
(*called* MICHAEL JAMES), *a publican*	Arthur Sinclair
MARGARET FLAHERTY	
(*called* PEGEEN MIKE), *his daughter*	Maire O'Neill
SHAWN KEOGH, *her second cousin, a young farmer*	F. J. Fay
PHILLY CULLEN ⎱ *small farmers*	J. A. O'Rourke
JIMMY FARRELL ⎰	J. M. Kerrigan
WIDOW QUIN	Sara Allgood
SARA TANSEY ⎱	Brigit O'Dempsey
SUSAN BRADY ⎬ *village girls*	Alice O'Sullivan
HONOR BLAKE ⎰	Mary Craig
PEASANTS	Harry Young
	U. Wright

The week that followed the first performance of *Playboy* was a continuous riot. In *Our Irish Theatre*, Lady Gregory described the response:

> There was a battle of a week. Every night protestors with their trumpets came and raised a din. Every night the police carried some of them off to the police courts. Every afternoon the paper gave reports of the trial before a magistrate who had not heard or read the play and who insisted on being given details of its incidents by the accused and by the police . . . There was a very large audience on the first night . . . Synge was there, but Mr Yeats was giving a lecture in Scotland. The first act got its applause, and the second, though one felt that the audience were a little puzzled, a little

shocked at the wild language. Near the end of the third act there was some hissing. We had sent a telegram to Mr Yeats after the end of the first act 'Play great success'; but at the end we sent another – 'Audience broke up in disorder at the word shift.'

On his return, Yeats was able to witness the disturbances for himself but they were not to be restricted to the first production:

Picturesque, poetical, fantastical, a masterpiece of style and of music, the supreme work of our dialect theatre, his *Playboy* roused the populace to fury. We played it under police protection, seventy police in the theatre the last night, and five hundred, some newspaper said, keeping order in the streets outside. It is never played before any Irish audience for the first time without something or other being flung at the players. In New York a currant cake and a watch were flung, the owner of the watch claiming it at the stage-door afterwards. The Dublin audience has, however, long since accepted the play. (*Autobiographies*)

The Playboy, which in the opinion of many is the greatest Irish play, has been produced in countries throughout the world.

Selected Bibliography

J. M. Synge: Collected Works, Oxford University Press, 1961–8, Robin Skelton (General Editor), 4 vols. Vols. III and IV (ed. Ann Saddlemyer) contain the plays along with manuscript and notebook material. *The Complete Plays*, London: Methuen (World Dramatists series), 1981, T. R. Henn (Editor). A shortened paperback version of T. R. Henn's edition of *The Plays and Poems of J. M. Synge*, London: Methuen, 1963. *Plays, Poems and Prose*, London: J. M. Dent (Everyman), 1961, M. Mac Liammoir (Editor).

The Playboy of the
Western World

Preface

In writing 'The Playboy of the Western World', as in my other plays, I have used one or two words only that I have not heard among the country people of Ireland, or spoken in my own nursery before I could read the newspapers. A certain number of the phrases I employ I have heard also from herds and fishermen along the coast from Kerry to Mayo or from beggar-women and ballad-singers nearer Dublin; and I am glad to acknowledge how much I owe to the folk-imagination of these fine people. Anyone who has lived in real intimacy with the Irish peasantry will know that the wildest sayings and ideas in this play are tame indeed, compared with the fancies one may hear in any little hillside cabin in Geesala, or Carraroe, or Dingle Bay. All art is a collaboration; and there is little doubt that in the happy ages of literature, striking and beautiful phrases were as ready to the story-teller's or the playwright's hand, as the rich cloaks and dresses of his time. It is probable that when the Elizabethan dramatist took his ink-horn and sat down to his work he used many phrases that he had just heard, as he sat at dinner, from his mother or his children. In Ireland, those of us who know the people have the same privilege. When I was writing *The Shadow of the Glen*, some years ago, I got more aid than any learning could have given me from a chink in the floor of the old Wicklow house where I was staying, that let me hear what was being said by the servant girls in the kitchen. This matter, I think, is of importance, for in countries where the imagination of the people, and the language they use, is rich and living, it is possible for a writer to be rich and copious in his words, and at the same time to give the reality, which is the root of all poetry, in a comprehensive and natural form. In the modern literature of towns, however, richness is found only in sonnets, or prose poems, or in one or two elaborate books that are far away from the profound and common interests of life. One has, on one side, Mallarmé and Huysmans producing this literature; and on the other, Ibsen and Zola dealing with the reality of life in joyless and pallid works. On the stage one must have reality, and one must have joy; and that is why the intellectual modern drama has failed, and people have grown sick of the false joy of the musical comedy, that has been given them in place of the rich joy found only in what is superb and wild in reality. In a good play every speech should be as fully flavoured as a nut or apple, and such speeches cannot be written by any one who works among people who have shut their lips on poetry. In Ireland, for a few years more, we have a popular imagination that is fiery, and magnificent, and tender; so that those of us who wish to write start with a chance that is not given to writers in places where the springtime of the local life has been forgotten, and the harvest is a memory only, and the straw has been turned into bricks.

J.M.S.

21st January, 1907.

Persons in the Play

CHRISTOPHER MAHON
OLD MAHON, *his father, a squatter*
MICHAEL JAMES FLAHERTY (*called* MICHAEL JAMES), *a publican*
MARGARET FLAHERTY (*called* PEGEEN MIKE), *his daughter*
WIDOW QUIN, *a woman of about thirty*
SHAWN KEOGH, *her cousin, a young farmer*
PHILLY CULLEN *and* JIMMY FARRELL, *small farmers*
SARA TANSEY, SUSAN BRADY *and* HONOR BLAKE, *village girls*
A BELLMAN
SOME PEASANTS

The action takes place near a village, on a wild coast of Mayo. The first Act passes on an evening of autumn, the other two Acts on the following day.

ACT I

Country public house or shebeen, very rough and untidy. There is a sort of counter on the right with shelves, holding many bottles and jugs, just seen above it. Empty barrels stand near the counter. At back, a little to left of counter, there is a door into the open air, then, more to the left, there is a settle with shelves above it, with more jugs, and a table beneath a window. At the left there is a large open fireplace, with turf fire, and a small door into inner room. Pegeen, a wild-looking but fine girl, of about twenty, is writing at table. She is dressed in the usual peasant dress.

PEGEEN [*slowly as she writes*] Six yards of stuff for to make a yellow gown. A pair of lace boots with lengthy heels on them and brassy eyes. A hat is suited for a wedding day. A fine-tooth comb. To be sent with three barrels of porter in Jimmy Farrell's creel cart on the evening of the coming Fair to Mister Michael James Flaherty. With the best compliments of this season. Margaret Flaherty.

SHAWN KEOGH [*a fat and fair young man comes in as she sighs, looks around awkwardly, when he sees she is alone*] Where's himself?

PEGEEN [*without looking at him*] He's coming. [*She directs letter*] to Mister Sheamus Mulroy, Wine and Spirit Dealer, Castlebar.

SHAWN [*uneasily*] I didn't see him on the road.

PEGEEN. How would you see him [*licks stamp and puts it on letter*] and it dark night this half-hour gone by?

SHAWN [*turning towards door again*] I stood a while outside wondering would I have a right to pass on or to walk in and see you, Pegeen Mike [*comes to fire*], and I could hear the cows breathing and sighing in the stillness of the air, and not a step moving any place from this gate to the bridge.

PEGEEN [*putting letter in envelope*] It's above at the crossroads he is, meeting Philly Cullen and a couple more are going along with him to Kate Cassidy's wake.

SHAWN [*looking at her blankly*] And he's going that length in the dark night.

PEGEEN [*impatiently*] He is surely, and leaving me lonesome on the scruff of the hill. [*She gets up and puts envelope on dresser, then winds clock*]. Isn't it long the nights are now, Shawn Keogh, to be leaving a poor girl with her own self counting the hours to the dawn of day?

SHAWN [*with awkward humour*] If it is, when we're wedded in a short while you'll have no call to complain, for I've little will to be walking off to wakes or weddings in the darkness of the night.

PEGEEN [*with rather scornful good humour*] You're making mighty certain, Shaneen, that I'll wed you now.

SHAWN. Aren't we after making a good bargain, the way we're only waiting these days on Father Reilly's dispensation from the bishops, or the Court of Rome.

PEGEEN [*looking at him teasingly, washing up at dresser*] It's a wonder, Shaneen, the Holy Father'd be taking notice of the likes of you; for if I was him I wouldn't bother with this place where you'll meet none but Red Linahan, has a squint in his eye, and Patcheen is lame in his heel, or the mad Mulrannies were driven from California and they lost in their wits. We're a queer lot these times to go troubling the Holy Father on his sacred seat.

SHAWN [*scandalized*] If we are, we're as good this place as another, maybe, and as good these times as we were for ever.

PEGEEN [*with scorn*] As good it is? Where now will you meet the like of Daneen Sullivan knocked the eye from a peeler; or Marcus Quin, God rest him, got six months for maiming ewes, and he a great warrant to tell stories of holy Ireland till he'd have the old women shedding down tears about their feet. Where will you find the like of them, I'm saying?

SHAWN [*timidly*] If you don't, it's a good job, maybe; for [*with peculiar emphasis on the words*] Father Reilly has small conceit to have that kind walking around and talking to the girls.

PEGEEN [*impatiently throwing water from basin out of the door*] Stop tormenting me with Father Reilly [*imitating his voice*] when I'm asking only what way I'll pass these twelve hours of dark, and not take my death with the fear. [*Looking out of door*].

SHAWN [*timidly*] Would I fetch you the Widow Quin, maybe?

PEGEEN. Is it the like of that murderer? You'll not, surely.

SHAWN [*going to her, soothingly*] Then I'm thinking himself will stop along with you when he sees you taking on; for it'll be a long night-time with great darkness, and I'm after feeling a kind of fellow above in the furzy ditch, groaning wicked like a maddening dog, the way it's good cause you have, maybe, to be fearing now.

PEGEEN [*turning on him sharply*] What's that? Is it a man you seen?

SHAWN [*retreating*] I couldn't see him at all; but I heard him groaning out, and breaking his heart. It should have been a young man from his words speaking.

PEGEEN [*going after him*] And you never went near to see was he hurted or what ailed him at all?

SHAWN. I did not, Pegeen Mike. It was a dark, lonesome place to be hearing the like of him.

PEGEEN. Well, you're a daring fellow, and if they find his corpse stretched above in the dews of dawn, what'll you say then to the peelers, or the Justice of the Peace?

SHAWN [*thunderstruck*] I wasn't thinking of that. For the love of God, Pegeen Mike, don't let on I was speaking of him. Don't tell your father and the men is coming above; for if they heard that story they'd have great blabbing this night at the wake.

PEGEEN. I'll maybe tell them, and I'll maybe not.

SHAWN. They are coming at the door. Will you whisht, I'm saying?

PEGEEN. Whisht yourself.

She goes behind counter. Michael James, fat, jovial publican, comes in followed by Philly Cullen, who is thin and mistrusting, and Jimmy Farrell, who is fat and amorous, about forty-five.

MEN [*together*] God bless you! The blessing of God on this place!

PEGEEN. God bless you kindly.

MICHAEL [*to men, who go to the counter*] Sit down now, and take your rest. [*Crosses to Shawn at the fire*]. And how is it you are, Shawn Keogh? Are you coming over the sands to Kate Cassidy's wake?

SHAWN. I am not, Michael James. I'm going home the short cut to my bed.

PEGEEN [*speaking across the counter*] He's right, too, and have you no shame, Michael James, to be quitting off for the whole night, and leaving myself lonesome in the shop?

MICHAEL [*good-humouredly*] Isn't it the same whether I go for the whole night or a part only? and I'm thinking it's a queer daughter you are if you'd have me crossing backward through the Stooks of the Dead Women, with a drop taken.

PEGEEN. If I am a queer daughter, it's a queer father'd be leaving me lonesome these twelve hours of dark, and I piling the turf with the dogs barking, and the calves mooing, and my own teeth rattling with the fear.

JIMMY [*flatteringly*] What is there to hurt you, and you a fine, hardy girl would knock the heads of any two men in the place?

PEGEEN [*working herself up*] Isn't there the harvest boys with their tongues red for drink, and the ten tinkers is camped in the east glen, and the thousand militia – bad cess to them! – walking idle through the land. There's lots surely to hurt me, and I won't stop alone in it, let himself do what he will.

MICHAEL. If you're that afeard, let Shawn Keogh stop along with you. It's the will of God, I'm thinking, himself should be seeing you now. [*They all turn on Shawn*].

SHAWN [*in horrified confusion*] I would and welcome, Michael James, but I'm afeard of Father Reilly; and what at all would the Holy Father and the Cardinals of Rome be saying if they heard I did the like of that?

MICHAEL [*with contempt*] God help you! Can't you sit in by the hearth with the light lit and herself beyond in the room? You'll do that surely, for I've heard tell there's a queer fellow above, going mad or getting his death, maybe, in the gripe of the ditch, so she'd be safer this night with a person here.

SHAWN [*with plaintive despair*] I'm afeard of Father Reilly, I'm saying. Let you not be tempting me, and we near married itself.

PHILLY [*with cold contempt*] Lock him in the west room. He'll stay then and have no sin to be telling to the priest.

MICHAEL [*to Shawn, getting between him and the door*] Go up, now.

SHAWN [*at the top of his voice*] Don't stop me, Michael James. Let me out of the door, I'm saying, for the love of the Almighty God. Let me out. [*Trying to dodge past him*]. Let me out of it, and may God grant you His indulgence in the hour of need.

MICHAEL [*loudly*] Stop your noising, and sit down by the hearth. [*Gives him a push and goes to counter laughing*].

SHAWN [*turning back, wringing his hands*] Oh, Father Reilly, and the saints of God, where will I hide myself today? Oh, St Joseph and St Patrick and St Brigid and St James, have mercy on me now!

Shawn turns round, sees door clear, and makes a rush for it.

MICHAEL [*catching him by the coat-tail*] You'd be going, is it?

SHAWN [*screaming*] Leave me go, Michael James, leave me go, you old Pagan, leave me go, or I'll get the curse of the priests on you, and of the scarlet-coated bishops of the Courts of Rome.

With a sudden movement he pulls himself out of his coat, and disappears out of the door, leaving his coat in Michael's hands.

MICHAEL [*turning round, and holding up coat*] Well, there's the coat of a Christian man. Oh, there's sainted glory this day in the lonesome west; and by the will of God I've got you a decent man, Pegeen, you'll have no call to be spying after if you've a score of young girls, maybe, weeding in your fields.

PEGEEN [*taking up the defence of her property*] What right have you to be making game of a poor fellow for minding the priest, when it's your own the fault is, not paying a penny pot-boy to stand along with me and give me courage in the doing of my work. [*She snaps the coat away from him, and goes behind counter with it*].

MICHAEL [*taken aback*] Where would I get a pot-boy? Would you have me send the bell-men screaming in the streets of Castlebar?

SHAWN [*opening the door a chink and putting in his head, in a small voice*] Michael James!

MICHAEL [*imitating him*] What ails you?

SHAWN. The queer dying fellow's beyond looking over the ditch. He's come up, I'm thinking, stealing your hens. [*Looks over his shoulder*]. God help me, he's following me now [*he runs into room*], and if he's heard what I said, he'll be having my life, and I going home lonesome in the darkness of the night.

For a perceptible moment they watch the door with curiosity. Someone coughs outside. Then Christy Mahon, a slight young man, comes in very tired and frightened and dirty.

CHRISTY [*in a small voice*] God save all here!

MEN. God save you kindly!

CHRISTY [*going to the counter*] I'd trouble you for a glass of porter, woman of the house. [*He puts down coin*].

PEGEEN [*serving him*] You're one of the tinkers, young fellow, is beyond camped in the glen?

CHRISTY. I am not; but I'm destroyed walking.

MICHAEL [*patronizingly*] Let you come up then to the fire. You're looking famished with the cold.

CHRISTY. God reward you. [*He takes up his glass and goes a little way across to the left, then stops and looks about him*]. Is it often the polis do be coming into this place, master of the house?

MICHAEL. If you'd come in better hours, you'd have seen 'Licensed for the Sale of Beer and Spirits, to be Consumed on the Premises', written in white letters above the door, and what would the polis want spying on me, and not a decent house within four miles, the way every living Christian is a bona fide, saving one widow alone?

CHRISTY [*with relief*] It's a safe house, so.

He goes over to the fire, sighing and moaning. Then he sits down, putting his glass beside him, and begins gnawing a turnip, too miserable to feel the others staring at him with curiosity.

MICHAEL [*going after him*] Is it yourself is fearing the polis? You're wanting, maybe?

CHRISTY. There's many wanting.

MICHAEL. Many, surely, with the broken harvest and the ended wars. [*He picks up some stockings, etc., that are near the fire, and carries them away furtively*]. It should be larceny, I'm thinking?

CHRISTY [*dolefully*] I had it in my mind it was a different word and a bigger.

PEGEEN. There's a queer lad. Were you never slapped in school, young fellow, that you don't know the name of your deed?

CHRISTY [*bashfully*] I'm slow at learning, a middling scholar only.

MICHAEL. If you're a dunce itself, you'd have a right to know that larceny's robbing and stealing. Is it for the like of that you're wanting?

CHRISTY [*with a flash of family pride*] And I the son of a strong farmer [*with a sudden qualm*], God rest his soul, could have bought up the whole of your old house a while since, from the butt of his tail-pocket, and not have missed the weight of it gone.

MICHAEL [*impressed*] If it's not stealing, it's maybe something big.

CHRISTY [*flattered*] Aye; it's maybe something big.

JIMMY. He's a wicked-looking young fellow. Maybe he followed after a young woman on a lonesome night.

CHRISTY [*shocked*] Oh, the saints forbid, mister; I was all times a decent lad.

PHILLY [*turning on Jimmy*] You're a silly man, Jimmy Farrell. He said his father was a farmer a while since, and there's himself now in a poor state. Maybe the land was grabbed from him, and he did what any decent man would do.

MICHAEL [*to Christy, mysteriously*] Was it bailiffs?

CHRISTY. The divil a one.

MICHAEL. Agents?

CHRISTY. The divil a one.

MICHAEL. Landlords?

CHRISTY [*peevishly*] Ah, not at all, I'm saying. You'd see the like of them stories on any little paper of a Munster town. But I'm not calling to mind any person, gentle, simple, judge or jury, did the like of me.

They all draw nearer with delighted curiosity.

PHILLY. Well, that lad's a puzzle-the-world.

JIMMY. He'd beat Dan Davies's circus, or the holy missioners making sermons on the villainy of man. Try him again, Philly.

PHILLY. Did you strike golden guineas out of solder, young fellow, or shilling coins itself?

CHRISTY. I did not, mister, not sixpence nor a farthing coin.

JIMMY. Did you marry three wives maybe? I'm told there's a sprinkling have done that among the holy Luthers of the preaching north.

CHRISTY [*shyly*] I never married with one, let alone with a couple or three.

PHILLY. Maybe he went fighting for the Boers, the like of the man beyond, was judged to be hanged, quartered, and drawn. Were you off east, young fellow, fighting bloody wars for Kruger and the freedom of the Boers?

CHRISTY. I never left my own parish till Tuesday was a week.

PEGEEN [*coming from counter*] He's done nothing, so. [*To Christy*]. If you didn't commit murder or a bad, nasty thing; or false coining, or robbery, or butchery, or the like of them, there isn't anything that would be worth your troubling for to run from now. You did nothing at all.

CHRISTY [*his feelings hurt*] That's an unkindly thing to be saying to a poor orphaned traveller, has a prison behind him, and hanging before, and hell's gap gaping below.

PEGEEN [*with a sign to the men to be quiet*] You're only saying it. You did nothing at all. A soft lad the like of you wouldn't slit the wind pipe of a screeching sow.

CHRISTY [*offended*] You're not speaking the truth.

PEGEEN [*in mock rage*] Not speaking the truth, is it? Would you have me knock the head of you with the butt of the broom?

CHRISTY [*twisting round on her with a sharp cry of horror*] Don't strike me. I killed my poor father, Tuesday was a week, for doing the like of that.

PEGEEN [*with blank amazement*] Is it killed your father?

CHRISTY [*subsiding*] With the help of God I did, surely, and that the Holy Immaculate Mother may intercede for his soul.

PHILLY [*retreating with Jimmy*] There's a daring fellow.

JIMMY. Oh, glory be to God!

MICHAEL [*with great respect*] That was a hanging crime, mister honey. You should have had good reason for doing the like of that.

CHRISTY [*in a very reasonable tone*] He was a dirty man, God forgive him, and he getting old and crusty, the way I couldn't put up with him at all.

PEGEEN. And you shot him dead?

CHRISTY [*shaking his head*] I never used weapons. I've no licence, and I'm a law-fearing man.

MICHAEL. It was with a hilted knife maybe? I'm told, in the big world, it's bloody knives they use.

CHRISTY [*loudly, scandalized*] Do you take me for a slaughter-boy?

PEGEEN. You never hanged him, the way Jimmy Farrell hanged his dog from the licence, and had it screeching and wriggling three hours at the butt of a string, and himself swearing it was a dead dog, and the peelers swearing it had life?

CHRISTY I did not, then. I just riz the loy and let fall the edge of it on the ridge of his skull, and he went down at my feet like an empty sack, and never let a grunt or groan from him at all.

MICHAEL [*making a sign to Pegeen to fill Christy's glass*] And what way weren't you hanged, mister? Did you bury him then?

CHRISTY [*considering*] Aye. I buried him then. Wasn't I digging spuds in the field?

MICHAEL. And the peelers never followed after you the eleven days that you're out?

CHRISTY [*shaking his head*] Never a one of them, and I walking forward facing hog, dog, or divil on the highway of the road.

PHILLY [*nodding wisely*] It's only with a common weekday kind of murderer them lads would be trusting their carcass, and that man should be a great terror when his temper's roused.

MICHAEL. He should then. [*To Christy*]. And where was it, mister honey, that you did the deed?

CHRISTY [*looking at him with suspicion*] Oh, a distant place, master of the house, a windy corner of high, distant hills.

PHILLY [*nodding with approval*] He's a close man, and he's right, surely.

PEGEEN. That'd be a lad with the sense of Solomon to have for a pot-boy, Michael James, if it's the truth you're seeking one at all.

PHILLY. The peelers is fearing him, and if you'd that lad in the house there isn't one of them would come smelling around if the dogs itself were lapping poteen from the dung-pit of the yard.

JIMMY. Bravery's treasure in a lonesome place, and a lad would kill his father, I'm thinking, would face a foxy divil with a pitchpike on the flags of hell.

PEGEEN. It's the truth they're saying, and if I'd that lad in the house, I wouldn't be fearing the loosèd khaki cut-throats, or the walking dead.

CHRISTY [*swelling with surprise and triumph*] Well, glory be to God!

MICHAEL [*with deference*] Would you think well to stop here and be pot-boy, mister honey, if we gave you good wages, and didn't destroy you with the weight of work.

SHAWN [*coming forward uneasily*] That'd be a queer kind to bring into a decent, quiet household with the like of Pegeen Mike.

PEGEEN [*very sharply*] Will you whisht? Who's speaking to you?

SHAWN [*retreating*] A bloody-handed murderer the like of . . .

PEGEEN [*snapping at him*] Whisht, I am saying; we'll take no fooling from your like at all. [*To Christy, with a honeyed voice*]. And you, young fellow, you'd have a right to stop, I'm thinking, for we'd do our all and utmost to content your needs.

CHRISTY [*overcome with wonder*] And I'd be safe this place from the searching law?

MICHAEL. You would, surely. If they're not fearing you, itself, the peelers in this place is decent, drouthy poor fellows, wouldn't touch a cur dog and not give warning in the dead of night.

PEGEEN [*very kindly and persuasively*] Let you stop a short while anyhow. Aren't you destroyed by walking with your feet in bleeding blisters, and your whole skin needing washing like a Wicklow sheep.

CHRISTY [*looking round with satisfaction*] It's a nice room, and if it's not humbugging me you are, I'm thinking that I'll surely stay.

JIMMY [*jumps up*] Now, by the grace of God, herself will be safe this night, with a man killed his father holding danger from the door, and let you come on, Michael James, or they'll have the best stuff drunk at the wake.

MICHAEL [*going to the door with men*] And begging your pardon, mister, what name will we call you, for we'd like to know?

CHRISTY. Christopher Mahon.

MICHAEL. Well, God bless you, Christy, and a good rest till we meet again when the sun'll be rising to the noon of the day.

CHRISTY. God bless you all.

MEN. God bless you.

They go out, except Shawn, who lingers at the door.

SHAWN [*to Pegeen*] Are you wanting me to stop along with you and keep you from harm?

PEGEEN [*gruffly*] Didn't you say you were fearing Father Reilly?

SHAWN. There'd be no harm staying now, I'm thinking, and himself in it too.

PEGEEN. You wouldn't stay when there was need for you, and let you step off nimble this time when there's none.

SHAWN. Didn't I say it was Father Reilly . . .

PEGEEN. Go on, then, to Father Reilly [*in a jeering tone*], and let him put you in the holy brotherhoods, and leave that lad to me.

SHAWN. If I meet the Widow Quin . . .

PEGEEN. Go on, I'm saying, and don't be waking this place with your noise. [*She hustles him out and bolts door*]. That lad would wear the spirits from the saints of peace. [*Bustles about, then takes off her apron and pins it up in the window as a blind, Christy watching her timidly. Then she comes to him and speaks with bland good humour*]. Let you stretch out now by the fire, young fellow. You should be destroyed travelling.

CHRISTY [*shyly again, drawing off his boots*] I'm tired surely, walking wild eleven days, and waking fearful in the night.

He holds up one of his feet, feeling his blisters, and looking at them with compassion.

PEGEEN [*standing beside him, watching him with delight*] You should have had great people in your family, I'm thinking, with the little, small feet you have, and you with a kind of a quality name, the like of what you'd find on the great powers and potentates of France and Spain.

CHRISTY [*with pride*] We were great, surely, with wide and windy acres of rich Munster land.

PEGEEN. Wasn't I telling you, and you a fine, handsome young fellow with a noble brow?

CHRISTY [*with a flush of delighted surprise*] Is it me?

PEGEEN. Aye. Did you never hear that from the young girls where you come from in the west or south?

CHRISTY [*with venom*] I did not, then. Oh, they're bloody liars in the naked parish where I grew a man.

PEGEEN. If they are itself, you've heard it these days, I'm thinking, and you walking the world telling out your story to young girls or old.

CHRISTY. I've told my story no place till this night, Pegeen Mike, and it's foolish I was here, maybe, to be talking free; but you're decent people, I'm thinking, and yourself a kindly woman, the way I wasn't fearing you at all.

PEGEEN [*filling a sack with straw*] You've said the like of that, maybe, in every cot and cabin where you've met a young girl on your way.

CHRISTY [*going over to her, gradually raising his voice*] I've said it nowhere till this night, I'm telling you; for I've seen none the like of you the eleven long days I am walking the world, looking over a low ditch or a high ditch on my north or south, into stony, scattered fields, or scribes of bog, where you'd see young, limber girls, and fine, prancing women making laughter with the men.

PEGEEN. If you weren't destroyed travelling, you'd have as much talk and streeleen, I'm thinking, as Owen Roe O'Sullivan or the poets of the Dingle Bay; and I've heard all times it's the poets are your like – fine, fiery fellows with great rages when their temper's roused.

CHRISTY [*drawing a little nearer to her*] You've a power of rings, God bless you, and would there be any offence if I was asking are you single now?

PEGEEN. What would I want wedding so young?

CHRISTY [*with relief*] We're alike so.

PEGEEN [*she puts sack on settle and beats it up*] I never killed my father. I'd be afeared to do that, except I was the like of yourself with blind rages tearing me within, for I'm thinking you should have had great tussling when the end was come.

CHRISTY [*expanding with delight at the first confidential talk he has ever had with a woman*] We had not then. It was a hard woman was come over the hill; and if he was always a crusty kind, when he'd a hard woman setting him on, not the divil himself or his four fathers could put up with him at all.

PEGEEN [*with curiosity*] And isn't it a great wonder that one wasn't fearing you?

CHRISTY [*very confidentially*] Up to the day I killed my father, there wasn't a person in Ireland knew the kind I was, and I there drinking, waking, eating, sleeping, a quiet, simple poor fellow with no man giving me heed.

PEGEEN [*getting a quilt out of cupboard and putting it on the sack*] It was the girls were giving you heed, maybe, and I'm thinking it's most conceit you'd have to be gaming with their like.

CHRISTY [*shaking his head with simplicity*] Not the girls itself, and I won't tell you a lie. There wasn't any one heeding me in that place saving only the dumb beasts of the field.

He sits down at fire.

PEGEEN [*with disappointment*] And I thinking you should have been living the like of a king of Norway or the eastern world.

She comes and sits beside him after placing bread and mug of milk on the table.

CHRISTY [*laughing piteously*] The like of a king, is it? and I after toiling, moiling, digging, dodging from the dawn till dusk; with never a sight of joy or sport saving only when I'd be abroad in the dark night poaching rabbits on hills, for I was a divil to poach, God forgive me [*very naïvely*], and I near got six months for going with a dung fork and stabbing a fish.

PEGEEN. And it's that you'd call sport, is it, to be abroad in the darkness with yourself alone?

CHRISTY. I did, God help me, and there I'd be as happy as the sunshine of St Martin's Day, watching the light passing the north or the patches of fog, till I'd hear a rabbit starting to screech and I'd go running in the furze. Then, when I'd my full share, I'd come walking down where you'd see the ducks and geese stretched sleeping on the highway of the road, and before I'd pass the dunghill, I'd hear himself snoring out – a loud, lonesome snore he'd be making all times, the while he was sleeping; and he a man'd be raging all times, the while he was waking, like a gaudy officer you'd hear cursing and damning and swearing oaths.

PEGEEN. Providence and Mercy, spare us all!

CHRISTY. It's that you'd say surely if you seen him and he after drinking for weeks, rising up in the red dawn, or before it maybe, and going out into the yard as naked as an ash-tree in the moon of May, and shying clods against the visage of the stars till he'd put the fear of death into the banbhs and the screeching sows.

PEGEEN. I'd be well-nigh afeard of that lad myself, I'm thinking. And there was no one in it but the two of you alone?

CHRISTY. The divil a one, though he'd sons and daughters walking all great states and territories of the world, and not a one of them, to this day, but would say their seven curses on him, and they rousing up to let a cough or sneeze, maybe, in the deadness of the night.

PEGEEN [*nodding her head*] Well, you should have been a queer lot. I never cursed my father the like of that, though I'm twenty and more years of age.

CHRISTY. Then you'd have cursed mine, I'm telling you, and he a man never gave peace to any, saving when he'd get two months or three, or be locked in the asylums for battering peelers or assaulting men [*with depression*], the way it was a bitter life he led me till I did up a Tuesday and halve his skull.

PEGEEN [*putting her hand on his shoulder*] Well, you'll have peace in this place, Christy Mahon, and none to trouble you, and it's near time a fine lad like you should have your good share of the earth.

CHRISTY. It's time surely, and I a seemly fellow with great strength in me and bravery of . . .

Someone knocks.

CHRISTY [*clinging to Pegeen*] Oh, glory! it's late for knocking, and this last while I'm in terror of the peelers, and the walking dead.

Knocking again.

PEGEEN. Who's there?

VOICE [*outside*] Me.

PEGEEN. Who's me?

VOICE. The Widow Quin.

PEGEEN [*jumping up and giving him the bread and milk*] Go on now with your supper, and let on to be sleepy, for if she found you were such a warrant to talk, she'd be stringing gabble till the dawn of day.

He takes bread and sits shyly with his back to the door.

PEGEEN [*opening door, with temper*] What ails you, or what is it you're wanting at this hour of the night?

WIDOW QUIN [*coming in a step and peering at Christy*] I'm after meeting Shawn Keogh and Father Reilly below, who told me of your curiosity man, and they fearing by this time he was roaring, romping on your hands with drink.

PEGEEN [*pointing to Christy*] Look now is he roaring, and he stretched out drowsy with his supper and his mug of milk. Walk down and tell that to Father Reilly and to Shaneen Keogh.

WIDOW QUIN [*coming forward*] I'll not see them again, for I've their word to lead that lad forward to lodge with me.

PEGEEN [*in blank amazement*] This night is it?

WIDOW QUIN [*going over*] This night, 'It isn't fitting,' says the priesteen, 'to have his likeness lodging with an orphaned girl.' [*To Christy*]. God save you mister!

CHRISTY [*shyly*] God save you kindly!

WIDOW QUIN [*looking at him with half amused curiosity*] Well, aren't you a little smiling fellow? It should have been great and bitter torments did rouse your spirits to a deed of blood.

CHRISTY [*doubtfully*] It should, maybe.

WIDOW QUIN. It's more than 'maybe' I'm saying, and it'd soften my heart to see you sitting so simple with your cup and cake, and you fitter to be saying your catechism than slaying your da.

PEGEEN [*at counter, washing glasses*] There's talking when any'd see he's fit to be holding his head high with the wonders of the world. Walk on from this, for I'll not have him tormented, and he destroyed travelling since Tuesday was a week.

WIDOW QUIN [*peaceably*] We'll be walking surely when his supper's done, and you'll find we're great company, young fellow, when it's of the like of you and me you'd hear the penny poets singing in an August Fair.

CHRISTY [*innocently*] Did you kill your father?

PEGEEN [*contemptuously*] She did not. He hit himself with a worn pick, and the rusted poison did corrode his blood the way he never overed it, and died after. That was a sneaky kind of murder did win small glory with the boys itself.

She crosses to Christy's left.

WIDOW QUIN [*with good humour*] If it didn't, maybe all knows a widow woman has buried her children and destroyed her man is a wiser comrade for a young lad than a girl, the like of you, who'd go helter-skeltering after any man would let you a wink upon the road.

PEGEEN [*breaking out into wild rage*] And you'll say that, Widow Quin, and you gasping with the rage you had racing the hill beyond to look on his face.

WIDOW QUIN [*laughing derisively*] Me, is it? Well, Father Reilly has cuteness to divide you now. [*She pulls Christy up*]. There's great temptation in a man did slay his da, and we'd best be going, young fellow; so rise up and come with me.

PEGEEN [*seizing his arm*] He'll not stir. He's pot-boy in this place, and I'll not have him stolen off and kidnapped while himself's abroad.

WIDOW QUIN. It'd be a crazy pot-boy'd lodge him in the shebeen where he works by day, so you'd have a right to come on, young fellow, till you see my little houseen, a perch off on the rising hill.

PEGEEN. Wait till morning, Christy Mahon. Wait till you lay eyes on her leaky thatch is growing more pasture for her buck goat than her square of fields, and she without a tramp itself to keep in order her place at all.

WIDOW QUIN. When you see me contriving in my little gardens, Christy Mahon, you'll swear the Lord God formed me to be living lone, and that there isn't my match in Mayo for thatching, or mowing, or shearing a sheep.

PEGEEN [*with noisy scorn*] It's true the Lord God formed you to contrive indeed. Doesn't the world know you reared a black ram at your own breast, so that the Lord Bishop of Connaught felt the elements of a Christian, and he eating it after in a kidney stew? Doesn't the world know you've been seen shaving the foxy skipper from France for a threepenny-bit and a sop of grass tobacco would wring the liver from a mountain goat you'd meet leaping the hills?

WIDOW QUIN [*with amusement*] Do you hear her now, young fellow? Do you hear the way she'll be rating at your own self when a week is by?

PEGEEN [*to Christy*] Don't heed her. Tell her to go on into her pigsty and not plague us here.

WIDOW QUIN. I'm going; but he'll come with me.

PEGEEN [*shaking him*] Are you dumb, young fellow?

CHRISTY [*timidly to Widow Quin*] God increase you; but I'm pot-boy in this place, and it's here I liefer stay.

PEGEEN [*triumphantly*] Now you have heard him, and go on from this.

WIDOW QUIN [*looking round the room*] It's lonesome this hour crossing the hill, and if he won't come along with me, I'd have a right maybe to stop this night with yourselves. Let me stretch out on the settle, Pegeen Mike; and himself can lie by the hearth.

PEGEEN [*short and fiercely*] Faith, I won't. Quit off or I will send you now.

WIDOW QUIN [*gathering her shawl up*] Well, it's a terror to be aged a score. [*To Christy*]. God bless you now, young fellow, and let you be wary, or there's right torment will await you here if you go romancing with her like, and she waiting only, as they bade me say, on a sheepskin parchment to be wed with Shawn Keogh of Killakeen.

CHRISTY [*going to Pegeen as she bolts door*] What's that she's after saying?

PEGEEN. Lies and blather, you've no call to mind. Well, isn't Shawn Keogh an impudent fellow to send up spying on me? Wait till I lay hands on him. Let him wait, I'm saying.

CHRISTY. And you're not wedding him at all?

PEGEEN. I wouldn't wed him if a bishop came walking for to join us here.

CHRISTY. That God in glory may be thanked for that.

PEGEEN. There's your bed now. I've put a quilt upon you I'm after quilting a while since with my own two hands, and you'd best stretch out now for your sleep, and may God give you a good rest till I call you in the morning when the cocks will crow.

CHRISTY [*As she goes to inner room*] May God and Mary and St Patrick bless you and reward you for your kindly talk. [*She shuts the door behind her. He settles his bed slowly, feeling the quilt with immense satisfaction*]. Well, it's a clean bed and soft with it, and it's great luck and company I've won me in the end of time – two fine women fighting for the likes of me – till I'm thinking this night wasn't I a foolish fellow not to kill my father in the years gone by.

[CURTAIN]

ACT II

Scene as before. Brilliant morning light. Christy, looking bright and cheerful, is cleaning a girl's boots.

CHRISTY [*to himself, counting jugs on dresser*] Half a hundred beyond. Ten there. A score that's above. Eighty jugs. Six cups and a broken one. Two plates. A power of glasses. Bottles, a schoolmaster'd be hard set to count, and enough in them, I'm thinking, to drunken all the wealth and wisdom of the county Clare. [*He puts down the boot carefully*]. There's her boots now, nice and decent for her evening use, and isn't it grand brushes she has? [*He puts them down and goes by degrees to the looking-glass*]. Well, this'd be a fine place to be my whole life talking out with swearing Christians, in place of my old dogs and cat; and I stalking around, smoking my pipe and drinking my fill, and never a day's work but drawing a cork an odd time, or wiping a glass, or rinsing out a shiny tumbler for a decent man. [*He takes the looking-glass from the wall and puts it on the back of a chair; then sits down in front of it and begins washing his face*]. Didn't I know rightly, I was handsome, though it was the divil's own mirror we had beyond, would twist a squint across an angel's brow; and I'll be growing fine from this day, the way I'll have a soft lovely skin on me and won't be the like of the clumsy young fellows do be ploughing all times in the earth and dung. [*He starts*]. Is she coming again? [*He looks out*]. Stranger girls. God help me, where'll I hide myself away and my long neck naked to the world? [*He looks out*]. I'd best go to the room maybe till I'm dressed again.

He gathers up his coat and the looking-glass, and runs into the inner room. The door is pushed open, and Susan Brady looks in, and knocks on door.

SUSAN. There's nobody in it. [*Knocks again*]

NELLY [*pushing her in and following her, with Honor Blake and Sara Tansey*] It'd be early for them both to be out walking the hill.

SUSAN. I'm thinking Shawn Keogh was making game of us, and there's no such man in it at all.

HONOR [*pointing to straw and quilt*] Look at that. He's been sleeping there in the night. Well, it'll be a hard case if he's gone off now, the way we'll never set our eyes on a man killed his father, and we after rising early and destroying ourselves running fast on the hill.

NELLY. Are you thinking them's his boots?

SARA [*taking them up*] If they are, there should be his father's track on them. Did you never read in the papers the way murdered men do bleed and drip?

SUSAN. Is that blood there, Sara Tansey?

SARA [*smelling it*] That's bog water, I'm thinking; but it's his own they are, surely, for I never seen the like of them for whitey mud, and red mud, and turf on them, and the fine sands of the sea. That man's been walking, I'm telling you.

She goes down right, putting on one of his boots.

SUSAN [*going to window*] Maybe he's stolen off to Belmullet with the boots of Michael James, and you'd have a right so to follow after him, Sara Tansey, and you the one yoked the ass-cart and drove ten miles to set your eyes on the man bit the yellow lady's nostril on the northern shore. [*She looks out*].

SARA [*running to window, with one boot on*] Don't be talking, and we fooled today. [*Putting on the other boot*]. There's a pair do fit me well and I'll be keeping them for walking to the priest, when you'd be ashamed this place, going up winter and summer with nothing worth while to confess at all.

HONOR [*who has been listening at door*] Whisht! there's someone inside the room. [*She pushes door a chink open*]. It's a man.

Sara kicks off boots and puts them where they were. They all stand in a line looking through chink.

SARA. I'll call him. Mister! Mister! [*He puts in his head*] Is Pegeen within?

CHRISTY [*coming in as meek as a mouse, with the looking-glass held behind his back*] She's above on the cnuceen, seeking the nanny goats, the way she'd have a sup of goats' milk for to colour my tea.

SARA. And asking your pardon, is it you's the man killed his father?

CHRISTY [*sidling toward the nail where the glass was hanging*] I am, God help me!

SARA [*taking eggs she has brought*] Then my thousand welcomes to you, and I've run up with a brace of duck's eggs for your food today, Pegeen's ducks is no use, but these are the real rich sort. Hold out your hand and you'll see it's no lie I'm telling you.

CHRISTY [*coming forward shyly, and holding out his left hand*] They're a great and weighty size.

SUSAN. And I run up with a pat of butter, for it'd be a poor thing to have you eating your spuds dry, and you after running a great way since you did destroy your da.

CHRISTY. Thank you kindly.

HONOR. And I brought you a little cut of a cake, for you should have a thin stomach on you, and you that length walking the world.

NELLY. And I brought you a little laying pullet – boiled and all she is – was crushed at the fall of night by the curate's car. Feel the fat of the breast, mister.

CHRISTY. It's bursting, surely.

He feels it with the back of his hand, in which he holds the presents.

SARA. Will you pinch it? Is your right hand too sacred for to use at all? [*She slips round behind him*]. It's a glass he has. Well, I never seen to this day a man with a looking-glass held to his back. Them that kills their fathers is a vain lot surely. [*Girls giggle*].

CHRISTY [*smiling innocently and piling presents on glass*] I'm very thankful to you all today . . .

WIDOW QUIN [*coming in quietly, at door*] Sara Tansey, Susan Brady, Honor Blake! What in glory has you here at this hour of day!

GIRLS [*giggling*] That's the man killed his father.

WIDOW QUIN [*coming to them*] I know well it's the man; and I'm after putting him down in the sports below for racing, leaping, pitching, and the Lord knows what.

SARA [*exuberantly*] That's right, Widow Quin. I'll bet my dowry that he'll lick the world.

WIDOW QUIN. If you will, you'd have a right to have him fresh and nourished in place of nursing a feast. [*Taking presents*]. Are you fasting or fed, young fellow?

CHRISTY. Fasting, if you please.

WIDOW QUIN [*loudly*] Well, you're the lot. Stir up now and give him his breakfast. [*To Christy*] Come here to me [*she puts him on bench beside her while the girls make tea and get his breakfast*], and let you tell us your story before Pegeen will come, in place of grinning your ears off like the moon of May.

CHRISTY [*beginning to be pleased*] It's a long story; you'd be destroyed listening.

WIDOW QUIN. Don't be letting on to be shy, a fine, gamy, treacherous lad the like of you. Was it in your house beyond you cracked his skull?

CHRISTY [*shy but flattered*] It was not. We were digging spuds in his cold, sloping, stony, divil's patch of a field.

WIDOW QUIN. And you went asking money of him, or making talk of getting a wife would drive him from his farm?

CHRISTY. I did not, then; but there I was, digging and digging, and 'You squinting idiot,' says he, 'let you walk down now and tell the priest you'll wed the Widow Casey in a score of days.'

WIDOW QUIN. And what kind was she?

CHRISTY [*with horror*] A walking terror from beyond the hills, and she two score and five years, and two hundred weights and five pounds in the weighing scales, with a limping leg on her, and a blinded eye, and she a woman of noted misbehaviour with the old and young.

GIRLS [*clustering round him, serving him*] Glory be.

WIDOW QUIN. And what did he want driving you to wed with her? [*She takes a bit of the chicken*].

CHRISTY [*eating with growing satisfaction*] He was letting on I was wanting a protector from the harshness of the world, and he without a thought the whole while but how he'd have her hut to live in and her gold to drink.

WIDOW QUIN. There's maybe worse than a dry hearth and a widow woman and your glass at night. So you hit him then?

CHRISTY [*getting also excited*] I did not. 'I won't wed her,' says I, 'when all know she did suckle me for six weeks when I came into the world, and she a hag this day with a tongue on her has the crows

and seabirds scattered, the way they wouldn't cast a shadow on her
garden with the dread of her curse.'

WIDOW QUIN [*teasingly*] That one should be right company.

SARA [*eagerly*] Don't mind her. Did you kill him then?

CHRISTY. 'She's too good for the like of you,' says he, 'and go on
now or I'll flatten you out like a crawling beast has passed under a
dray.' 'You will not if I can help it,' says I. 'Go on,' says he, 'or I'll
have the divil making garters of your limbs tonight.' 'You will not if
I can help it,' says I. [*He sits up brandishing his mug*].

SARA. You were right surely.

CHRISTY [*impressively*] With that sun came out between the cloud and
the hill, and it shining green in my face. 'God have mercy on your
soul,' says he, lifting a scythe. 'Or on your own,' says I, raising the
loy.

SUSAN. That's a grand story.

HONOR. He tells it lovely.

CHRISTY [*flattered and confident, waving bone*] He gave a drive with the
scythe, and I gave a lep to the east. Then I turned around with my
back to the north, and I hit a blow on the ridge of his skull, laid him
stretched out, and he split to the knob of his gullet.

He raises the chicken bone to his Adam's apple.

GIRLS [*together*] Well, you're a marvel! Oh, God bless you! You're the
lad, surely!

SUSAN. I'm thinking the Lord God sent him this road to make a
second husband to the Widow Quin, and she with a great yearning
to be wedded, though all dread her here. Lift him on her knee,
Sara Tansey.

WIDOW QUIN. Don't tease him.

SARA [*going over to dresser and counter very quickly and getting two glasses
and porter*] You're heroes, surely, and let you drink a supeen with
your arms linked like outlandish lovers in the sailor's song. [*She
links their arms and gives them the glasses*]. There now. Drink a health
to the wonders of the western world, the pirates, preachers, poteen-
makers, with the jobbing jockies; parching peelers, and the juries
fill their stomachs selling judgments of the English law. [*Brandishing
the bottle*].

WIDOW QUIN. That's a right toast, Sara Tansey. Now, Christy.

They drink with their arms linked, he drinking with his left hand, she with her right. As they are drinking, Pegeen Mike comes in with a milk-can and stands aghast. They all spring away from Christy. He goes down left. Widow Quin remains seated.

PEGEEN [*angrily to Sara*] What is it you're wanting?

SARA [*twisting her apron*] An ounce of tobacco.

PEGEEN. Have you tuppence?

SARA. I've forgotten my purse.

PEGEEN. Then you'd best be getting it and not be fooling us here. [*To the Widow Quin, with more elaborate scorn*]. And what is it you're wanting, Widow Quin?

WIDOW QUIN [*insolently*] A penn'orth of starch.

PEGEEN [*breaking out*] And you without a white shift or a shirt in your whole family since the dying of the flood. I've no starch for the like of you, and let you walk on now to Killamuck.

WIDOW QUIN [*turning to Christy, as she goes out with the girls*] Well, you're mighty huffy this day, Pegeen Mike, and you, young fellow, let you not forget the sports and racing when the noon is by. [*They go out*].

PEGEEN [*imperiously*] Fling out that rubbish and put them cups away. [*Christy tidies away in great haste*]. Shove in the bench by the wall [*He does so*]. And hang that glass on the nail. What disturbed it at all?

CHRISTY [*very meekly*] I was making myself decent only, and this a fine country for young lovely girls.

PEGEEN [*sharply*] Whisht your talking of girls [*Goes to counter on right*].

CHRISTY. Wouldn't any wish to be decent in a place . . .

PEGEEN. Whisht, I'm saying.

CHRISTY [*looks at her face for a moment with great misgivings, then as a last effort takes up a loy, and goes towards her, with feigned assurance*] It was with a loy the like of that I killed my father.

PEGEEN [*still sharply*] You've told me that story six times since the dawn of day.

CHRISTY [*reproachfully*] It's a queer thing you wouldn't care to be hearing it and them girls after walking four miles to be listening to me now.

PEGEEN [*turning round astonished*] Four miles?

CHRISTY [*apologetically*] Didn't himself say there were only bona fides living in the place?

PEGEEN. It's bona fides by the road they are, but that lot came over the river lepping the stones. It's not three perches when you go like that, and I was down this morning looking on the papers the post-boy does have in his bag. [*With meaning and emphasis*]. For there was great news this day, Christopher Mahon. [*She goes into room on left*].

CHRISTY [*suspiciously*] It is news of my murder?

PEGEEN [*inside*] Murder, indeed.

CHRISTY [*loudly*] A murdered da?

PEGEEN [*coming in again and crossing right*] There was not, but a story filled half a page of the hanging of a man. Ah, that should be a fearful end, young fellow, and it worst of all for a man destroyed his da; for the like of him would get small mercies, and when it's dead he is they'd put him in a narrow grave, with cheap sacking wrapping him round, and pour down quicklime on his head, the way you'd see a woman pouring any frish-frash from a cup.

CHRISTY [*very miserably*] Oh, God help me. Are you thinking I'm safe? You were saying at the fall of night I was shut of jeopardy and I here with yourselves.

PEGEEN [*severely*] You'll be shut of jeopardy no place if you go talking with a pack of wild girls the like of them do be walking abroad with the peelers, talking whispers at the fall of night.

CHRISTY [*with terror*] And you're thinking they'd tell?

PEGEEN [*with mock sympathy*] Who knows, God help you?

CHRISTY [*loudly*] What joy would they have to bring hanging to the likes of me?

PEGEEN. It's queer joys they have, and who knows the thing they'd do, if it'd make the green stones cry itself to think of you swaying and swinging at the butt of a rope, and you with a fine, stout neck. God bless you! the way you'd be a half an hour, in great anguish, getting your death.

CHRISTY [*getting his boots and putting them on*] If there's that terror of them it'd be best, maybe, I went on wandering like Esau or Cain and Abel on the sides of Neifin or the Erris plain.

PEGEEN [*beginning to play with him*] It would maybe, for I've heard the circuit judges this place is a heartless crew.

CHRISTY [*bitterly*] It's more than judges this place is a heartless crew. [*Looking up at her*]. And isn't it a poor thing to be starting again, and I a lonesome fellow will be looking out on women and girls the way the needy fallen spirits do be looking on the Lord?

PEGEEN. What call have you to be that lonesome when there's poor girls walking Mayo in their thousands now?

CHRISTY [*grimly*] It's well you know what call I have. It's well you know it's a lonesome thing to be passing small towns with the lights shining sideways when the night is down, or going in strange places with a dog noising before you and a dog noising behind, or drawn to the cities where you'd hear a voice kissing and talking deep love in every shadow of the ditch, and you passing on with an empty, hungry stomach failing from your heart.

PEGEEN. I'm thinking you're an odd man, Christy Mahon. The oddest walking fellow I ever set my eyes on to this hour today.

CHRISTY. What would any be but odd men and they living lonesome in the world?

PEGEEN. I'm not odd, and I'm my whole life with my father only.

CHRISTY [*with infinite admiration*] How would a lovely, handsome woman the like of you be lonesome when all men should be thronging around to hear the sweetness of your voice, and the little infant children should be pestering your steps, I'm thinking, and you walking the roads.

PEGEEN. I'm hard set to know what way a coaxing fellow the like of yourself should be lonesome either.

CHRISTY. Coaxing?

PEGEEN. Would you have me think a man never talked with the girls would have the words you've spoken today? It's only letting on you are to be lonesome, the way you'd get around me now.

CHRISTY. I wish to God I was letting on; but I was lonesome all times, and born lonesome, I'm thinking, as the moon of dawn. *Going to door.*

PEGEEN [*puzzled by his talk*] Well, it's a story I'm not understanding at all why you'd be worse than another, Christy Mahon, and you a fine lad with the great savagery to destroy your da.

CHRISTY. It's little I'm understanding myself, saving only that my heart's scalded this day, and I going off stretching out the earth between us, the way I'll not be waking near you another dawn of the year till the two of us do arise to hope or judgment with the saints of God, and now I'd best be going with my wattle in my hand for hanging is a poor thing [*turning to go*], and it's little welcome only is left me in this house today.

PEGEEN [*sharply*] Christy. [*He turns round*]. Come here to me. [*He goes towards her*]. Lay down that switch and throw some sods on the fire. You're pot-boy in this place, and I'll not have you mitch off from us now.

CHRISTY. You were saying I'd be hanged if I stay.

PEGEEN [*quite kindly at last*] I'm after going down and reading the fearful crimes of Ireland for two weeks or three, and there wasn't a word of your murder. [*Getting up and going over to the counter*]. They've likely not found the body. You're safe so with ourselves.

CHRISTY [*astonished, slowly*] It's making game of me you were [*following her with fearful joy*], and I can stay so, working at your side, and I not lonesome from this mortal day.

PEGEEN. What's to hinder you staying, except the widow woman or the young girls would inveigle you off?

CHRISTY [*with rapture*] And I'll have your words from this day filling my ears, and that look is come upon you meeting my two eyes, and I watching you loafing around in the warm sun, or rinsing your ankles when the night is come.

PEGEEN [*kindly, but a little embarrassed*] I'm thinking you'll be a loyal young lad to have working around, and if you vexed me a while since with your leaguing with the girls, I wouldn't give a thraneen for a lad hadn't a mighty spirit in him and a gamy heart.

Shawn Keogh runs in carrying a cleeve on his back, followed by the Widow Quin.

SHAWN [*to Pegeen*] I was passing below, and I seen your mountainy sheep eating cabbages in Jimmy's field. Run up or they'll be bursting surely.

PEGEEN. Oh, God, mend them!

She puts a shawl over her head and runs out.

CHRISTY [*looking from one to the other. Still in high spirits*] I'd best go to her aid maybe. I'm handy with ewes.

WIDOW QUIN [*closing the door*] She can do that much, and there is Shaneen has long speeches for to tell you now. [*She sits down with an amused smile*].

SHAWN [*taking something from his pocket and offering it to Christy*] Do you see that, mister?

CHRISTY [*looking at it*] The half of a ticket to the Western States!

SHAWN [*trembling with anxiety*] I'll give it to you and my new hat [*pulling it out of hamper*]; and my breeches with the double seat [*pulling it out*]; and my new coat is woven from the blackest shearings for three miles around [*giving him the coat*]; I'll give you the whole of them, and my blessing, and the blessing of Father Reilly itself, maybe, if you'll quit from this and leave us in the peace we had till last night at the fall of dark.

CHRISTY [*with a new arrogance*] And for what is it you're wanting to get shut of me?

SHAWN [*looking to the Widow for help*] I'm a poor scholar with middling faculties to coin a lie, so I'll tell you the truth, Christy Mahon. I'm wedding with Pegeen beyond, and I don't think well of having a clever fearless man the like of you dwelling in her house.

CHRISTY [*almost pugnaciously*]. And you'd be using bribery for to banish me?

SHAWN [*in an imploring voice*] Let you not take it badly, mister honey; isn't beyond the best place for you, where you'll have golden chains and shiny coats and you riding upon hunters with the ladies of the land.

He makes an eager sign to the Widow Quin to come to help him.

WIDOW QUIN [*coming over*] It's true for him, and you'd best quit off and not have that poor girl setting her mind on you, for there's Shaneen thinks she wouldn't suit you, though all is saying that she'll wed you now.

Christy beams with delight.

SHAWN [*in terrified earnest*] She wouldn't suit you, and with the divil's own temper the way you'd be strangling one another in a score of days. [*He makes the movement of strangling with his hands*]. It's the like of me only that she's fit for; a quiet simple fellow wouldn't raise a hand upon her if she scratched itself.

WIDOW QUIN [*putting Shawn's hat on Christy*] Fit them clothes on you anyhow, young fellow, and he'd maybe loan them to you for the sports. [*Pushing him towards inner door*]. Fit them on and you can give your answer when you have them tried.

CHRISTY [*beaming, delighted with the clothes*] I will then. I'd like herself to see me in them tweeds and hat.

He goes into room and shuts the door.

SHAWN [*in great anxiety*] He'd like herself to see them. He'll not leave us, Widow Quin. He's a score of divils in him the way it's well-nigh certain he will wed Pegeen.

WIDOW QUIN [*jeeringly*] It's true all girls are fond of courage and do hate the like of you.

SHAWN [*walking about in desperation*] Oh, Widow Quin, what'll I be doing now? I'd inform again him, but he'd burst from Kilmainham and he'd be sure and certain to destroy me. If I wasn't so God-fearing, I'd near have courage to come behind him and run a pike into his side. Oh, it's a hard case to be an orphan and not to have your father that you're used to, and you'd easy kill and make yourself a hero in the sight of all. [*Coming up to her*]. Oh, Widow Quin, will you find me some contrivance when I've promised you a ewe?

WIDOW QUIN. A ewe's a small thing, but what would you give me if I did wed him and did save you so?

SHAWN [*with astonishment*] You?

WIDOW QUIN. Aye. Would you give me the red cow you have and the mountainy ram, and the right of way across your rye path, and a load of dung at Michaelmas, and turbary upon the western hill?

SHAWN [*radiant with hope*] I would, surely, and I'd give you the wedding-ring I have, and the loan of a new suit, the way you'd have him decent on the wedding-day. I'd give you two kids for your dinner, and a gallon of poteen, and I'd call the piper on the long car to your wedding from Crossmolina or from Ballina. I'd give you . . .

WIDOW QUIN. That'll do, so, and let you whisht, for he's coming now again.

Christy comes in, very natty in the new clothes. Widow Quin goes to him admiringly.

WIDOW QUIN. If you seen yourself now, I'm thinking you'd be too proud to speak to at all, and it'd be a pity surely to have your like sailing from Mayo to the western world.

CHRISTY [*as proud as a peacock*] I'm not going. If this is a poor place itself, I'll make myself contented to be lodging here.

Widow Quin makes a sign to Shawn to leave them.

SHAWN. Well, I'm going measuring the racecourse while the tide is low, so I'll leave you the garments and my blessing for the sports today. God bless you!

He wriggles out.

WIDOW QUIN [*admiring Christy*] Well, you're mighty spruce, young fellow. Sit down now while you're quiet till you talk with me.

CHRISTY [*swaggering*] I'm going abroad on the hillside for to seek Pegeen.

WIDOW QUIN. You'll have time and plenty for to seek Pegeen, and you heard me saying at the fall of night the two of us should be great company.

CHRISTY. From this out I'll have no want of company when all sorts is bringing me their food and clothing [*he swaggers to the door, tightening his belt*], the way they'd set their eyes upon a gallant orphan cleft his father with one blow to the breeches belt. [*He opens door, then staggers back*] Saints of Glory! Holy angels from the throne of light!

WIDOW QUIN [*going over*] What ails you?

CHRISTY. It's the walking spirit of my murdered da!

WIDOW QUIN [*looking out*] Is it that tramper?

CHRISTY [*wildly*] Where'll I hide my poor body from that ghost of hell?

The door is pushed open, and old Mahon appears on threshold. Christy darts in behind door.

WIDOW QUIN [*in great amazement*] God save you, my poor man.

MAHON [*gruffly*] Did you see a young lad passing this way in the early morning or the fall of night?

WIDOW QUIN. You're a queer kind to walk in not saluting at all.

MAHON. Did you see the young lad?

WIDOW QUIN [*stiffly*] What kind was he?

MAHON. An ugly young streeler with a murderous gob on him, and a little switch in his hand. I met a tramper seen him coming this way at the fall of night.

WIDOW QUIN. There's harvest hundreds do be passing these days for the Sligo boat. For what is it you're wanting him, my poor man?

MAHON. I want to destroy him for breaking the head on me with the clout of a loy. [*He takes off a big hat, and shows his head in a mass of bandages and plaster, with some pride*]. It was he did that, and amn't I a great wonder to think I've traced him ten days with that rent in my crown?

WIDOW QUIN [*taking his head in both hands and examining it with extreme delight*] That was a great blow. And who hit you? A robber maybe?

MAHON. It was my own son hit me, and he the divil a robber, or anything else, but a dirty, stuttering lout.

WIDOW QUIN [*letting go his skull and wiping her hands in her apron*] You'd best be wary of a mortified scalp, I think they call it, lepping around with that wound in the splendour of the sun. It was a bad blow, surely, and you should have vexed him fearful to make him strike that gash in his da.

MAHON. Is it me?

WIDOW QUIN [*amusing herself*] Aye. And isn't it a great shame when the old and hardened do torment the young?

MAHON [*raging*] Torment him, is it? And I after holding out with the patience of a martyred saint till there's nothing but destruction on, and I'm driven out in my old age with none to aid me.

WIDOW QUIN [*greatly amused*] It's a sacred wonder the way that wickedness will spoil a man.

MAHON. My wickedness, is it? Amn't I after saying it is himself has me destroyed, and he a liar on walls, a talker of folly, a man you'd see stretched the half of the day in the brown ferns with his belly to the sun.

WIDOW QUIN. Not working at all?

MAHON. The divil a work, or if he did itself, you'd see him raising up a haystack like the stalk of a rush, or driving our last cow till he broke her leg at the hip, and when he wasn't at that he'd be fooling over little birds he had – finches and felt – or making mugs at his own self in the bit of glass we had hung on the wall.

WIDOW QUIN [*looking at Christy*] What way was he so foolish? It was running wild after the girls maybe?

MAHON [*with a shout of derision*] Running wild, is it? If he seen a red petticoat coming swinging over the hill, he'd be off to hide in the sticks, and you'd see him shooting out his sheep's eyes between the little twigs and the leaves, and his two ears rising like a hare looking out through a gap. Girls, indeed!

WIDOW QUIN. It was drink maybe?

MAHON. And he a poor fellow would get drunk on the smell of a pint. He'd a queer rotten stomach, I'm telling you, and when I gave him three pulls from my pipe a while since, he was taken with contortions till I had to send him in the ass-cart to the females' nurse.

WIDOW QUIN [*clasping her hands*] Well, I never, till this day, heard tell of a man the like of that!

MAHON. I'd take a mighty oath you didn't, surely, and wasn't he the laughing joke of every female woman where four baronies meet, the way the girls would stop their wedding if they seen him coming the road to let a roar at him, and call him the loony of Mahon's?

WIDOW QUIN. I'd give the world and all to see the like of him. What kind was he?

MAHON. A small, low fellow.

WIDOW QUIN. And dark?

MAHON. Dark and dirty.

WIDOW QUIN [*considering*] I'm thinking I seen him.

MAHON [*eagerly*] An ugly young blackguard.

WIDOW QUIN. A hideous, fearful villain, and the spit of you.

MAHON. Which way is he fled?

WIDOW QUIN. Gone over the hills to catch a coasting steamer to the north or south.

MAHON. Could I pull up on him now?

WIDOW QUIN. If you'll cross the sands below where the tide is out, you'll be in it as soon as himself, for he had to go round ten miles by the top of the bay. [*She points to the door*]. Strike down by the head beyond and then follow on the roadway to the north and east.

Mahon goes abruptly.

WIDOW QUIN [*shouting after him*] Let you give him a good vengeance
when you come up with him, but don't put yourself in the power of
the law, for it'd be a poor thing to see a judge in his black cap
reading out his sentence on a civil warrior the like of you. [*She
swings the door to and looks at Christy, who is cowering in terror, for a
moment, then she bursts into a laugh*]. Well, you're the walking Playboy
of the Western World, and that's the poor man you had divided to
his breeches belt.

CHRISTY [*looking out; then, to her*] What'll Pegeen say when she hears
that story? What'll she be saying to me now?

WIDOW QUIN. She'll knock the head of you, I'm thinking, and drive
you from the door. God help her to be taking you for a wonder, and
you a little schemer making up a story you destroyed your da.

CHRISTY [*turning to the door, nearly speechless with rage, half to himself*]
To be letting on he was dead, and coming back to his life, and
following after me like an old weasel tracing a rat, and coming in
here laying desolation between my own self and the fine women of
Ireland, and he a kind of carcass that you'd fling upon the sea . . .

WIDOW QUIN [*more soberly*] There's talking for a man's one only son.

CHRISTY [*breaking out*] His one son, is it? May I meet him with one
tooth and it aching, and one eye to be seeing seven and seventy
divils in the twists of the road, and one old timber leg on him to
limp into the scalding grave. [*Looking out*]. There he is now crossing
the strands, and that the Lord God would send a high wave to wash
him from the world.

WIDOW QUIN [*scandalized*] Have you no shame? [*Putting her hand on
his shoulder and turning him round*]. What ails you? Near crying, is it?

CHRISTY [*in despair and grief*] Amn't I after seeing the love-light of
the star of knowledge shining from her brow, and hearing words
put you thinking of the holy Brigid speaking to the infant saints,
and now she'll be turning again, and speaking hard words to me,
like an old woman with a spavindy ass she'd have, urging on a hill.

WIDOW QUIN. There's poetry talk for a girl you'd see itching and
scratching, and she with a stale stink of poteen on her from selling
in the shop.

CHRISTY [*impatiently*] It's her like is fitted to be handling merchandise in the heavens above, and what'll I be doing now, I ask you, and I a kind of wonder was jilted by the heavens when a day was by.

There is a distant noise of girls' voices. Widow Quin looks from window and comes to him, hurriedly.

WIDOW QUIN. You'll be doing like myself, I'm thinking, when I did destroy my man, for I'm above many's the day, odd times in geat spirits, abroad in the sunshine, darning a stocking or stitching a shift; and odd times again looking out on the schooners, hookers, trawlers is sailing the sea, and I thinking on the gallant hairy fellows are drifting beyond, and myself long years living alone.

CHRISTY [*interested*] You're like me, so.

WIDOW QUIN. I am your like, and it's for that I'm taking a fancy to you, and I with my little houseen above where there'd be myself to tend you, and none to ask were you a murderer or what at all.

CHRISTY. And what would I be doing if I left Pegeen?

WIDOW QUIN. I've nice jobs you could be doing – gathering shells to make a whitewash for our hut within, building up a little goose-house, or stretching a new skin on an old curagh I have, and if my hut if far from all sides, it's there you'll meet the wisest old men, I tell you, at the corner of my wheel, and it's there yourself and me will have great times whispering and hugging . . .

VOICES [*outside, calling far away*] Christy! Christy Mahon! Christy!

CHRISTY. Is it Pegeen Mike?

WIDOW QUIN. It's the young girls, I'm thinking, coming to bring you to the sports below, and what is it you'll have me to tell them now?

CHRISTY. Aid me to win Pegeen. It's herself only that I'm seeking now. [*Widow Quin gets up and goes to window*]. Aid me for to win her, and I'll be asking God to stretch a hand to you in the hour of death, and lead you short cuts through the Meadows of Ease, and up the floor of heaven to the Footstool of the Virgin's Son.

WIDOW QUIN. There's praying!

VOICES [*nearer*] Christy! Christy Mahon!

CHRISTY [*with agitation*] They're coming! Will you swear to aid and save me, for the love of Christ?

WIDOW QUIN [*looks at him for a moment*] If I aid you, will you swear to give me a right of way I want, and a mountainy ram, and a load of dung at Michaelmas, the time that you'll be master here?

CHRISTY. I will, by the elements and stars of night.

WIDOW QUIN. Then we'll not say a word of the old fellow, the way Pegeen won't know your story till the end of time.

CHRISTY. And if he chances to return again?

WIDOW QUIN. We'll swear he's a maniac, and not your da. I could take an oath I seen him raving on the sands today.

Girls run in.

SUSAN. Come on to the sports below. Pegeen says you're to come.

SARA TANSEY. The lepping's beginning, and we've a jockey's suit to fit upon you for the mule race on the sands below.

HONOR. Come on, will you?

CHRISTY. I will then if Pegeen's beyond.

SARA. She's in the boreen making game of Shaneen Keogh.

CHRISTY. Then I'll be going to her now.

He runs out, followed by the girls.

WIDOW QUIN. Well, if the worst comes in the end of all, it'll be great game to see there's none to pity him but a widow woman, the like of me, has buried her children and destroyed her man.

She goes out.

[CURTAIN]

ACT III

Scene as before. Later in the day. Jimmy comes in, slightly drunk.

JIMMY [*calls*] Pegeen! [*Crosses to inner door*]. Pegeen Mike! [*Comes back again into the room*]. Pegeen! [*Philly comes in in the same state – To Philly*]. Did you see herself?

PHILLY. I did not; but I sent Shawn Keogh with the ass-cart for to bear him home. [*Trying cupboards, which are locked*]. Well, isn't he a nasty man to get into such staggers at a morning wake; and isn't herself the divil's daughter for locking, and she so fussy after that young gaffer, you might take your death with drouth and none to heed you?

JIMMY. It's little wonder she'd be fussy, and he after bringing bankrupt ruin on the roulette man, and the trick-o'-the-loop man, and the breaking the nose of the cockshot-man, and winning all in the sports below, racing, lepping, dancing, and the Lord knows what! He's right luck, I'm telling you.

PHILLY. If he has, he'll be rightly hobbled yet, and he not able to say ten words without making a brag of the way he killed his father, and the great blow he hit with the loy.

JIMMY. A man can't hang by his own informing, and his father should be rotten by now.

Old Mahon passes window slowly.

PHILLY. Supposing a man's digging spuds in that field with a long spade, and supposing he flings up the two halves of that skull, what'll be said then in the papers and the courts of law?

JIMMY. They'd say it was an old Dane, maybe, was drowned in the flood. [*Old Mahon comes in and sits down near door listening*]. Did you never hear tell of the skulls they have in the city of Dublin, ranged out like blue jugs in a cabin of Connaught?

PHILLY. And you believe that?

JIMMY [*pugnaciously*] Didn't a lad see them and he after coming from harvesting in the Liverpool boat? 'They have them there,' says he, 'making a show of the great people there was one time walking the world. White skulls and black skulls and yellow skulls, and some with full teeth, and some haven't only but one.'

PHILLY. It was no lie, maybe, for when I was a young lad there was a graveyard beyond the house with the remnants of a man who had thighs as long as your arm. He was a horrid man, I'm telling you, and there was many a fine Sunday I'd put him together for fun, and he with shiny bones, you wouldn't meet the like of these days in the cities of the world.

MAHON [*getting up*] You wouldn't, is it? Lay your eyes on that skull, and tell me where and when there was another the like of it, is splintered only from the blow of a loy.

PHILLY. Glory be to God! And who hit you at all?

MAHON [*triumphantly*] It was my own son hit me. Would you believe that?

JIMMY. Well, there's wonders hidden in the heart of man!

PHILLY [*suspiciously*] And what way was it done?

MAHON [*wandering about the room*] I'm after walking hundreds and long scores of miles, winning clean beds and the fill of my belly four times in the day, and I doing nothing but telling stories of that naked truth. [*He comes to them a little aggressively*]. Give me a supeen and I'll tell you now.

Widow Quin comes in and stands aghast behind him. He is facing Jimmy and Philly, who are on the left.

JIMMY. Ask herself beyond. She's the stuff hidden in her shawl.

WIDOW QUIN [*coming to Mahon quickly*] You here, is it? You didn't go far at all?

MAHON. I seen the coasting steamer passing, and I got a drouth upon me and a cramping leg, so I said: 'The divil go along with him,' and turned again [*Looking under her shawl*]. And let you give me a supeen, for I'm destroyed travelling since Tuesday was a week.

WIDOW QUIN [*getting a glass, in a cajoling tone*] Sit down then by the fire and take your ease for a space. You've a right to be destroyed indeed, with your walking, and fighting, and facing the sun. [*Giving him poteen from a stone jar she has brought in*]. There now is a drink for you, and may it be to your happiness and length of life.

MAHON [*taking glass greedily, and sitting down by fire*] God increase you!

WIDOW QUIN [*taking men to the right stealthily*] Do you know what? That man's raving from his wound today, for I met him a while since telling a rambling tale of a tinker had him destroyed. Then he heard of Christy's deed, and he up and says it was his son had cracked his skull. Oh, isn't madness a fright, for he'll go killing someone yet, and he thinking it's the man has struck him so?

JIMMY [*entirely convinced*] It's a fright surely. I knew a party was kicked in the head by a red mare, and he went killing horses a great while, till he eat the insides of a clock and died after.

PHILLY [*with suspicion*] Did he see Christy?

WIDOW QUIN. He didn't. [*With a warning gesture*]. Let you not be putting him in mind of him, or you'll be likely summoned if there's murder done. [*Looking round at Mahon*]. Whisht! He's listening. Wait now till you hear me taking him easy and unravelling all. [*She goes to Mahon*]. And what way are you feeling, mister? Are you in contentment now?

MAHON [*slightly emotional from his drink*] I'm poorly only, for it's a hard story the way I'm left today, when it was I did tend him from his hour of birth, and he a dunce never reached his second book, the way he'd come from school, many's the day, with his legs lamed under him, and he blackened with his beatings like a tinker's ass. It's a hard story, I'm saying, the way some do have their next and nighest raising up a hand of murder on them, and some is lonesome getting their death with lamentation in the dead of night.

WIDOW QUIN [*not knowing what to say*] To hear you talking so quiet, who'd know you were the same fellow we seen pass today?

MAHON. I'm the same surely. The wrack and ruin of threescore years; and it's a terror to live that length, I tell you, and to have your sons going to the dogs against you, and you wore out scolding them, and skelping them, and God knows what.

PHILLY [*to Jimmy*] He's not raving. [*To Widow Quin*]. Will you ask him what kind was his son?

WIDOW QUIN [*to Mahon, with a peculiar look*] Was your son that hit you a lad of one year and a score maybe, a great hand at racing and lepping and licking the world?

MAHON [*turning on her with a roar of rage*] Didn't you hear me say he was the fool of men, the way from this out he'll know the orphan's lot, with old and young making game of him, and they swearing, raging, kicking at him like a mangy cur.

A great burst of cheering outside, some way off.

MAHON [*putting his hands to his ears*] What in the name of God do they want roaring below?

WIDOW QUIN [*with the shade of a smile*] They're cheering a young lad, the champion Playboy of the Western World.

More cheering.

MAHON [*going to window*] It'd split my heart to hear them, and I with pulses in my brain-pan for a week gone by. Is it racing they are?

JIMMY [*looking from door*] It is, then. They are mounting him for the mule race will be run upon the sands. That's the playboy on the winkered mule.

MAHON [*puzzled*] That lad, is it? If you said it was a fool he was, I'd have laid a mighty oath he was the likeness of my wandering son. [*Uneasily, putting his hand to his head*]. Faith, I'm thinking I'll go walking for to view the race.

WIDOW QUIN [*stopping him, sharply*] You will not. You'd best take the road to Belmullet, and not be dilly-dallying in this place where there isn't a spot you could sleep.

PHILLY [*coming forward*] Don't mind her. Mount there on the bench and you'll have a view of the whole. They're hurrying before the tide will rise, and it'd be near over if you went down the pathway through the crags below.

MAHON [*mounts on bench, Widow Quin beside him*] That's a right view again the edge of the sea. They're coming now from the point. He's leading. Who is he at all?

WIDOW QUIN. He's the champion of the world, I tell you, and there isn't a ha'p'orth isn't falling lucky to his hands today.

PHILLY [*looking out; interested in the race*] Look at that. They're pressing him now.

JIMMY. He'll win it yet.

PHILLY. Take your time, Jimmy Farrell. It's too soon to say.

WIDOW QUIN [*shouting*] Watch him taking the gate. There's riding.

JIMMY [*cheering*] More power to the young lad!

MAHON. He's passing the third.

JIMMY. He'll lick them yet.

WIDOW QUIN. He'd lick them if he was running races with a score itself.

MAHON. Look at the mule he has, kicking the stars.

WIDOW QUIN. There was a lep! [*Catching hold of Mahon in her excitement*]. He's fallen? He's mounted again! Faith, he's passing them all!

JIMMY. Look at him skelping her!

PHILLY. And the mountain girls hooshing him on!

JIMMY. It's the last turn! The post's cleared for them now!

MAHON. Look at the narrow place. He'll be into the bogs! [*With a yell*]. Good rider! He's through it again!

JIMMY. He's neck and neck!

MAHON. Good boy to him! Flames, but he's in!

Great cheering, in which all join.

MAHON [*with hesitation*] What's that? They're raising him up. They're coming this way. [*With a roar of rage and astonishment*]. It's Christy, by the stars of God! I'd know his way of spitting and he astride the moon.

He jumps down and makes a run for the door, but Widow Quin catches him and pulls him back.

WIDOW QUIN. Stay quiet, will you? That's not your son. [*To Jimmy*]. Stop him, or you'll get a month for the abetting of manslaughter and be fined as well.

JIMMY. I'll hold him.

MAHON [*struggling*] Let me out! Let me out, the lot of you, till I have my vengeance on his head today.

WIDOW QUIN [*shaking him, vehemently*] That's not your son. That's a man is going to make a marriage with the daughter of this house, a place with fine trade, with a licence, and with poteen too.

MAHON [*amazed*] That man marrying a decent and a moneyed girl! Is it mad yous are? Is it in a crazy-house for females that I'm landed now?

WIDOW QUIN. It's mad yourself is with the blow upon your head. That lad is the wonder of the western world.

MAHON. I see it's my son.

WIDOW QUIN. You seen that you're mad. [*Cheering outside*]. Do you hear them cheering him in the zigzags of the road? Aren't you after saying that your son's a fool, and how would they be cheering a true idiot born?

MAHON [*getting distressed*] It's maybe out of reason that that man's himself. [*Cheering again*]. There's none surely will go cheering him. Oh, I'm raving with a madness that would fright the world! [*He sits down with his hand to his head*]. There was one time I seen ten scarlet divils letting on they'd cork my spirit in a gallon can; and one time I seen rats as big as badgers sucking the lifeblood from the butt of my lug; but never till this day confused that dribbling idiot with a likely man. I'm destroyed surely.

WIDOW QUIN. And who'd wonder when it's your brain-pan that is gaping now?

MAHON. Then the blight of the sacred drouth upon myself and him, for I never went mad to this day, and I not three weeks with the Limerick girls drinking myself silly and parlatic from the dusk to dawn. [*To Widow Quin, suddenly*]. Is my visage astray?

WIDOW QUIN. It is, then. You're a sniggering maniac, a child could see.

MAHON [*getting up more cheerfully*] Then I'd best be going to the union beyond, there'll be a welcome before me. I tell you [*with great pride*], and I a terrible and fearful case, the way that there I was one time, screeching in a straightened waistcoat, with seven doctors writing out my sayings in a printed book. Would you believe that?

WIDOW QUIN. If you're a wonder itself, you'd best be hasty, for them lads caught a maniac one time and pelted the poor creature till he ran out, raving and foaming, and was drowned in the sea.

MAHON [*with philosophy*] It's true mankind is the divil when your head's astray. Let me out now and I'll slip down the boreen, and not see them so.

WIDOW QUIN [*showing him out*] That's it. Run to the right, and not a one will see.

He runs off.

PHILLY [*wisely*] You're at some gaming, Widow Quin; but I'll walk after him and give him his dinner and a time to rest, and I'll see then if he's raving or as sane as you.

WIDOW QUIN [*annoyed*] If you go near that lad, let you be wary of your head, I'm saying. Didn't you hear him telling he was crazed at times?

PHILLY. I heard him telling a power; and I'm thinking we'll have right sport before night will fall.

He goes out.

JIMMY. Well, Philly's a conceited and foolish man. How could that madman have his senses and his brain-pan slit? I'll go after them and see him turn on Philly now.

He goes; Widow Quin hides poteen behind counter. Then hubbub outside.

VOICES. There you are! Good jumper! Grand lepper! Darlint boy! He's the racer! Bear him on, will you!

Christy comes in, in jockey's dress, with Pegeen Mike, Sara, and other girls and men.

PEGEEN [*to crowd*] Go on now, and don't destroy him, and he drenching with sweat. Go along, I'm saying, and have your tug-of-warring till he's dried his skin.

CROWD. Here's his prizes! A bagpipes! A fiddle was played by a poet in the years gone by! A flat and three-thorned blackthorn would lick the scholars out of Dublin town!

CHRISTY [*taking prizes from the men*] Thank you kindly, the lot of you. But you'd say it was little only I did this day if you'd seen me a while since striking my one single blow.

TOWN CRIER [*outside ringing a bell*] Take notice, last event of this day! Tug-of-warring on the green below! Come on, the lot of you! Great achievements for all Mayo men!

PEGEEN. Go on and leave him for to rest and dry. Go on, I tell you, for he'll do no more.

She hustles crowd out; Widow Quin following them.

MEN [*going*] Come on, then. Good luck for the while!

PEGEEN [*radiantly, wiping his face with her shawl*] Well, you're the lad, and you'll have great times from this out when you could win that wealth of prizes, and you sweating in the heat of noon!

CHRISTY [*looking at her with delight*] I'll have great times if I win the crowning prize I'm seeking now, and that's your promise that you'll wed me in a fortnight, when our banns is called.

PEGEEN [*backing away from him*] You've right daring to go ask me that, when all knows you'll be starting to some girl in your own townland, when your father's rotten in four months, or five.

CHRISTY [*indignantly*] Starting from you, is it? [*He follows her*]. I will not, then, and when the airs is warming in four months or five, it's then yourself and me should be pacing Neifin in the dews of night, the times sweet smells do be rising, and you'd see a little, shiny new moon, maybe sinking on the hills.

PEGEEN [*looking at him playfully*] And it's that kind of a poacher's love you'd make, Christy Mahon, on the sides of Neifin, when the night is down?

CHRISTY. It's little you'll think if my love's a poacher's or an earl's itself, when you'll feel my two hands stretched around you, and I squeezing kisses on your puckered lips, till I'd feel a kind of pity for the Lord God is all ages sitting lonesome in His golden chair.

PEGEEN. That'll be right fun, Christy Mahon, and any girl would walk her heart out before she'd meet a young man was your like for eloquence, or talk at all.

CHRISTY [*encouraged*] Let you wait, to hear me talking, till we're astray in Erris, when Good Friday's by, drinking a sup from a well, and making mighty kisses with our wetted mouths, or gaming in a gap of sunshine, with yourself stretched back unto your necklace, in the flowers of the earth.

PEGEEN [*in a low voice, moved by his tone*] I'd be nice so, is it?'

CHRISTY [*with rapture*] If the mitred bishops seen you that time, they'd be the like of the holy prophets, I'm thinking, do be straining the bars of paradise to lay eyes on the Lady Helen of Troy, and she abroad, pacing back and forward, with a nosegay in her golden shawl.

PEGEEN [*with real tenderness*] And what is it I have, Christy Mahon, to make me fitting entertainment for the like of you, that has such poet's talking, and such bravery of heart?

CHRISTY [*in a low voice*] Isn't there the light of seven heavens in your heart alone, the way you'll be an angel's lamp to me from this out, and I abroad in the darkness, spearing salmons in the Owen or the Carrowmore?

PEGEEN. If I was your wife I'd be along with you those nights, Christy Mahon, the way you'd see I was a great hand at coaxing bailiffs, or coining funny nicknames for the stars of night.

CHRISTY. You, is it? Taking your death in the hailstones, or in the fogs of dawn.

PEGEEN. Yourself and me would shelter easy in a narrow bush [*with a qualm of dread*]; but we're only talking, maybe, for this would be a poor, thatched place to hold a fine lad is the like of you.

CHRISTY [*putting his arm round her*] If I wasn't a good Christian, it's on my naked knees I'd be saying my prayers and paters to every jackstraw you have roofing your head, and every stony pebble is paving the laneway to your door.

PEGEEN [*radiantly*] If that's the truth I'll be burning candles from this out to the miracles of God that have brought you from the south today, and I with my gowns bought ready, the way that I can wed you, and not wait at all.

CHRISTY. It's miracles, and that's the truth. Me there toiling a long while, and walking a long while, not knowing at all I was drawing all times nearer to this holy day.

PEGEEN. And myself, a girl, was tempted often to go sailing the seas till I'd marry a Jew-man, with ten kegs of gold, and I not knowing at all there was the like of you drawing nearer, like the stars of God.

CHRISTY. And to think I'm long years hearing women talking that talk, to all bloody fools, and this the first time I've heard the like of your voice talking sweetly for my own delight.

PEGEEN. And to think it's me is talking sweetly, Christy Mahon, and I the fright of seven townlands for my biting tongue. Well, the heart's a wonder; and, I'm thinking, there won't be our like in Mayo, for gallant lovers, from this hour today. [*Drunken singing is heard outside*]. There's my father coming from the wake, and when he's had his sleep we'll tell him for he's peaceful then.

They separate.

MICHAEL [*singing outside*]

        The jailer and the turnkey
        They quickly ran us down,

And brought us back as prisoners
Once more to Cavan town

He comes in supported by Shawn.

There we lay bewailing
All in a prison bound . . .

He sees Christy. Goes and shakes him drunkenly by the hand, while Pegeen and Shawn talk on the left.

MICHAEL [*to Christy*] The blessing of God and the holy angels on your head, young fellow. I hear tell you're after winning all in the sports below; and wasn't it a shame I didn't bear you along with me to Kate Cassidy's wake, a fine, stout lad, the like of you, for you'd never see the match of it for flows of drink, the way when we sunk her bones at noonday in her narrow grave, there were five men, aye, and six men, stretched out retching speechless on the holy stones.

CHRISTY [*Uneasily, watching Pegeen*] Is that the truth?

MICHAEL. It is, then; and aren't you a louty schemer to go burying your poor father unbeknownst when you'd a right to throw him on the crupper of a Kerry mule and drive him westwards, like holy Joseph in the days gone by, the way we could have given him a decent burial, and not have him rotting beyond, and not a Christian drinking a smart drop to the glory of his soul?

CHRISTY [*gruffly*] It's well enough he's lying, for the likes of him.

MICHAEL [*slapping him on the back*] Well, aren't you a hardened slayer? It'll be a poor thing for the household man where you go sniffing for a female wife; and [*pointing to Shawn*] look beyond at that shy and decent Christian I have chosen for my daughter's hand, and I after getting the gilded dispensation this day for to wed them now.

CHRISTY. And you'll be wedding them this day, is it?

MICHAEL [*drawing himself up*] Aye. Are you thinking, if I'm drunk itself, I'd leave my daughter living single with a little frisky rascal is the like of you?

PEGEEN [*breaking away from Shawn*] Is it the truth the dispensation's come?

MICHAEL [*triumphantly*] Father Reilly's after reading it in gallous Latin, and 'It's come in the nick of time,' says he; 'so I'll wed them in a hurry, dreading that young gaffer who'd capsize the stars.'

PEGEEN [*fiercely*] He's missed his nick of time, for it's that lad, Christy Mahon, that I'm wedding now.

MICHAEL [*loudly, with horror*] You'd be making him a son to me, and he wet and crusted with his father's blood?

PEGEEN. Aye. Wouldn't it be a bitter thing for a girl to go marrying the like of Shaneen, and he a middling kind of a scarecrow, with no savagery or fine words in him at all?

MICHAEL [*gasping and sinking on a chair*] Oh, aren't you a heathen daughter to go shaking the fat of my heart, and I swamped and drowned with the weight of drink? Would you have them turning on me the way that I'd be roaring to the dawn of day with the wind upon my heart? Have you not a word to aid me, Shaneen? Are you not jealous at all?

SHAWN [*in great misery*] I'd be afeard to be jealous of a man did slay his da.

PEGEEN. Well, it'd be a poor thing to go marrying your like. I'm seeing there's a world of peril for an orphan girl, and isn't it a great blessing I didn't wed you before himself came walking from the west or south?

SHAWN. It's a queer story you'd go picking a dirty tramp up from the highways of the world.

PEGEEN [*playfully*] And you think you're a likely beau to go straying alone with the shiny Sundays of the opening year, when it's sooner on a bullock's liver you'd put a poor girl thinking than on the lily or the rose?

SHAWN. And have you no mind of my weight of passion, and the holy dispensation, and the drift of heifers I'm giving, and the golden ring?

PEGEEN. I'm thinking you're too fine for the like of me, Shawn Keogh of Killakeen, and let you go off till you'd find a radiant lady with droves of bullocks on the plains of Meath, and herself bedizened in the diamond jewelleries of Pharaoh's ma. That'd be your match, Shaneen. So God save you now!

She retreats behind Christy.

SHAWN. Won't you hear me telling you . . .?

CHRISTY [*with ferocity*] Take yourself from this, young fellow, or I'll maybe add a murder to my deeds today.

MICHAEL [*springing up with a shriek*] Murder is it? Is it mad yous are? Would you go making murder in this place, and it piled with poteen for our drink tonight? Go on to the foreshore if it's fighting you want, where the rising tide will wash all traces from the memory of man.

Pushing Shawn towards Christy.

SHAWN [*shaking himself free, and getting behind Michael*] I'll not fight him, Michael James, I'd liefer live a bachelor, simmering in passions to the end of time, than face a lepping savage the like of him has descended from the Lord knows where. Strike him yourself, Michael James, or you'll lose my drift of heifers and my blue bull from Sneem.

MICHAEL. Is it me fight him, when it's father-slaying he's bred to now? [*Pushing Shawn*]. Go on, you fool, and fight him now.

SHAWN [*coming forward a little*] Will I strike him with my hand?

MICHAEL. Take the loy is on your western side.

SHAWN. I'd be afeard of the gallows if I struck with that.

CHRISTY [*taking up the loy*] Then I'll make you face the gallows or quit off from this.

Shawn flies out of the door.

CHRISTY. Well, fine weather be after him [*going to Michael, coaxingly*], and I'm thinking you wouldn't wish to have that quaking blackguard in your house at all. Let you give us your blessing and hear her swear her faith to me, for I'm mounted on the spring-tide of the stars of luck, the way it'll be good for any to have me in the house.

PEGEEN [*at the other side of Michael*] Bless us now, for I swear to God I'll wed him, and I'll not renege.

MICHAEL [*standing up in the centre, holding on to both of them*] It's the will of God, I'm thinking, that all should win an easy or a cruel end, and it's the will of God that all should rear up lengthy families for the nurture of the earth. What's a single man, I ask you, eating a bit in one house and drinking a sup in another, and he with no place of his own, like an old braying jackass strayed upon the rocks? [*To Christy*]. It's many would be in dread to bring your like into their house for to end them, maybe, with a sudden end; but I'm a decent man of Ireland, and I liefer face the grave untimely and I seeing a score of grandsons growing up little gallant swearers by the name of God, than go peopling my bedside with puny weeds the like of what you'd breed, I'm thinking, out of Shaneen Keogh. [*He joins their hands*]. A daring fellow is the jewel of the world, and a man did split his father's middle with a single clout should have the bravery of ten, so may God and Mary and St Patrick bless you, and increase you from this mortal day.

CHRISTY and PEGEEN. Amen, O Lord!

Hubbub outside. Old Mahon rushes in, followed by all the crowd, and Widow Quin. He makes a rush at Christy, knocks him down, and begins to beat him.

PEGEEN [*dragging back his arm*] Stop that, will you? Who are you at all?

MAHON. His father, God forgive me!

PEGEEN [*drawing back*] Is it rose from the dead?

MAHON. Do you think I look so easy quenched with the tap of a loy?

Beats Christy again.

PEGEEN [*glaring at Christy*] And it's lies you told, letting on you had him slitted, and you nothing at all.

CHRISTY [*catching Mahon's stick*] He's not my father. He's a raving maniac would scare the world. [*Pointing to Widow Quin*]. Herself knows it is true.

CROWD. You're fooling, Pegeen! The Widow Quin seen him this day, and you likely knew! You're a liar!

CHRISTY [*dumbfounded*] It's himself was a liar, lying stretched out with an open head on him, letting on he was dead.

MAHON. Weren't you off racing the hills before I got my breath with the start I had seeing you turn on me at all?

PEGEEN. And to think of the coaxing glory we had given him, and he after doing nothing but hitting a soft blow and chasing northward in a sweat of fear. Quit off from this.

CHRISTY [*piteously*] You've seen my doings this day, and let you save me from the old man; for why would you be in such a scorch of haste to spur me to destruction now?

PEGEEN. It's there your treachery is spurring me, till I'm hard set to think you're the one I'm after lacing in my heart-strings half an hour gone by. [*To Mahon*]. Take him on from this, for I think bad the world should see me raging for a Munster liar, and the fool of men.

MAHON. Rise up now to retribution, and come on with me.

CROWD [*jeeringly*] There's the playboy! There's the lad thought he'd rule to roost in Mayo! Slate him now, mister.

CHRISTY [*getting up in shy terror*] What is it drives you to torment me here, when I'd asked the thunders of the might of God to blast me if I ever did hurt to any saving only that one single blow.

MAHON [*loudly*] If you didn't, you're a poor good-for-nothing, and isn't it by the like of you the sins of the whole world are committed?

CHRISTY [*raising his hands*] In the name of the Almighty God . . .

MAHON. Leave troubling the Lord God. Would you have Him sending down droughts, and fevers, and the old hen and the cholera morbus?

CHRISTY [*to Widow Quin*] Will you come between us and protect me now?

WIDOW QUIN. I've tried a lot, God help me, and my share is done.

CHRISTY [*looking round in desperation*] And I must go back into my torment is it, or run off like a vagabond straying through the unions with the dust of August making mudstains in the gullet of my throat; or the winds of March blowing on me till I'd take an oath I felt them making whistles of my ribs within?

SARA. Ask Pegeen to aid you. Her like does often change.

CHRISTY. I will not, then, for there's torment in the splendour of her like, and she a girl any moon of midnight would take pride to meet, facing southwards on the heaths of Keel. But what did I want crawling forward to scorch my understanding at her flaming brow?

PEGEEN [*to Mahon, vehemently, fearing she will break into tears*] Take him on from this or I'll set the young lads to destroy him here.

MAHON [*going to him, shaking his stick*] Come on now if you wouldn't have the company to see you skelped.

PEGEEN [*half laughing, through her tears*] That's it, now the world will see him pandied, and he an ugly liar was playing off the hero, and the fright of men.

CHRISTY [*to Mahon, very sharply*] Leave me go!

CROWD. That's it. Now, Christy. If them two set fighting, it will lick the world.

MAHON [*making a grab at Christy*] Come here to me.

CHRISTY [*more threateningly*] Leave me go, I'm saying.

MAHON I will, maybe, when your legs is limping, and your back is blue.

CROWD. Keep it up, the two of you. I'll back the old one. Now the playboy.

CHRISTY [*in low and intense voice*] Shut your yelling, for if you're after making a mighty man of me this day by the power of a lie, you're setting me now to think if it's a poor thing to be lonesome it's worse, maybe, go mixing with the fools of earth.

Mahon makes a movement towards him.

CHRISTY [*almost shouting*] Keep off . . . lest I do show a blow unto the lot of you would set the guardian angels winking in the clouds above.

He swings round with a sudden rapid movement and picks up a loy.

CROWD [*half frightened, half amused*] He's going mad! Mind yourselves! Run from the idiot!

CHRISTY. If I am an idiot, I'm after hearing my voice this day saying words would raise the top-knot on a poet in a merchant's town. I've won your racing, and your lepping, and . . .

MAHON. Shut your gullet and come on with me.

CHRISTY. I'm going, but I'll stretch you first.

He runs at old Mahon with the loy, chases him out of the door, followed by crowd and Widow Quin. There is a great noise outside, then a yell, and dead silence for a moment. Christy comes in, half dazed, and goes to fire.

WIDOW QUIN [*coming in hurriedly, and going to him*] They're turning again you. Come on, or you'll be hanged, indeed.

CHRISTY. I'm thinking from this out, Pegeen'll be giving me praises, the same as in the hours gone by.

WIDOW QUIN [*impatiently*] Come by the back door. I'd think bad to have you stifled on the gallows tree.

CHRISTY [*indignantly*] I will not, then. What good'd be my lifetime if I left Pegeen?

WIDOW QUIN. Come on, and you'll be no worse than you were last night; and you with a double murder this time to be telling to the girls.

CHRISTY. I'll not leave Pegeen Mike.

WIDOW QUIN [*impatiently*] Isn't there the match of her in every parish public, from Binghamstown unto the plain of Meath? Come on, I tell you, and I'll find you finer sweethearts at each waning moon.

CHRISTY. It's Pegeen I'm seeking only, and what'd I care if you brought me a drift of chosen females, standing in their shifts itself, maybe, from this place to the eastern world?

SARA [*runs in, pulling off one of her petticoats*] They're going to hang him. [*Holding out petticoat and shawl*]. Fit these upon him, and let him run off to the east.

WIDOW QUIN. He's raving now; but we'll fit them on him, and I'll take him in the ferry to the Achill boat.

CHRISTY [*struggling feebly*] Leave me go, will you? when I'm thinking of my luck today, for she will wed me surely, and I a proven hero in the end of all.

They try to fasten petticoat round him.

WIDOW QUIN. Take his left hand and we'll pull him now. Come on, young fellow.

CHRISTY [*suddenly starting up*] You'll be taking me from her? You're jealous, is it, of her wedding me? Go on from this.

He snatches up a stool, and threatens them with it.

WIDOW QUIN [*going*] It's in the madhouse they should put him, not in jail, at all. We'll go by the back door to call the doctor, and we'll save him so.

She goes out, with Sara, through inner room. Men crowd in the doorway. Christy sits down again by the fire.

MICHAEL [*in a terrified whisper*] Is the old lad killed surely?

PHILLY. I'm after feeling the last gasps quitting his heart.

They peer in at Christy.

MICHAEL [*with a rope*] Look at the way he is. Twist a hangman's knot on it, and slip it over his head, while he's not minding at all.

PHILLY. Let you take it, Shaneen. You're the soberest of all that's here.

SHAWN. Is it me to go near him, and he the wickedest and worst with me? Let you take it, Pegeen Mike.

PEGEEN. Come on, so.

She goes forward with the others, and they drop the double hitch over his head.

CHRISTY. What ails you?

SHAWN [*triumphantly, as they pull the rope tight on his arms*] Come on to the peelers, till they stretch you now.

CHRISTY. Me!

MICHAEL. If we took pity on you the Lord God would, maybe, bring us ruin from the law today, so you'd best come easy, for hanging is an easy and a speedy end.

CHRISTY. I'll not stir. [*To Pegeen*]. And what is it you'll say to me, and I after doing it this time in the face of all?

PEGEEN. I'll say, a strange man is a marvel, with his mighty talk; but what's a squabble in your back yard, and the blow of a loy, have taught me that there's a great gap between a gallous story and a dirty deed. [*To men*]. Take him on from this, or the lot of us will be likely put on trial for his deed today.

CHRISTY [*with horror in his voice*] And it's yourself will send me off, to have a horny-figured hangman hitching slip-knots at the butt of my ear.

MEN [*pulling rope*] Come on, will you?

He is pulled down on the floor.

CHRISTY [*twisting his legs round the table*] Cut the rope, Pegeen, and I'll quit the lot of you, and live from this out, like the madman of Keel, eating muck and green weeds on the faces of the cliffs.

PEGEEN. And leave us to hang, is it, for a saucy liar, the like of you? [*To men*]. Take him on, out from this.

SHAWN. Pull a twist on his neck, and squeeze him so.

PHILLY. Twist yourself. Sure he cannot hurt you, if you keep your distance from his teeth alone.

SHAWN. I'm afeard of him. [*To Pegeen*]. Lift a lighted sod, will you, and scorch his leg.

PEGEEN [*blowing the fire with a bellows*] Leave go now, young fellow, or I'll scorch your shins.

CHRISTY. You're blowing for to torture me. [*His voice rising and growing stronger*]. That's your kind, is it? Then let the lot of you be wary, for, if I've to face the gallows, I'll have a gay march down, I tell you, and shed the blood of some of you before I die.

SHAWN [*in terror*] Keep a good hold, Philly. Be wary, for the love of God. For I'm thinking he would liefest wreak his pains on me.

CHRISTY [*almost gaily*] If I do lay my hands on you, it's the way you'll be at the fall of night, hanging as a scarecrow for the fowls of hell. Ah, you'll have a gallous jaunt, I'm saying, coaching out through limbo with my father's ghost.

SHAWN [*to Pegeen*] Make haste, will you? Oh, isn't he a holy terror, and isn't it true for Father Reilly, that all drink's a curse that has the lot of you so shaky and uncertain now?

CHRISTY. If I can wring a neck among you, I'll have a royal judgment looking on the trembling jury in the courts of law. And won't there be crying out in Mayo the day I'm stretched upon the rope, with ladies in their silks and satins snivelling in their lacy kerchiefs, and they rhyming songs and ballads on the terror of my fate?

He squirms round on the floor and bites Shawn's leg.

SHAWN [*shrieking*] My leg's bit on me. He's the like of a mad dog, I'm thinking, the way that I will surely die.

CHRISTY [*delighted with himself*] You will, then, the way you can shake out hell's flags of welcome for my coming in two weeks or three, for I'm thinking Satan hasn't many have killed their da in Kerry, and in Mayo too.

Old Mahon comes in behind on all fours and looks on unnoticed.

MEN [*to Pegeen*] Bring the sod, will you?

PEGEEN [*coming over*] God help him so.

Burns his leg.

CHRISTY [*kicking and screaming*] Oh, glory to be God!

He kicks loose from the table, and they all drag him towards the door.

JIMMY [*seeing old Mahon*] Will you look what's come in?

They all drop Christy and run left.

CHRISTY [*scrambling on his knees face to face with old Mahon*] Are you coming to be killed a third time, or what ails you now?

MAHON. For what is it they have you tied?

CHRISTY. They're taking me to the peelers to have me hanged for slaying you.

MICHAEL [*apologetically*] It is the will of God that all should guard their little cabins from the treachery of law, and what would my daughter be doing if I was ruined or was hanged itself?

MAHON [*grimly, loosening Christy*] It's little I care if you put a bag on her back, and went picking cockles till the hour of death; but my son and myself will be going our own way, and we'll have great times from this out telling stories of the villainy of Mayo, and the fools is here. [*To Christy, who is freed*]. Come on now.

CHRISTY. Go with you, is it? I will then, like a gallant captain with his heathen slave. Go on now and I'll see you from this day stewing my oatmeal and washing my spuds, for I'm master of all fights from now. [*Pushing Mahon*]. Go on, I'm saying.

MAHON. Is it me?

CHRISTY. Not a word out of you. Go on from this.

MAHON [*walking out and looking back at Christy over his shoulder*] Glory be to God! [*With a broad smile*]. I am crazy again.

Goes.

CHRISTY. Ten thousand blessings upon all that's here, for you've turned me a likely gaffer in the end of all, the way I'll go romancing through a romping lifetime from this hour to the dawning of the Judgment Day.

He goes out.

MICHAEL. By the will of God, we'll have peace now for our drinks. Will you draw the porter, Pegeen?

SHAWN [*going up to her*] It's a miracle Father Reilly can wed us in the end of all, and we'll have none to trouble us when his vicious bite is healed.

PEGEEN [*hitting him a box on the ear*] Quit my sight. [*Putting her shawl over her head and breaking out into wild lamentations*]. Oh, my grief, I've lost him surely. I've lost the only Playboy of the Western World.

[CURTAIN]

W. B. YEATS

On Baile's Strand

W. B. Yeats (1865–1939)

William Butler Yeats was born in Sandymont, a suburb of Dublin, 13 June 1865. He was the son of John Butler Yeats, the distinguished painter and man of letters. For three years he studied art and developed an interest in mystic religion and the supernatural. Yeats came under the influence of the Irish literary revival of the 1890's and began to make plans for an Irish theatre and wrote his nationalistic verse plays, *The Countess Cathleen* (1892), *The Land of Heart's Desire* (1894), and the prose drama *Cathleen ni Houlihan* (1902). In 1899 Yeats worked with Lady Gregory to found the Irish Literary Theatre, the group became known in 1902 as the Irish National Theatre Society; and in 1904 it was established in its own building as the Abbey Theatre. Yeats remained an active manager and playwright of the Abbey, encouraging and defending new playwrights, until his death.

At 23, Yeats fell in love with Maude Gonne, a young woman totally committed to the cause of Irish independence. For a short time he became involved in the national movement but, following Gonne's marriage to a political activist, he broke with politics. His three outstanding tragedies are *On Baile's Strand* (1904), *Deirdre* (1907) and *Purgatory* (1939). His other plays include: *At the Hawk's Well* (1917), *The Only Jealousy of Emer* (1919) strongly influenced by Japanese *noh* plays and termed 'Plays for Dancers'. These were followed by one-act verse plays such as *The Dreaming of the Bones* (1919), *Calvary* (1920), *The Cat and the Moon* (1926), *The Resurrection* (1931), *The King of the Great Clock Tower* (1934), *A Full Moon in March* and *The Death of Cuchulain* (1939). His other publications include collections of essays, anthologies and many fine selections of his poetry including *The Wild Swans at Coole* (1917) and *The Winding Stair* (1929). In 1917 Yeats married an Englishwoman, Georgie Hyde-Lees, from 1922–28 he served as a senator in the Irish Free State and in 1923 he was awarded the Nobel Prize for literature. He died in 1939.

On Baile's Strand

The first version of this play was produced at the Abbey Theatre on 27 December 1904. It was performed by the Irish National Theatre Society, with the following cast:

CUCHULAIN	Frank Fay
CONCHUBAR	George Roberts
DAIRE, *an old king*	G. Mac Donald
THE BLIND MAN	Seamus O'Sullivan
THE FOOL	William Fay
THE YOUNG MAN	P. Mac Siubhlaigh

The old and young Kings were played by the following: R. Nash, N. Power, U. Wright, E. Kegan, Emma Vernon, Doreen Gunning, Sara Allgood. Yeats himself, in his *Notes*, gives us further information about the play. He is talking about it, a few months after its first production.

It was revived by the National Theatre Society, Ltd., in a somewhat altered version at Oxford, Cambridge, and London a few months later. I then entirely rewrote it up to the entrance of the Young Man, and changed it a good deal from that on to the end, and this new version was played at the Abbey Theatre in April, 1906. It is now as right as I can make it with my present experience, but it must always be a little over-complicated when played by itself. It is one of a cycle of plays dealing with Cuchulain, with his friends and enemies. One of these plays will have Aoife as its central character, and the principal motive of another will be the power of the witches over Cuchulain's life. The present play is a kind of cross-road where too many interests meet and jostle for the hearer to take them in at a first hearing unless he listens carefully, or knows something of the story of the other plays of the cycle. Mr Herbert Hughes has written the music for the Fool's song in the opening dialogue, and another friend a little tune for the three women. These songs, like all other songs in our plays, are sung so as to preserve as far as possible the intonation and speed of ordinary

passionate speech, for nothing can justify the degradation of an
element of life even in the service of an art. Very little of the words
of the song of the three women can be heard, for they must be for
the most part a mere murmur under the voices of the men. It
seemed right to take some trouble over them, just as it is right to
finish off the statue where it is turned to the wall, and besides there
is always the reader and one's own pleasure.

Joseph Holloway attended the dress rehearsal for the first production on 16 December 1904:

On entering the stage door of the Abbey Theatre, I stepped down
onto the stage and found it set for *On Baile's Strand* and with no
one about – only the stage hands. The effect produced by the
simple and novel setting, I thought, was very good and just the thing
for rich costumed figures to disport themselves before.

Having viewed the scene from the front, I went up to the
gentlemen's dressing room where I found all the actors in the
confusion of dressing for their parts for the first time. The chaos of
the whole thing was delightful to behold. I secured a corner out of
the way and watched the transformation of the company into kings,
warriors and beggars. One propped up a mirror against a barber's
block as he built a whisker round his youthful face, transforming it
into an aged countenance of a king; another wrestled with a tunic
turning the wrong side forward; while others amid a din of 'Where's
my wig?' or 'Where's my cloak?' or 'Did anyone see my helmet?'
kept going hither and thither in the large dressing room until things
began to straighten themselves out and the actors presented a truly
strange sight in the gorgeous, if strange, fantastical robes. Frequent
tappings and inquiries at the door during the enactment of this
scene told that the ladies in a neighbouring dressing room suffered
the same confusion. Such questions as, 'Did you see the Young
Kings' cloaks?' etc., were frequently heard, on the door being partly
opened in answer to the gentle tapping of Mrs Esposito, who kindly
acted as wardrobe mistress to the company and played the part
excellently.

The rehearsal proceeded smoothly, but many of the costumes,
especially those of the old kings and the long, streaky hair worn by

them, were found to border on the grotesque or eccentric, and at
the conclusion of the play the entire company was recalled on the
stage, and an exciting and amusing exchange of difference of
opinion took place between author Yeats and designer Miss Horniman. He with his eye on the effect created as an author, and she as
the designer of the colour scheme of the costumes. Yeats likened
some of the kings to 'extinguishers,' their robes were so long and
sloped so from the shoulders. Father Christmas was another of his
comparisons. He wished the cloaks away, but the lady would have
none of his suggestions. Then commenced a lively scene in which
the actors played the part of lay figures, and Yeats and Miss
Horniman treated them as such in discussing the costumes. The
red-robed kings were told to take off their cloaks, which they did,
and then the green-clad ones followed. After much putting on and
taking off, and an abundance of plain speaking as to the figures or
lack of them among the players, a compromise was arrived at, and
the 'grey fur' on the green costumes was 'made fly,' and the red-
clad kings were allowed to carry their cloaks on their arms, though
Miss Horniman was of opinion that the red unrelieved, somewhat
marred the colour scheme she had intended. . . . Candidly I thought
some of the costumes trying, though all of them were exceedingly
rich in material and archaeologically correct. 'Hang archaeology!'
said the great W. B. Yeats. 'It's effect we want on the stage!' And
that settled it!

(Reprinted in 'The Noble Drama of W. B. Yeats' *by Liam Miller,*
Humanities Press, Atlantic Highlands, 1977.)

Selected Bibliography

Collected Plays, London and New York, Macmillan, 1952; *The Variorum Edition of the Plays of W. B. Yeats*, ed., Russel K. Alspach, London and New York, Macmillan, corrected second printing 1966; *Collected Poems*, London and New York, Macmillan, 1956; *The Variorum Editions of the Poems of W. B. Yeats*, ed., Peter Allt and Russell Alspach, London and New York, Macmillan, corrected third printing 1966. Special reference: 'The Countess Cathleen', London, T. Fisher Unwin, 1892; 'The Shadowy Waters', London, Hodder & Stoughton, 1900; 'Cathleen ni Houlihan', London, A. H. Bullen; 1902; 'The Hour Glass', London, Heinemann, 1903; *'The King's Threshold'* and *'On Baile's Strand'*, London, A. H. Bullen, 1904; *Deirdre*, London, A. H. Bullen; Dublin, Maunsel: 1907; 'At the Hawk's Well' in *The Wild Swans at Coole*, Dundrum, Cuala Press, 1917; *Two Plays for Dancers* ('The Dreaming of the Bones', 'The Only Jealousy of Emer'), Dublin, Cuala Press, 1919; *Plays in Prose and Verse*, New York, Macmillan 1928; 'The Words upon the Windowpane', Dublin, Cuala Press, 1934; 'Fighting the Waves,' in *Wheels and Butterflies*, London, Macmillan, 1934; *Last Poems and Two Plays* ('Purgatory', 'The Death of Cuchulain'), Dublin, Cuala Press, 1939. Other works: *Autobiographies*, London, Macmillan, 1956; *Essays and Introductions*, London, Macmillan, 1961; *Explorations*, London, Macmillan, 1962; *Memoirs*, ed. Denis Donoghue, London, Macmillan, 1972; ed. *Poems and Translations by J. M. Synge*, Dundrum, Cuala Press, 1909; *Uncollected Prose*, I, ed. John P. Frayne; II, ed. John P. Frayne and Colton Johnston, London, Macmillan, 1970, 1975: *Letters*, ed. Allan Wade, London, Macmillan, 1954.

On Baile's Strand

To
William Fay
because of the beautiful
fantasy of his
playing in the character
of the Fool

Persons in the Play

A FOOL
A BLIND MAN
CUCHULAIN, *King of Muirthemne*
CONCHUBAR, *High King of Uladh*
A YOUNG MAN, *son of Cuchulain*
KINGS *and* SINGING WOMEN

On Baile's Strand

A great hall at Dundealgan, not 'Cuchulain's great ancient house' but an assembly-house nearer to the sea. A big door at the back, and through the door misty light as of sea-mist. There are many chairs and one long bench. One of these chairs, which is towards the front of the stage, is bigger than the others. Somewhere at the back there is a table with flagons of ale upon it and drinking-horns. There is a small door at one side of the hall. A Fool and Blind Man, both ragged, and their features made grotesque and extravagant by masks, come in through the door at the back. The Blind Man leans upon a staff.

FOOL. What a clever man you are though you are blind! There's nobody with two eyes in his head that is as clever as you are. Who but you could have thought that the henwife sleeps every day a little at noon? I would never be able to steal anything if you didn't tell me where to look for it. And what a good cook you are! You take the fowl out of my hands after I have stolen it and plucked it, and you put it into the big pot at the fire there, and I can go out and run races with the witches at the edge of the waves and get an appetite, and when I've got it, there's the hen waiting inside for me, done to the turn.

BLIND MAN [*who is feeling about with his stick*]. Done to the turn.

FOOL [*putting his arm round Blind Man's neck*]. Come now, I'll have a leg and you'll have a leg, and we'll draw lots for the wish-bone. I'll be praising you, I'll be praising you while we're eating it, for your good plans and for your good cooking. There's nobody in the world like you, Blind Man. Come, come. Wait a minute. I shouldn't have closed the door. There are some that look for me, and I wouldn't like them not to find me. Don't tell it to anybody, Blind Man. There are some that follow me. Boann herself out of the river and Fand out of the deep sea. Witches they are, and they come by in the wind, and they cry, 'Give a kiss, Fool, give a kiss,' that's what they cry. That's wide enough. All the witches can come in now. I wouldn't have them beat at the door and say, 'Where is the Fool? Why has he put a lock on the door?' Maybe they'll hear the bubbling of the pot and come in and sit on the ground. But we won't give them any of the fowl. Let them go back to the sea, let them go back to the sea.

BLIND MAN [*feeling legs of big chair with his hands*] Ah! [*Then, in a louder voice as he feels the back of it*]. Ah – ah –

FOOL. Why do you say 'Ah-ah'?

BLIND MAN. I know the big chair. It is to-day the High King Conchubar is coming. They have brought out his chair. He is going to be Cuchulain's master in earnest from this day out. It is that he's coming for.

FOOL. He must be a great man to be Cuchulain's master.

BLIND MAN. So he is. He is a great man. He is over all the rest of the kings of Ireland.

FOOL. Cuchulain's master! I thought Cuchulain could do anything he liked.

BLIND MAN. So he did, so he did. But he ran too wild, and Conchubar is coming to-day to put an oath upon him that will stop his rambling and make him as biddable as a housedog and keep him always at his hand. He will sit in this chair and put the oath upon him.

FOOL. How will he do that?

BLIND MAN. You have no wits to understand such things. [*The Blind Man has got into the chair*]. He will sit up in this chair and he'll say: 'Take the oath, Cuchulain. I bid you take the oath. Do as I tell you. What are your wits compared with mine, and what are your riches compared with mine? And what sons have you to pay your debts and to put a stone over you when you die? Take the oath, I tell you. Take a strong oath.'

FOOL [*crumpling himself up and whining*] I will not. I'll take no oath. I want my dinner.

BLIND MAN. Hush, hush! It is not done yet.

FOOL. You said it was done to a turn.

BLIND MAN. Did I, now? Well, it might be done, and not done. The wings might be white, but the legs might be red. The flesh might stick hard to the bones and not come away in the teeth. But, believe me, Fool, it will be well done before you put your teeth in it.

FOOL. My teeth are growing long with the hunger.

BLIND MAN. I'll tell you a story – the kings have story-tellers while they are waiting for their dinner – I will tell you a story with a fight in it, a story with a champion in it, and a ship and a queen's son that has his mind set on killing somebody that you and I know.

FOOL. Who is that? Who is he coming to kill?

BLIND MAN. Wait, now, till you hear. When you were stealing the fowl, I was lying in a hole in the sand, and I heard three men coming with a shuffling sort of noise. They were wounded and groaning.

FOOL. Go on. Tell me about the fight.

BLIND MAN. There had been a fight, a great fight, a tremendous great fight. A young man had landed on the shore, the guardians of the shore had asked his name, and he had refused to tell it, and he had killed one, and others had run away.

FOOL. That's enough. Come on now to the fowl. I wish it was bigger. I wish it was as big as a goose.

BLIND MAN. Hush! I haven't told you all. I know who that young man is. I heard the men who were running away say he had red hair, that he had come from Aoife's country, that he was coming to kill Cuchulain.

FOOL. Nobody can do that.

> [*To a tune*]
> Cuchulain had killed kings,
> Kings and sons of kings,
> Dragons out of the water,
> And witches out of the air,

Banachas and Bonachas and people of the woods.

BLIND MAN. Hush! hush!

FOOL [*still singing*]

> Witches that steal the milk,
> Fomor that steal the children,
> Hags that have heads like hares,

> Hares that have claws like witches,
> All riding a-cock-horse
> [*Spoken*]

Out of the very bottom of the bitter black North.

BLIND MAN. Hush, I say!

FOOL. Does Cuchulain know that he is coming to kill him?

BLIND MAN. How would he know that with his head in the clouds?
He doesn't care for common fighting. Why would he put himself
out, and nobody in it but that young man? Now if it were a white
fawn that might turn into a queen before morning –

FOOL. Come to the fowl. I wish it was as big as a pig; a fowl with
goose grease and pig's crackling.

BLIND MAN. No hurry, no hurry. I know whose son it is. I wouldn't
tell anybody else, but I will tell you, – a secret is better to you than
your dinner. You like being told secrets.

FOOL. Tell me the secret.

BLIND MAN. That young man is Aoife's son. I am sure it is Aoife's
son, it flows in upon me that it is Aoife's son. You have often heard
me talking of Aoife, the great woman-fighter Cuchulain got the
mastery over in the North?

FOOL. I know, I know. She is one of those cross queens that live in
hungry Scotland.

BLIND MAN. I am sure it is her son. I was in Aoife's country for a
long time.

FOOL. That was before you were blinded for putting a curse upon the
wind.

BLIND MAN. There was a boy in her house that had her own red
colour on him, and everybody said he was to be brought up to kill
Cuchulain, that she hated Cuchulain. She used to put a helmet on
a pillar-stone and call it Cuchulain and set him casting at it. There
is a step outside – Cuchulain's step.

Cuchulain passes by in the mist outside the big door.

FOOL. Where is Cuchulain going?

BLIND MAN. He is going to meet Conchubar that has bidden him to
take the oath.

FOOL. Ah, an oath, Blind Man. How can I remember so many things
at once? Who is going to take an oath?

BLIND MAN. Cuchulain is going to take an oath to Conchubar who is High King.

FOOL. What a mix-up you make of everything, Blind Man! You were telling me one story, and now you are telling me another story . . . How can I get the hang of it at the end if you mix everything at the beginning? Wait till I settle it out. There now, there's Cuchulain [*He points to one foot*], and there is the young man [*He points to the other foot*] that is coming to kill him, and Cuchulain doesn't know. But where's Conchubar? [*Takes bag from side*]. That's Conchubar with all his riches – Cuchulain, young man, Conchubar. – And where's Aoife? [*Throws up cap*]. There is Aoife, high up on the mountains in high hungry Scotland. Maybe it is not true after all. Maybe it was your own making up. It's many a time you cheated me before with your lies. Come to the cooking-pot, my stomach is pinched and rusty. Would you have it to be creaking like a gate?

BLIND MAN. I tell you it's true. And more than that is true. If you listen to what I say, you'll forget your stomach.

FOOL. I won't.

BLIND MAN. Listen. I know who the young man's father is, but I won't say. I would be afraid to say. Ah, Fool, you would forget everything if you could know who the young man's father is.

FOOL. Who is it? Tell me now quick, or I'll shake you. Come, out with it, or I'll shake you.

A murmur of voices in the distance.

BLIND MAN. Wait, wait. There's somebody coming . . . It is Cuchulain is coming. He's coming back with the High King. Go and ask Cuchulain. He'll tell you. It's little you'll care about the cooking-pot when you have asked Cuchulain, that . . .

Blind Man goes out by side door.

FOOL. I'll ask him. Cuchulain will know. He was in Aoife's country. [*Goes up stage*]. I'll ask him. [*Turns and goes down stage*]. But, no, I won't ask him, I would be afraid. [*Going up again*]. Yes. I will ask him. What harm in asking? The Blind Man said I was to ask him. [*Going down*]. No, no. I'll not ask him. He might kill me. I have but killed hens and geese and pigs. He has killed kings. [*Goes up again almost to big door*]. Who says I'm afraid? I'm not afraid. I'm no coward. I'll ask him. No, no, Cuchulain, I'm not going to ask you.

He has killed kings,
Kings and the sons of kings,
Dragons out of the water,
And witches out of the air,

Banachas and Bonachas and people of the woods.

*Fool goes out by side door, the last words being heard outside. Cuchulain
and Conchubar enter through the big door at the back. While they are still
outside, Cuchulain's voice is heard raised in anger. He is a dark man,
something over forty years of age. Conchubar is much older and carries a
long staff, elaborately carved or with an elaborate gold handle.*

CUCHULAIN. Because I have killed men without your bidding
And have rewarded others at my own pleasure,
Because of half a score of trifling things,
You'd lay this oath upon me, and now – and now
You add another pebble to the heap,
And I must be your man, well-nigh your bondsman,
Because a youngster out of Aoife's country
Has found the shore ill-guarded.

CONCHUBAR.   He came to land
While you were somewhere out of sight and hearing,
Hunting or dancing with your wild companions.

CUCHULAIN. He can be driven out. I'll not be bound.
I'll dance or hunt, or quarrel or make love,
Wherever and whenever I've a mind to.
If time had not put water in your blood,
You never would have thought it.

CONCHUBAR.   I would leave
A strong and settled country to my children.

CUCHULAIN. And I must be obedient in all things;
Give up my will to yours; go where you please;
Come when you call; sit at the council-board
Among the unshapely bodies of old men;
I whose mere name has kept this country safe,
I that in early days have driven out
Maeve of Cruachan and the northern pirates,
The hundred kings of Sorcha, and the kings
Out of the Garden in the East of the World.

Must I, that held you on the throne when all
Had pulled you from it, swear obedience
As if I were some cattle-raising king?
Are my shins speckled with the heat of the fire,
Or have my hands no skill but to make figures
Upon the ashes with a stick? Am I
So slack and idle that I need a whip
Before I serve you?

CONCHUBAR.   No, no whip, Cuchulain,
But every day my children come and say:
'This man is growing harder to endure.
How can we be at safety with this man
That nobody can buy or bid or bind?
We shall be at his mercy when you are gone;
He burns the earth as if he were a fire,
And time can never touch him.'

CUCHULAIN.   And so the tale
Grows finer yet; and I am to obey
Whatever child you set upon the throne,
As if it were yourself!

CONCHUBAR.   Most certainly.
I am High King, my son shall be High King;
And you for all the wildness of your blood,
And though your father came out of the sun,
Are but a little king and weigh but light
In anything that touches government,
If put into the balance with my children.

CUCHULAIN. It's well that we should speak our minds out plainly,
For when we die we shall be spoken of
In many countries. We in our young days
Have seen the heavens like a burning cloud
Brooding upon the world, and being more
Than men can be now that cloud's lifted up,
We should be the more truthful. Conchubar,
I do not like your children – they have no pith,
No marrow in their bones, and will lie soft
Where you and I lie hard.

CONCHUBAR.   You rail at them
  Because you have no children of your own.
CUCHULAIN. I think myself most lucky that I leave
  No pallid ghost or mockery of a man
  To drift and mutter in the corridors
  Where I have laughed and sung.
CONCHUBAR.   That is not true,
  For all your boasting of the truth between us;
  For there is no man having house and lands,
  That have been in the one family, called
  By that one family's name for centuries,
  But is made miserable if he know
  They are to pass into a stranger's keeping,
  As yours will pass.
CUCHULAIN.   The most of men feel that,
  But you and I leave names upon the harp.
CONCHUBAR. You play with arguments as lawyers do,
  And put no heart in them. I know your thoughts,
  For we have slept under the one cloak and drunk
  From the one wine-cup. I know you to the bone,
  I have heard you cry, aye, in your very sleep,
  'I have no son', and with such bitterness
  That I have gone upon my knees and prayed
  That it might be amended.
CUCHULAIN.   For you thought
  That I should be as biddable as others
  Had I their reason for it; but that's not true;
  For I would need a weightier argument
  Than one that marred me in the copying,
  As I have that clean hawk out of the air
  That, as men say, begot this body of mine
  Upon a mortal woman.
CONCHUBAR.   Now as ever
  You mock at every reasonable hope,
  And would have nothing, or impossible things.
  What eye has ever looked upon the child
  Would satisfy a mind like that?

CUCHULAIN. I would leave
My house and name to none that would not face
Even myself in battle.

CONCHUBAR. Being swift of foot,
And making light of every common chance,
You should have overtaken on the hills.
Some daughter of the air, or on the shore
A daughter of the Country-under-Wave.

CUCHULAIN. I am not blasphemous.

CONCHUBAR. Yet you despise
Our queens, and would not call a child your own,
If one of them had borne him.

CUCHULAIN. I have not said it.

CONCHUBAR. Ah! I remember I have heard you boast,
When the ale was in your blood, that there was one
In Scotland, where you had learnt the trade of war,
That had a stone-pale cheek and red-brown hair;
And that although you had loved other women,
You'd sooner that fierce woman of the camp
Bore you a son than any queen among them.

CUCHULAIN. You call her a 'fierce woman of the camp',
For, having lived among the spinning-wheels,
You'd have no woman near that would not say,
'Ah! how wise!' 'What will you have for supper?'
'What shall I wear that I may please you, sir?'
And keep that humming through the day and night
For ever. A fierce woman of the camp!
But I am getting angry about nothing.
You have never seen her. Ah! Conchubar, had you seen her
With that high, laughing, turbulent head of hers
Thrown backward, and the bowstring at her ear,
Or sitting at the fire with those grave eyes
Full of good counsel as it were with wine,
Or when love ran through all the lineaments
Of her wild body – although she had no child,
None other had all beauty, queen or lover,
Or was so fitted to give birth to kings.

CONCHUBAR. There's nothing I can say but drifts you farther
    From the one weighty matter. That very woman –
    For I know well that you are praising Aoife –
    Now hates you and will leave no subtlety
    Unknotted that might run into a noose
    About your throat, no army in idleness
    That might bring ruin on this land you serve.
CUCHULAIN. No wonder in that, no wonder at all in that.
    I never have known love but as a kiss
    In the mid-battle, and a difficult truce
    Of oil and water, candles and dark night,
    Hillside and hollow, the hot-footed sun
    And the cold, sliding, slippery-footed moon –
    A brief forgiveness between opposites
    That have been hatreds for three times the age
    Of this long-'stablished ground.
CONCHUBAR.   Listen to me.
    Aoife makes war on us, and every day
    Our enemies grow greater and beat the walls
    More bitterly, and you within the walls
    Are every day more turbulent; and yet,
    When I would speak about these things, your fancy
    Runs as it were a swallow on the wind.

*Outside the door in the blue light of the sea-mist are many old and young
Kings; among them are three Women, two of whom carry a bowl of fire. The
third, in what follows, puts from time to time fragrant herbs into the fire so
that it flickers up into brighter flame.*

    Look at the door and what men gather there –
    Old counsellors that steer the land with me,
    And younger kings, the dancers and harp-players
    That follow in your tumults, and all these
    Are held there by the one anxiety.
    Will you be bound into obedience
    And so make this land safe for them and theirs?
    You are but half a king and I but half;
    I need your might of hand and burning heart,
    And you my wisdom.

CUCHULAIN [*going near to door*] Nestling of a high nest,
   Hawks that have followed me into the air
   And looked upon the sun, we'll out of this
   And sail upon the wind once more. This king
   Would have me take an oath to do his will,
   And having listened to his tune from morning,
   I will no more of it. Run to the stable
   And set the horses to the chariot-pole,
   And send a messenger to the harp-players.
   We'll find a level place among the woods,
   And dance awhile.
A YOUNG KING.   Cuchulain, take the oath.
   There is none here that would not have you take it.
CUCHULAIN. You'd have me take it? Are you of one mind?
THE KINGS. All, all, all, all!
A YOUNG KING.   Do what the High King bids you.
CONCHUBAR. There is not one but dreads this turbulence
   Now that they're settled men.
CUCHULAIN.   Are you so changed,
   Or have I grown more dangerous of late?
   But that's not it. I understand it all.
   It's you that have changed. You've wives and children now,
   And for that reason cannot follow one
   That lives like a bird's flight from tree to tree. –
   It's time the years put water in my blood
   And drowned the wildness of it, for all's changed,
   But what unchanged – I'll take what oath you will:
   The moon, the sun, the water, light, or air,
   I do not care how binding.
CONCHUBAR.   On this fire
   That has been lighted from your hearth and mine;
   The older men shall be my witnesses,
   The younger, yours. The holders of the fire
   Shall purify the thresholds of the house
   With waving fire, and shut the outer door,
   According to the custom; the sing rhyme.
   That has come down from the old law-makers

To blow the witches out. Considering
That the wild will of man could be oath-bound,
But that a woman's could not, they bid us sing
Against the will of woman as its wildest
In the Shape-Changers that run upon the wind.
Conchubar has gone on to his throne.

THE WOMEN [*They sing in a very low voice after the first few words so
that the others all but drown their words*]
                    May this fire have driven out
                    The Shape-Changers that can put
                    Ruin on a great king's house
                    Until all be ruinous.
                    Names whereby a man has known
                    The threshold and the hearthstone,
                    Gather on the wind and drive
                    The women none can kiss and thrive,
                    For they are but whirling wind,
                    Out of memory and mind.
                    They would make a prince decay
                    With light images of clay
                    Planted in the running wave;
                    Or, for many shapes they have,
                    They would change them into hounds
                    Until he had died of his wounds,
                    Though the change were but a whim;
                    Or they'd hurl a spell at him,
                    That he follow with desire
                    Bodies that can never tire
                    Or grow kind, for they anoint
                    All their bodies, joint by joint,
                    With a miracle-working juice
                    That is made out of the grease
                    Of the ungoverned unicorn.
                    But the man is thrice forlorn,
                    Emptied, ruined, wracked, and lost,
                    That they follow, for at most
                    They will give him kiss for kiss

> While they murmur, 'After this
> Hatred may be sweet to the taste'.
> Those white hands that have embraced
> All his body can but shove
> At the burning wheel of love
> Till the side of hate comes up.
> Therefore in this ancient cup
> May the sword-blades drink their fill
> Of the home-brew there, until
> They will have for masters none
> But the threshold and hearthstone.

CUCHULAIN [*speaking, while they are singing*] I'll take and keep this
    oath, and from this day
  I shall be what you please, my chicks, my nestlings.
  Yet I had thought you were of those that praised
  Whatever life could make the pulse run quickly,
  Even though it were brief, and that you held
  That a free gift was better than a forced –
  But that's all over – I will keep it, too;
  I never gave a gift and took it again.
  If the wild horse should break the chariot-pole,
  It would be punished. Should that be in the oath?

*Two of the Women, still singing, crouch in front of him holding the bowl
over their heads. He spreads his hands over the flame.*

  I swear to be obedient in all things
  To Conchubar, and to uphold his children.

CONCHUBAR. We are one being, as these flames are one:
  I give my wisdom, and I take your strength.
  Now thrust the swords into the flame, and pray
  That they may serve the threshold and the hearthstone
  With faithful service.

*The Kings kneel in a semicircle before the two Women and Cuchulain,
who thrusts his sword into the flame. They all put the points of their swords
into the flame. The third Woman is at the back near the big door.*

CUCHULAIN.   O pure, glittering ones
  That should be more than wife or friend or mistress,

Give us the enduring will, the unquenchable hope,
The friendliness of the sword! –

*The song grows louder, and the last words ring out clearly. There is a loud
knocking at the door, and a cry of* 'Open! open!'.

CONCHUBAR. Some king that has been loitering on the way.
Open the door, for I would have all know
That the oath's finished and Cuchulain bound,
And that the swords are drinking up the flame.

*The door is opened by the third Woman, and a Young Man with a drawn
sword enters.*

YOUNG MAN. I am of Aoife's country.

The Kings rush towards him. Cuchulain throws himself between.

CUCHULAIN.   Put up your swords.
He is but one. Aoife is far away.

YOUNG MAN. I have come alone into the midst of you
To weigh this sword against Cuchulain's sword.

CONCHUBAR. And are you noble? for if of common seed,
You cannot weigh your sword against his sword
But in mixed battle.

YOUNG MAN.   I am under bonds
To tell my name to no man; but it's noble.

CONCHUBAR. But I would know your name and not your bonds.
You cannot speak in the Assembly House,
If you are not noble.

FIRST OLD KING.   Answer the High King!

YOUNG MAN. I will give no other proof than the hawk gives
That it's no sparrow!

He is silent for a moment, then speaks to all.

                              Yet look upon me, kings.
I, too, am of that ancient seed, and carry
The signs about this body and in these bones.

CUCHULAIN. To have shown the hawk's grey feather is enough,
And you speak highly, too. Give me that helmet.
I'd thought they had grown weary sending champions.
That sword and belt will do. This fighting's welcome.
The High King there has promised me his wisdom;
But the hawk's sleepy till its well-beloved

Cries out amid the acorns, or it has seen
Its enemy like a speck upon the sun.
What's wisdom to the hawk, when that clear eye
Is burning nearer up in the high air?
Looks hard at Young Man; then comes down steps and grasps Young Man
by shoulder.
Hither into the light.
[*To Conchubar*].   The very tint
Of her that I was speaking of but now.
Not a pin's difference.
[*To Young Man*].   You are from the North,
Where there are many that have that tint of hair –
Red-brown, the light red-brown. Come nearer, boy,
For I would have another look at you.
There's more likeness – a pale, stone-pale cheek.
What brought you, boy? Have you no fear of death?

YOUNG MAN. Whether I live or die is in the gods' hands.

CUCHULAIN. That is all words, all words; a young man's talk.
I am their plough, their harrow, their very strength;
For he that's in the sun begot this body
Upon a mortal woman, and I have heard tell
It seemed as if he had outrun the moon
That he must follow always through waste heaven,
He loved so happily. He'll be but slow
To break a tree that was so sweetly planted.
Let's see that arm. I'll see it if I choose.
That arm had a good father and a good mother,
But it is not like this.

YOUNG MAN.   You are mocking me;
You think I am not worthy to be fought.
But I'll not wrangle but with this talkative knife.

CUCHULAIN. Put up your sword; I am not mocking you.
I'd have you for my friend, but if it's not
Because you have a hot heart and a cold eye,
I cannot tell the reason.
[*To Conchubar*].   He has got her fierceness,
And nobody is as fierce as those pale women.

But I will keep him with me, Conchubar,
That he may set my memory upon her
When the day's fading – You will stop with us,
And we will hunt the deer and the wild bulls;
And, when we have grown weary, light our fires
Between the wood and water, or on some mountain
Where the Shape-Changers of the morning come.
The High King there would make a mock of me
Because I did not take a wife among them.
Why do you hang your head? It's a good life:
The head grows prouder in the light of the dawn,
And friendship thickens in the murmuring dark
Where the spare hazels meet the wool-white foam.
But I can see there's no more need for words
And that you'll be my friend from this day out.

CONCHUBAR. He has come hither not in his own name
But in Queen Aoife's, and has challenged us
In challenging the foremost man of us all.

CUCHULAIN. Well, well, what matter?

CONCHUBAR.   You think it does not matter,
And that a fancy lighter than the air,
A whim of the moment, has more matter in it.
For, having none that shall reign after you,
You cannot think as I do, who would leave
A throne too high for insult.

CUCHULAIN.   Let your children
Re-mortar their inheritance, as we have,
And put more muscle on – I'll give you gifts,
But I'd have something too – that arm-ring, boy.
We'll have this quarrel out when you are older.

YOUNG MAN. There is no man I'd sooner have my friend
Than you, whose name has gone about the world
As if it has been the wind, but Aoife'd say
I had turned coward.

CUCHULAIN.   I will give you gifts
That Aoife'll know, and all her people know,
To have come from me.   [Showing cloak].

My father gave me this.
He came to try me, rising up at dawn
Out of the cold dark of the rich sea.
He challenged me to battle, but before
My sword had touched his sword, told me his name,
Gave me this cloak, and vanished. It was woven
By women of the Country-under-Wave
Out of the fleeces of the sea. O! tell her
I was afraid, or tell her what you will.
No; tell her that I heard a raven croak
On the north side of the house, and was afraid.

CONCHUBAR. Some witch of the air has troubled Cuchulain's mind.

CUCHULAIN. No witchcraft. His head is like a woman's head
I had a fancy for.

CONCHUBAR.   A witch of the air
Can make a leaf confound us with memories.
They run upon the wind and hurl the spells
That make us nothing, out of the invisible wind.
They have gone to school to learn the trick of it.

CUCHULAIN. No, no — there's nothing out of common here;
The winds are innocent — That arm-ring, boy.

A KING. If I've your leave I'll take this challenge up.

ANOTHER KING. No, give it me, High King, for this wild Aoife
Has carried off my slaves.

ANOTHER KING.   No, give it me,
For she has harried me in house and herd.

ANOTHER KING. I claim this fight.

OTHER KINGS [together].   And I! And I! And I!

CUCHULAIN. Back! back! Put up your swords! Put up your swords!
There's none alive that shall accept a challenge
I have refused. Laegaire, put up your sword!

YOUNG MAN. No, let them come. If they've a mind for it,
I'll try out with any two together.

CUCHULAIN. That's spoken as I'd have spoken it at your age.
But you are in my house. Whatever man
Would fight with you shall fight it out with me.
They're dumb, they're dumb. How many of you would meet

[Draws sword].

This mutterer, this old whistler, this sand-piper,
This edge that's greyer than the tide, this mouse
That's gnawing at the timbers of the world,
This, this – Boy, I would meet them all in arms
If I'd a son like you. He would avenge me
When I have withstood for the last time the men
Whose fathers, brothers, sons, and friends I have killed
Upholding Conchubar, when the four provinces
Have gathered with the ravens over them.
But I'd need no avenger. You and I
Would scatter them like water from a dish.

YOUNG MAN. We'll stand by one another from this out.
Here is the ring.

CUCHULAIN.   No, turn and turn about.
But my turn's first because I am the older.
[Spreading out cloak].
Nine queens out of the Country-under-Wave
Have woven it with the fleeces of the sea
And they were long embroidering at it. – Boy,
If I had fought my father, he'd have killed me,
As certainly as if I had a son
And fought with him, I should be deadly to him;
For the old fiery fountains are far off
And every day there is less heat o' the blood.

CONCHUBAR [*in a loud voice*] No more of this. I will not have this
friendship.
Cuchulain is my man, and I forbid it.
He shall not go unfought, for I myself –

CUCHULAIN. I will not have it.

CONCHUBAR.   You lay commands on me?

CUCHULAIN [*seizing Conchubar*] You shall not stir, High King. I'll
hold you there.

CONCHUBAR. Witchcraft has maddened you.

THE KINGS [*shouting*].   Yes, witchcraft! witchcraft!

FIRST OLD KING. Some witch has worked upon your mind,
Cuchulain.

The head of that young man seemed like a woman's
You'd had a fancy for. Then of a sudden
You laid your hands on the High King himself!

CUCHULAIN. And laid my hands on the High King himself?

CONCHUBAR. Some witch is floating in the air above us.

CUCHULAIN. Yes, witchcraft! witchcraft! Witches of the air!

[*To Young Man*]. Why did you? Who was it set you to this work?

Out, out! I say, for now it's sword on sword!

YOUNG MAN. But . . . but I did not.

CUCHULAIN.   Out, I say, out, out!

Young Man goes out followed by Cuchulain. The Kings follow them out with confused cries, and words one can hardly hear because of the noise. Some cry, 'Quicker, quicker!' 'Why are you so long at the door?' 'We'll be too late!' 'Have they begun to fight?' 'Can you see if they are fighting?' *and so on. Their voices drown each other. The three Women are left alone.*

FIRST WOMAN. I have seen, I have seen!

SECOND WOMAN.   What do you cry aloud?

FIRST WOMAN. The Ever-living have shown me what's to come.

THIRD WOMAN. How? Where?

FIRST WOMAN.   In the ashes of the bowl.

SECOND WOMAN. While you were holding it between your hands?

THIRD WOMAN. Speak quickly!

FIRST WOMAN.   I have seen Cuchulain's roof-tree
Leap into fire, and the walls split and blacken.

SECOND WOMAN. Cuchulain has gone out to die.

THIRD WOMAN.   O! O!

SECOND WOMAN. Who could have thought that one so great as he
Should meet his end at this unnoted sword!

FIRST WOMAN. Life drifts between a fool and a blind man
To the end, and nobody can know his end.

SECOND WOMAN. Come, look upon the quenching of this greatness.

The other two go to the door, but they stop for a moment upon the threshold and wail.

FIRST WOMAN. No crying out, for there'll be need of cries
And rending of the hair when it's all finished.

The Women go out. There is the sound of clashing swords from time to time during what follows.

Enter the Fool, dragging the Blind Man.

FOOL. You have eaten it, you have eaten it! You have left me nothing but the bones.

He throws Blind Man down by big chair.

BLIND MAN. O, that I should have to endure such a plague! O, I ache all over! O, I am pulled to pieces! This is the way you pay me all the good I have done you.

FOOL. You have eaten it! You have told me lies. I might have known you had eaten it when I saw your slow, sleepy walk. Lie there till the kings come. O, I will tell Conchubar and Cuchulain and all the kings about you!

BLIND MAN. What would have happened to you but for me, and you without your wits? If I did not take care of you, what would you do for food and warmth?

FOOL. You take care of me? You stay safe, and send me into every kind of danger. You sent me down the cliff for gulls' eggs while you warmed your blind eyes in the sun; and then you ate all that were good for food. You left me the eggs that were neither egg nor bird. [*Blind Man tries to rise; Fool makes him lie down again*]. Keep quiet now, till I shut the door. There is some noise outside – a high vexing noise, so that I can't be listening to myself. [*Shuts the big door*]. Why can't they be quiet? Why can't they be quiet? [*Blind Man tries to get away*]. Ah! you would get away, would you? [*Follows Blind Man and brings him back.*] Lie there! lie there! No, you won't get away! Lie there till the kings come. I'll tell them all about you. I will tell it all. How you sit warming yourself, when you have made me light a fire of sticks, while I sit blowing it with my mouth. Do you not always make me take the windy side of the bush when it blows, and the rainy side when it rains?

BLIND MAN. O, good Fool! listen to me. Think of the care I have taken of you. I have brought you to many a warm hearth, where there was a good welcome for you, but you would not stay there; you were always wandering about.

FOOL. The last time you brought me in, it was not I who wandered away, but you that got put out because you took the crubeen out of the pot when nobody was looking. Keep quiet, now!

CUCHULAIN [*rushing in*] Witchcraft! There is no witchcraft on the earth, or among the witches of the air, that these hands cannot break.

FOOL. Listen to me, Cuchulain. I left him turning the fowl at the fire. He ate it all, though I had stolen it. He left me nothing but the feathers.

CUCHULAIN. Fill me a horn of ale!

BLIND MAN. I gave him what he likes best. You do not know how vain this Fool is. He likes nothing so well as a feather.

FOOL. He left me nothing but the bones and feathers. Nothing but the feathers, though I had stolen it.

CUCHULAIN. Give me that horn. Quarrels here, too! [*Drinks*]. What is there between you two that is worth a quarrel? Out with it!

BLIND MAN. Where would he be but for me? I must be always thinking – thinking to get food for the two of us, and when we've got it, if the moon is at the full or the tide on the turn, he'll leave the rabbit in the snare till it is full of maggots, or let the trout slip back through his hands into the stream.

The Fool has begun singing while the Blind Man is speaking.

FOOL [*singing*]

> When you were an acorn on the tree-top,
>   Then was I an eagle-cock;
> Now that you are a withered old block,
>   Still am I an eagle-cock.

BLIND MAN. Listen to him, now. That's the sort of talk I have to put up with day out, day in.

The Fool is putting the feathers into his hair. Cuchulain takes a handful of feathers out of a heap the Fool has on the bench beside him, and out of the Fool's hair, and begins to wipe the blood from his sword with them.

FOOL. He has taken my feathers to wipe his sword. It is blood that he is wiping from his sword.

CUCHULAIN [*goes up to door at back and throws away feathers*] They are standing about his body. They will not awaken him, for all his witchcraft.

BLIND MAN. It is that young champion that he has killed. He that came out of Aoife's country.

CUCHULAIN. He thought to have saved himself with witchcraft.

FOOL. That Blind Man there said he would kill you. He came from Aoife's country to kill you. That Blind Man said they had taught him every kind of weapon that he might do it. But I always knew that you would kill him.

CUCHULAIN [to the Blind Man] You knew him, then?

BLIND MAN. I saw him, when I had my eyes, in Aoife's country.

CUCHULAIN. You were in Aoife's country?

BLIND MAN. I knew him and his mother there.

CUCHULAIN. He was about to speak of her when he died.

BLIND MAN. He was a queen's son.

CUCHULAIN. What queen? what queen? [Seizes Blind Man, who is now sitting upon the bench]. Was it Scathach? There were many queens. All the rulers there were queens.

BLIND MAN. No, not Scathach.

CUCHULAIN. It was Uathach, then? Speak! speak!

BLIND MAN. I cannot speak; you are clutching me too tightly. [Cuchulain lets him go]. I cannot remember who it was. I am not certain. It was some queen.

FOOL. He said a while ago that the young man was Aoife's son.

CUCHULAIN. She? No! no! She had no son when I was there.

FOOL. That Blind Man there said that she owned him for her son.

CUCHULAIN. I had rather he had been some other woman's son. What father had he? A soldier out of Alba? She was an amorous woman – a proud, pale, amorous woman.

BLIND MAN. None knew whose son he was.

CUCHULAIN. None knew! Did you know, old listener at doors?

BLIND MAN. No, no; I knew nothing.

FOOL. He said a while ago that he heard Aoife boast that she'd never but the one lover, and he the only man that had overcome her in battle.   [Pause].

BLIND MAN. Somebody is trembling, Fool! The bench is shaking. Well are you trembling? Is Cuchulain going to hurt us? It was not I who told you, Cuchulain.

FOOL. It is Cuchulain who is trembling. It is Cuchulain who is shaking the bench.

BLIND MAN. It is his own son he has slain.

CUCHULAIN. 'Twas they that did it, the pale windy people.
Where? where? where? My sword against the thunder!
But no, for they have always been my friends;
And though they love to blow a smoking coal
Till it's all flame, the wars they blow aflame
Are full of glory, and heart-uplifting pride,
And not like this. The wars they love awaken
Old fingers and the sleepy strings of harps.
Who did it then? Are you afraid? Speak out!
For I have put you under my protection,
And will reward you well. Dubthach the Chafer?
He'd an old grudge. No, for he is with Maeve.
Laegaire did it! Why do you not speak?
What is this house? [*Pause*]. Now remember all.
Comes before Comchubar's chair, and strikes out with his sword, as if Conchubar was sitting upon it.
'Twas you who did it – you who sat up there
With your old rod of kinship, like a magpie
Nursing a stolen spoon. No, not a magpie,
A maggot that is eating up the earth!
Yes, but a magpie, for he's flown away.
Where did he fly to?

BLIND MAN. He is outside the door.

CUCHULAIN. Outside the door?

BLIND MAN. Between the door and the sea.

CUCHULAIN. Conchubar, Conchubar! the sword into your heart!
He rushes out. Pause. Fool creeps up to the big door and looks after him.

FOOL. He is going up to King Conchubar. They are all about the young man. No, no, he is standing still. There is a great wave going to break, and he is looking at it. Ah! now he is running down to the sea, but he is holding up his sword as if he were going into a fight. [*Pause*]. Well struck! well struck!

BLIND MAN. What is he doing now?

FOOL. O! he is fighting the waves!

BLIND MAN. He sees King Conchubar's crown on every one of them.

FOOL. There, he has struck at a big one! He has struck the crown off it; he has made the foam fly. There again, another big one!

BLIND MAN. Where are the kings? What are the kings doing?

FOOL. They are shouting and running down to the shore, and the people are running out of the houses. They are all running.

BLIND MAN. You say they are running out of the houses? There will be nobody left in the houses. Listen, Fool!

FOOL. There, he is down! He is up again. He is going out in the deep water. There is a big wave. It has gone over him. I cannot see him now. He has killed kings and giants, but the waves have mastered him, the waves have mastered him!

BLIND MAN. Come here, Fool!

FOOL. The waves have mastered him.

BLIND MAN. Come here!

FOOL. The waves have mastered him.

BLIND MAN. Come here, I say.

FOOL [coming towards him, but looking backwards towards the door]. What is it?

BLIND MAN. There will be nobody in the houses. Come this way; come quickly! The ovens will be full. We will put our hands into the ovens. [They go out].

SEAN O'CASEY

The Silver Tassie

Sean O'Casey (1880–1964)

Sean O'Casey was born in Dublin in 1880. The youngest of thirteen children, he never went to school but taught himself to read at the age of fourteen, becoming successively a newspaper-seller, docker, stone-breaker, railway-worker and builder's labourer. In 1913 he helped to organise the Irish Citizen Army and wrote for *The Irish Worker*. The production at the Abbey Theatre of his early plays translated his experiences into art and brought him international acclaim. Among his later works are the plays, *The Silver Tassie, Red Roses for Me, Cock-a-Doodle Dandy* and *The Drums of Father Ned*. Like many other great Irish writers, Sean O'Casey was an exile from Ireland, living for many years in Devon, where he died in 1964.

The Silver Tassie

The Silver Tassie was first produced at the Apollo Theatre, London, on 11 October 1929. Included in the cast were: Charles Laughton as Harry Heegan, Barry Fitzgerald as Sylvester Heegan, and Sidney Morgan as Simon Norton. The performance was directed by Raymond Massey and the set was designed by Gladys Calthorp and Augustus John (Act II).

The Silver Tassie marked the end of O'Casey's close association with the Abbey Theatre. The play was rejected by W. B. Yeats, on behalf of the Abbey, and so it became the first of O'Casey's plays to be published before it received a production – a pattern which was to continue throughout his life and a situation which, as an experimental playwright, he was to find frustrating and inhibiting. Eventually the play was taken up by the producer C. B. Cochran and opened at the Apollo.

The rejection of the play by W. B. Yeats prompted a lively correspondence with O'Casey, which was published in the *Observer* 3 June 1928 and reprinted with further comments by the other Abbey directors and O'Casey in the *Irish Statesman* in June. The exchange demonstrates the impact of what O'Casey described as the 'curse of the Abbey's rejection'. Yeats first wrote to O'Casey turning down the play in April 1928:

My dear Casey ... I had looked forward with great hope and excitement to reading your play, and not merely because of my admiration for your work, for I bore in mind that the Abbey owed its recent prosperity to you. If you had not brought us your plays just at that moment I doubt if it would now exist. I read the first act with admiration, I thought it was the best first act you had written, and told a friend that you had surpassed yourself. The next night I read the second and third acts, and tonight I have read the fourth. I am sad and discouraged; you have no subject. You were interested in the Irish Civil War, and at every moment of those plays wrote out of your own amusement with life or your sense of its tragedy;

you were excited, and we all caught your excitement; you were exasperated almost beyond endurance by what you had seen or heard, as a man is by what happens under his window, and you moved us as Swift moved his contemporaries.

But you are not interested in the great war; you never stood on its battlefields or walked its hospitals, and so write out of your opinions. You illustrate those opinions by a series of almost unrelated scenes, as you might in a leading article; there is no dominating character, no dominating action, neither psychological unity nor unity of action; and your great power of the past has been the creation of some unique character who dominated all about him and was himself a main impulse in some action that filled the play from beginning to end.

The mere greatness of the world war has thwarted you; it has refused to become mere background, and obtrudes itself upon the stage as so much dead wood that will not burn with the dramatic fire. Dramatic action is a fire that must burn up everything but itself; there should be no room in a play for anything that does not belong to it; the whole history of the world must be reduced to wallpaper in front of which the characters must pose and speak.

Among the things that dramatic action must burn up are the author's opinions; while he is writing he has no business to know anything that is not a portion of that action. Do you suppose for one moment that Shakespeare educated Hamlet and King Lear by telling them what he thought and believed? As I see it, Hamlet and Lear educated Shakespeare, and I have no doubt that in the process of that education he found out that he was an altogether different man to what he thought himself, and had altogether different beliefs. A dramatist can help his characters to educate him by thinking and studying everything that gives them the language they are groping for through his hands and eyes, but the control must be theirs, and that is why the ancient philosophers thought a poet or dramatist Daimon-possessed. . . .

W. B. Yeats, letter to Sean O'Casey, 20 April 1928

O'Casey was determined to weather the storm of this rejection in the full glare of publicity:

Lady Gregory in her kind way again enclosed portion of a letter from W. B. Yeats which unfolds the suggestion that the directorate would be willing to allow me to 'withdraw for revision and let that be known to the Press saying that he himself has become dissatisfied and had written to ask it back'. This to save my dignity and to deliver me from the curse of the Abbey's rejection when dealing with an English Manager. If W. B. Yeats had known me as faintly as he thinks he knows me well, he wouldn't have wasted his time – and mine – making such a suggestion. I am too big for this sort of mean and petty shuffling, this lousy perversion of the truth. There is going to be no damned secrecy with me surrounding the Abbey's rejection of the play. Does he think that I would practice in my life the prevarication and wretchedness that I laugh at in my plays?

O'Casey, letter to Lennox Robinson, 2 May 1928

The play's reception in London was overshadowed by its history:

Cochran's production of *The Silver Tassie* . . . was of the utmost significance for Sean. He was desperately anxious to vindicate his work of the shame of rejection. But he knew the *Tassie* was open to adverse criticism, that he had broken some of the traditional rules of dramaturgy, that he had completely altered mood and style with his symbolic and satirical second act, and had ignored continuity and convention. Before we started rehearsals he said to me with a twinkle in those poor, weak eyes, 'I can be of no help to you with the second act, but I do believe that the play will act well when you get it on its feet'. He was right. With the aid of an inspired cast and contributions from several talents in the art world, *The Silver Tassie* achieved a triumph at its opening . . . George Bernard Shaw summed it up in his tribute to a fellow Irishman, 'It's a hell of a play!' he shouted as he stood with cheering first-nighters.

Raymond Massey,
letter to *The Sean O'Casey Review*, IV 2 (1978)

Lady Gregory saw the production and wrote in her *Journals*: 'we ought to have taken it and done our best to put it on.' Charles

Morgan, who reviewed the play for *The Times* (12 October 1929) was equally convinced:

> Many years may pass before Mr O'Casey's art ceases to produce confusion in the mind of an audience accustomed by long theatrical usage to consistency of mood. Hitherto it has commonly been demanded of a play that it be tragic, or that it be comic, or, if by profession a tragi-comedy, that the contrasted elements should remain distinct, the one appearing as a 'relief' to the other. This theory Mr O'Casey has definitely abandoned, and has substituted for it another, still very unfamiliar in the theatre, though having its now recognised counterpart in the novels of Mr Aldous Huxley. We are no longer invited to give attention to one aspect of life and to consider it dominant for the time being. The unity of the work of art is no longer to depend upon the consistency of its material. Instead, as if the drama were being rolled over and tossed in air before our eyes like a diamond, we are so to observe its facets of tragedy, comedy, and open farce that their flashing becomes at last one flash and perhaps, by imaginative and symbolic transition, one spiritual light. Unity is to spring from diversity. The elements of drama are to be compounded – not separated, not mixed.
>
> Mr O'Casey's experimental practice of this theory is of absorbing interest, and it is not less interesting because he has not perfected it. Of even greater value is his attempt to break free from the bonds of naturalism by the bold use of verse. . . .
>
> Mr O'Casey's attempt to make his play take wings from naturalistic earth succeeds; we move in a new plane of imagination. Yet the scene is not a masterpiece. The elements are not truly compounded ... And more important and more disastrous is the discovery, which we begin to make as the scene advances, that the greater part of its effect springs from the setting, the leaning crucifix, the shadowy gun, the grouping of the men, and the rhythm of language – the rhythm of language, not the substance of it. Though the use of poetry has lifted the play from earth to dream, the poetry itself has not force enough to sustain so great a suspense. The scene is filled with a kind of wonder. It is, in the theatre, a new wonder; it is exciting and, at intervals, moving; but little proceeds

from it. Mr O'Casey has not been able to give a full answer to his own challenge.

The other acts are more limited in their range. They are not, as the second act is, a brilliant failure that might have been the core of a masterpiece. But in them also Mr O'Casey is working at his proper experiment, twirling his diamond, leaping suddenly from a music-hall turn at a telephone to a transcendental dialogue between a blind man and a cripple. . . . This method of compression does not and cannot yield the full, naturalistic portraits that arise from drama of a different kind . . . But the method and not the drawing of character is the central interest of this play. It is rash; it is extravagant; it fails sometimes with a great tumbling failure. But it is a method with a future.

The Times 12 October 1929

And George Bernard Shaw had no reservations:

Whitehall Court
London

Charles B. Cochran
Apollo Theatre
London

My dear Cochran,

I really must congratulate you on *The Silver Tassie* before it passes into the classical repertory. It is a magnificent play; and it was a magnificent gesture of yours to produce it. The highbrows should have produced it; you, the unpretentious showman, did, as you have done so many other noble and rash things on your Sundays. This, I think, will rank as the best of them. I hope you have not lost too much by it, especially as I am quite sure you have done your best in that direction by doing the thing as extravagantly as possible. That is the worst of operating on your colossal scale; you haven't time to economise; and you lose the habit of thinking it worth while.

No matter! a famous achievement. There is a new drama rising from unplumbed depths to sweep the nice little bourgeois efforts of myself and my contemporaries into the dustbin; and your name will live as that of the man who didn't run away. If only someone would build you a huge Woolworth Theatre (all seats 6*d*) to start with O'Casey and O'Neill, and no plays by men who had ever seen a £5 note before they were 30 or been inside a school after they were 13, you would be buried in Westminster Abbey. Bravo!

G.B.S.
(from *The Times*, 26 Nov 1929)

In 1972, when the play was revived at the Abbey, its initial rejection was a live issue still:

Whatever one's reaction to *The Silver Tassie*, no one who is deeply interested in the theatre will dispute the validity of Sean O'Casey's final comment on the rejection of his play: 'Dramatists cannot go on imitating themselves, and when they get tired of that, imitating others. They must change, must experiment, must develop their power, or try to, if the drama is to live.' Brecht would have agreed with that; and so, too, would the seemingly placid Lady Gregory who as long ago as 1914 had written: 'The desire to experiment is like fire in the blood.' This possibility was the reason why, of the three directors concerned, she was waveringly on the side of the rejected playwright. But for Sean O'Casey and the Abbey Theatre, things were never quite the same again.

Gabriel Fallon,
programme note to the Abbey Theatre revival, 1972

Selected Bibliography

The Complete Plays of Sean O'Casey 1. London: Macmillan, 1984. [*Juno and the Paycock, The Shadow of a Gunman, The Plough and the Stars, The End of the Beginning, A Pound on Demand*.] *The Complete Plays of Sean O'Casey 2*. London: Macmillan, 1984. [*The Silver Tassie, Within the Gates, The Star Turns Red*.] *The Complete Plays of Sean O'Casey 3*. London: Macmillan, 1984. [*Purple Dust, Red Roses for Me, Hall of Healing*.] *The Complete Plays of Sean O'Casey 4*. London: Macmillan, 1984. [*Oak Leaves and Lavender, Cock-a-Doodle Dandy, Bedtime Story, Time to Go*.] *The Complete Plays of Sean O'Casey 5*. London: Macmillan, 1984. [*The Bishop's Bonfire, The Drums of Father Ned, Behind the Green Curtains, Figuro in the Night, The Moon Shines on Kylenamoe, The Harvest Festival, Kathleen Listens In, Nannie's Night Out*.]

The Silver Tassie

A Tragi-Comedy in Four Acts
STAGE VERSION

To
Eileen
with the yellow daffodils
in the green vase

Notes

The Croucher's make-up should come as close as possible to a death's head, a skull; and his hands should show like those of a skeleton's. He should sit somewhere *above* the group of Soldiers; preferably to one side, on the left, from view-point of audience, so as to overlook the Soldiers. He should look languid, as if very tired of life.

The group of Soldiers – Scene Two – should enter in a close mass, as if each was keeping the other from falling, utterly weary and tired out. They should appear as if they were almost locked together.

The Soldiers' last response to the Staff Wallah's declaration, namely, 'To the Guns!' should have in these three words the last high notes of 'The Last Post'.

The song sung at the end of the play should be given to the best two (or one) singers in the cast. If, on the other hand, there be no passable singer among the players, the song should be omitted.

Perhaps a more suitable Spiritual than 'Sweet Chariot' would be chosen for Harry to sing. For instance, 'Keep Inchin' Along', or 'Keep Me from Sinkin' Down.'

The Chants in the play are simple Plain Song. The first chant is given in full as an example of the way in which they are sung. In the others, the dots . . . indicate that the note preceding them should be sustained till the music indicates a change. There are three parts in each chant; the Intonation; the Meditation; and the Ending. After a little practice, they will be found to be easy to sing. The Soldiers having the better voices should be selected to intone the chants, irrespective of the numbers allotted to them as characters in the book of the play.

Persons in the Play

(As they appear)

SYLVESTER HEEGAN
MRS HEEGAN, *his wife*
SIMON NORTON
SUSIE MONICAN
MRS FORAN
TEDDY FORAN, *her husband*
HARRY HEEGAN, D.C.M., *Heegan's son*
JESSIE TAITE
BARNEY BAGNAL
THE CROUCHER
1ST SOLDIER
2ND SOLDIER
3RD SOLDIER
4TH SOLDIER
THE CORPORAL
THE VISITOR
THE STAFF WALLAH
1ST STRETCHER-BEARER
2ND STRETCHER-BEARER
1ST CASUALTY
2ND CASUALTY
SURGEON FORBY MAXWELL
THE SISTER OF THE WARD

ACT   I. – Room in Heegan's home.
ACT II. – Somewhere in France (*later on*).
ACT III. – Ward in a Hospital (*a little later on*).
ACT IV. – Room in Premises of Avondale Football Club
                (*later on still*).

ACT I

The eating, sitting, and part sleeping room of the Heegan family. A large window at back looks on to a quay, from which can be seen the centre mast of a steamer, at the top of which gleams a white light. Another window at right looks down on a side street. Under the window at back, plump in the centre, is a stand, the legs gilded silver and the top gilded gold; on the stand is a purple velvet shield on which are pinned a number of silver medals surrounding a few gold ones. On each side of the shield is a small vase holding a bunch of artificial flowers. The shield is draped with red and yellow ribbons. To the left of the stand is a bed covered with a bedspread of black striped with vivid green. To the right of the stand is a dresser and chest of drawers combined. The fireplace is to the left. Beside the fireplace is a door leading to a bedroom, another door which gives access to the rest of the house and the street, on the right. At the corner left is a red coloured stand resembling an easel, having on it a silver-gilt framed picture photograph of Harry Heegan in football dress, crimson jersey with yellow collar and cuffs and a broad yellow belt, black stockings, and yellow football boots. A table on which are a half-pint bottle of whisky, a large parcel of bread and meat sandwiches, and some copies of English illustrated magazines.

Sylvester Heegan and Simon Norton are sitting by the fire. Sylvester Heegan is a stockily built man of sixty-five; he has been a docker all his life since first the muscles of his arms could safely grip a truck, and even at sixty-five the steel in them is only beginning to stiffen.

Simon Norton is a tall man, originally a docker too, but by a little additional steadiness, a minor effort towards self-education, a natural, but very slight superior nimbleness of mind, has risen in the Company's estimation and has been given the position of checker, a job entailing as many hours of work as a docker, almost as much danger, twice as much responsibility, and a corresponding reduction in his earning powers. He is not so warmly, but a little more circumspectly dressed than Sylvester, and in his manner of conduct and speech there is a hesitant suggestion of greater refinement than in those of Sylvester, and a semi-conscious sense of superiority, which Simon sometimes forgets, is shown frequently by a complacent stroking of a dark beard which years are beginning to humiliate. The night is cold, and Simon and Sylvester occasionally stretch longingly towards the fire. They are fully dressed and each has his topcoat and hat beside him, as if ready to go out at a moment's notice. Susie Monican is standing at the table polishing a Lee-Enfield rifle with a chamois cloth; the butt of the rifle is resting on the table. She is a girl of twenty-two, well-shaped limbs, challenging breasts, all of which are defiantly hidden by a rather long dark blue skirt and bodice buttoning up to the throat, relieved by a crimson scarf around her neck, knotted in front and falling down her bosom like a man's tie. She is undeniably pretty, but her charms are almost completely hidden by her sombre, ill-fitting dress, and the rigid manner in which she has made her hair up declares her unflinching and uncompromising modesty. Just now she is standing motionless, listening intently, looking towards the door on right.

Mrs Heegan is standing at the window at right, listening too, one hand pulling back the curtains, but her attention, taken from the window, is attracted to the door. She is older than Sylvester, stiffened with age and rheumatism; the end of her life is unknowingly lumbering towards a rest: the impetus necessity has given to continual toil and striving is beginning to slow down, and everything she has to do is done with a quiet mechanical persistence. Her inner ear cannot hear even a faint echo of a younger day. Neither Sylvester nor Simon has noticed the attentive attitude of Mrs Heegan or Susie, for Sylvester, with one arm outstretched crooked at the elbow, is talking with subdued intensity to Simon.

SYLVESTER. I seen him do it, mind you. I seen him do it.

SIMON. I quite believe you, Sylvester.

SYLVESTER. Break a chain across his bisseps! [*With pantomime action*]. Fixes it over his arm . . . bends it up . . . a little strain . . . snaps in two . . . right across his bisseps!

SUSIE. Shush you, there!

Mrs Heegan goes out with troubled steps by door. The rest remain still for a few moments.

SYLVESTER. A false alarm.

SIMON. No cause for undue anxiety; there's plenty of time yet.

SUSIE [*chanting as she resumes the polishing of gun*]:
Man walketh in a vain shadow, and disquieteth himself in vain:
He heapeth up riches, and cannot tell who shall gather them.

She sends the chant in the direction of Sylvester and Simon, Susie coming close to the two men and sticking an angry face in between them.

SUSIE. When the two of yous stand quiverin' together on the dhread day of the Last Judgment, how will the two of yous feel if yous have nothin' to say but 'he broke a chain across his bisseps'? Then the two of you'll know that the wicked go down into hell, an' all the people who forget God!

She listens a moment, and leaving down the rifle, goes out by door left.

SYLVESTER. It's persecutin', that tambourine theology of Susie's. I always get a curious, sickenin' feelin', Simon, when I hear the Name of the Supreme Bein' tossed into the quietness of a sensible conversation.

SIMON. The day he won the Cross Country Championship of County Dublin, Syl, was a day to be chronicled.

SYLVESTER. In a minor way, yes, Simon. But the day that caps the chronicle was the one when he punched the fear of God into the heart of Police Constable 63 C under the stars of a frosty night on the way home from Terenure.

SIMON. Without any exaggeration, without any exaggeration, mind you, Sylvester, that could be called a memorable experience.

SYLVESTER. I can see him yet [*he gets up, slides from side to side, dodging and parrying imaginary blows*] glidin' round the dazzled Bobby, cross-ey'd tryin' to watch him.

SIMON [*tapping his pipe resolutely on the hob*] Unperturbed, mind you, all the time.

SYLVESTER. An' the hedges by the road-side standin' stiff in the silent cold of the air, the frost beads on the branches glistenin' like toss'd-down diamonds from the breasts of the stars, the quietness of the night stimulated to a fuller stillness by the mockin' breathin' of Harry, an' the heavy, ragin' pantin' of the Bobby, an' the quickenin' beats of our own hearts afraid, of hopin' too little or hopin' too much.

During the last speech by Sylvester, Susie has come in with a bayonet, and has commenced to polish it.

SUSIE. We don't go down on our knees often enough; that's why we're not able to stand up to the Evil One: we don't go down on our knees enough . . . I can hear some persons fallin' with a splash of sparks into the lake of everlastin' fire . . . An account of every idle word shall be given at the last day.

She goes out again with rifle.

SUSIE [*bending towards Simon and Sylvester as she goes*] God is listenin' to yous; God is listenin' to yous!

SYLVESTER. Dtch, dtch, dtch. People ought to be forcibly restrained from constant cannonadin' you with the name of the Deity.

SIMON. Dubiety never brush'd a thought in my mind, Syl, while I was waiting' for the moment when Harry would stretch the Bobby hors dee combaa on the ground.

SYLVESTER [*resuming his pantomime actions*] There he was staggerin', beatin' out blindly, every spark of energy panted out of him, while Harry feinted, dodg'd, side-stepp'd, then suddenly sail'd in an' put him asleep with . . .

SIMON. A right-handed hook to the jaw! ⎫
SYLVESTER. A left-handed hook to the jaw! ⎬ [*together*].
⎭

SYLVESTER [*after a pause*] A left-handed hook to the jaw, Simon.

SIMON. No, no, Syl, a right-handed hook to the jaw.

Mrs Foran runs quickly in by the door with a frying-pan in her hand, on which is a steak. She comes to the fire, pushing, so as to disturb the two men. She is one of the many gay, careworn women of the working-class.

MRS FORAN [*rapidly*] A pot of clothes is boilin' on the fire above, an' I knew yous wouldn't mind me slappin' a bit of a steak on here for a second to show him, when he comes in before he goes away, that we're mindful of his needs, an' I hopeful of a dream to-night that the sea's between us, not lookin' very haggard in the mornin' to find the dream a true one. [*With satisfied anticipation*].

For I'll be single again, yes, I'll be single again;
An' I eats what I likes, . . . an' I drinks what I likes,
An' I likes what I likes, when I'm –

[*Stopping suddenly*]. What's the silence for?

SYLVESTER [*slowly and decidedly*] I was at the fight, Simon, an' I seen him givin' a left-handed hook to the jaw.

MRS FORAN. What fight?

SIMON [*slowly and decidedly*] I was there too, an' I saw him down the Bobby with a right-handed hook to the jaw.

MRS FORAN. What Bobby?   [*A pause*].

SYLVESTER. It was a close up, an' I don't know who'd know better if it wasn't the boy's own father.

MRS FORAN. What boy . . . what father?

SYLVESTER. Oh, shut up, woman, an' don't be smotherin' us with a shower of questions.

SUSIE [*who has entered on the last speech, and has started to polish a soldier's steel helmet*] Oh, the miserableness of them that don't know the things that belong unto their peace. They try one thing after another, they try everything, but they never think of trying God. [*Coming nearer to them*]. Oh, the happiness of knowing that God's hand has pick'd you out for heaven. [*To Mrs Foran*]. What's the honey-pot kiss of a lover to the kiss of righteousness and peace?
Mrs Foran, embarrassed, goes over to the window.

SUSIE [*turning to Simon*] Simon, will you not close the dandy door of the public-house and let the angels open the pearly gates of heaven for you?

SYLVESTER. We feel very comfortable where we are, Susie.

SUSIE. Don't mock, Sylvester, don't mock. You'd run before a great wind, tremble in an earthquake, and flee from a fire; so don't treat lightly the still, small voice calling you to repentance and faith.

SYLVESTER [*with appeal and irritation*] Oh, do give over worryin' a man, Susie.

SUSIE. God shows His love by worrying, and worrying, and worrying the sinner. The day will come when you will call on the mountains to cover you, and then you'll weep and gnash your teeth that you did not hearken to Susie's warning. [*Putting her hands appealingly on his shoulders*]. Sylvester, if you pray long enough, and hard enough, and deep enough, you'll get the power to fight and conquer Beelzebub.

MRS FORAN. I'll be in a doxological mood tonight, not because the kingdom of heaven'll be near me, but because my husband'll be far away, and tomorrow [*singing*]:

I'll be single again, yes, single again;
An' I goes where I likes, an' I does what I likes,
An' I likes what I likes now I'm single again!

SIMON. Go on getting Harry's things ready, Susie, and defer the dosing of your friends with canticles till the time is ripe with rest for them to listen quietly.

Simon and Sylvester are very self-conscious during Susie's talk to them. Simon empties his pipe by tapping the head on the hob of the grate. He then blows through it. As he is blowing through it, Sylvester is emptying his by tapping it on the hob; as he is blowing it Simon taps his again; as Simon taps Sylvester taps with him, and then they look into the heads of the pipes and blow together.

SUSIE. It must be mercy or it must be judgement: if not mercy today it may be judgement tomorrow. He is never tired of waiting and waiting and waiting; and watching and watching and watching; and knocking and knocking and knocking for the sinner – you, Sylvester, and you, Simon – to turn from his wickedness and live. Oh, if the two of you only knew what it was to live! Not to live leg-staggering an' belly-creeping among the pain-spotted and sin-splashed desires of the flesh; but to live, oh, to live swift-flying from a holy peace to a holy strength, and from holy strength to a holy joy, like the flashing flights of a swallow in the deep beauty of a summer sky.

Simon and Sylvester shift about, self-conscious and uneasy.

SUSIE [*placing her hand first on Simon's shoulder and then on Sylvester's*] The two of you God's elegant swallows; a saved pair; a loving pair strong-wing'd, freed from the gin of the snarer, tip of wing to tip of wing, flying fast or darting swift together to the kingdom of heaven.

SIMON [*expressing a protecting thought to Sylvester*] One of the two of us should go out and hunt back the old woman from the perishing cold of watching for the return of Harry.

SYLVESTER. She'll be as cold as a naked corpse, an' unstinted watchin' won't bring Harry back a minute sooner. I'll go an' drive her back. [*He rises to go*]. I'll be back in a minute, Susie.

SIMON [*hurriedly*] Don't bother, Syl, I'll go; she won't be farther than the corner of the street; you go on toasting yourself where you are. [*He rises*]. I'll be back in a minute, Susie.

MRS FORAN [*running to the door*] Rest easy the two of you, an' I'll go, so as to give Susie full time to take the sin out of your bones an' put you both in first-class form for the kingdom of heaven.

She goes out.

SUSIE. Sinners that jeer often add to the glory of God: going out, she gives you, Sylvester, and you, Simon, another few moments, precious moments – oh, how precious, for once gone, they are gone for ever – to listen to the warning from heaven.

SIMON [*suddenly*] Whisht, here's somebody coming, I think?

SYLVESTER. I'll back this is Harry comin' at last.

A pause as the three listen.

SYLVESTER. No, it's nobody.

SIMON. Whoever it was's gone by.

SUSIE. Oh, Syl, oh, Simon, don't try to veil the face of God with an evasion. You can't, you can't cod God. This may be your last chance before the pains of hell encompass the two of you. Hope is passing by; salvation is passing by, and glory arm-in-arm with her. In the quietness left to you go down on your knees and pray that they come into your hearts and abide with you for ever . . . [*With fervour, placing her left hand on Simon's shoulder and her right hand on Sylvester's, and shaking them*]. Get down on your knees, get down on your knees, get down on your knees and pray for conviction of sin, lest your portion in David become as the portion of the Canaanites, the Amorites, the Perizzites and the Jebusites!

SYLVESTER. Eh, eh, Susie; cautious now – you seem to be forgettin' yourself.

SIMON. Desist, Susie, desist. Violence won't gather people to God. It only engenders hostility to what you're trying to do.

SYLVESTER. You can't batter religion into a man like that.

SIMON. Religion is love, but that sort of thing is simply a nullification of religion.

SUSIE. Bitterness and wrath in exhortation is the only hope of rousing the pair of yous into a sense of coming and everlasting penalties.

SYLVESTER. Well, give it a miss, give it a miss to me now. Don't try to claw me into the kingdom of heaven. An' you only succeed in distempering piety when you try to mangle it into a man's emotions.

SIMON. Heaven is all the better, Susie, for being a long way off.

SYLVESTER. If I want to pray, I do it voluntarily, but I'm not going to be goaded an' goaded into it.

SUSIE. I go away in a few days to help to nurse the wounded, an' God's merciful warnings may depart along with me, then sin'll usher the two of you into Gehenna for all eternity. Oh, if the two of you could only grasp the meaning of the word eternity! [*Bending down and looking up into their faces*]. Time that had no beginning and never can have an end – an' there you'll be – two cockatrices creeping together, a desolation, an astonishment, a curse and a hissing from everlasting to everlasting.   [*She goes into room*].

SYLVESTER. Cheerful, what! Cockatrices – be-God, that's a good one, Simon!

SIMON. Always a trying thing to have to listen to one that's trying to push the kingdom of God into a reservation of a few yards.

SYLVESTER. A cockatrice! Now where did she manage to pick up that term of approbation, I wonder?

SIMON. From the Bible. An animal somewhere mentioned in the Bible, I think, that a serpent hatched out of a cock's egg.

SYLVESTER. A cock's egg! It couldn't have been the egg of an ordinary cock. Not the male of what we call a hen?

SIMON. I think so.

SYLVESTER. Well, be-God, that's a good one! You know Susie'll have to be told to disintensify her soul-huntin', for religion even isn't an excuse for saying that a man'll become a cockatrice.

SIMON. In a church, somehow or other, it seems natural enough, and even in the street it's alright, for one thing is as good as another in the wide-open ear of the air, but in the delicate quietness of your own home it, it –

SYLVESTER. Jars on you!

SIMON. Exactly!

SYLVESTER. If she'd only confine her glory-to-God business to the festivals, Christmas, now, or even Easter, Simon, it would be recommendable; for a few days before Christmas, like the quiet raisin' of a curtain, an' a few days after, like the gentle lowerin' of one, there's nothing more . . . more –

SIMON. Appropriate . . .

SYLVESTER. Exhilaratin' than the singin' of the Adestay Fidellis.

SIMON. She's damned pretty, an' if she dressed herself justly, she'd lift some man's heart up, an' toss down many another. It's a mystery now, what affliction causes the disablement, for most women of that kind are plain, an' when a woman's born plain she's born good. I wonder what caused the peculiar bend in Susie's nature? Narrow your imagination to the limit and you couldn't call it an avocation.

SYLVESTER [giving the head of his pipe a sharp, quick blow on the palm of his hand to clear it] Adoration.

SIMON. What?

SYLVESTER. Adoration, Simon, accordin' to the flesh . . . She fancied Harry and Harry fancied Jessie, so she hides her rage an' loss in the love of a scorchin' Gospel.

SIMON. Strange, strange.

SYLVESTER. Oh, very curious, Simon.

SIMON. It's a problem, I suppose.

SYLVESTER. An inconsolable problem, Simon.

Mrs Foran enters by door, helping in Mrs Heegan, who is pale and shivering with cold.

MRS HEEGAN [shivering and shuddering] U-u-uh, I feel the stream of blood that's still trickling through me old veins icifyin' fast; u-uh.

MRS FORAN. Madwoman, dear, to be waitin' out there on the quay an' a wind risin' as cold as a stepmother's breath, piercin' through your old bones, mockin' any effort a body would make to keep warm, an' [suddenly rushing over to the fireplace in an agony of dismay, scattering Simon and Sylvester, and whipping the frying-pan off the fire]. – The steak, the steak; I forgot the blasted steak an' onions fryin' on the fire! God Almighty, there's not as much as a bead of juice left in either of them. The scent of the burnin' would penetrate to the street, an' not one of you'd stir a hand to lift them out of danger. Oh, look at the condition they're in. Even the gospel-gunner couldn't do a little target practice by helpin' the necessity of a neighbour. [As she goes out]. I can hear the love for your neighbours almost fizzlin' in your hearts.

MRS HEEGAN [*pushing in to the fire, to Simon and Sylvester*] Push to the right and push to the left till I get to the fosterin' fire. Time eatin' his heart out, an' no sign of him yet. The two of them, the two of my legs is numb ... an' the wind's risin' that'll make the sea heave an' sink under the boat tonight, under shaded lights an' the submarines about. [*Susie comes in, goes over to window, and looks out*]. Hours ago the football match must have been over, an' no word of him yet, an' all drinkin' if they won, an' all drinkin' if they lost; with Jessie hitchin' on after him, an' no one thinkin' of me an' the maintenance money.

SYLVESTER. He'll come back in time; he'll have to come back; he must come back.

SIMON. He got the goals, Mrs Heegan, that won the last two finals, and it's only fair he'd want to win this, which'll mean that the Cup won before two –

SYLVESTER [*butting in*] Times hand runnin'.

SIMON. Two times consecutively before, makin' the Cup the property of the Club.

SYLVESTER. Exactly.

MRS HEEGAN. The chill's residin' in my bones, an' feelin's left me just the strength to shiver. He's overstayed his leave a lot, an' if he misses now the tide that's waitin', he skulks behind desertion from the colours.

SUSIE. On Active Service that means death at dawn.

MRS HEEGAN. An' my governmental money grant would stop at once.

SUSIE. That would gratify Miss Jessie Taite, because you put her weddin' off with Harry till after the duration of the war, an' cut her out of the allowances.

SYLVESTER [*with a sickened look at Simon*] Dtch, dtch, dtch, the way the women wag the worst things out of happenings! [*To the women*]. My God Almighty, he'll be back in time an' fill yous all with disappointment.

MRS HEEGAN. She's coinin' money workin' at munitions, an' doesn't need to eye the little that we get from Harry; for one evening hurryin' with him to the pictures she left her bag behind, an' goin' through it what would you think I found?

SUSIE. A saucy book, now, or a naughty picture?

MRS HEEGAN. Lion and Unicorn standin' on their Jew ay mon draw. With all the rings an' dates, an' rules an' regulations.

SIMON. What was it, Mrs Heegan?

MRS HEEGAN. Spaced an' lined; signed an' signatured; nestlin' in a blue envelope to keep it warm.

SYLVESTER [*testily*] Oh, sing it out, woman, an' don't be takin' the value out of what you're goin' to tell us.

MRS HEEGAN. A Post Office Savings Bank Book.

SYLVESTER. Oh, hairy enough, eh?

SIMON. How much, Mrs Heegan?

MRS HEEGAN. Pounds an' shillings with the pence missin'; backed by secrecy, an' security guaranteed by Act of Parliament.

SYLVESTER [*impatiently*] Dtch, dtch. Yes, yes, woman, but how much was it?

MRS HEEGAN. Two hundred an' nineteen pounds, sixteen shillings, an' no pence.

SYLVESTER. Be-God, a nice little nest egg, right enough!

SUSIE. I hope in my heart that she came by it honestly, and that she remembers that it's as true now as when it was first spoken that it's harder for a camel to go through the eye of a needle than for a rich person to enter the kingdom of heaven.

SIMON. And she hidin' it all under a veil of silence, when there wasn't the slightest fear of any of us bein' jealous of her.

A tumult is heard on the floor over their heads, followed by a crash of breaking delf. They are startled, and listen attentively.

MRS HEEGAN [*breaking the silence*] Oh, there he's at it again. An' she sayin' that he was a pattern husband since he came home on leave, merry-making with her an' singin' dolorously the first thing every mornin'. I was thinkin' there'd be a rough house sometime over her lookin' so well after his long absence ... you'd imagine now, the trenches would have given him some idea of the sacredness of life!

Another crash of breaking delfware.

MRS HEEGAN. An' the last week of his leave she was too fond of breakin' into song in front of him.

SYLVESTER. Well, she's gettin' it now for goin' round heavin' her happiness in the poor man's face.

A crash, followed by screams from Mrs Foran.

SUSIE. I hope he won't be running down here as he often does.

SIMON [*a little agitated*] I couldn't stay here an' listen to that; I'll go up and stop him: he might be killing the poor woman.

MRS HEEGAN. Don't do anything of the kind, Simon; he might down you with a hatchet or something.

SIMON. Phuh, I'll keep him off with the left and hook him with the right. [*Putting on his hat and coat as he goes to the door*]. Looking prim and careless'll astonish him. Monstrous to stay here, while he may be killing the woman.

MRS HEEGAN [*to Simon as he goes out*] For God's sake mind yourself, Simon.

SYLVESTER [*standing beside closed door on right with his ear close to one of the panels, listening intently*] Simon's a tidy little man with his fists, an' would make Teddy Foran feel giddy if he got home with his left hook. [*Crash*]. I wonder is that Simon knockin' down Foran, or Foran knockin' down Simon?

MRS HEEGAN. If he came down an' we had the light low, an' kept quiet, he might think we were all out.

SYLVESTER. Shush. I can hear nothin' now. Simon must have awed him. Quiet little man, but when Simon gets goin'. Shush? No, nothin' . . . Something unusual has happened. O, oh, be-God!

The door against which Sylvester is leaning bursts suddenly in. Sylvester is flung headlong to the floor, and Mrs Foran, her hair falling wildly over her shoulders, a cut over her eye, frantic with fear, rushes in and scrambles in a frenzy of haste under the bed. Mrs Heegan, quickened by fear, runs like a good one, followed by Susie, into the room, the door of which they bang after them. Sylvester hurriedly fights his way under the bed with Mrs Foran.

MRS FORAN [*speaking excitedly and jerkily as she climbs under the bed*] Flung his dinner into the fire – and started to smash the little things in the room. Tryin' to save the dresser, I got a box in the eye. I locked the door on him as I rushed out, an' before I was half-way down, he had one of the panels flyin' out with – a hatchet!

SYLVESTER [*under the bed – out of breath*] Whythehell didn'tyou sing out beforeyousent thedoor flyin' inontop o' me!

MRS FORAN. How could I an' I flyin' before danger to me – life?

SYLVESTER. Yes, an'you'vegot meinto a nice extremity now!

MRS FORAN. An' I yelled to Simon Norton when he had me – down, but the boyo only ran the faster out of the – house!

SYLVESTER. Oh, an' the regal like way he went out to fight! Oh, I'm findin' out that everyone who wears a cocked hat isn't a Napoleon!

Teddy Foran, Mrs Foran's husband, enters by door, with a large, fancy, vividly yellow-coloured bowl, ornamented with crimson roses, in one hand and a hatchet in the other. He is big and powerful, rough and hardy. A man who would be dominant in a public-house, and whose opinions would be listened to with great respect. He is dressed in khaki uniform of a soldier home on leave.

TEDDY. Under the bed, eh? Right place for a guilty conscience. I should have thrown you out of the window with the dinner you put before me. Out with you from under there, an' come up with your husband.

SUSIE [*opening suddenly door right, putting in her head, pulling it back and shutting door again*] God is looking at you, God is looking at you!

MRS FORAN. I'll not budge an inch from where I am.

TEDDY [*looking under the bed and seeing Sylvester*] What are you doin' there encouragin' her against her husband?

SYLVESTER. You've no right to be rippin' open the poor woman's life of peace with violence.

TEDDY [*with indignation*] She's my wife, isn't she?

MRS FORAN. Nice thing if I lose the sight of my eye with the cut you gave me.

TEDDY. She's my wife, isn't she? An' you've no legal right to be harbourin' her here, keepin' her from her household duties. Stunned I was when I seen her lookin' so well after me long absence. Blowin' her sighin' in me face all day, an' she sufferin' the tortures of hell for fear I'd miss the boat!

SYLVESTER. Go on up to your own home; you've no right to be violatin' this place.

TEDDY. You'd like to make her your cheery amee, would you? It's napoo, there, napoo, you little pip-squeak. I seen you an' her goin' down the street arm-in-arm.

SYLVESTER. Did you expect to see me goin' down the street leg-in-leg with her?

TEDDY. Thinkin' of her Ring-papers instead of her husband. [*To Mrs*

Foran]. I'll teach you to be rippling with joy an' your husband goin'
away! [*He shows the bowl*]. Your weddin' bowl, look at it; pretty, isn't
it? Take your last eyeful of it now, for it's goin' west quick!

SUSIE [*popping her head in again*] God is watching, God is watching
you!

MRS FORAN [*appealingly*] Teddy, Teddy, don't smash the poor
weddin' bowl.

TEDDY [*smashing the bowl with a blow of the hatchet*] It would be a
pity, wouldn't it? Damn it, an' damn you. I'm off now to smash
anything I missed, so that you'll have a gay time fittin' up the little
home again by the time your loving husband comes back. You can
come an' have a look, an' bring your mon amee if you like.

*He goes out, and there is a pause as Mrs Foran and Sylvester peep
anxiously towards the door.*

SYLVESTER. Cautious, now cautious; he might be lurking outside the
door there, read to spring on you the minute you show'd your nose!

MRS FORAN. Me lovely little weddin' bowl, me lovely little weddin'
bowl!

Teddy is heard breaking things in the room above.

SYLVESTER [*creeping out from under the bed*] Oh, he is gone up. He was
a little cow'd, I think, when he saw me.

MRS FORAN. Me little weddin' bowl, wrapp'd in tissue paper, an' only
taken out for a few hours every Christmas – me poor little weddin'
bowl.

SUSIE [*popping her head in*] God is watching – oh, he's gone!

SYLVESTER [*jubilant*] Vanished! He was a little cow'd, I think, when
he saw me.

Mrs Heegan and Susie come into the room.

MRS FORAN. He's makin' a hash of every little thing we have in the
house, Mrs Heegan.

MRS HEEGAN. Go inside to the room, Mrs Foran, an' if he comes
down again, we'll say you ran out to the street.

MRS FORAN [*going into room*] My poor little weddin' bowl that I might
have had for generations!

SUSIE [*who has been looking out of the window, excitedly*] They're comin',
they're comin': a crowd with a concertina; some of them carrying
Harry on their shoulders, an' others are carrying that Jessie Taite

too, holding a silver cup in her hands. Oh, look at the shameful way
she's showing her legs to all who like to have a look at them!

MRS HEEGAN. Never mind Jessie's legs — what we have to do is to
hurry him out in time to catch the boat.

*The sound of a concertina playing in the street outside has been heard, and
the noise of a marching crowd. The crowd stop at the house. Shouts are
heard — 'Up the Avondales!'; 'Up Harry Heegan and the Avondales!' Then
steps are heard coming up the stairs, and first Simon Norton enters, holding
the door ceremoniously wide open to allow Harry to enter, with his arm
around Jessie, who is carrying a silver cup joyously, rather than reverentially,
elevated, as a priest would elevate a chalice. Harry is wearing khaki trousers,
a military cap stained with trench mud, a vivid orange-coloured jersey with
black collar and cuffs. He is twenty-three years of age, tall, with the sinewy
muscles of a manual worker made flexible by athletic sport. He is a typical
young worker, enthusiastic, very often boisterous, sensible by instinct rather
than by reason. He has gone to the trenches as unthinkingly as he would go
to the polling booth. He isn't naturally stupid; it is the stupidity of persons
in high places that has stupefied him. He has given all to his masters, strong
heart, sound lungs, healthy stomach, lusty limbs, and the little mind that
education has permitted to develop sufficiently to make all the rest a little
more useful. He is excited now with the sweet and innocent insanity of a fine
achievement, and the rapid lowering of a few drinks.*

*Jessie is twenty-two or so, responsive to all the animal impulses of life.
Ever dancing around, in and between the world of the flesh, and the devil.
She would be happy climbing with a boy among the heather on Howth Hill,
and could play ball with young men on the swards of the Phœnix Park. She
gives her favour to the prominent and popular. Harry is her favourite: his
strength and speed has won the Final for his club, he wears the ribbon of the
D.C.M. It is a time of spiritual and animal exaltation for her].*

*Barney Bagnal, a soldier mate of Harry's, stands a little shyly near the
door, with a pleasant, good-humoured grin on his rather broad face. He is
the same age as Harry, just as strong, but not so quick, less finely formed,
and not so sensitive; able to take most things quietly, but savage and wild
when he becomes enraged. He is fully dressed, with topcoat buttoned on him,
and he carries Harry's on his arm.*

HARRY [*joyous and excited*] Won, won, won, be-God; by the odd goal
in five. Lift it up, lift it up, Jessie, sign of youth, sign of strength,
sign of victory!

MRS HEEGAN [*to Sylvester*] I knew, now, Harry would come back in time to catch the boat.

HARRY [*to Jessie*] Leave it here, leave it down here, Jessie, under the picture, the picture of the boy that won the final.

MRS HEEGAN. A parcel of sandwiches, a bottle of whisky, an' some magazines to take away with you an' Barney, Harry.

HARRY. Napoo sandwiches, an' napoo magazines: look at the cup, eh? The cup that Harry won, won by the odd goal in five! [*To Barney*]. The song that the little Jock used to sing, Barney, what was it? The little Jock we left shrivellin' on the wire after the last push.

BARNEY. 'Will ye no come back again?'

HARRY. No, no, the one we all used to sing with him, 'The Silver Tassie'. [*Pointing to the cup*]. There it is, the Silver Tassie, won by the odd goal in five, kicked by Harry Heegan.

MRS HEEGAN. Watch your time, Harry, watch your time.

JESSIE. He's watching it, he's watching it – for God's sake don't get fussy, Mrs Heegan.

HARRY. They couldn't take their beatin' like men . . . Play the game, play the game, why the hell couldn't they play the game? [*To Barney*]. See the President of the Club, Dr Forby Maxwell, shaking hands with me, when he was giving me the cup, 'Well done, Heegan!' The way they yell'd and jump'd when they put in the equalizing goal in the first half!

BARNEY. Ay, a fluke, that's what it was; a losy fluke.

MRS HEEGAN [*holding Harry's coat up for him to put it on*] Here, your coat, Harry, slip it on while you're talkin'.

HARRY [*putting it on*] Alright, keep smiling, don't fuss. [*To the rest*]. Grousing the whole time they were chasing the ball; an' when they lost it, 'Referee, referee, offside, referee . . . foul there; ey, open your eyes referee!'

JESSIE. And we scream'd and shout'd them down with 'Play the game, Primrose Rovers, play the game!'

BARNEY. You ran them off their feet till they nearly stood still.

MRS FORAN [*has been peeping twice in timidly from the room and now comes in to the rest*] Somebody run up an' bring Teddy down for fear he'd be left behind.

SYLVESTER [*to Harry*] Your haversack an' trench tools, Harry; haversack first, isn't it?

HARRY [*fixing his haversack*] Haversack, haversack, don't rush me. [*To the rest*]. But when I got the ball, Barney, once I got the ball, the rain began to fall on the others. An' the last goal, the goal that put us one ahead, the winning goal, that was a-a-eh-a-stunner!

BARNEY. A beauty, me boy, a hot beauty.

HARRY. Slipping by the back rushing at me like a mad bull, steadying a moment for a drive, seeing in a flash the goalie's hands sent with a shock to his chest by the force of the shot, his half-stunned motion to clear, a charge, and then carrying him, the ball and all with a rush into the centre of the net!

BARNEY [*enthusiastically*] Be-God, I did get a thrill when I seen you puttin' him sittin' on his arse in the middle of the net!

MRS FORAN [*from the door*] One of yous do go up an' see if Teddy's ready to go.

MRS HEEGAN [*to Harry*] Your father'll carry your kit-bag, an' Jessie'll carry your rifle as far as the boat.

HARRY [*irritably*] Oh, damn it, woman, give your wailin' over for a minute!

MRS HEEGAN. You've got only a few bare minutes to spare, Harry.

HARRY. We'll make the most of them, then. [*To Barney*]. Out with one of them wine-virgins we got in 'The Mill in the Field', Barney, and we'll rape her in a last hot moment before we set out to kiss the guns!

Simon has gone into room and returned with a gun and a kit-bag. He crosses to where Barney is standing.

BARNEY [*taking a bottle of wine from his pocket*] Empty her of her virtues, eh?

HARRY. Spill it out, Barney, spill it out ... [*Seizing Silver Cup, and holding it towards Barney*]. Here, into the cup, be-God. A drink out of the cup, out of the Silver Tassie!

BARNEY [*who has removed the cap and taken out the cork*] Here she is now ... Ready for anything, stripp'd to the skin!

JESSIE. No double-meaning talk, Barney.

SUSIE [*haughtily, to Jessie*] The men that are defending us have leave

to bow themselves down in the House of Rimmon, for the men that
go with the guns are going with God.

Barney pours wine into the cup for Harry and into a glass for himself.

HARRY [*to Jessie*] Jessie, a sup for you. [*She drinks from the cup*]. An' a
drink for me. [*He drinks*]. Now a kiss while our lips are wet. [*He
kisses her*]. Christ, Barney, how would you like to be retreating from
the fairest face and [*lifting Jessie's skirt a little*] – and the trimmest,
slimmest little leg in the parish? Napoo, Barney, to everyone but
me!

MRS FORAN. One of you go up, an' try to get my Teddy down.

BARNEY [*lifting Susie's skirt a little*] Napoo, Harry, to everyone but –

SUSIE [*angrily, pushing Barney away from her*] You khaki-cover'd ape,
you, what are you trying to do? Man-handle the lassies of France, if
you like, but put on your gloves when you touch a woman that
seeketh not the things of the flesh.

HARRY [*putting an arm round Susie to mollify her*] Now, Susie, Susie,
lengthen your temper for a passing moment, so that we may bring
away with us the breath of a kiss to the shell-bullied air of the
trenches . . . Besides, there's nothing to be ashamed of – it's not a
bad little leggie at all.

SUSIE [*slipping her arm round Harry's neck, and looking defiantly at
Barney*] I don't mind what Harry does; I know he means no harm,
not like other people. Harry's different.

JESSIE. You'll not forget to send me the German helmet home from
France, Harry?

SUSIE [*trying to rest her head on Harry's breast*] I know Harry, he's
different. It's his way. I wouldn't let anyone else touch me, but in
some way or another I can tell Harry's different.

JESSIE [*putting her arm round Harry under Susie's in an effort to dislodge
it*] Susie, Harry wants to be free to keep his arm round me during
his last few moments here, so don't be pulling him about!

SUSIE [*shrinking back a little*] I was only saying that Harry was different.

MRS FORAN. For God's sake, will someone go up for Teddy, or he
won't go back at all!

TEDDY [*appearing at door*] Damn anxious for Teddy to go back! Well,
Teddy's goin' back, an' he's left everything tidy upstairs so that
you'll not have much trouble sortin' things out. [*To Harry*]. The

Club an' a crowd's waitin' outside to bring us to the boat before they go to the spread in honour of the final. [*Bitterly*]. A party for them while we muck off to the trenches!

HARRY [*after a slight pause, to Barney*] Are you game, Barney?

BARNEY. What for?

HARRY. To go to the spread and hang the latch for another night?

BARNEY [*taking his rifle from Simon and slinging it over his shoulder*] No, no, napoo desertin' on Active Service. Deprivation of pay an' the rest of your time in the front trenches. No, no. We must go back!

MRS HEEGAN. No, no, Harry. You must go back.

SIMON
SYLVESTER } [*together*] You must go back.
and SUSIE

VOICES OF CROWD OUTSIDE. They must go back!

The ship's siren is heard blowing.

SIMON. The warning signal.

SYLVESTER. By the time they get there, they'll be unslinging the gangways!

SUSIE [*handing Harry his steel helmet*] Here's your helmet, Harry.

He puts it on.

MRS HEEGAN. You'll all nearly have to run for it now!

SYLVESTER. I've got your kit-bag, Harry.

SUSIE. I've got your rifle.

SIMON. I'll march in front with the cup, after Conroy with the concertina.

TEDDY. Come on: ong, avong to the trenches!

HARRY [*recklessly*] Jesus, a last drink, then! [*He raises the Silver Cup, singing*]:
    Gae bring to me a pint of wine,
    And fill it in a silver tassie;

BARNEY [*joining in vigorously*]:
    . . . a silver tassie.

HARRY:
    That I may drink before I go,
    A service to my bonnie lassie.

BARNEY:
    . . . bonnie lassie.

HARRY:

 The boat rocks at the pier o' Leith,
 Full loud the wind blows from the ferry;
 The ship rides at the Berwick Law,
 An' I must leave my bonnie Mary!

BARNEY:

 . . . leave my bonnie Mary!

HARRY:

 The trumpets sound, the banners fly,
 The glittering spears are ranked ready;

BARNEY:

 . . . glittering spears are ranked ready;

HARRY:

 The shouts of war are heard afar,
 The battle closes thick and bloody.

BARNEY:

 . . . closes thick and bloody.

HARRY:

 It's not the roar of sea or shore,
 That makes me longer wish to tarry,
 Nor shouts of war that's heard afar –
 It's leaving thee, my bonnie lassie!

BARNEY:

 . . . leaving thee, my bonnie lassie!

TEDDY. Come on, come on. [*Simon, Sylvester, and Susie go out*].

VOICES OUTSIDE:

 Come on from your home to the boat;
 Carry on from the boat to the camp.

Teddy and Barney go out. Harry and Jessie follow; as Harry reaches the door, he takes his arm from round Jessie and comes back to Mrs Heegan.

VOICES OUTSIDE. From the camp up to the lines to the trenches.

HARRY [*shyly and hurriedly kissing Mrs Heegan*] Well, goodbye, old woman.

MRS HEEGAN. Goodbye, my son.

Harry goes out. The chorus of 'The Silver Tassie', accompanied by a concertina, can be heard growing fainter till it ceases. Mrs Foran goes out timidly. Mrs Heegan pokes the fire, arranges the things in the room, and then goes to the window and looks out. After a pause, the loud and long blast of the ship's siren is heard. The light on the masthead, seen through the window, moves slowly away, and Mrs Heegan with a sigh, 'Ah dear', goes over to the fire and sits down. A slight pause, then Mrs Foran returns to the room.

MRS FORAN. Every little bit of china I had in the house is lyin' above in a mad an' muddled heap like the flotsam an' jetsam of the seashore!

MRS HEEGAN [*with a deep sigh of satisfaction*] Thanks be to Christ that we're after managin' to get the three of them away safely.

ACT II

In the war zone: a scene of jagged and lacerated ruin of what was once a monastery. At back a lost wall and window are indicated by an arched piece of broken coping pointing from the left to the right, and a similar piece of masonry pointing from the right to the left. Between these two lacerated fingers of stone can be seen the country stretching to the horizon where the front trenches are. Here and there heaps of rubbish mark where houses once stood. From some of these, lean, dead hands are protruding. Further on, spiky stumps of trees which were once a small wood. The ground is dotted with rayed and shattered shell holes. Across the horizon in the red glare can be seen the criss-cross pattern of the barbed wire bordering the trenches. In the sky sometimes a green star, sometimes a white star, burns. Within the broken archway to the left is an arched entrance to another part of the monastery, used now as a Red Cross Station. In the wall, right, near the front is a stained-glass window, background green, figure of the Virgin, white-faced, wearing a black robe, lights inside making the figure vividly apparent. Further up from this window is a life-size crucifix. A shell has released an arm from the cross, which has caused the upper part of the figure to lean forward with the released arm outstretched towards the figure of the Virgin. Underneath the crucifix on a pedestal, in red letters, are the words:
PRINCEPS PACIS. *Almost opposite the crucifix is a gunwheel to which Barney is tied. At the back, in the centre, where the span of the arch should be, is the shape of a big howitzer gun, squat, heavy underpart, with a long, sinister barrel now pointing towards the front at an angle of forty-five degrees. At the base of the gun a piece of wood is placed on which is chalked,* HYDE PARK CORNER. *On another piece of wood near the entrance of the Red Cross Station is chalked,* NO HAWKERS OR STREET CRIES PERMITTED HERE. *In the near centre is a brazier in which a fire is burning. Crouching above, on a ramp, is a soldier whose clothes are covered with mud and splashed with blood. Every feature of the scene seems a little distorted from its original*

appearance. Rain is falling steadily; its fall worried now and again by fitful gusts of a cold wind. A small organ is heard playing slow and stately notes as the curtain rises.

After a pause, the Croucher, without moving, intones dreamily:

CROUCHER. And the hand of the Lord was upon me, and carried me out in the spirit of the Lord, and set me down in the midst of a valley.

And I looked and saw a great multitude that stood upon their feet, an exceeding great army.

And he said unto me, Son of man, can this exceeding great army become a valley of dry bones?

[*The music ceases, and a voice, in the part of the monastery left standing, intones*: Kyr ... ie ... e ... eleison. Kyr ... ie ... e ... eleison, *followed by the answer*: Christe ... eleison].

CROUCHER [*resuming*] And I answered, O Lord God, thou knowest. And he said, prophesy and say unto the wind, come from the four winds a breath and breathe upon these living that they may die.

[*As he pauses the voice in the monastery is heard again*]: Gloria in excelsis Deo et in terra pax hominibus bonae voluntatis.]

CROUCHER [*resuming*]. And I prophesied, and the breath came out of them, and the sinews came away from them, and behold a shaking, and their bones fell asunder, bone from his bone, and they died, and the exceeding great army became a valley of dry bones.

[*The voice from the monastery is heard, clearly for the first half of the sentence, then dying away towards the end*]. Accendat in nobis Dominus ignem sui amoris, et flammam aeternae caritatis].

[*A group of soldiers come in from fatigue, bunched together as if for comfort and warmth. They are wet and cold, and they are sullen-faced. They form a circle around the brazier and stretch their hands towards the blaze*].

1ST SOLDIER. Cold and wet and tir'd.

2ND SOLDIER. Wet and tir'd and cold.

3RD SOLDIER. Tir'd and cold and wet.

4TH SOLDIER [*very like Teddy*] Twelve blasted hours of ammunition transport fatigue!

1ST SOLDIER. Twelve weary hours.

2ND SOLDIER. And wasting hours.

3RD SOLDIER. And hot and heavy hours.

1ST SOLDIER. Toiling and thinking to build the wall of force that blocks the way from here to home.

2ND SOLDIER. Lifting shells.

3RD SOLDIER. Carrying shells.

4TH SOLDIER. Piling shells.

1ST SOLDIER. In the falling, pissing rine and whistling wind.

2ND SOLDIER. The whistling wind and falling, drenching rain.

3RD SOLDIER. The God-dam rain and blasted whistling wind.

1ST SOLDIER. And the shirkers sife at home coil'd up at ease.

2ND SOLDIER. Shells for us and pianos for them.

3RD SOLDIER. Fur coats for them and winding-sheets for us.

4TH SOLDIER. Warm.

2ND SOLDIER. And dry.

1ST SOLDIER. An' 'appy.   [*A slight pause*].

BARNEY. An' they call it re-cu-per-at-ing!

1ST SOLDIER [*reclining near the fire*] Gawd, I'm sleepy.

2ND SOLDIER [*reclining*] Tir'd and lousy.

3RD SOLDIER [*reclinging*] Damp and shaking.

4TH SOLDIER [*murmuringly, the rest joining him*] Tir'd and lousy, an' wet an' sleepy, but mother call me early in the morning.

1ST SOLDIER [*dreamily*] Wen I thinks of 'ome, I thinks of a field of dysies.

THE REST [*dreamily*] Wen 'e thinks of 'ome, 'e thinks of a field of dysies.

1ST SOLDIER [*chanting dreamily*]:

> I sees the missus paryding along Walham Green,
> Through the jewels an' silks on the costers' carts,
> Emmie a-pulling her skirt an' muttering,
> 'A balloon, a balloon, I wants a balloon',
> The missus a-tugging 'er on, an' sying,
> 'A balloon, for shime, an' your father fighting:
> You'll wait till 'e's 'ome, an' the bands a-plying!'   [*He pauses*].

[*Suddenly*] But wy'r we 'eer, wy'r we 'ere – that's wot we wants to know!

2ND SOLDIER. God only knows – or else, perhaps, a red-cap.

1ST SOLDIER [*chanting*]:

Tabs'll murmur, 'em an' 'aw, 'an sy: 'You're 'ere because you're
Point nine double o, the sixth platoon an' forty-eight battalion,
The Yellow Plumes that pull'd a bow at Crecy,
And gave to fame a leg up on the path to glory;
Now with the howitzers of the Twenty-first Division,
Tiking life easy with the Army of the Marne,
An' all the time the battered Conchie squeals,
"It's one or two men looking after business"'

3RD SOLDIER. An' saves his blasted skin!

1ST SOLDIER [*chanting*] The padre gives a fag an' softly whispers:

'Your king, your country an' your muvver 'as you 'ere.'
An' last time 'ome on leave, I awsks the missus:
'The good God up in heaven, Bill, 'e knows,
An' I gets the seperytion moneys reg'lar.'   [*He sits up suddenly*].
But wy'r we 'ere, wy'r we 'ere, – that's wot I wants to know?

THE REST [*chanting sleepily*] Why 's 'e 'ere, why 's 'e 'cre – that's wot
'e wants to know!

BARNEY [*singing to the air of second bar in chorus of 'Auld Lang Syne'*]

We're here because we're here, because we're here, because we're here!

*Each slides into an attitude of sleep – even Barney's head droops a little.
The Corporal, followed by the Visitor, appears at back. The Visitor is a portly
man with a rubicund face; he is smiling to demonstrate his ease of mind, but
the lines are a little distorted with an ever-present sense of anxiety. He is
dressed in a semi-civilian, semi-military manner – dark worsted suit,
shrapnel helmet, a haversack slung round his shoulder, a brown belt round
his middle, black top boots and spurs, and he carries a cane. His head is bent
between his shoulders, and his shoulders are crouched a little.*

VISITOR. Yes, to-morrow, I go a little further. Penetrate a little deeper
into danger. Foolish, yes, but then it's an experience; by God, it's
an experience. The military authorities are damned strict – won't
let a . . . man . . . plunge!

CORPORAL. In a manner of speakin', sir, only let you see the arses of the guns.

VISITOR [*not liking the remark*] Yes, no; no, oh yes. Damned strict, won't let a . . . man . . . plunge! [*Suddenly, with alarm*]. What's that, what was that?

CORPORAL. Wha' was what?

VISITOR. A buzz, I thought I heard a buzz.

CORPORAL. A buzz?

VISITOR. Of an aeroplane.

CORPORAL. Didn't hear. Might have been a bee.

VISITOR. No, no; don't think it was a bee. [*Arranging helmet with his hands*]. Damn shrapnel helmet; skin tight; like a vice; hurts the head. Rather be without it; but regulations, you know. Military authorities damn particular – won't let a . . . man . . . plunge!

VISITOR [*seeing Barney*] Aha, what have we got here, what have we got here?

CORPORAL [*to Barney*] 'Tshun! [*To the Visitor*]. Regimental misdemeanour, sir.

VISITOR [*to Barney*] Nothing much, boy, nothing much?

BARNEY [*chanting softly*]:
A Brass-hat pullin' the bedroom curtains
Between himself, the world an' the Estaminay's daughter,
In a pyjama'd hurry ran down an' phon'd
A Tommy was chokin' an Estiminay cock,
An' I was pinch'd as I was puttin' the bird
Into a pot with a pint of peas.

CORPORAL [*chanting hoarsely*]:
And the hens all droop, for the loss has made
The place a place of desolation!

VISITOR [*reprovingly, to the Corporal*] Seriously, Corporal, seriously, please. Sacred, sacred: property of the citizen of a friendly State, sacred. On Active Service, serious to steal a fowl, a cock. [*To Barney*]. The uniform, the cause, boy, the corps. Infra dignitatem, boy, infra dignitatem.

BARNEY. Wee, wee.

VISITOR [*pointing to reclining soldiers*] Taking it easy, eh?

CORPORAL. Done in; transport fatigue; twelve hours.

VISITOR. Um, not too much rest, corporal. Dangerous. Keep 'em moving much as possible. Too much rest – bad. Sap, sap, sap.

CORPORAL [*pointing to the left*] Bit of monastery left intact. Hold services there; troops off to front line. Little organ plays.

VISITOR. Splendid. Bucks 'em up. Gives 'em peace.

A Staff Officer enters suddenly, passing by the Visitor with a springing hop, so that he stands in the centre with the Visitor on his right and the Corporal on his left. He is prim, pert, and polished, superfine khaki uniform, gold braid, crimson tabs, and gleaming top boots. He speaks his sentences with a gasping importance.

CORPORAL [*stiffening*] 'Shun! Staff!

SOLDIERS [*springing to their feet – the Croucher remains as he is, with a sleepy alertness*] Staff! 'Shun!

CORPORAL [*bellowing at the Croucher*] Eh, you there: 'shun! Staff!

CROUCHER [*calmly*] Not able. Sick. Privilege. Excused duty.

STAFF WALLAH [*reading document*]:

Battery Brigade Orders, F.A., 31 D 2.

Units presently recuperating, parade eight o'clock P.M.

Attend Lecture organised by Society for amusement and mental development, soldiers at front.

Subject: Habits of those living between Frigid Zone and Arctic Circle.

Lecturer: Mr Melville Sprucer.

Supplementary Order: Units to wear gas masks.

As you were.

The Staff Wallah departs as he came with a springing hop. The Visitor and the Corporal relax, and stroll down towards the R.C. Station. The soldiers relax too, seeking various positions of ease around the fire.

VISITOR [*indicating R.C. Station*]. Ah, in here. We'll just pop in here for a minute. And then pops out again. [*He and the Corporal go into the R.C. Station. A pause*].

1ST SOLDIER [*chanting and indicating that he means the Visitor by looking in the direction of the R.C. Station*]:

The perky bastard's cautious nibbling

In a safe, safe shelter at danger queers me.

Furiously feeling he's up to the neck in

The whirl and the sweep of the front-line fighting.

2ND SOLDIER [*chanting*]:
  In his full-blown, chin-strapp'd, shrapnel helmet,
  He'll pat a mug on the back and murmur,
  'Here's a stand-fast Tauntonshire before me',
  And the mug, on his feet, 'll whisper 'yessir'.

3RD SOLDIER [*chanting*]:
  Like a bride, full-flush'd, 'e'll sit down and listen
  To every word of the goddam sermon,
  From the cushy-soul'd, word-spreading, yellow-streaked dud.

BARNEY [*chanting*] Who wouldn't make a patch on a Tommy's backside. [*A pause*].

1ST SOLDIER. 'Ow long have wee been resting 'ere?

2ND SOLDIER. A month.

3RD SOLDIER. Twenty-nine days, twenty-three hours and [*looking at watch*] twenty-three minutes.

4TH SOLDIER. Thirty-seven minutes more'll make it thirty days.

CROUCHER:
  Thirty days hath September, April, June, and November –
  November – that's the month when I was born – November.
  Not the beginning, not the end, but the middle of November.
  Near the valley of the Thames, in the middle of November.
  Shall I die at the start, near the end, in the middle of November?

1ST SOLDIER [*nodding towards the Croucher*] One more scrap, an' 'e'll be Ay one in the kingdom of the bawmy.

2ND SOLDIER. Perhaps they have forgotten.

3RD SOLDIER. Forgotten.

4TH SOLDIER. Forgotten us.

1ST SOLDIER. If the blighters at the front would tame their grousing.

THE REST. Tame their grousing.

2ND SOLDIER. And the wounded cease to stare their silent scorning.

THE REST. Passing by us, carried cushy on the stretchers.

3RD SOLDIER. We have beaten out the time upon the duck-board.

4TH SOLDIER. Stiff standing watch'd the sunrise from the firestep.

2ND SOLDIER. Stiff standing from the firestep watch'd the sunset.

3RD SOLDIER. Have bless'd the dark wiring of the top with curses.

2ND SOLDIER. And never a ray of leave.

3RD SOLDIER. To have a quiet drink.

1ST SOLDIER. Or a mad moment to rustle a judy.

3rd Soldier takes out a package of cigarettes; taking one himself he hands the package round. Each takes one, and the man nearest to Barney, kneeling up, puts one in his mouth and lights it for him. They all smoke silently for a few moments, sitting up round the fire.

2ND SOLDIER [*chanting very earnestly and quietly*]:
Would God I smok'd an' walk'd an' watch'd th'
Dance of a golden Brimstone butterfly,
To the saucy pipe of a greenfinch resting
In a drowsy, brambled lane in Cumberland.

1ST SOLDIER:
Would God I smok'd and lifted cargoes
From the laden shoulders of London's river-way;
Then holiday'd, roaring out courage and movement
To the muscled machines of Tottenham Hotspur.

3RD SOLDIER:
To hang here even a little longer,
Lounging through fear-swell'd, anxious moments;
The hinderparts of the god of battles
Shading our war-tir'd eyes from his flaming face.

BARNEY:
If you creep to rest in a clos'd-up coffin,
A tail of comrades seeing you safe home;
Or be a kernel lost in a shell exploding –
It's all, sure, only in a lifetime.

ALL TOGETHER:
Each sparrow, hopping, irresponsible,
Is indentur'd in God's mighty memory;
And we, more than they all, shall not be lost
In the forgetfulness of the Lord of Hosts.

The Visitor and the Corporal come from the Red Cross Station.

VISITOR [*taking out a cigarette case*]. Nurses too gloomy. Surgeons too serious. Doesn't do.

CORPORAL. All lying-down cases, sir. Pretty bad.

VISITOR [*who is now standing near the crucifix*] All the more reason make things merry and bright. Lift them out of themselves. [*To the soldiers*]. See you all to-morrow at lecture?

1ST SOLDIER [*rising and standing a little sheepishly before the Visitor*] Yessir, yessir.

THE REST. Yessir, yessir.

THE VISITOR. Good. Make it interesting. [*Searching in pocket*]. Damn it, have I none? Ah, saved.

He takes a match from his pocket and it about to strike it carelessly on the arm of the crucifix, when the 1st Soldier, with a rapid frightened movement, knocks it out of his hand.

1ST SOLDIER [*roughly*] Blarst you, man, keep your peace-white paws from that!

2ND SOLDIER. The image of the Son of God.

3RD SOLDIER. Jesus of Nazareth, the King of the Jews.

1ST SOLDIER [*reclining by the fire again*] There's a Gawd knocking abaht somewhere.

4TH SOLDIER. Wants Him to be sending us over a chit in the shape of a bursting shell.

THE VISITOR. Sorry put it across you. [*To Corporal*]. Too much time to think. Nervy. Time to brood, brood; bad. Sap. Sap. Sap. [*Walking towards where he came in*]. Must return quarters; rough and ready. Must stick it. There's a war on. Cheerio. Straight down road instead of round hill: shorter?

CORPORAL. Less than half as long.

THE VISITOR. Safe?

CORPORAL. Yes. Only drop shells off and on, cross roads. Ration party wip'd out week ago.

THE VISITOR. Go round hill. No hurry. General Officer's orders, no unnecessary risks. Must obey. Military Authorities damned particular – won't let a . . . man . . . plunge!

He and the Corporal go off. The soldiers in various attitudes are asleep around the fire. After a few moments' pause, two Stretcher-Bearers come in slowly from left, carrying a casualty. They pass through the sleeping soldiers, going towards the Red Cross Station. As they go they chant a verse, and as the verse is ending, they are followed by another pair carrying a second casualty.

1ST BEARERS [*chanting*]:
 Oh, bear it gently, carry it softly –
 A bullet or a shell said stop, stop, stop.
 It's had its day, and it's left the play,
 Since it gamboll'd over the top, top, top.
 It's had its day and it's left the play,
 Since it gamboll'd over the top.

2ND BEARERS [*chanting*]:
 Oh, carry it softly, bear it gently –
 The beggar has seen it through, through, through.
 If it 'adn't been 'im, if it 'adn't been 'im,
 It might 'ave been me or you, you, you.
 If it 'adn't been 'im, if it 'adn't been 'im,
 It might 'ave been me or you.

VOICE [*inside R.C. Station*] Easy, easy there; don't crowd.

1ST STRETCHER-BEARER [*to man behind*] Woa, woa there, Bill, 'ouse
 full.

STRETCHER-BEARER [*behind, to those following*] Woa, woa; traffic
 blocked. [*They leave the stretchers on the ground*].

THE WOUNDED ON THE STRETCHERS [*chanting*]:
 Carry on, carry on to the place of pain,
 Where the surgeon spreads his aid, aid, aid.
 And we show man's wonderful work, well done,
 To the image God hath made, made, made,
 And we show man's wonderful work, well done,
 To the image God hath made!

 When the future hours have all been spent,
 And the hand of death is near, near, near,
 Then a few, few moments and we shall find
 There'll be nothing left to fear, fear, fear,
 Then a few, few moments and we shall find
 There'll be nothing left to fear.

 The power, the joy, the pull of life,
 The laugh, the blow, and the dear kiss,
 The pride and hope, the gain and loss,

Have been temper'd down to this, this, this,
The pride and hope, the gain and loss,
Have been temper'd down to this.

1ST STRETCHER-BEARER [*to Barney*] Oh, Barney, have they liced you up because you've kissed the Colonel's judy?

BARNEY. They lit on me stealin' Estaminay poulthry.

1ST STRETCHER-BEARER. A hen?

2ND STRETCHER-BEARER. A duck, again, Barney?

3RD STRETCHER-BEARER. A swan this time.

BARNEY [*chanting softly*]:
A Brass-hat pullin' the bedroom curtains
Between himself, the world an' the Estaminay's daughter,
In a pyjama'd hurry ran down and phon'd
A Tommy was chokin' an Estaminay cock;
An' I was pinch'd as I was puttin' the bird
Into a pot with a pint of peas.

1ST STRETCHER-BEARER. The red-tabb'd squit!

2ND STRETCHER-BEARER. The lousey map-scanner!

3RD STRETCHER-BEARER. We must keep up, we must keep up the morale of the awrmy.

2ND STRETCHER-BEARER [*loudly*] Does 'e eat well?

THE REST [*in chorus*] Yes, 'e eats well!

2ND STRETCHER-BEARER. Does 'e sleep well?

THE REST [*in chorus*] Yes, 'e sleeps well!

2ND STRETCHER-BEARER. Does 'e whore well?

THE REST [*in chorus*] Yes, 'e whores well!

2ND STRETCHER-BEARER. Does 'e fight well?

THE REST [*in chorus*] Napoo; 'e 'as to do the thinking for the Tommies!

VOICE [*from the R.C. Station*] Stretcher Party – carry on!

The Bearers stoop with precision, attach their supports to the stretchers, lift them up and march slowly into the R.C. Station, chanting.

STRETCHER-BEARERS [*chanting*]:
Carry on – we've one bugled reason why –
We've 'eard and answer'd the call, call, call.
There's no more to be said, for when we are dead,
We may understand it all, all, all.

There's no more to be said, for when we are dead,
We may understand it all.

*They go out, leaving the scene occupied by the Croucher and the soldiers
sleeping around the fire. The Corporal re-enters. He is carrying two parcels.
He pauses, looking at the sleeping soldiers for a few moments, then shouts.*

CORPORAL [*shouting*] Hallo, there, you sleepy blighters! Number 2, a
parcel; and for you, Number 3. Get a move on – parcels! [*The
Soldiers wake up and spring to their feet*].

CORPORAL. For you, Number 2. [*He throws a parcel to 2nd Soldier*].
Number 3. [*He throws the other parcel to 3rd Soldier*].

3RD SOLDIER [*taking paper from around his parcel*] Looks like a bundle
of cigarettes.

1ST SOLDIER. Or a pack of cawds.

4TH SOLDIER. Or a prayer book.

3RD SOLDIER [*astounded*] Holy Christ, it is!

THE REST. What?

3RD SOLDIER. A prayer book!

4TH SOLDIER. In a green plush cover with a golden cross.

CROUCHER. Open it at the Psalms and sing that we may be saved
from the life and death of the beasts that perish.

BARNEY. Per omnia saecula saeculorum.

2ND SOLDIER [*who has opened his parcel*] A ball, be God!

4TH SOLDIER. A red and yellow coloured rubber ball.

1ST SOLDIER. And a note.

2ND SOLDIER [*reading*] To play your way to the enemies' trenches
when you all go over the top. Mollie.

1ST SOLDIER. See if it 'ops.

*The 2nd Soldier hops the ball, and then kicks it from him. The Corporal
intercepts it, and begins to dribble it across the stage. The 3rd Soldier tries to
take it from him. The Corporal shouts 'Offside, there!' They play for a few
minutes with the ball, when suddenly the Staff-Wallah springs in and stands
rigidly in centre.*

CORPORAL [*stiff to attention as he sees the Staff-Wallah*] 'Shun. Staff!
All the soldiers stiffen. The Croucher remains motionless.

CORPORAL [*shouting to the Croucher*] You: 'shun. Staff!

CROUCHER. Not able. Sick. Excused duty.

STAFF-WALLAH [*reading document*]:

Brigade Orders, C/X 143. B/Y 341. Regarding gas-masks. Gas-masks to be worn round neck so as to lie in front 2½ degrees from socket of left shoulder-blade, and 2¾ degrees from socket of right shoulder-blade, leaving bottom margin to reach ¼ of an inch from second button of lower end of tunic. Order to take effect from 6 A.M. following morning of date received. Dismiss! [*He hops out again, followed by Corporal*].

1ST SOLDIER [*derisively*] Comprenneemoy.

3RD SOLDIER. Tray bong.

2ND SOLDIER [*who is standing in archway, back, looking scornfully after the Staff-Wallah, chanting*]:

Jazzing back to his hotel he now goes gaily,
Shelter'd and safe where the clock ticks tamely.
His backside warming a cushion, downfill'd,
Green clad, well splash'd with gold birds redbeak'd.

1ST SOLDIER:

His last dim view of the front-line sinking
Into the white-flesh'd breasts of a judy;
Cuddling with proud, bright, amorous glances
The thing salved safe from the mud of the trenches.

2ND SOLDIER:

His tunic reared in the lap of comfort,
Peeps at the blood-stain'd jackets passing,
Through colour-gay bars of ribbon jaunty,
Fresh from a posh shop snug in Bond Street.

CROUCHER:

Shame and scorn play with and beat them,
Till we anchor in their company;
Then the decorations of security
Become the symbols of self-sacrifice.

[*A pause*].

2ND SOLDIER:

A warning this that we'll soon be exiles
From the freedom chance of life can give,
To the front where you wait to be hurried breathless,
Murmuring how, how do you do, to God.

3RD SOLDIER:

Where hot with the sweat of mad endeavour,
Crouching to scrape a toy-deep shelter,
Quick-tim'd by hell's fast, frenzied drumfire
Exploding in flaming death around us.

2ND SOLDIER:

God, unchanging, heart-sicken'd, shuddering,
Gathereth the darkness of the night sky
To mask His paling countenance from
The blood dance of His self-slaying children.

3RD SOLDIER:

Stumbling, swiftly cursing, plodding,
Lumbering, loitering, stumbling, grousing,
Through mud and rain, and filth and danger,
Flesh and blood seek slow the front line.

2ND SOLDIER:

Squeals of hidden laughter run through
The screaming medley of the wounded –
Christ, who bore the cross, still weary,
Now trails a rope tied to a field gun.

*As the last notes of the chanting are heard the Corporal comes rapidly in;
he is excited but steady; pale-faced and grim.*

CORPORAL. They attack. Along a wide front the enemy attacks. If
they break through it may reach us even here.

SOLDIERS [*in chorus as they all put on gas-masks*] They attack. The
enemy attacks.

CORPORAL. Let us honour that in which we do put our trust.

SOLDIERS [*in chorus*]:

That it may not fail us in our time of need.

*The Corporal goes over to the gun and faces towards it, standing on the
bottom step. The soldiers group around, each falling upon one knee, their
forms crouched in a huddled act of obeisance. They are all facing the gun
with their backs to the audience. The Croucher rises and joins them.*

CORPORAL [*singing*]:

Hail cool-hardened tower of steel emboss'd
With the fever'd, figment thoughts of man;

Guardian of our love and hate and fear,
Speak for us to the inner ear of God!

SOLDIERS:

We believe in God and we believe in thee.

CORPORAL:

Dreams of line, of colour, and of form;
Dreams of music dead for ever now;
Dreams in bronze and dreams in stone have gone
To make thee delicate and strong to kill.

SOLDIERS:

We believe in God and we believe in thee.

CORPORAL:

Jail'd in thy steel are hours of merriment
Cadg'd from the pageant-dream of children's play;
Too soon of the motley stripp'd that they may sweat
With them that toil for the glory of thy kingdom.

SOLDIERS:

We believe in God and we believe in thee.

CORPORAL:

Remember our women, sad-hearted, proud-fac'd,
Who've given the substance of their wombs for shadows;
Their shrivel'd, empty breasts war tinselléd
For patient gifts of graves to thee.

SOLDIERS:

We believe in God and we believe in thee.

CORPORAL:

Dapple those who are shelter'd with disease,
And women labouring with child,
And children that play about the streets,
With blood of youth expiring in its prime.

SOLDIERS:

We believe in God and we believe in thee.

CORPORAL:

Tear a gap through the soul of our mass'd enemies;
Grant them all the peace of death;
Blow them swiftly into Abram's bosom,
And mingle them with the joys of paradise!

SOLDIERS:

For we believe in God and we believe in thee.

The sky has become vexed with a crimson glare, mixed with yellow streaks, and striped with pillars of rising brown and black smoke. The Staff-Wallah rushes in, turbulent and wild, with his uniform disordered.

STAFF-WALLAH:

The enemy has broken through, broken through, broken through!

Every man born of woman to the guns, to the guns.

SOLDIERS:

To the guns, to the guns, to the guns!

STAFF-WALLAH:

Those at prayer, all in bed, and the swillers drinking deeply in the pubs.

SOLDIERS:

To the guns, to the guns.

STAFF-WALLAH:

All the batmen, every cook, every bitch's son that hides

A whiff of courage in his veins,

Shelter'd vigour in his body,

That can run, or can walk, even crawl –

Dig him out, dig him out, shove him on –

SOLDIERS:

To the guns!

The Soldiers hurry to their places led by the Staff-Wallah to the gun. The gun swings around and points to the horizon; a shell is swung into the breech and a flash indicates the firing of the gun, searchlights move over the red glare of the sky; the scene darkens, stabbed with distant flashes and by the more vivid flash of the gun which the Soldiers load and fire with rhythmical movements while the scene is closing. Only flashes are seen; no noise is heard.

ACT III

The upper end of an hospital ward. At right angles from back wall are two beds, one covered with a red quilt and the other with a white one. From the centre of the head of each bed is an upright having at the top a piece like a swan's neck, curving out over the bed, from which hangs a chain with a wooden cross-piece to enable weak patients to pull themselves into a sitting posture. To the left of these beds is a large glass double-door which opens on to the ground: one of the doors is open and a lovely September sun, which is setting, gives a glow to the garden.

Through the door two poplar trees can be seen silhouetted against the sky. To the right of this door is another bed covered with a black quilt. Little white discs are fixed to the head of each bed: on the first is the number 26, on the second 27, and on the third 28. Medical charts hang over each on the wall. To the right is the fireplace, facing down the ward. Farther on, to the right of the fire, is a door of a bathroom. In the corner, between the glass door and the fire, is a pedestal on which stands a statue of the Blessed Virgin; under the statue is written, 'Mater Misericordiae, ora pro nobis'. An easy-chair, on which are rugs, is near the fire. In the centre is a white, glass-topped table on which are medicines, drugs, and surgical instruments. On one corner is a vase of flowers. A locker is beside the head, and a small chair by the foot of each bed. Two electric lights, green shaded, hang from the ceilings, and a bracket light with a red shade projects from the wall over the fireplace. It is dusk, and the two lights suspended from the ceiling are lighted. The walls are a brilliant white.

Sylvester is in the bed marked '26'; he is leaning upon his elbow looking towards the glass door.

Simon, sitting down on the chair beside bed numbered '27', is looking into the grounds.

SYLVESTER [after a pause] Be God, isn't it a good one!
SIMON. Almost, almost, mind you, Sylvester, incomprehensible.

SYLVESTER. To come here and find Susie Monican fashion'd like a Queen of Sheba. God moves in a mysterious way, Simon.

SIMON. There's Surgeon Maxwell prancing after her now.

SYLVESTER [*stretching to see*] Heads together, eh? Be God, he's kissing her behind the trees! Oh, Susannah, Susannah, how are the mighty fallen, and the weapons of war perished!

Harry Heegan enters crouched in a self-propelled invalid chair; he wheels himself up to the fire. Sylvester slides down into the bed, and Simon becomes interested in a book that he takes off the top of his locker. Harry remains for a few moments beside the fire, and then wheels himself round and goes out as he came in; Sylvester raises himself in the bed, and Simon leaves down the book to watch Harry.

SYLVESTER. Down and up, up and down.

SIMON. Up and down, down and up.

SYLVESTER. Never quiet for a minute.

SIMON. Never able to hang on to an easy second.

SYLVESTER. Trying to hold on to the little finger of life.

SIMON. Half-way up to heaven.

SYLVESTER. And him always thinking of Jessie.

SYLVESTER. And Jessie never thinking of him.

Susie Monican, in the uniform of a V.A.D. nurse, enters the ward by the glass door. She is changed, for it is clear that she has made every detail of the costume as attractive as possible. She has the same assertive manner, but dignity and a sense of importance have been added. Her legs, encased in silk stockings, are seen (and shown) to advantage by her short and smartly cut skirt. Altogether she is now a very handsome woman. Coming in she glances at the bed numbered 28, then pauses beside Sylvester and Simon.

SUSIE. How is Twenty-eight?

SIMON and SYLVESTER [*together*] Travelling again.

SUSIE. Did he speak at all to you?

SYLVESTER. Dumb, Susie, dumb.

SIMON. Brooding, Susie; brooding, brooding.

SYLVESTER. Cogitatin', Susie, cogitatin', cogitatin'.

SUSIE [*sharply, to Sylvester*] It's ridiculous, Twenty-six, for you to be in bed. The Sister's altogether too indulgent to you. Why didn't you pair of lazy devils entice him down to sit and cogitate under the warm wing of the sun in the garden?

SYLVESTER. Considerin' the low state of his general health.

SIMON. Aided by a touch of frost in the air.

SYLVESTER. Thinkin' it over we thought it might lead –

SIMON. To him getting an attack of double pneumonia.

SYLVESTER and SIMON [*together*] An' then he'd go off like – [*they blow through their lips*] poof – the snuff of a candle!

SUSIE. For the future, during the period you are patients here, I am to be addressed as 'Nurse Monican', and not as 'Susie'. Remember that, the pair of you, please.

Harry wheels himself in again, crossing by her, and, going over to the fire, looks out into the grounds.

SUSIE [*irritatedly, to Sylvester*] Number Twenty-six, look at the state of your quilt. You must make an effort to keep it tidy. Dtch, dtch, dtch, what would the Matron say if she saw it!

SIMON [*with a nervous giggle*] He's an uneasy divil, Nurse Monican.

SUSIE [*hotly, to Simon*] Yours is as bad as his, Twenty-seven. You mustn't lounge on your bed; it must be kept perfectly tidy [*she smoothes the quilts*]. Please don't make it necessary to mention this again. [*To Harry*]. Would you like to go down for a little while into the garden, Twenty-eight?

Harry crouches silent and moody.

SUSIE [*continuing*] After the sober rain of yesterday it is good to feel the new grace of the yellowing trees, and to get the fresh smell of the grass.

Harry wheels himself round and goes out by the left.

SUSIE [*to Sylvester as she goes out*] Remember, Twenty-six, if you're going to remain in a comatose condition, you'll have to keep your bed presentable.   [*A pause*].

SYLVESTER [*mimicking Susie*] Twenty-six, if you're going to remeen in a comatowse condition, you'll have to keep your bed in a tidy an' awdahly mannah.

SIMON. Dtch, dtch, dtch, Twenty-seven, it's disgriceful. And as long as you're heah, in the capacity of a patient, please remember I'm not to be addressed as 'Susie', but as 'Nurse Monican'.

SYLVESTER. Twenty-seven, did you tike the pills the doctah awdahed?

VOICE OF SUSIE, LEFT. Twenty-six!

SYLVESTER. Yes, nurse?

VOICE OF SUSIE. Sister says you're to have a bawth at once; and you, Twenty-seven, see about geting it ready for him.

[*A fairly long pause*].

SYLVESTER [*angrily*] A bawth: well, be God, that's a good one! I'm not in a fit condition for a bath!   [*Another pause*].

SYLVESTER [*earnestly, to Simon*] You haven't had a dip now for nearly a week, while I had one only the day before yesterday in the late evening: it must have been you she meant, Simon.

SIMON. Oh, there was no dubiety about her bellowing out Twenty-six, Syl.

SYLVESTER [*excitedly*] How the hell d'ye know, man, she didn't mix the numbers up?

SIMON. Mix the numbers up! How could the woman mix the numbers up?

SYLVESTER. How could the woman mix the numbers up! What could be easier than to say Twenty-six instead of Twenty-seven? How could the woman mix the numbers up! Of course the woman could mix the numbers up!

SIMON. What d'ye expect me to do – hurl myself into a bath that was meant for you?

SYLVESTER. I don't want you to hurl yourself into anything; but you don't expect me to plunge into a bath that maybe wasn't meant for me?

SIMON. Nurse Monican said Twenty-six, and when you can alter that, ring me up and let me know.

A pause; then Simon gets up and goes toward bathroom door.

SYLVESTER [*snappily*] Where are you leppin' to now?

SIMON. I want to get the bath ready.

SYLVESTER. You want to get the bawth ready! Turn the hot cock on, and turn the cold cock on for Number Twenty-six, mixin' them the way a chemist would mix his medicines – sit still, man, till we hear the final verdict.

Simon sits down again. Susie comes in left, and, passing to the door leading to grounds, pauses beside Simon and Sylvester.

SUSIE [*sharply*] What are the two of you doing? Didn't I tell you, Twenty-six, that you were to take a bawth; and you, Twenty-seven, that you were to get it ready for him?

SYLVESTER [*sitting brightly in bed*] Oh, just goin' to spring up, Nurse Monican, when you popped in.

SUSIE. Well, up with you, then, and take it. [*To Simon*]. You go and get it ready for him.

Simon goes into the bathroom.

SYLVESTER [*venturing a last hope as Susie goes towards the entrance to grounds*] I had a dip, Nurse, only the day before yesterday in the late evening.

SUSIE [*as she goes out*] Have another one now, please.

The water can be heard flowing in the bathroom, and a light cloud of steam comes out by the door which Simon has left open.

SYLVESTER [*mimicking Susie*] Have another one, now, please! One to be taken before and after meals. The delicate audacity of the lip of that one since she draped her shoulders with a crimson cape!

Simon appears and stands leaning against the side of the bathroom door.

SIMON [*gloating*] She's steaming away now, Sylvester, full cock.

SYLVESTER [*scornfully, to Simon*] Music to you, the gurgling of the thing, music to you. Gaugin' the temperature for me. Dtch, dtch, dtch [*sitting up*], an hospital's the last place that God made. Be damn it, I wouldn't let a stuffed bird stay in one!

SIMON. Come on, man, before the hot strength bubbles out of it.

SYLVESTER [*getting out of bed*] Have you the towels hot an' everything ready for me to spring into?

SIMON [*with a bow*] Everything's ready for your enjoyment, Sir.

SYLVESTER [*as he goes towards the bathroom*] Can't they be content with an honest to God cleanliness, an' not be tryin' to gild a man with soap and water.

SIMON [*with a grin, as Sylvester pauses*] Can I do anything more for you, Sir?

SYLVESTER [*almost inarticulate with indignation, as he goes in*] Now I'm tell' you, Simon Norton, our cordiality's gettin' a little strained!

Harry wheels himself in, goes again to the fireplace, and looks into grounds. Simon watches him for a moment, takes a package of cigarettes from his pocket and lights one.

SIMON [*awkwardly, to Harry*] Have a fag, Harry, oul' son?

HARRY. Don't want one; tons of my own in the locker.

SIMON. Like me to get you one?

HARRY. I can get them myself if I want one. D'ye think my arms are lifeless as well as my legs?

SIMON. Far from that. Everybody's remarking what a great improvement has taken place in you during the last few days.

HARRY. Everybody but myself.

SIMON. What with the rubbing every morning and the rubbing every night, and now the operation to-morrow as a grand finally, you'll maybe be in the centre of the football field before many months are out.

HARRY [*irritably*] Oh, shut up, man! It's a miracle I want – not an operation. The last operation was to give life to my limbs, but no life came, and again I felt the horrible sickness of life only from the waist up. [*Raising his voice*]. Don't stand there gaping at me, man. Did you never before clasp your eyes on a body dead from the belly down? Blast you, man, why don't you shout at me, 'While there's life there's hope!'

Simon edges away to his corner. Susie comes in by the glass door and goes over to the table.

HARRY [*to Susie*] A package of fags. Out of the locker. Will you, Susie?

Susie goes to Harry's locker, gets the cigarettes and gives them to him. As he lights the cigarette, his right arm gives a sudden jerk.

SUSIE. Steady. What's this?

HARRY [*with a nervous laugh*] Barred from my legs it's flowing back into my arms. I can feel it slyly creeping into my fingers.

VOICE OF PATIENT, OUT LEFT [*plaintively*] Nurse!

SUSIE [*turning her head in direction of the voice*] Shush, you Twenty-three; go asleep, go asleep.

HARRY. A soft, velvety sense of distance between my fingers and the things I touch.

SUSIE. Stop thinking of it. Brooding checks the chance of your recovery. A good deal may be imagination.

HARRY [*peevishly*] Oh, I know the different touches of iron [*he touches the bed rail*]; of wood [*he touches the chair*]; of flesh [*he touches his cheek*]; and to my fingers they're giving the same answers – a feeling of numb distance between me and the touches of them all.

VOICE OF PATIENT, OUT LEFT. Nurse!

SUSIE. Dtch, dtch, Go asleep, Twenty-three.

VOICE, OUT LEFT. The stab in the head is worse than ever, Nurse.

SUSIE. You've got your dose of morphia, and you'll get no more. You'll just have to stick it.

Resident Surgeon Forby Maxwell enters from the grounds. He is about thirty years of age, and good-looking. His white overalls are unbuttoned, showing war ribbons on his waistcoat, flanked by the ribbons of the D.S.O. He has a careless, jaunty air, and evidently takes a decided interest in Susie. He comes in singing softly.

SURGEON MAXWELL:

    Stretched on the couch, Jessie fondled her dress,
    That hid all her beauties just over the knee;
    And I wondered and said, as I sigh'd, 'What a shame,
    That there's no room at all on the couch there for me.'

SUSIE [*to Surgeon Maxwell*] Twenty-three's at it again.

SURGEON MAXWELL. Uh, hopeless case. Half his head in Flanders. May go on like that for another month.

SUSIE. He keeps the patients awake at night.

SIMON. With his 'God have mercys on me', running after every third or fourth tick of the clock.

HARRY. 'Tisn't fair to me, 'tisn't fair to me; I must get my bellyful of sleep if I'm ever going to get well.

SURGEON MAXWELL. Oh, the poor devil won't trouble any of you much longer. [*Singing*]:

    Said Jess, with a light in the side of her eyes,
    'A shrewd, mathematical fellow like you,
    With an effort of thought should be able to make
    The couch wide enough for the measure of two.'

SUSIE. Dtch, dtch, Surgeon Maxwell.

SURGEON MAXWELL [*singing*]:

    I fixed on a plan, and I carried it through,
    And the eyes of Jess gleam'd as she whisper'd to me:
    'The couch, made for one, that was made to hold two,
    Has, maybe, been made big enough for three!'

Surgeon Maxwell catches Susie's hand in his. Sylvester bursts in from the bathroom, and rushes to his bed, colliding with the Surgeon as he passes him.

SURGEON MAXWELL. Hallo, hallo there, what's this?

SYLVESTER [*flinging himself into bed, covering himself rapidly with the clothes, blowing himself warm*] Pooh, pooh, I feel as if I was sittin' on the doorstep of pneumonia! Pooh, oh!

SURGEON MAXWELL [*to Sylvester*] We'll have a look at you in a moment, Twenty-six, and see what's wrong with you.

Sylvester subsides down into the bed, and Simon edges towards the entrance to grounds, and stands looking into the grounds, or watching Surgeon Maxwell examining Sylvester.

SURGEON MAXWELL [*to Harry, who is looking intently out into the grounds*] Well, how are we to-day, Heegan?

HARRY. I imagine I don't feel quite so dead in myself as I've felt these last few days back.

SURGEON MAXWELL. Oh, well, that's something.

HARRY. Sometimes I think I feel a faint, fluttering kind of a buzz in the tops of my thighs.

SURGEON MAXWELL [*touching Harry's thigh*] Where, here?

HARRY. No; higher up, doctor; just where the line is that leaves the one part living and the other part dead.

SURGEON MAXWELL. A buzz?

HARRY. A timid, faint, fluttering kind of buzz.

SURGEON MAXWELL. That's good. There might be a lot in that faint, fluttering kind of buzz.

HARRY [*after a pause*] I'm looking forward to the operation to-morrow.

SURGEON MAXWELL. That's the way to take it. While there's life there's hope [*with a grin and a wink at Susie*]. And now we'll have a look at Twenty-six.

Harry, when he hears 'while there's life there's hope', wheels himself madly out left; half-way out he turns his head and stretches to look out into the grounds, then he goes on.

SUSIE. Will the operation to-morrow be successful?

SURGEON MAXWELL. Oh, of course; very successful.

SUSIE. Do him any good, d'ye think?

SURGEON MAXWELL. Oh, blast the good it'll do him.

Susie goes over to Sylvester in the bed.

SUSIE [*to Sylvester*] Sit up, Twenty-six, Surgeon Maxwell wants to examine you.

SYLVESTER [*sitting up with a brave effort but a woeful smile*] Righto. In the pink!

Surgeon Maxwell comes over, twirling his stethoscope. Simon peeps round the corner of the glass door.

SUSIE [*to Surgeon Maxwell*] What was the cause of the row between the Matron and Nurse Jennings? [*To Sylvester*]. Open your shirt, Twenty-six.

SURGEON MAXWELL [*who has fixed the stethoscope in his ears, removing it to speak to Susie*] Caught doing the tango in the Resident's arms in the Resident's room. Naughty girl, naughty girl. [*To Sylvester*]. Say 'ninety-nine'.

SYLVESTER. Ninety-nine.

SUSIE. Oh, I knew something like that would happen. Daughter of a Dean, too.

SURGEON MAXWELL [*to Sylvester*] Say 'ninety-nine'.

SYLVESTER. Ninety-nine. U-u-uh, it's gettin' very cold here, sitting up!

SURGEON MAXWELL [*to Sylvester*] Again. Don't be frightened; breathe quietly.

SYLVESTER. Ninety-nine. Cool as a cucumber, Doctor. Ninety-nine.

SURGEON MAXWELL [*to Susie*] Damn pretty little piece. Not so pretty as you, though.

SYLVESTER [*to Surgeon Maxwell*] Yesterday Doctor Joyce, givin' me a run over, said to a couple of medical men that were with him lookin' for tips, that the thing was apparently yieldin' to treatment, and that an operation wouldn't be necessary.

SURGEON MAXWELL. Go on; ninety-nine, ninety-nine.

SYLVESTER. Ninety-nine, ninety-nine.

SURGEON MAXWELL [*to Susie*] Kicks higher than her head, and you should see her doing the splits.

SYLVESTER [*to Surgeon Maxwell*] Any way of gettin' rid of it'll do for me, for I'm not one of them that'll spend a night before an operation in a crowd of prayers.

SUSIE. Not very useful things to be doing and poor patients awaiting attention.

SURGEON MAXWELL [*putting stethoscope into pocket*] He'll do alright; quite fit. Great old skin. [*To Sylvester*]. You can cover yourself up, now. [*To Susie*]. And don't tell me, Nurse Susie, that you've never felt a thrill or left a bedside for a kiss in a corner. [*He tickles her under the arm*]. Kiss in a corner, Nurse!

SUSIE [*pleased, but coy*] Please don't, Doctor Maxwell, please.

SURGEON MAXWELL [*tickling her again as they go out*] Kiss in a corner; ta-ra-ra-ra, kiss in a corner!   [*A pause*].

SYLVESTER [*to Simon*] Simon, were you listenin' to that conversation.

SIMON. Indeed I was.

SYLVESTER. We have our hands full, Simon, to keep alive. Think of sinkin' your body to the level of a hand that, ta-ra-ra-ra, would plunge a knife into your middle, haphazard, hurryin' up to run away after a thrill from a kiss in a corner. Did you see me dizzied an' wastin' me time pumpin' ninety-nines out of me, unrecognised, quiverin' with cold an' equivocation!

SIMON. Everybody says he's a very clever fellow with the knife.

SYLVESTER. He'd gouge out your eye, saw off your arm, lift a load of vitals out of your middle, rub his hands, keep down a terrible desire to cheer lookin' at the ruin, an say, 'Twenty-six, when you're a little better, you'll feel a new man!'

Mrs Heegan, Mrs Foran, and Teddy enter from the grounds. Mrs Foran is leading Teddy, who has a heavy bandage over his eyes, and is dressed in the blue clothes of military hospitals.

MRS FORAN [*to Teddy*] Just a little step here, Ted; upsh! That's it; now we're on the earth again, beside Simon and Sylvester. You'd better sit here.

She puts him sitting on a chair.

SYLVESTER [*to Mrs Heegan, as she kisses him*] Well, how's the old woman, eh?

MRS HEEGAN. A little anxious about poor Harry.

SIMON. He'll be alright. Tomorrow'll tell a tale.

SUSIE [*coming in, annoyed*] Who let you up here at this hour? Twenty-eight's to have an operation tomorrow, and shouldn't be disturbed.

MRS HEEGAN. Sister Peter Alcantara said we might come up, Nurse.

MRS FORAN [*loftily*] Sister Peter Alcantara's authority ought to be good enough, I think.

MRS HEEGAN. Sister Peter Alcantara said a visit might buck him up a bit.

MRS FORAN. Sister Peter Alcantara knows the responsibility she'd incur by keeping a wife from her husband and a mother from her son.

SUSIE. Sister Peter Alcantara hasn't got to nurse him. And remember, nothing is to be said that would make his habit of introspection worse than it is.

MRS FORAN [*with dignity*] Thanks for the warnin', Nurse, but them kind of mistakes is unusual with us.

Susie goes out left, as Harry wheels himself rapidly in. Seeing the group, he stops suddenly, and a look of disappointment comes on to his face.

MRS HEEGAN [*kissing Harry*] How are you, son?

MRS FORAN. I brought Teddy, your brother in arms, up to see you, Harry.

HARRY [*impatiently*] Where's Jessie? I thought you were to bring her with you?

MRS HEEGAN. She's comin' after us in a moment.

HARRY. Why isn't she here now?

MRS FORAN. She stopped to have a word in the grounds with someone she knew.

HARRY. It was Barney Bagnal, was it? Was it Barney Bagnal?

TEDDY. Maybe she wanted to talk to him about gettin' the V.C.

HARRY. What V.C.? Who's gettin' the V.C.?

TEDDY. Barney. Did he not tell you? [*Mrs Foran prods his knee*]. What's up?

HARRY [*intensely, to Teddy*] What's he gettin' it for? What's he gettin' the V.C. for?

TEDDY. For carryin' you wounded out of the line of fire. [*Mrs Foran prods his knee*]. What's up?

HARRY [*in anguish*] Christ Almighty, for carryin' me wounded out of the line of fire!

MRS HEEGAN [*rapidly*] Harry, I wouldn't be thinkin' of anything till we see what the operation'll do tomorrow.

SIMON [*rapidly*] God, if it gave him back the use even of one of his legs.

MRS FORAN [*rapidly*] Look at all the places he could toddle to, an' all the things he could do then with the prop of a crutch.

MRS HEEGAN. Even at the worst, he'll never be dependin' on anyone, for he's bound to get the maximum allowance.

SIMON. Two quid a week, isn't it?

SYLVESTER. Yes, a hundred per cent total incapacitation.

HARRY. She won't come up if one of you don't go down and bring her up.

MRS HEEGAN. She's bound to come up, for she's got your ukelele.

HARRY. Call her up, Simon, call her up – I must see Jessie.

Simon goes over to the door leading to the grounds, and looks out.

MRS FORAN [*bending over till her face is close to Harry's*] The drawn look on his face isn't half as bad as when I seen him last.

MRS HEEGAN [*bending and looking into Harry's face*] Look, the hollows under his eyes is fillin' up, too.

TEDDY. I'm afraid he'll have to put Jessie out of his head, for when a man's hit in the spine ... [*Mrs Foran prods his knee*]. What's up, woman?

HARRY [*impatiently, to Simon*] Is she coming? Can you see her anywhere?

SIMON. I see someone like her in the distance, under the trees.

HARRY. Call her; can't you give her a shout, man?

SIMON [*calling*] Jessie. Is that you, Jessie! Jessic-e!

MRS HEEGAN [*to Harry*] What time are you goin' under the operation?

HARRY [*to Simon*] Call her again, call her again, can't you!

SIMON [*calling*] Jessie; Jessie-e!

TEDDY. Not much of a chance for an injury to the spine, for ...

MRS FORAN [*putting her face close to Teddy's*] Oh, shut up, you!

HARRY. Why did you leave her in the grounds? Why didn't you wait till she came up with you?

MRS FORAN [*going over to Simon and calling*] Jessie, Jessie-e!

JESSIE'S VOICE, IN DISTANCE. Yehess!

MRS FORAN [*calling*] Come up here at once; we're all waiting' for you!

JESSIE'S VOICE. I'm not going up!

MRS FORAN [*calling*] Bring up that ukelele here at once, miss!

JESSIE'S VOICE. Barney'll bring it up!

Harry, who has been listening intently, wheels himself rapidly to where Simon and Mrs Foran are, pushing through them hurriedly.

HARRY [*calling loudly*] Jessie! Jessie! Jessie-e!

MRS FORAN. Look at that now; she's runnin' away, the young rip!

HARRY [*appealingly*] Jessie, Jessie-e!

Susie enters quickly from left. She goes over to Harry and pulls him back from the door.

SUSIE [*indignantly*] Disgraceful! Rousing the whole ward with this commotion! Dear, dear, dear, look at the state of Twenty-eight. Come along, come along, please; you must all go at once.

HARRY. Jessie's coming up for a minute, Nurse.

SUSIE. No more to come up. We've had enough for one night, and you for a serious operation tomorrow. Come on, all out, please.

Susie conducts Mrs Heegan, Mrs Foran, and Teddy out left.

MRS FORAN [*going out*] We're goin', we're goin', thank you. A nice way to treat the flotssm and jetssm of the battlefields!

SUSIE [*to Harry*] To bed now, Twenty-eight, please. [*To Simon*]. Help me get him to bed, Twenty-seven.

Susie pushes Harry to his bed, right; Simon brings portion of a bed-screen which he places around Harry, hiding him from view.

SUSIE [*turning to speak to Sylvester, who is sitting up in bed, as she arranges the screen*] You're going to have your little operation in the morning, so you'd better go to sleep too.

Sylvester goes pale and a look of dismay and fear crawls over his face.

SUSIE. Don't funk it now. They're not going to turn you inside out. It'll be over in ten minutes.

SYLVESTER [*with a groan*] When they once get you down your only hope is in the infinite mercy of God!

SIMON. If I was you, Sylvester, I wouldn't take this operation too seriously. You know th' oul' song – Let Me like a Soldier Fall! If I was you, I'd put it completely out of me mind.

SYLVESTER [*subsiding on to the pillow – with an agonised look on his face*] Let me like a soldier fall! Did anyone ever hear th' equal o' that! Put it out of me mind completely! [*He sits up, and glares at Simon*]. Eh, you, look! If you can't think sensibly, then thry to think without talkin'! [*He sinks back on the pillow again*]. Let me like a soldier fall. Oh, it's not a fair trial for a sensible man to be stuck down in a world like this!

Sylvester slides down till he lies prone and motionless on the bed. Harry is in bed now. Simon removes the screen, and Susie arranges Harry's quilt for the night.

SUSIE [*to Simon*] Now run and help get the things together for supper. [*Simon goes out left*]. [*Encouragingly to Harry*]. After the operation, a stay in the air of the Convalescent may work wonders.

HARRY. If I could mingle my breath with the breeze that blows from every sea, and over every land, they wouldn't widen me into anything more than the shrivell'd thing I am.

SUSIE [*switching off the two hanging lights, so that the red light over the fireplace alone remains*] Don't be foolish, Twenty-eight. Wheeling yourself about among the beeches and the pines, when the daffodils are hanging out their blossoms, you'll deepen your chance in the courage and renewal of the country.

The bell of a Convent in grounds begins to ring for Compline.

HARRY [*with intense bitterness*] I'll say to the pine, 'Give me the grace and beauty of the beech'; I'll say to the beech, 'Give me the strength and stature of the pine'. In a net I'll catch butterflies in bunches; twist and mangle them between my fingers and fix them wriggling on to mercy's banner. I'll make my chair a Juggernaut, and wheel it over the neck and spine of every daffodil that looks at me, and strew them dead to manifest the mercy of God and the justice of man!

SUSIE [*shocked*] Shush, Harry, Harry!

HARRY. To hell with you, your country, trees, and things, you jibbering jay!

SUSIE [*as she is going out*] Twenty-eight!

HARRY [*vehemently*] To hell with you, your country, trees, and things, you jibbering jay!

Susie looks at him, pauses for a few moments, as if to speak, and then goes out.

A pause; then Barney comes in by door from grounds. An overcoat covers his military hospital uniform of blue. His left arm is in a sling. Under his right arm he carries a ukelele, and in his hand he has a bunch of flowers. Embarrassed, he goes slowly to Harry's bed, drops the flowers at the foot, then he drops the ukelele there.

BARNEY [*awkwardly*] Your ukelele. An' a bunch of flowers from Jessie. *Harry remains motionless on the bed.*

BARNEY. A bunch of flowers from Jessie, and . . . your . . . ukelele.

The Sister of the Ward enters, left, going to the chapel for Compline. She wears a cream habit with a white coif; a large set of Rosary beads hangs from her girdle. She pauses on her way, and a brass Crucifix flashes on her bosom.

SISTER [*to Harry*] Keeping brave and hopeful, Twenty-eight?

HARRY [*softly*] Yes, Sister.

SISTER. Splendid. And we've got a ukelele too. Can you play it, my child?

HARRY. Yes, Sister.

SISTER. Splendid. You must play me something when you're well over the operation. [*To Barney*]. Standing guard over your comrade, Twenty-two, eh?

BARNEY [*softly and shyly*] Yes, Sister.

SISTER. Grand. Forasmuch as ye do it unto the least of these my brethren, ye do it unto me. Well, God be with you both, my children. [*To Harry*]. And Twenty-eight, pray to God, for wonderful He is in His doing toward the children of men.

Calm and dignified she goes out into the grounds.

BARNEY [*pausing as he goes out left*] They're on the bed; the ukelele, and the bunch of flowers from . . . Jessie.

The Sisters are heard singing in the Convent the hymn of Salve Regina.

SISTERS:

Salve Regina, mater misericordiae;

Vitae dulcedo et spes nostra, salve!

Ad te clamamus, exules filii Hevae;

Ad te suspiramus, gementes et flentes in hac lacrymarum valle.

Eia ergo Advocata nostra,

Illos tuos misericordes oculos ad nos converte,

Et Jesum, benedictum fructum ventris tui –

HARRY. God of the miracles, give a poor devil a chance, give a poor devil a chance!

SISTERS:

Nobis post hoc exsilium ostende,

O clemens, o pia, o dulcis Virgo Maria!

ACT IV

A room of the dance hall of the Avondale Football Club. At back, left, cutting corners of the back and side walls, is the arched entrance, divided by a slim pillar, to the dance hall. This entrance is hung with crimson and black striped curtains; whenever these are parted the dancers can be seen swinging or gliding past the entrance if a dance be taking place at the time. Over the entrance is a scroll on which is printed: 'Up the Avondales!' The wall back has a wide, tall window which opens to the garden, in which the shrubs and some sycamore trees can be seen. It is hung with apple-green casement curtains, which are pulled to the side to allow the window to be open as it is at present. Between the entrance to hall and the window is a Roll of Honour containing the names of five members of the Club killed in the war. Underneath the Roll of Honour a wreath of laurel tied with red and black ribbon. To the front left is the fireplace. Between the fireplace and the hall entrance is a door on which is an oval white enamel disc with 'Caretaker' painted on it. To the right a long table, covered with a green cloth, on which are numerous bottles of wine and a dozen glasses. On the table, too, is a telephone. A brown carpet covers the floor. Two easy and one ordinary chairs are in the room. Hanging from the ceiling are three lanterns; the centre one is four times the length of its width, the ones at the side are less than half as long as the centre lantern and hang horizontally; the lanterns are black, with a broad red stripe running down the centre of the largest and across those hanging at each side, so that, when they are lighted, they suggest an illuminated black cross with an inner one of gleaming red. The hall is vividly decorated with many coloured lanterns, looped with coloured streamers.

When the scene is revealed the curtains are drawn, and the band can be heard playing a fox-trot. Outside in the garden, near the window, Simon and Sylvester can be seen smoking, and Teddy is walking slowly up and down the path. The band is heard playing for a few moments, then the curtains are pulled aside, and Jessie, with Barney holding her hand, comes

*in and walks rapidly to the table where the wine is standing. They are
quickly followed by Harry, who wheels himself a little forward, then stops,
watching them. The curtains part again, and Mrs Heegan is seen watching
Harry. Simon and Sylvester, outside, watch those in the room through the
window. Barney wears a neat navy-blue suit, with a rather high, stiff collar
and black tie. Pinned on the breast of his waistcoat are his war medals,
flanked by the Victoria Cross. Harry is also wearing his medals. Jessie has
on a very pretty, rather tight-fitting dance frock, with the sleeves falling
widely to the elbow, and cut fairly low on her breast. All the dancers, and
Harry too, wear coloured, fantastically shaped paper hats.*

JESSIE [*hot, excited, and uneasy, as with a rapid glance back she sees the
curtains parted by Harry*] Here he comes prowling after us again! His
watching of us is pulling all the enjoyment out of the night. It makes
me shiver to feel him wheeling after us.

BARNEY. We'll watch for a chance to shake him off, an' if he starts
again we'll make him take his tangled body somewhere else. [*As
Harry moves forward from the curtained entrance*]. Shush, he's comin'
near us. [*In a louder tone to Jessie*]. Red wine, Jessie, for you, or
white wine?

HARRY. Red wine first, Jessie, to the passion and the power and the
pain of life, an' then a drink of white wine to the melody that is in
them all!

JESSIE. I'm so hot.

HARRY. I'm so cold; white wine for the woman warm to make her
cold; red wine for the man that's cold to make him warm!

JESSIE. White wine for me.

HARRY. For me the red wine till I drink to men puffed up with pride
of strength, for even creeping things can praise the Lord!

BARNEY [*gently to Harry, as he gives a glass of wine to Jessie*] No more
for you now, Harry.

HARRY [*mockingly*] Oh, please, your lusty lordship, just another, an' if
I seek a second, smack me well. [*Wheeling his chair viciously against
Barney*]. Get out, you trimm'd-up clod. There's medals on my
breast as well as yours! [*He fills a glass*].

JESSIE. Let us go back to the dancing, Barney. [*Barney hesitates*].
Please, Barney, let us go back to the dancing!

HARRY. To the dancing, for the day cometh when no man can play. And legs were made to dance, to run, to jump, to carry you from one place to another; but mine can neither walk, nor run, nor jump, nor feel the merry motion of a dance. But stretch me on the floor fair on my belly, and I will turn over on my back, then wriggle back again on to my belly; and that's more than a dead, dead man can do!

BARNEY. Jessie wants to dance, an' so we'll go, and leave you here a little.

HARRY. Cram pain with pain, and pleasure cram with pleasure. I'm going too. You'd cage me in from seeing you dance, and dance, and dance, with Jessie close to you and you so close to Jessie. Though you wouldn't think it, yes, I have – I've hammer'd out many a merry measure upon a polish'd floor with a sweet, sweet heifer. [*As Barney and Jessie are moving away he catches hold of Jessie's dress*]. Her name? Oh, any name will do – we'll call her Jessie!

JESSIE. Oh, let me go. [*To Barney*]. Barney, make him let me go, please.

Barney, without a word, removes Harry's hand from Jessie's dress. Jessie and Barney then go out to the dance hall through the curtained entrance. After a while Mrs Heegan slips away from the entrance into the hall. After a moment's pause Harry follows them into the hall. Simon and Sylvester come in from the garden, leaving Teddy still outside smoking and walking to and fro in the cautious manner of the blind. Simon and Sylvester sit down near the fire and puff in silence for a few moments.

SYLVESTER [*earnestly*] I knew it. I knew it, Simon – strainin', an' strainin' his nerves; driftin', an' driftin' towards an hallucination!

SIMON. Jessie might try to let him down a little more gently, but it would have been better, I think, if Harry hadn't come here tonight.

SYLVESTER. I concur in that, Simon. What's a decoration to an hospital is an anxiety here.

SIMON. To carry life and colour to where there's nothing but the sick and helpless is right; but to carry the sick and helpless to where there's nothing but life and colour is wrong.

The telephone bell rings.

SYLVESTER. There's the telephone bell ringing.

SIMON. Oh, someone'll come in and answer it in a second.

SYLVESTER. To join a little strength to a lot of weakness is what I call sensible; but to join a little weakness to a lot of strength is what I call a . . .

SIMON. A cod.

SYLVESTER. Exactly.   [*The telephone continues to ring*].

SYLVESTER. There's that telephone ringin' still.

SIMON. Oh, someone'll come in and answer it in a second.

Teddy has groped his way to French window.

TEDDY. The telephone's tinklin', boys.

SYLVESTER. Thanks, Teddy. We hear it, thanks. [*To Simon*]. When he got the invitation from the Committay to come, wearin' his decorations, me an' the old woman tried to persuade him that, seein' his condition, it was better to stop at home, an' let me represent him, but [*with a gesture*] no use!

Teddy resumes his walk to and fro.

SIMON. It was natural he'd want to come, since he was the means of winning the Cup twice before for them, leading up to their keeping the trophy for ever by the win of a year ago.

SYLVESTER. To bring a boy so helpless as him, whose memory of agility an' strength time hasn't flattened down, to a place wavin' with joy an' dancin', is simply, simply –

SIMON. Devastating, I'd say.

SYLVESTER. Of course it is! Is that god-damn telephone goin' to keep ringin' all night?

Mrs Foran enters from hall quickly.

MRS FORAN. Miss Monican says that one of you is to answer the telephone, an' call her if it's anything important.

SYLVESTER [*nervously*] I never handled a telephone in my life.

SIMON. I chanced it once and got so hot and quivery that I couldn't hear a word, and didn't know what I was saying myself.

MRS FORAN. Have a shot at it and see.

The three of them drift over to the telephone.

SYLVESTER. Chance it again, Simon, an' try to keep steady.

As Simon stretches his hand to the receiver.

SYLVESTER. Don't rush, don't rush, man, an' make a mess of it. Take it in your stride.

SIMON [*pointing to receiver*] When you lift this down, you're connected, I think.

SYLVESTER. No use of thinkin' on this job. Don't you turn the handle first?

SIMON [*irritably*] No, you don't turn no handle, man!

MRS FORAN. Let Simon do it now; Simon knows.

Simon tremblingly lifts down the receiver, almost letting it fall.

SYLVESTER. Woa, woa, Simon; careful, careful!

SIMON [*speaking in receiver*] Eh, hallo! Eh, listen there. Eh, hallo! listen.

SYLVESTER. You listen, man, an' give the fellow at the other end a chance to speak.

SIMON. If you want me to manipulate the thing, let me manipulate it in tranquility.

MRS FORAN [*to Sylvester*] Oh, don't be puttin' him out, Sylvester.

SIMON [*waving them back*] Don't be crushing in on me; give me room to manipulate the thing.

Dead silence for some moments.

MRS FORAN. Are you hearin' anything from the other end?

SIMON. A kind of buzz and a roaring noise.

Sylvester suddenly gives the cord a jerk and pulls the receiver out of Simon's hand.

[*Angrily*]. What the hell are you trying to do, man? You're after pulling it right out of my mit.

SYLVESTER [*heatedly*] There was a knot or a twist an' a tangle in it that was keepin' the sound from travellin'.

SIMON. If you want me to work the thing properly, you'll have to keep yourself from interfering. [*Resuming surlily*]. Eh, hallo, listen, yes? Ha! ha! ha! ha! Yes, yes, yes. No, no, no. Cheerio! Yes. Eh, hallo, listen, eh. Hallo.

SYLVESTER. What is it? What're they sayin'?

SIMON [*hopelessly, taking the receiver from his ear*] I don't seem to be able to hear a damn sound.

SYLVESTER. An' Holy God, what are you yessin' and noin' and cheerioin' out of you for then?

SIMON. You couldn't stand here like a fool and say nothing, could you?

SYLVESTER. Show it to me, Simon, show it to me – you're not holdin' it at the proper angle.

MRS FORAN. Give it to Syl, Simon; it's a delicate contrivance that needs a knack in handlin'.

SYLVESTER [*as he is taking the receiver from Simon and carefully placing it to his ear*] You have always to preserve an eqwee-balance between the speakin' mouth and the hearin' ear. [*Speaking into receiver*]. Hallo! Anybody there at the other end of this? Eh, wha's that? Yes, yes, I've got you [*taking the receiver from his ear and speaking to Simon and Mrs Foran*]: Something like wine, or dine, or shine, or something – an' a thing that's hummin'.

SIMON. I can see no magnificent meaning jumping out of that!

MRS FORAN. They couldn't be talkin' about bees, could they?

SYLVESTER [*scornfully*] Bees! No, they couldn't be talkin' about bees! That kind of talk, Mrs Foran, only tends to confuse matters. Bees! Dtch, dtch, dtch – the stupidity of some persons is . . . terrifyin'!

SIMON. Ask them quietly what they want.

SYLVESTER [*indignantly*] What the hell's the use of askin' them that, when I can hear something only like a thing that's hummin'?

MRS FORAN. It wouldn't be, now, comin', or even bummin'?

SYLVESTER. It might even possibly be drummin'. Personally, Mrs Foran, I think, since you can't help, you might try to keep from hinderin'.

SIMON. Put it back, Syl, where it was, an' if it rings again, we'll only have to slip quietly out of this.

MRS FORAN. Yes, put it back, an' say it never rang.

SYLVESTER. Where was it? Where do I put it back?

SIMON. On that thing stickin' out there. Nice and gently now.

Sylvester cautiously puts receiver back. They look at the telephone for a few moments, then go back to the fire, one by one. Sylvester stands with his back to it; Simon sits in a chair, over the back of which Mrs Foran leans.

MRS FORAN. Curious those at the other end of the telephone couldn't make themselves understood.

SIMON. Likely they're not accustomed to it, and it's a bit difficult if you're not fully conscious of its manipulation.

SYLVESTER. Well, let them study an' study it then, or abide by the consequences, for we can't be wastin' time teachin' them.

The curtains at entrance of dance hall are pulled aside, and Teddy, who has disappeared from the garden a little time before, comes in. As he leaves the curtains apart, the dancers can be seen gliding past the entrance in the movements of a tango. Teddy comes down, looks steadily but vacantly towards the group around the fire, then goes over carefully to the table, where he moves his hand about till it touches a bottle, which he takes up in one hand, feeling it questioningly with the other.

SIMON. How goes it, Teddy?

TEDDY [*with a vacant look towards them*] Sylvester – Simon – well. What seest thou, Teddy? Thou seest not as man seeth. In the garden the trees stand up; the green things showeth themselves and fling out flowers of divers hues. In the sky the sun by day and the moon and the stars by night – nothing. In the hall the sound of dancing, the eyes of women, grey and blue and brown and black, do sparkle and dim and sparkle again. Their white breasts rise and fall, and rise again. Slender legs, from red and black, and white and green, come out, go in again – nothing. Strain as you may, it stretches from the throne of God to the end of the hearth of hell.

SIMON. What?

TEDDY. The darkness.

SIMON [*knowing not what to say*] Yes, oh yes.

TEDDY [*holding up a bottle of wine*] What colour, Syl? It's all the same, but I like the red the best.

MRS FORAN [*going over to Teddy*]. Just one glass, dear, and you'll sit down quietly an' take it in sips.

Mrs Foran fills a glass of wine for Teddy, leads him to a chair, puts him sitting down, and gives the glass of wine carefully to him. The band in the hall has been playing and through the parted curtains the dancers are seen gliding past. Jessie moves by now in the arms of Barney, and in a few moments is followed along the side of the hall by Harry wheeling himself in his chair and watching them. Mrs Foran and the two men look on and become more attentive when among the dancers Susie, in the arms of Surgeon Maxwell, Jessie partnered with Barney, and Harry move past.

SYLVESTER [*as Susie goes by*] Susie Monican's lookin' game enough to-night for anything.

SIMON. Hardly remindful of her one-time fear of God.

SYLVESTER [*as Jessie goes by followed by Harry*] There he goes, still followin' them.

SIMON. And Jessie's looking as if she was tired of her maidenhood, too.

MRS FORAN. The thin threads holdin' her dress up sidelin' down over her shoulders, an' her catchin' them up again at the tail end of the second before it was too late.

SIMON [*grinning*] And Barney's hand inching up, inching up to pull them down a little lower when they're sliding down.

MRS FORAN. Astonishin' the way girls are advertisin' their immodesty. Whenever one of them sits down, in my heart I pity the poor men havin' to view the disedifyin' sight of the full length of one leg couched over another.

TEDDY [*forgetful*] A damn nice sight, all the same, I think.

MRS FORAN [*indignantly*] One would imagine such a thought would jar a man's mind that had kissed goodbye to the sight of his eyes.

TEDDY. Oh, don't be tickin' off every word I say!

MRS FORAN [*after an astonished pause, whipping the glass out of Teddy's hand*] Damn the drop more, now, you'll get for the rest of the evenin'.

The band suddenly stops playing, and the couples seen just then through the doorway stop dancing and look attentively up the hall. After a slight pause, Harry in his chair, pushed by Susie, comes in through the entrance; his face is pale and drawn, his breath comes in quick fast gasps, and his head is leaning sideways on the back of the chair. Mrs Heegan is on one side of Harry, and Surgeon Maxwell, who is in dinner-jacket style of evening dress, wearing his medals, including the D.S.O., walks on the other. Harry is wheeled over near the open window. Barney and Jessie, standing in the entrance, look on and listen.

MAXWELL. Here near the window. [*To Mrs Heegan*]. He'll be all right, Mrs Heegan, in a second; a little faint – too much excitement. When he recovers a little, I'd get him home.

HARRY [*faintly but doggedly*] Napoo home, napoo. Not yet. I'm all right. I'll spend a little time longer in the belly of an hour bulgin' out with merriment. Carry on.

MAXWELL. Better for you to go home, Heegan.

HARRY. When they drink to the Club from the Cup – the Silver

Tassie – that I won three times, three times for them – that first was filled to wet the lips of Jessie and of me – I'll go, but not yet. I'm all right; my name is yet only a shadow on the Roll of Honour.

MRS HEEGAN. Come home, Harry; you're gettin' your allowance only on the understandin' that you take care of yourself.

HARRY. Get the Cup. I'll mind it here till you're ready to send it round to drink to the Avondales – on the table here beside me. Bring the Cup; I'll mind it here on the table beside me.

MAXWELL. Get the Cup for him, someone.

Simon goes to the hall and returns with the Cup, which he gives to Harry.

HARRY [*holding the Cup out*] A first drink again for me, for me alone this time, for the shell that hit me bursts for ever between Jessie and me. [*To Simon*]. Go on, man, fill out the wine!

MAXWELL [*to Simon*] A little – just a glass. Won't do him any harm. [*To Harry*]. Then you'll have to remain pefectly quiet, Heegan.

HARRY. The wine – fill out the wine!

SIMON [*to Harry*] Red wine or white?

HARRY. Red wine, red like the faint remembrance of the fires in France; red wine like the poppies that spill their petals on the breasts of the dead men. No, white wine, white like the stillness of the millions that have removed their clamours from the crowd of life. No, red wine; red like the blood that was shed for you and for many for the commission of sins! [*He drinks the wine*]. Steady, Harry, and lift up thine eyes unto the hills. [*Roughly to those around him*]. What are you all gaping at?

MAXWELL. Now, now, Heegan – you must try to keep quiet.

SUSIE. And when you've rested and feel better, you will sing for us a Negro Spiritual, and point the melody with the ukelele.

MRS HEEGAN. Just as he used to do.

SYLVESTER. Behind the trenches.

SIMON. In the Rest Camps.

MRS FORAN. Out in France.

HARRY. Push your sympathy away from me, for I'll have none of it. [*He wheels his chair quickly towards the dance hall*]. Go on with the dancing and keep the ball a-rolling. [*Calling loudly at the entrance*]. Trumpets and drum begin! [*The band begins to play*]. Dance and dance and dance. [*He listens for a moment*]. Sink into merriment again, and sling

your cares to God! [*He whirls round in the chair to the beat of the tune.
Dancers are seen gliding past entrance*]. Dear God, I can't. [*He sinks
sideways on his chair*]. I must, must rest. [*He quietly recites*]

> For a spell here I will stay,
> Then pack up my body and go –
> For mine is a life on the ebb,
> Yours a full life on the flow!

*Harry goes over to far side of window and looks out into garden. Mrs
Heegan is on his right and Teddy on his left; Simon and Sylvester a little
behind, looking on. Mrs Foran to the right of Mrs Heegan. Surgeon Maxwell
and Susie, who are a little to the front, watch for a moment, then the
Surgeon puts his arm round Susie and the pair glide off into the dance hall.*

*When Surgeon Maxwell and Susie glide in to the motions of the dance
through the entrance into the dance hall, the curtains are pulled together. A
few moments' pause. Teddy silently puts his hand on Harry' shoulder, and
they both stare into the garden.*

SIMON. The air'll do him good.

SYLVESTER. An' give him breath to sing his song an' play the ukelele.

MRS HEEGAN. Just as he used to do.

SYLVESTER. Behind the trenches.

SIMON. In the Rest Camps.

MRS FORAN. Out in France.

HARRY. I can see, but I cannot dance.

TEDDY. I can dance, but I cannot see.

HARRY. Would that I had the strength to do the things I see.

TEDDY. Would that I could see the things I've strength to do.

HARRY. The Lord hath given and the Lord hath taken away.

TEDDY. Blessed be the name of the Lord.

MRS FORAN. I do love the ukelele, especially when it goes tinkle,
tinkle, tinkle in the night-time.

SYLVESTER. Bringin' before you glistenin' bodies of blacks, coilin'
themselves an' shufflin' an' prancin' in a great jungle dance; shakin'
assegais an' spears to the rattle, rattle, rattle an' thud, thud, thud of
the tom-toms.

MRS FORAN. There's only one possible musical trimmin' to the air of
a Negro Spiritual, an' that's the tinkle, tinkle, tinkle of a ukelele.

HARRY. The rising sap in trees I'll never feel.

TEDDY. The hues of branch or leaf I'll never see.

HARRY. There's something wrong with life when men can walk.

TEDDY. There's something wrong with life when men can see.

HARRY. I never felt the hand that made me helpless.

TEDDY. I never saw the hand that made me blind.

HARRY. Life came and took away the half of life.

TEDDY. Life took from me the half he left with you.

HARRY. The Lord hath given and the Lord hath taken away.

TEDDY. Blessed be the name of the Lord.

Susie comes quickly in by entrance, goes over to the table and, looking at several bottles of wine, selects one. She is going hurriedly back, when, seeing Harry, she goes over to him.

SUSIE [*kindly*] How are you now, Harry?

HARRY. All right, thank you.

SUSIE. That's good.

Susie is about to hurry away, when Mrs Foran stops her with a remark.

MRS FORAN [*with a meaning gesture*] He's takin' it cushy till you're ready to hear him singin' his Negro Spiritual, Miss.

SUSIE. Oh, God, I'd nearly forgotten that. They'll be giving out the balloons at the next dance, and when that fox-trot's over he'll have to come in and sing us the Spiritual.

MRS HEEGAN. Just as he used to do.

SIMON. Behind the trenches.

SYLVESTER. In the Rest Camps.

MRS FORAN. Out in France.

SUSIE. As soon as the Balloon Dance is over, Harry, out through the garden and in by the front entrance with you, so that you'll be ready to start as they all sit down. And after the song, we'll drink to the Club from the Silver Tassie.

She hurries back to the hall with the bottle of wine.

MRS FORAN. I'm longin' to hear Harry on the ukelele.

HARRY. I hope I'll be able to do justice to it.

MRS HEEGAN. Of course you will, Harry.

HARRY [*nervously*] Before a crowd. Forget a word and it's all up with you.

SIMON. Try it over now, softly; the sound couldn't carry as far as the hall.

SYLVESTER. It'll give you confidence in yourself.

HARRY [*to Simon*] Show us the ukelele, Simon.

Simon gets the ukelele and gives it to Harry.

TEDDY. If I knew the ukelele it might wean me a little way from the darkness.

Harry pulls a few notes, tuning the ukelele, then he softly sings.

HARRY:

Swing low, sweet chariot, comin' for to carry me home,

Swing low, sweet chariot, comin' for to carry me home.

I looked over Jordan, what did I see, comin' for to carry me home?

A band of angels comin' after me – comin' for to carry me home.

A voice in the hall is heard shouting through a megaphone.

VOICE. Balloons will be given out now! Given out now – the balloons!

MRS FORAN [*excitedly*] They're goin' to send up the balloons! They're going to let the balloons fly now!

HARRY [*singing*]:

Swing low, sweet chariot, comin' for to carry me home.

Swing low, sweet chariot, comin' for to carry me home.

MRS FORAN [*as Harry is singing*] Miss Monican wants us all to see the flyin' balloons.

She catches Teddy's arm and runs with him into the hall.

SIMON. We must all see the flyin' balloons.

MRS HEEGAN [*running into hall*] Red balloons and black balloons.

SIMON [*following Mrs Heegan*] Green balloons and blue balloons.

SYLVESTER [*following Simon*] Yellow ballons and puce balloons.

All troop into the hall, leaving the curtains apart, and Harry alone with his ukelele. Through the entrance various coloured balloons that have been tossed into the air can be seen, mid sounds of merriment and excitement.

HARRY [*softly*] Comin' for to carry me home.

He throws the ukelele into an arm-chair, sits still for a moment, then goes to the table, takes up the silver cup, and wheels himself into the garden.

After a pause Barney looks in, then enters pulling Jessie by the hand, letting the curtains fall together again. Then he goes quickly to window, shuts and bolts it, drawing-to one half of the curtains, goes back to Jessie, catches

*her hand again, and tries to draw her towards room on the left. During the
actions that follow the dance goes merrily on in the hall.*

JESSIE [*holding up a broken shoulder-strap and pulling back towards the
hall*] Barney, no. God, I'd be afraid he might come in on us alone.

*Hands part the curtains and throw in coloured streamers that encircle
Jessie and Barney.*

BARNEY. Damn them! . . . He's gone, I tell you, to sing the song an'
play the ukelele.

JESSIE [*excited and afraid*] See, they're watching us. No, Barney. You
mustn't. I'll not go! [*Barney seizes Jessie in his arms and forces her
towards the door on the left*]. You wouldn't be good. I'll not go into
that room.

BARNEY. I will be good, I tell you! I just want to be alone with you for
a minute.

*Barney loosens Jessie's other shoulder-strap, so that her dress leaves her
shoulders and bosom bare.*

JESSIE [*near the door left, as Barney opens it*] You've loosened my dress –
I knew you weren't going to be good. [*As she kisses him passionately*].
Barney, Barney – you shouldn't be making me do what I don't want
to do!

BARNEY [*holding her and trying to pull her into room*] Come on, Jessie,
you needn't be afraid of Barney – we'll just rest a few minutes from
the dancing.

*At that part of the window uncurtained Harry is seen peering in. He then
wheels his chair back and comes on to the centre of the window-frame with a
rush, bursting the catch and speeding into the room, coming to a halt, angry
and savage, before Barney and Jessie.*

HARRY. So you'd make merry over my helplessness in front of my
face, in front of my face, you pair of cheats! You couldn't wait till
I'd gone, so that my eyes wouldn't see the joy I wanted hurrying
away from me over to another? Hurt her breast pulling your hand
quick out of her bodice, did you? [*To Jessie*]. Saved you in the nick
of time, my lady, did I? [*To Barney*]. Going to enjoy yourself on the
same little couch where she, before you formed an image in her
eye, acted the part of an amateur wife, and I acted the part of an
amateur husband – the black couch with the green and crimson

butterflies, in the yellow bushes, where she and me often tired of the things you're dangling after now!

JESSIE. He's a liar, he's a liar, Barney! He often tried it on with coaxing first and temper afterwards, but it always ended in a halt that left him where he started.

HARRY. If I had my hands on your white neck I'd leave marks there that crowds of kisses from your Barney wouldn't moisten away.

BARNEY. You half-baked Lazarus, I've put up with you all the evening, so don't force me now to rough-handle the bit of life the Jerrics left you as a souvenir!

HARRY. When I wanted to slip away from life, you brought me back with your whispered 'Think of the tears of Jess, think of the tears of Jess', but Jess has wiped away her tears in the ribbon of your Cross, and this poor crippled jest gives a flame of joy to the change; but when you get her, may you find in her the pressed down emptiness of a whore!

BARNEY [*running over and seizing Harry*] I'll tilt the leaking life out of you, you jealous, peering pimp!

JESSIE [*trying to hold Barney back*] Barney, Barney, don't! don't!

HARRY [*appealingly*] Barney, Barney! My heart – you're stopping it!

JESSIE [*running to entrance and shouting in*] Help! help! They're killing each other!

In the hall the dance stops. Surgeon Maxwell runs in, followed by Susie, Simon, Sylvester, Mrs Foran, Mrs Heegan, and lastly Teddy finding his way over to the window. Dancers gather around entrance and look on.

Surgeon Maxwell, running over, separates Barney from Harry.

MAXWELL. What's this? Come, come – we can't have this sort of thing going on.

MRS HEEGAN. He was throttlin' him, throttlin' a poor helpless creature, an' if anything happens, he and that painted slug Jessie Taite'll be held accountable!

MAXWELL. This can't be allowed to go on. You'll have to bring him home. Any more excitement would be dangerous.

MRS HEEGAN. This is what he gets from Jessie Taite for sittin' on the stairs through the yawnin' hours of the night, racin' her off to the play an' the pictures, an' plungin' every penny he could keep from me into presents for the consolation of the courtship!

MAXWELL. Bring the boy home, woman, bring the boy home.

SYLVESTER [*fiercely to Jessie*] And money of mine in one of the gewgaws scintillatin' in her hair!

JESSIE. What gewgaw? What gewgaw?

Coloured streamers are thrown in by those standing at entrance, which fall on and encircle some of the group around Harry.

SYLVESTER. The tiarara I gave you two Christmases ago with the yellow berries and the three flutterin' crimson swallows!

HARRY [*faintly and bitterly, with a hard little laugh*] Napoo Barney Bagnal and napoo Jessie Taite. A merry heart throbs coldly in my bosom; a merry heart in a cold bosom – or is it a cold heart in a merry bosom? [*He gathers a number of the coloured streamers and winds them round himself and chair*]. Teddy! [*Harry catches Teddy by the sleeve and winds some more streamers round him*]. Sing a song, man, and show the stuff you're made of!

MAXWELL [*catching hold of Mrs Heegan's arm*] Bring him home, woman. [*Maxwell catches Sylvester's arm*]. Get him home, man.

HARRY. Dear God, this crippled form is still your child. [*To Mrs Heegan*]. Dear mother, this helpless thing is still your son. Harry Heegan, me, who, on the football field, could crash a twelve-stone flyer off his feet. For this dear Club three times I won the Cup, and grieve in reason I was just too weak this year to play again. And now, before I go, I give you all the Cup, the Silver Tassie, to have and to hold for ever, evermore. [*From his chair he takes the Cup with the two sides hammered close together, and holds it out to them*]. Mangled and bruised as I am bruised and mangled. Hammered free from all its comely shape. Look, there is Jessie writ, and here is Harry, the one name safely separated from the other. [*He flings it on the floor*]. Treat it kindly. With care it may be opened out, for Barney there to drink to Jess, and Jessie there to drink to Barney.

TEDDY. Come, Harry, home to where the air is soft. No longer can you stand upon a hill-top; these empty eyes of mine can never see from one. Our best is all behind us – what's in front we'll face like men, dear comrade of the blood-fight and the battle-front!

HARRY. What's in front we'll face like men! [*Harry goes out by the window, Sylvester pushing the chair, Teddy's hand on Harry's shoulder, Mrs Heegan slowly following. Those left in the room watch them going out*

*through the garden, turning to the right till they are all out of sight. As he
goes out of window*]. The Lord hath given and man hath taken away!

TEDDY [*heard from the garden*] Blessed be the name of the Lord!

The band in the hall begin to play again. Those in hall being to dance.

MAXWELL. Come on, all, we've wasted too much time already.

SUSIE [*to Jessie, who is sitting quietly in a chair*] Come on, Jessie – get
your partner; [*roguishly*] you can have a quiet time with Barney later
on.

JESSIE. Poor Harry!

SUSIE. Oh nonsense! If you'd passed as many through your hands as
I, you'd hardly notice one. [*To Jessie*]. Jessie, Teddy Foran and
Harry Heegan have gone to live their own way in another world.
Neither I nor you can lift them out of it. No longer can they do the
things we do. We can't give sight to the blind or make the lame
walk. We would if we could. It is the misfortune of war. As long as
wars are waged, we shall be vexed by woe; strong legs shall be made
useless and bright eyes made dark. But we, who have come through
the fire unharmed, must go on living. [*Pulling Jessie from the chair*].
Come along, and take your part in life! [*To Barney*]. Come along,
Barney, and take your partner into the dance!

*Barney comes over, puts his arm round Jessie, and they dance into the
hall. Susie and Surgeon Maxwell dance together. As they dance the Waltz
'Over the Waves,' some remain behind drinking. Two of these sing the song
to the same tune as the dance.*

MAXWELL:

> Swing into the dance,
> Take joy when it comes, ere it go;
> For the full flavour of life
> Is either a kiss or a blow.
> He to whom joy is a foe,
> Let him wrap himself up in his woe;
> For he is a life on the ebb,
> We a full life on the flow!

*All in the hall dance away with streamers and balloons flying. Simon and
Mrs Foran sit down and watch the fun through the entrance. Mrs Foran
lights a cigarette and smokes. A pause as they look on.*

MRS FORAN. It's a terrible pity Harry was too weak to stay an' sing his song, for there's nothing I love more than the ukelele's tinkle, tinkle, tinkle in the night-time.

SONGS AND CHANTS IN
THE SILVER TASSIE

1st CHANT.

Intonation

I sees the mis-sus paryd-ing a-long Wal-ham Green, Through the jewels

Mediation

an' silks on the cos-ters' carts, Em-mie a-pull-ing her skirt

Ending

an' mut-ter-ing, "A bal-loon, a bal-loon, I wants a bal-loon",

The mis-sus ... an' your fa-ther fight-ing : You'll wait ... that's wot I wants to know !

Tabs 'll ... for-ty-eight bat-ta-lion, The Yel-low ... leg up on the path to glo-ry ;

Now with ... Ar-my of the Marne, An' all the time ... two men looking after business.

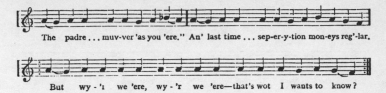

The padre ... muv-ver 'as you 'ere." An' last time ... sep-er-y-tion mon-eys reg'-lar.

But wy-'ı we 'ere, wy-'r we 'ere—that's wot I wants to know?

2nd CHANT.

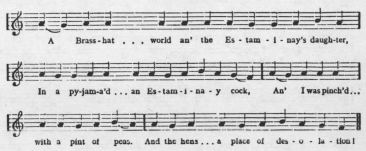

A Brass-hat ... world an' the Es-tam-i-nay's daugh-ter,

In a py-jam-a'd ... an Es-tam-i-na-y cock, An' I was pinch'd ...

with a pint of peas. And the hens ... a place of des-o-la-tion!

3rd CHANT.

The perk-y ... queers me. Furi-ous-ly feel-ing ... front-line fight-ing.

In his full-blown, ... mur-mur, "Here's a stand-fast ... whis-per "yes-sir".

Like a bride, ... ser-mon, From the cush-y ... Tom-my's back-side.

4th CHANT.

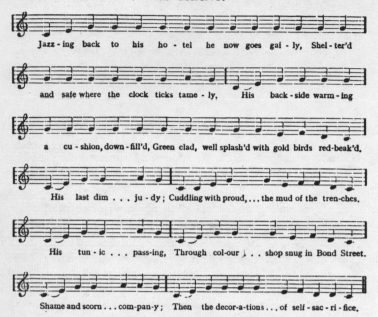

Jazz - ing back to his ho - tel he now goes gai - ly, Shel - ter'd

and safe where the clock ticks tame - ly, His back - side warm - ing

a cu - shion, down - fill'd, Green clad, well splash'd with gold birds red-beak'd.

His last dim . . . ju - dy; Cuddling with proud, . . . the mud of the tren-ches.

His tun - ic . . . pass-ing, Through col-our ⌡ . . shop snug in Bond Street.

Shame and scorn . . . com-pan-y; Then the decor-a-tions . . . of self - sac - ri - fice.

5th CHANT.

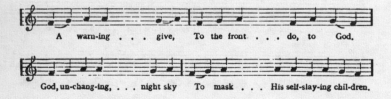

A warn-ing . . . give, To the front . . . do, to God.

God, un-chang-ing, . . . night sky To mask . . . His self-slay-ing chil-dren.

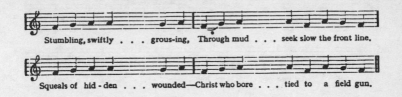

Stumbling, swiftly . . . grous-ing, Through mud . . . seek slow the front line.

Squeals of hid-den . . . wounded—Christ who bore . . . tied to a field gun.

THE ENEMY HAS BROKEN THROUGH.

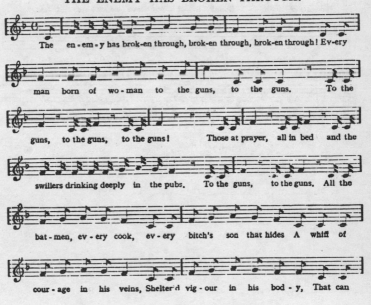

The en-em-y has brok-en through, brok-en through, brok-en through! Ev-ery

man born of wo-man to the guns, to the guns. To the

guns, to the guns, to the guns! Those at prayer, all in bed and the

swillers drinking deeply in the pubs. To the guns, to the guns. All the

bat-men, ev-ery cook, ev-ery bitch's son that hides A whiff of

cour-age in his veins, Shelter'd vig-our in his bod-y, That can

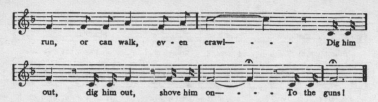

run,   or can walk,   ev - en   crawl—   ·   ·   Dig him

out,   dig him out,   shove him on—   ·   ·   To the guns!

SONG TO THE GUN.

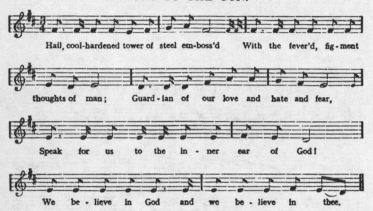

Hail, cool-hardened tower of steel em-boss'd   With the fever'd, fig - ment

thoughts of man;   Guard - ian of   our   love and   hate and fear,

Speak   for   us   to   the   in - ner   ear   of   God!

We   be - lieve   in   God   and   we   be - lieve in   thee.

WOULD GOD, I SMOK'D.

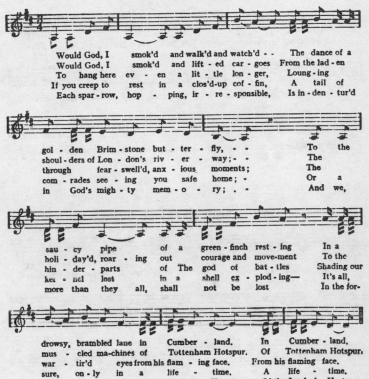

Would God, I smok'd and walk'd and watch'd - - The dance of a
Would God, I smok'd and lift - ed car - goes From the lad - en
To hang here ev - en a lit - tle lon - ger, Loung - ing
If you creep to rest in a clos'd-up cof - fin, A tail of
Each spar - row, hop - ping, ir - re - sponsible, Is in - den - tur'd

gol - den Brim - stone but - ter - fly, - - To the
shoul - ders of Lon - don's riv - er - way; - - The
through fear - swell'd, anx - ious moments; The
com - rades see - ing you safe home; - Or a
in God's migh - ty mem - o - ry; . . And we,

sau - cy pipe of a green - finch rest - ing In a
holi - day'd, roar - ing out courage and move-ment To the
hin - der - parts of The god of bat - tles Shading our
ker - nel lost in a shell ex - plod - ing— It's all,
more than they all, shall not be lost In the for-

drowsy, brambled lane in Cumber - land. In Cumber - land,
mus - cled ma-chines of Tottenham Hotspur. Of Tottenham Hotspur,
war - tir'd eyes from his flam - ing face. From his flaming face,
sure, on - ly in a life - time. A life - time,
get - ful - ness of the Lord of Hosts. Of the Lord of Hosts,

SURGEON'S SONG.

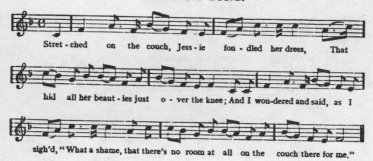

Stret - ched on the couch, Jess - ie fon - dled her dress, That

hid all her beaut - ies just o - ver the knee; And I won-dered and said, as I

sigh'd, "What a shame, that there's no room at all on the couch there for me."

STRETCHER-BEARERS' SONG.

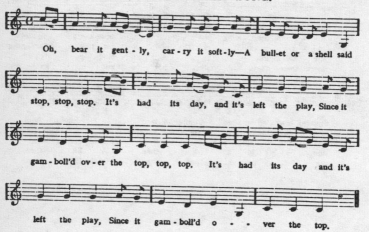

Oh, bear it gent - ly, car - ry it soft - ly—A bull-et or a shell said

stop, stop, stop. It's had its day, and it's left the play, Since it

gam - boll'd ov - er the top, top, top. It's had its day and it's

left the play, Since it gam - boll'd o - - ver the top.

DENIS JOHNSTON

The Old Lady Says 'No!'

Denis Johnston (1901–84)

William Denis Johnston, playwright, critic, director of the Dublin Gate Theatre, and mystical philosopher. He is best known for his plays, which include *The Old Lady Says 'No!'* (1929), *A Bride for the Unicorn* (1925), *The Moon in the Yellow River* (1935), his adaptation of Toller's *Die Blinde Göttin* as *Blind Man's Buff* (1938) and *The Scythe and the Sunset* (1958). He wrote many plays for radio and television, and his non-dramatic writings include *In Search of Swift* (1959) and *The Brazen Horn* (1976).

The Old Lady Says 'No!'

This remarkable play was submitted to the Abbey Theatre under the title *Shadowdance*. W. B. Yeats outlined his ideas on the play to Denis Johnston, saying that the scenes were too long and – after a thoughtful pause – there were too many scenes. Lady Gregory turned up her nose at the play and the words indicating her rejection became the play's title. The Old Lady did indeed say 'No!'. The play was produced at the Gate Theatre on 3 July 1929, with the following cast:

THE SPEAKER (Robert Emmet)	Micheál MacLiammóir
SARAH CURRAN	Meriel Moore
MAJOR SIRR	Hilton Edwards
FIRST REDCOAT	Johann Manning
SECOND REDCOAT	Mitchel Cogley

THE OTHER ONES: Gearóid O'Lochlainn, Coralie Carmichael, Michael Scott, Dorothy Casey, Fred Johnson, Hazel Ellis, Dudley Walsh, Florence Lynch, Art O'Murnaghan, Ida Moore, Dom. Bowe, Kay Scannell, Pauline Besson, Susan Hunt

The play produced and lit by Hilton Edwards; the settings designed and executed by Micheál MacLiammóir; costumes designed by Micheál MacLiammóir and made up by Bougwaine Wilson.

Selected Bibliography

The Dramatic Works of Denis Johnston, vol. I (General Introduction; *The Old Lady Says 'No!'' A Note on what happened; The Scythe and the Sunset; Storm Song; The Dreaming Dust; Strange Occurrence on Ireland's Eye*); Vol. II (Preface; *A Bride for the Unicorn; The Moon in the Yellow River; A Fourth for Bridge; The Golden Cuckoo; The Tain – a Pageant;* 'Introducing the enigmatic Dean Swift'); Gerrards Cross, Colin Smythe, 1977, 1979. Johnston contributes the General Introduction, 'Note', Preface, and prefatory remarks on each play. Special reference: Plays. *The Old Lady Says 'No!'*, *The Moon in the Yellow River, Two Plays*, London, Jonathan Cape, 1932; *Storm Song and A Bride for the Unicorn*, London, Johathan Cape, 1935; *The Golden Cuckoo and other plays*, London, Jonathan Cape, 1954. Other works: *Nine Rivers from Jordan*, London, Derek Verschoyle, 1953; *In Search of Swift*, Dublin, Allen Figgis, 1959, *The Brazen Horn*, Dublin, Dolmen, 1977.

The Old Lady Says 'No!'

A Romantic Play in Two Parts
with Choral Interludes

Opus One

One of the best loved figures of Irish romantic literature is Robert Emmet. The story of his rebellion of 1803 has all of the elements that make for magic. It was very high-minded, and completely unsuccessful. It was picturesquely costumed and insufficiently organized. Its leader – a young protestant university man of excellent social background – having failed to achieve anything more than an armed street riot, remained behind to bid goodbye to his forbidden sweetheart, instead of taking flight as any sensible rebel should do. In consequence of this, he was captured by an ogre of melodrama called Major Sirr, and was hanged after making one of the finest speeches from the dock in the annals of the criminal courts – and we have had some pretty good ones in Ireland.

So we all love Robert Emmet. Yeats and De Valera loved him, each in his own fashion. I do too; and so did Sarah Curran. Even the hoardings along the Canal have been known to display a chalked inscription, 'UP EMMET'. We all agree that it was a pity that some of his supporters had to murder one of the most liberal judges on the bench, Lord Kilwarden, and that the only practical outcome of his affray was to confirm the Union with England for about a hundred and twenty years. Our affection is not affected by these details.

The tragedy of his love has been immortalized by Tom Moore in one of his finest ballads:

> She is far from the land
> Where her young hero sleeps,
> And lovers around her are sighing.
> But coldly she turns from their gaze, and weeps,
> For her heart in his grave is lying.

Who cares that this reason for her absence from the land is the fact that she subsequently married an English officer, and ended her days happily with him elsewhere? For us, her heart will always be lying in Robert's grave. And lying is the operative word.

The whole episode has got that delightful quality of story-book unreality that creates a glow of satisfaction without any particular reference to the facts of life. To put it into conflict with those facts ought to be an easy proposition in the theatre, and particularly so back in 1926, when several years of intermittent and unromantic civil war had soured us all a little towards the woes of Cathleen ni Houlihan. It was inevitable that such a play would be written in Ireland by someone or other at about that time.

Although it is by no means my favourite play, and is my only work that might fairly be described as anti-Irish, it is by far the best spoken-of in its native habitat. In Dublin it is now generally regarded as a strongly nationalistic piece, full of sound popular sentiments and provided with a title calculated to annoy Lady Gregory and the Abbey Theatre. It is true that on the occasion of its first production at the Gate, some tentative efforts were made to have me prosecuted – for what, I cannot at present remember. But those days are long past, and the only acrimony that the play evokes today is among the cast, the older members of which argue strongly during rehearsals over business and movements that were used on previous occasions, and must not now be altered.

As for the title, I cannot be held responsible for this. It was written by somebody on a sheet of paper attached to the front of the first version, when it came back to me from the Abbey. Whether it was intended to inform me that the play had been rejected, or whether it was being offered as an alternative to my own coy little name for the play – *Shadowdance* – is a question that I never liked to ask. So it remained, thereafter, as the title of the work – a definite improvement for which I have always been grateful. Lennox Robinson used to complain bitterly about any suggestion that Lady G. was against the play, but all I know of the matter is the distaste she expressed to me in the back sitting-room of her hotel in Harcourt Street. I was never invited to Gort.

It is, of course, a director's play, written very much in the spirit of 'Let's see what would happen' if we did this or that. We were tired of the conventional three-act shape, of conversational dialogue, and of listening to the tendentious social sentiments of the stage of the 'twenties, and we wanted to know whether the emotional appeal of music could be made use of in terms of theatrical prose, and an opera constructed that did not have to be sung. Could dialogue be used in lieu of some of the scenery, or as a shorthand form of character-delineation? Could the associations and thought-patterns already connected with the songs and slogans of our city be used deliberately to evoke a planned reaction from a known audience?

The opening playlet – which was felt by Lady G. to be an all-too-brief preliminary to a vein of 'coarseness' that was to follow – is made up almost entirely from lines by Mangan, Moore, Ferguson, Kickham, Todhunter, and the romantic school of nineteenth-century Irish poets, still well known to everybody although no longer imitated. So too, the final speech of the play contains some easily recognizable sections of Pearse's funeral oration for O'Donovan Rossa, together with a large portion of Emmet's actual speech from the dock, which concludes:

'When my country takes her place amongst the nations of the earth, then, and not till then, let my epitaph by written.'

There are both handicaps and benefits to be derived from writing for so specialized an audience. I phrase such as 'When in the course of human events' will spontaneously call up an association-pattern when uttered in the United States, where it belongs. An Englishman, prodded with the expression 'Kiss me, Hardy', may react in a variety of ways, but some response is usually noticeable. On the other hand, outside Ireland, a reference to 'my four beautiful green fields' will not wring any withers, but becomes instead a mere literary reference that may or may not be recognized as an echo from Yeats.

Thus, although written in a language common to all three countries, *The Old Lady* is not quite the same play in London or New York as it is in Dublin. Across the sea its intentional clichés are no longer clichés, and the various daggers concealed within its lacy sentiments find no flesh into which to probe. For this reason, apart from one production in New York, a couple in London, and a few presentations in colleges with *avant garde* theatre departments, it has never been performed outside Ireland. There the pattern devised by Hilton Edwards and Micheál MacLiammóir for its first production in 1929 has become as much an integral part of the play as is the text.

Although many of its expressionist tricks are now commonplace, especially in radio production, it was, at the time of writing, a fairly original type of play, and technically it owes less to other dramatists that anything I have written since. The play's actual foster parents are neither Evreinov, O'Neill nor Georg Kaiser. Nor has Joyce got much to do with it, although I gratefully acknowledge the presence of his finger in the stirring of some of my later pies. I have once or twice been written to by students of the drama who feel that they can trace the influence of *Finnegans Wake* upon *The Old Lady*. This is a book that I first attempted to read through about ten years ago, and the only part of it that has got into my play did so by a most circuitous route. This is the *Thuartpeatrick* phrase, misspelled *St Peetrick* by me in the party scene. Its presence there is a surprising reminder that Tuohy, the artist who painted both Joyce and his old father, had sentences from Joyce's own lips that he was bandying around Dublin as early as the Nine Arts Ball of 1925. In this very second-hand condition the expression has found its way into my text, as a quotation from a section of a book that had then hardly been begun. There are, of course, two short quotes from *Ulysses* in *The Old Lady*, together with a phrase or two, such as 'Jacobs Vobiscuits'. But any resemblances to the *Wake* have nothing to do with me.

The two plays to which this experiment does owe something are, firstly Kaufman and Connelly's *Beggar on Horseback* – a superb piece of American expressionism that I have always admired – and secondly, a Continental satire called *The Land of Many Names* that I once saw in the 'twenties. Who wrote it, and where it came from, I have often since wondered. I think it may have been one of the Capeks.

Persons in the Play

(in this version)

SARAH CURRAN *and* FLOWER WOMAN*
THE SPEAKER (ROBERT EMMET)
FIRST REDCOAT *and* GENERAL*
SECOND REDCOAT
MAJOR SIRR *and* GRATTAN*
STAGE HAND *and* MINISTER FOR ARTS AND CRAFTS*
DOCTOR
BLIND MAN
CHORUS: VOICES AND FORMS, NEWSBOYS, PASSER-BY, BUS
    MAN, FLAPPER, MEDICAL, WELL-DRESSED WOMAN, BUSI-
    NESSMAN, CARMEL, BERNADETTE, AN OLDER MAN, TWO
    TOUTS, HANDSHAKERS, YOUNGER MAN, A MAN, SECOND
    MAN, JOE, MAEVE, LADY TRIMMER, O'COONEY, O'MOO-
    NEY, O'ROONEY, MINISTER'S WIFE, HE, SHE.
FIRST SHADOW, SECOND SHADOW, THIRD SHADOW, FOURTH
    SHADOW.

* Both characters to be played by the same performer.

The action of the play opens in the garden of The Priory, the home of John Philpot Curran, close to Rathfarnham (now a suburb of Dublin), on the night of August 25th, 1803.

PART ONE

To the left the dark gable of a building can be seen with a light burning behind the blind in the first-floor window. It is the house of John Philpot Curran, The Priory, close to Rathfarnham, a village outside Dublin. To the centre and to the right are the trees of the garden, and behind them the profile of Kilmashogue and the hills beyond. It is the night of August 25th in the year 1803, and the sound of men's voices is dying away into the distance as the Curtain rises.

VOICES.

With their pikes in good repair,
Says the Shan Van Vocht,
To the Curragh of Kildare
The boys they will repair,
And Lord Edward will be there,
Says the Shan Van Vocht.

The window opens and Sarah Curran gazes out towards the mountains.

SARAH.

The air is rich and soft – the air is mild and bland.
Her woods are tall and straight, grove rising over grove.
Trees flourish in her glens below and on her heights above,
Oh, the fair hills of Eire, oh.
Down from the high cliffs the rivulet is teeming
To wind around the willow banks that lure him from above.
Ah, where the woodbines with sleepy arms have wound him ...
She starts.
Who is there? I heard a rustling in the trees!
Who is there, I say?

The Speaker emerges from among the trees. He is dressed as Robert Emmet in a green tunic, white-plumed hat, white breeches and Wellington boots with gold tassels. At his side hangs a large cavalry sword.

SPEAKER [*with an appropriate gesture*] Hush beloved, it is I.

SARAH. Robert! I think, oh my love, 'tis thy voice from the kingdom of souls!

SPEAKER. Was ever light of beauty shed on loveliness like thine!

SARAH. Oh, Robert, Robert, why have you ventured down? You are in danger.

SPEAKER. My bed was the ground, my roof the greenwood above: and the wealth that I sought, one far, kind glance from my love.

SARAH. My love, for a vision of fanciful bliss to barter thy calm life of labour and peace!

SPEAKER. What matters life! Deirdre is mine: she is my queen, and no man now can rob me!

SARAH. The redcoats are everywhere. Last night they were around the house and they will come again.

SPEAKER. Let them come! A million a decade! Let me be persuaded that my springing soul may meet the eagle on the hills, and I am free.

SARAH. Ah, go, forget me. Why should sorrow o'er that brow a shadow fling?

SPEAKER. My strong ones have fallen from the bright eye of day. Their graves are red, but their souls are with God in glory.

SARAH. Ah, love, love! Where is thy throne? It is gone in the wind!

SPEAKER. A dark chain of silence is thrown o'er the deep. No streak of dawning is in the sky. It is still unriven, that clanking chain. Yet, am I the slave they say?

SARAH. A lost dream to us now in our home! Ullagone! Gall to our heart!

SPEAKER. But there is lightning in my blood – red lightning tightening in my blood! Oh, if there was a sword in every Irish hand! If there was a flame in every Irish heart to put an end to slavery and shame! Oh, I would end these things!

SARAH. It is too late! Large, large affliction unto me and mine, that one his majestic bearing, his fair and stately form, should thus be tortured and o'erborne – that this unsparing storm should wreak its wrath on head like this!

SPEAKER [*softly*] My earthly comforter, whose love so indefeasible might be! Your holy, delicate, white hands shall girdle me with steel. You'll pray for me, my flower of flowers! You'll think of me through daylight hours, my virgin flower!

SARAH. At least I'll love thee till I die.

SPEAKER. How long, ah, Sarah, can I say how long my life will last?

SARAH. Cease boding doubt, my gentlest love; be hushed that struggling sigh.

SPEAKER. When he who adores thee has left but a name, ah say, wilt thou weep?

SARAH. I shall not weep. I shall not breathe his name. For my heart in his grave will be lying. I shall sing a lament for the Sons of Usnach.

SPEAKER. But see, she smiles, she smiles! Her rosy mouth dimples with hope and joy; her dewy eyes are full of pity!

SARAH. Ah, Robert, Robert, come to me.

SPEAKER [*climbing up*] I have written my name in letters of fire across the page of history. I have unfurled the green flag in the streets and cried aloud from the high places to all the people of the Five Kingdoms: 'Men of Eire, awake to be blest! Rise, Arch of the Occan and Queen of the West!' I have dared all for Ireland and I will dare all again for Sarah Curran. Ah, it is a glorious thing to dare!

He is about to touch her outstretched hand when –.

A VOICE. Halt! Who gocs there?

SARAH. Ah God! The yeomen!

VOICES.   The countersign.
            Stand.
            Front point.
            Advance.

SPEAKER. The flint-hearted Saxon!

He makes a gesture to her. She disappears and the light goes out.

SARAH. . . . in their fearful red array!

FIRST REDCOAT [*rushing forward*] Hold! Surrender or I fire!

SECOND REDCOAT. We hold this house for our lord the King.

FIRST REDCOAT. Amen, says I. May all traitors swing.

SPEAKER [*springing down and folding his arms*] Slaves and dastards, stand aside!

Major Sirr enters.

SIRR. Spawn of treason, bow down thy humbled head to him, the King!

SPEAKER. A nation's voice, a nation's voice, 'tis stronger than the King.

SIRR. Silence rebel! Do you know who I am?

SPEAKER. A jackal of the Pale.

SIRR. Major Sirr.

SPEAKER. Who trapped Lord Edward?

SIRR. The same.

SPEAKER [*drawing his sword*] I am honoured. Ireland will remember. Look well to your soul, Major Sirr, for the dawn of the Gael is still to break; when they that are up will be down and they that are down will be up. I tell you, Major Sirr, we'll be a glorious nation yet – redeemed, erect, alone!

He leaps upon them. One of the Redcoats clubs his musket and strikes him a resounding blow upon the head. The lights flicker momentarily and he lies still. Sarah Curran appears once more at the window.

SARAH. A star is gone! There is a blank in heaven. The last great tribune of the world is dead.

SIRR [*seemingly a little surprised*]

The sport of fools – the scoff of knaves,

Dead ere they blossomed, barren blighted.

They came, whose counsels wrapped the land in foul rebellion's flame,

Their hearts unchastened by remorse, their cheeks untinged by shame,

To sue for a pity they shall not – shall not –

Er –

One of the Redcoats kneels beside the Speaker and shakes him by the shoulder. Sirr looks helplessly into the wings from which he receives a whispered prompt.

PROMPT. Find.

FIRST REDCOAT. Ay!

SECOND REDCOAT. What's up?

SIRR [*to the wings*]. Curtain . . . curtain . . . I say.

STAGE HAND. Is he hurted!

VOICES. He's hurt. Hurt. He's hurt. Hurted.

FIRST REDCOAT. It wasn't my fault. I only . . .

SIRR. Curtain, please. Do stand back for a moment and give him a chance.

VOICES. Loosen his collar. What do you think you're doing? How did it happen? What's the matter? He'll be all right. Give him brandy. Take those boots off. Stand back, please. Did you see the skelp he gave him? Can I help?

The Curtain comes jerkily down and there is a heavy tramping behind upon the stage. Presently Sirr comes through the Curtain. House lights up.

SIRR [*beckoning to someone in the audience*] Is there a doctor in . . . I say . . . can you?

DOCTOR. Me?

SIRR. Just come through for a minute. I think he'll be all right.

DOCTOR. It looked a heavy enough . . .

SIRR. I don't think it is . . .

DOCTOR. . . . blow from the front.

SIRR. . . . very serious, really.

DOCTOR. I hope not. Anyhow you had better see whether you can't . . .

They disappear through the Curtain, talking. Presently Sirr re-appears.

SIRR. Ladies and Gentlemen . . . he . . . er . . . the doctor would like the curtain up again . . . the draught blows through from the scene dock when it's across. We're really very sorry that the performance should be held up . . . but you see . . . it's nothing really . . . He . . . er . . . says he will be all right in a moment if he's kept quiet and not moved . . . if you would only be so good as to keep your seats and stay perfectly quiet for a few moments . . . just a few moments . . . while the doctor is . . . er . . . busy . . . I'm sure we'll be able to go on . . . if you don't mind . . . curtain please . . . quite quiet please . . . just for a few minutes . . . thank you so much.

He hurries off. The Curtain is slowly drawn again, disclosing the Speaker where we left him, now attended by the Doctor, the Stage Hand and one of the Redcoats. A black gauze curtain has been drawn behind him through which we can see dim figures moving about and hear the thumping of heavy weights.

DOCTOR. That's better now. Can you get them off?

STAGE HAND. Yes, Sir. They're coming now.

He draws off one of the Speaker's boots.

REDCOAT. How could I know anyway? It wasn't my fault. I tell you I only . . .

DOCTOR. That's all right. Hold up his head a little. That's better. Oh, they've got it up.

He refers to the Curtain.

REDCOAT. Ah, God, isn't it awful!

DOCTOR. Ask those people to keep quiet there while he's coming round.

STAGE HAND. Ay, Barnie, tell them to shut up! Give us a hand with this boot. I can't get a grip on it at all.

REDCOAT. I don't know how it could have happened at all. You pull now.

STAGE HAND. Ah, will you hold on? How the hell . . .

DOCTOR. Ssssssh!

STAGE HAND. There she comes.

DOCTOR. See if you can get something to cover his legs with. He must be kept warm. And ask them to turn down that light a bit. He'll be all right soon if he's kept quiet and allowed to come round.

The Stage Hand goes out obligingly.

REDCOAT. I swear to God I hit him no harder than I was shown yesterday. I only . . . look . . .

DOCTOR. Ah, be quiet you, and be off. You're more of a hindrance than a help.

REDCOAT. It's all very well blaming me, but I only did what I was shown bef . . .

DOCTOR. Sssssssh!

The Redcoat goes off muttering protestations. The lights are dimmed, making the forms behind the gauze clearer still. Presently the Stage Hand enters with a pair of gaudy carpet slippers.

STAGE HAND. Would these be any use? They were all I could find. They belong to Mr . . . er . . .

DOCTOR. He's stirring a little.

He examines the Speaker while the Stage Hand puts the slippers on his feet.

STAGE HAND. Is the lights OK now?

DOCTOR. What's that? Oh, fine. You'd better . . .

STAGE HAND. I brought a sup of brandy.

DOCTOR. Brandy! Good heavens, no! He has a slight concussion.

STAGE HAND. Is that a fact? A what?

DOCTOR. But I tell you what. Go and see if you can manage to get a little ice.

STAGE HAND [*dubiously*] An ice?

DOCTOR. Yes. You know. In a basin of cold water. For a compress.

STAGE HAND. Oh, for a . . . Oh I see.

He goes out slowly.

DOCTOR. And . . . [*He notices the slippers*]. My God, what are those? I told you to bring something for his legs. Do you hear? A rug. [*He rises and crosses*]. Has anybody got a rug? [*He goes off and his voice is heard faintly*]. A rug for his legs. Ah, thanks so much. That will . . .

Silence. The figures behind the Curtain have ceased to move and are clustered in a silent group peering through towards the spot where the Speaker is lying. Presently the latter stirs and his lips begin to move. There is a dim and distant boom-boom-boom as of someone tapping on a big drum. The lights pulse.

SPEAKER. Redeemious . . . Oh . . . be a redeemious . . . re . . . warmest core I said . . . we'll [*He opens his eyes and stares weakly ahead*]. . . . I love thee . . . love thee bosom my head bosom my head's all . . . Oh, God! [*There is a pause while he stares out into the auditorium*]. They that are down will be down . . . down . . . up . . . erect . . . redeemiable . . . love thee, Sarah . . . redeemiablecurran . . . I see you. [*Pause – then with a great effort*]. I am the Speaker . . . Deadbosom I see you.

THE FORMS [*answering on behalf of the audience with unctuous friendliness*].

A.	Quirke	present
B.	Quinn	present
C.	Foley	present
D.	Byrne	present
E.	Ryan	present
F.	Carrol	present
G.	Lynch	present
H.	Dwyer	present
I.	Burke	present
J.	Farrell	present

K. Gleeson   present
L. Mooney   present
M. Quigley   present

SPEAKER [*holding up his hand peremptorily*] Stop! [*Pause. He bows solemnly*]. Thank you.

THE FORMS [*whispering in rhythm*]

Poor poor poor poor
Hit him hit him
With a gun
Butt end butt end
Dirty dirty
Give him water
For a compress
Calf's foot jelly
Fever fever
Ninty-nine point ninety ninety
Fahrenheit Centigrade
Centigrade Fahrenheit
Very unsettled unsettled unsettled
Take his boots off
Milk and soda
Patrick Dun's and
Cork Street Mater
Adelaide and
Vincent's Elpis
Baggot Street and
Mercer's Meath and
Is he better?
How's the headache?
Ambulance ambulance
S.O.S.
S.O.S. S.O.S.
Tut tut tut tut
tut tut tut tut
Poor poor poor poor . . .

SPEAKER [*with an impatient flap of his hand*] Slaves and dastards stand aside, a nation's voice . . . a nation's voice is stronger than a Speaker

... I am an honoured gloriable nationvoice your Sirrflinthearted Saxons ... Oh! ... if it would only stop going round ... round ... round ... up ... down ... up will be down ... O God, I am the Unspeakerable.

THE FORMS [*relentlessly*]
> On with the performance
> Programmes Tenpence
> No Smoking
> Spitting Coughing
> Nobody admitted
> Till after the Performance
> After nine
> Point ninety ninety
> For further particulars
> Apply to the Manager
> N. Moore
> O. Callan
> Q. O'Reilly
> R. Donovan
> S. Muldoon

SPEAKER [*with the rhythm*] Yes ... yes ... yes ... yes ...

THE FORMS.
> T. Cosgrave
> U. O'Toole
> V. Kelly
> W. Fogarty

SPEAKER.
Red lightning tightening through my blood.
Red tightening lightning tightening through my blood
My tightening blood ...

The voices are merged in a clunking, shrieking, concatenation that swells up ... the throb of petrol engines, the hoot of motor horns, the rattle and pounding of lorries, and, above all, the cry of the newsboys.

NEWSBOYS.
> Hegler Press
> Late Buff Hegler Press
> Weekly Honesty
> Hegler Press

SPEAKER [*commencing to act again, at the top of his voice*] Their graves
are red but their souls are with God in glory. A dark chain of silence
is thrown o'er the deep. Silence ... silence I say O Ireland, Ireland,
it is still unriven, that clanking chain ... still unriven. O Ireland,
Ireland, no streak of dawning is in the sky.

*As he has been declaiming the crowd break up and passes to and fro as in
the street. The gauze parts. Headlights of motor cars. A policeman with a
white baton is directing the traffic, while behind him upon a pedestal stands
Grattan with arm outstretched. He has the face of Major Sirr.*

SPEAKER [*now in the midst of the traffic*] Men of Eire, awake to be
blest! Do you hear? [*He fiercely accosts a Passer-by*]. Do you hear?
Awake!

PASSER-BY [*politely disengaging himself*] Sorry. The banks close at half
two.

SPEAKER. At the loud call of freedom why don't they awake? Come
back! ... Rise Arch of the Ocean ... Let me be persuaded that my
springing soul may meet the eagle on the hills ... the hills ... the
hills ... I say ... [*He shouts*]. I say! Look here!

The Stage Hand enters with the scripts.

STAGE HAND. What's the trouble?

SPEAKER. The hills!

STAGE HAND. What hills?

SPEAKER. Yes, what hills? Where?

STAGE HAND. Where's which?

SPEAKER. Don't be so stupid. You know I must have them. The eagle
on the ...

STAGE HAND. Did the Artistic Director say you were to have hills?

SPEAKER. I don't know what you mean. I can't go on like this. This is
not right.

STAGE HAND. Well it's the first I heard of it. Wait now till I get the
place.

SPEAKER. Down from the high cliff the rivulet is teeming. Go away!
Be off!

STAGE HAND. Where had you got to?

SPEAKER. Not very far. I was with Sarah. She was up there. I was
talking to her.

STAGE HAND [*producing a dirty programme*] Scene One. Wait now till I see. Who did you say you were?

SPEAKER. Robert Emmet. See there.

STAGE HAND. Oh is that you? I thought I rekernized the unyform.

SPEAKER. 'The action of the play opens in the garden of "The Priory", the home of John Philpot Curran close to Rathfarnham.' You see. This is not Rathfarnham.

STAGE HAND. No. I suppose not.

SPEAKER. I can't go on here. Can't you stop this noise?

STAGE HAND. Well you know I'd be glad to do all I can, but . . . well, you see, it's all very well telling me now.

SPEAKER. The air is rich and soft, the air is mild and bland, her woods are tall and straight, grove rising over grove . . .

STAGE HAND. Yes, I know, but I don't know what I can do. You should have told me sooner. You see the shops is all shut now . . .

SPEAKER. And Sarah . . . Sarah Curran is gone too. Clear all this away!

STAGE HAND. Ay, you can't touch that! That's wanted for the dancing class.

SPEAKER. Stop them! My play! Rathfarnham!

STAGE HAND. Ah you know I'm doing my best for you. But as a matter of fact I have to be off now.

SPEAKER. Off where?

STAGE HAND. I'm due at my Irish class this half hour.

SPEAKER. And what am I to do?

STAGE HAND. Ah sure aren't you doing well enough. You're very particular all of a sudden.

SPEAKER. Come back, damn you!

STAGE HAND. Ah, they won't know the difference. It's good enough for that gang. Ta-ta now or I'll be late.

SPEAKER. Stop! You must tell me . . .

STAGE HAND. You'll get a Rathfarnham bus over there at the corner. Goodbye-ee!

He goes.

SPEAKER. Here! Oh my head! At the corner where? Rathfarnham.

BUS MAN. Rathfarnham bus. No. 17 Rathfarnham. Step along now please.

SPEAKER. Are you going to Rathfarnham?

BUS MAN. This bus's full. Full, I tell ya. You'll have to wait for the next.

SPEAKER. Nonsense . . . there's lot of room. See . . .

BUS MAN. The bus's full. D'ye want to get me into trouble? Let go the bar now there's room for no more here. There'll be another along behind.

SPEAKER. I tell you there's nobody there.

Ding Ding Ding.

BUS MAN. Fares please. [*And he moves off mysteriously*].

SPEAKER. There's nobody there! Liar! Cheat! You're all a lot of . . . a lot of . . . I shall speak to the stage manager about . . . [*His voice breaks*]. Oh my head! I wish I wasn't so tired. I wish I wasn't so terribly tired!

He sinks down upon something in the centre of the state. The passers-by thin out and the noise dies away, first into a low hum and then into complete silence. There is nobody left but the figure of Grattan and an old tattered Flower Woman in a black straw hat who sits crouching at the base of the pedestal.

SPEAKER [*mumbling*] My bed was the ground – my way the greenwood above, and the wealth I sought . . . I sought . . . the wealth . . . Oh, what is it?

GRATTAN. How long, O Lord, how long?

Pause.

SPEAKER [*without looking round*] What was that?

GRATTAN. This place stifles me. The thick, sententious atmosphere of this little hell of babbling torment! Sometimes the very breath seems to congeal in my throat and I can scarce keep from choking.

SPEAKER [*nodding gravely*] I might have known it.

WOMAN. Penny a bunch th' violets.

GRATTAN. God forgive me, but it is hard sometimes. Very hard.

SPEAKER. All the same I will not allow this. It is the voice of Major Sirr. It is not my part.

GRATTAN. Your part? Ah yes! More play-acting. Go on, go on.

SPEAKER. I am Robert Emmet and I . . .

GRATTAN. A young man playing Robert Emmet! Yes, yes they all come here.

SPEAKER. I am Robert Emmet. I have written my name in letters of fire across the page of history. I have unfurled the green flag . . .

GRATTAN. Letters of fire?

SPEAKER. Their graves are red but their souls . . .

GRATTAN. Ah yes, the graves are red . . . the grave of one poor helpless old man, the justest judge in Ireland . . . dragged from his coach by the mob and slaughtered in the road.

SPEAKER. Kilwarden!

GRATTAN. Kilwarden's grave is red.

SPEAKER. Who said that? I did my best to save him, but the people were mad . . .

GRATTAN. 'Let no man perish in consequence of my death,' he cried, as his lifeblood stained the cobbles crimson . . .

SPEAKER. . . . maddened by long centuries of oppression and injustice. I did my best to save him. What more could I do?

GRATTAN. 'Let no man perish, save by the regular operation of the laws.' And with that, pierced by a dozen patriot pikes, he died, at the feet of his gallant countrymen.

SPEAKER. It was horrible. But it was war.

GRATTAN. Eighty tattered turncocks from the Coombe; a plumed hat, and a silver sword. War, for the liberation of Erin!

WOMAN. Me four bewtyful gre-in fields. Me four bewtyful gre-in fields.

SPEAKER. Men of Eire, awake to be blest!

GRATTAN. The full long years of my life I gave for her, with the harness weighing on my shoulders and my heart bleeding for my country's woes.

SPEAKER. Rise, Arch of the Ocean!

GRATTAN. Full fifty years I worked and waited, only to see my country's new-found glory melt away at the bidding of the omniscient young Messiahs with neither the ability to work nor the courage to wait.

SPEAKER. I have the courage to go on.

GRATTAN. Oh, it is an easy thing to draw a sword and raise a barricade. It saves working, it saves waiting. It saves everything but blood! And blood is the cheapest thing the good God has made.

WOMAN. Two apples a penny. Penny a bunch th' gre-in fields.

SPEAKER. Listen! Something is telling me that I must go on. I must march proudly through to the final act. Look! [*Pointing*]. The people are waiting for me, watching me.

GRATTAN. Fool, fool, strutting upon the stage! Go out, into the cold night air, before you crucify yourself in the blind folly of your eternal play-acting.

SPEAKER [*to the audience*] He is an old man. He does not understand the way we do. He can only doubt . . . while we believe . . . believe with heart and soul and every fibre of our tired bodies. Therefore I am not afraid to go on. I will kiss my wounds in the last act. I will march proudly through, head high, even if it must be to my grave. That is the only test.

GRATTAN. Ah, the love of death, creeping like a mist at the heels of my countrymen! Death is the only art in which we own no masters. Death is the only voice that can be heard in this distressful land where no man's word is taken, no man's message heeded, no man's prayer answered except it be his epitaph. Out into every quarter of the globe we go, seeking for a service in which to die: saving the world by dying for a good cause just as readily as we will damn it utterly by dying for a bad one. It is all the same to us. It is the only thing that we can understand.

The Woman laughs shortly and shrilly and breaks into a wheezy cough.

SPEAKER. What is that woman doing here?

WOMAN. God bless ye, lovely gentleman, spare a copper for a cuppa tea. Spare a copper for yer owin old lady, for when th' trouble is on me I must be talkin' te me friends.

GRATTAN. A copper, lovely gentleman, for your own old lady.

SPEAKER. Go away! There is something horrible about your voice.

GRATTAN.

> Young she is, and fair she is
> And would be crowned a Queen.

SPEAKER. What can I do in this place? I can't even remember my lines!

WOMAN. Yer lines, ducky. Ay Jack, pull them up on ye!

SPEAKER. I must go back to Rathfarnham. They will understand there.

GRATTAN. A shadowy land has appeared.

SPEAKER. Sally!

GRATTAN.

> Men thought it a region of Sunshine and Rest,
> And they call it 'Rathfarnham', the Land of the Blest.

SPEAKER. Oh if the will had wings, how fast I'd fly to the home of my heart!

GRATTAN. Poor weary footsore fool. And we are all the same, every one of us, whether we look to the foreigner for our sovereign or for our salvation. All of us fit to lead, and none of us fit to serve.

SPEAKER.

> If wishes were power, if words were spells,
> I'd be this hour where my true love dwells!

GRATTAN. Driven blindly on by the fury of our spurious moral courage! Is there to be no rest for Ireland from her soul? What monstrous blasphemy has she committed to be condemned to drift for ever like the wandering Jew after a Heaven that can never be?

WOMAN [*crooning softly to herself*]

> She's a darlin', she's a daisy,
> She has all the neighbours crazy,
> And she's arrums an' legs upon her like a man.
> But no matter where she goes,
> Sure everybody knows
> That she's Mick Magilligan's daughter, Mary Ann.

GRATTAN. In my day Dublin was the second city of a mighty Empire. What is she now?

SPEAKER. No! No!

GRATTAN [*with unutterable scorn*] Free!

He bursts into a wild peal of laughter.

SPEAKER. You are lying! It is the voice of Major Sirr! You are trying to torment me . . . torture me . . . Ghosts out of Hell, that's what you are.

The figures are blotted out by black curtains which sweep across behind the Speaker, entrapping him in their folds.

SPEAKER. But I'm not afraid! Heads up! One allegiance only! Robert Emmet is not afraid! I know what I want and I'm going on. [*Feverishly fumbling with the folds*].

> God save Ireland cried the heroes,
> God save Ireland cry we all,
> Whether on the scaffold high –
> Whether on the scaffold high
> The scaffold high . . .!

Come out! Come out! Where are you? Oh, where am I? Come out! I . . . can't . . . remember . . . my lines . . .!

And old blind man, tap-tapping with his stick, passes slowly across the stage, a mug outstretched and a fiddle under his arm.

SPEAKER. If only I could get through. Where's the way through?

A Flapper and a Trinity Medical appear.

FLAPPER. No, I don't like the floor there, the Metropole's much better. As for that Buttery basement up and down and down and up Grafton Street. Tea for two and two for tea on one enchanted evening in the Dewdrop Inn. Do you like my nails this shade? Heart's Despair it's called.

MEDICAL. Play wing three for Monkstown. Four caps in the last couple of seasons. Pity they've put those glass doors in the Capitol boxes.

FLAPPER. Brown Thomas for panty-bras and Elizabeth Arden to rebuild drooping tissues. Max Factor, Chanel Number Five and Mum's the Word. Has your car got a strap round the bonnet?

MEDICAL. Well let's go up to Mother Mason's and hold hands. She needs decarbonizing probably. Botany Bay, you can be sure. Number twenty-one is my number.

SPEAKER. Can I get through here?

FLAPPER. Brittas Bay in a yellow MG.

SPEAKER. I beg your pardon.

MEDICAL. Would you like a part in the Trinity Players?

SPEAKER. What?

FLAPPER. Tennis at Fitzwilliam all through the summer. We all go to Alexandra where the Lady Ardilaun lectures on Gilbert and Sullivan are quite indescribable. See you at the Carrickmines Mixed Singles. The Aga Khan is playing.

MEDICAL. Tyson's ties tie tightly. Going to crew next week for Dr Snufflebottom. Coming in left, Wanderers. Use your feet!

BOTH [*singing as they disappear*]
> Kitty she was witty, Kitty she was pretty,
> Down in the valley where they tried to pull her leg.
> One of the committee thought he would be witty,
> So he hit her in the titty with a hard boiled egg.

SPEAKER. What was that?

A Well-Dressed Woman and a Businessman appear.

WELL-DRESSED WOMAN. This is the way to the Ringsend Baby Club. Double three Clubs. You are requested to attend a meeting of the Peamount After-care Committee. Ballsbridge, at 11.30 A.M. *She yawns loudly.*

BUSINESSMAN. Dame Street to Clarinda Park East Kingstown not Dun Laoghaire. Second National Loan Deferred Preference is now at thirty under proof. And only last Saturday I went round the Island in twenty-five and a bisque. Service not self I always say. Telegrams: 'Stability' Dublin. Have you got a *Herald*?

SPEAKER. Please . . . please! Can't you tell me the way out of here?

WELL-DRESSED WOMAN. Cover the milk. Do keep the milk covered, there's a good man.

Goes.

BUSINESSMAN [*making a secret sign*] Past Grand High Deacon for the Fitzwilliam Lodge. Honorary Treasurer of the Sandycove and District Philatelic Society. House Committee, Royal St George. Assistant District Commissioner, South County Dublin Boy Scouts. Achievement. [*Goes*].

Two Young Things from somewhere up Phibsboro' way appear.

CARMEL. Down at the Girls's Club a Parnell Square. Janey Mac, such gas as we had!

BERNADETTE. Ah God, if I'd only a known! I couldn't get out a Tuesday. Were the fellas in?

CARMEL. They were. The Grocers' and Vintners' Assistants Assocation. D'ye know?

BERNADETTE. An' I suppose you had the Wet Dreams to play?

CARMEL. We had. The Gorgeous Wrecks were on in the Banba Hall. But listen, D'ye know the fella out a Cusack's a Dorset Street?

BERNADETTE. Is it that awful-lookin' iabeck with the red hair?

CARMEL. He ain't an awful lookin' iabeck, Bernadette, an' his hair's auburrin.

BERNADETTE. Yer taste's in yer mouth, duckie. Anyway . . . eyes off. He's walkin' out with Sarah Morrissy for I seen them meself last Sunday week a-clickin' on the Cab-ar-a Road.

CARMEL. Well wait now till I tell ya. He asked me for an AP at the Depot next Sunday an' he said to bring a pal an' he'll get her a fella, will ye come?

BERNADETTE. Will I come? Te th' Depot? Looka Carmel, I'll be there in me best Viyella.

CARMEL. Looka I'm off up to meet him a half five a Doyle's. He said th' Phib, but I think he has one eye on the Courtin' Park if I know that laddo. Do ye know?

BERNADETTE [giggling] Ah such gas! Sarah'll be wild when I tell her.

CARMEL. That one! You'd think she was someone.

SPEAKER [politely] I beg your pardon.

Bernadette nudges Carmel.

SPEAKER. Did I hear you mention Sarah?

BERNADETTE. There's a fella tryin' to click.

CARMEL. Where? What sort of a fella?

BERNADETTE. Behind you. A queer-lookin' skin.

SPEAKER. If you would be so good? I'd be very much obliged.

Carmel queries Bernadette with her eyebrows. The latter thinks not.

BERNADETTE. Give him the back of yer hand, Carmel. I'm not on.

SPEAKER. Could you tell me . . .?

CARMEL [turning with great dignity] Chase yerself Jiggs or I'll call the Guards.

SPEAKER. Please don't misunderstand me. I only want to make an inquiry.

The two girls look knowingly at one another.

BERNADETTE [in a hoarse whisper] One of the Foresters.

CARMEL. Aw yes, well ye didn't meet me in Bray last summer. So goodbye-ee.

SPEAKER. In Bray? I said . . .

Bernadette giggles hysterically.

CARMEL [to Bernadette] That's th' stuff to give th' trupes. Well, I'll have to be off now or I'll be late. He'll be wild as it is. So long love.

BERNADETTE. Corner a Prussia Street a Sunday?

CARMEL. Mind yer there a half seven. Ta-ta so.

SPEAKER. Listen . . . I must speak. I will not have this!

CARMEL. Egs-scuse me! But may I ask who you're addressin' in that tone a voice?

BERNADETTE [*fluttering*] Ay – ay!

SPEAKER. I can't have this.

He tries to restrain her with a hand.

BERNADETTE. Ay, give us a hand someone!

CARMEL. Oh ye can't have this so ye can't, then listen to me, me Mountjoy Masher, ye'll have the flat of me fist across yer puss if ye can't conduct yerself when addressin' a lady, an' I'll thank ye to take that big slab from fingerin' me bawneen before I have ye run in the way God knows ye ought to be pesterin' an' pursuin' a pair of decent girls in th' public thoroughfare!

SPEAKER. Stop! For God's sake!

BERNADETTE. Ay-ay! Help! Help!

CARMEL. It's not safe for a respectable woman to leave th' shadda of her own door, so it's not, for the dirty gowgers that would be after them like . . . [*He tries to place his hand over her mouth. She bites him. Bernadette screams*]. Looka, I suppose you think yer face is yer fortune, but God knows at that rate some of us should be on the dole!

VOICES. Ay, what's up. What's the matter?

CARMEL. I declare to God I'd be ashamed of meself. A big lowsey yuck the like of you, why can't ye get a job a honest work and not be annoyin' young girls in th' street. It's lucky for your skin me fella's on th' far side of the Tolka River this minnit d'ye hear that now!

VOICES.

What did he do?

Is that him?

What's up?

Ay, can't ye leave the girl alone?

Rows of heads, hatted and becapped. The Curtains part again, disclosing a street.

BERNADETTE [*breathlessly*] Laida – laid aholt of us he did . . . an' says he, didn't I meet you in Bray last summer? says he, didn't I meet you in Bray? . . . An' then he takes her by the arm and says he . . .

SPEAKER. I did nothing of the sort!

VOICES.
Hold that fella.
Disgusting.
Put him out.

SPEAKER. I was only asking the way.

CARMEL [*choking*] Askin' th' way! Now d'ye hear that? . . . only askin' th' – looka what sort of a brass neck has that one got at all!

BERNADETTE. Look at what wants to ask th' way!

VOICES [*raucously – laughing*] To ask the way! 'Will any lady show a gentleman how who doesn't know the way?'

AN OLDER MAN. Ay, see here now. You ought to know better at your age. You'd better leave the girls alone or maybe some of these days you'll be finding your way where you least expect. This is a decent country.

VOICES.
Still dear. No longer dirty.
Keep to the right.
Does your mother know yer out?

SPEAKER.
How shall I reach the land that I love?
Through the way of the wind, the high hills above?
Down by the blue wide ways of the sea?

Pause.

OLDER MAN. What's that?

CARMEL. God blessus, he's up the spout!

SPEAKER. That this unsparing storm should wreak its wrath . . .

OLDER MAN. Ay, give over. What's up with ye?

CARMEL. Well ye won't see me in his bewty chorus!

General laughter.

OLDER MAN. Be quiet youse! I'm lookin' after this. What's yer name?

SPEAKER. I am Robert Emmet.

A VOICE. Robert Emmet?

A VOICE. Who?

A VOICE. Any relation to Paddy Emmet of Clonakilty?

OLDER MAN. Ssssh!

VOICES. Ssssh!

SPEAKER. I could explain it all in a moment if only you thought it worth while to give me a chance.

OLDER MAN. Oh if you're Robert Emmet you'll get every chance you want here. This is a free country. Is this true what you say?

SPEAKER. It is.

BERNADETTE. Well, d'ye hear that?

CARMEL. Who did he say?

BERNADETTE. Emmet. D'ye know. That fella.

A VOICE [as fingers point] That's Robert Emmet.

VOICES.
Emmet.
Emmet.
That's him.
Ay, d'ye know.

OLDER MAN. If yer Robert Emmet it must be all right.

SPEAKER. Won't you let me explain?

OLDER MAN. You can speak yer mind here without fear or favour.

VOICES.
Nor sex, nor creed, nor class.
One for all and all for one.
Can laws forbid the blades of grass
From growing as they grow?
That's right.
A free country.
Up freedom!

SPEAKER. I knew I would be all right when I told you. And it will be so much better for all of us.

OLDER MAN. Let him have his way. I'll see that justice is done.

VOICES.
Without fear or favour.
That's right.
It's Robert Emmet.
Fair play for all.
Let him have his way.

He's all right.
Be reasonable.
Justice.
Free speech.
All right. All right.

OLDER MAN [*fussing round as if putting everybody into their seats*] Sit down now all. Be easy. I'll look after this. I'll see you through. Leave it all to me now an' we'll fix it all up for you in half a jiffy. Isn't that right?

General clapping. The Older Man assumes an air of platform importance, coughs, and comes forward to address the audience.

OLDER MAN. Ladies and gents . . . we are very fortunate . . . in having with us tonight . . . one, who . . . I am sure . . . will need no introduction from me to a Dublin audience . . . His fair fame . . . his manly bearing . . . his zeal in the cause of the Gael . . . his upright character . . . his unbounded enthusiasm for the old cause . . . whatever it may or may not have been . . . his Christian charity . . . his wide experience . . . his indefatigable courage . . . his spotless reputation – and his kindness to the poor of the city . . . have made his name a household word wherever th' ole flag flies.

CARMEL [*shrilly*] Who wounded Maud McCutcheon?

OLDER MAN [*tolerantly*] Now, now, we mustn't touch on controversial matters . . . In introducing him to you this evening . . . I can say with confidence . . . that you will one and all listen to what he has to say . . . whatever it may be . . . and I am sure we are all looking forward to it very much indeed . . . with the greatest interest and with the deepest respect . . . The views which he has at heart . . . are also very near to the hearts of every one of us in this hall . . . and before calling upon him to address you I would just like to say that the committee will be glad to see any or all of you at the Central Branch Whist Drive in Ierne Hall next Friday and the treasurer will be waiting in the passage as you pass out for those members who have not yet paid their subs. Ladies and gents, Mr – er – er –

A VOICE. Emmet.

OLDER MAN. Mr Robert Ellis.

Applause.

SPEAKER. Don't gape at me like that. It is you who are confused – not I. It is only in this place that I am mocked. But I will carry you away to where the spirit is triumphant . . . where the streets have no terrors and the darkness no babbling torment of voices . . . where all will be plain . . . clear and simple . . . as God's sky above, and the chains will fall from your souls at the first sound of her voice from the lighted window. Which of you would not be free?

BERNADETTE. Up the Repubbelick!

SPEAKER. We know only one definition of freedom. It is Tone's definition; it is Mitchell's definition; it is Rossa's definition. Let no man blaspheme the cause that the dead generations of Ireland served, by giving it any other name and definition than their name and their definition. Life springs from death, and from the graves of patriot men and women spring living nations. Men and women of Eire, who is with me?

VOICES.

Up Emmet!

We are with you! Up the Partisans!

Fuck a bal la! Emmet leads!

SPEAKER. But hark, a voice in thunder spake! I knew it. Slaves and dastards, stand aside!

VOICES [*with great waving of arms*] Rathfarnham! Rathfarnham! *Singing*.

> Yes, Ireland shall be free
> From the centre to the sea,
> Then hurrah for Liberty!
> Says the Shan Van Vocht.

Terrific enthusiasm. A queue forms.

OLDER MAN [*ringing a hand-bell*] Line up, line up, ladies and gents. This way for Rathfarnham. All aboard for the Priory. Leaving An Lar every three minutes. Plenty of room on top. No waiting. This way ladies and gents. Seats for Rathfarnham.

TWO TOUTS [*distributing handbills*] Next bus leaves in ten minutes. All aboard for Tir-na-n'Og. Special reduced return fares at single and a third. The Radio Train for Hy Brasail. No waits. No stops. Courtesy, efficiency and punctuality. Joneses Road, Walsh Road,

Philipsburg Avenue, Clontarf, Clonturk, Curran's Cross and the
New Jerusalem.

OLDER MAN. Now then, quietly, quietly please. There is room for
one and all. Step this way please. All those in favour will say 'Taw'.

> Put your troubles on the shelf.
> Country life restores the health.

*Many gentlemen and ladies shake hands with the Speaker as they file
past.*

TWO TOUTS. Schoolchildren, under twelve half price. Senior Citizens
free. Uniformed social workers will meet young girls travelling
alone. Special Whit facilities when not on strike. Penalty for
improper use, five pounds. Empyrean Express, Park in Paradise,
Hearts' Desire Non-stop picks up and sets down passengers only at
the white pole. Please do not spit in or on the conductor.

HANDSHAKERS.

Proud to meet you, sir.

Look us up any time you're in Sandymount.

Jacobs Vobiscuits.

The country is with you.

My! how you've grown!

Remember me to the boys.

D'ye vanta vuya vatch?

Magnificent, sir!

Would you sign a snap?

Have ye e'er a Green Stamp?

TWO TOUTS. Excursions for schools and colleges. Boy Scouts and
Girl Guides in uniform admitted free. Tea and boiled eggs may be
had from the conductor. Special comfort facilities on all vehicles,
except when standing in the station.

*The queue queues. Presently the Speaker finds himself shaking hands with
the old Flower Woman. There is silence.*

WOMAN. Wait, my love, an' I'll be with ye.

SPEAKER. You!

WOMAN. I thought I heard th' noise I used to hear when me friends
come to visit me.

> Oh, she doesn't paint nor powdher,
> An' her figger-is-all-her-owin.
> Hoopsie-daisie! The walk of a Quee-in!

SPEAKER. Hurry on please.

WOMAN [*patting him roguishly on the shoulder*] Ah, conduct yerself. We're all friends here. Have ye nothing for me, lovely gentleman?

SPEAKER. What do you want?

WOMAN. It's not food or drink that I want. It's not silver that I want. Ochone.

SPEAKER. I have no time to waste talking to you.

WOMAN. What is it he called it? . . . the cheapest thing the good God has made . . . eh? He-he-he. That's all. For your own old lady.

SPEAKER. I've nothing for you.

WOMAN. Gimme me rights . . . me rights first!

SPEAKER. Go away!

WOMAN. Me rights! Me rights first . . . or I'll bloody well burst ye!

VOICES. Get on! Get on!

WOMAN [*turning on the crowd*] Aw ye have a brave haste about ye. Ye have a grand wild spirit to be up an' somewheres, haven't ye! Ye'll be off to a betther land will yez? Ye will . . . in me eye!

VOICES.
    Ah, dry up!
    What's she talking about?
    Up Emmet!

WOMAN. An' a nice lot of bowsy scuts youse are, God knows! Emmet! He-he-he! Up Emmet! Let me tell youse that fella's not all he says he is!

VOICES. What's that? Not Emmet?

WOMAN. Look at him, ye gawms! Use yer eyes an' ask him for yourselves.

A VOICE. But the costume?

WOMAN. Five bob a day from Ging.

She disappears into the crowd, whispering and pointing.

SPEAKER. My friends . . .

OLDER MAN. Is this true?

SPEAKER. My friends – we must go on . . . at once.

OLDER MAN. I asked you a question.

VOICES.
    Look at him.
    Well, what about it?

Perhaps she's right.

SPEAKER. We can wait no longer.

VOICES. Can't you answer the gentleman's question?

OLDER MAN. Are these charges true?

SPEAKER. What are you talking about?

YOUNGER MAN [*in a beret*] What's all this?

OLDER MAN. This chap says he's Robert Emmet.

SPEAKER. I am

OLDER MAN. Oh, you are, are you?

SPEAKER. I am.

OLDER MAN. Well answer me this then. *What's happened to your boots?*

VOICES.

Ah-ha!

Look!

What about his boots?

SPEAKER. My boots!

OLDER MAN. He comes here an' says he's Robert Emmet, and where are his boots?

VOICES.

That's right.

Such an idea.

He's an impostor.

Throw him out!

SPEAKER. I don't know . . . I thought they were . . . I see your point . . . I . . .

VOICES. Well?

SPEAKER. Perhaps I had better explain . . . You see . . . someone took them from me when I was playing Robert Emmet and . . .

OLDER MAN [*with heavy sarcasm*] Oh so you were *playing* Robert Emmet? A play-actor are you? Some of this high-brow stuff I suppose?

SPEAKER. Oh no, not at all.

VOICES. High brow! Ha!

OLDER MAN. I suppose you consider yourself a member of the so-called Intelligentsia? One of the Smart Set.

SPEAKER. Me?

VOICES. Smart Set! Ha! Ha!

OLDER MAN. A self-appointed judge of good taste, eh?

SPEAKER. I don't want to judge anything.

VOICES. Good taste. Ha! Ha! Ha!

OLDER MAN. You want to pose before the world as representative of the Irish people? Eh?

SPEAKER. I only want to . . .

VOICES. Representative. Ha! Ha! Ha! Ha!

OLDER MAN. Tell me [*suddenly*] how much do you get for this?

SPEAKER. That's none of your business!

VOICES.

A job! A job!

He does it for a job!

He's related to someone!

And has a job!

OLDER MAN. Honest friends and anti-jobbers! This so-called leader, this self-appointed instructor of the Irish people, is owney linin' his pocket at the expense of the poor. His downy couch, debauched with luxury is watered with the sweat of the humble. A traitor's pillory in the hearts of his countrymen would be a proper reward for such an abattoir of licentiousness.

SPEAKER [*assuming a Parnellesque attitude*] Who is the master of this party?

OLDER MAN. Who is the mistress of this party?

SPEAKER. Until the party deposes of me I am leader.

A VOICE. You are not our leader. You are a dirty trickster.

A VOICE. Committee Room Fifteen!

SPEAKER. So you won't follow me any longer?

VOICES. No!

SPEAKER [*after a pause*] Very well. I shall just have to go on by myself.

OLDER MAN. Oh no you don't. You're not going out of this.

SPEAKER. Who's going to stop me?

OLDER MAN. We are. You're not going to be allowed to hold up this country to disgrace and ridicule in the eyes of the world. Throwing mud and dirt at the Irish people.

VOICE. Give him a taste of backwoodsman's law.

SPEAKER [*to Younger Man*] Tell him to get out of my way. You won't allow this.

YOUNGER MAN. It's nothing to do with me. The army has no interest in civilian affairs. All the same I don't like to see my country insulted by indecent plays.

OLDER MAN. That's right.

YOUNGER MAN. A high-spirited race resents being held up to scorn before the world, and it shows its resentment [*He takes out a revolver and hands it to the Older Man*]. in various ways. But as I say it has nothing to do with me.

He walks away.

OLDER MAN [*with revolver*] Take off that uniform.

SPEAKER. Put up that revolver. I warn you, I am serious.

He stretches out his hand and gently takes it from him. The crowd slowly closes in upon him with sheeplike heedlessness.

SPEAKER. Stand back or I will have to shoot. I warn you I won't be interfered with, I am going on at all costs.

VOICES. Traitor. Spy. Cheat. Cur.

SPEAKER [*hidden in their midst*] Back! Back! Slaves and dastards, stand aside! Back! Back! or I'll . . .

The revolver emits a dull pop. The crowd melts away to the side and he is disclosed standing there alone with the smoking weapon still clenched in his fist. There is a deathlike silence.

A VOICE. Oh, my God!

OLDER MAN [*very quietly*] Now you've done it.

SPEAKER. Done what?

OLDER MAN. You've plugged somebody.

A VOICE. Oh, my God! My God!

SPEAKER. I've what?

A MAN [*looking out*] It's Joe.

SECOND MAN. Joe?

FIRST MAN. He's got it in the breast.

YOUNGER MAN. [*reappearing*] Who fired that shot?

OLDER MAN. Joe's got it. Right through the left lung. He can't last long.

SECOND MAN. Christ!

FIRST MAN. It wasn't any of us, Tom. It was this chap.

SPEAKER. Stand back, stand back, I tell you. I'm fighting. This is war.

YOUNGER MAN [*quite unperturbed*] There's a man out there. You've put a bullet through his breast.

OLDER MAN. God rest his soul!

SPEAKER. I warned you – I warned you all.

YOUNGER MAN. He's going to die. You did it. That's what comes of having guns.

VOICES.

He's going to die.

You did it.

You did it.

SPEAKER. I had to. It wasn't my gun.

Two men appear bearing between them the body of another. The people take off their hats and stand mutely with bowed heads.

JOE. It's welling out over me shirt, boys . . . Can't anybody stop . . . it?

YOUNGER MAN. A good man . . . a true man . . . That is what you did.

OLDER MAN. That is what he did.

VOICES.

You did.

He did.

Robert Emmet did.

Who did it?

He did it.

He there.

SPEAKER. I had to . . . [*All hands point*].

JOE. Give me . . . me beads . . . before the life . . . has ebbed out of me . . . I can't breathe . . . oh, lads, I'm going . . .

SPEAKER. What could I do? I ask you, what could I do? It was war. I didn't mean to hurt him.

OLDER MAN. Joe, old scout. We're sorry . . . we're . . . O God!

JOE. God bless you boys . . . sure I know . . . I know well . . . it wasn't any of . . . you . . .

SPEAKER [*flinging down the revolver*] Shoot back then! It is war. Shoot! I can die too!

YOUNGER MAN. Will that give him back the warm blood you have stolen from him?

OLDER MAN. Ah, leave him alone, Tom, leave him alone.

VOICES [*whispering*]
Leave him alone.
He shot Joe.
Through the breast.
Poor Joe.
Leave him alone.

JOE [*as he is carried off, followed by the crowd*] O my God ... I am heartily ... sorry ... for having offended ... Thee ... and ... I ...

VOICES [*chanting*]

> *Lacrymosa dies illa*
> *Qua resurget ex favilla*
> *Judicandus homo reus.*
> *Huic ergo parce Deus;*
> *Pie Jesu Domine*
> *Dona eis requiem*   Amen.

FLOWER WOMAN [*appearing in the shadows, but speaking with the voice of Sarah Curran*]

> Do not make a great keening
> When the graves have been dug tomorrow.
> Do not call the white-scarfed riders
> To the burying ...

[*Hoarsely*]. Ay misther – spare a copper for a cuppa tea – spare a copper for a poor old lady – a cuppa tea – [*Whisper*]. a copper for your own ole lady, lovely gentleman.
She fades away.

SPEAKER. Sally! Sally! – where are you? – where are you? Sally!

[CURTAIN]

PART TWO

Through the Curtain, amidst a hearty round of applause, comes the Minister's talented daughter, Maeve. She has on a nice white dress with a white bow to match in her long, loose, black hair which reaches quite to her waist. Around her neck on a simple gold chain hangs a religious medal. She curtsies in charming embarrassment and commences to recite.

MAEVE.

> Kingth Bweakfatht.
> The King athed de Queen
> And de Queen athed de Dar-med
> Could – I [*a little breathlessly*] – se – butter
> For-de-roy – – – thlaice – a – bwead?
> Queen athed de Dar-med
> De Dar-med thed Thertinley
> Ah goan tell – Cow now
> For he goeth tebed . . .

She continues this amusing piece to the very end, when the Curtain parts amid general applause disclosing a fantastically respectable drawing-room loud with the clatter of tea things. A party is in progress under the aegis of the Minister for Arts and Crafts and his nice little Wife. The guests consist of one of the Redcoats, now a General in a green uniform, the Statue of Grattan, rather a nice woman called Lady Trimmer – one of those people whose expression of pleased expectancy never for a moment varies, the old Flower Woman who is seated unobtrusively in the background eating an orange, and a small but enthusiastic Chorus. Side by side upon the sofa reading from right to left are O'Cooney the well-known dramatist, O'Mooney the rising portrait painter, and O'Rooney the famous novelist. O'Cooney wears a cloth cap, blue sweater and a tweed coat. O'Mooney has a red shirt and horn-rimmed spectacles, while O'Rooney is dressed in full saffron kilt

*together with Russian boots. The Minister himself bears a strange resemblance
to the Stage Hand. It is all very nice indeed.*

CHORUS.

Oh very nice nice

Oh very nice nice nice

How old how nice how very nice don't you think so

Oh yes indeed yes very nice indeed I do think so indeed don't you
    indeed.

Teaspoons clink.

LADY TRIMMER. What was that one, my dear?

MAEVE. Kingth Bweakfatht pleathe.

LADY TRIMMER. Very nice indeed, Maeve. I must teach that one to
    my two chicks. Where do you learn, my dear?

MAEVE. The Banba Thcool of Acting, Lower Abbey Thweet.

CHORUS. The Banba School of Acting, Lower Abbey Street.

O'COONEY. Wasn't that bloody awful?

O'MOONEY. The question is, is she an aartist? A real aartist?

O'ROONEY. O'Mooney sounds better with his mouth shut.

WIFE. Of course, she hasn't been learning very long. But she has the
    language, and that's half the battle these days. Show them,
    Maeve.

MAEVE. *Caed mile failte.*

LADY TRIMMER. Oh very good indeed. But of course, she has her
    father's talent.

MINISTER. Ah, well, now . . .

WIFE [*pleased*] Oh, Lady Trimmer!

MINISTER. Well, now, all the same I don't know about that. But mind
    you I do say this, Talent is what the country wants. Politics may
    be all OK in their way, but what I say to *An Taoischach* is this,
    until we have Talent and Art in the country we have no National
    Dignity. We must have Talent and Art. Isn't that right?

CHORUS. We must have Art have Talent and Art.

LADY TRIMMER. Quite. And cultivated people of taste. You mustn't
    forget them, Mr Minister. Art cannot live you know by taking in
    its own washing – if I may put it that way.

O'COONEY. Aw Holy God!

O'MOONEY [*ruminatively*] The reel aartist must be fundamental. Like Beethoven. Now, *I'm* fundamental.

O'ROONEY. Fundament, all right.

MINISTER. Now see here. I'm Minister of Arts and Crafts, you see. Well, a young fellow comes along to me and he says, Now look, Liam, here's some Art I'm after doing . . . it might be a book you see, or a drawing, or even a poem . . . and can you do anything for me, he says? Well, with that, I do . . . if he deserves it, mind you, only if he deserves it, under Section 15 of the Deserving Artists' [Support] Act, No. 65 of 1926. And there's none of this favouritism at all.

CHORUS. The State supports the Artist.

GRATTAN. And the Artist supports the State.

CHORUS. Very satisfactory for everybody and no favouritism at all.

MINISTER [*confidentially*] And of course, then you see, it helps us to keep an eye on the sort of stuff that's turned out, you understand.

CHORUS. Clean and pure Art for clean and pure people.

LADY TRIMMER. What we need most is a small Salon.

GENERAL. That's right. A small Art Saloon.

WIFE. We often have people in on Sunday evenings for music and things. Won't you sing something now, General?

GENERAL. Aw, I have no voice at all.

O'COONEY. He's bloody well right there.

O'MOONEY. The question is . . . Is he fundamental?

LADY TRIMMER. Just somewhere where the nicest people . . . the people one wants to meet . . . like Mr O'Cooney and Mr O'Mooney . . .

O'ROONEY [*suspiciously*] And Mr O'Rooney.

LADY TRIMMER. *And* Mr O'Rooney, can get together quietly and discuss Art and common interests.

WIFE. Haven't you brought your music?

CHORUS. You must have brought your music.

GENERAL. Well now . . . if you insist. Maybe I might find something.

O'COONEY [*to o'Mooney*] Ay, have *you* put my cap somewhere?

WIFE. Do, General.

GENERAL. I don't know for sure, mind you. I might . . . just happen to have something on me.

He produces a roll of music from inside his tunic.

CHORUS. The General's going to sing.

GENERAL. Ah, but . . . sure there's no one to play th' accompanyment.

WIFE. Maeve will play. Won't you, darling?

MAEVE. Yeth mammy.

Signs of distress from the sofa.

WIFE. Of course you will dear. Give her the music, General.

CHORUS. Ssssh!

The General gives her the music rather doubtfully and they are opening the performance, when there comes a loud, peremptory knock at the door. General surprise.

WIFE [*bravely but apprehensively*] What can that be?

LADY TRIMMER. Strange!

MINISTER. A knock at the door?

GENERAL. Ah now, isn't that too bad!

CARMEL [*entering*] There's a gentleman at the door, ma'am, looking for the Rathfarnham bus.

WIFE. What kind of a gentleman, Carmel?

CARMEL. A gentleman in a uniform, ma'am.

MINISTER. A uniform? Tell me, does he look like the start of a Daring Outrage?

CHORUS. Possibly the Garda Síothchána.

CARMEL. He has a sword, sir.

MINISTER. A sword?

CARMEL [*primly*] And a pair of slippers.

WIFE. Slippers?

GENERAL. I don't think I know that unyform.

CHORUS. Can't be the Garda Síothchána after all.

WIFE. Did he give any name, Carmel?

CARMEL. Yes, ma'am. A Mr Emmet.

LADY TRIMMER. Not *the* Mr Emmet?

CARMEL. I don't know I'm sure, ma'am.

MINISTER. Ah, yes I remember. That's him all right.

GENERAL. Aw, the hard Emmet.

MINISTER. The old Scout.

WIFE. The gentleman who is far from the land. Show him up at once, Carmel.

CARMEL. Yes, ma'am [*She goes, muttering*]. Doesn't look like a sailor to me.

LADY TRIMMER. How nice of him to call.

WIFE. Yes, indeed, but you know we can't be too careful since the Trouble.

MINISTER. Emmet's all right. I know him well. Used to work with him in the old days.

MINISTER. Aw, the rare old Emmet.

LADY TRIMMER. You know I've wanted to meet him for such a long time. My husband always says that we of the old regime ought to get into touch with those sort of people as much as possible. We can assist each other in so many ways.

MINISTER. That's right. We must all get together for the good of the country.

WIFE. I wonder has he brought his music too?

GRATTAN. I expect he has.

Carmel enters, cocking her head contemptuously towards the Speaker, who follows her with a strange, hunted look in his eye. He glances round apprehensively as though prepared for the worst and yet hoping against hope.

CHORUS. Oh how do you how do you how do you how do you how . . .

WIFE. How do you do? Bring another cup, Carmel.

CARMEL. Yes, ma'am. [*She goes, muttering*] I'll have to wash one first.

SPEAKER. Excuse . . . me

WIFE. Come and sit down and let me introduce you to everybody. It was nice of you to call. Liam has just been speaking about your work.

SPEAKER. I only came in to ask . . .

CHORUS. Have you brought your music?

WIFE. This is Lady Trimmer, Mr Emmet.

CHORUS. Of the old regime.

LADY TRIMMER. Dee do.

SPEAKER [*after peering closely into her face*] No, ah, no.

LADY TRIMMER. You must come and visit us too, Mr Emmet. First Fridays. Now promise.

WIFE. And General O'Gowna of the *Oglaigh na h-Eireann*.

GENERAL [*affably*] And many of them.

SPEAKER. It was you who hit me.

WIFE. And of course you know my husband, the Minister for Arts and Crafts.

CHORUS. Vote *Fianna na Poblacht*.

MINISTER. *A chara.*

The Speaker tries to remonstrate but is hurried on.

WIFE. And Mr Grattan's statue from College Green.

GRATTAN. Welcome Don Quixote Alighieri. Did I speak the truth?

The Speaker's head goes up.

WIFE. And this is Mr O'Cooney, the great dramatist.

SPEAKER. Cap?

WIFE. Oh, Mr O'Cooney always wears his cap in the drawing-room.

O'COONEY. And why the bloody hell shouldn't I wear my cap in the drawing-room?

General laughter.

SPEAKER. I see.

O'MOONEY. Now me.

WIFE. This is Mr O'Mooney, the artist, if you can remember everybody.

O'MOONEY. The reel Aartist.

O'COONEY. The owl cod.

WIFE. Oh, please, Mr O'Cooney!

CHORUS. I love the way he talks, don't you?

O'MOONEY. Oh, don't mind O'Cooney. He's a great friend of mine, really.

O'COONEY. He is not!

WIFE. And this is Mr O'Rooney, the well-known novelist. Now I think you know everybody.

SPEAKER [*indicating the costume*] You play the pipes?

O'Mooney laughs shrilly.

O'ROONEY. I do not. I do not believe in political Nationalism. Do you not see my Russian boots?

WIFE. Mr O'Rooney believes in the workers.

O'ROONEY. I do not believe in the workers. Nor do I believe in the Upper Class nor in the Bourgeoisie. It should be perfectly clear by now what I do not believe in, unless you wish me to go over it again?

LADY TRIMMER [*archly*] Mr O'Rooney, you dreadful man!

SPEAKER. I'm sorry.

WIFE. Sit down now and have a nice cup of tea.

Carmel meanwhile has been back with a dirty cup.

CHORUS. I do like a nice cup of tea.

SPEAKER. So she is here, too!

WIFE. What's that?

SPEAKER. That damned old flower woman who turned them all against me!

WOMAN. Ay, mister, have ye e'er an old hempen rope for a neckcloth?

WIFE. You're joking, Mr Emmet. There's no old flower woman.

SPEAKER. I mean . . . look there.

WIFE. Have some tea, Mr Emmet. You're a little tired, no doubt.

SEMICHORUS. Delightful drink.

SEMICHORUS. Pity it tans the stomach.

WIFE. You'll feel much the better of it. And we'll have a little music afterwards. We often have music in the evenings.

MINISTER. Are you interested in Art, Mr Emmet?

LADY TRIMMER. I suppose you're a member of the Nine Arts Club?

WIFE. And the Royal Automobile Academy?

CHORUS. Celebrity Concerts. The Literary Literaries.

SPEAKER. I don't feel very . . . Did you say that statue of Grattan was there?

WIFE. Oh yes, that's Mr Grattan's statue from College Green. We always have a few of the nicest statues in on Sunday evening. My husband is Minister of Arts and Crafts, you know.

LADY TRIMMER. Just to form a little group you know. A few people of taste.

WIFE. Of course we're only amateurs, but we're doing our best.

Pause.

SPEAKER [*suddenly*] Let me be persuaded that my springing soul may meet the . . .

Pause.

LADY TRIMMER. I beg your pardon?

SPEAKER. Let me be per – [*He shakes his head hopelessly*]. I am Robert Emmet.

GRATTAN. You are not.

SPEAKER. Who are you to question me?

GRATTAN. You are only a play-actor.

SPEAKER. Look well to your own soul, Major Sirr!

GRATTAN. Have you found your Holy Curran, Galahad?

WIFE. I always say to Liam, Liam you really *must* get a proper statue of Mr Emmet. It's positively disgraceful that we haven't got a good one, don't you think?

MINISTER. Ah, well, dear, you know, expense, expense.

LADY TRIMMER. What a nice uniform! Tell me, do you admire the plays of Chekhov?

WIFE. Perhaps he acts for the Civil Service Dramatics.

SPEAKER. Act? . . . No. No cake, thank you.

CHORUS. Benevente Strindberg Toller Euripides Pirandello Tolstoy Calderon O'Neill.

LADY TRIMMER. I'm sure you'd be good.

CHORUS. An annual subscription of one guinea admits a member to all productions and to all At Homes.

MINISTER [*confidentially*] Say the word and I'll get you into the Rathmines and Rathmines. I know the man below.

LADY TRIMMER. Now do tell us, Mr Emmet, about your wonderful experiences in the Trouble.

The Speaker spills his tea and looks around wild-eyed.

SPEAKER. What do you mean?

GRATTAN. Ah – ha!

WIFE. Never mind. It's quite all right. I'll pour you out another cup.

LADY TRIMMER [*hastily*] You must have had such interesting times all through the fighting.

SPEAKER. I shall never fight again!

He buries his face in his hands.

MINISTER. Oh come, Mr Emmet! What's the matter?

WIFE. Are you not feeling well?

LADY TRIMMER [*aside*] Ssssh! Don't pay any attention. I understand. Do tell us about it, Mr Emmet. Talk. Talk someone.

SPEAKER. God have pity on me.

CHORUS. Oh the fighting everyone talk don't pay any attention wonderful experiences those were the attention fighting days how wonderful to tell us about the fighting days interesting and wonderful.

SPEAKER. It was I who shot him and you all know it! You all know! Isn't it enough for you? Haven't I suffered enough?

CHORUS [*louder*] Oh tuttut poor man don't talk do talk as hard as you can fighting wonderful pay no attention shellshock probably to have seen it all wonderful is he better yet poor man everybody pretend not to fighting notice.

SPEAKER. They trapped me! A good man ... a true man ... and I did it!

WIFE. Well what if you did shoot somebody? Everybody's shot somebody nowadays. That'll soon be over.

LADY TRIMMER. Yes, yes; of course we didn't approve of it at the time, but it's all so interesting now.

SPEAKER. Interesting!

CHORUS. Perhaps we had better how is he change the subject change the subject getting on what's the wonderful experiences matter with him matter with him at all?

WIFE. How about a little song?

CHORUS. How about a little little song song song?

WIFE. Do you sing, Mr Emmet?

SPEAKER. What do you all want with me?

LADY TRIMMER. Nothing, nothing at all, Mr Emmet. Perhaps you'd like to act us a little snippet from your play?

WIFE. We often have plays on Sunday evenings. Poor man. There, there. We are all friends here.

LADY TRIMMER. The General has just obliged us.

GENERAL. I have not. I was interrupted before I got going.

WIFE. You're better now, I'm sure. Of course you are. Aren't you?

MINISTER. Well, I believe in supporting Art and acting's Art. So you have *my* consent anyhow.

WIFE. You'll act something for us, Mr Emmet, won't you?

GRATTAN. Oh, leave him alone. Can't you see he's beaten.

SPEAKER. That voice! That voice.

GRATTAN. I said that you were beaten. You should have taken my advice from the first; but you would go on with your play-acting.

Now, perhaps you know better. Rathfarnham! Ha! Sarah Curran! Ha-ha-ha!

SPEAKER [*slowly rising*] I am not beaten. I still believe. I will go on.

CHORUS. Oh good, he's going to do something for us.

WIFE. Oh do, Mr Emmet.

GENERAL. But look here . . .

GRATTAN. Don't be a fool. Do you imagine that they'll listen to you if you do?

MINISTER. Nothing political. That's barred of course.

O'COONEY. For God's sake make it short anyhow.

O'MOONEY. Nothing Iberian. There's no Iberian real Art.

O'ROONEY. See that it's not pompous. That would be an insult to the people of this country.

GENERAL. Hey, what about my song?

GRATTAN. Go on. Tell them all to go to hell.

SPEAKER. Please, please . . . if you want to do it . . .

CHORUS. Oh yes yes, do Mr Emmet.

MINISTER. I suppose it will be all right. I wouldn't like anything by somebody with the slave mind, you know.

SPEAKER. Nobody can object to my play.

MINISTER. Or calculated to excite you-know-what.

CHORUS. Emmet's play is all right.

GENERAL. Well you needn't expect me to sit down quietly under this sort of behaviour. When you ask a man to sing . . .

SPEAKER [*advancing towards the audience*] It's very hard without Sally. It may seem a little strange here . . . but I'll do it.

GRATTAN. Very well. Have it your own way.

LADY TRIMMER. Did I hear him mention somebody called . . . er, Sally Somebody?

WIFE [*confidentially*] I think it must be his young lady.

LADY TRIMMER. How charming.

GENERAL [*determinedly*] One of Moore's Melodies entitled 'She is Far from the Land'.
He bows.

O'COONEY. Aw, this'll be bloody awful. [*Settles down*]. D'ye remember that night, Liam, when the two of us hid in the chimbley from the Tans?

MINISTER. Will I ever forget it? Ah, those were the days, Seamus.

SPEAKER. I had got to the part where I am arrested, hadn't I? No. I think I was . . .

WIFE. We always have music and things on Sunday evenings.

LADY TRIMMER. Just a nucleus. A few nice people.

GENERAL [*to Maeve*] Have you got the place?

MAEVE. Mammy.

WIFE. Yes, dear?

MAEVE. Why ith that man wearing hith thlipperth in the dwawing woom?

WIFE. Hush, dear, you mustn't ask questions. You must be a good girl.

MAEVE [*plaintively*] You never let me –

GENERAL. Ah, go on when I tell you!

Maeve commences the introduction to 'She is Far from the Land'.

SPEAKER.

The air is rich and soft – the air is mild and bland.

Her woods are tall and straight, grove rising over grove.

Trees flourish in her glens below and on her heights above,

Oh, the fair hills of Eire, oh.

O'ROONEY. Will you move up on the sofa and breathe into yourself.

O'MOONEY. We'd be better off if your hips were as soft as your head.

Simultaneously.

SPEAKER.	GENERAL [*singing*].
Down from the high cliffs the rivulet is teeming	She is far from the land where her young hero sleeps
To wind around the willow banks that lure me from above;	And lovers around her are sighing:
Ah, where the woodbines with sleepy arms have wound me.	But coldly she turns from their gaze and weeps
	For her heart in his grave is lying.

MINISTER [*solo*] And do you remember the day Seamus, of the big round-up in Moore Street when the 'G' man tried to plug me getting out of the skylight?

Speaker, General, and O'Cooney [*simultaneously*].

SPEAKER [*louder*].

But there is a lightning in my blood; red lightning tightening in my blood. Oh! if there was a sword in every Irish hand! If there was a flame in every Irish heart to put an end to slavery and shame! Oh, I would end these things!

GENERAL.

She sings the wild songs of her dear native plains,
Every note which he loved awaking.
Ah! little they think, who delight in her strains,
How the heart of the ministrel is breaking.

O'COONEY.

Aw, Jesus, and the evenings down in the old I.R.B. in Talbot Street, picking out the 'Soldiers' Song' on the blackboard.

Speaker, Minister, and General [*simultaneously*].

I have written my name in letters of fire across the page of history. I have unfurled the green flag in the streets and cried aloud from the high places to the people of the Five Kingdoms: Men of Eire, awake to be blest! to be blest!

He had lived for his love, for his country he died,
They were all that to life had entwined him;
Nor soon shall the tears of his country be dried,
Nor long will his love stay behind him.

MINISTER

Sometimes I wish I was back again on the run with the old flying column out by the glen of Aherlow.

O'Mooney and O'Rooney join in in low undertones.

O'ROONEY.

My good woman, I said, I'll tell you what's wrong with you. Virginity, my good woman, that's all. And believe me, its nothing to be proud of.

O'MOONEY.

Saint Peetric d'ye see because Saint Peter was the rock and Saint Patrick was the seed. That makes Saint Peetric, d'ye see. For the rock is underneath and the seed lies above, so Saint Peter and Saint Patrick are Saint Peetric.

At the same time.

O'COONEY

And that night waiting up on the North Circular for word of the executions. Ah, not for
all the wealth of the world would I give up the
maddenin' minglin' memories of the past . . .

SPEAKER.	GENERAL.
Rise, Arch of the Ocean and Queen of the West! I have dared all for Ireland, I will dare all again for Sarah Curran. Their graves are red. O make her a maddening mingling glorious morrow . . .	O! make her a grave where the sunbeams rest When they promise a glorious morrow . . .

The black curtain closes behind the Speaker, blotting out the room, and the voices fade away. The Speaker himself has somehow chimed in upon the last few lines of the song, and is left singing it by himself.

SPEAKER.

They'll shine o 'er her sleep like a smile from the west,
From her own loved island of sorrow . . .

The Blind Man comes tap-tapping with a fiddle under his arm and a tin mug in his hand. He bumps lightly into the Speaker.

BLIND MAN [*feeling with his stick*] Peek-a-boo! Peek-a-boo!

SPEAKER. Damn your eyes!

BLIND MAN [*looking up*] That's right.

SPEAKER. You're . . . blind?

BLIND MAN [*with a chuckle*]. That's what they say.

SPEAKER. I didn't know. I didn't mean to hurt you.

BLIND MAN. Ah, not at all. I'm not so easy hurted. [*Feeling him over*].
Oh, a grand man. A grand man. A grand man surely, from the feel
of his coat.

SPEAKER. Do you know where I am?

BLIND MAN. Well, isn't that a rare notion now! Asking the way of an
old dark fiddler, and him tip-tappin' over the cold sets day in and
day out with never sight nor sign of the blessed sun above.

SPEAKER. I give it up.

BLIND MAN. And where might you be bound for, stranger?

SPEAKER. The Priory.

BLIND MAN [*with a start*] Ah, so! So you're bound for them parts, are you, stranger dear?

SPEAKER. Yes.

BLIND MAN. Up the glen maybe as far as the edge of the white mist, and it hanging soft around the stones of Mount Venus, eh stranger? He-he-he!

SPEAKER. That's right.

BLIND MAN. Oh, I know you. I know you. Sure all the Queer Ones of the twelve counties do be trysting around them hills beyond the Priory.

SPEAKER. The blessed hills!

BLIND MAN. It's sad I am, stranger, for my light words of greeting and the two of us meeting for the first time. Take my arm now, and walk with me for a while and I'll put you on your way. Come – take my arm! Why should you not take my arm, stranger, for I'm telling you, my fathers are Kings in Thomond so they are.

SPEAKER [*taking his arm gingerly*] There.

BLIND MAN. That's better now. He-he-he. 'Tis proud I am to be walking arm in arm with the likes of you, stranger. Tell me now, or am I wrong? Would you by any chance be Mr Robert Emmet?

SPEAKER. You know me?

BLIND MAN. Uh! I thought I recognized them words I heard you singing.

SPEAKER. Yes. I am Robert Emmet. He said that I wasn't. But I am. It was the voice of Major Sirr.

BLIND MAN. Ah, poor Bob Emmet. He died for Ireland. God rest his soul.

SPEAKER. He died. I died?

BLIND MAN. You did indeed. You remember the old song we used to sing?

They sit down together.

SPEAKER. You mean 'The Struggle is Over'.

BLIND MAN. That's right. Ah, the rare old lilt of it. How does it go, now? [*He sings*].

The struggle is over, our boys are defeated,
And Erin surrounded with silence and gloom.
We were betrayed and shamefully treated

And I, Robert Emmet, awaiting my doom.

Hanged, drawn and quartered, sure that was my sentence,

But soon I will show them, no coward am I.

My crime was the love of the land I was born in.

A hero I've lived and a hero I'll die.

BOTH.

Bold Robert Emmet, the darling of Erin,

Bold Robert Emmet will die with a smile.

Farewell companions, both loyal and daring,

I'll lay down my life for the Emerald Isle.

Pause. From somewhere comes faint dance music.

BLIND MAN. Ah, them are the songs. Them are the songs.

SPEAKER. He died for Ireland, I died. I?

BLIND MAN. High Kings in Thomond, my fathers are. Lords of the Gael. You'll know them, stranger.

SPEAKER. How can I have died for Ireland? What is that I hear?

BLIND MAN. Ah, never mind that. That's nothing. Nothing at all.

A young man in evening dress and a pretty girl are walking out of the darkness into the edge of the light. It is the Trinity Medical and his friend, now a little older. They are smoking and laughing together.

SPEAKER. Go away.

BLIND MAN. Never heed them stranger. That's nobody at all.

SPEAKER. And I am dead this hundred years and more?

BLIND MAN. What would the likes of you have to do with the likes of them? He-he-he.

HE. I remember when I was a kid in Clyde Road how wonderful I thought a private dance was.

SHE. Now I suppose you've quite grown out of us all.

HE [*laughing*] Oh, well, I wouldn't say that. But of course when one's lived abroad things do seem a little different, when you come back.

SHE. I suppose so.

HE. Small in a way and rather provincial. But that's to be expected.

SPEAKER. I wonder is Sally dead too?

BLIND MAN. Dust to dust and ashes to ashes.

HE. Of course, there have been a lot of improvements. But over there . . . well, after all, it takes over an hour and a half to get into the country.

SHE. And you like that?

HE. Well, you know how it is. It makes one feel one's sort of *in* the world. Everything seems more serious, somehow.

SHE. While we and the old days never seemed serious at all.

HE. Oh well, I didn't quite mean it that way.

SPEAKER. O God help me!

BLIND MAN. Coming and going on the mailboat. And they thinking themselves the real ones – the strong ones! I do have to laugh sometimes and I hearing the wings of the Queer Ones beating under the arch of the sky.

HE. Of course I liked the old days. We had some jolly good times together, didn't we?

SHE. I liked them too.

HE. I was crazy about you.

SHE. My eye and Betty Martin.

HE. I was. I was, really. I often think about it all. It's a bit lonely sometimes over there, and often – Oh, I don't know. Do you ever think about me?

SHE. Sometimes.

HE. I hope you do. You know, Daphne, sometimes I wonder whether you and I oughtn't to have . . .

SHE. Have what?

HE. I think we ought to have . . . maybe we still could . . .
The music stops. There is a pause.

HE. Hello. The music's stopped.

SHE. Yes. I suppose it has.

HE. Like to go in and have a drink?

SHE. I think we might as well.

HE [*briskly*] Funny, you know, how the old place can get you for a bit. But after all, one can't get away from the fact that it's all so damned depressing – [*They vanish*].

SPEAKER. O God, make speed to save us! I cannot tell what things are real and what are not!

BLIND MAN. Oh, but it is not myself that is dark at all, but them – blind and drunk with the brave sight of their own eyes. For why would they care that the winds is cold and the beds is hard and the sewers do be stinking and steaming under the stone sets of the streets, when they can see a bit of a rag floating in the wild wind, and they dancing their bloody Ceilidhes over the lip of Hell! Oh, I have my own way of seeing surely. It takes a dark man to see the will-o'-the-wisps and the ghosts of the dead and the half dead and them that will never die while they can find lazy, idle hearts ready to keep their venom warm.

SPEAKER [*up*] Out of the depths I have cried to Thee, O Lord: Lord, hear my voice!

BLIND MAN. In every dusty corner lurks the living word of some dead poet, and it waiting for to trap and to snare them. This is no City of the Living: but of the Dark and the Dead!

SPEAKER. I am mad – mad – mad! Sally!

During his speech the stage darkens until both figures are blotted out and the speaker is left groping in the dark.

SARAH'S VOICE. Robert! Robert!

SPEAKER. What was that?

SARAH'S VOICE [*singing*]

>She stretched forth her arms,
>Her mantle she flung to the wind,
>And swam o'er Loch Leane
>Her outlawed lover to find . . .

SPEAKER. Sally! Sally! Where are you?

SARAH'S VOICE. Why don't you come to me, Robert? I have been waiting for you so long.

SPEAKER. I have been searching for you so long.

SARAH'S VOICE. I thought you had forgotten me.

SPEAKER. Forgotten you! Forgotten you, Sally! Is that your hand, dear? *A cuisle geal mo chroidhe* – 'Tis you shall have a silver throne – Her sunny mouth dimples with hope and joy: her dewy eyes are full of pity. It is you, Sally – Deirdre is mine: she is my Queen, and no man now can rob me!

The lights go up. He is in the dingy room of a tenement house. The plaster is peeling off the walls. On a bed in the corner a young man with the face of Joe is lying with an expression of serene contentment upon his pale, drawn features. Two men – the Older and the Younger Man – are playing cards at a table opposite, upon which stands a bottle with a candle perched rakishly in the neck. The Speaker himself is affectionately clasping the arm of the old Flower Woman. When he sees her he bursts into hysterical laughter.

WOMAN. Ah, me lovely gentleman, is it me yer calling?

SPEAKER. Well done! Well done! The joke is on me! Well done!

WOMAN. The Lord love ye, an' how's the poor head?

SPEAKER. Robert Emmet knows when the joke is on him! Kiss me, lovely Sarah Curran!

WOMAN [*archly*] Ah, go on owa that! D'jever hear the like!

OLDER MAN [*looking up from his game*] Drunk.

YOUNGER MAN. Aw, disgustin'.

WOMAN. Sit down now. Ah, go along with ye! Sit down now there, an' take no heed a them ignerant yucks . . . an' I'll get ye a small drop.

SPEAKER. My lovely Sarah Curran! Sweet Sally!

WOMAN [*aside to the Older Man*] Ye bloody rip! I'll twist the tongue of ye, that's what I will.

SPEAKER. Her sunny mouth dimples with hope and joy.

YOUNGER MAN. Ho, yes, you'll do the hell of a lot, ma . . . in me eye!

WOMAN. Don't heed them. Don't heed them at all mister. He's no son of mine that has ne'er a soft word in his heart for th' old mudher that reared him in sickness and in sorra te be a heart-scaldin' affliction an' a theef a honest names.

OLDER MAN. Now ye can say what ye like, but there's a Man! There's a man! Drunk, an' it's hours after closin'! Drunk, an' in th' old green coat! [*Singing*]. Oh, wrap the green flag round me, boys.

SPEAKER [*joins in*] Ta-ra-ra-ra-ra-ra, Ra! Ra!

WOMAN. Sure, he's not drunk are ye, gentleman, an' if he was itself it's none a your concern. [*To Speaker*]. Isn't that right, son?

OLDER MAN. And why the hell shouldn't he be drunk? Tell me that. We're a Free State, aren't we? Keep open the pubs. That's my motto. What man says we're not a Free State?

YOUNGER MAN. I say it, ye drunken bastard!

OLDER MAN. Drunken bastard . . . hell! I declare to God I'm sober'n you are, me bold, water-drinkin' Diehard. God knows I'm cold an odd time, but sure a true Patriot is always drunk.

YOUNGER MAN. Have you no love for Ireland?

SPEAKER. God save Ireland!

OLDER MAN. Ho yes – 'The Republic still lives'. Aw – go te hell!

YOUNGER MAN. I've been to hell all right, never fear. I went down into hell shouting 'Up the living Republic', and I came up out of hell still shouting 'Up the living Republic'. Do you hear me? Up the Republic!

SPEAKER. Up the Priory!

OLDER MAN. Oh, I hear you well enough. But you'll not convince me for all your bridge blasting. Looka here, I stand for the status q-oh, and I'll not be intimidated by the gun.

WOMAN [*handing the Speaker a precious black bottle*] Here, have another sup and never heed that old chat of them!

SPEAKER. A health, Sarah Curran! A toast to the woman with brave sons!

WOMAN. Aw God . . . If I was young again!

YOUNGER MAN. And who needs to convince you?

OLDER MAN. Oh, you needn't think . . .

YOUNGER MAN. Every day and every night while you were lying on your back snoring, wasn't I out in the streets shouting 'Up the living Republic'?

OLDER MAN. Ah, don't we remember that too well.

SPEAKER. Up the living Departed!

YOUNGER MAN. Every morning and every night while you were sitting in the old snug, wasn't I out on the hills shouting 'Up the living Republic'?

SPEAKER. Up the pole!

OLDER MAN. Well?

YOUNGER MAN. Every hour of the day that you spent filling your belly and gassing about your status q-oh, wasn't I crying 'Republic, Republic, Republic'?

OLDER MAN. May God give ye a titther a sense some day.

SPEAKER. Up the blood-red Phlegethon! Up Cocytus, frozen lake of Hell!

OLDER MAN [*turning for a moment*] Aw, wouldn't that languidge disgust ye!

YOUNGER MAN. So one day, me laddo, you woke up and found that the Republic did live after all. And would you like to know why?

OLDER MAN. 'Tell me not in mournful numbers' . . .

YOUNGER MAN. Just because I and my like had said so, and said so again, while you were too drunk and too lazy and too thick in the head to say anything at all. That's why. And then, with the rest of your kidney you hunched your shoulders, spat on your hands, and went back to your bed mumbling 'Up the Status q-oh'. So why the hell should I try to convince you?

SPEAKER. A long speech. A strong speech. A toast to the son that speaks. A toast to the son that swills!

OLDER MAN. Aw, that's all words. Nothing but bloody words. You can't change the world by words.

YOUNGER MAN. That's where you fool yourself! What other way can you change it? I tell you, we can make this country – this world – whatever we want it to be by saying so, and saying so again. I tell you it is the knowledge of this that is the genius and glory of the Gael!

SPEAKER. Up the Primum Mobile! Up the graters of verdigreece. Up the Apes Pater Noster.

JOE.
  Cupping the crystal jewel-drops
  Girdling the singing of the silver stream . . .
He tries to scribble on the wall.
  What was it? . . . the singing of the silver stream.
  Damp acid-cups of meadows sweet . . .

SPEAKER. Hello! There's the fellow I shot. Is he not gone yet? A toast to the son that dies!

WOMAN. Ay . . . are ye lookin' for a bit of sport tonight?

SPEAKER. I have had brave sport this night!

WOMAN. Aw, mister . . . have a heart!

SPEAKER [*flaring up*] A heart!
Joe gives a short, contented laugh.

SPEAKER. Do not do that. That is not the way to laugh.

YOUNGER MAN. I tell you, what the likes of me are saying tonight, the likes of you will be saying tomorrow.

OLDER MAN. Is that a fact? And may I be so bold as to in-quire what awtority you have for makin' that observation?

YOUNGER MAN. Because we're the lads that make the world.

OLDER MAN. You don't say!

SPEAKER [*passionately*] Then why have you made it as it is? Then will you stand before the Throne and justify your handiwork? Then will you answer to me for what I am?

YOUNGER MAN. What are *you* talking about? You're only a bloody play-actor. If you were a man and not satisfied with the state of things, you'd alter them for yourself.

OLDER MAN [*holding out a bottle*] Aw, have a sup and dry up for God's sake!

Joe laughs again.

SPEAKER. That blasphemous laugh! Do you know you're going to die?

JOE [*laughing again*]
     Soft radiance of the shy new moon
     Above the green gold cap of Kilmashogue
     Where . . .

SPEAKER. Kilmashogue!

JOE.
     Where of a summer's evening I have danced
     A saraband.

SPEAKER. What of Kilmashogue? Look around you. Here! Don't you know me? I shot you.

JOE. Well, please don't interrupt. [*He coughs*].

WOMAN. It's the cough that shivers ye, isn't it, son? Me poor lamb, will ye tell the gentleman . . . [*She goes as if to touch him*].

JOE [*through his teeth*] Strumpet! Strumpet!

WOMAN. Blast ye! ye'd use that word t'yer own mudher, would ye! God, I'll throttle ye with me own two hands for the dirty scut ye are!

SPEAKER. Go back!

YOUNGER MAN [*seizing her from behind and flinging her away*] Away to hell, ye old trollop!

OLDER MAN. Ah, leave her alone.

WOMAN. Awlright! Awlright! Yer all agin me. But it won't be th' cough will have th' stiffenin' of him not if I lay me hands on his dirty puss before he's gone. When I get a holt a ye I'll leave me mark on ye never fear.

YOUNGER MAN. Aw, shut yer mouth, ma!

JOE. I'd like to do it all again ... That's right ... Again ... It's good ... to feel the wind ... in your hair ...
He laughs weakly.

SPEAKER. Don't! Don't do that I tell you!

JOE.

> Stench of the nut-brown clay
> Piled high around the headstones and the yews,
> My fingers clotted with the crusted clay,
> My heart is singing ... in the skies ...

He coughs again. The Blind Fiddler enters slowly through the door.

OLDER MAN. You know, some of that stuff is very hard to follow. I'd sooner have the old stuff any day.

> 'Oh I met with Nappy Tandy
> An' he took me by the hand.'

SPEAKER. Sssssh!

YOUNGER MAN. What do you want here?

BLIND MAN. Wouldn't I have a right to pay my respects to one, and he passin' into the ranks of the Government? Isn't it a comely thing for me to be hopin' that he'll remember a poor old dark man an' he sittin' in the seats of the mighty in his kingdom out beyond?

JOE [*very soft*] Well ... so long, lads. It was ... a grand life ... so long, lad ... that plugged me ... So long ... [*He dies*].

WOMAN. Burn ye! Burn ye!

BLIND MAN. Be silent now, and a new shadow after being born! Do you not know, woman, that this land belongs not to them that are on it, but to them that are under it.

YOUNGER MAN. He's gone. Stiffening already, poor chap. Hats off, lads.

SPEAKER. Gone! And I am only a play-actor – unless I dare to contradict the dead! Must I do that?

BLIND MAN. Let them build their capitols on Leinster Lawn. Let them march their green battalions out by the Park Gate. Out by Glasnevin there's a rattle of bones and a bit of a laugh where the presidents and senators of Ireland are dancing hand in hand, with no one to see them but meself an' I with the stick an' the fiddle under me arm.

OLDER MAN. Well ... a wake's a wake, anyhow. So pass over the bottle and give us a tune on the ole instrument.

BLIND MAN [*tuning up*] It's many's the year an' I fiddled at a wake.

WOMAN. One son with th' divil in hell, an' two more with th' divils on earth. [*She spits*]. God forgive me for weanin' a brood a sorry scuts!

The Speaker is seated silently at the foot of the bed, staring at the body with his back to the audience. There is a knock at the door.

WOMAN. Wha's that?

The Younger Man goes to the door, pauses, and flings it open. On the threshold stands Maeve.

MAEVE. My mammy thez ...

WOMAN. Ah love, is it yerself?

MAEVE. My mammy thez I'm to play the accompaniment of 'The Thruggle Ith Over'.

WOMAN. Come on in, duckie. God love ye an' welcome. The ole pianner's waiting for ye, love.

MAEVE. Yeth pleathe. My mammy ...

She comes in and, catching sight of the Speaker, she points, and bursts into tears.

WOMAN. There, there! What's the matter, lamb? Ah God help her! What ails ye at all?

MAEVE [*gulping*] Thlipperth ...

WOMAN. There, there now ...

OLDER MAN. Aw, will ye dry up?

WOMAN [*with an impatient flap of the hand*] There's the pianner, so do what yer mammy says before I slaughter ye.

BLIND MAN. Play on now, young one. And when you've played, 'tis meself will fiddle for the shadows and they dancing at the wake.

MAEVE [*sniffling*] My mammy thez ...

Maeve sits at an old cracked piano, upon which presently she commences to thump out carefully 'The Struggle Is Over'.

WOMAN. There now. Ah God, hasn't she the gorgus touch on th' ole instrument!

Another knock at the door. The Younger Man opens it. The Minister for Arts and Crafts is on the threshold in top hat, frock coat, and carrying one of those hemispherical glass cases full of white flowers.

MINISTER. Deep concern – Government grieved to learn – struck down in prime – Requiem Mass – life for Erin – send a gunboat – bitter loss – token of our regard. [*He presents the case*].

WOMAN [*very unctuous*] Ah, aren't ye the kind-hearted Goverment, and isn't them th' gorgus flowers. God will reward ye, sir; He will indeed at the next election, for th' blessed pity ye've shown to a poor woman in her sorra.

Another knock at the door. The Younger Man opens it. Lady Trimmer, dressed in widow's weeds, enters.

LADY TRIMMER. So sad! So sad indeed! I can't simply say how sad it is. Quite a poet, too, I hear. Can any of his books be purchased?

WOMAN. At Hodges an' Figgis ma'am. Be sure ye get the name right. Come in, come in!

Before the Younger Man has the door properly closed there comes another knock. He abandons it, leaving it open. The Statue of Grattan is on the threshold.

GRATTAN. A word-spinner dying gracefully, with a cliché on his lips. The symbol of Ireland's genius. Never mind. He passed on magnificently. He knew how to do that.

WOMAN [*her head quite turned*] An' he was me favrit', too lady . . . never a bitter word . . . never a hard glance. Sure, it's them we love th' best is took th' first, God help us. Ullagone! Ullagone! Ochone-a-ree!

Enter the General with crape upon his arm.

GENERAL. . . . a grand song called 'Home to Our Mountains'. No. 17 bus passes the door or a bus to Ballyboden, whenever the road's not up. But of course if you don't want me to sing, I won't force myself on you. Won't I?

WOMAN.

> Low lie your heads this day
> My sons! My sons
> The strong in their pride go by me
> Saying, 'Where are thy sons!'

O'Cooney, O'Mooney and O'Rooney enter, all in black gloves and top hats.

ALL THREE. Who's a twister? I'm a twister? You're a twister? He's taken a header into the Land of Youth. Anyhow, he was a

damn sight better man than some I could name, and there's no
blottin' it out.

LADY TRIMMER. So yellow-haired Donough is dead! Dear, dear!

*A few more stray figures crush in, chattering and pressing forward in file
before the body.*

WOMAN.

> Gall to our heart! Oh, gall to our heart!
> Ullagone! Ochone-a-ree!
> A lost dream to us now in our home!

MAEVE [*stopping her playing*] Will that do, Daddy?

BLIND MAN [*mounting upon a chair*] The shadows are gathering,
gathering. They're coming to dance at a wake. An' I playin' for
them on the gut box. Are yez ready all?

*He tunes up. The lights in front have dimmed, leaving a great sheet of
brightness flooding from the sides upon the back-cloth. The walls of the room
seem to fade apart while the crowd darts aside and seats itself upon the floor
and upon all sides of the stage. The Speaker has vanished.*

THE VOICES OF THE CROWD. The Shadows are gathering, gathering: he says they must dance at a wake. Seats for the Shadows the
gathering Shadows . . . The Shadows that dance at a wake.

The Blind Man commences to fiddle a jig in the whole-tone scale.

THE VOICES.

Overture started
Seats for the Shadows
Gathering, gathering
Dance at a wake
Loosen his collar
Basin of water
Dance Shadows
Oooooooh!

*Upon the back-cloth two great Shadows appear gesturing and posturing in
time with the music.*

THE FIRST SHADOW [*stopping his dance and striking an attitude*]

> Come clear of the nets of wrong and right;
> Laugh, heart, again in the grey twilight,
> Sigh, heart, again in the dew of the morn.
> Your Mother Eire is always young . . .

Hand clapping. The Second Shadow jostles the First aside and points one long arm vaguely in the direction of the Flower Woman.

THE SECOND SHADOW. Stone traps of dead builders. Warrens of weasel rats! How serene does she now arise! Queen among the Pleiades, in the penultimate antelucan hour: shod in sandals of bright gold: coifed with a veil of gossamer.

Applause. Amidst shrieks of laughter the Flower Woman rises, curtsies and dances hilariously once round the foreground. Two more Shadows have elbowed the first pair aside and are now dancing to the music.

THE VOICES.

Dance! Dance!

Speak, Shadows, speak!

THE THIRD SHADOW. It is difficult not to be unjust to what one loves. Is not He who made misery wiser than thou?

Applause, mingled with some booing. The Third Shadow throws up its arms and flees.

THE FOURTH SHADOW. Every dream is a prophecy: every jest an earnest in the womb of time.

Shouts of laughter and applause. The Shadows change into a tumbling mass of blackness.

THE VOICES.

Dance! Dance!

Speak, Shadows, speak!

A VOICE. There are no Shadows left to speak.

BLIND MAN. Speak, great Shadow! Shadow of Ireland's Heart.

VOICES [*whispering*] We see him. He is here.

The shadow of the Speaker precedes him as he comes slowly in from the back.

BLIND MAN. Speak, shadow of Robert Emmet.

SPEAKER. I know whom you are calling. I am ready.

BLIND MAN. The eyes of the people are fixed on your face.

VOICES. Justify! Justify! Shadow of the Speaker, speak!

VOICES. Sssh!

SPEAKER. The souls in the seven circles of Purgatory cry out, Deliver us O Lord from the mouth of the Lion that Hell may not swallow us up. The Word Made Flesh shall break the chains that bind me. Three armies may be robbed of their leader – no wretch can be robbed of his will.

Yes, there is darkness now, but I can create light, I can separate the waters of the deep, and a new world will be born out of the void. A challenge, Norns! A gage flung down before you! Justify! Justify!

VOICES. Justify! Justify!

The Speaker continues to address the audience.

SPEAKER [*continues*] Race of men with dogs' heads! Panniers filled with tripes and guts! Thelemites! Cenobites! Flimflams of the law! Away! while Niobe still weeps over her dead children. I have heard the angels chanting the Beatitudes to the souls in Malebolge, and I have done with you.

I do not fear to approach the Omnipotent Judge to answer for the conduct of my short life and am I to stand appalled here before this mere remnant of mortality? I do not imagine that Your Lordships will give credit to what I utter. I have no hopes that I can anchor my character in the breast of this court. I only wish Your Lordships may suffer it to float down your memories until it has found some more hospitable harbour to shelter it.

Voices, shuffling, applause.

SPEAKER [*continues*] For now is the axe put to the root of the tree. My fan is in my hand, and I will burn the chaff with unquenchable fire.

VOICES.

Up Emmet!

Rathfarnham!Up the Up that won't be Down!

He draws his sword and turns upon them all. During the following commination the Voices give the responses in unison and the Figures in turn fling up their arms and take flight before him. The light fades, gradually blotting out all vestiges of the room.

SPEAKER. Cursed be he who values the life above the dream.

VOICES. Amen.

SPEAKER. Cursed be he who builds but does not destroy.

VOICES. Amen.

SPEAKER. Cursed be he who honours the wisdom of the wise.

VOICES. Amen.

SPEAKER. Cursed be the ear that heeds the prayer of the dead.

VOICES. Amen.

SPEAKER. Cursed be the eye that sees the heart of a foe.

VOICES. Amen.

SPEAKER. Cursed be prayers that plough not, praises that reap not, joys that laugh not, sorrows that weep not.

VOICES [*dying away*] Amen. Amen. Ah – men.

The last of the Figures fling up their arms and vanish. As the Speaker comes down stage they come creeping back again, crouching in the darkness and watching him with many eyes. It is dark.

SPEAKER. I will take this earth in both my hands and batter it into the semblance of my heart's desire! See, there by the trees is reared the gable of the house where sleeps my dear one. Under my feet the grass is growing, soft and subtle, in the evening dew. The cool, clean wind is blowing down from Killakee, kissing my hair and dancing with the flowers that fill the garden all around me. And Sarah . . . Sarah Curran . . . you are there . . . waiting for Robert Emmet.

I know this garden well for I have called it into being with the Credo of the Invincibles: I believe in the might of Creation, the majesty of the Will, the resurrection of the Word, and Birth Everlasting.

He flings aside his sword and looks around him in triumph. It is very dark, so dark that for all we know perhaps it may be the garden of the first scene. Perhaps those may be the trees and the mountains beyond the Priory. For a moment we hear the tramp of feet and the distant sound of the Shan Van Vocht. His voice falters and he staggers wearily.

SPEAKER. My ministry is now ended. Shall we sit down together for a while? Here on the hillside . . . where we can look down over the city, and watch the lights twinkle and wink to each other . . . Our city . . . our wilful, wicked old city . . .

The gauze curtains close slowly behind him.

I think . . . I would like to sleep . . . What? . . . On your shoulder? . . . Ah, I was so right to go on!

His head sinks drowsily and his eyes stare out into the auditorium. He is lying just where the Doctor left him some time ago.

Strumpet city in the sunset.

Suckling the bastard brats of Scots, of Englishry, of Huguenot.

Brave sons breaking from the womb, wild sons fleeing from their
    Mother.
Wilful city of savage dreamers,
So old, so sick with memories!
Old Mother
Some they say are damned,
But you, I know, will walk the streets of Paradise
Head high, and unashamed.
His eyes close. He speaks very softly.
There now. Let my epitaph be written.
There is silence for a moment and then the Doctor speaks off.
DOCTOR . . . do, fine.
*He appears bearing a large and gaudy rug. He looks towards the audience,
places one finger to his lips, and makes a sign for the front curtains to be
drawn. When last we see him he is covering the unconscious Speaker with
his rug. That is the end of this play.*

BLOOMSBURY, 1926 – DALKEY, 1976.

A Note on What Happened

(The following note was originally written nearly fifty years ago in advance of the production of the play in the United States. It is published here for the first time.)

Walking back from Sorrento with Mr Yeats he gave me what was probably the most incisive criticism this play has received. 'I liked your play,' he said, 'but it has one or two faults. The first is, the scenes are too long.' He was silent for a time, while we both gazed with some signs of embarrassment at a cargo boat rounding Dalkey Island. 'Then', he added finally and after considerable thought, 'there are too many scenes'.

Needless to say I was grateful for this opinion.

To say that the scenes are too long and that there are too many of them goes right to the root of the matter. Why do it at all? And if it does mean anything, isn't it better left unsaid?

A distinguished member of the audience who sat through most of the performance with his eyes closed remarked very aptly as he took himself home, 'I suppose people must have nightmares, but why inflict them on us?' I am afraid I can supply very little in the way of an answer. Perhaps nightmares – or dreams, if you're that kind – don't really mean very much, and probably a good many of them would be better left unremembered. Ireland is spiritually in a poor condition at the moment and I don't know that homoeopathic treatment is the best for her complaint. A young lady having seen the play said of it that it made her blush. Not because of its vulgarity – ordinary vulgarity was a commonplace on the stage. But this was different. She had blushed for me – that such thoughts should ever have entered my head.

This play, if plays must be about something, is about what Dublin has made a good many of us feel. And if it is a very wrong and vulgar feeling that could only have been experienced by people with nasty minds, we aren't worth bothering about anyway. But it is no good saying that it isn't true, because we happen to know that it is.

I was warned during rehearsals by various friends that the play would be denounced as anti-National, or as Republican propaganda, or as a personal reflection on so-and-so – opinions which were given with the best of good will but whose only common denominator was that the play would be denounced. In this they were right, but only in their conclusions. For as it turned out when the production was complete the assault came from a most unexpected quarter. It was well patronised by *l'ancien regime* and was stoutly defended in the press and elsewhere by more than one physical force Intransigentist. But exception was taken to the play on the ground that it was blasphemous.

It appeared that the language of the Holy Writ was used in obscene circumstances – ranted and raved by a mad actor to the accompaniment of a chorus of curses and swearwords – that the scene in which some of these lines were spoken was a brothel – and that the final Commination was a ribald parody of Jesus driving the money-changers from the Temple.

I need hardly say that I was not prepared for this, although I was ready to be philosophic about the charge that I was trying to write a silly lampoon of living persons. But now that I come to think of it, I have noticed before that the words of Holy Writ when used in circumstances in which they are liable to be taken seriously sometimes incur the suspicion of being either insanity or blasphemy.

I can quite appreciate the point of view which holds that the ethics of religion are solely a matter for the pulpit and have no place upon the stage.

But granted that we have persuaded all those members of the audience to leave the theatre if they are the kind who experience a shock on discovering that their own theological ideas have a human and a dramatic meaning as well as a symbolic one; how then, are we to express on the stage the idea of the triumph of the Word over environment – the dogma of the Resurrection? It seems to me that the most straightforward way – especially in a play where all other ideas are conveyed by the thematic method – is to call up the desired association of ideas by suggesting the words of the Liturgy.

Whether or not I have succeeded in doing this myself is another matter, but the fact that I appear to have suggested to the minds of some of my critics the picture of the expulsion of the money-changers from the Temple – an analogy which was not before my own mind – would indicate that I have not entirely failed.

And lest it should be thought that criticisms of this kind are not of much consequence these days, I should add that nearly every night indignant women walked out during the last act, and strong representations were made to the authorities to have a blasphemy prosecution set on foot. Needless to say the authorities had no time to waste on such small fry as the little Gate Theatre or myself, but the threat had high ramifications and results that it would be amusing but totally wrong of me to disclose.

* * *

I think that it must be a result of the long predominance of narrative drama to the exclusion of all else that people get so worried when one cannot tell them what a play is about. Yet the dithyrambic outbursts from which both western and eastern theatrical conventions have developed had nothing to do with a plot. It would be difficult to interpret the religious ecstasy of a mediaeval miracle play or the intricacies of a No Play of Japan for inclusion in French's 'Guide to Selecting Plays'.

It seems to me that the real play must be regarded as what goes on in the mind of the audience. What, therefore, a play is about depends entirely on who is listening to it.

Anybody who has done any acting will know that a performance to an audience is quite a different affair from the most complete Dress Rehearsal – as different as War is from Salisbury Plain. And furthermore, a good play – that is to say, a play which is succeeding in registering its effect whether we personally approve of it or not – is a different play from night to night according as the reflex of the House varies.

And these ideas and emotions can be stimulated without the assistance of a narrative plot at all, whether melodically as in music, by direct statement as in continental Expressionism, or by simple association of ideas. Strindberg in some of his later work provides one of the best modern examples of the fact that dramatic experience is not dependent on physical actuality and is in fact hampered by it. In the 'Spook Sonata' there is for example, the wretched wife who sits all day in a dark cupboard from which she cries like a parrot, 'Pretty

Polly! Pretty Polly!' This genius with which he conveys an attitude of mind in terms of a fantastic physical reality has, on me at any rate, a most real and horrifying effect, but the intention of the author is completely defeated if the audience insists on regarding the picture as one of narrative fact.

The melodic method has been greatly developed since the War by the Russians, principally in the Constructivist Theatre of Meierhold and in the Moscow Jewish Art Theatre, where an attempt is made to stimulate the desired attitude of mind by means of acrobatics and dancing and the elimination of all unnecessary detail in the way of stage decor or scenery. The development of electric lighting has of course opened up limitless possibilities in all those directions.

Toller and Kaiser taking the dangerous course of direct statement have so simplified the stage by throwing out unnecessary lumber that nothing will convince a British audience, schooled to the loud technical camouflage of Mr St. John Irvine, that they are really saying anything at all. They have however discredited their school to some extent in the eyes of non-industrial audiences by a complete absence of humour and by the Frankenstein complex that seems to have dominated the stage of Central Europe ever since the War.

In English-speaking countries on the other hand, the tradition of Pinero, Barker and Shaw, culminating in the 'Problem Play', is still well entrenched in the path of any further development of the theatre. We have the Play that leaves you with a Thought. What would I do if I met an Escaped Convict? How would I like it if Father married a Prostitute? Is War Right? I need hardly say that as a natural consequence nobody can go to an ostensibly serious play without feeling that he must concentrate upon what it is all About.

But surely this is all wrong, just as it would be in the case of music! All that is needed to enjoy and appreciate a work such as E. E. Cummings, 'Him' is a simple faith, a little human experience, and a receptive state of mind attained by a process the reverse of concentration. This being the normal condition of my own mind I need hardly say that I find little difficulty in preferring Strindberg's 'Dream Play' to 'Emperor and Galilean'.

* * *

The Old Lady says "No"! is not an expressionist play and ought never to have been mistaken for one. I have attempted to evolve a thematic method based on simple association of ideas, a process which has as many disadvantages as the opposite. For it presupposes at the start a set of recognisable figments in the minds of the audience – figments which from their very nature are bound to be somewhat local. In consequence of this, the play to be intelligible to a non-Irish audience requires to some extent to be translated.

The theme of the Romantic temperament seeking for an environment in which to express himself is a universal one, but everybody cannot be expected to know about Robert Emmet. When an old lady appears upon the stage and maunders about her four beautiful green fields, it is too much to expect of a London audience that it will recognise the traditional figure of romantic Nationalism for whom Mangan and Pearse sighed. It is only in the Free State that the O'Donovan Rossa speech and Committee Room 15 (where Parnell was betrayed) can be relied upon to call up any recollections without the aid of a footnote.

Yet the search for the Land of Heart's Desire is as old and as universal as the Holy Grail. The tale might also be the tale of such diverse figures as Juan Ponce de Leon, of the great Danton, of Abelard, of John Brown of Harper's Ferry and even of poor William Blake. Every land has had its store of Emmets, preaching their burning messages to the accompaniment of farmyard noises, and Ireland has more than her share.

It was Plato who first told us that if we don't like our environment it is up to us to alter it for ourselves, and the vigorous philosophy of Nietzsche's Man-Gott and the biology of Buffon and Lamarck are in somewhat the same line of business. If the Emmets in particular or if intransigent Irish Republicanism in general are to be taken as having made any contribution to the world of applied philosophy I feel that it is this characteristic attitude of mind. 'The Republic still lives' is not the expression of a pious hope, but is in itself a creative act, as England knows to her cost.

I understand that there is a correct psychological explanation of all this. Ned Stephens, for instance, tells me that the play represents the breaking down of something called a 'synthetic personality' by contact with reality and the creation of a new one in its stead. I am much too scared of Freud, Adler and McDougall ever to have attempted any such thing, but I feel that if a play is true to experience in its emotional aspect it may well have a sound psychological meaning thrown in as well. As a small boy I used to make pictures for myself with a box of blocks. When the work was completed I used to find that by turning the whole over you found another finished picture constructed on the other side.

But I should add that all this is not intended to be by way of explanation. All that I do wish to do is to answer the objection levelled at much of the post-war spirit both in art and in letters; that it is insincere, intentionally obscure and that it lacks fundamentality. Lucidity seems to me to be the *sine qua non* of any effort of this kind. It has not been my desire to detract attention from my lack of craftsmanship by muddling people's minds. Neither have I any desire that the play should be unjustly enhanced by the 'false glitter of quotations', as one critic very threateningly put it. The method is thematic and a motif in the realm of thought is carried best by a name or a quotation.

Some years ago I used to have to play a game where some large, blindfold person, groping round with a cushion, would sit on my knee and tell me to 'Make a noise like a camel'. Well in this play when I want to make a noise like the Old Ireland, I do it in what seems to me to be the easiest way – by means of a potted anthology of the 'Erin a tear and a smile' school that preceded Geoffrey Phibbs. The play with which the first part opens, and which crops up again at intervals, is almost entirely composed of well-known lines from Mangan, Moore, Callinan, Blacker, Griffin, Ferguson, Kickham, Todhunter and a dozen more. The voices of the Shadows are the easily recognisable words of some of Dublin's greatest contributors to the World's knowledge of itself. The long speech with which the play concludes contains suggestions from Emmet's speech from the dock, the resurrection thesis of the Litany, and the magnificent, though sadly neglected, Commination Service of the Anglican Church.

I have already drawn attention to the Old Woman's lines. For the rest I have not consciously or wilfully bowdlerised anybody, except one line of Blake's which I freely admit I am not entitled to, but which is too apt to be surrendered. You may have it if you can find it!

But whatever may be said of the play, there can be no two opinions as to the merits of Hilton Edward's production. It was staged on a space roughly 16 feet by 12 feet – an incredible feat, when it is remembered that at several points there are mass movements of crowds that have to be carried out in a manner not dissimilar to a ballet, and that sets have to be changed while the action is proceeding.

The rhythmatic chanting of the Choruses was carried out to the throb of a drum, for which purpose a considerable portion of the dialogue had practically to be scored – the parts coming in one on top of the other as in instrumental music or a madrigal. It was an unusual and amusing sight at rehearsals to see the spoken lines being conducted from the front by the Producer. It would be invidious to refer to the players. The elan of Michael MacLiammoir as the Speaker, the virtuosity of Meriel Moore in the difficult double role of Sarah Curran and the old woman, and the very trying work of the Chorus were the real cause of the play's success.

May I respectively thank them – not forgetting to include my friend Kate Curling for her help and for her contribution.

PERTISAU, 1929.

SAMUEL BECKETT

All That Fall

Samuel Beckett (1906–   )

Samuel Beckett was born in Foxrock, south of Dublin in 1906. He studied Modern Languages at Trinity College, Dublin, and became a teacher in Paris in 1928. The following ten years were divided between Ireland and France. Beckett was poor but eked out a living with short stories, criticism and translation. His first novel *Murphy* was published in 1935. In 1938 he met and later married Suzanne Dechevaux-Dumesmil. They remained in France during the war, and were active in the Resistance. After a period of hiding, he joined the Irish Red Cross medical unit. He was awarded the Croix de Guerre and the Medaille de la Resistance in 1945. After the war Beckett wrote several novels in English and French. *En Attendant Godot* was finished in 1949. It was premiered in Paris in 1953, London at the Royal Court Theatre as *Waiting for Godot* in 1955 and New York in 1956. London productions followed of *Fin de Partie* (1957), *All that Fall* (1957), *Endgame* (1958), *Krapp's Last Tape* (1958) *Happy Days* (1961). Beckett continued writing poetry, short pieces, plays and a film followed attracting a number of prizes around the world.

In 1969 he was awarded the Nobel Prize for Literature for 'a body of work that, in new forms of fiction and the theatre, has transmuted the destitution of modern man into his exaltation.' In 1972 he wrote *Not I* and *That Time*; *Footfalls* in 1976, *Rockaby* (1980) and *Catastrophe* (1982).

All That Fall

'It is a text written to come out of the dark.'
(Beckett)

All That Fall was written between June and November 1956, at the suggestion of a friend in the BBC.

The play was published in England by Faber and Faber, London, 1957; in France by Editions de Minuit, 1957; in America by Grove Press, New York, 1957. It was commissioned and first broadcast in England by the BBC Third Programme on 13 January 1957. It was directed by Donald McWhinnie. The cast was as follows:

MRS ROONEY	Mary O'Farrell
CHRISTY	Allan McClelland
MR TYLER	Brian O'Higgins
MR SLOCUM	Pat Magee
TOMMY	Jack MacGowran
MR BARRELL	Harry Hutchinson
MISS FITT	Sheila Ward
A FEMALE VOICE	Peggy Marshall
MR ROONEY	J. G. Devlin
JERRY	Terrance Farrell

and members of the BBC Drama Repertory Company

First broadcast in Francy by ORTF, Paris, 19 December 1959 and directed by Alain Trutat. The cast included Marise Paillet as Mme Rooney and Roger Blin as M Rooney.

First televised in France by ORTF, Paris, 25 February 1963, directed by Michel Mitrani. Mme Rooney was played by Alic Sapricht, and M Rooney by Guy Tréjean.

First broadcast in Ireland RTE, Dublin, 26 January 1969, directed by Dan Treston. The cast was as follows:

MRS ROONEY	Neasa Ní Annracháin
CHRISTY	Dermot Crowley

MR TYLER	Eamonn Keane
MR SLOCUM	Aidan Grennell
TOMMY	Michael Campion
MR BARRELL	Brian O'Higgins
MISS FITT	Deirdre O'Meara
A FEMALE VOICE	Patricia Moloney
MR ROONEY	Thomas Studley
JERRY	Bosco Hogan

A stage version was given, with special permission from Beckett, by the Reading Players, on 20 June 1967, at the Whiteknights Theatre, Reading University, England.

Never thought about a radio play technique ... but in the dead of t'other night got a nice gruesome idea full of cartwheels and dragging feet and puffing and panting which may or may not lead to something.

Beckett, letter to Nancy Cunard, 5 July 1956.

What raises this play, also, above the mere desolating wit of *Fin de partie* is the Irish love of extravagant language that runs through it. . . . There is a warmth in the incidental humour, though it may be unintended warmth. . . . This is a play by a man at the end of his tether; but that tether, tying Mr Beckett, perhaps reluctantly, to sympathy with those who fall and those who are bowed down, has not yet been broken.

Times Literary Supplement, 6 Sept. 1957, p.528.

Selected Bibliography

Plays:
All That Fall. London: Faber & Faber, 1957. *Breath*. *Gambit*, IV, 16 (1970), pp. 8–9. *Collected Shorter Plays*. London, Boston: Faber & Faber, 1984. *Come and Go*. London: Calder & Boyars, 1967. *Eh Joe, Act Without Words II, Film*. London: Faber & Faber, 1967. *Endgame and Act Without Words I*. London: Faber & Faber, 1958. *Ends and Odds*. London: Faber & Faber, 1977. *Happy Days*. London: Faber & Faber, 1962. *Human Wishes*. In *Disjecta*, ed. Ruby Cohn (London: John Calder, 1983), pp. 153–166. *Krapp's Last Tape and Embers*. London: Faber & Faber, 1959. *Play, Words and Music, Cascando*. London: Faber & Faber, 1967. *Waiting for Godot*. London: Faber & Faber, 1965.

Other works:
'Beckett's Letters on *Endgame*'. *Village Voice*, 19 March 1958, pp. 8, 15. 'Dante . . . Brune . Vico . . Joyce', in *Our Examination Round His Factification for Incamination of Work in Progress*. New York: New Directions, 1962. *How It Is*. London: Calder & Boyars, 1964. *More Pricks Than Kicks*. London: Calder & Boyars, 1970. *Murphy*. London: Calder & Boyars, 1963. *No's Knife*. London: Calder & Boyars, 1967. *Poems in English*. London: Calder & Boyars, 1961. *Proust and Three Dialogues with Georges Dutbuit*. London: Calder & Boyars, 1965. *Three Novels (Molloy, Malone Dies, The Unnamable)*. London: Calder & Boyars, 1959. *Watt*. London: Calder & Boyars, 1963.

All That Fall

A Play for Radio

Persons in the Play

MRS ROONEY (Maddy) *a lady in her seventies*
CHRISTY *a carter*
MR TYLER *a retired bill-broker*
MR SLOCUM *Clerk of the Racecourse*
TOMMY *a porter*
MR BARRELL *a station-master*
MISS FITT *a lady in her thirties*
A FEMALE VOICE
DOLLY *a small girl*
MR ROONEY (Dan) *husband of Mrs Rooney, blind*
JERRY *a small boy*

Rural sounds. Sheep, bird, cow, cock, severally, then together.
Silence.
Mrs Rooney advances along country road towards railway-station. Sound of her dragging feet.
Music faint from house by way. 'Death and the Maiden.' The steps slow down, stop.

MRS ROONEY. Poor woman. All alone in that ruinous old house.
Music louder. Silence but for music playing. The steps resume. Music dies. Mrs Rooney murmurs, melody. Her murmur dies. Sound of approaching cartwheels. The cart stops.
The steps slow down, stop.
MRS ROONEY. Is that you, Christy?
CHRISTY. It is, Ma'am.
MRS ROONEY. I thought the hinny was familiar. How is your poor wife?
CHRISTY. No better, Ma'am.
MRS ROONEY. Your daughter then?
CHRISTY. No worse, Ma'am.
Silence.
MRS ROONEY. Why do you halt? [*Pause*]. But why do I halt?
Silence.
CHRISTY. Nice day for the races, Ma'am.
MRS ROONEY. No doubt it is. [*Pause*]. But will it hold up?
[*Pause. With emotion*]. Will it hold up?
Silence.
CHRISTY. I suppose you wouldn't –
MRS ROONEY. Hist! [*Pause*]. Surely to goodness that cannot be the up mail I hear already.

Silence. The hinny neighs. Silence.

CHRISTY. Damn the mail.

MRS ROONEY. Oh thank God for that! I could have sworn I heard it, thundering up the track in the far distance. [*Pause*]. So hinnies whinny. Well, it is not surprising.

CHRISTY. I suppose you wouldn't be in need of a small load of dung?

MRS ROONEY. Dung? What class of dung?

CHRISTY. Stydung.

MRS ROONEY. Stydung . . . I like your frankness, Christy. [*Pause*]. I'll ask the master. [*Pause*]. Christy.

CHRISTY. Yes, Ma'am.

MRS ROONEY. Do you find anything . . . bizarre about my way of speaking? [*Pause*]. I do not mean the voice. [*Pause*]. No, I mean the words. [*Pause. More to herself*]. I use none but the simplest words, I hope, and yet I sometimes find my way of speaking very . . . bizarre. [*Pause*]. Mercy! What was that?

CHRISTY. Never mind her, Ma'am, she's very fresh in herself today. *Silence.*

MRS ROONEY. Dung? What would we want with dung, at our time of life? [*Pause*]. Why are you on your feet down on the road? Why do you not climb up on the crest of your manure and let yourself be carried along? Is it that you have no head for heights? *Silence.*

CHRISTY [*to the hinny*] Yep! [*Pause. Louder*]. Yep wiyya to hell owwa that! *Silence.*

MRS ROONEY. She does not move a muscle. [*Pause*]. I too should be getting along, if I do not wish to arrive late at the station. [*Pause*]. But a moment ago she neighed and pawed the ground. And now she refuses to advance. Give her a good welt on the rump. [*Sound of welt. Pause*]. Harder! [*Sound of welt. Pause*]. Well! If someone were to do that for me I should not dally. [*Pause*]. How she gazes at me to be sure, with her great moist cleg-tormented eyes! Perhaps if I were to move on, down the road, out of her field of vision . . . [*Sound of welt*]. No, no, enough! Take her by the snaffle and pull her eyes away from me. Oh this is awful! [*She moves on. Sound of her dragging feet*]. What have I done to deserve all this, what, what?

[*Dragging feet*]. So long ago . . . No! No! [*Dragging feet. Quotes*]. 'Sigh out a something something tale of things, Done long ago and ill done.' [*She halts*]. How can I go on, I cannot. Oh let me just flop down flat on the road like a big fat jelly out of a bowl and never move again! A great big slop thick with grit and dust and flies, they would have to scoop me up with a shovel. [*Pause*]. Heavens, there is that up mail again, what will become of me! [*The dragging steps resume*]. Oh I am just a hysterical old hag I know, destroyed with sorrow and pining and gentility and church-going and fat and rheumatism and childlessness. [*Pause. Brokenly*]. Minnie! Little Minnie! [*Pause*]. Love, that is all I asked, a little love, daily, twice daily, fifty years of twice daily love like a Paris horse-butcher's regular, what normal woman wants affection? A peck on the jaw at morning, near the ear, and another at evening, peck, peck, till you grow whiskers on you. There is that lovely laburnum again

Dragging feet. Sound of bicycle-bell. It is old Mr Tyler coming up behind her on his bicycle, on his way to the station. Squeak of brakes. He slows down and rides abreast of her.

MR TYLER. Mrs Rooney! Pardon me if I do not doff my cap, I'd fall off. Divine day for the meeting.

MRS ROONEY. Oh, Mr Tyler, you startled the life out of me stealing up behind me like that like a deer-stalker! Oh!

MR TYLER [*playfully*] I rang my bell, Mrs Rooney, the moment I sighted you I started tinkling my bell, now don't you deny it.

MRS ROONEY. Your bell is one thing, Mr Tyler, and you are another. What news of your poor daughter?

MR TYLER. Fair, fair. They removed everything, you know, the whole . . . er . . . bag of tricks. Now I am grandchildless.

Dragging feet.

MRS ROONEY. Gracious how you wobble! Dismount, for mercy's sake, or ride on.

MR TYLER. Perhaps if I were to lay my hand lightly on your shoulder, Mrs Rooney, how would that be?

[*Pause*]. Would you permit that?

MRS ROONEY. No, Mr Rooney, Mr Tyler I mean, I am tired of light old hands on my shoulders and other senseless places, sick and tired of them. Heavens, here comes Connolly's van! [*She halts.*

Sound of motor-van. It approaches, passes with thunderous rattles, recedes]. Are you all right, Mr Tyler? [*Pause*]. Where is he? [*Pause*]. Ah there you are! [*The dragging steps resume*]. That was a narrow squeak.

MR TYLER. I alit in the nick of time.

MRS ROONEY. It is suicide to be abroad. But what is it to be at home, Mr Tyler, what is it to be at home? A lingering dissolution. Now we are white with dust from head to foot. I beg your pardon?

MR TYLER. Nothing, Mrs Rooney, nothing, I was merely cursing, under my breath, God and man, under my breath, and the wet Saturday afternoon of my conception. My back tyre has gone down again. I pumped it hard as iron before I set out. And now I am on the rim.

MRS ROONEY. Oh what a shame!

MR TYLER. Now if it were the front I should not so much mind. But the back. The back! The chain! The oil! The grease! The hub! The brakes! The gear! No! It is too much!

Dragging steps.

MRS ROONEY. Are we very late, Mr Tyler? I have not the courage to look at my watch.

MR TYLER [*bitterly*] Late! I on my bicycle as I bowled along was already late. Now therefore we are doubly late, trebly, quadrupedly late. Would I had shot by you, without a word.

Dragging feet.

MRS ROONEY. Whom are you meeting, Mr Tyler?

MR TYLER. Hardy. [*Pause*]. We used to climb together. [*Pause*]. I saved his life once. [*Pause*]. I have not forgotten it.

Dragging feet. They stop.

MRS ROONEY. Let us halt a moment and let this vile dust fall back upon the viler worms.

Silence. Rural sounds.

MR TYLER. What sky! What light! Ah in spite of all it is a blessed thing to be alive in such weather, and out of hospital.

MRS ROONEY. Alive?

MR TYLER. Well half alive shall we say?

MRS ROONEY. Speak for yourself, Mr Tyler. I am not half alive nor anything approaching it. [*Pause*]. What are we standing here for?

This dust will not settle in our time. And when it does some great roaring machine will come and whirl it all skyhigh again.

MR TYLER. Well, shall we be getting along in that case?

MRS ROONEY. No.

MR TYLER. Come, Mrs Rooney –

MRS ROONEY. Go, Mr Tyler, go on and leave me, listening to the cooing of the ringdoves. [*Cooing*]. If you see my poor blind Dan tell him I was on my way to meet him when it all come over me again, like a flood. Say to him, Your poor wife, she told me to tell you it all came flooding over her again and . . . [*the voice breaks*] . . . she simply went back home . . . straight back home . . .

MR TYLER. Come, Mrs Rooney, come, the mail has not yet gone up, just take my free arm and we'll be there with time and to spare.

MRS ROONEY [*sobbing*]. What? What's all this now? [*Calmer*].

Can't you see I'm in trouble? [*With anger*].

Have you no respect for misery? [*Sobbing*].

Minnie! Little Minnie!

MR TYLER. Come, Mrs Rooney, come, the mail has not yet gone up, just take my free arm and we'll be there with time and to spare.

MRS ROONEY [*brokenly*]. In her forties now she'd be, I don't know, fifty girding up her lovely little loins, getting ready for the change . . .

MR TYLER. Come, Mrs Rooney, come, the mail –

MRS ROONEY [*exploding*]. Will you get along with you, Mr Rooney, Mr Tyler I mean, will you get along with you now and cease molesting me? What kind of a country is that where a woman can't weep her heart out on the highways and byways without being tormented by retired bill-brokers! [*Mr Tyler prepares to mount his bicycle*]. Heavens you're not going to ride her flat! [*Mr Tyler mounts*]. You'll tear your tube to ribbons! [*Mr Tyler rides off. Receding sound of bumping bicycle. Silence. Cooing*]. Venus birds! Billing in the woods all the long summer long. [*Pause*]. Oh cursed corset! If I could let it out, without indecent exposure. Mr Tyler! Mr Tyler! Come back and unlace me behind the hedge! [*She laughs wildly, ceases*]. What's wrong with me, what's wrong with me, never tranquil, seething out of my dirty old pelt, out of my skull, oh to be atoms in atoms! [*Frenziedly*]. ATOMS! [*Silence. Cooing. Faintly*]. Jesus! [*Pause*]. Jesus!

Sound of car coming up behind her. It slows down and draws up beside her, engine running. It is Mr Slocum, the Clerk of the Racecourse.

MR SLOCUM. Is anything wrong, Mrs Rooney? You are bent all double. Have you a pain in the stomach?

Silence. Mrs Rooney laughs wildly. Finally.

MRS ROONEY. Well if it isn't my old admirer the Clerk of the Course, in his limousine.

MR SLOCUM. May I offer you a lift, Mrs Rooney? Are you going in my direction?

MRS ROONEY. I am, Mr Slocum, we all are. [*Pause*]. How is your poor mother?

MR SLOCUM. Thank you, she is fairly comfortable. We manage to keep her out of pain. That is the great thing, Mrs Rooney, is it not?

MRS ROONEY. Yes, indeed, Mr Slocum, that is the great thing, I don't know how you do it. [*Pause. She slaps her cheek violently*]. Ah these wasps!

MR SLOCUM [*coolly*] May I then offer you a seat, Madam?

MRS ROONEY [*with exaggerated enthusiasm*] Oh that would be heavenly, Mr Slocum, just simply heavenly. [*Dubiously*]. But would I ever get in, you look very high off the ground today, these new balloon tyres I presume. [*Sound of door opening and Mrs Rooney trying to get in*]. Does this roof never come off? No? [*Efforts of Mrs Rooney*]. No . . . I'll never do it . . . you'll have to get down, Mr Slocum, and help me from the rear. [*Pause*]. What was that? [*Pause. Aggrieved*]. This is all your suggestion, Mr Slocum, not mine. Drive on, Sir, drive on.

MR SLOCUM [*switching off the engine*] I'm coming, Mrs Rooney, I'm coming, give me time, I'm as stiff as yourself.

Sound of Mr Slocum extracting himself from driver's seat.

MRS ROONEY. Stiff! Well I like that! And me heaving all over back and front. [*To herself*]. The dry old reprobate!

MR SLOCUM [*in position behind her*] Now, Mrs Rooney, how shall we do this?

MRS ROONEY. As if I were a bale, Mr Slocum, don't be afraid. [*Pause. Sounds of effort*]. That's the way! [*Effort*]. Lower! [*Effort*]. Wait! [*Pause*]. No, don't let go! [*Pause*]. Suppose I do get up, will I ever get down?

MR SLOCUM [*breathing hard*] You'll get down, Mrs Rooney, you'll get

down. We may not get you up, but I warrant you we'll get you
down.

He resumes his efforts. Sound of these.

MRS ROONEY. Oh! . . . Lower! . . . Don't be afraid! . . . We're past
the age when . . . There! . . . Now! . . . Get your shoulder under it
. . . Oh! . . . [*Giggles*]. Oh glory! . . . Up! Up! . . . Ah! . . . I'm in!
[*Panting of Mr Slocum. He slams the door. In a scream*]. My frock!
You've nipped my frock! [*Mr Slocum opens the door. Mrs Rooney frees
her frock. Mr Slocum slams the door. His violent unintelligible muttering
as he walks round to the other door. Tearfully*]. My nice frock! Look
what you've done to my nice frock! [*Mr Slocum gets into his seat,
slam's driver's door, presses starter. The engine does not start. He releases
starter*]. What will Dan say when he sees me?

MR SLOCUM. Has he then recovered his sight?

MRS ROONEY. No, I mean when he knows, what will he say when he
feels the hole? [*Mr Slocum presses starter. As before. Silence*]. What are
you doing, Mr Slocum?

MR SLOCUM. Gazing straight before me, Mrs Rooney, through the
windscreen, into the void.

MRS ROONEY. Start her up, I beseech you, and let us be off. This is
awful!

MR SLOCUM [*dreamily*] All morning she went like a dream and now
she is dead. That is what you get for a good deed. [*Pause. Hopefully*].
Perhaps if I were to choke her. [*He does so, presses the starter. The
engine roars. Roaring to make himself heard*]. She was getting too
much air!

*He throttles down, grinds in his first gear, moves off, changes up in a
grinding of gears.*

MRS ROONEY [*in anguish*] Mind the hen! [*Scream of brakes. Squawk of
hen*]. Oh, mother, you have squashed her, drive on, drive on! [*The
car accelerates. Pause*]. What a death! One minute picking happy at
the dung, on the road, in the sun, with now and then a dust bath,
and then – bang! – all her troubles over. [*Pause*]. All the laying and
the hatching. [*Pause*]. Just one great squawk and then . . . peace.
[*Pause*]. They would have slit her weasand in any case. [*Pause*].
Here we are, let me down. [*The car slows down, stops, engine running.
Mr Slocum blows his horn. Pause. Louder. Pause*]. What are you up to

now, Mr Slocum? We are at a standstill, all danger is past and you blow your horn. Now if instead of blowing it now you had blown it at that unfortunate –

Horn violently. Tommy the porter appears at top of station steps.

MR SLOCUM [*calling*] Will you come down, Tommy, and help this lady out, she's stuck. [*Tommy descends the steps*]. Open the door, Tommy, and ease her out. *Tommy opens the door.*

TOMMY. Certainly, sir. Nice day for the races, sir. What would you fancy for –

MRS ROONEY. Don't mind me. Don't take any notice of me. I do not exist. The fact is well known.

MR SLOCUM. Do as you're asked, Tommy, for the love of God.

TOMMY. Yessir. Now, Mrs Rooney.

He starts pulling her out.

MRS ROONEY. Wait, Tommy, wait now, don't bustle me, just let me wheel round and get my feet to the ground. [*Her efforts to achieve this*]. Now.

TOMMY [*pulling her out*] Mind your feather, Ma'am. [*Sounds of effort*]. Easy now, easy.

MRS ROONEY. Wait, for God's sake, you'll have me beheaded.

TOMMY. Crouch down, Mrs Rooney, crouch down, and get your head in the open.

MRS ROONEY. Crouch down! At my time of life! This is lunacy!

TOMMY. Press her down, sir.

Sounds of combined efforts.

MRS ROONEY. Pity!

TOMMY. Now! She's coming! Straighten up, Ma'am! There! *Mr Slocum slams the door.*

MRS ROONEY. Am I out?

The voice of Mr Barrell, the station-master, raised in anger.

MR BARRELL. Tommy! Tommy! Where the hell is he?

Mr Slocum grinds in his gear.

TOMMY [*hurriedly*] You wouldn't have something for the Ladies Plate, sir? I was given Flash Harry.

MR SLOCUM [*scornfully*] Flash Harry! That carthorse!

MR BARRELL [*at top of steps, roaring*] Tommy! Blast your bleeding bloody – [*He sees Mrs Rooney*]. Oh, Mrs Rooney ... [*Mr Slocum drives away in a grinding of gears*]. Who's that crucifying his gearbox, Tommy?

TOMMY. Old Cissy Slocum.

MRS ROONEY. Cissy Slocum! That's a nice way to refer to your betters. Cissy Slocum! And you an orphan!

MR BARRELL [*angrily to Tommy*] What are you doing stravaging down here on the public road? This is no place for you at all! Nip up there on the platform now and whip out the truck! Won't the twelve thirty be on top of us before we can turn round?

TOMMY [*bitterly*] And that's the thanks you get for a Christian act.

MR BARRELL [*violently*] Get on with you now before I report you! [*Slow feet of Tommy climbing steps*]. Do you want me to come down to you with the shovel! [*The feet quicken, recede, cease*]. Ah God forgive me, it's a hard life. [*Pause*]. Well, Mrs Rooney, it's nice to see you up and about again. You were laid up there a long time.

MRS ROONEY. Not long enough, Mr Barrell. [*Pause*]. Would I were still in bed, Mr Barrell. [*Pause*]. Would I were lying stretched out in my comfortable bed, Mr Barrell, just wasting slowly, painlessly away, keeping up my strength with arrowroot and calves-foot jelly, till in the end you wouldn't see me under the blankets any more than a board. [*Pause*]. Oh no coughing or spitting or bleeding or vomiting, just drifting gently down into the higher life, and remembering, remembering . . . [*the voice breaks*] . . . all the silly unhappiness . . . as though . . . it had never happened . . . What did I do with that handkerchief? [*Sound of handkerchief loudly applied*]. How long have you been master of this station now, Mr Barrell?

MR BARRELL. Don't ask me, Mrs Rooney, don't ask me.

MRS ROONEY. You stepped into your father's shoes, I believe, when he took them off.

MR BARRELL. Poor Pappy! [*Reverent pause*]. He didn't live long to enjoy his ease.

MRS ROONEY. I remember him clearly. A small ferrety purple-faced widower, deaf as a doornail, very testy and snappy. [*Pause*]. I suppose you'll be retiring soon yourself, Mr Barrell, and growing your roses. [*Pause*]. Did I understand you to say the twelve thirty would soon be upon us?

MR BARRELL. Those were my words.

MRS ROONEY. But according to my watch which is more or less right
– or was – by the eight o'clock news the time is now coming up to
twelve . . . [*pause as she consults her watch*] . . . thirty-six. [*Pause*]. And
yet upon the other hand the up mail has not yet come through.
[*Pause*]. Or has it sped by unbeknown to me? [*Pause*]. For there was
a moment there, I remember now, I was so plunged in sorrow I
wouldn't have heard a steam roller go over me. [*Pause. Mr Barrell
turns to go*]. Don't go, Mr Barrell! [*Mr Barrell goes. Loud*]. Mr
Barrell! [*Pause. Louder*]. Mr Barrell!
Mr Barrell comes back.

MR BARRELL [*testily*] What is it, Mrs Rooney, I have my work to do.
Silence. Sound of wind.

MRS ROONEY. The wind is getting up. [*Pause. Wind*]. The best of the
day is over. [*Pause. Wind. Dreamily*]. Soon the rain will begin to fall
and go on falling, all afternoon. [*Mr Barrell goes*]. Then at evening
the clouds will part, the setting sun will shine an instant, then sink,
behind the hills. [*She realizes Mr Barrell has gone*]. Mr Barrell! Mr
Barrell! [*Silence*]. I estrange them all. They come towards me,
uninvited, bygones bygones, full of kindness, anxious to help . . .
[*the voice breaks*] . . . genuinely pleased . . . to see me again . . .
looking so well . . . [*Handkerchief*]. A few simple words . . . from my
heart . . . and I am all alone . . . once more . . . [*Handkerchief.
Vehemently*]. I should not be out at all! I should never leave the
grounds! [*Pause*]. Oh there is that Fitt woman, I wonder will she
bow to me. [*Sound of Miss Fitt approaching, humming a hymn. She
starts climbing the steps*]. Miss Fitt! [*Miss Fitt halts, stops humming*].
Am I then invisible, Miss Fitt? Is this cretonne so becoming to me
that I merge into the masonry? [*Miss Fitt descends a step*]. That is
right, Miss Fitt, look closely and you will finally distinguish a once
female shape.

MISS FITT. Mrs Rooney! I saw you, but I did not know you.

MRS ROONEY. Last Sunday we worshipped together. We knelt side
by side at the same altar. We drank from the same chalice. Have I
so changed since then?

MISS FITT [*shocked*] Oh but in church, Mrs Rooney, in church I am
alone with my Maker. Are you not? [*Pause*]. Why even the sexton
himself, you know, when he takes up the collection, knows it is

useless to pause before me. I simply do not see the plate, or bag, whatever it is they use, how could I? [*Pause*]. Why even when all is over and I go out into the sweet fresh air, why even then for the first furlong or so I stumble in a kind of daze as you might say, oblivious to my co-religionists. And they are very kind I must admit – the vast majority – very kind and understanding. They know me now and take no umbrage. There she goes, they say, there goes the dark Miss Fitt, alone with her Maker, take no notice of her. And they step down off the path to avoid my running into them. [*Pause*]. Ah yes, I am distray, very distray, even on week-days. Ask Mother, if you do not believe me. Hetty, she says, when I start eating my doily instead of the thin bread and butter. Hetty, how can you be so distray? [*Sighs*]. I suppose the truth is I am not there, Mrs Rooney, just not really there at all. I see, hear, smell, and so on, I go through the usual motions, but my heart is not in it, Mrs Rooney, but heart is in none of it. Left to myself, with no one to check me, I would soon be flown . . . home. [*Pause*]. So if you think I cut you just now, Mrs Rooney, you do me an injustice. All I saw was a big pale blur, just another big pale blur. [*Pause*]. Is anything amiss, Mrs Rooney, you do not look normal somehow. So bowed and bent.

MRS ROONEY [*ruefully*]. Maddy Rooney, née Dunne, the big pale blur. [*Pause*]. You have piercing sight, Miss Fitt, if you only knew it, literally piercing.

Pause.

MISS FITT. Well . . . is there anything I can do, now that I am here?

MRS ROONEY. If you would help me up the face of this cliff, Miss Fitt, I have little doubt your Maker would requite you, if no one else.

MISS FITT. Now, now, Mrs Rooney, don't put your teeth in me. Requite! I make these sacrifices for nothing – or not at all. [*Pause. Sound of her descending steps*]. I take it you want to lean on me, Mrs Rooney.

MRS ROONEY. I asked Mr Barrell to give me his arm, just give me his arm. [*Pause*]. He turned on his heel and strode away.

MISS FITT. Is it my arm you want then? [*Pause. Impatiently*]. Is it my arm you want, Mrs Rooney, or what is it?

MRS ROONEY [*exploding*] Your arm! Any arm! A helping hand! For
five seconds! Christ what a planet!

MISS FITT. Really . . . Do you know what it is, Mrs Rooney, I do not
think it is wise of you to be going about at all.

MRS ROONEY [*violently*] Come down here, Miss Fitt, and give me
your arm, before I scream down the parish!
Pause. Wind. Sound of Miss Fitt descending last steps.

MISS FITT [*resignedly*] Well, I suppose it is the Protestant thing to do.

MRS ROONEY. Pismires do it for one another. [*Pause*]. I have seen
slugs do it. [*Miss Fitt proffers her arm*]. No, the other side, my dear,
if it's all the same to you, I'm left-handed on top of everything else.
[*She takes Miss Fitt's right arm*]. Heavens, child, you're just a bag of
bones, you need building up. [*Sound of her toiling up steps on Miss
Fitt's arm*]. This is worse than the Matterhorn, were you ever up
the Matterhorn, Miss Fitt, great honeymoon resort. [*Sound of
toiling*]. Why don't they have a handrail? [*Panting*]. Wait till I get
some air. [*Pause*]. Don't let me go! [*Miss Fitt hums her hymn. After a
moment Mrs Rooney joins in with the words*]. . . . the encircling gloo-
oom . . . [*Miss Fitt stops humming*] . . . tum tum me on. [*Forte*]. The
night is dark and I am far from ho-ome, tum tum—

MISS FITT [*hysterically*] Stop it, Mrs Rooney, stop it, or I'll drop you!

MRS ROONEY. Wasn't it that they sung on the *Lusitania*? Or Rock of
Ages? Most touching it must have been. Or was it the *Titanic*?
*Attracted by the noise a group, including Mr Tyler, Mr Barrell and
Tommy, gathers at top of steps.*

MR BARRELL. What the –
Silence.

MR TYLER. Lovely day for the fixture.
*Loud titter from Tommy cut short by Mr Barrell with backhanded blow
in the stomach. Appropriate noise from Tommy.*

FEMALE VOICE [*shrill*] Oh look, Dolly, look!

DOLLY. What, Mamma?

FEMALE VOICE. They are stuck! [*Cackling laugh*]. They are stuck!

MRS ROONEY. Now we are the laughing-stock of the twenty-six
counties. Or is it thirty-six?

MR TYLER. That is a nice way to treat your defenceless subordinates,
Mr Barrell, hitting them without warning in the pit of the stomach.

MISS FITT. Has anybody seen my mother?

MR BARRELL. Who is that?

TOMMY. The dark Miss Fitt.

MR BARRELL. Where is her face?

MRS ROONEY. Now, deary, I am ready if you are. [*They toil up remaining steps*]. Stand back, you cads!

Shuffle of feet.

FEMALE VOICE. Mind yourself, Dolly!

MRS ROONEY. Thank you, Miss Fitt, thank you, that will do, just prop me against the wall like a roll of tarpaulin and that will be all, for the moment. [*Pause*]. I am sorry for all this ramdam, Miss Fitt, had I known you were looking for your mother I should not have importuned you, I know what it is.

MR TYLER [*in marvelling aside*] Ramdam!

FEMALE VOICE. Come, Dolly darling, let us take up our stand before the first class smokers. Give me your hand and hold me tight, one can be sucked under.

MR TYLER. You have lost your mother, Miss Fitt?

MISS FITT. Good morning, Mr Tyler.

MR TYLER. Good morning, Miss Fitt.

MR BARRELL. Good morning, Miss Fitt.

MISS FITT. Good morning, Mr Barrell.

MR TYLER. You have lost your mother, Miss Fitt?

MISS FITT. She said she would be on the last train.

MRS ROONEY. Do not imagine, because I am silent, that I am not present, and alive, to all that is going on.

MR TYLER [*to Miss Fitt*] When you say the last train—

MRS ROONEY. Do not flatter yourself for one moment, because I hold aloof, that my sufferings have ceased. No. The entire scene, the hills, the plain, the racecourse with its miles and miles of white rails and three red stands, the pretty little wayside station, even you yourselves, yes, I mean it, and over all the clouding blue, I see it all, I stand here and see it all with eyes . . . [*the voice breaks*] . . . through eyes . . . oh if you had my eyes . . . you would understand . . . the things they have seen . . . and not looked away . . . this is nothing . . . nothing . . . what did I do with that handkerchief?

Pause.

MR TYLER [*to Miss Fitt*]. When you say the last train – [*Mrs Rooney blows her nose violently and long*] – when you say the last train, Miss Fitt, I take it you mean the twelve thirty.

MISS FITT. What else could I mean, Mr Tyler, what else could I *conceivably* mean?

MR TYLER. Then you have no cause for anxiety, Miss Fitt, for the twelve thirty has not yet arrived. Look. [*Miss Fitt looks*]. No, up the line. [*Miss Fitt looks, Patiently*]. No, Miss Fitt, follow the direction of my index. [*Miss Fitt looks*]. There. You see now. The signal. At the bawdy hour of nine. [*In rueful afterthought*]. Or three alas! [*Mr Barrell stifles a guffaw*]. Thank you, Mr Barrell.

MISS FITT. But the time is now getting on for—

MR TYLER [*patiently*] We all know, Miss Fitt, we all know only too well what the time is now getting on for, and yet the cruel fact remains that the twelve thirty has not yet arrived.

MISS FITT. Not an accident, I trust! [*Pause*]. Do not tell me she has left the track! [*Pause*]. Oh darling mother! With the fresh sole for lunch!

Loud titter from Tommy, checked as before by Mr Barrell.

MR BARRELL. That's enough old guff out of you. Nip up to the box now and see has Mr Case anything for me.

Tommy goes.

MRS ROONEY. Poor Dan!

MISS FITT [*in anguish*] What terrible thing has happened?

MR TYLER. Now now, Miss Fitt, do not—

MRS ROONEY [*with vehement sadness*]. Poor Dan!

MR TYLER. Now now, Miss Fitt, do not give way ... to despair, all will come right ... in the end. [*Aside to Mr Barrell*]. What *is* the situation, Mr Barrell? Not a collision surely?

MRS ROONEY [*enthusiastically*] A collision! Oh that would be wonderful!

MISS FITT [*horrified*] A collision! I knew it!

MR TYLER. Come, Miss Fitt, let us move a little up the platform.

MRS ROONEY. Yes, let us all do that. [*Pause*]. No? [*Pause*]. You have changed your mind? [*Pause*]. I quite agree, we are better here, in the shadow of the waiting-room.

MR BARRELL. Excuse me a moment.

MRS ROONEY. Before you slink away, Mr Barrell, please, a statement of some kind, I insist. Even the slowest train on this brief line is not ten minutes and more behind its scheduled time without good cause, one imagines. [*Pause*]. We all know your station is the best kept of the entire network, but there are times when that is not enough, just not enough. [*Pause*]. Now, Mr Barrell, leave off chewing your whiskers, we are waiting to hear from you – we the unfortunate ticket-holders' nearest if not dearest.
Pause.

MR TYLER [*reasonably*] I do think we are owed some kind of explanation, Mr Barrell, if only to set our minds at rest.

MR BARRELL. I know nothing. All I know is there has been a hitch. All traffic is retarded.

MRS ROONEY [*derisively*] Retarded! A hitch! Ah these celibates! Here we are eating our hearts out with anxiety for our loved ones and he calls that a hitch! Those of us like myself with heart and kidney trouble may collapse at any moment and he calls that a hitch! In our ovens the Saturday roast is burning to a shrivel and he calls that—

MR TYLER. Here comes Tommy, running! I am glad I have been spared to see this.

TOMMY [*excitedly, in the distance*] She's coming. [*Pause. Nearer*]. She's at the level-crossing!
Immediately exaggerated station sounds. Falling signals. Bells. Whistles. Crescendo of train whistle approaching. Sound of train rushing through station.

MRS ROONEY [*above rush of train*] The up mail! The up mail! [*The up mail recedes, the down train approaches, enters the station, pulls up with great hissing of steam and clashing of couplings. Noise of passengers descending, doors banging, Mr Barrell shouting 'Boghill! Boghill!', etc. Piercingly*]. Dan! . . . Are you all right? . . . Where is he? . . . Dan! . . . Did you see my husband? . . . Dan! . . . [*Noise of station emptying. Guard's whistle. Train departing, receding. Silence*]. He isn't on it! The misery I have endured, to get here, and he isn't on it! . . . Mr Barrell! . . . Was he not on it? [*Pause*]. Is anything the matter, you look as if you had seen a ghost. [*Pause*]. Tommy! . . . Did you see the master?

TOMMY. He'll be along, Ma'am, Jerry is minding him.

*Mr Rooney suddenly appears on platform, advancing on small boy Jerry's
arm. He is blind, thumps the ground with his stick and pants incessantly.*

MRS ROONEY. Oh, Dan! There you are! [*Her dragging feet as she
hastens towards him. She reaches him. They halt*].

Where in the world were you?

MR ROONEY [*coolly*] Maddy.

MRS ROONEY. Where were you all this time?

MR ROONEY. In the men's.

MRS ROONEY. Kiss me!

MR ROONEY. Kiss you? In public? On the platform? Before the boy?
Have you taken leave of your senses?

MRS ROONEY. Jerry wouldn't mind. Would you, Jerry?

JERRY. No, Ma'am.

MRS ROONEY. How is your poor father?

JERRY. They took him away, Ma'am.

MRS ROONEY. Then you are all alone?

JERRY. Yes, Ma'am.

MR ROONEY. Why are you here? You did not notify me.

MRS ROONEY. I wanted to give you a surprise. For your birthday.

MR ROONEY. My birthday?

MRS ROONEY. Don't you remember? I wished you your happy returns
in the bathroom.

MR ROONEY. I did not hear you.

MRS ROONEY. But I have you a tie! You have it on!
Pause.

MR ROONEY. How old am I now?

MRS ROONEY. Now never mind about that. Come.

MR ROONEY. Why did you not cancel the boy. Now we shall have to
give him a penny.

MRS ROONEY [*miserably*]. I forgot! I had such a time getting here!
Such horrid nasty people! [*Pause. Pleading*]. Be nice to me, Dan, be
nice to me today!

MR ROONEY. Give the boy a penny.

MRS ROONEY. Here are two halfpennies, Jerry. Run along now and
buy yourself a nice gobstopper.

JERRY. Yes, Ma'am.

MR ROONEY. Come for me on Monday, if I am still alive.

JERRY. Yessir.

He runs off.

MR ROONEY. We could have saved sixpence. We have saved five pence. [*Pause*]. But at what cost?

They move off along platform arm in arm. Dragging feet, panting, thudding stick.

MRS ROONEY. Are you not well?

They halt, on Mr Rooney's initiative.

MR ROONEY. Once and for all, do not ask me to speak and move at the same time. I shall not say this in this life again.

They move off. Dragging feet, etc. They halt at top of steps.

MRS ROONEY. You are not—

MR ROONEY. Let us get this precipice over.

MRS ROONEY. Put your arm around me.

MR ROONEY. Have you been drinking again? [*Pause*]. You are quivering like a blanc-mange. [*Pause*]. Are you in a condition to lead me? [*Pause*]. We shall fall into the ditch.

MRS ROONEY. Oh, Dan! It will be like old times!

MR ROONEY. Pull yourself together or I shall send Tommy for the cab. Then instead of having saved sixpence, no, fivepence, we shall have lost . . . [*calculating mumble*] . . . two and three less six one and no plus one one and no plus three one and nine and one ten and three two and one . . . [*normal voice*] two and one, we shall be the poorer to the tune of two and one. [*Pause*]. Curse that sun, it has gone in. What is the day doing?

Wind.

MRS ROONEY. Shrouding, shrouding, the best of it is past. [*Pause*]. Soon the first great drops will fall slashing in the dust.

MR ROONEY. And yet the glass was firm. [*Pause*]. Let us hasten home and sit before the fire. We shall draw the blinds. You will read to me. I think Effie is going to commit adultery with the Major. [*Brief drag of feet*]. Wait! [*Feet cease. Stick tapping at steps*]. I have been up and down these steps five thousand times and still I do not know how many there are. When I think there are six there are four or five or seven or eight and when I remember there are five there are three or four or six or seven and when finally I realize there are seven there are five or six or eight or nine. Sometimes I wonder if they do not change them in the night. [*Pause. Irritably*]. Well? How many do you make them today?

MRS ROONEY. Do not ask me to count, Dan, not now.

MR ROONEY. Not count! One of the few satisfactions in life!

MRS ROONEY. Not steps. Dan, please, I always get them wrong. Then you might fall on your wound and I would have that on my manure-heap on top of everything else. No, just cling to me and all will be well.

Confused noise of their descent. Panting, stumbling, ejaculations, curses. Silence.

MR ROONEY. Well! That is what you call well!

MRS ROONEY. We are down. And little the worse. [*Silence. A donkey brays. Silence*]. That was a true donkey. Its father and mother were donkeys.

Silence.

MR ROONEY. Do you know what it is, I think I shall retire.

MRS ROONEY [*appalled*] Retire! And live at home? On your grant!

MR ROONEY. Never tread these cursed steps again. Trudge this hellish road for the last time. Sit at home on the remnants of my bottom counting the hours − till the next meal. [*Pause*]. The very thought puts life in me! Forward, before it does!

They move on. Dragging feet, panting, thudding stick.

MR ROONEY. Now mind, here is the path ... Up! ... Well done! Now we are in safety and a straight run home.

MR ROONEY [*without halting, between gasps*] A straight ... run! ... She calls that ... a straight ... run! ...

MRS ROONEY. Hush! Do not speak as you go along, you know it is not good for your coronary. [*Dragging steps, etc*]. Just concentrate on putting one foot before the next or whatever the expression is. [*Dragging feet, etc*]. That is the way, now we are doing nicely. [*Dragging feet, etc. They suddenly halt, on Mrs Rooney's initiative*]. Heavens! I knew there was something! With all the excitement! I forgot!

MR ROONEY [*quietly*] Good God.

MRS ROONEY. But you must know, Dan, of course, you were on it. Whatever happened? Tell me!

MR ROONEY. I have never known anything to happen.

MRS ROONEY. But you must—

MR ROONEY [*violently*] All this stopping and starting again is devilish, devilish! I get a little way on me and begin to be carried along when suddenly you stop dead! Two hundred pounds of unhealthy fat! What possessed you to come out at all? Let go of me!

MRS ROONEY [*in great agitation*] No, I must know, we won't stir from here till you tell me. Fifteen minutes late! On a thirty minute run! It's unheard of!

MR ROONEY. I know nothing. Let go of me before I shake you off.

MRS ROONEY. But you must know! You were on it! Was it at the terminus? Did you leave on time? Or was it on the line? [*Pause*]. Did something happen on the line? [*Pause*]. Dan! [*Brokenly*]. Why won't you tell me!
Silence. They move off. Dragging feet, etc. They halt. Pause.

MR ROONEY. Poor Maddy! [*Pause. Children's cries*]. What was that?
Pause for Mrs Rooney to ascertain.

MRS ROONEY. The Lynch twins jeering us.
Cries.

MR ROONEY. Will they pelt us with mud today, do you suppose?
Cries.

MRS ROONEY. Let us turn and face them. [*Cries. They turn. Silence*]. Threaten them with your stick. [*Silence*]. They have run away.
Pause.

MR ROONEY. Did you ever wish to kill a child? [*Pause*]. Nip some young doom in the bud. [*Pause*]. Many a time at night, in winter, on the black road home, I nearly attacked the boy. [*Pause*]. Poor Jerry! [*Pause*]. What restrained me then? [*Pause*]. Not fear of man. [*Pause*]. Shall we go on backwards now a little?

MRS ROONEY. Backwards?

MR ROONEY. Yes. Or you forwards and I backwards. The perfect pair. Like Dante's damned, with their faces arsy-versy. Our tears will water our bottoms.

MRS ROONEY. What is the matter, Dan? Are you not well?

MR ROONEY. Well! Did you ever know me to be well? The day you met me I should have been in bed. The day you proposed to me the doctors gave me up. You knew that, did you not? The night you married me they came for me with an ambulance. You have not

forgotten that, I suppose? [*Pause*]. No, I cannot be said to be well. But I am no worse. Indeed I am better than I was. The loss of my sight was a great fillip. If I could go deaf and dumb I think I might pant on to be a hundred. Or have I done so? [*Pause*]. Was I a hundred today? [*Pause*]. Am I a hundred, Maddy?
Silence.

MRS ROONEY. All is still. No living soul in sight. There is no one to ask. The world is feeding. The wind – [*brief wind*] – scarcely stirs the leaves and the birds – [*brief chirp*] – are tired singing. The cows – [*brief moo*] – and sheep – [*brief baa*] – ruminate in silence. The dogs – [*brief bark*] – are hushed and the hens – [*brief cackle*] – sprawl torpid in the dust. We are alone. There is no one to ask.
Silence.

MR ROONEY [*clearing his throat, narrative tone*] We drew out on the tick of time, I can vouch for that. I was –

MRS ROONEY. How can you vouch for it?

MR ROONEY [*normal tone, angrily*]. I can vouch for it, I tell you! Do you want my relation or don't you? [*Pause. Narrative tone*]. On the tick of time. I had the compartment to myself, as usual. At least I hope so, for I made no attempt to restrain myself. My mind – [*Normal tone*]. But why do we not sit down somewhere? Are we afraid we should never rise again?

MRS ROONEY. Sit down on what?

MR ROONEY. On a bench, for example.

MRS ROONEY. There is no bench.

MR ROONEY. Then on a bank, let us sink down upon a bank.

MRS ROONEY. There is no bank.

MR ROONEY. Then we cannot. [*Pause*]. I dream of other roads, in other lands. Of another home, another – [*he hesitates*] – another home. [*Pause*]. What was I trying to say?

MRS ROONEY. Something about your mind.

MR ROONEY [*startled*] My mind? Are you sure. [*Pause. Incredulous*]. My mind? . . . [*Pause*]. Ah yes. [*Narrative tone*]. Alone in the compartment my mind began to work, as so often after office hours, on the way home, in the train, to the lilt of the bogeys. Your season-ticket, I said, costs you twelve pounds a year and you earn, on an average, seven and six a day, that is to say barely enough to keep you alive and twitching with the help of food, drink, tobacco and periodicals until you finally reach home and fall into bed. Add to this – or subtract from it – rent, stationery, various subscriptions, tramfares to and fro, light and heat, permits and licences, hairtrims and shaves, tips to escorts, upkeep of premises and appearances, and a thousand unspecifiable sundries, and it is clear that by lying at home in bed, day and night, winter and summer, with a change of pyjamas once a fortnight, you would add very considerably to your income. Business, I said – [*A cry. Pause. Again. Normal tone*]. Did I hear a cry?

MRS ROONEY. Mrs Tully I fancy. Her poor husband is in constant pain and beats her unmercifully.

Silence.

MR ROONEY. That was a short knock. [*Pause*]. What was I trying to get at?

MRS ROONEY. Business.

MR ROONEY. Ah yes, business. [*Narrative tone*]. Business, old man, I said, retire from business, it has retired from you. [*Normal tone*]. One has these moments of lucidity.

MRS ROONEY. I feel very cold and weak.

MR ROONEY [*narrative tone*]. On the other hand, I said, there are the horrors of home life, the dusting, sweeping, airing, scrubbing, waxing, waning, washing, mangling, drying, mowing, clipping, raking, rolling, scuffling, shovelling, grinding, tearing, pounding, banging and slamming. And the brats, the happy little healthy little howling neighbours' brats. Of all this and much more the week-end, the Saturday intermission and then the day of rest, have given you some idea. But what must it be like on a working-day? A Wednesday? A Friday! What must it be like on a Friday! And I fell to thinking of my silent, backstreet, basement office, with its obliterated plate, rest-couch and velvet hangings, and what it means to be buried there alive, if only from ten to five, with convenient to the one hand a bottle of light pale ale and to the other a long ice-cold fillet of hake. Nothing, I said, not even fully certified death, can ever take the place of that. It was then I noticed we were at a standstill. [*Pause. Normal tone, Irritably*]. Why are you hanging out of me like that? Have you swooned away?

MRS ROONEY. I feel very cold and faint. The wind – [*whistling wind*] – is whistling through my summer frock as if I had nothing on over my bloomers. I have had no solid food since my elevenses.

MR ROONEY. You have ceased to care. I speak – and you listen to the wind.

MRS ROONEY. No no, I am agog, tell me all, then we shall press on and never pause, never pause, till we come safe to haven.
Pause.

MR ROONEY. Never pause ... safe to haven ... Do you know, Maddy, sometimes one would think you were struggling with a dead language.

MRS ROONEY. Yes indeed, Dan, I know full well what you mean, I often have that feeling, it is unspeakably excruciating.

MR ROONEY. I confess I have it sometimes myself, when I happen to overhear what I am saying.

MRS ROONEY. Well, you know, it will be dead in time, just like our own poor dear Gaelic, there is that to be said.
Urgent baa.

MR ROONEY [*startled*] Good God!

MRS ROONEY. Oh the pretty little woolly lamb, crying to suck its mother! Theirs has not changed, since Arcady.
Pause.

MR ROONEY. Where was I in my composition?

MRS ROONEY. At a standstill.

MR ROONEY. Ah yes. [*Clears his throat. Narrative tone*]. I concluded naturally that we had entered a station and would soon be on our way again, and I sat on, without misgiving. Not a sound. Things are very dull today, I said, nobody getting down, nobody getting on. Then as time flew by and nothing happened I realized my error. We had not entered a station.

MRS ROONEY. Did you not spring up and poke your head out of the window?

MR ROONEY. What good would that have done me?

MRS ROONEY. Why to call out to be told what was amiss.

MR ROONEY. I did not care what was amiss. No, I just sat on, saying, If this train were never to move again I should not greatly mind. Then gradually a – how shall I say – a growing desire to – er – you know – welled up within me. Nervous probably. In fact now I am sure. You know, the feeling of being confined.

MRS ROONEY. Yes yes, I have been through that.

MR ROONEY. If we sit here much longer, I said, I really do not know what I shall do. I got up and paced to and fro between the seats, like a caged beast.

MRS ROONEY. That is a help sometimes.

MR ROONEY. After what seemed an eternity we simply moved off. And the next thing was Barrell bawling the abhorred name. I got down and Jerry led me to the men's, or Fir as they call it now, from Vir Viris I suppose, the V becoming F, in accordance with Grimm's Law. [*Pause*]. The rest you know. [*Pause*]. You say nothing? [*Pause*]. Say something. Maddy. Say you believe me.

MRS ROONEY. I remember once attending a lecture by one of these new mind doctors. I forget what you call them. He spoke—

MR ROONEY. A lunatic specialist?

MRS ROONEY. No no, just the troubled mind. I was hoping he might shed a little light on my lifelong preoccupation with horses' buttocks.

MR ROONEY. A neurologist.

MRS ROONEY. No no, just mental distress, the name will come back to me in the night. I remember his telling us the story of a little girl, very strange and unhappy in her ways, and how he treated her unsuccessfully over a period of years and was finally obliged to give up the case. He could find nothing wrong with her, he said. The only thing wrong with her as far as he could see was that she was dying. And she did in fact die, shortly after he washed his hands of her.

MR ROONEY. Well? What is there so wonderful about that?

MRS ROONEY. No, it was just something he said, and the way he said it, that have haunted me ever since.

MR ROONEY. You lie awake at night, tossing to and fro and brooding on it.

MRS ROONEY. On it and other . . . wretchedness. [*Pause*]. When he had done with the little girl he stood there motionless for some time, quite two minutes I should say, looking down at his table. Then he suddenly raised his head and exclaimed, as if he had had a revelation. The trouble with her was she had never been really born! [*Pause*]. He spoke throughout without notes. [*Pause*]. I left before the end.

MR ROONEY. Nothing about your buttocks? [*Mrs Rooney weeps. In affectionate remonstrance*]. Maddy!

MRS ROONEY. There is nothing to be done for those people!

MR ROONEY. For which is there? [*Pause*]. That does not sound right somehow. [*Pause*]. What way am I facing?

MRS ROONEY. What?

MR ROONEY. I have forgotten what way I am facing.

MRS ROONEY. You have turned aside and are bowed down over the ditch.

MR ROONEY. There is a dead dog down there.

MRS ROONEY. No no, just the rotting leaves.

MR ROONEY. In June? Rotting leaves in June?

MRS ROONEY Yes, dear, from last year, and from the year before last, and from the year before that again. [*Silence. Rainy wind. They move on. Dragging steps, etc.*] There is that lovely laburnam again. Poor thing, it is losing all its tassels. [*Dragging steps, etc.*] There are the first drops. [*Rain. Dragging feet, etc*]. Golden drizzle. [*Dragging steps, etc*]. Do not mind me, dear, I am just talking to myself. [*Rain heavier. Dragging steps, etc*]. Can hinnies procreate, I wonder?
They halt.

MR ROONEY. Say that again.

MRS ROONEY. Come on, dear, don't mind me, we are getting drenched.

MR ROONEY [*forcibly*]. Can what what?

MRS ROONEY. Hinnies procreate. [*Silence*]. You know, hinnies, or jinnies, aren't they barren, or sterile, or whatever it is? [*Pause*]. It wasn't as ass's colt at all, you know. I asked the Regius Professor.
Pause.

MR ROONEY. He should know.

MRS ROONEY. Yes, it was a hinny, he rode into Jerusalem or wherever it was on a hinny. [*Pause*]. That must mean something. [*Pause*]. It's like the sparrows, than many of which we are of more value, they weren't sparrows at all.

MR ROONEY. Than many of which! . . . You exaggerate, Maddy.

MRS ROONEY [*with emotion*] They weren't sparrows at all!

MR ROONEY. Does that put our price up?

Silence. They move on. Wind and rain. Dragging feet, etc. They halt.

MRS ROONEY. Do you want some dung? [*Silence. They move on. Wind and rain, etc. They halt*]. Why do you stop? Do you want to say something?

MR ROONEY. No.

MRS ROONEY. Then why do you stop?

MR ROONEY. It is easier.

MRS ROONEY. Are you very wet?

MR ROONEY. To the buff.

MRS ROONEY. The buff?

MR ROONEY. The buff. From buffalo.

MRS ROONEY. We shall hang up all our things in the hot-cupboard and get into our dressing-gowns. [*Pause*]. Put your arm round me. [*Pause*]. Be nice to me! [*Pause. Gratefully*]. Ah, Dan! [*They move on. Wind and rain. Dragging feet, etc. Faintly some music as before. They halt. Music clearer. Silence but for music playing. Music dies*]. All day the same old record. All alone in that great empty house. She must be a very old woman now.

MR ROONEY [*indistinctly*] Death and the Maiden.

Silence.

MRS ROONEY. You are crying. [*Pause*]. Are you crying?

MR ROONEY [*violently*] Yes! [*They move on. Wind and rain. Dragging feet, etc. They halt. They move on. Wind and rain. Dragging feet, etc. They halt*]. Who is the preacher tomorrow? The incumbent?

MRS ROONEY. No.

MR ROONEY. Thank God for that. Who?

MRS ROONEY. Hardy.

MR ROONEY. 'How to be Happy though Married'?

MRS ROONEY. No no, he died, you remember. No connexion.

MR ROONEY. Has he announced his text?

MRS ROONEY. 'The Lord upholdeth all that fall and raiseth up all those that be bowed down.' [*Silence. They join in wild laughter. They move on. Wind and rain. Dragging feet, etc*]. Hold me tighter, Dan! [*Pause*]. Oh yes!

They halt.

MR ROONEY. I hear something behind us.
Pause.
MRS ROONEY. It looks like Jerry. [*Pause*]. It is Jerry.
Sound of Jerry's running steps approaching. He halts beside them, panting.
JERRY [*panting*] You dropped—
MRS ROONEY. Take your time, my little man, you will burst a blood-
vessel.
JERRY [*panting*] You dropped something, sir. Mr Barrell told me to
run after you.
MRS ROONEY. Show. [*She takes the object*]. What is it? [*She examines
it*]. What is this thing, Dan?
MR ROONEY. Perhaps it is not mine at all.
JERRY. Mr Barrell said it was, sir.
MRS ROONEY. It looks like a kind of ball. And yet it is not a ball.
MR ROONEY. Give it to me.
MRS ROONEY [*giving it*] What *is* it, Dan?
MR ROONEY. It is a thing I carry about with me.
MRS ROONEY. Yes, but what –
MR ROONEY [*violently*] It is a thing I carry about with me!
Silence. Mrs Rooney looks for a penny.
MRS ROONEY. I have no small money. Have you?
MR ROONEY. I have none of any kind.
MRS ROONEY. We are out of change, Jerry. Remind Mr Rooney on
Monday and he will give you a penny for your pains.
JERRY. Yes, Ma'am.
MR ROONEY. If I am alive.
JERRY. Yessir.
Jerry starts running back towards the station.
MRS ROONEY. Jerry! [*Jerry halts*]. Did you hear what the hitch was?
[*Pause*]. Did you hear what kept the train so late?
MR ROONEY. How would he have heard? Come on.
MRS ROONEY. What was it, Jerry?
JERRY. It was a –
MR ROONEY. Leave the boy alone, he knows nothing! Come on!
MRS ROONEY. What was it Jerry?
JERRY. It was a little child, Ma'am.
Mr Rooney groans.

MRS ROONEY. What do you mean, it was a little child?

JERRY. It was a little child fell out of the carriage, Ma'am. [*Pause*]. On to the line, Ma'am. [*Pause*]. Under the wheels, Ma'am.

Silence, Jerry runs off. His steps die away. Tempest of wind and rain. It abates. They move on. Dragging steps, etc. They halt. Tempest of wind and rain.

BRENDAN BEHAN

The Quare Fellow

Brendan Behan (1923–1964)

Brendan Behan was born in Dublin in 1923, while his father, a housepainter and republican activist, was in jail. Behan left school at fourteen but spent two years in Borstal and a further four (1942–46) in prison for political activities. Out of these experiences came his autobiography, *Borstal Boy* (1958), and his first stage play, *The Quare Fellow* (1954). His first radio plays were broadcast in Ireland in 1952 and he was writing a column for the Irish Press in 1954; but it was with the enormous success of Joan Littlewood's London productions of *The Quare Fellow* (in 1956) and *The Hostage* (in 1958), combined with Behan's much publicised drinking bouts, that he achieved international fame. A third play, *Richard's Cork Leg*, was left almost complete at his death in 1964 and was edited and directed by Alan Simpson for the 1972 Dublin Theatre Festival.

The Quare Fellow

The Quare Fellow was premièred at the Pike Theatre Club, Dublin, on 19 November 1954 with the following cast (listed in order of appearance):

WARDER DONELLY	Denis Hickie
PRISONER A.	Austin Byrne
PRISONER B.	Pat Nolan
DUNLAVIN	John McDarby
SCHOLARA } *Juvenile Prisoners* {	Art O'Phelan
SHAYBO	Patrick Duggan
THE LIFER, *a reprieved murderer*	Herbert Thomas
THE OTHER FELLOW	Patrick Clarke
NEIGHBOUR	Dermot Kelly
A MEDICAL ORDERLY	Gilbert McIntyre
MR HELY, *an Official of the Department*	David Kelly
WARDER REGAN	Gearoid O'Lochlainn
THE CHAPLAIN	Alan Barry
PRISONER C., *a young Kerry Boy*	Derry Power
MICKSER	David Kelly
THE VOICE OF AN ENGLISHMAN ON REMAND	Art O'Phelan
A COOK FROM THE HOSPITAL	Gilbert McIntyre
THE CHIEF WARDER	Bob Lepler
A PRINCIPAL WARDER	Liam Shanahan
THE SPEAKING VOICE OF A PRISONER IN THE PUNISHMENT CELLS	Derry Power
PRISONER D., *a middle-aged bourgeois*	Geoffrey Mackay
WARDER CRINNIN	Alan Barry
A HANGMAN	James Tinkler
FIRST WARDER	Tom Nolan
SECOND WARDER	Patrick Duggan
THE GOVERNOR	Tom Willoughby
ASSISTANT HANGMAN, ENOCH JENKINSON	Patrick Clarke

ASSISTANT HANGMAN,
CHRISTMAS HALLIWELL   Gilbert McIntyre
The Recorded Singing Voice of the Prisoner in the Punishment Cells by
Brendan Behan

Production and lighting directed by Alan Simpson
Settings designed by Alan Simpson and constructed by John O'Shea
Assistant producer: Carolyn Swift

This version of *The Quare Fellow* was first presented by Theatre
Workshop at the Theatre Royal, Stratford, London, E.15, on 24 May
1956, with the following cast:

PRISONERS

DUNLAVIN	Maxwell Shaw
NEIGHBOUR	Gerard Dynevor
PRISONER A. (*Hard Case*)	Glynn Edwards
PRISONER B. (*The Man of Thirty*)	Brian Murphy
LIFER	Bill Grover
THE OTHER FELLOW	Ron Brooker
MICKSER	Eric Ogle
ENGLISH VOICE	John Rutley
SCHOLARA } *Juvenile Prisoners* {	Timothy Harley
SHAYBO } {	George Eugeniou
PRISONER C. (*The Boy from the Island*)	Henry Livings
PRISONER D. (*The Embezzler*)	Barry Clayton
PRISONER E. (*The Bookie*)	Brian Murphy

WARDERS

CHIEF WARDER	Maxwell Shaw
REGAN	Dudley Foster
CRIMMIN	Brian Nunn
DONELLY (*Warder 1*)	Clive Goodwin
THE NEW ONE (*Warder 2*)	Fred Cooper

THE PRISON GOVERNOR	Robert Henderson
HOLY HEALEY	Barry Clayton

THE HANGMAN   Gerry Raffles
JENKINSON   Brian Murphy

The play directed by Joan Littlewood

The London production was extremely well received:

In Brendan Behan's tremendous new play language is out on a
spree, ribald, dauntless and spoiling for a fight ... with superb
dramatic tact, the tragedy is concealed beneath layer after layer of
rough comedy.

Kenneth Tynan in the *Observer*.

Brendan Behan is the most exciting new talent to enrich our theatre
since the war, and his play is a marvellous combination of passion
and humour which dwarfs anything else to be seen at present in
London, West or East. It is not in mortals to command sucess.
Brendan Behan has done more, at one bound, he has achieved
immortality.

Bernard Levin in *The Times*

In *The Theatre Workshop Story*, Howard Goorney, a member of the
Company for over 30 years, gives an account of the production:

I recall Joan's enthusiasm for a script she had received from a
Dublin playwright called Brendan Bchan, and which had been
rejected by the Abbey Theatre. Set in a prison, it was a rambling
story of the last twenty-four hours in a condemned man's life, seen
through the eyes of the wardens and his fellow prisoners. It would
need cutting and shaping, but was full of wonderful characters and
humour. I knew a lot of hard work was involved and I was tired and
couldn't face it. So I opted out for a few weeks and, feeling rather
pleased with myself, went to do a special week at St Helens Rep. in
a well-tried Lancashire comedy. All I had to do was more or less
learn the lines. Then on to a broadcast in Manchester where I
didn't need to learn them at all. However, it was clear from the
reviews on the Sunday after *The Quare Fellow* opened that Joan's
enthusiasm had been well founded, and I felt less pleased with

myself. The critics were unanimous and fulsome in their praise. During the run of *The Quare Fellow* the Company received £10 a week – the first time wages at Stratford reached double figures.

The achievement was the result of a great deal of hard work, even more than I had imagined. Rehearsals were well under way before the cast were given scripts or told what parts they were playing. They had just to set about creating the atmosphere of prison life, marching round and round the flat roof of the Theatre Royal as prisoners on exercise. The day to day routines were improvised, cleaning out cells, the quick smoke, the furtive conversation, trading tobacco and the boredom and meanness of prison life were explored. The improvisations had, of course, been selected by Joan with the script in mind, and when it was finally introduced, the situation and the relationships had been well explored. The bulk of the work had been done and the groundwork laid for any cutting and shaping that was necessary. Brendan welcomed this way of working and commented on the finished play – 'Christ, I'm a bloody genius' and in his curtain speech on the first night – 'Miss Littlewood's company has performed a better play than I wrote.'

Brendan was well supported by his fellow countrymen on the first night at Stratford. In the audience were three IRA men who had been barred from the country, more than fifteen recognised leaders of the Republican Movement, men whose prison sentences totalled three hundred years, and two Special Branch detectives. When the Irish National Anthem was played in the course of the action, half the audience stood to attention. This, of course, was in 1956, long before the terrorist campaign of the IRA had begun. Brendan became overnight the darling of the media, and his fondness for drink, which was to eventually kill him, made good copy for the popular press. One unfortunate result, amongst several, was a completely incoherent interview on television with Malcolm Muggeridge, which led to scores of outraged viewers ringing in to protest at the spectacle and the language.

Brendan was not spurred on by the success of *The Quare Fellow*. On the contrary, it rather overwhelmed him, and getting a second play, *The Hostage*, out of him was to prove a long and painful process.

Selected Bibliography

The Complete Plays (Introduction by Alan Simpson), London, Eyre Methuen, 1978. Contains *The Quare Fellow, The Hostage, Richard's Cork Leg,* and three radio plays, *Moving Out, The Garden Party, The Big House.* Special reference: Plays. *The Quare Fellow,* London, Methuen, 1956. *The Hostage,* London, Methuen, 1958. Other work: *Borstal Boy,* London, Hutchinson, 1958.

The Quare Fellow

A Comedy-Drama

All enquiries concerning performing rights, professional or amateur, should be directed to Tessa Sayle Literary and Dramatic Agency, 11 Jubilee Place, London SW3 3TE.

Persons in the Play

Prisoners

DUNLAVIN
NEIGHBOUR
PRISONER A. (*Hard Case*)
PRISONER B. (*The Man of Thirty*)
LIFER
THE OTHER FELLOW
MICKSER
ENGLISH VOICE
SCHOLARA ⎱
SHAYBO ⎰ (*Young Prisoners*)
PRISONER C. (*The Boy from the Island*)
PRISONER D. (*The Embezzler*)
PRISONER E. (*The Bookie*)

Warders

CHIEF WARDER
REGAN
CRIMMIN
DONELLY (*Warder 1*)
THE NEW ONE (*Warder 2*)

THE PRISON GOVERNOR
HOLY HEALEY
THE HANGMAN
JENKINSON

ACT I

A prisoner sings: he is in one of the punishment cells.
>A hungry feeling came o'er me stealing
>And the mice were squealing in my prison cell,
>And that old triangle
>Went jingle jangle.
>Along the banks of the Royal Canal.
>>*The curtain rises.*

The scene is the bottom floor or landing of a wing in a city prison, 'B.1'. The cell doors are of metal with a card giving the name, age and religion of the occupant. Two of the cells have no cards. The left of the stage leads to the circle, the administrative heart of the prison, and on the right, in the wall and at right angles to the audience, is a window, from which a view may be had of the laundry yard of the women's prison. On the wall and facing the audience is printed in large block shaded Victorian lettering the word 'SILENCE'.

PRISONER.

>To begin the morning
>The warder bawling
>Get out of bed and clean up your cell;
>And that old triangle
>Went jingle jangle,
>Along the banks of the Royal Canal.

A triangle is beaten, loudly and raucously. A warder comes briskly and, swinging a bunch of keys, goes to the vacant cells, looks in the spyholes, takes two white cards from his pocket, and puts one on each door. Then he goes to the other doors, looks in the spyholes and unlocks them.

Meanwhile the singer in the base punishment cells is on his third verse:

>The screw was peeping
>And the lag was weeping . . .

But this only gets as far as the second line, for the warder leans over the stairs and shouts down . . .

WARDER. The screw is listening as well as peeping, and you'll be bloody well weeping if you don't give over your moaning. We might go down there and give you something to moan about. [*The singing stops and he turns and shouts up and down the landing*]. B. Wings: two, three and one. Stand to your doors. Come on, clean up your cells there. [*He goes off R.*]

Prisoners a. and b. come out of their cells, collect buckets and brushes, and start the morning's chores. a. is a man of 40, he has done two 'laggings', a sentence of five years or more, and some preventive detention. b. is a gentle-looking man and easy-going.

PRISONER A. Nice day for the races.

PRISONER B. Don't think I can make it today. Too much to do in the office. Did you hear the commotion last night round in D. Wing? A reprieve must have come through.

PRISONER A. Aye, but there's two for a haircut and shave, I wonder which one's been chucked?

PRISONER B. Dunlavin might know; give him a call there.

PRISONER A. Dunlavin!

VOICE [*from cell*]

> There are hands that will welcome you in
> There are lips that I am burning to kiss
> There are two eyes that shine . . .

PRISONER A. Hey, Dunlavin, are you going to scrub that place of yours away?

VOICE.

> Far away where the blue shadows fall
> I will come to contentment and rest,
> And the toils of the day
> Will be all charmed away . . .

PRISONER A. Hey, Dunlavin.

Dunlavin appears in the door of the cell polishing a large enamel chamber pot with a cloth. An old man, he has spent most of his life in jail. Unlike most old lags he has not become absolutely dulled from imprisonment.

DUNLAVIN. . . . . In my little grey home in the West.

PRISONER A. What do you think that is you're polishing – the Railway Cup?

DUNLAVIN. I'm shining this up for a special visitor. Healey of the Department of Justice is coming up today to inspect the cells.

PRISONER A. Will he be round again so soon?

DUNLAVIN. He's always round the day before an execution. I think he must be in the hanging and flogging section.

PRISONER B. Dunlavin, there you are, at the corner of the wing, with the joints in the hot-water pipes bringing you news from every art and part, any time you put your ear to it.

DUNLAVIN. Well? Well?

PRISONER B. Well, what was the commotion last night round in D. Wing? Did the quare fellow get a reprieve?

DUNLAVIN. Just a minute till I put back me little bit of china, and I'll return and tell all. Now which quare fellow do you mean? The fellow beat his wife to death with the silver-topped cane, that was a presentation to him from the Combined Staffs, Excess and Refunds branch of the late Great Southern Railways, was reprieved, though why him any more than the other fellow is more nor I can tell.

PRISONER A. Well, I suppose they looked at it, he only killed her and left it at that. He didn't cut the corpse up afterwards with a butcher's knife.

DUNLAVIN. Yes, and then of course the other fellow used a meat-chopper. Real bog-man act. Nearly as bad as a shotgun, or getting the weed-killer mixed up in the stirabout. But a man with a silver-topped cane, that's a man that's a cut above meat-choppers whichever way you look at it.

PRISONER A. Well, I suppose we can expect Silver-top round soon to start his life.

PRISONER B. Aye, we've a couple of vacancies.

PRISONER A. There's a new card up here already.

DUNLAVIN. I declare to God you're right. [*Goes to read one of the cards*]. It's not him at all, it's another fellow, doing two years, for . . . oh, the dirty beast, look what the dirty man-beast is in for. 'Clare to God, putting the likes of that beside me. They must think this is the bloody sloblands.

PRISONER B. There's another fellow here.

DUNLAVIN. I hope it's not another of that persuasion. [*Reads the card*]. Ah, no, it's only the murderer, thanks be to God.

The others have a read of the card and skip back to their own cells.

DUNLAVIN. You wouldn't mind old Silver-top. Killing your wife is a natural class of a thing could happen to the best of us. But this other dirty animal on me left . . .

PRISONER B. Ah well, now he's here he'll just have to do his birdlime like anyone else.

DUNLAVIN. That doesn't say that he should do it in the next flowery dell to me. Robbers, thieves and muderers I can abide, but when it comes to that class of carry-on – Good night, Joe Doyle.

PRISONER A. [*indicates 22*] This fellow was dead lucky.

PRISONER B. Live lucky.

PRISONER A. Two fellows waiting to be topped and he's the one that gets away. As a general rule they don't like reprieving one and topping the other.

DUNLAVIN. So as to be on the safe side, and not to be making fish of one and flesh of the other, they usually top both. Then, of course, the Minister might have said, enough is as good as a feast.

They rest on their brooms.

PRISONER B. It must be a great thing to be told at the last minute that you're not going to be topped after all. To be lying there sweating and watching. The two screws for the death watch coming on at twelve o'clock and the two going off shaking hands with you, and you go to bed, and stare up at the ceiling.

DUNLAVIN. And the two screws nod to each other across the fire to make a sup of tea, but to do it easy in case they wake you, and you turn round in the bed towards the fire and you say 'I'll take a sup as you're at it' and one of the screws says 'Ah, so you're awake, Mick. We were just wetting it; isn't it a good job you spoke up in time.'

PRISONER A. And after that, the tea is drunk and they offer you cigarettes, though the mouth is burned off you from smoking and anyway you've more than they have, you've got that many you'll be leaving them after you, and you lie down and get up, and get up and lie down, and the two screws not letting on to be minding you and not taking their eyes off you for one half-minute, and you walk up and down a little bit more . . .

PRISONER B. And they ask you would you like another game of draughts or would you sooner write a letter, and getting on to morning you hear a bell out in the city, and you ask them the time, but they won't tell you.

DUNLAVIN. But they put a good face on it, and one says 'There's that old watch stopped again' and he says to the other screw 'Have you your watch, Jack?' and the other fellow makes a great joke of it, 'I'll have to take a run up as far as the North City Pawn shop and ask them to let me have a look at it.' And then the door is unlocked and everyone sweats blood, and they come in and ask your man to stand up a minute, that's if he's able, while they read him something: 'I am instructed to inform you that the Minister has, he hasn't, he has, he hasn't recommended to the President, that . . .'

PRISONER A. And the quare fellow says 'Did you say "has recommended or has not recommended . . .?" I didn't quite catch that.'

DUNLAVIN. My bloody oath but he catches it. Although I remember once in a case like now when there were two fellows to be topped over two different jobs, didn't the bloody fellow from the Prison Board, as it was then, in old Max Greeb's time, didn't he tell the wrong man he was reprieved? Your man was delighted for a few hours and then they had to go back and tell him 'Sorry, my mistake, but you're to be topped after all'?

PRISONER B. And the fellow that was reprieved, I bet he was glad.

DUNLAVIN. Of course he was glad, anyone that says that a condemned man would be better off hung than doing life, let them leave it to his own discretion. Do you know who feels it worse going out to be topped?

PRISONER A. Corkmen and Northerners . . . they've such bloody hard necks.

DUNLAVIN. I have to do me funny half-hour for Holy Healey. I'm talking serious now.

PRISONER A. All right, come on, let's have it –

DUNLAVIN. The man that feels it worst, going into that little house with the red door and the silver painted gates at the bottom of D. Wing, is a man that has been in the nick before, when some other merchant was topped; or he's heard screws or old lags in the bag shop or at exercise talking about it. A new chap that's never done anything but murder, and that only once, is usually a respectable man, such as this Silver-top here. He knows nothing about it, except the few lines that he'd see in the papers. 'Condemned man entered the hang-house at seven fifty-nine. At eight three the doctor pronounced life extinct.'

PRISONER B. That's a lot of mullarkey. In the first place the doctor has his back turned after the trap goes down, and doesn't turn to face it until a screw has caught the rope and stopped it wriggling. Then they go out and lock up the shop and have their breakfast and don't come back for an hour. Then they cut your man down and the doctor slits the back of his neck to see if the bones are broken. Who's to know what happens in the hour your man is swinging there, maybe wriggling to himself in the pit.

PRISONER A. You're right there. When I was in the nick in England, there was a screw doing time, he'd been smuggling out medical reports on hangings and selling them to the Sunday papers, and he told me that one bloke had lived seventeen minutes at the end of a rope.

DUNLAVIN. I don't believe that! Seventeen minutes is a bloody long time to be hanging at the end of a rope.

PRISONER A. It was their own medical report.

PRISONER B. I'll lay odds to a make that Silver-top isn't half charmed with himself if he's not going with the meat-chopper in the morning.

DUNLAVIN. You could sing that if you had an air to it.

PRISONER A. They'll have him down to reception, changed into Fry's and over here any time now.

DUNLAVIN. Him and this other jewel here. Bad an' all as Silver-top was to beat his wife's brains out, I'd as lief have him near to me as this article. Dirty beast! I won't have an hour's luck for the rest of me six months, and me hoping to touch Uncle Healey today for a letter to the Room-Keepers for when I'd go out.

PRISONER B. Eh, Dunlavin, is the Department trying to reform, reconstruct and rehabilitate you in your old age?

DUNLAVIN. Ah no, it's nothing to do with the Department. Outside his job in the Department, Uncle Healey's in some holy crowd, that does good be stealth. They never let the right hand know what the left hand doeth, as the man said. Of course they never put either hand in their pocket, so you'd never get money off them, but they can give letters to the Prisoners' Aid and the Room-Keepers. Mind you. Healey's not here today as a holy man. He'll just be fixing up the man that's getting hung in the morning, but if I can get on the right side of him, he might mix business with pleasure and give me a letter for when I get out.

PRISONER B. Now we know the cause of all the spring-cleaning.

DUNLAVIN. And a fellow in the kitchen told us they're doing a special dinner for us on account of Uncle Healey's visit.

PRISONER A. Do you mean we're getting food with our meals today?

DUNLAVIN. That's right, and I can't be standing yapping to youse. I've to hang up my holy pictures and think up a few funny remarks for him. God, what Jimmie O'Dea is getting thousands for I've to do for a pair of old socks and a ticket for the Prisoners' Aid.

Dunlavin goes into his cell. Two young prisoners aged about seventeen go past with sweeping brushes in front of them, singing softly in unison.

YOUNG PRISONERS.

Only one more cell inspection
We go out next Saturday,
Only one more cell inspection
And we go far, far away.

PRISONER A. What brings you fellows round here this morning?

YOUNG PRISONER 1. Our screw told us to sweep all round the Juvenile Wing and then come round here and give it a bit of a going over.

PRISONER B. And have you your own wing done?

YOUNG PRISONER 2. No, but if we did our wing first, we'd miss the mots hanging out the laundry. You can't see them from our wing.

PRISONER A. Just as well, maybe; you're bad enough as it is.

YOUNG PRISONER 1. But I tell you what you will see from our wing this morning. It's the carpenter bringing up the coffin for the quare fellow and leaving it over in the mortuary to have it handy for the morning. There's two orderlies besides us over in Juveniles, and we were going to toss up who'd come over here, but they're country fellows and they'd said they'd sooner see the coffin. I'd sooner pike at a good-looking mot than the best coffin in Ireland, wouldn't you, Shaybo?

YOUNG PRISONER 2. Certainly I would, and outside that, when you're over here, there's always a chance of getting a bit of education about screwing jobs, and suchlike, from experienced men. Do you think Triplex or celluloid is the best for Yale locks, sir?

YOUNG PRISONER 1. Do you carry the stick all the time, sir?

PRISONER A. If I had a stick I'd know where to put it, across your bloody . . .

YOUNG PRISONER 2. Scholara, get sweeping, here's the screw.

They drift off sweeping and singing softly.

PRISONER B. He's bringing one of 'em. Is it Silver-top or the other fellow?

PRISONER A. Silver-top. I remember him being half carried into the circle the night he was sentenced to death.

PRISONER B. He has a right spring in his step this morning then.

PRISONER A. He's not looking all that happy. Still, I suppose he hasn't got over the shock yet.

Warder and a prisoner come on l. The prisoner is in early middle age; when he speaks he has a 'good accent'. He is carrying a pillow slip which contains his sheets and other kit. The warder halts him.

WARDER REGAN. Stand by the door with your name on it. Later on when you've seen the doctor these fellows will show you how to lay your kit. [*He goes. There is a pause, while the prisoners survey the newcomer*].

PRISONER B. He'll bloody well cheer the place up, won't he?

LIFER. Have any of you got a cigarette?

PRISONER A. That's a good one. You're not in the condemned cell now, you know. No snout allowed here.

PRISONER B. Unless you manage to scrounge a dog-end off the remands.

PRISONER A. Or pick one up in the exercise yard after a man the like of yourself that's allowed them as a special concession. Not, by God, that we picked up much after you. What did you do with your dog ends? .

LIFER. Threw them in the fire.

PRISONER B. You what!

PRISONER A. How was it the other poor bastard, that's got no reprieve and is to be topped in the morning – how was it he was always able to leave a trail of butts behind him when he went off exercise?

LIFER. I've never been in prison before; how was I to know?

PRISONER A. You're a curse of God liar, my friend, you did know; for it was whispered to him by the fellows from the hospital bringing over the grub to the condemened cell. He never gave them as much as a match! And he couldn't even bring his dog-ends to the exercise yard and drop them behind for us to pick up when we came out later.

PRISONER B. I bet you're charmed with yourself that you're not going through the iron door tomorrow morning.

The lifer doesn't speak, but looks down at his suit.

PRISONER A. Aye, you're better off in that old suit, bad as it is, than the wooden overcoat the quare fellow is going to get tomorrow morning.

PRISONER B. The longest you could do would be twenty years. More than likely you'll get out in half of that. Last man to finish up in the Bog, he done eleven.

LIFER. Eleven. How do you live through it?

PRISONER A. A minute at a time.

PRISONER B. You haven't got a bit of snout for him, have you? [PRISONER A. *shakes his head*]. Maybe Dunlavin has. Hey, Dunlavin, have you e'er a smoke you'd give this chap? Hey, Dunlavin.

DUNLAVIN [*coming from his cell*] Yes, what is it? Anyone there the name of headache?

PRISONER B. Could you manage to give this chap something to smoke? E'er a bit of snout at all.

DUNLAVIN. There's only one brand of tobacco allowed here – 'Three Nuns'. None today, none tomorrow, and none the day after.

He goes back into his cell.

PRISONER B. Eh, Dunlavin, come back to hell out of that.

DUNLAVIN. Well, what?

PRISONER B. This poor chap after being smoking about sixty a day . . .

DUNLAVIN. Where?

PRISONER B. In the condemned cell – where else?

DUNLAVIN. Now I have you. Sure I thought you were the other fellow, and you're not, you're only the murderer. God comfort you. [*Shakes hands*]. Certainly so. [*Takes off his jacket, looks up and down the wing, undoes his trousers and from the depths of his combinations he produces cigarette end, and a match, and presents them to the lifer*].

Reprieved in the small hours of this morning. Certainly so. The dead arose and appeared to many, as the man said, but you'll be getting yourself a bad name standing near that other fellow's door. This is your flowery dell, see? It has your name there on that little card. And all your particulars. Age forty-three. Religion RC.

LIFER [*reads*] Life.

DUNLAVIN. And a bloody sight better than death any day of the week.

PRISONER B. It always says that. The Governor will explain it all to you later this morning.

DUNLAVIN. Or maybe they'll get holy Uncle Healey to do it.

PRISONER B. Go into your cell and have a smoke for yourself. Bring in your kit bag. [*Passes in kit to lifer*]. Have a quiet burn there before the screw comes round; we'll keep nick. [*Lifer closes the door of his cell*].

DUNLAVIN. God knows I got the pick of good neighbours. Lovely people. Give me a decent murderer though, rather then the likes of this other fellow. Well, I'll go into me little place and get on with me bit of dobying so as to have it all nice for Healey when he comes round [He *goes back to his cell*].

PRISONER B. [*to lifer*] Don't light up yet! Here's the screw coming.

PRISONER A. With the other fellow.

Warder Regan and another prisoner, 'the other fellow', an anxious-faced man, wearing prison clothes and carrying a kit bag, come on l.

WARDER REGAN. Yes, this is your flowery dell. Leave in your kitbag and stand at your door and wait for the doctor. These other fellows will show you where to go when he comes.

OTHER FELLOW. Right, sir. Very good, sir.

Warder Regan goes, the other fellow has a look round.

PRISONER B. There's a bloke in the end cell getting himself a quiet burn. Why don't you join him before the screws get back?

The other fellow notices the card on lifer's cell.

OTHER FELLOW. My God! Is this what I've come to, mixing with murderers! I'd rather not, thank you, though I could do with a smoke. I'll have to spend long months here, even if I get my remission, with murderers and thieves and God knows what! You're not all murderers are you? You haven't killed anyone, have you?

PRISONER B. Not for a while, I haven't.

OTHER FELLOW. I cannot imagine any worse crime than taking a life, can you?

PRISONER B. It'd depend whose life.

OTHER FELLOW. Of course. I mean, a murderer would be justified in taking his own life, wouldn't he? 'We send him forth' says Carlisle – you've heard of Carlisle haven't you? – 'We send him forth, back to the void, back to the darkness far out beyond the stars. Let him go from us.'

DUNLAVIN [*head out of the door of cell*] Oh. [*Looks at other fellow*]. I thought it was Healey from the Department or someone giving it out of them.

PRISONER A. Looks like this man is a bit of an intellectual.

DUNLAVIN. Is that what they call it now?

LIFER. Thanks for the smoke, Mr Dunlavin.

DUNLAVIN. Not at all, sure, you're welcome, call again when you're passing. But remember the next wife you kill and you getting forty fags a day in the condemned cell, think of them as is not so fortunate as yourself and leave a few dog-ends around the exercise yard after you. Here's these noisy little gets again.

The two young prisoners come round from the left, their sweeping brushes in front of them and singing their song. The other fellow stands quite still at his door.

YOUNG PRISONERS.

Only one more cell inspection
We go out next Saturday
Only one more cell inspection
Then we go far far away.
[*They are sweeping near the lifer.*]
Only one more cell inspection
We go out next Saturday
Only one more cell . . .

LIFER. For God's sake shut up that squeaking . . .

YOUNG PRISONER 1. We've as much right to open our mouth as what you have, and you only a wet day in the place.

PRISONER B. Leave the kids alone. You don't own the place, you know. They're doing no harm [*To the young prisoners*]. You want to sweep this bit of floor away?

DUNLAVIN. What brings you round here so often? If you went over to the remand wings you might pick up a bit of snout or a look at the paper.

YOUNG PRISONER 1. We get a smoke and the *Mail* every day off a limey on our road that's on remand. He's in over the car smuggling. But round here this morning you can see the mots from the laundry over on the female side hanging out the washing in the exercise yard. Do youse look at them? I suppose when you get old, though, you don't much bother about women.

PRISONER B. I'm thirty-six, mac.

YOUNG PRISONER 1. Ah, I thought that. Don't suppose you care if you never see a mot. There's Shaybo there and he never thinks of anything else. Do you think of anything else but women, Shaybo?

YOUNG PRISONER 2. Yes. Robbing and stealing, Scholara. You go to the window and keep an eye out for them and I'll sweep round here till you give us a call.

YOUNG PRISONER 1. Right, Shaybo, they should be nearly out now. [*Goes up and stands by window*].

PRISONER B. I forgot about the women.

DUNLAVIN. I didn't. It's a great bit of a treat today – that and having me leg rubbed. Neighbour and I wait in for it.

YOUNG PRISONER 1 [*from the window, in a coarse whisper*]. Shaybo, you can see them now.

YOUNG PRISONER 2. The blondy one from North Crumlin?

YOUNG PRISONER 1. Yes, and there's another one with her. I don't know her.

YOUNG PRISONER 2. Must be a country mot. Scholara doesn't know her. Women.

DUNLAVIN. Women.

PRISONER A. I see the blondy one waving.

YOUNG PRISONER 1. If it's all one to you, I'd like you to know that's my mot and it's me she's waving at.

PRISONER A. I'll wave you a thick ear.

DUNLAVIN. Hey, Neighbour! Where the hell is he this morning? Neighbour!

AN OLD MAN'S CREAKING VOICE. Here I am, Neighbour, here I am.

Neighbour, a bent old man, comes from l., hobbling as quickly as he can on a stick.

DUNLAVIN. Ah, you lost mass.

NEIGHBOUR. What are they gone in already?

DUNLAVIN. No, but they're finished hanging up the top row of clothes. There'll be no stretching or reaching off chairs.

NEIGHBOUR. Still, thanks be to God for small mercies. They'll be out again this day week.

PRISONER A. If you lives to see it.

NEIGHBOUR. Why wouldn't I live to see it as well as what you would? This is not the nearest I was to fine women, nor are they the first good-looking ones I saw.

PRISONER A. With that old cough of yours they could easy be the last.

NEIGHBOUR. God, you're a desperate old gas bag. We remember better-looking women than ever they were, don't we, Dunlavin? Meena La Bloom, do you remember her?

DUNLAVIN. Indeed and I do; many's the seaman myself and Meena gave the hey and a do, and Mickey Finn to.

NEIGHBOUR. And poor May Oblong.

DUNLAVIN. Ah, where do you leave poor May? The Lord have mercy on her, wasn't I with her one night in the digs, and there was a Member of Parliament there, and May after locking him in the back room and taking away his trousers, with him going over the north wall that morning to vote for Home Rule. 'For the love of your country and mine,' he shouts under the door to May, 'give me back me trousers.' 'So I will,' says May, 'if you shove a fiver out under the door.'

NEIGHBOUR. He had the wad hid? Dirty suspicious old beast.

DUNLAVIN. That's right. He was cute enough to hide his wad somewhere, drunk and all as he was the previous night. All we got in his trousers was a locket of hair of the patriotic plumber of Dolphin's barn that swore to let his hair grow till Ireland was free.

NEIGHBOUR. Ah, poor May, God help her, she was the heart of the roll.

DUNLAVIN. And when she was arrested for carrying on after the curfew, the time of the trouble, she was fined for having concealed about her person two Thompson sub-machine guns. 1921 pattern, three Mills bombs, and a stick of dynamite.

NEIGHBOUR. And will you ever forget poor Lottie L'Estrange, that got had up for pushing the soldier into Spencer Dock?

DUNLAVIN. Ah, God be with the youth of us.

NEIGHBOUR. And Cork Annie, and Lady Limerick.

DUNLAVIN. And Julia Rice and the Goofy One.

NEIGHBOUR [*turns towards window*] Hey, you, move out of the way there and give us a look. Dunlavin, come up here before they go, and have a look at the blondy one.

YOUNG PRISONER 1. Go 'long, you dirty old dog. That's my mot you're speaking about. [*Shoves neighbour*]. You old heap of dirt, to wave at a decent girl.

PRISONER A. Hey, snots, d'you think you own the bloody place?

YOUNG PRISONER 1. Would you like it, to have that dirty old eyebox looking at your mot?

PRISONER B. He's not going to eat her.

DUNLAVIN [*from behind*]. No, but he'd like to.

YOUNG PRISONER 2. That's right, and Scholara is nearly married to her. At least she had a squealer for him and he has to pay her money every week. Any week he's outside like, to give it, or her to get it.

YOUNG PRISONER 1 [*blows a kiss*] That's right, and I have him putting his rotten old eye on her.

OTHER FELLOW [*at his doorway*] God preserve us.

PRISONER A. Well, you don't own the bloody window. [*Shoves young prisoner 1 out of the way and brings over neighbour*]. Come on, you, if you want to see the May procession.

NEIGHBOUR. Ah, thanks, butty, your blood's worth bottling.

PRISONER A. I didn't do it on account of you, but if you let them young pups get away with too much they'd be running the place.

YOUNG PRISONER 2. Come on, Scholara, we'll mosey back. The screw will think we're lost.

They go back down the stairs, pick up their brushes, and start sweeping again and singing . . .

YOUNG PRISONER 1.

> Only one more cell inspection
> We go out next Saturday

YOUNG PRISONER 2. Only one more cell inspection . . .

LIFER. Shut your bloody row, can't you?

DUNLAVIN. Shut up yourself; you're making more noise than any of them.

YOUNG PRISONER I. Don't tell us to shut up, you bastard.

PRISONER B. Ah leave him alone; he started life this morning.

YOUNG PRISONER I. Ah, we're sorry, mister, ain't we, Shaybo?

YOUNG PRISONER 2. God, we are. Go over and take a pike at the female yard. They hang up the clothes now and Scholara's mot is over there. You can have a look at her. Scholara won't mind, will you, Schol?

YOUNG PRISONER I. Certainly and I won't. Not with you going to the Bog to start life in a couple of days, where you won't see a woman.

YOUNG PRISONER 2. A child.

YOUNG PRISONER I. A dog.

YOUNG PRISONER 2. A fire.

PRISONER A. Get to hell out of that round to your own wing. Wouldn't you think a man would know all that forbye you telling it to him?

YOUNG PRISONER 2. We were going anyway. We've seen all we wanted to see. It wasn't to look at a lot of old men we came here, but to see mots hanging out the washing.

YOUNG PRISONER I. And eitherways, we'll be a lot nearer the women than you'll be next Saturday night. Think of us when you're sitting locked up in the old flowery, studying the Bible, Chapter I, verse 2, and we trucking round in chase of charver.

They samba out with their brushes for partners, humming the Wedding Samba.

PRISONER A. Them young gets have too much old gab out of them altogether. I was a YP in Walton before the war and I can tell you they'd be quiet boys if they got the larrying we used to get.

OTHER FELLOW. And talking so disrespectfully about the Bible.

NEIGHBOUR. Belied and they needn't; many's the time the Bible was a consolation to a fellow all alone in the old cell. The lovely thin paper with a bit of mattress coir in it, if you could get a match or a bit of tinder or any class of light, was a good a smoke as ever I tasted. Am I right, Dunlavin?

DUNLAVIN. Damn the lie, Neighbour. The first twelve months I done, I smoked my way half-way through the book of Genesis and three inches of my mattress. When the Free State came in we were afraid of our life they were going to change the mattresses for feather beds. And you couldn't smoke feathers, not, be God, if they were rolled in the Song of Solomon itself. But sure, thanks to God, the Free State didn't change anything more than the badge on the warders' caps.

OTHER FELLOW. Can I be into my cell for a while?

PRISONER B. Until the doctor calls you [*Goes into his cell*].

PRISONER A. Well, I'm going to have a rest. It's hard work doing a lagging.

LIFER. A lagging? That's penal servitude, isn't it?

DUNLAVIN. Three years or anything over.

LIFER. Three years is a long time.

DUNLAVIN. I wouldn't like to be that long hanging.

NEIGHBOUR. Is he the . . .

DUNLAVIN [*sotto voice*] Silver-top! [*Aloud*]. Started life this morning.

NEIGHBOUR. So they're not going to top you after all? Well, you're a lucky man. I worked one time in the hospital, helping the screw there, and the morning of the execution he gave me two bottles of stout to take the hood off the fellow was after being topped. I wouldn't have done it a second time for two glasses of malt, no, nor a bottle of it. I cut the hood away; his head was all twisted and his face black, but the two eyes were the worst; like a rabbit's; it was fear that had done it.

LIFER. Perhaps he didn't feel anything. How do you know?

NEIGHBOUR. I only seen him. I never had a chance of asking him. [NEIGHBOUR *goes to the murderer's door*]. Date of expiration of sentence, life. In some ways I wouldn't mind if that was my lot. What do you say?

DUNLAVIN. I don't know; it's true we're too old and bet for lobbywatching and shaking down anywhere, so that you'd fall down and sleep on the pavement of a winter's night and not know but you were lying snug and comfortable in the Shelbourne.

NEIGHBOUR. Only then to wake up on some lobby and the hard floorboards under you, and a lump of hard filth for your pillow, and the cold and the drink shaking you, wishing it was morning for the market pubs to open, where if you had the price of a drink you could sit in the warm anyway. Except, God look down on you, if it was Sunday.

DUNLAVIN. Ah, there's the agony. No pub open, but the bells battering your bared nerves and all you could do with the cold and the sickness was to lean over on your side and wish that God would call you.

LIFER. If I was outside my life wouldn't be like that.

NEIGHBOUR. No, but ours would.

DUNLAVIN [quietly] See, we're selfish, mister, like everyone else.

WARDER [shouts off] Medical applications and receptions. Fall in for the doctor. [Lifer looks lost].

DUNLAVIN. Yes, that's you. Go up there to the top of the wing and wait till the screw tells you to go in. Neighbour, call them other fellows.

Exit lifer.

NEIGHBOUR. Come on – the vet's here.

DUNLAVIN [calling in to the Other fellow] Hey, come out and get gelded.

Other fellow and prisoners a. and b. come out of cells.

NEIGHBOUR. You're for the doctor. Go on up there with the rest of them. Me and Dunlavin don't go up. We only wait to be rubbed.

DUNLAVIN. Don't have any chat at all with that fellow. D'you see what he's in for?

Neighbour goes and looks. Exit other fellow and prisoners a. and b.

NEIGHBOUR. What the hell does that mean?

DUNLAVIN. A bloody sex mechanic.

NEIGHBOUR. I didn't know.

DUNLAVIN. Well, you know now. I'll go in and get me chair. You can sit on it after me. It'll save you bringing yours out.

NEIGHBOUR. Well, if you go first and have a chance of a go at the spirit bottle, don't swig the bloody lot. Remember I'm for treatment too.

DUNLAVIN. Don't be such an old begrudger. He'll bring a quart bottle of it, and who could swallow that much methylated spirit in the few drops you'd get at it?

NEIGHBOUR. You could, or a bucket of it, if it was lying anywhere handy. I seen you do it, bluestone and all, only buns to a bear as far as you were concerned.

DUNLAVIN. Do you remember the old doctor they had here years ago?

NEIGHBOUR. The one they used to call Crippen.

DUNLAVIN. The very man. There was one day I was brought in for drinking the chat and I went to court that morning and was here in the afternoon still as drunk as Pontius Pilate. Crippen was examining me. 'When I put me hand there you cough,' and all to that effect. 'Did you ever have VD?' says he. 'I haven't got your habits,' says I to him. These fellows weren't long.

Re-enter prisoners a. and b.

NEIGHBOUR. What did he give youse?

PRISONER B. [*passing into cell*] Extra six ounces of bread. Says we're undernourished.

PRISONER A. Is the bar open yet?

NEIGHBOUR. Never you mind the bar. I've cruel pains in my leg that I want rubbed to take out the rheumatics, not to be jeered at, and I've had them genuine since the war.

PRISONER A. What war? The economic war?

NEIGHBOUR. Ah, you maggot. It's all your fault, Dunlavin, telling them fellows we do get an odd sup out of the spirit bottle. Letting everyone know our business.

Prisoners a. and b. go into cells and shut the doors.

DUNLAVIN. No sign of Holy Healey yet.

NEIGHBOUR. You're wasting your time chasing after old Healey. He told me here one day, and I trying to get myself an old overcoat out of him, that he was here only as a head man of the Department of Justice, and he couldn't do other business of any sort or size whatever, good, bad or indifferent. It's my opinion that old Healey does be half-jarred a deal of the time anyway.

DUNLAVIN. The likes of Healey would take a sup all right, but being a high-up civil servant, he wouldn't drink under his own name. You'd see the likes of Healey nourishing themselves with balls of malt, at eleven in the morning, in little back snug round Merrion Row. The barman would lose his job if he so much as breathed their name. It'd be 'Mr H. wants a drop of water but not too much.' 'Yes, Mr O.' 'No, sir, Mr Mac wasn't in this morning.' 'Yes, Mr D. Fine morning; it will be a lovely day if it doesn't snow.' Educated drinking, you know. Even a bit of chat about God at an odd time, so as you'd think God was in another department, but not long off the Bog, and they was doing Him a good turn to be talking well about Him.

NEIGHBOUR. Here's the other two back. The MO will be down to us soon.

Lifer and other fellow go into cells and shut the doors.

DUNLAVIN. That other fellow's not looking as if this place is agreeing with him.

NEIGHBOUR. You told me a minute ago that I wasn't even to speak to him.

DUNLAVIN. Ah, when all is said and done, he's someone's rearing after all, he could be worse, he could be a screw or an official from the Department.

Warder Regan comes on with a bottle marked 'methylated spirit'.

WARDER REGAN. You're the two for rubs, for your rheumatism.

DUNLAVIN. That's right, Mr Regan sir, old and bet, sir, that's us. And the old pain is very bad with us these times, sir.

WARDER REGAN. Not so much lip, and sit down whoever is first for treatment.

DUNLAVIN. That's me, sir. Age before ignorance, as the man said. [*Sits in the chair*].

WARDER REGAN. Rise the leg of your trousers. Which leg is it?

DUNLAVIN. The left, sir.

WARDER REGAN. That's the right leg you're showing me.

DUNLAVIN. That's what I was saying, sir. The left is worst one day and the right is bad the next. To be on the safe side, you'd have to do two of them. It's only the mercy of God I'm not a centipede, sir, with the weather that's in it.

WARDER REGAN. Is that where the pain is?

DUNLAVIN [*bending down slowly towards the bottle*] A little lower down, sir, if you please. [*Grabs the bottle and raises it to his mouth*]. Just a little lower down, sir, if it's all equal to you.

Regan rubs, head well bent, and Dunlavin drinks long and deeply and as quickly lowers the bottle on to the floor again, wiping his mouth and making the most frightful grimaces, for the stuff doesn't go down easy at first. He goes through the pantomime of being burnt inside for Neighbour's benefit and rubs his mouth with the back of his hand.

DUNLAVIN. Ah, that's massive, sir. 'Tis you that has the healing hand. You must have desperate luck at the horses; I'd only love to be with you copying your dockets. [*Regan turns and pours more spirit on his hands*]. Ah, that's it, sir, well into me I can feel it going. [*Reaches forward towards the bottle again, drinks*]. Ah, that's it, I can feel it going right into me. And doing me all the good in the world. [*Regan reaches and puts more spirit on his hand and sets to rubbing again*]. That's it, sir, thorough does it; if you're going to do a thing at all you might as well do it well. [*Reaches forward for the bottle again and raises it. Neighbour looks across in piteous appeal to him not to drink so much, but he merely waves the bottle in elegant salute, as if to wish him good health, and takes another drink*]. May God reward you, sir, you must be the seventh son of the seventh son of one of the Lees from Limerick on your mother's side maybe. [*Drinks again*]. Ah, that's the cure for the cold of the wind and the world's neglectment.

WARDER REGAN. Right, now you.

Neighbour comes forward.

WARDER DONELLY [*offstage*] All present and correct, Mr Healey, sir.

DUNLAVIN. Holy Healey!

Enter Warder Donelly.

WARDER DONELLY. This way, Mr Healey.

WARDER REGAN. Attention! Stand by your doors.

DUNLAVIN. By the left, laugh.

WARDER DONELLY. This way.

Enter Mr Healey, an elegantly dressed gentleman.

HEALEY. Good morning.

WARDER DONELLY. Any complaints?

PRISONER A. No, sir.

HEALEY. Good morning!

WARDER DONELLY. Any complaints?

OTHER FELLOW. ⎱
PRISONER B. ⎰ No, sir.

HEALEY. Good morning all! Well, now, I'm here representing the Department of Justice, if there are any complaints now is the time to make them.

SEVERAL PRISONERS. No complaints, sir.

WARDER REGAN. All correct, sir. Two receiving medical treatment here, sir.

DUNLAVIN. Just getting the old leg rubbed, sir, Mr Healey.

HEALEY. Well, well, it almost smells like a bar.

DUNLAVIN. I'm near drunk myself on the smell of it, sir.

HEALEY. Don't let me interrupt the good work.

DUNLAVIN. Ah, the old legs. It's being out in all weathers that does it, sir. Of course we don't have that to contend with while we're here, sir.

HEALEY. Out in all weathers, I should think not indeed. Well, my man, I will be inspecting your cell amongst others in due course.

DUNLAVIN. Yes, sir.

HEALEY. It's always a credit to you, I must say that [He turns to Regan]. Incorrigible some of these old fellows, but rather amusing.

WARDER REGAN. Yes, sir.

HEALEY. It's Regan, isn't it?

WARDER REGAN. Yes, sir.

HEALEY. Ah yes, you're helping the Canon at the execution tomorrow morning, I understand.

WARDER REGAN. Well, I shall be with the condemned man sir, seeing that he doesn't do away with himself during the night and that he goes down the hole with his neck properly broken in the morning, without making too much fuss about it.

HEALEY. A sad duty.

WARDER REGAN. Neck breaking and throttling, sir? [Healey gives him a sharp look]. You must excuse me, sir. I've seen rather a lot of it. They say familiarity breeds contempt.

HEALEY. Well, we have one consolation, Regan, the condemned man gets the priest and the sacraments, more than his victim got maybe. I venture to suggest that some of them die holier deaths than if they had finished their natural span.

WARDER REGAN. We can't advertise 'Commit a murder and die a happy death,' sir. We'd have them all at it. They take religion very seriously in this country.

HEALEY. Quite, quite so! Now, I understand you have the reprieved man over here, Regan.

WARDER REGAN. No. Twenty-six sir.

DUNLAVIN. Just beside me, sir.

HEALEY. Ah, yes! So here we are! Here's the lucky man, eh? Well, now, the Governor will explain your position to you later in the day. Your case will be examined every five years. Meanwhile I thought you might like a holy picture to hang up in your cell. Keep a cheerful countenance, my friend. God gave you back your life and the least you can do is to thank him with every breath you draw! Right? Well, be of good heart. I will call in and see you again, that is, if duty permits. [*He moves to Dunlavin's cell*].

HEALEY [*at Dunlavin's cell*]. Very creditable. Hm.

DUNLAVIN Well, to tell the truth, sir, it's a bit extra special today. You see, we heard you was here.

HEALEY. Very nice.

DUNLAVIN. Of course I do like to keep my little place as homely as I can with the little holy pictures you gave me of Blessed Martin, sir.

HEALEY. I see you don't recognize the colour bar.

DUNLAVIN. The only bar I recognize, sir, is the Bridge Bar or the Beamish House the corner of Thomas Street.

HEALEY. Well, I must be off now, and I'm glad to see you're being well looked after.

DUNLAVIN. It's neither this nor that, but if you could spare a minute, sir?

HEALEY. Yes, what is it? But hurry; remember I've a lot to do today.

DUNLAVIN. It's like this, sir. I won't always be here, sir, having me leg rubbed and me bit of grub brought to me. As it says in the Bible, sir, have it yourself or be without it and put ye by for the rainy day, for thou knowest not the night thou mayest be sleeping in a lobby.

HEALEY. Yes, yes, but what is it you want?

DUNLAVIN. I've a chance of a little room up round Buckingham

Street, sir, if you could only give me a letter to the Room-Keepers after I go out, for a bit of help with the rent.

HEALEY. Well, you know, when I visit the prison, I'm not here as a member of any outside organization of which I may be a member but simply as an official of the Department of Justice.

DUNLAVIN. Yes, but where else would I be likely to meet you, sir? I'd hardly bump into you in the Bridge Bar when I'd be outside, would I, sir?

HEALEY. No, no, certainly not. But you know the Society offices in the Square. See me there any Friday night, between eight and nine.

DUNLAVIN. Thank you, sir, and a bed in heaven to you, sir.

HEALEY. And the same to you. [*Goes to next cell*].

DUNLAVIN. And many of them, and I hope we're all here this time next year [*venomously after Mr Healey*] that it may choke you.

Warder Donelly bangs on Lifer's closed door, then looks in.

WARDER DONELLY. Jesus Christ, sir. He's put the sheet up! Quick.

Regan and Donelly go into Lifer's cell. He is hanging. They cut him down.

WARDER REGAN. Gently does it.

They lay him down in the passage and try to restore him.

HEALEY. What a dreadful business and with this other coming off tomorrow.

The prisoners crowd out of line.

WARDER DONELLY. Get back to your cells!

HEALEY. Is he still with us?

WARDER REGAN. He'll be all right in an hour or two. Better get the MO, Mr Donelly.

The triangle sounds.

WARDER DONELLY. B. Wing, two, three and one. Stand by your doors. Right, lead on. Now come on, come on, this is no holiday. Right sir, over to you. Lead on, B.1.

Warder Regan and Healey are left with the unconscious Lifer.

HEALEY. Dear, dear. The Canon will be very upset about this.

WARDER REGAN. There's not much harm done, thank God. They don't have to put a death certificate against the receipt for his live body.

HEALEY. That doesn't seem a very nice way of looking at it, Regan.

WARDER REGAN. A lot of people mightn't consider ours a very nice job, sir.

HEALEY. Ours?

WARDER REGAN. Yes, ours, sir. Mine, the Canon's, the hangman's, and if you don't mind my saying so, yours, sir.

HEALEY. Society cannot exist without prisons, Regan. My job is to bring what help and comfort I can to these unfortunates. Really, a man with your outlook, I cannot see why you stay in the service.

WARDER REGAN. It's a soft job, sir, between hangings.

The triangle is heard. The MO comes on with two stretcher-bearers.

[CURTAIN]

ACT II

The prison yard, a fine evening.

VOICE OF PRISONER [*off-stage, singing*]

> A hungry feeling came o'er me stealing
> And the mice were squealing in my prison cell
> And the old triangle
> Went jingle jangle
> Along the banks of the Royal Canal.

WARDER DONELLY. B.1. B.2. B.3. Head on for exercise, right! Lead on, B.1. All one, away to exercise.

The prisoners file out, Warder Donelly with them.

> On a fine spring evening,
> The lag lay dreaming
> The seagulls wheeling high above the wall,
> And the old triangle
> Went jingle jangle
> Along the banks of the Royal Canal.
> The screw was peeping
> The lag was sleeping,

The prisoners wander where they will; most go and take a glance at the half-dug grave.

> While he lay weeping for the girl Sal,

WARDER DONELLY. Who's the bloody baritone? Shut up that noise, you. Where do you think you are?

NEIGHBOUR. It's not up here, sir; it's one of the fellows in the basement, sir, in the solitary.

WARDER DONELLY. He must be getting birdseed with his bread and water. I'll bloody well show him he's not in a singing house. [*Song is still going on*]. Hey, shut up that noise! Shut up there or I'll leave you weeping. Where do you think you are? [*Song stops*]. You can get sitting down any of you that wants it. [*Dunlavin sits*].

NEIGHBOUR [*at the grave*] They'll have to bottom out another couple of feet before morning.

PRISONER B. They! Us you mean; they've got four of us in a working party after tea.

NEIGHBOUR. You want to get that clay nice and neat for filling in. [*He spits and wanders away*].

PRISONER B. We'll get a couple of smokes for the job at least. *They wander.*

NEIGHBOUR. How are you, Neighbour?

DUNLAVIN. Dying.

NEIGHBOUR. If you are itself, it's greed that's killing you. I only got a sup of what was left.

DUNLAVIN. I saved your life then; it was very bad meths.

PRISONER B. What did Regan say when he caught youse lying in the cell?

NEIGHBOUR. He wanted to take us up for drinking it on him, but Dunlavin said we were distracted with the events of the morning and didn't know what we were doing. So he just told us to get to hell out of it and he hoped it would destroy us for life.

DUNLAVIN. May God forgive him.

NEIGHBOUR. I thought it was as good a drop of meths as ever I tasted. It would never come up to the pre-war article, but between the spring-time and the warmth of it, it would put new life into you. Oh, it's a grand evening and another day's work behind us.

PRISONER B. With the winter over, Neighbour, I suppose you don't feel a day over ninety.

NEIGHBOUR. If you'd have done all the time I have you wouldn't look so young.

PRISONER A. What time? Sure, you never done a lagging in your life. A month here and a week there for lifting the collection box out of a chapel or running out of a chemist's with a bottle of cheap wine. Anything over six months would be the death of you.

NEIGHBOUR. Oh, you're the hard chaw.

PRISONER A. Two laggings, I've done. Five years and seven, and a bit of Preventive Detention, on the Moor and at Parkhurst.

NEIGHBOUR. What for? Ferocious begging?

PRISONER A. I've never been a grasshopper or a nark for the screws anyway, wherever I was; and if you were in a lagging station I know what they'd give you, shopping the poor bastard that was singing in the chokey. He was only trying to be company for himself down there all alone and not knowing whether it was day or night.

NEIGHBOUR. I only did it for his own good. If the screw hadn't checked him the Principal might have been coming out and giving him an extra few days down there.

DUNLAVIN. Will youse give over the pair of youse for God's sake. The noise of youse battering me bared nerves is unhuman. Begod, an Englishman would have more nature to a fellow lying with a sick head. A methylated martyr, that's what I am.

NEIGHBOUR [to prisoner a.] Meself and that man sitting there, we done time before you came up. In Kilmainham, and that's where you never were. First fourteen days without a mattress, skilly three times a day. None of your sitting out in the yard like nowadays. I got my toe amputated by one of the old lags so I could go into hospital for a feed.

DUNLAVIN [looks up and feebly moans] A pity you didn't get your head amputated as you were at it. It would have kept you quiet for a bit.

NEIGHBOUR. I got me mouth to talk, the same as the next man. Maybe we're not all that well up, that we get up at the Christmas concert and do the electrocutionist performance, like some I could mention.

DUNLAVIN. It's neither this nor that, Neighbour, but if you would only give over arguing the toss about nothing and change over to a friendly subject of mutual interest – like the quare fellow that's to be topped in the morning.

NEIGHBOUR. True, true, Dunlavin, and a comfortable old flowery dell he'll have down there. [He prods the grave with his stick]. We'll be eating the cabbages off that one in a month or two.

PRISONER A. You're in a terrible hurry to get the poor scut under the cabbages. How do you know he won't get a reprieve, like old Silver-top?

LIFER. Jesus, Mary and Joseph, you'd like to see me in there, wouldn't you! [He moves violently away from them].

NEIGHBOUR. Your man doesn't like any talk about hanging.

PRISONER A. No more would you, if you'd tried to top yourself this morning.

NEIGHBOUR. Anyway he's gone now and we can have a chat about it in peace. Sure we must be saying something and it's better than scandalizing our neighbours.

PRISONER B. You never know what might happen to the quare fellow. God is good.

PRISONER C. And has a good mother.

They look in surprise at the young person who has quietly joined them.

DUNLAVIN. No, no, it's too late now for him to be chucked.

PRISONER A. It has been known, a last-minute reprieve, you know.

NEIGHBOUR. He bled his brother into a crock, didn't he, that had been set aside for the pig-slaughtering and mangled the remains beyond all hope of identification.

PRISONER C. Go bfoirdh Dia reinn.

NEIGHBOUR. He hasn't got a chance, never in a race of cats. He'll be hung as high as Guilderoy.

PRISONER A. You're the life of the party, aren't you? You put me in mind of the little girl who was sent in to cheer her father up. She was so good at it that he cut his throat.

PRISONER E. Ah, sure he was only computing the odds to it. He'll be topped.

NEIGHBOUR. I'd lay me Sunday bacon on it if anyone would be idiot enough to take me up.

Prisoner e., a bookie, has been listening.

PRISONER E. I wouldn't take your bacon, but I'll lay it off for you if you like.

Another prisoner watches for the screws. Prisoner e. acts as if he were a tick-tack man at the races.

PRISONER E. The old firm. Here we are again. Neighbour lays his Sunday bacon the quare fellow will be topped tomorrow morning. Any takers.

PRISONER D. Five snout.

PRISONER E. Away home to your mother.

MICKSER. Half a bacon.

PRISONER E. Half a . . .

NEIGHBOUR. Even bacons.

PRISONER E. Even bacons. Even bacons any takers? Yourself, sir, come on now, you look like a sportsman.

PRISONER A. I wouldn't eat anything after he'd touched it, not if I were starving.

NEIGHBOUR. Is that so . . .

PRISONER E. Now, now, now, don't interrupt the betting. Any takers?

DUNLAVIN. I'll take him up if only to shut his greedy gob.

NEIGHBOUR. You won't! You having me on!

DUNLAVIN. No, I'll bet you my Sunday bacon that a reprieve will come through before morning. I feel it in my bones.

NEIGHBOUR. That's the rheumatics.

PRISONER E. Is he on, Neighbour?

NEIGHBOUR. He is.

PRISONER E. Shake on it, the two of youse!

DUNLAVIN. How d'ye do, Lord Lonsdale!

NEIGHBOUR. Never mind all that. The minute the trap goes down tomorrow morning your Sunday bacon is mine.

PRISONER A. God leave you health to enjoy it.

NEIGHBOUR. He'll be topped all right.

PRISONER E. And if he isn't. I'm the very man will tell him you bet your bacon on his life.

NEIGHBOUR. You never would.

PRISONER A. Wouldn't I?

NEIGHBOUR. You'd never be bad enough.

PRISONER A. And what would be bad about it?

NEIGHBOUR. Causing a dissension and a disturbance.

The two young prisoners enter.

PRISONER A. You mean he mightn't take it for a joke.

PRISONER B. Here's them two young prisoners; they've the life of Reilly, rambling round the place. Where youse wandering off to now?

SCHOLARA. We came over here to see a chiner of ours. He turned twenty the day before yesterday, so they shifted him away from the juveniles to here. [*He sees prisoner c*]. Ah, there you are. We were over in the hospital being examined for going out on Saturday and we had a bit of snout to give you [*Takes out a Woodbine package, extracts a cigarette from it and gives it to prisoner c., who shyly stands and takes it].*

PRISONER C. [*quietly*] Thanks.

SCHOLARA. Gurra morra gut, you mean.

PRISONER C. [*smiles faintly*] Go raibh maith agat.

SCHOLARA [*grandly*] Na bac leis. [*To the other prisoners*]. Talks Irish to beat the band. Comes from an island between here and America. And Shaybo will give you a couple of strikers.

SHAYBO [*reaches in the seams of his coat and takes out a match which he presents to prisoner c*]. Here you are. It's a bloody shame to shove you over here among all these old men even if you are twenty itself, but maybe you won't be long after us, and you going home.

PRISONER C. [*Kerry accent*] I will, please God. It will be summer-time and where I come from is lovely when the sun is shining.

They stand there, looking embarrassed for a moment].

DUNLAVIN. Go on, why don't you kiss him good-bye.

SHAYBO. Eh, Schol, let's have a pike at the grave before the screw comes out.

SCHOLARA. Ah, yes, we must have a look at the grave.

They dive into the grave, the old men shout at them, but Warder Donelly comes to the door of the hospital.

WARDER DONELLY. Get up to hell out of that and back to your own wing, youse two. [*Shouts to the warders in the prison wing*]. Two on you there, pass them fellows into the juveniles. Get to hell out of that!

Scholara and Shaybo samba off, give the so-called V-sign, slap the right biceps with the left palm, and turning lightly, run in through the door.

NEIGHBOUR. Aren't they the impudent pups? Too easy a time they have of it. I'd tan their pink backsides for them. That'd leave them fresh and easy. Impudent young curs is going these days. No respect for God nor man, pinch anything that wasn't nailed down.

PRISONER B. Neighbour, the meths is rising in you.

DUNLAVIN. He might as well rave there as in bed.

ENGLISH VOICE [*from one of the cell windows*] I say, I say, down there in the yard.

DUNLAVIN. The voice of the Lord!

PRISONER A. That's the geezer from London that's in over the car smuggling.

ENGLISH VOICE. I say, down there.

PRISONER B. Hello, up there.

NEIGHBOUR. How are you fixed for fillet?

PRISONER B. Shut up a minute. Wait till we hear what is it he wants.

ENGLISH VOICE. Is there any bloke down there going out this week?

PRISONER B. Mickser is going out tomorrow. He's on this exercise. [*Shouts*]. Hold on a minute [*Looks round*]. Hey, Mickser.

MICKSER. What's up?

PRISONER B. That English fellow that's on remand over the cars, he wants to know if there's anyone going out this week. You're going out tomorrow, ain't you?

MICKSER. Yes, I am I'm going out in the morning. [*To English prisoner*]. What do you want?

ENGLISH VOICE. I want you to go up and contact my mate. He's in Dublin. It's about bail for me. I can write his name and address here and let it down to you on my string. I didn't want the law to get his address in Dublin, so I can't write to him. I got a quid in with me, without the screw finding it, and I'll let it down with the address if you'll do it.

MICKSER. Good enough. Let down the address and the quid.

ENGLISH VOICE. My mate will you give you some more when you see him.

MICKSER. That's all right. Let the quid down now and the address before the screw comes out of the hospital. I'm going out tomorrow and I'll see him for you, soon as we get out of the market pubs at half two.

PRISONER B. He's letting it down now.

MICKSER. There's the quid anyway. [*Reading the note. Neighbour gets to his feet and goes behind and peers over his shoulder. Mickser sees him*]. Get to hell out of it, you.

NEIGHBOUR. I only just wanted to have a look at what he wrote.

MICKSER. And have his mate in the Bridewell, before the day was out. I know you, you bloody old stag.

NEIGHBOUR. I saw the day you wouldn't say the like of that.

MICKSER [*proferring him the pound*] Here, get a mass said for yourself.

NEIGHBOUR. It wouldn't do you much harm to put yourself under the hand of a priest either.

MICKSER [*laughs at him*] That's for sinners. Only dirty people has to wash.

NEIGHBOUR. A man of your talent and wasting your time here.

MICKSER [*going back to walk with the prisoners behind*] Good luck now, Neighbour. I'll call up and see you in the hospice for the dying.

NEIGHBOUR. [*stands and calls loudly after him*] You watch yourself. I saw the quare fellow in here a couple of years ago. He was a young hard chaw like you in all the pride of his strength and impudence. He was kicking a ball about over in A yard and I was walking around with poor old Mockridge, neither of us minding no one. All of a sudden I gets such a wallop on the head it knocks the legs from under me and very nigh cuts off my ear. 'You headed that well', says he, and I deaf for three days after it! Who's got the best of it now, young as he is and strong as he is? How will his own ear feel tomorrow morning, with the washer under it, and whose legs will be the weakest when the trap goes down and he's slung into the pit? And what use is the young heart?

Some of the prisoners walking round stop and listen to him, but Mickser gives him a contemptuous look and walks on, shouting at him in passing.

MICKSER. Get along with you, you dirty half animal.

A warder passes, sounds of the town heard, factory sirens, distant ships. Some of the prisoners pace up and down like caged animals.

NEIGHBOUR. Dunlavin, have you the loan of a pencil for a minute?

DUNLAVIN. What do you want it for?

NEIGHBOUR. I just want to write something to that English fellow about his bail.

DUNLAVIN. You'd better hurry, before the screw comes back out.

Neighbour writes.

NEIGHBOUR. Hey, you up there that's looking for the bail.

ENGLISH VOICE. Hello, you got the quid and the address?

PRISONER A. What's the old dog up to?

DUNLAVIN. Ah, leave him alone. He's a bit hasty, but poor old Neighbour has good turns in him.

PRISONER A. So has a corkscrew.

NEIGHBOUR. Let down your string and I'll send you up this bit of a message.

ENGLISH VOICE [*his hands can be seen at the window holding the note*] 'Get a bucket and bail yourself out.' [*Shouts in rage*]. You dirty bastard bleeder to take my quid and I'll tell the bloody screw I will; I'll shop you, you bleeding . . .

MICKSER. What's up with you?

NEIGHBOUR. Get a bucket and bail yourself out. [*Laughing an old man' cackle*].

ENGLISH VOICE. You told me to get a bucket and bail myself out, but I'll tell the screws; I'll shop you about that quid.

MICKSER [*shouts up to the window*] Shut your bloody big mouth for a minute. I told you nothing.

PRISONER A. It was this old get here.

MICKSER. I sent you no message; it was this old pox bottle.

NEIGHBOUR [*ceases to laugh, is alarmed at the approach of Mickser*] Now, now, Mickser, take a joke, can't you, it was only a bit of a gas.

MICKSER [*advancing*] I'll give you gas.

Mickser advances on neighbour. The lags stop and look – suddenly Mickser seizes the old man and, yelling with delight, carries neighbour over to the grave and thrusts him into it. The prisoners all crowd around kicking dirt on to the old man and shouting 'Get a bucket and bail yourself out'.

PRISONER D. Nick, Mickser, nick, nick here's the screw.

PRISONER A. It's only the cook with the quare fellow's tea.

A prisoner comes through the hospital gate and down the steps. He wears a white apron, carries a tray and is surrounded by an interested band, except for the lifer, who stands apart, and Dunlavin, who lies prone on the front asleep. From the prisoners around the food arises an excited chorus:

PRISONER A. Rashers and eggs.

PRISONER B. He got that last night.

MICKSER. Chicken.

NEIGHBOUR. He had that for dinner.

PRISONER B. Sweet cake.

PRISONER A. It's getting hung he is, not married.

NEIGHBOUR. Steak and onions.

MICKSER. Sausages and bacon.

PRISONER B. And liver.

PRISONER A. Pork chops.

PRISONER B. Pig's feet.

PRISONER A. Salmon.

NEIGHBOUR. Fish and chips.

MICKSER. Jelly and custard.

NEIGHBOUR. Roast lamb.

PRISONER A. Plum pudding.

PRISONER B. Turkey.

NEIGHBOUR. Goose.

PRISONERS A., B. AND NEIGHBOUR. Rashers and eggs.

ALL. Rashers and eggs, rashers and eggs, and eggs and rashers and eggs and rashers it is.

COOK [*desperate*] Ah, here, lads.

PRISONERS. Here give us a look, lift up the lid, eh, here, I never seen it.

The cook struggles to protect his cargo, the prisoners mill round in a loose scrum of excitement and greed, their nostrils mad almost to the point of snatching a bit. There is a roar from the gate.

WARDER DONELLY [*from inside the hospital gate*] Get to hell out of that. What do youse think you are on?

The prisoners scatter in a rush.

The cook with great dignity carries on.

NEIGHBOUR [*sitting down*] Oh, the two eggs, the yolk in the middle like ... a bride's eye under a pink veil, and the grease of the rashers ... pale and pure like melted gold.

DUNLAVIN. Oh, may God forgive you, as if a body wasn't sick enough as it is.

NEIGHBOUR. And the two big rashers.

PRISONER A. Go along, you begrudging old dog. Maybe when you go back the standard of living in your town residence, No. 1 St James Street, might be gone up. And they'll be serving rashers and eggs. You'd do a lot for them, when you'd begrudge them to a man for his last meal on this earth.

NEIGHBOUR. Well, it's not his last meal if you want to know. He'll get supper tonight and a breakfast in the morning, and I don't begrudge him the little he'll eat of that, seeing the rope stew to follow, and lever pudding and trap door doddle for desert. And anyway didn't you run over the same as the rest of us to see what he was getting?

PRISONER A. And if I did, it wasn't to begrudge it to the man.

PRISONER B. Sure we all ran over, anything to break the monotony in a kip like this.

The triangle is heard.

PRISONER A. [*gloomily*] I suppose you're right. In Strangeways, Manchester, and I in it during the war, we used to wish for an air-raid. We had one and we were left locked up in our cells. We stood up on our tables and took the blackouts off the windows and had a grand-stand view of the whole city burning away under us. The screws were running round shouting in the spy-holes at us to get down from the windows, but they soon ran off down the shelters. We had a great view of the whole thing till a bomb landed on the Assize Court next door, and the blast killed twenty of the lags. They were left standing on their tables without a mark on them, stone dead. Sure anyway, we all agreed it broke the monotony.

Enter Warder Donelly.

WARDER DONELLY. Right, fall in there!

PRISONER B. Don't forget the bet. Neighbour.

WARDER DONELLY. Come on, get in line there.

PRISONER A. And don't forget what I'm going to tell the quare fellow.

WARDER DONELLY. Silence there. [*Search begins*]. What's this you've got in your pocket? A file? Scissors out of the bag shop? No? A bit of rope? Oh, your handkerchief, so it is. [*Searching next prisoner*]. You here, what's this? A bit of wax end, you forgot to leave in the bag shop? Well, don't forget the next time. What's this? [*Man takes out two inches of rope*]. What's this for? You were roping mail bags today, and after all they don't rope themselves. Ah, you forgot to leave it behind? Well, go easy, save as much as that each time and in five years' time you'd have enough to make a rope ladder. Oh, you're only doing six months? Well maybe you want to save the taxpayers a few quid and hang yourself. Sorrow the loss if you did, but they'd want to know where you got the rope from. [*Prisoners laugh as they are expected to do*]. Come on, next man. [*He hurries along now*]. Come along now, no mailbags, scissors, needles, knives, razor blades, guns, hatchets or empty porter bottles. No? [*To the last prisoner*]. Well, will you buy a ticket to the Police Ball?

Prisoners laugh dutifully.

WARDER REGAN [*voice from prison wing*] All done, sir?

PRISONER A. Don't forget, Neighbour.

WARDER DONELLY. Right, sir, on to you, sir [*Gate swings open*]. Right, lead on, B.1.

NEIGHBOUR. Anyway, his grave's dug and the hangman's on his way.

PRISONER A. That doesn't mean a thing, they always dig the grave, just to put the wind up them –

WARDER DONELLY. Silence!

The prisoners march, the gate clangs behind them; the tramp of their feet is heard as they mark time inside.

WARDER REGAN [*voice from the prison wing*] Right, B. Wing, bang out your doors. B.1, get in off your steps and bang out your doors, into your cells and bang out your doors. Get locked up. BANG THEM DOORS! GET INSIDE AND BANG OUT THEM DOORS!

The last door bangs lonely on its own and then there is silence.

VOICE FROM BELOW [*singing*]

> The wind was rising.
> And the day declining
> As I lay pining in my prison cell
> And that old triangle
> Went jingle jangle

The triangle is beaten, the gate of the prison wing opens and the Chief and Warder Donelly come down the steps and approach the grave.

> Along the banks of the Royal Canal.

CHIEF [*resplendent in silver braid*] Who's that singing?

WARDER DONELLY. I think it's one of the prisoners in the chokey, sir.

CHIEF. Where?

WARDER DONELLY. In the punishment cells, sir.

CHIEF. That's more like it. Well, tell him to cut it out.

SONG.

> In the female prison
> There are seventy women . . .

WARDER DONELLY. [*goes down to the area and leans and shouts*] Hey, you down there, cut it out, or I'll give you jingle jangle.

The song stops. Warder Donelly walks back.

CHIEF. Is the quare fellow finished his tea?

WARDER DONELLY. He is. He is just ready to come out for exercise, now. The wings are all clear. They're locked up having their tea. He'll be along any minute.

CHIEF. He's coming out here?

WARDER DONELLY. Yes, sir.

CHIEF [*exasperated*] Do you want him to see his grave, bloody well half dug? Run in quick and tell those bloody idiots to take him out the side door, and exercise him over the far side of the stokehold, and tell them to keep him well into the wall where he'll be out of sight of the cell windows. Hurry and don't let him hear you. Let on it's something about another duty. Warders! You'd get better in Woolworths.

He goes to the area and shouts down.

Hey, you down there. You in the cell under the steps. You do be singing there to keep yourself company? You needn't be afraid, it's only the Chief. How long you doing down there? Seven days No. 1 and twenty-one days No. 2. God bless us and love us, you must have done something desperate. I may be able to do something for you, though God knows you needn't count on it, I don't own the place. You what? With who? Ah sure, I often have a bit of a tiff with the same man myself. We'll see what we can do for you. It's a long time to be stuck down there, no matter who you had the tiff with.

Enter Warder Donelly.

CHIEF. Well?

WARDER DONELLY. It's all right, they've brought him out the other way.

They look out beyond the stage.

CHIEF. Looks as if they're arguing the toss about something.

WARDER DONELLY. Football.

CHIEF. Begod, look at them stopping while the quare fellow hammers his point home.

WARDER DONELLY. I was down in the condemned cell while he was getting his tea. I asked him if it was all right. He said it was, and 'Aren't the evenings getting a grand stretch?' he says.

CHIEF. Look at him now, putting his nose to the air.

WARDER DONELLY. He's a grand evening for his last.

CHIEF. I took the name of the fellow giving the concert in the punishment cells. In the morning when we get this over, see he's shifted to Hell's gates over the far side. He can serenade the stokehold wall for a change if he's light enough to make out his music.

Warder Donelly copies the name and number.

CHIEF. I have to attend to every mortal thing in this place. None of youse seem to want to do a hand's turn, bar draw your money – you're quick enough at that. Well, come on, let's get down to business.

Warder Donelly goes and uncovers the grave.

CHIEF [*looking off*] Just a minute. It's all right. They've taken him round the back of the stokehold. [*Looking at the grave*]. Not so bad, another couple of feet out of the bottom and we're elected. Regan should be down with the working party any minute, as soon as the quare fellow's finished his exercise.

WARDER DONELLY. There, he's away in now, sir. See him looking at the sky?

CHIEF. You'd think he was trying to kiss it good-bye. Well, that's the last he'll see of it.

WARDER DONELLY. No chance of a reprieve, sir?

CHIEF. Not a chance. Healey never even mentioned fixing up a line with the Post Office. If there'd been any chance of developments he'd have asked us to put a man on all night. All he said was 'The Governor will get the last word before the night's out.' That means only one thing. Go ahead.

Warders Reagan and Crimmin come out with prisoners a. b. c. and d.

WARDER REGAN. Working party all correct, sir. Come on, get those boards off. Bottom out a couple more feet and leave the clay at the top, nice and neat.

CHIEF. O, Mr Regan.

WARDER REGAN. Take over, Mr Crimmin.

CHIEF. Mr Regan. All I was going to say was – why don't you take yourself a bit of a rest while these fellows are at work on the grave. It's a long old pull till eight tomorrow morning.

WARDER REGAN. Thank you, sir.

CHIEF. Don't mention it. I'll see you before you go down to the cell. Get yourself a bit of a smoke, in the hospital. Don't forget now.

He and Warder Donelly go back in.

WARDER REGAN. Mr Crimmin. The Chief, a decent man, he's after giving us his kind permission to go into the hospital and have a sit down and a smoke for ourselves when these fellows have the work started. He knew we'd go in anyway, so he saw the chance of being floochalach, at no expense to the management. Here [*Takes out a packet of cigarettes, and takes some from it*]. here's a few fags for the lads.

CRIMMIN. I'll give them some of mine too.

WARDER REGAN. Don't do anything of the sort. One each is enough, you can slip them a couple when they're going to be locked up, if you like, but if these fellows had two fags each, they'd not work at all but spend the time out here blowing smoke rings in the evening air like lords. I'll slip in now, you come in after me. Tell them not to have them in their mouths if the Chief or the Governor comes out.

He goes up the steps to the hospital.

CRIMMIN [*calls prisoner c.*] Hey!

PRISONER C. [*comes to him*] Seadh a Thomais?

CRIMMIN [*gives him cigarettes and matches*] Seo, cupla toitin* Taim fhein is an scew eile ag dul isteach chuig an cispeadeal, noimeat. Roinn amach na toitini siud, is glacfhaidh sibh gal. Mathagann an Governor no'n Chief no an Principal, na biodh in bhur moeil agaibh iad. A' tuigeann tu?

PRISONER C. Tuigim, a Thomais, go raibh maith agat.

CRIMMIN [*officially*] Right, now get back to work.

PRISONER C. Yes, sir.

Crimmin goes up the hospital steps.

PRISONER C. He gave me some cigarettes.

Prisoner d. has gone straight to the grave, prisoner b. is near it.

* For translation of the Gaelic dialogue see page 539

PRISONER A. May I never dig a grave for less! You two get on and do a bit of digging while we have a quiet burn, then we'll take over.

PRISONER C. He said to watch out for the chief and them.

PRISONER B. Pass down a light to your man. He says he'd enjoy it better down there, where he can't be seen! Decent of him and Regan wasn't it?

PRISONER A. They'd have you dead from decency. That same Regan was like a savage in the bag shop today, you couldn't get a word to the fellow next to you.

PRISONER C. I never saw him like that before.

PRISONER B. He's always the same at a time like this, hanging seems to get on his nerves.

PRISONER A. Why should he worry, he won't feel it.

PRISONER B. He's on the last watch. Twelve till eight.

PRISONER A. Till death do us part.

PRISONER C. The quare fellow asked for him, didn't he?

PRISONER A. They all do.

PRISONER C. He asked to have Mr Crimmin too.

PRISONER A. It'll break that young screw up and him only a wet day in the place.

PRISONER B. Funny the way they all ask for Regan. Perhaps they think he'll bring them good luck, him being good living.

PRISONER A. Good living! Whoever heard of a good living screw? Did you never hear of the screw, married the prostitute?

PRISONER B. No, what happened to him?

PRISONER A. He dragged her down to his own level.

PRISONER B. He told me once that if I kept off the beer I need never come back here. I asked him what about himself, and he told me he was terrible hardened to it and would I pray for him.

PRISONER C. When I was over in the Juveniles he used to talk like that to us. He said that the Blessed Virgin knew us better than the police or the judges – or ourselves even. We might think we were terrible sinners but she knew we were good boys only a bit wild . . .

PRISONER A. Bloody mad he is.

PRISONER C. And that we were doing penance here for the men who took us up, especially the judges, they being mostly rich old men with great opportunity for vice.

Prisoner d. appears from the grave.

PRISONER A. The dead arose and appeared to many.

Prisoner a. goes and rearranges the work which prisoner d. has upset.

PRISONER B. What's brought you out of your fox hole?

PRISONER D. I thought it more discreet to remain in concealment while I smoked but I could not stop down there listening to talk like that, as a ratepayer, I couldn't stand for it, especially those libellous remarks about the judiciary.

He looks accusingly at the boy.

PRISONER C. I was only repeating what Mr Regan said, sir.

PRISONER D. He could be taken up for it. According to that man, there should be no such thing as law and order. We could all be murdered in our beds, the innocent prey of every ruffian that took it into his head to appropriate our goods, our lives even. Property must have security! What do you think society would come to without police and judges and suitable punishments? Chaos! In my opinion hanging's too good for 'em.

PRISONER C. Oh, Mr Regan doesn't believe in capital punishment, sir.

PRISONER D. My God, the man's an atheist! He should be dismissed from the public service. I shall take it up with the Minister when I get out of here. I went to school with his cousin.

PRISONER A. Who the hell does he think he is, a bloody high court judge?

PRISONER D. Chaos!

PRISONER B. He's in for embezzlement, there were two suicides and a bye-election over him.

PRISONER D. There are still a few of us who care about the state of the country, you know. My family's national tradition goes back to the Land War. Grandfather did four weeks for incitement to mutiny – and we've never looked back since. One of my young nephews, as a matter of fact, has just gone over to Sandhurst.

PRISONER B. Isn't that where you done your four years?

PRISONER A. No, that was Parkhurst.

PRISONER C. [*to others*] A college educated man in here, funny, isn't it?

PRISONER D. I shall bring all my influence to bear to settle this Regan fellow.

PRISONER C. You must be a very important man, sir.

PRISONER D. I am one of the Cashel Carrolls, my boy, related on my mother's side to the Killens of Killcock.

PRISONER B. Used to wash for our family.

PRISONER C. Go bhfoiridh Dia 'rainn.

PRISONER D. Irish speaking?

PRISONER C. Yes, sir.

PRISONER D. Then it might interest you to know that I took my gold medal in Irish.

PRISONER C. Does that mean he speaks Irish?

PRISONER D. Of course.

PRISONER C. Oh sir. Ta Gaeilge go leor agamsa. O'n gcliabhain amach, sir.

PRISONER A. That's fixed you.

PRISONER D. Quite. Tuigim tu.

PRISONER A. The young lad's from Kerry, from an island where they don't speak much else.

PRISONER D. Kerry? Well of course you speak with a different dialect to the one I was taught.

PRISONER A. The young screw Crimmin's from the same place. He sneaks up to the landing sometimes when the other screws aren't watching and there they are for hours talking through the spy hole, all in Irish.

PRISONER D. Most irregular,

PRISONER B. There's not much harm in it.

PRISONER D. How can there be proper discipline between warder and prisoner with that kind of familiarity?

PRISONER C. He does only be giving me the news from home and who's gone to America or England; he's not long up here and neither am I . . . the two of us do each be as lonely as the other.

PRISONER B. The lad here sings an old song betimes. It's very nice. It makes the night less lonely, each man alone and sad maybe in the old cell. The quare fellow heard him singing and after he was sentenced to death he sent over word he'd be listening every night around midnight for him.

PRISONER A. You'd better make a big effort tonight, kid, for his last concert.

PRISONER C. Ah, God help him! Sure, you'd pity him all the same. It must be awful to die at the end of a swinging rope and a black hood over his poor face.

PRISONER A. Begod, he's not being topped for nothing – to cut his own brother up and butcher him like a pig.

PRISONER D. I must heartily agree with you, sir, a barbarian if ever there was one.

PRISONER C. Maybe he did those things, but God help him this minute and he knowing this night his last on earth. Waiting over there he is, to be shaken out of his sleep and rushed to the rope.

PRISONER A. What sleep will he take? They won't have to set the alarm clock for a quarter to eight, you can bet your life on that.

PRISONER C. May he find peace on the other side.

PRISONER A. Or his brother waiting to have a word with him about being quartered in such an unmannerly fashion.

PRISONER C. None of us can know for certain.

PRISONER D. It was proved in a court of law that this man had experience as a pork butcher and put his expert knowledge to use by killing his brother with an axe and dismembering the body, the better to dispose of it.

PRISONER C. Go bfoirdh. Dia rainn.

PRISONER A. I wouldn't put much in the court of law part of it, but I heard about it myself from a fellow in from his part of the country. He said he had the brother strung up in an outhouse like a pig.

PRISONER D. Actually he was bleeding him into a farmhouse vessel according to the evidence. He should be hung three or four times over.

PRISONER A. Seeing your uncle was at school with the President's granny, perhaps he could fix it up for you.

PRISONER C. I don't believe he is a bad man. When I was on remand he used to walk around with me at exercise every day and he was sad when I told him about my brother, who died in the Yank's army, and my father, who was buried alive at the demolition of Manchester ... He was great company for me who knew no one, only jackeens would be making game of me, and I'm sorry for him.

PRISONER A. Sure, it's a terrible pity about you and him. Maybe the jackeens should spread out the red carpet for you and every other bog barbarian that comes into the place.

He moves away irritably.

Let's get a bit more off this bloody hole.

PRISONER B. Nick. Nick.

WARDER REGAN [*entering with Crimmin*] I've been watching you for the last ten minutes and damn the thing you've done except yap, yap, yap, the whole time. The Chief or the Governor or any of them could have been watching you. They'd have thought it was a bloody mothers' meeting. What with you and my other bald mahogany gas pipe here.

PRISONER D. We werc merely exchanging a few comments, sir.

WARDER REGAN. That's a lie and it's not worth a lie.

PRISONER A. All right! So we were caught talking at labour. I didn't ask to be an undertaker's assistant. Go on, bang me inside and case me in the morning! Let the Governor give me three days of No. 1.

WARDER REGAN. Much that'd worry you.

PRISONER A. You're dead right.

WARDER REGAN. Don't be such a bloody big baby. We all know you're a hard case. Where did you do your lagging? On the bog?

PRISONER A. I did not. Two laggings I done! At Parkhurst and on the Moor.

WARDER REGAN. There's the national inferiority complex for you. Our own Irish cat-o-nine-tails and the batons of the warders loaded with lead from Carrick mines aren't good enough for him. He has to go Dartmooring and Parkhursting it. It's a wonder you didn't go further while you were at it, to Sing Sing or Devil's Island.

PRISONER A. [*stung*] I'm not here to be made a mock of, whether I done a lagging in England or not.

WARDER REGAN. Who said a word about it, only yourself – doing the returned Yank in front of these other fellows? Look, the quare fellow's got to be buried in the morning, whether we like it or not so cut the mullarkey and get back to work.

PRISONER A. I don't let anyone make game of me!

WARDER REGAN. Well, what are you going to do about it? Complain to Holy Healey's department? He's a fine bloody imposter, isn't he?

Like an old IRA man with a good agency in the Sweep now. Recommend me to the respectable people! Drop it for Christ's sake man. It's a bad night for all of us. Fine job, isn't it, for a young fellow like him, fresh from his mother's apron strings. You haven't forgotten what it's like to come from a decent home, have you, with the family rosary said every night?

PRISONER A. I haven't any time for that kind of gab. I never saw religion do anything but back up the screws. I was in Walton last Christmas Eve, when the clergyman came to visit a young lad that had been given eighteen strokes of the cat that morning. When the kid stopped moaning long enough to hear what he had to say, he was told to think on the Lord's sufferings, then the cell door closed with a bang, leaving a smell of booze that would have tripped you up.

He takes a look at the quare fellow's side of the stage and, muttering to himself, goes back to work.

WARDER REGAN. You should pray for a man hardened in drink. Get back to it, all of you, and get that work a bit more advanced. Myself and Crimmin here have a long night ahead of us; we don't want to be finishing off your jobs for you.

They get into the grave.

PRISONER A. I never seen a screw like that before.

PRISONER B. Neither did anyone else.

They work.

CRIMMIN. What time is it, sir?

WARDER REGAN. Ten to seven.

CRIMMIN. Is himself here yet?

WARDER REGAN. Yes, he came by last night's boat. He's nervous of the 'plane, says it isn't natural. He'll be about soon. He's been having a sleep after the trip. We'll have to wait till he's measured the quare fellow for the drop, then we can go off till twelve.

CRIMMIN. Good.

WARDER REGAN. And for Christ's sake try to look a bit more cheerful when you come back on.

CRIMMIN. I've never seen anyone die, Mr Regan.

WARDER REGAN. Of course, I'm a callous savage that's used to it.

CRIMMIN. I didn't mean that.

WARDER REGAN. I don't like it now any more than I did the first time.

CRIMMIN. No sir.

WARDER REGAN. It was a little Protestant lad, the first time; he asked me if he could be walked backwards into the hanghouse so as he wouldn't see the rope.

CRIMMIN. God forgive them.

WARDER REGAN. May He forgive us all. The young clergyman that was on asked if the prison chaplain could accompany him; it was his first hanging too. I went to the Canon to ask him, a fine big man he was. 'Regan,' he says, 'I thought I was going to escape it this time, but you never escape. I don't suppose neither of us ever will. Ah well,' he says, 'maybe being hung twenty times will get me out of purgatory a minute or two sooner.'

CRIMMIN. Amen, a Thighearna Dhia.

WARDER REGAN. The young clergyman was great; he read a bit of the Bible to the little Protestant lad while they waited and he came in with him, holding his hand and telling him, in their way, to lean on God's mercy that was stronger than the power of men. I walked beside them and guided the boy on to the trap and under the beam. The rope was put round him and the washer under his ear and the hood pulled over his face. And still the young clergyman called out to him, in a grand steady voice, in through the hood: 'I declare to you, my living Christ this night . . .' and he stroked his head till he went down. Then he fainted; the Canon and myself had to carry him out to the Governor's office.

A pause. We are aware of the men working at the grave.

WARDER REGAN. The quare fellow asked for you especially, Crimmin; he wanted you because you're a young lad, not yet practised in badness. You'll be a consolation to him in the morning when he's surrounded by a crowd of bigger bloody ruffians than himself, if the truth were but told. He's depending on you, and you're going to do your best for him.

CRIMMIN. Yes, Mr Regan.

Regan walks to the grave.

WARDER REGAN. How's it going?

PRISONER A. Just about done, sir.

WARDER REGAN. All right, you can leave it.

They get up.

WARDER REGAN. Leave your shovels; you'll be wanting them in the morning. Go and tell the warder they've finished, Mr Crimmin. I'll turn them over.

He searches the prisoners, finds a cigarette end on a. and sniffs it.

Coffin nail. Most appropriate. [*He goes towards exit and calls*]. You needn't bother searching them, sir. I've turned them over.

PRISONER A. [*aside*] He's as mad as a coot.

PRISONER C. But charitable.

WARDER REGAN. Right, lead on there!

PRISONER D. This is no place for charity, on the taxpayers' money.

PRISONER A. Take it up with your uncle when you get back into your stockbroker's trousers.

WARDER REGAN. Silence. Right, sir, working party off.

As the prisoners march off, the hangman comes slowly down the steps.

CRIMMIN. Is this . . .

WARDER REGAN. Himself.

HANGMAN. It's Mr Regan, isn't it? Well, as the girl said to the soldier 'Here we are again.'

WARDER REGAN. Nice evening. I hope you had a good crossing.

HANGMAN. Not bad. It's nice to get over to old Ireland you know, a nice bit of steak and a couple of pints as soon as you get off the boat. Well, you'll be wanting to knock off, won't you? I'll just pop down and have a look, then you can knock off.

WARDER REGAN. We were just waiting for you.

HANGMAN. This young man coming with us in the morning?

CRIMMIN. Yes, sir.

HANGMAN. Lend us your cap a minute, lad.

CRIMMIN. I don't think it would fit you, sir.

HANGMAN. We don't have to be so particular. Mr Regan's will do. It ought to fit me by this time, and he won't catch cold the time I'll be away.

He goes out.

CRIMMIN. What does he want the cap for?

WARDER REGAN. He gets the quare fellow's weight from the doctor so as he'll know what drop to give him, but he likes to have a look at him as well, to see what build he is, how thick his neck is, and so on. He says he can judge better with the eye. If he gave him too much one way he'd strangle him instead of breaking his neck, and too much the other way he'd pull the head clean off his shoulders.

CRIMMIN. Go bhfoiridh Dia 'rainn.

WARDER REGAN. You should have lent him your cap. When he lifts the corner of the spy-hole all the quare fellow can see is the peak of a warder's cap. It could be you or me or anyone looking at him. Himself has no more to do with it than you or I or the people that pay us, and that's every man or woman that pays taxes or votes in elections. If they don't like it, they needn't have it.

The hangman comes back.

HANGMAN. Well set up lad. Twelve stone, fine pair of shoulders on him. Well, I expect you'll give us a call this evening over at the hospital. I'm in my usual apartments. This young man is very welcome, too, if he wants to join the company.

WARDER REGAN. Right, sir.

HANGMAN. See you later.

He goes out.

WARDER REGAN. Right, Crimmin. Twelve o'clock and look lively. The quare fellow's got enough on his plate without putting him in the blue jigs altogether. As the old Home Office memorandum says 'An air of cheerful decorum is indicated, as a readiness to play such games as draughts, ludo, or snakes and ladders; a readiness to enter into conversation on sporting topics will also be appreciated.'

CRIMMIN. Yes, sir.

WARDER REGAN [*as they go*] And, Crimmin . . .

CRIMMIN. Yes, sir?

WARDER REGAN. Take off your watch.

They go out.

NEIGHBOUR [*from his cell*] Hey, Dunlavin. Don't forget that Sunday bacon. The bet stands. They're after being at the grave. I just heard them. Dunlavin, do you hear me?

PRISONER A. Get down on your bed, you old Anti-Christ. You sound like something in a week-end pass out of Hell.

ENGLISH PRISONER. Hey, you bloke that's going out in the morning. Don't forget to see my chiner and get him to bail me out.

NEIGHBOUR. Get a bucket and bail yourself out.

SONG.   The day was dying and the wind was sighing,
        As I lay crying in my prison cell.
        And the old triangle
        Went jingle jangle
        Along the banks of the Royal Canal.

                    [CURTAIN]

ACT III

Scene One

Later the same night. Cell windows lit. A blue lamp in the courtyard. A faint tapping is heard intermittently.

As the curtain rises, two warders are seen, One is Donelly, the other a fellow new to the job.

WARDER 1. Watch the match.

WARDER 2. Sorry.

WARDER 1. We're all right for a couple of minutes, the Chief'll have plenty to worry him tonight; he's not likely to be prowling about.

WARDER 2. Hell of a job, night patrol, at any time.

WARDER 1. We're supposed to pass each cell every half-hour tonight, but what's the use? Listen to 'em.

The tapping can be distinctly heard.

WARDER 2. Yap, yap, yap. It's a wonder the bloody old hot-water pipes aren't worn through.

Tapping.

WARDER 1. Damn it all, they've been yapping in association since seven o'clock.

Tapping.

WARDER 2. Will I go round the landings and see who it is?

WARDER 1. See who it is? Listen.

WARDER 2. Do you think I should go?

WARDER 1. Stay where you are and get yourself a bit of a burn. Devil a bit of use it'd be anyway. As soon as you lifted the first spy-hole, the next fellow would have heard you and passed it on to the whole landing. Mind the cigarette, keep it covered. Have you ever been in one of these before?

WARDER 2. No.

WARDER 1. They'll be at it from six o'clock tomorrow morning, and when it comes a quarter to eight it'll be like a running commentary in the Grand National.

Tapping.

WARDER 1 [*quietly*] Shut your bloody row! and then the screeches and roars of them when his time comes. They say it's the last thing the fellow hears.

Tapping dies down.

WARDER 2. Talk about something else.

Tapping.

WARDER 1. They're quietening down a bit. You'd think they'd be in the humour for a read or a sleep, wouldn't you?

WARDER 2. It's a hell of a job.

WARDER 1. We're in for the three P's, boy, pay, promotion and pension, that's all that should bother civil servants like us.

WARDER 2. You're quite right.

WARDER 1. And without doing the sergeant major on you, I'm senior man of us two, isn't that right, now?

WARDER 2. I know what you mean.

WARDER 1. Well, neither bragging nor boasting – God gives us the brains and no credit to ourselves – I think I might speak to you as a senior man, if you don't mind.

WARDER 2. Not at all. Any tip you could give me I'd be only too grateful for it. Sure it'd only be a thick wouldn't improve his knowledge when an older man would be willing to tell him something that would be of benefit to him in his career.

WARDER 1. Well now, would I be right in saying that you've no landing of your own?

WARDER 2. Quite right, quite right. I'm only on here, there or any old where when you or any other senior man is wanting me.

WARDER 1. Well, facts is facts and must be faced. We must all creep before we can walk, as the man said; but I may as well tell you straight, what I told the Principal about you.

WARDER 2. Tell me face to face. If it's fault you found in me I'd as lief hear it from me friend as from me enemy.

WARDER 1. It was no fault I found in you. If I couldn't do a man a good turn – I'd be sorry to do him a bad one.

WARDER 2. Ah, sure I know that.

WARDER 1. What I said to the Pricipal about you was: that you could easily handle a landing of your own. If it happened that one was left vacant. And I don't think I'm giving official information away, when I say that such a vacancy may occur in the near future. Before the month is out. Have you me?

WARDER 2. I have you, and I'm more than grateful to you. But sure I'd expect no less from you. You're all nature.

WARDER 1. It might happen that our Principal was going to the Bog on promotion, and it might happen that a certain senior officer would be promoted in his place.

WARDER 2. Ah, no.

WARDER 1. But ah, yes.

WARDER 2. But there's no one in the prison but'd be delighted to serve under you. You've such a way with you. Even with the prisoners.

WARDER 1. Well, I hope I can do my best by me fellow men, and that's the most any can hope to do, barring a double-dyed bloody hypocrite like a certain party we needn't mention. Well, him and me have equal service and it's only the one of us can be made Principal, and I'm damn sure they're not going to appoint a half-lunatic that goes round asking murderers to pray for him.

WARDER 2. Certainly they're not, unless they're bloody-well half-mad themselves.

WARDER 1. And I think they know him as well as I do.

WARDER 2. Except the Canon, poor man; he has him well recommended.

WARDER 1. You can leave out the 'poor man' part of it. God forgive me and I renounce the sin of it, the Lord says 'touch not my annointed', but the Canon is a bloody sight worse than himself, if you knew only the half of it.

WARDER 2. Go to God.

WARDER 1. Right, I'll tell you now. He was silenced for something before he came here and this is the *only* job he can get. Something terrible he did, though God forgive us, maybe it's not right to talk of it.

WARDER 2. You might sing it.

WARDER 1. I hear it was the way that he made the housekeeper take a girl into the house, the priest's house, to have a baby, an illegitimate!

WARDER 2. And could a man like that be fit to be a priest!

WARDER 1. He'd hardly be fit to be a prison chaplain, even. Here's the Chief or one of them coming. Get inside quick and let on you're looking for them fellows talking on the hot-water pipes, and not a rod about what I said. That's between ourselves.

WARDER 2. Ah sure I know that's under foot. Thanks anyway.

WARDER 1. You're more than welcome. Don't be surprised if you get your landing sooner than you expected. Thirty cells all to yourself before you're fifty.

WARDER 2. I'll have the sister's children pray for you.

Enter Chief Warder.

WARDER 1. All correct, sir.

CHIEF. What the hell do you mean, 'All correct, sir'? I've been watching you this half-hour yapping away to that other fellow.

WARDER 1. There were men communicating on the hot-water pipes, sir, and I told him ten times if I told him once to go inside the landing and scc who it was; it's my opinion, sir, thc man is a bit thick.

CHIEF. It's your opinion. Well, you're that thick yourself you ought to be a fair judge. And who the bloody hell are you to tell anyone to do anything? You're on night patrol the same as what he is.

WARDER 1. I thought, sir, on account of the night that's in it.

CHIEF. Why, is it Christmas? Listen here, that there is an execution in the morning is nothing to do with you. It's not your job to care, and a good job too, or you'd probably trip over the rope and fall through the bloody trap. What business have you out here, anyway?

WARDER 1. I thought I had to patrol by the grave, sir.

CHIEF. Afraid somebody might pinch it? True enough, this place is that full of thieves, you can leave nothing out of your hand. Get inside and resume your patrol. If you weren't one of the old hands I'd report you to the Governor. Get along with you and we'll forget about it.

WARDER 1. Very good, sir, and thank you, sir.

Tapping.

CHIEF. And stop that tapping on the pipes.

WARDER 1. I will, sir, and thanks again, sir.

First warder salutes, goes up the steps to the prison gates, which open. The Governor comes in in evening dress. The first warder comes sharply to attention, salutes and goes off. The Governor continues down the steps and over the the chief warder.

CHIEF. All correct, sir.

GOVERNOR. Good. We had final word about the reprieve this afternoon. But you know how these things are, Chief, hoping for last-minute developments. I must say I should have been more than surprised had the Minister made a recommendation. I'll go down and see him before the Canon comes in. It makes them more settled for confession when they know there is absolutely no hope. How is he?

CHIEF. Very well, sir. Sitting by the fire and chatting to the warders. He says he might go to bed after he sees the priest.

GOVERNOR. You'll see that there's a good breakfast for himself and the two assistants?

CHIEF. Oh, yes, sir, he's very particular about having two rashers and eggs. Last time they were here, some hungry pig ate half his breakfast and he kicked up murder.

GOVERNOR. See it doesn't happen this time.

CHIEF. No indeed. There's a fellow under sentence of death next week in the Crumlin; we don't want him going up to Belfast and saying we starved him.

GOVERNOR. Have they come back from town yet?

CHIEF [*looks at his watch*] It's after closing time. I don't expect they'll be long now. I put Clancy on the side gate to let them in. After he took the quare fellow's measurements he went over to the place he drinks in. Some pub at the top of Grafton Street. I believe he's the life of the bar there, sir; the customers think he's an English traveller. The publican knows who he is, but then they're both in the pub business, and sure that's as tight a trade as hanging.

GOVERNOR. I suppose his work here makes him philosophical, and they say that drink is the comfort of the philosophers.

CHIEF. I wouldn't doubt but you'd be right there, sir. But he told me himself he only takes a drink when he's on a job. The rest of the time he's serving behind his own bar.

GOVERNOR. Is Jenkinson with him?

CHIEF. Yes, sir. He likes to have him with him, in case he gets a bit jarred. Once he went straight from the boat to the pubs and spent the day in them, and when he got here wasn't he after leaving the black box with his rope and his washers and his other little odds and ends behind him in a pub and forgot which one it was he left them in.

GOVERNOR. Really.

CHIEF. You could sing it. You were in Limerick at the time, sir, but here we were, in a desperate state. An execution coming off in the morning and we without the black box that had all his tools in it. The Governor we had then, he promised a novena to St Anthony and two insertions in the *Messenger* if they were found in time. And sure enough after squad cars were all over the city, the box was got in a pub down the North Wall, the first one he went into. It shows you the power of prayer, sir.

GOVERNOR. Yes, I see what you mean.

CHIEF. So now he always brings Jenkinson with him. You see, Jenkinson takes nothing, being very good living. A street preacher he is, for the Methodists or something. Himself prefers TTs. He had an Irishman from Clare helping one time, but he sacked him over the drink. In this Circus, he said, there's only one allowed to drink and that's the Ringmaster.

GOVERNOR. We advertised for a native hangman during the Economic War. Must be fluent Irish speaker. Cailíoctaí de réir Meamram V. a seacht. There were no suitable applicants.

CHIEF. By the way, sir, I must tell you that the warders on night patrol were out here conversing, instead of going round the landings.

GOVERNOR. Remind me to make a note of it tomorrow.

CHIEF. I will, sir, and I think I ought to tell you that I heard the principal warder make a joke about the execution.

GOVERNOR. Good God, this sort of thing is getting out of hand. I was at my School Union this evening. I had to leave in sheer embarrassment; supposedly witty remarks made to me at my own table. My eldest son was furious with me for going at all. He was at a table with a crowd from the University. They were even worse. One young pup went so far as to ask him if he thought I would oblige with a rendering of 'The night before Larry was stretched'. I shall certainly tell the Principal that there's at least one place in this city where an execution is taken very seriously indeed. Good night to you.

CHIEF. Good night, sir.

Tapping. The Chief Warder walks up and down, Regan enters.

Ah, Mr Regan, the other man coming along?

WARDER REGAN. He'll be along in a minute.

CHIEF. I don't know what we'd do without you, Regan, on these jobs. Is there anything the Governor or I could do to make things easier?

WARDER REGAN. You could say a decade of the rosary.

CHIEF. I could hardly ask the Governor to do that.

WARDER REGAN. His prayers would be as good as anyone else's.

CHIEF. Is there anything on the practical side we could send down?

WARDER REGAN. A bottle of malt.

CHIEF. Do you think he'd drink it?

WARDER REGAN. No, but I would.

CHIEF. Regan, I'm surprised at you.

WARDER REGAN. I was reared among people that drank at a death or prayed. Some did both. You think the law makes this man's death someway different, not like anyone else's. Your own, for instance.

CHIEF. I wasn't found guilty of murder.

WARDER REGAN. No, nor no one is going to jump on you in the morning and throttle the life out of you, but it's not him I'm thinking of. It's myself. And you're not going to give me that stuff about just shoving over the lever and bob's your uncle. You forget the times the fellow gets caught and has to be kicked off the edge of the trap hole. You never heard of the warders down below swinging on his legs the better to break his neck, or jumping on his back when the drop was too short.

CHIEF. Mr Regan, I'm surprised at you.

WARDER REGAN. That's the second time tonight.

Tapping. Enter Crimmin.

CRIMMIN. All correct, sir.

CHIEF. Regan, I hope you'll forget those things you mentioned just now. If talk the like of that got outside the prison . . .

WARDER REGAN [*almost shouts*] I think the whole show should be put on in Croke Park; after all, it's at the public expense and they let it go on. They should have something more for their money than a bit of paper stuck up on the gate.

CHIEF. Good night, Regan. If I didn't know you, I'd report what you said to the Governor.

WARDER REGAN. You will anyway.

CHIEF. Good night, Regan.

WARDER REGAN [*to Crimmin*] Crimmin, there you are. I'm going into the hospital to fix up some supper for us. An empty sack won't stand, as the man said, nor a full one won't bend.

He goes. Crimmin strolls. Traffic is heard in the distance, drowning the tapping. A drunken crowd are heard singing. Donelly and the new warder appear in the darkness.

WARDER 1. It that young Mr Crimmin?

CRIMMIN. Yes, it's me.

WARDER 1. You've a desperate job for a young warder this night. But I'll tell you one thing, you've a great man with you. Myself and this other man here are only after being talking about him.

WARDER 2. That's right, so we were. A grand man and very good living.

WARDER 1. There's someone coming. Too fine a night to be indoors. Good night, Mr Crimmin.

CRIMMIN. Good night, sir.

WARDER 1 [*as they go off*] Come on, let's get a sup of tea.

Crimmin waits. Tapping heard. Warder Regan re-enters.

WARDER REGAN. Supper's fixed. It's a fine clear night. Do you hear the buses? Fellows leaving their mot's home, after the pictures or coming from dances, and a few old fellows well jarred but half sober for fear of what herself will say when they get in the door. Only a hundred yards up there on the bridge, and it might as well be a hundred miles away. Here they are back from the pub.

Voices are heard in the dark approaching. Enter hangman and Jenkins.

HANGMAN [*sings*]

'She was lovely and fair like the rose of the summer,
Though 'twas not her beauty alone that won me,

Oh, no, 'twas the truth in her eyes ever shining,
That made me love Mary the Rose of Tralee.'
Don't see any signs of Regan.

JENKINSON. He's probably had to go on duty. You've left it too late.

HANGMAN. Well, if the mountain won't come to M'ammed then the M'ammed must go to the mountain.

WARDER REGAN [*from the darkness*] As the girl said to the soldier.

HANGMAN. As the girl said to the soldier. Oh, it's you, Regan. Will you have a drink?

WARDER REGAN. I'm afraid we've got to be off now.

HANGMAN. Never mind off now. Have one with me. It's a pleasure to see you again. We meet all too seldom. You have one with me. Adam, give him a bottle of stout.

He sings again.

'Oh, no, 'twas the truth in her eyes ever shining,
That made me love Mary the Rose of Tralee.'

Not bad for an old 'un. Lovely song, in't it? Very religious though. 'The Poor Christian Fountain.' I'm very fond of the old Irish songs; we get a lot of Irish in our place on a Saturday night, you know.

WARDER REGAN. Is it what they call a sporting pub?

HANGMAN. That's just what it is, and an old sport behind the bar counter an' all. All the Irish come in, don't they, Adam?

JENKINSON [*gloomily*] Reckon they do. Perhaps because no one else would go in it.

HANGMAN. What do you mean? It's the best beer in the district. Not that you could tell the difference.

WARDER REGAN. Good health.

HANGMAN. May we never do worse. [*To Jenkinson*]. You're in a right cut, aren't you, making out there's nobody but Irish coming into my pub? I've never wanted for friends. Do you know why? Because I'd go a 'undred mile to do a man a good turn. I've always tried to do my duty.

JENKINSON. And so have I.

HANGMAN. Do you remember the time I got out from a sickbed to 'ang a soldier at Strangeways, when I thought you and Christmas 'adn't enough experience?

JENKINSON. Aye, that's right enough.

HANGMAN. I'm not going to quarrel with you. Here, go and fetch your concertina and sing 'em that hymn you composed.

Jenkinson hesitates.

HANGMAN. Go. It's a grand tune, a real credit to you. Go on, lad.

JENKINSON. Well, only for the hymn, mind.

He goes off to fetch it.

HANGMAN. 'E's a good lad is our Adam, but 'e's down in the dumps at the moment. 'Im and Christmas, they used to sing on street corners with the Band of Holy Joy, every Saturday night, concertina and all. But some of the lads found out who they were and started putting bits of rope in collection boxes; it's put them off outdoor testimony. But this 'ymn's very moving about hanging and mercy and so forth. Brings tears to your eyes to 'ear Adam and Christmas singing it.

Jenkinson returns.

JENKINSON. Right?

HANGMAN. Right!

JENKINSON [*sings*].
> My brother, sit and think
> While yet some time is left to thee
> Kneel to thy God who from thee does not shrink
> And lay thy sins on Him who died for thee.

HANGMAN. Take a fourteen-stone man as a basis for giving him a drop of eight foot ...

JENKINSON.
> Men shrink from thee but not I,
> Come close to me I love my erring sheep.
> My blood can cleanse thy sins of blackest dye,
> I understand if thou canst only weep.

HANGMAN. Every half-stone lighter would require a two-inch longer drop, so for weight thirteen and a half stone – drop eight feet two inches, and for weight thirteen stone – drop eight feet four inches.

JENKINSON.
> Though thou hast grieved me sore,
> My arms of mercy still are open wide,
> I still hold open Heaven's shining door
> Come then, take refuge in my wounded side.

HANGMAN. Now he's only twelve stone so he should have eight foot, eight, but he's got a thick neck on him, so I'd better give him another couple of inches. Yes, eight foot ten.

JENKINSON.

　　　　　Come now, time is short.

　　　　　Longing to pardon and bless I wait.

　　　　　Look up to me, my sheep so dearly bought

　　　　　And say, forgive me, ere it is too late.

HANGMAN. Divide 412 by the weight of the body in stones, multiply by two gives the length of the drop in inches. [*He looks up and seems sobered*]. 'E's an RC, I suppose, Mr Regan? [*Puts book in his pocket*].

WARDER REGAN. That's right.

HANGMAN. That's all, then. Good night.

JENKINSON. Good night.

WARDER REGAN. Good night. [*The hangman and Jenkinson go off*]. Thanks for the hymn. Great night for stars. If there's life on any of them, I wonder do the same things happen up there? Maybe some warders on a planet are walking across a prison yard this minute amd some fellow up there waiting on the rope in the morning, and looking out through the bars, for a last look at our earth and the moon for the last time. Though I never saw them to bother much about things like that. It's nearly always letters to their wives or mothers, and then we don't send them – only throw them into the grave after them. What'd be the sense of broadcasting such distressful rubbish?

PRISONER C. [*sings from his cell window*] Is e fath mo bhuartha na bhfhaghaim cead chuarta.

WARDER REGAN. Regular choir practice going on around here tonight.

CRIMMIN. He's singing for . . . for . . .

WARDER REGAN. For the quare fellow.

CRIMMIN. Yes. Why did the Englishman ask if he was a Catholic?

WARDER REGAN. So as they'd know to have the hood slit to annoint him on the rope, and so as the fellows below would know to take off his boots and socks for the holy oil on his feet when he goes down.

PRISONER C. [*sings*] Ni'l gaoth adthuaidh ann, ni'l sneachta cruaidh ann . . .

WARDER REGAN. We'd better be getting in. The other screws will be hopping mad to get out; they've been there since four o'clock today.

PRISONER C. [*sings*] Mo mhuirnin bhan . . .

His song dies away and the empty stage is gradually lightened for

Scene Two

The prison yard. It is morning.

WARDER 1. How's the time?

WARDER 2. Seven minutes.

WARDER 1. As soon as it goes· five to eight they'll start. You'd think they were working with stop watches. I wish I was at home having my breakfast. How's the time?

WARDER 2. Just past six minutes.

MICKSER'S VOICE. Bail o dhis orribh go leir a chairdre.

WARDER 1. I knew it. That's that bloody Mickser. I'll fix him this time.

MICKSER'S VOICE. And we take you to the bottom of D. Wing.

WARDER 1. You bastard, I'll give you D. Wing.

MICKSER'S VOICE. We're ready for the start, and in good time, and who do I see lined up for the off but the High Sheriff of this ancient city of ours, famous in song and story as the place where the pig ate the whitewash brushes and – [*The warders remove their caps*]. We're off, in this order: the Governor, the Chief, two screws Regan and Crimmin, the quare fellow between them, two more screws and three runners from across the Channel, getting well in front, now the Canon. He's making a big effort for the last two furlongs. He's got the white pudding bag on his head, just a short distance to go. He's in. [*A clock begins to chime the hour. Each quarter sounds louder*]. His feet to the chalk line. He'll be pinioned, his feet together. The bag will be pulled down over his face. The screws come off the trap and steady him. Himself goes to the lever and . . .

The hour strikes. The warders cross themselves and put on their caps. From the prisoners comes a ferocious howling.

PRISONERS. One off, one away, one off, one away.

WARDER I. Shut up there.

WARDER 2. Shut up, shut up.

WARDER I. I know your windows, I'll get you. Shut up.

The noise dies down and at last ceases altogether.

Now we'll go in and get that Mickser. [*Grimly*]. I'll soften his cough. Come on . . .

Warder Regan comes out.

WARDER REGAN. Give us a hand with this fellow.

WARDER I. We're going after that Mickser.

WARDER REGAN. Never mind that now, give us a hand. He fainted when the trap was sprung.

WARDER I. These young screws, not worth a light.

They carry Crimmin across the yard.

NEIGHBOUR'S VOICE. Dunlavin, that's a Sunday bacon you owe me. Your man was topped, wasn't he?

PRISONER A'S VOICE. You won't be long after him.

DUNLAVIN'S VOICE. Don't mind him, Neighbour.

NEIGHBOUR'S VOICE. Don't forget that bacon, Dunlavin.

DUNLAVIN'S VOICE. I forgot to tell you, Neighbour.

NEIGHBOUR'S VOICE. What did you forget to tell me?

ENGLISH VOICE. Where's the bloke what's going out this morning?

NEIGHBOUR'S VOICE. He's up in Nelly's room behind the clock. What about that bacon, Dunlavin?

ENGLISH VOICE. You bloke that's going out this morning, remember to see my chiner and tell him to 'ave me bailed out.

NEIGHBOUR'S VOICE. Get a bucket and bail yourself out. What about me bacon, Dunlavin?

ENGLISH VOICE. Sod you and your bleeding bacon.

DUNLAVIN'S VOICE. Shut up a minute about your bail, till I tell Neighbour about his bet.

NEIGHBOUR'S VOICE. You lost it, that's all I know.

DUNLAVIN'S VOICE. Yes, but the doctor told me that me stomach was out of order; he put me on a milk diet.

CHIEF [*comes through prison gates and looks up*]. Get down from those windows. Get down at once. [*He beckons inside and prisoners a., b., c., and d. file past him and go down on the steps. Prisoner b. is carrying a cold hammer and chisel*]. Hey, you there in front, have you the cold chisel and hammer?

PRISONER B. Yes, sir.

CHIEF. You other three, the shovels are where you left them; get to work there and clear the top and have it ready for filling in.

They go on to the canvas, take up the shovels from behind and begin work.
prisoner b. stands on the foot of the steps with his cold chisel while the chief studies his paper to give final instructions.

CHIEF. Yes, that's it. You're to carve E.777. Got that?

PRISONER B. Yes, sir. E.777.

CHIEF. That's it. It should be E.779 according to the book, but a '7' is easier for you to do than a '9'. Right, the stone in the wall that's nearest to the spot. Go ahead now. [*Raising his voice*]. There's the usual two bottles of stout a man, but only if you work fast.

WARDER I. I know the worst fellow was making the noise, sir. It was Mickser, sir. I'm going in to case him now. I'll take an hour's overtime to do it, sir.

CHIEF. You're a bit late. He was going out this morning and had his civilian clothing on in the cell. We were only waiting for this to be over to let him out.

WARDER I. But . . . Sir, he was the whole cause.

WARDER 2. Well, what do you want me to do, run down the Circular Road after him? He went out on remission. We could have stopped him. But you were too bloody slow for that.

WARDER I. I was helping to carry . . .

CHIEF. You were helping to carry . . . Warders! I'd get better in Woolworths.

WARDER 2. To think of that dirty savage getting away like that. Shouting and a man going to his God.

WARDER I. Never mind that part of it. He gave me lip in the woodyard in '42, and I couldn't do anything because he was only on remand. I've been waiting years to get that fellow.

WARDER 2. Ah, well, you've one consolation. He'll be back.

At the grave prisoner a. is the only one visible over the canvas.

PRISONER B. Would you say that this was the stone in the wall nearest to it?

PRISONER A. It'll do well enough. It's only for the records. They're not likely to be digging him up to canonize him.

PRISONER B. Fair enough. E.777.

Regan drops the letters into the grave, and goes.

PRISONER A. Give us them bloody letters. They're worth money to one of the Sunday papers.

PRISONER B. So I understood you to say yesterday.

PRISONER A. Well, give us them.

PRISONER D. They're not exclusively your property any more than anyone else's.

PRISONER B. There's no need to have a battle over them. Divide them. Anyone that likes can have my share and I suppose the same goes for the kid.

PRISONER D. Yes, we can act like business men. There are three. One each and toss for the third. I'm a businessman.

PRISONER A. Fair enough. Amn't I a businessman myself? For what's a crook, only a businessman without a shop.

PRISONER D. What side are you on? The blank side or the side with the address?

VOICE OF PRISONER BELOW [*singing*].

> In the female prison
> There are seventy women
> I wish it was with them that I did dwell,
> Then that old triangle
> Went jingle jangle
> Along the banks of the Royal Canal.

[CURTAIN]

Translation of Passages in Gaelic

Act II, page 513
PRISONER C. [*comes to him*], Yes, Thomas?
CRIMMIN. [*gives him cigarettes and matches*] Here, a couple of cigarettes. Myself and the other screw are going into the hospital for a moment. Divide these cigarettes and let you take a smoke. If the Governor or the Chief or the Principal come, let you not have them in your mouths. Do you understand?
PRISONER C. I understand, Thomas, thanks.

Act II, page 516
PRISONER C. God look down on us.
PRISONER C. Oh sir. I have Irish galore. From the cradle up, sir.
PRISONER D. Quite. I understand you.

Act II, page 522
CRIMMIN. God look down on us.

Act III, page 529
GOVERNOR. Qualifications in accordance with Memorandum Seven . . .

Act III, page 534–535
PRISONER C. [*sings from his cell window*] It is the cause of my sorrow that I have not permission to visit.
PRISONER C. [*sings*] There is no north wind there, there is no hard snow there . . .
PRISONER C. [*sings*] My white darling mavourneen.